Hope in Ancient Literature, History, and Art

Trends in Classics –
Supplementary Volumes

Edited by
Franco Montanari and Antonios Rengakos

Associate Editors
Evangelos Karakasis · Fausto Montana · Lara Pagani
Serena Perrone · Evina Sistakou · Christos Tsagalis

Scientific Committee
Alberto Bernabé · Margarethe Billerbeck
Claude Calame · Jonas Grethlein · Philip R. Hardie
Stephen J. Harrison · Richard Hunter · Christina Kraus
Giuseppe Mastromarco · Gregory Nagy
Theodore D. Papanghelis · Giusto Picone
Tim Whitmarsh · Bernhard Zimmermann

Volume 63

Hope in Ancient Literature, History, and Art

Ancient Emotions I

Edited by
George Kazantzidis and Dimos Spatharas

DE GRUYTER

Ancient Emotions, edited by George Kazantzidis and Dimos Spatharas within the series *Trends in Classics. Supplementary Volumes*, investigates the history of emotions in classical antiquity, providing a home for interdisciplinary approaches to ancient emotions, and exploring the interfaces between emotions and significant aspects of ancient literature and cultures.

ISBN 978-3-11-071013-7
e-ISBN (PDF) 978-3-11-059825-4
e-ISBN (EPUB) 978-3-11-059710-3
ISSN 1868-4785

Library of Congress Control Number: 2018944696

Bibliographic information published by the Deutsche Nationalbibliothek
The Deutsche Nationalbibliothek lists this publication in the Deutsche Nationalbibliografie; detailed bibliographic data are available on the Internet at http://dnb.dnb.de.

© 2020 Walter de Gruyter GmbH, Berlin/Boston
This volume is text- and page-identical with the hardback published in 2018.
Editorial Office: Alessia Ferreccio and Katerina Zianna
Logo: Christopher Schneider, Laufen
Printing and binding: CPI books GmbH, Leck

www.degruyter.com

Preface

This volume arose from the Crete/Patras *Ancient Emotions I Conference* (Rethymno, December 11–13, 2015). It is the first in the sub-series *Trends in Classics-Ancient Emotions*. Despite the sinister conceptualizations of 'hope' —Greek *elpis* and Latin *spes*— in the ancient world, we do hope that this volume will be a useful addition to the burgeoning literature on the history of ancient emotions, a research area that may plausibly be described as a sub-field of Classics. The contributions that constitute this volume explore scripts of 'hope' in ancient literary and non-literary texts, history, and art. If and to what extent 'hope' is an emotion is a topic that we discuss in our Introduction. We take the view, that, although hope does not display the rich affective repertoire of other, more prototypical emotions, say anger, fear or disgust, some of its phenomenological aspects present interfaces with other members of the category 'emotion'. The fact that hope is not self-evidently identified as an emotion raises questions concerning the category 'emotion' itself, but also indicates saliently the methodological affinities between the study of ancient emotions and the study of concepts —an object of investigation at which classicists are particularly adept.

Although several book-length studies and many articles focus on the implications of hope for individual authors and their work(s) or for significant aspects of ancient cultures, e.g. religion and politics, as far as we know this is the first volume dedicated to ancient hope, especially affective, passionate hope. With some notable exceptions, classicists' attention is usually attracted by 'negative' emotions —indeed, on account of the distractions that they cause these emotions are attention-seekers. Although our ancient sources describe hope as deceptive, 'empty', or even dangerous, and, thereby, do not share our (mainly Christian) culturally specific understanding of hope as something good (and recently an anti-depressant), Greeks and Romans were also able to experience passionate 'hope' as a kind of comfort and solace. As evolutionists would aver, moderate hope is necessary for humans' survival. No Greek or Roman would prefer despair to hope, because it is hope, not despair, that serves as a motivational drive that guides and sustains (or causes the failure of) individuals' or groups of individuals' action.

Our decision to discuss hope in the first volume of this series was directly relevant to the sentiments of despair and uncertainty that tormented people in the country that we live in during the time of the 'debt crisis'. Ελπίδα played a predominant role in the public discourse in 2015, the year of our first *Ancient Emotions Conference*. As several contributors suggest, *elpis* and *spes* were central to ancient politics or political propaganda. We have learned much from the conference presentations and the process of editing this volume. We are indeed grateful to our distinguished contributors. It is primarily thanks to them that this volume materialized. We would also like to extend our thanks to the *Trends in Classics* general editors, Professors Franco Montanari and Antonios Rengakos, for encouraging us to join forces with them and making the *Ancient Emotions* sub-series and this volume possible. We also wish to thank warmly Laurel Fulkerson who read our Introduction and offered useful suggestions —naturally, we are responsible for the remaining mistakes.

George Kazantzidis
Dimos Spatharas

Contents

Preface —— V

George Kazantzidis and Dimos Spatharas
Introductory: 'Hope', *elpis*, *spes*: Affective and Non-affective Expectancy —— 1

Part I: *Elpis*. 'Hope' in Greek Literature

Alexandre Johnston
"Poet of Hope": *Elpis* in Pindar —— 35

Nick Fisher
Hope and Hopelessness in Euripides —— 53

Niall W. Slater
Up from Tragicomedy: The Growth of Hope in Greek Comedy —— 85

Natalia Tsoumpra
The Politics of Hopelessness: Thucydides and Aristophanes' *Knights* —— 111

Donald Lateiner
***Elpis* as Emotion and Reason (Hope and Expectation) in Fifth-century Greek Historians** —— 131

Part II: *Spes*. 'Hope' in Latin Literature

Laurel Fulkerson
***Deos speravi* (*Miles* 1209): Hope and the Gods in Roman Comedy** —— 153

Michael Paschalis
uestras spes uritis*: Hope and Empire in Virgil's *Aeneid —— 171

Andreas N. Michalopoulos
Hope Dies Last at Tomis —— 183

Antony Augoustakis
Quaenam spes hominum*? Dashed Hopes in Statius' *Thebaid —— 197

Sophia Papaioannou
'A Historian Utterly Without Hope': Literary Artistry and Narratives of Decline in Tacitus' *Historiae* I —— 213

Part III: Scripts of 'Hope' in History, Art, and Inscriptions

Costas Vlassopoulos
Hope and Slavery —— 235

Andrew Stiles
Velleius Paterculus, the Adoptions of 4 CE, and the *Spes* Race —— 259

Antti Lampinen
Against Hope? The Untimely *elpis* of Northern Barbarians —— 275

Keely Elizabeth Heuer
The Face of Hope: Isolated Heads in South Italian Visual Culture —— 297

Olympia Bobou
Hope and the Sub-adult —— 329

Angelos Chaniotis
***Elpis* in the Greek Epigraphic Evidence, from Rational Expectation to Dependence from Authority** —— 351

List of Contributors —— 365
Index Rerum et Nominum —— 369
Index Auctorum Antiquorum et Locorum —— 373
Epigraphic and Papyrological Sources —— 395

Introductory: 'Hope', *elpis*, *spes*: Affective and Non-affective Expectancy

The first volume in the series *Trends in Classics-Ancient Emotions* explores Greek *elpis* and Latin *spes* in ancient literature, history, and art. In recent years, 'hope' —roughly corresponding to the affective aspects of *elpis* and *spes*, i.e. instances in which these words designate desiderative and motivational hope rather than just expectation—[1] acquired prominence in the political communication of several countries. In his 2008 electoral campaign, Barack Obama identified himself with the hopes of his nation —the presidential campaign poster consisted of a portrait of Obama with the word HOPE below. In addition, as Douglas Cairns points out in the preliminary remarks of a recent publication on Greek metaphors for hope (2016, 13), "a contest between fear and hope" shaped the public discussion about the consequences of or the benefits from voting in favour of Scotland's independence. Hope was also pivotal to current Greek PM's, Alexis Tsipras' anti-austerity rhetoric in his 2015 electoral campaign. In the days that preceded the referendum on the third 'adjustment programme', hope and fear about the country's uncertain future —especially under the threat of the so-called Grexit— reflected contrasting perceptions of what a 'yes' or a 'no' would mean: a catastrophe or a difficult, but brighter future? The ways in which voters responded to this dilemma depended on individual personality traits, political and ideological predilections, and more realistic calculations, though rarely expressed, that revolved around personal interest. But 'collective' emotions also became the object of ethical, political, and social evaluations. Hope was criticized on the grounds that it was enlisted in support of a deceptive and populist rhetoric exploiting voters' despair (or even stupidity)— as Thucydides would say, imaginative hope is not a strategy—,[2] while fear's real name was prudence. As Thucydides would also aver, in times of crisis appraisive concepts change their meanings.[3]

Just like other (more prototypical) emotions, say envy, disgust, or indignation, the scripts of 'hope' that we find in our ancient sources reflect wider cultural or ideological understandings and normative ethical concerns. The extent to which individuals, groups of individuals, or indeed mankind (as Pandora's ambiguous myth indicates) find solace in hope suggests their degree of displeasure

---

[1] Not all authors of this volume are native speakers of English. We use the label 'hope' because English is the language in which the volume's contributions are written.
[2] On Thucydides and hope, see Lateiner, Tsoumpra in this volume, with further literature.
[3] Thucydides' comments concern the *stasis* at Corcyra (3.82.4).

with their present situation. The desired outcomes that hope promises indicate the conditions, external or personal, which hurdle the bettering of an individual's or a social group's current state of being and the extent to which one's own agency impinges on conditions which are beyond one's control. E.g. humans' knowledge of death's inescapability yields anticipatory representations which others deem as mere fantasies and others as a motivational drive.

As several contributions in the present volume suggest, ancient 'hope', especially Greek *elpis*, is more elusive, more deceptive and, thereby, less trustworthy than its modern counterpart. Hesiod's myth of Pandora (*Op.* 90–105), whose exact meaning remains unfathomable, encapsulates in a prototypical fashion the ambivalence of hope in Greek thought.[4] Furthermore, if hope is fundamental to Christian metaphysics, in ancient anti-emotionalist ethical writings, especially those of the Stoics (see discussion below), it is a passion that, along with fear is conceived as an immobilizing power. Fear for possible calamities and hopes about our desired goals are, in Seneca's mind (see p. 11), like the chains that fasten prisoners. Thucydides' narrative emphasizes the desiderative aspects of *elpis* in contexts that thematize the unrealistic calculations on which over-ambitious undertakings rely. As we shall see, even in cases where *elpis* is viewed positively, its blessings are presented as limited.

So far, we have been referring to hope as an emotion. Yet, the question of whether English 'hope' or its modern Greek equivalent, ελπίδα, belong to the category 'emotion' does not afford sweeping answers. First, no two scholars, thinkers, or researchers who work on emotions agree on what emotions are.[5] The category 'emotion' is surrounded by indeterminacy and, although definitions of the term are abundant, we are far from reaching consensus. Furthermore, and this is perhaps more relevant to the history of emotions, the term EMOTION has a relatively short life in the language of concepts. As Dixon (2003) has shown, the word is not in use before the 19th century and when it emerged it displaced other, "more differentiated typologies" expressed with the words 'sentiments', 'passions', and 'appetites' (25).

Although ancient systematic approaches to emotions, e.g. Aristotle's definitions of *pathe* in the *Rhetoric*, present salient affinities with modern, appraisal-oriented treatments of the phenomenon, it would be wrong to assume that the undefined, but phenomenogically recognizable category 'emotion' encompasses

---

[4] For an overview of the different interpretations of Pandora's myth and its reception in antiquity, see Musäus 2004, esp. 13–30.
[5] Excellent discussions of methodological questions concerning the study of emotions are offered by Cairns 2008 and Cairns and Fulkerson 2015.

all the possible ways in which different cultural models in antiquity conceptualized 'emotions' (*pathos, motus animi* etc). Both ancient and modern systematic approaches to individual emotions offer prototypical and to some degree arbitrary definitions reflecting the different perspectives from which the category 'emotion' is viewed. As Aristotle claims, in their attempts to explain the eliciting factors of individual emotions philosophers and natural philosophers endorse radically different approaches: a philosopher would define anger as a response to slight, whereas a 'natural philosopher' would emphasize physiological changes in the body. The bipolar pairs mind/body, nature/culture are still salient in modern interpretations of emotions.[6]

The difficulties involved in defining the category 'emotion', pronounced by some a 'scandal',[7] should not, however, induce us to assume that emotions are not good to think about or with. The very fact that we can identify more and less obvious members of the category 'emotion' —contrast for example anger to contempt—, indicates that emotions share recognizable phenomenological aspects which distinguish them from other categories, e.g. desire, or sexual appetite, which, may, of course, be constituents of or intensify emotions. We may be unable to define a tree but we can still describe its leaves. Hence, the question of whether hope is (culturally) perceived as an emotion can be approached by comparing it with other, more prototypical members of the category, and by investigating the ways in which the cultures that we study represent, verbally or visually, its phenomenology. Hence, our approach to hope, or indeed other emotions, is not seriously affected by the fact that we do not have an all-encompassing definition of emotions. Indeed, the very fact that *elpis* and *spes* commonly appear with fear indicates that ancient 'hope' is conceived as an emotion.[8] As Eric Hobsbawm writes in an essay on peasants and politics, "A good deal of the effort of definition is, of course, significant for theoretical rather than for practical reasons. It may well be a very complex matter for a zoologist to define a horse, but this does not normally mean that there is any real difficulty about recognizing one" (1999, ch. 11).

Modern expert approaches in the field of psychology fairly commonly treat hope as a (controllable) state of mind rather than as an emotion. Snyder's theory for example (1989, 1994, 2002), construes hope primarily as a motivational force,

---

6 Διαφερόντως δ' ἂν ὁρίσαιντο φυσικός τε καὶ διαλεκτικὸς ἕκαστον αὐτῶν, οἷον ὀργὴ τί ἐστίν· ὁ μὲν γὰρ ὄρεξιν ἀντιλυπήσεως ἤ τι τοιοῦτον, ὁ δὲ ζέσιν τοῦ περὶ καρδίαν αἵματος καὶ θερμοῦ (*De. an.* 403a29–b1).
7 Russell 2012. See the criticism of Cairns and Fulkerson 2015, 2–3.
8 On this point, see Fulkerson's analysis of *elpis* in the Greek novel (2016).

in so far as it facilitates the achievement of one's goals through assessments of one's resources, what he calls 'pathway thinking'. Snyder's influential hope theory, however, emphasizes positive expectations rather than desiderative hope and is thereby offered as a medium of personal success. His emphasis on positive expectations revolving around attainable goals is more akin to optimism rather than hope, as is the stress that he lays on personal agency which he views as a medium of self-efficacy. Self-efficacy means that I have reasons to be optimistic about a desired outcome, because I sense that I am in control of the situation.[9] And, conversely, I may well be aware of the limitations of my personal agency and, therefore, be pessimistic about the attainment of a goal, but still hope that in the end I will succeed. Indeed, it is hope's inherent potentiality to make unlikely outcomes appear as possible that fixes an agent's *attention* to desired outcomes thereby necessitating action —or, conversely, inspiring a counter-intuitive, sedating self-confidence.[10] As several of this volume's contributions show, it is this strongly desirative aspect of hope and its impact on one's anticipatory evaluations that underlie the deceptive potential of hope in Greek thought.

Unlike systematic approaches, like Snyder's, which, 'canonize' the meaning of hope and reflect culturally specific idealizations of personal achievement (athletics and academic distinction are some of the domains emphasized by Snyder), folk psychology enables us to investigate how cultural models determine the qualities required for a concept's membership in the category 'emotion'. In a recent study (2016), Douglas Cairns explored ancient Greek metaphors for *elpis* and concluded that in cases where it is expressed metaphorically, it "is an affective state with a substantial goal-directed and desirative aspect" (32). Unlike dispassionate expectation, also signified with the label *elpis*, passionate *elpis* is relatively coextensive with modern 'hope'. In so far as the source domain of metaphors for emotions are typically informed by the apparatus of our complex physiology —e.g. one 'boils with anger', while *elpis* keeps one warm—, on which different cultures write their own distinct scripts, the embodied metaphors for hope that Cairns investigates indicate that Greeks construe passionate *elpis* as an emotion.[11]

A study conducted by Averill (1975) found that on a 7-point scale (a rating of 1 meant that in participants' view a specific label would in no way refer to 'emotion') hope received a rating of 5.42 —placing it ahead of labels such as 'proud',

---

9 See Miceli-Castelfranchi 2015, 161.
10 On this point, see Miceli-Castelfranchi 2015, 164. As Johnston shows in his present analysis of hope in Pindar, excessively desiderative *elpis* may result in painful, obsessive fixation.
11 On emotion metaphors, see Kövecses 2000; Theodoropoulou 2012.

'contemptuous', or 'amazed'. According to the findings of this study, participants claimed that hope is an emotion or feeling like anger and love. Interestingly, they mentioned that hope is more representative of emotion than emotions such as disgust which specialists classify in 'basic' emotions.[12] Furthermore, in a recent folk-conceptual study, Bruininks and Malle (2005) concluded that their participants found hope to be more closely related to wishing and, by being an emotion, distinct from optimism. Unlike optimism, hope revolves around more unlikely outcomes and it involves less personal control.

The implications of the discrepancies between expert and folk understandings are particularly important for our approach to hope, ancient and modern, because they indicate the dangers involved in applying systematic definitions to the study of emotions. Theoretical insights are extremely useful, but classicists' adeptness at interpreting concepts in their wider contexts, textual and cultural, is particularly important for the study of emotions.

Richard Lazarus' definition of hope can serve as a basis of comparison that may allow us to investigate the extent to which Greek *elpis* is semantically coextensive with modern hope. According to Lazarus (1999), "to hope is to believe that something positive, which does not presently apply to one's life, could still materialize, and so we yearn for it" (653). On this definition, hope is typically characterized by two constituent elements: an evaluative process involving positive anticipatory representations concerning the achievement of a goal which we deem to be important for us and a strong desire (a yearning, in Lazarus' definition) to achieve this goal. The extent to which we have or we believe to have control over the achievement of the desired outcome is directly relevant to the emotion's intensity. Hope thrives in cases where the desired outcome is possible rather than probable.[13] Real or perceived unbridgeable gaps between hoped-for outcomes and their achievement are crucial to many scripts of hope.

Lazarus' definition corresponds to "a distinct and prototypical" meaning of Greek *elpis* (Cairns 2016, 44), and, hence, does not encompass the many instances in which ἐλπίς and the verbs ἐλπίζω or ἔλπομαι convey one's dispassionate, i.e. non-desirative and non-motivational evaluations concerning possible future outcomes. Hence, unlike modern hope, ancient Greek *elpis* is sometimes used of unwanted, negative outcomes or positive outcomes to which one responds dispassionately, i.e. without yearning for them. In these cases, *elpis* is propositional rather than desiderative, even as in several scripts, the limits between 'hope' and

---

[12] See Averill 1975, 43 n.1. One of the volume's editors realized that disgust is an emotion only after he started working on its history in antiquity (see Lateiner/Spatharas 2017).
[13] On this point, see Lazarus 1999, 674 and Aspinwall/Leaf 2002, 281–282.

'positive expectation' are blurred. The contributions that constitute this volume focus primarily on affective *elpis* and *spes*, because, on account of its (sometimes excessively) desiderative and motivational nature it yields more interesting scenarios reflecting various responses to despair, frustration, and hardships. This is particularly obvious in scenarios emphasizing the repercussions of mistaking hoped-for outcomes with rationally deducted positive expectations.

The fact that the lexical marker *elpis* has both an affective and a propositional meaning indicates the methodological problems involved in approaches relying on emotion labels, namely approaches that emphasize lexical equivalents.[14] *Elpis* is not always 'hope'. In order to determine the different meanings of Greek *elpis* we must, as is generally the case with the study of emotions, investigate scripts, i.e. contextualized instances of emotional experience, providing information about a sentiment's phenomenology: the causes that prompt it, the ways in which it is expressed (verbally and physically), agents' attempts to control it, or the actions that it prompts.

Let us examine some examples indicating the main semantic varieties of *elpis*. In his work *On Memory*, Aristotle says that while memory concerns past events, *elpis* centers on the future. *Elpis* is here mere expectation, because, unlike affective 'hope', it is not characterized by intentionality. In other words, this *elpis* does not incorporate anticipations to which the agent ties his or her well-being (*Mem.* 449b 27–28). It is just expectation of good and evil alike. In other passages, Aristotle uses *elpis* to express mere expectation. Similarly, in a passage from the *Nichomachean Ethics* where Aristotle explains why villains want to be constantly in the company of others, he says that they are tormented by unpleasant memories of the past and expect (ἐλπίζουσι) that more unpleasant things will happen in the future. Hence, they prefer not to be by themselves and are thus constantly in need of others' comforting companion (*EN* 1166b 16). This *elpis* is expectation of bad (indeed, the script corresponds to what we would label as 'anxiety'). The good man by contrast, Aristotle says earlier, desires the company of himself because his memories of the past are pleasant and, thereby he expects good things in the future (καὶ τῶν μελλόντων ἐλπίδες ἀγαθαί, αἱ τοιαῦται δ' ἡδεῖαι, *EN* 1166a 25–26). The virtuous man's *elpides* for an agreeable future mirror the pleasant memories of his past (note that the good man has no reason to be remorseful) and, hence, his anticipations are characterized by some certainty. His confidence in himself thus constructs a script of expectation. At the same time, however, his

---

14 On the methodological problems involved in reductionist approaches, relying heavily on labels, see Cairns 2008, 46–47, 51–58, who also discusses the important issue of the translatability of emotion words.

elpides may reasonably be taken to involve a desire for a good future or, in any case, a future which is as good as his fondly remembered past. The degree of certainty with which future outcomes are viewed determines the nature of one's anticipatory representations. As Cairns (2016) suggests, in some cases "it is difficult to distinguish between anticipation of a future good and positive longing for it. The semantic range of *elpis* seems to have made that distinction somewhat less salient than it might be for us" (24).[15]

Neutral, propositional *elpis* is commonly easy to detect. No doctor would want the deterioration of his patient's health and, hence, when the author of the *Prognosticon* says that a rapid motion in patients' pupils indicates an *elpis* of madness (μανῆναι τούτους ἐλπίς, 7), he surely means that madness must be expected as a negative outcome. A less straightforward example, indicating the importance of contexts for the conceptual distinction between expectation and hope is provided in the proem of Lysias 3, a speech of defence delivered in the Areopagus. In the *captatio benevolentiae* that we find here (2), the defendant uses the verb ἐλπίζω to suggest that, thanks to the Areopagites' long experience as dikasts, he *expects* to be treated justly, i.e. be acquitted. No doubt, the defendant hopes for his acquittal, but it would be wrong to render ἐλπίζω as 'hope' in this context. Unlike the less experienced dikasts who man other Athenian courts, the Areopagites *can be trusted* because they are not easily deceived by false accusations. Hence, their favourable verdict is presented as almost certain, because the defendant knows and the Areopagites will surely conclude that he has not committed the crime that he is accused of.

The use of *elpis*-verbs to describe mere expectation appears as early as Homer. In his recent study, Cairns discusses several examples of 'expectation' from the epic, but, as he shows, a passage from the *Odyssey* reveals quite saliently how one's subjective perception of a future event determines the meaning of *elpis*:

> ἔλπεαι, αἴ χ' ὁ ξεῖνος Ὀδυσσῆος μέγα τόξον
> ἐντανύσῃ χερσίν τε βίηφί τε ἧφι πιθήσας,
> οἴκαδέ μ' ἄξεσθαι καὶ ἑὴν θήσεσθαι ἄκοιτιν;
> οὐδ' αὐτός που τοῦτό γ' ἐνὶ στήθεσσιν ἔολπε.
> (*Od.* 21.314–317)

---

15 See also the examples that he adduces under n. 41.

> Do you suppose that, if this stranger should string Odysseus's great bow, trusting in the strength of his hands, he would take me home and make me his wife? Not even he, I imagine, hopes for/expects that. (transl. D.L. Cairns)

Penelope's question introduced with ἔλπεαι is addressed to Antinous, who, of course, does not want the beggar to succeed in stringing Odysseus' bow and thereby take her as his wife. This *elpis* involves rational evaluation about a negative outcome and thus denotes expectation of bad. In anticipating Antinous' response, Penelope concludes that not even *he* hopes (ἔολπε) that their union will materialize. The outcome is here focalized though the beggar's perspective, who desires his union with Penelope, but, as the negative verb indicates, he deems the fulfillment of his desire almost impossible. Desire and uncertainty about the achievement of a desired goal construct a scenario of affective hope rather than a scenario of expectation —as the placement of hope into Antinous' heart also indicates.

Let us now turn our attention to 'hope', desiderative and motivational *elpis*. The first three lines of Emily Dickinson's poem 'Hope' run as follows: "Hope is the thing with feathers/That perches in the soul/And sings the tune without the words." Unlike mere expectation, affective hope is a 'tune without words' that only extreme hardships ('sore storms' in Dickinson's words) can silence. The wordlessness of hope's tune, one may assume, reflects passionate hope's lack of clear ideational content, a characteristic of dispassionate, rational, and sometimes coolly calculating positive expectation. Because hope revolves around possible rather than probable or likely outcomes and, hence, difficulties commonly intensify it, it does not readily lend itself to rational analysis —but still we find it comforting. Desire bridges the gap between hoped-for outcomes and their achievement and, as we saw, real or perceived limitations to personal agency conceptually at least contribute to hope's intensity. Indeed, probable or likely outcomes and a strong sense of self-efficacy make hope unnecessary. In cases of fatal illnesses, both doctors and patients may hope for the better, but doctors can typically substantiate their negative expectations on the basis of evidence concerning the illness's gravity and the limitations of possible treatments.

The desire for possible rather than probable or likely outcomes and, thus, the element of uncertainty that characterizes hope, may also explain why affective hope is proverbially 'the last to die'. Hope, not expectation, remains unaffected or rather relatively unaffected by disappointment. Like love, hope can stay with us, even if as a background sentiment ('a tune without words', as Dickinson puts it), for a long period of time. This does not, of course, mean that disappointed hopes are not painful. But they are, conceptually at least, less painful than unfulfilled positive expectations, i.e. instances in which personal agency can significantly contribute to the achievement of a desired goal. We say conceptually, because factors such as the nature of one's desired outcome (hoped-for retaliation is a good example), one's personality traits, the ways in which one perceives life's hardships, or indeed one's despair, may blur the limits between hope and positive expectation. Stores selling maps indicating the route to the fountain of eternal youth and the millions of voters in Greece who, after having lost their money in the stock market, were told by the Finance Minister that "the decline of the market has an expiry date, the election date" are examples that indicate how despair or the extent to which one invests in a desired outcome intensify hope by making fantasies look like positive expectations. As Lateiner and Tsoumpra show in their contributions, Thucydides was particularly observant to the fact that, on account of its desiderative and motivational qualities, hope engenders rationalizations that facilitate self-fulfilling prophecies. Hope enables rationalizations that make us perceive possible outcomes as likely or even certain. Too much hopefulness may either sedate or, conversely, lead to unreflective, precarious, or foolhardy action.

Tiger's evolutionist approach suggests that moderate hope serves as a necessary motivational force and (more graphically) is "an essential vitamin for social process" (1999, 622). As researchers have shown, hope contributes to the recovery from physical and mental illnesses.[16] Selective serotonin reuptake inhibitors and hope work together to make the depressed regain their enjoyment of life. Depression makes people more observant to life's harsh realities and facilitates our cognitive remapping (Welling 2003). But the sense of hopelessness and loss of motivation or interest in ordinary activities caused by depression are extremely painful (and sometimes dangerous) to be a choice. Yet, too much 'positive psychology' may also be harmful. As a researcher working on the affects of critically ill people shows, overdoses of psychotherapeutically injected hope are perceived by patients as a form of 'moral oppression': in situations of despair, 'positive psychology' may cause sentiments of anxiety, guilt, and self-blame (de Raeve 1997).

Ancient Greeks were generally less wholehearted than modern psychologists when they spoke positively about passionate *elpis*. To oversimplify, they took affective *elpis* to be as good as despair is bad. As the conceptual metaphors for *elpis* show, Greek 'hope' offers solace and comfort in times of despair, it is a nourishment, it keeps us warm when we are plagued by life's storms (to borrow Dickinson's wording). But still, in Greek thought, *elpis* (and its motivational aspects) is more commonly something that one resorts to when adversities limit one's ability

---

16 On the prominence of hope in psychologists' and psychiatrists' 'positive paradigm' approaches, see Miceli and Castelfranchi 2015, 159–160 with further literature.

to exert control over one's own life. In other words, in Greek thought scripts of *elpis* are commonly associated with situations in which individuals have a sense of limited self-efficacy and thus typically emphasize the external conditions which restrain personal agency. As Cairns points out (2016, 43) "Hope's motivational force is recognized, but often regarded as inadequate. This probably reflects a greater sense that important aspects of human existence and of human action depend upon factors beyond the control of the individual and a corresponding skepticism about the power of positive thinking in itself to ameliorate one's lot". Fisher's analysis in this volume, for example, shows that endurance, involving one's bitter realization of one's inability to change things by responding effectively to overpowering external conditions, is sometimes the only (tragic) alternative to failed hopes, i.e. hopes generated by despair. Hope is the last to die, but when it dies endurance becomes *arete*. And, as Slater shows in his contribution, the hopes of tragic heroes become the object of early comedians' mockery.

Several contributions in this volume indicate that the transition from *elpis* to *spes* involves some rather significant conceptual changes. "If *spes* is the expectation of something good, then we must conclude that fear (*metum*) is the expectation of something bad", says Cicero in *Tusculan Disputations* 4.80 (in the context of a detailed discussion of Stoic *pathe*[17] —and Aristotle would not disagree with him on this point). Cicero's axiomatic statement does not simply inscribe *spes* within an affective context; by placing it on the opposite side of *metus* (one of the four cardinal *pathe*, according to the Stoics[18]), it supports the assumption that *spes* is a *pathos* in and of itself (closely aligned to, if not interchangeable with Stoic *epithumia*).[19] In fact, *spes* and *metus* present one of the most common pairings of *pathe* in Latin literature[20] (*elpis* and *phobos*, on the other hand, are not so systematically linked in Greek[21]): this pairing can either take the form of a

---

17 See Graver 2002.
18 See Inwood 1985, 127ff.
19 See Leigh 1997, 15 n.12: "While Stoic *epithumia* is normally translated as libido, Cic. *Tusc.* 4.80... uses *spes* as an alternative, a practice followed by Seneca at *Constant.* 9.2; *Tro.* 399, *Phaed.* 492; *Thy.* 348–9".
20 See e.g. Cicero, *Verr.* 2.2.135 and 2.4.5; *Clu.* 176; *Red. Sen* 7; Livy 7.10.9, 8.13.17, 25.57.5, 26.37.1; Tacitus, *Ann.* 2.12.3, 3.69.2, 4.50.3; *Hist.* 1.62.2, 2.2.1, 4.59.1; *Ger.* 46.3; Virgil, *Aen.* 1.218; Ovid, *Fast.* 1.486; 3.362, *Ars Am.* 3.478; Seneca, *Ep.* 13.12, 82.18, 110.4; *Ben.* 4.11.5; 7.1.7, *Ag.* 283; *Phoen.* 516–7 and 631.
21 See e.g. Thucydides 2.89.10; 7.61.3; Euripides, *Ion* 1450–4. It should be noted that sometimes the association of *elpis* and *phobos* in Greek sources does not rest on a conceptual juxtaposition between the two (as is usually the case for *spes* and *metus*) but invites us to consider *elpis* as incidental to *phobos*, with the specific meaning of 'anticipating' —while being in a state of fear

definitional juxtaposition —as in the case of Cicero— or it can appear in an emotion script which blends both conditions more intimately, in a way which blurs the limits between the two. Citing Hecato of Rhodes, a Stoic pupil of Panaetius who flourished about 100 BC,[22] Seneca explains to Lucilius that hope and fear are 'inseparable' (*Ep.* 5.7–8):

> apud Hecatonem nostrum inveni cupiditatum finem etiam ad timoris remedia proficere. 'Desines' inquit 'timere, si sperare desieris.' Dices, 'quomodo ista tam diversa pariter sunt?' Ita est, mi Lucili: cum videantur dissidere, coniuncta sunt. Quemadmodum eadem catena et custodiam et militem copulat, sic ista quae tam dissimilia sunt pariter incedunt: spem metus sequitur. Nec miror ista sic ire: utrumque pendentis animi est, utrumque futuri exspectatione solliciti.
>
> I find in the writings of our Hecato that the limiting of desires helps also to cure fears: "Cease to hope," he says, "and you will cease to fear." "But how", you will reply, "can things so different go side by side?" In this way, my dear Lucilius: though they do seem at variance, yet they are really united. Just as the same chain fastens the prisoner and the soldier who guards him, so hope and fear, dissimilar as they are, keep step together; fear follows hope. I am not surprised that they proceed in this way; each alike belongs to a mind that is in suspense, a mind that is fretted by looking forward to the future.

Both Cicero's and Seneca's reference to hope should be located in a Stoic context. The philosophical background is important because it helps to explain the shift from *elpis*, with the meaning of mental expectation, to *spes* as a term assigned with a more discrete affective value. Prior to the Stoics, Aristotle mentions *elpis* as a component of emotion on various occasions, however, on closer inspection, it becomes clear that in several cases the word is used to denote expectation, in the specific sense of forming a mental picture (*phantasia*) whose realization appears possible —and not necessarily an affect-ladden process by itself.[23] Take, for instance, the famous definition of *orge* in book 2 of the *Rhetoric* (2.2.1378a31–3): "Let us define anger", Aristotle states, "as a desire, accompanied by pain, for a perceived revenge, on account of a perceived slight on the part of people who are not fit to slight one or one's own" (ἔστω δὴ ὀργὴ ὄρεξις μετὰ λύπης τιμωρίας φαινομένης διὰ φαινομένην ὀλιγωρίαν εἰς αὐτὸν ἤ τι τῶν αὐτοῦ, τοῦ ὀλιγωρεῖν μὴ προσήκοντος).[24] All *pathe* (with the exception of 'hatred') for Aristotle, are accompanied either by pain (*lupe*) or pleasure (*hedone*). And while it seems only

---
— a bad thing to happen; see e.g. Herodotus 8.12: οἱ δὲ στρατιῶται οἱ ταύτῃ ἀκούοντες ταῦτα **ἐς φόβον κατιστέατο, ἐλπίζοντες πάγχυ ἀπολέεσθαι** ἐς οἷα κακὰ ἧκον.
22 See Graver 2002, 155–6.
23 For a detailed discussion of 'hope' in Aristotle, see Gravlee 2000.
24 For a detailed discussion, see Konstan 2003.

fair to conceive of anger as a painful condition (hence μετὰ λύπης in its definition), as the discussion evolves, it becomes increasingly evident that there is also a considerable amount of pleasure to be felt by the angry person; such pleasure is intimately linked to *elpis*. According to Aristotle, every instance of *orge* is followed by 'some kind of *hedone*' which derives from the expectation (*elpis*) that revenge will be executed: "for it is pleasant to believe (*oiesthai*) that one can achieve the things that he desires; for no one desires the things that would seem impossible; in the same way, the man affected by *orge* desires what he believes it is possible for him to carry out" [i.e. to take his revenge] (1378b2ff.).[25] A close look at this passage suggests that *hedone* is incidental to *elpis*; as for *elpis* itself, the word appears to denote a cognitive process concerned with the future, just like 'remembering' (*mneme*) works with reference to the past or *aesthesis* with reference to the present (cf. *De memoria et reminiscentia* 449b: ἀλλὰ τοῦ μὲν παρόντος αἴσθησις, τοῦ δὲ μέλλοντος ἐλπίς, τοῦ δὲ γενομένου μνήμη, with discussion above; see also *Rhetoric* 1350b8–16). Thus, while memories can be sweet, and they can make us feel happy in retrospect, the very act of recalling something which happened in the past is not an affect itself; accordingly, to hope/expect that something good will take place in the future (that is, to create a mental picture and then project it to the future) can cause a considerable amount of pleasure but is not an emotion itself: *elpis* for Aristotle seems rather to be the cognitive carrier of, or prerequisite for our ability as humans to emote positively with reference to the future.

Stoicism marks a profoundly important shift in his respect—which is crucial for understanding also Roman *spes*. Overall, the Stoics are more willing to *equate* hope with desire, so much so that the two concepts become interchangeable. It is important to stress, for example, that in the passage of Seneca cited above, the opening reference is to *cupiditas*; when *sperare* appears a line below it seems to be glossing desire, rather than introducing a different concept. Similarly, Cicero's juxtaposition between fear (as *expectatio mali*) and hope (as *expectatio boni*) recalls the established contrast, in Stoic sources, between fear and desire: while all four Stoic passions (conventionally translated as 'desire', 'fear', 'sadness' and 'pleasure') are intertwined with each other on multiple levels, fear and desire create a consistent sub-set of affections in that they are both concerned with the future: thus, while *epithumia* is defined as a longing that is irrational, and originates from the belief that something good will happens to us (τὴν μὲν οὖν

---

25 καὶ πάσῃ ὀργῇ ἕπεσθαί τινα ἡδονήν, τὴν ἀπὸ τῆς ἐλπίδος τοῦ τιμωρήσασθαι· ἡδὺ μὲν γὰρ τὸ οἴεσθαι τεύξεσθαι ὧν ἐφίεται, οὐδεὶς δὲ τῶν φαινομένων ἀδυνάτων ἐφίεται αὑτῷ, ὁ δὲ ὀργιζόμενος ἐφίεται δυνατῶν αὑτῷ.

ἐπιθυμίαν λέγουσιν ὄρεξιν εἶναι ἀπειθῆ λόγῳ· αἴτιον δ' αὐτῆς τὸ δοξάζειν ἀγαθὸν ἐπιφέρεσθαι), fear is an irrational 'deflexion' caused by the impression that something bad will happen to us (φόβον δ' εἶναι ἔκκλισιν ἀπειθῆ λόγῳ, αἴτιον δ' αὐτοῦ τὸ δοξάζειν κακὸν ἐπιφέρεσθαι). Moreover, both fear and desire 'come before' pleasure and pain, since they are connected to anticipation while the last two derive from the experience of a present situation (ἐπιθυμίαν μὲν οὖν καὶ φόβον προηγεῖσθαι, τὴν μὲν πρὸς τὸ φαινόμενον ἀγαθόν, τὸν δὲ πρὸς τὸ φαινόμενον κακόν. ἐπιγίγνεσθαι δὲ τούτοις ἡδονὴν καὶ λύπην).[26]

A closer investigation of Stoic sources reveals that *elpis* undergoes in this context some rather significant changes. Aristotle, as we have seen above, states clearly that *elpis* is a condition from which pleasure can be derived, but he notes in the same context that 'hoping' is basically a cognitive process —essentially, it is presented as the ability to build in one's mind a positive scenario that looks feasible. Stoics, on the other hand, move a step further and they claim explicitly that hope can itself be a (preliminary) 'passion': in Philo's of Alexandria words, '*elpis* is a joy before a joy' (χαρά τις πρὸ χαρᾶς).[27] Clearly, the Stoic concept of *propatheiai* is here relevant, since it allows Philo to invest with an affective value (even though a 'preliminary' one) what in a different context could have appeared as primarily a *mental* expectation. But to think of *elpis* as a passion naturally creates, for a Stoic, the need to define explicitly this passion in terms of "what appears to be good or bad" (in the same way that *hedone* derives from the belief that something good is happening to us now and *lupe* originates from the belief that we are presently being affected in a negative way by a certain situation). Thus while Plato, in his discussion of *pathe* in book 1 of the *Laws*, divides *elpis* into *tharros* and *phobos* (which are characterized as opinions, *doxai*, about future pleasures and pains respectively; 1.644c–645a),[28] the Stoics narrow down

---

26 The Greek text cited comes from Stobaeus' informative summary of Stoic pathe at *Ecl.* 2.7.10ff. See Inwood 1985, 113ff. Cf. Long 2017, 32–3, illustrating the Stoic idea of passions as "movements contrary to reason". In his discussion of Galen, *PHP* 4.4.16–7 (which, in its turn, cites an excerpt from Chrysippus' *On Passions*) Long (p.33) notes that: "In the quoted passage Chrysippus' choice of desire and fear, rather than pleasure and distress, may be deliberate: it is rather easier to conceive of desire and fear as 'movements' or impulses, directed at what is currently unrealized".
27 See the important discussion in Graver 1999.
28 As Cairns (2016, 22–23) points out with reference to this passage, "though *elpis* is a matter of doxa, its subspecies are affects. But though the negative motive of avoiding pain is called fear, the positive one, that which pursues pleasure, is called not hope but confidence. It is possible that the choice of this term may have been at least partly influenced by a wish to avoid using *elpis* in both unmarked and marked senses".

the meaning of 'hope' (*qua* passion) into a positive thing —'positive' in the sense that it concerns something that 'looks good', *phainomenon agathon*. While in Greek literature (Hesiod, Thucydides etc.) *elpis* remains an ambivalent concept, with Stoicism it is clearly attached to a scenario in which we (a) desire strongly (since we believe that it will affect us in a positive way) and (b) given that desire is so strongly involved, we may experience it as a (preliminary) passion.

The conceptual categorization of *elpis* as a form of desire can also explain why in Stoicism hope turns into a more 'passionate' notion. Plato famously notes that desire, though 'similar in nature' (*homophues*) to the *thumoeides* (what accounts for emotions in people), should be assigned a distinct entity (*Republic* 4.439e–440a).[29] Aristotle, on the other hand, divides desire[30] (*orexis*) into three distinct forms that can be seen to map onto the reasoning, spirited and appetitive parts of Plato's tripartite division of the soul. Aristotle agrees with Plato that reason gives rise to desire, specifically desire for good, which he consistently calls *boulesis*. He also agrees with Plato that there are two specific kinds of non-rational desire: spirited or passionate desire (*thumos*) and appetitive desire (*epithumia*). As we read in the *Rhetoric* (1.1369a1–4): "Rational desire is wishing (*boulesis*), and wishing is a desire for something good —nobody wishes for anything unless he thinks it good. Non-rational desire is twofold: viz. spirit and appetite." Compared with this background, *epithumia* in Stoicism (and by implication, its sub-categories, such as *elpis*), becomes a predominantly affective concept: by using the word side by side with the other three cardinal *pathe* (*phobos, lupe, hedone*), the Stoics make it clear that all desire is non-rational, and it affects us in the same way that all other emotions do. While *elpis* in earlier Greek literature and philosophy retains a strong desiderative aspect (which can be combined with a state of rationally calculated expectation), its link with desire in Stoicism is sufficient to turn it into an irrational *pathos* altogether. In this sense, *elpis* changes its meaning partly because desire has in the meantime undergone a considerable, affective, enhancement.

These considerations can now help us place in a different context the repeated association of *metus* with *spes* by Roman authors. It would, of course, be an exaggeration to argue that every instance of Roman *spes* should be linked to a Stoic background; however, it would equally be a mistake to ignore Stoicism's pervasive influence in the conceptual inflexions of 'hope' in Latin literature. When Tacitus, for instance, in his so-called 'second preface', relates the reaction

---

[29] See the collection of essays in Barney/Brennan/Brittain 2012.
[30] For a book length discussion, see Pearson 2012.

of the Roman people at the news of Nero's death,[31] he describes the scene as follows (*Hist.* 1.4):

> finis Neronis ut laetus **primo gaudentium impetu** fuerat, ita **varios motus animorum** non modo in urbe apud patres aut populum aut urbanum militem, sed omnis legiones ducesque conciverat, evulgato imperii arcano posse principem alibi quam Romae fieri. sed patres laeti, usurpata statim libertate licentius ut erga principem novum et absentem; primores equitum proximi gaudio patrum; pars populi integra et magnis domibus adnexa, clientes libertique damnatorum et exulum **in spem erecti**: plebs sordida et circo ac theatris sueta, simul deterrimi servorum, aut qui adesis bonis per dedecus Neronis alebantur, maesti et rumorum avidi.

> Although Nero's death had at first been welcomed with outbursts of joy, it roused varying emotions, not only in the city among the senators and people and the city soldiery, but also among all the legions and generals; for the secret of empire was now revealed, that an emperor could be made elsewhere than at Rome. The senators rejoiced and immediately made full use of their liberty, as was natural, for they had to do with a new emperor who was still absent. The leading members of the equestrian class were nearly as elated as the senators. The respectable part of the common people and those attached to the great houses, the clients and freedmen of those who had been condemned and driven into exile, were all roused to hope. The lowest classes, addicted to the circus and theatre, and with them the basest slaves, as well as those men who had wasted their property and, to their shame, were wont to depend on Nero's bounty, were cast down and grasped at every rumour.[32]

The passage clearly demonstrates the general sense of elation experienced by the Roman people because of the hope they feel for a better future. Considering Tacitus' account, and the emphasis placed on the spontaneous 'outburst' of hope (*erectus* is used in contemporary sources to indicate the outburst of a strongly felt emotion e.g. Seneca, *Const.* 9.3: *erectus laetusque… continuo gaudio elatus*), it is safe to assume that hopefulness in this case carries with it a distinct affective value —it is almost synonymous to *gaudium* rather than its prerequisite or its result (cf. *erecti gaudio* in Livy, *AUC* 6.6.18). The reason why certain people are described as being 'sorrowful' (*maesti*) has precisely to do with the fact that they cannot share in the general feeling of elating hope that *affects* everyone else.[33] More importantly, the text opens with some distinct allusions to Stoic vocabulary: *impetus* (*primo gaudentium impetus*) in an affective context translates the

---

31 See Haynes 2003, 41–2.
32 Translation in Moore 1925.
33 On the association between *maestitia* and *desperatio* ('hopelessness', 'desperation'), see e.g. Caesar, *De Bello Gallico* 7.80.92 (*maesti prope victoria desperata*) and Cicero, *ad Fam.* 7.28.2: *cum meam maestitiam et desperationem.*

technical term *horme*, 'impulse',³⁴ while *motus animi* (*varios motus animorum*) is a reference to the Stoic conceptualization of *pathos* as a *kinesis* (in Cicero, *TD* 4.6.11, Stoic *pathos* is defined as *motus animi contra rationem*).³⁵ Tacitus could be exploring here the (Stoic) affectivity of *spes* as, constitutionally, an irrational passion — a blind impulse which has nothing to do with somber calculated anticipation; perhaps this can be explained as part of the historian's attempt to foreground that the hoped-for new emperor (Galba) will fail gravely to meet the people's expectations. Overall, the scene —particularly the way it embeds the contrasting states of *spes* and *maestitia*— comes in stark contrast with the end of Tacitus' *Germania* (ch. 46). Tacitus ends his narrative there with a description of the Fenni, a tribe of simple needs, whose "only dependence is on their arrows … They do not provide any other shelter for their infants from wild beasts and storms, than a covering of branches twisted together. This is the resort of youth; this is the receptacle of old age. Yet even this way of life is in their estimation happier than groaning over the plough; toiling in the erection of houses; subjecting their own fortunes and those of others to the agitations of alternate hope and fear. Secure against men, secure against the gods, they have attained the most difficult point, not to need even a wish" (…*sed beatius arbitrantur quam ingemere agris, inlaborare domibus, <u>suas alienasque fortunas spe metuque versare</u>: securi adversus homines, securi adversus deos rem difficillimam adsecuti sunt, ut illis <u>ne voto quidem opus esset</u>*). As Antti Lampinen shows in his contribution to this volume, Roman historiography systematically represents northern barbarians as being inhabited by hopes (hope for plunder or land, hope for revenge or hope for a general reversal of fortune against the oppressive control of Rome) which often remain unfulfilled because of lack of a proper plan. The Fenni, in this respect, constitute an exception —they are depicted as a golden-age tribe that is free from care: in contrast with the people at Rome who live in a constant state of political and emotional turmoil, the Fenni experience neither *spes* nor *metus* since they have succeeded in eliminating even the "need to wish."

The fact that *spes* can be felt in the context of Stoic *horme* and *kinesis*, combined with the observation that these 'motions' can occasionally turn rather violent, can also help to explain the intriguing association between *spes* and *furor* in

---

34 See Inwood 1993, 180–1; 2005, 219. Seneca, *Ep.* 118.9 associates *impetus animi* with *appetitio*. On the association between *impetus* and *instinctus* in Tacitus, *Hist.* 1.57, see Damon 2003, 217. *Instinctus* is often associated with *furor*, e.g. in Tac. *Hist.* 2.46.1: *furore quodam et instinctu flagrabant*.
35 Stobaeus, in the passage cited above, states that: πάθος δ' εἶναί φασιν ὁρμὴν πλεονάζουσαν καὶ ἀπειθῆ τῷ αἱροῦντι λόγῳ ἢ <u>κίνησιν</u> ψυχῆς ἄλογον παρὰ φύσιν.

Latin literature (on the contrary, *elpis*' association with insanity is not so prominent in Greek sources). The idea that strong emotions, when felt intensely, can lead to/be experienced as insanity, has a particularly Stoic flavor in Roman thought.[36] All Stoic passions fall into the category of *insania* which, as Cicero aptly notes, has a wider meaning and application (*patet latius*) when compared to *furor*, since it indicates the deviation from an optimal state of wisdom. *Furor*, on the other hand, carries with it the specific meaning of 'clinical' madness (*TD* 3.11).[37] But in some cases, Stoic *insania* (conceptualized as a strongly felt emotion) can lead to actual insanity. In *TD* 3.63, for instance, Cicero mentions the example of Hecuba who is driven mad (*rabiem*) because of her distress (*propter animi acerbitatem*) at the loss of her son. Seneca, in a similar vein, defines anger (*ira*) as a 'short fit of madness' (*brevis insania*) (*De ira* 1.1.2).

The fact that hope can have the same effect, i.e. it can inebriate people to the point of driving them mad, relies on the assumption that *spes* can be experienced as a violent passion *per se*; the mental image originally created as a form of anticipation (what Aristotle calls *phantasia*) may end up being a delusional state. The collocation *vana spes* in contexts which involve trickery and mental manipulation (e.g. in Virgil, *Aen*. 1.352: *vana spe lusit amantem*) reminds us that hallucinations too, in cases of actual madness, are 'vain' —they present themselves as the figments of a madman's imagination (see e.g. Celsus, *De medicina* 3.18.3).[38] At a crucial point in Virgil's *Aeneid* (see Paschalis in this volume), the blindness (*furor*) of the Trojan women's minds forces them to 'burn their hopes', *vestras spes uritis*, the ships of Aeneas. But often madness is nourished by 'hope' itself:[39] in the opening of *Ann*. 16.1 Tacitus hints at Nero's mental deterioration by stating that the emperor was 'deluded' by his vanity (*inlusit ... Neroni fortuna per vanitatem ipsius*); in 16.3, this delusional state is clearly linked to the emperor's 'inane hopes' (*gliscebat interim luxuria spe inani*; cf. Lucretius, *DRN* 4.1069: *inque dies gliscit furor*). Similarly, Suetonius (*Nero* 31) uses the word *furor* to describe the madness kindled by the hope of a vast hidden treasure in North Africa.[40]

---

36 For an illuminating discussion, see Gill 1997.
37 See the discussion in Kazantzidis 2013, 246–7.
38 *Phrenesis vero tum demum est, cum continua dementia esse incipit, cum aeger, quamvis adhuc sapiat, tamen quasdam vanas imagines accipit: perfecta est, ubi mens illis imaginibus addicta est.*
39 See Rimell 2015, 69.
40 *Ad hunc impendiorum furorem, super fiduciam imperii, etiam spe quadam repentina immensarum et reconditarum opum impulsus est ex indicio equitis R. pro comperto pollicentis thesauros antiquissimae gazae, quos Dido regina fugiens Tyro secum extulisset, esse in Africa vastissimis specubus abditos ac posse erui parvula molientium opera.*

But *spes* can also turn into *furor* in other, seemingly less violent contexts. It will suffice to mention at this point its occurrence as a 'deluding' force in instances of *eros*. In one of its only two occurrences in Lucretius' *DRN* (more on which below), *spes* is significantly opposed to *res*. In 4.1061–2 (a passage which is heavily indebted to Sappho's pathology of love outlined in fr. 31V)[41] Lucretius stresses the paradoxes of erotic absent presence as follows: "for if the object of your love is absent, yet images of it are present, and the sweet name sounds in your ears", *nam si abest quod ames, praesto simulacra tamen sunt / illius et nomen dulce obversatur as auris*. A few lines below, the poet associates the lover's 'hallucinating' state with *spes* (4.1086–90):

> namque **in eo spes est**, unde est ardoris origo,
> restingui quoque posse ab eodem corpore flammam.
> quod fieri contra totum natura repugnat;
> unaque **res haec est**, cuius quam plurima habemus,
> tam magis ardescit dira cuppedine pectus.

> For the hope is that the fire can be put out by the same body that is the source of the burning. Nature protests that entirely opposite is the case: this is the one thing, the more of which we have, the more our breasts burn with terrible desire.[42]

The contrast between *spes* and *res* is echoed by Leander's in Ovid's *Heroides* 18.178: *et res non semper, spes mihi semper adest*, "the object of my love is not always with me, but hope is always with me" (desire, it should be remembered, often tends to substitute, in erotic contexts, the very object of desire). *Spes* in Ovid's work can take an even more sinister tone; it can create actual images which blend the limits between reality and imagination and make it hard to distinguish what is real or false (even so, as Andreas Michalopoulos argues in this volume, in his exilic poetry, hope, *spes salutis*, stands as "the poet's most reliable companion and unfailing partner, along with love and nostalgia for his friends and family back in Rome"). So, for example, Narcissus —whose delusional state, as Philip Hardie has shown, owes a lot to the Lucretian theory of *simulacra* in *DRN* 4—[43] ends up falling in love with a 'hope' that has no body, i.e. his reflection on the water: *spem sine corpore amat* (*Met.* 3.417). *Spes* here is objectified: it does not simply appear as a mental expectation of touching one's lover; nor does it simply nourish the vain mental image of an absent lover; it actually creates a visible image which Narcissus, in his frenzied and desiring state, fails to identify for

---

41 The Sapphic intertext has been already alluded to in 3.152–8; see Fowler 2000, 23–4.
42 Translations of Lucretius are from Smith 1992.
43 See Hardie 2002, 152ff.

what it really is.⁴⁴ The Lucretian distinction between *spes* and *res* is taken by Ovid to an extreme: the contrast between the two in the case of Narcissus runs so deep that, in the end, reality is literally effaced by hope and hope materializes in the form of a reflected *corpus*. This substitution relies on the crucial, underlying assumption that *spes* can be a blinding force, just like all violent emotions are.

The reference to Lucretius —and given the attention that we have paid so far on Stoicism— naturally invites some thoughts on *spes* in the context of Roman Epicureanism. That the two should be discussed together is aptly demonstrated by the following passage in Lucan (*BC* 2.7–15):

> siue parens rerum, cum primum informia regna
> materiamque rudem flamma cedente recepit,
> fixit in aeternum causas, qua cuncta coercet
> se quoque lege tenens, et saecula iussa ferentem
> fatorum immoto diuisit limite mundum,
> siue nihil positum est, sed fors incerta uagatur
> fertque refertque uices et habet mortalia casus,
> sit subitum quodcumque paras; sit caeca futuri
> mens hominum fati; <u>liceat sperare timenti</u>.

> Perhaps when the Creator first took up his shapeless realm of raw matter after the conflagration had died down, he fixed causes for eternity, binding himself too by his all-controlling law, and with the immovable boundary of destiny arranged the universe to introduce prescribed ages. Or perhaps nothing is ordained, but Chance at random wanders bringing change after change, and accident is master of mortal affairs. Whatever you intend, let it be sudden; let men's minds be blind to future disaster; **let the fearful have hope!**⁴⁵

Several scholars have traced in these programmatic lines the contrasting trends of Stoicism (represented by an all-pervasive divine entity which subdues every single one of us to a personal destiny) and Epicureanism (a philosophy which proposes that nothing is ordained, and everything is subject to mere chance).⁴⁶ Interestingly enough, Lucan suggests that *spes* can find a place in both contexts: one would assume that in a Stoic universe fear can be balanced by the hope that

---

44 Cf. the case of Dido, on presence, absence and furor.
45 Translation in Braund 1992.
46 The same uncertainty as to what governs the universe can be traced in other parts of the poem; see Feeney 1991, 282. Hardie 2009, 250 argues that the philosophical uncertainty in these lines may have something to do with Lucretius' use of multiple explanations to illuminate things in the natural universe that cannot be positively linked to one cause alone.

things will turn out good for us because the divine will has decreed so;[47] in the case of Epicureanism, fear can be smoothed by the hope that chance (*casus*) will work to our favour, and since everything happens 'randomly', we may as well find comfort in the thought that it is (statistically) possible to avoid disaster and even attain happiness.

The link drawn by Lucan between hope and Epicureanism at this point looks plausible: *casus*, 'chance', is not necessarily linked to an unwanted result; though 'unforeseeable', the chance of nature (*casus naturalis*, 6.30) in Lucretius, for instance, has a positive outcome —it even creates patterns which reveal a certain, inherent order in them (*ordo certus*, 2.251; cf. *foedera naturai*, 1.586, 2.302). Consequently in a universe where the gods do not intervene and everything is contigent on the random clash between atoms, we might as well stop fearing and hope that we will have chance on our side. However, when we turn to Lucretius, our main source for Roman Epicureanism, *spes* is virtually absent as a concept — except for two, significantly problematic passages. To start with, the fact that *spes* occurs only two times in the poem (whereas, for instance, words such as *timor* and *metus* dominate the narrative) is telling in itself. *Spes*, as we have seen above, occurs one time (4.1068), describing the delusional state of passionate desire which comes in stark contrast with reality (*res*). While Lucretius clearly aims to deconstruct *spes* in a specifically erotic context,[48] the implications of his passage turn out to be wider: as Ovid's allusion to the text (in the case of Narcissus) indicates, *spes* is not simply about failed erotic hope; it can substitute reality itself,

---

47 Cf. Cicero, *De natura deorum* 3.14 — if we agree that the future is predetermined, it would be nonsensical to know it in advance; for if what is predestined for us happens to be unfortunate, we will spend our lives in misery, having been deprived of the hope that could keep us going in a state of ignorance: "The future follows upon the past, for no one can escape it. Indeed, it is often not even advantageous to know what is going to happen, for it is miserable to be tortured to no purpose, and to lose even the last, yet universal, solace of hope (*nec habere ne spei quidem extremum et tamen commune solacium*), all the more so as you also say that everything happens by fate, and that by fate is meant that which has always been true from all eternity. What help, then, or means of defence does it give to know that something will happen, when the fact that it is to happen is certain?"

48 It has been argued that Lucretius' diatribe against love and sexual infatuation at the end of book 4 is meant as a sustained polemic against the model of romanticized love promoted in contemporary erotic poetry, e.g. Catullus; see Kenney 2007, 324–5. One cannot ignore the fact, therefore, that *spes* is intrinsic as a concept to (the failed expectations of) erotic experience, e.g. in Catullus 64.140; 64.143–4 (*nunc iam nulla viro iuranti femina credat, / nulla viri speret sermones esse fideles*); 64.177; 64.186. Cf. Ovid, *Am*. 2.19.5 (*speremus pariter, pariter metuamus amantes*); Propertius, 3.17.11–12 (*semper enim vacuos nox sobria torquet amantes; / spesque timorque animos versat utraque modo*); and Tibullus 2.6.27.

thus casting doubt on the central Epicurean concept that our senses —what we see, hear, touch etc.— should be trusted. The second instance of *spes* in the *DRN* is equally problematic (1.921–28):

> Nunc age, quod superest, cognosce et clarius audi.
> nec me animi fallit quam sint obscura; sed **acri**
> **percussit** thyrso laudis **spes magna** meum cor
> et simul incussit suavem mi in pectus amorem
> Musarum, quo nunc instinctus mente vigenti
> avia Pieridum perago loca nullius ante
> trita solo. iuvat integros accedere fontes
> atque haurire

> Now learn what remains. Listen more attentively. I am well aware of how obscure these matters are, but an intense hope of fame has struck my heart and driven deep within my breast the sweet love of the Muses. Now, inspired by this love and hope, with a mind alert I traverse the pathless tracts of the Muses of Pieria that no human foot has touched before. It is a joy to approach untouched springs and drink from them.

The passage is usually discussed as one of Lucretius' most explicit allusions to Callimachean poetics (see e.g. the reference to 'untrodden paths' in 1.926–7).[49] However, its opening reference to (Dionysiac) *furor* —indicated by *thyrso* at 1.923 — seems rather unusual, especially if we take into account the emphasis placed throughout the poem on *ratio* as the only means by which Lucretius' philosophical enquiry can be conducted efficiently and to the benefit of the *DRN*'s readers.[50] More to the point, the fact that Lucretius presents himself as being 'inebriated' by hope comes in stark contrast with Callimachus' emphasis on 'plain water' which establishes, in the context of Hellenistic poetics the priority of *ars* over manic inspiration (Lucretius actually alludes to it in 1.927, *integros fontes*).[51] Significantly, 1.921–928 recalls a passage which comes before in book 1, where the poet describes the *destructive* power of the wind (1.271–76):

> Principio venti vis verberat incita corpus
> ingentisque ruit navis et nubila differt,
> inter dum rapido percurrens turbine campos
> arboribus magnis sternit montisque supremos
> silvifragis vexat flabris: ita **perfurit acri**
> cum fremitu saevitque minaci murmure pontus.

---

49 See Kenney 2007, 304; cf. Brown 2007.
50 See Gale 2000, 191; 2007, 70–1; cf. Volk 2002, 143.
51 See Fantuzzi/Hunter 2004, 448–9; cf. Acosta Hughes/Stephens 2012, 251.

The winds infuriate lash our face and frame, unseen, and swamp huge ships and rend the clouds, or, eddying wildly down, bestrew the plains with mighty trees, or scour the mountain tops with forest-crackling blasts. Thus on they rave with uproar shrill and ominous moan.

The imagery of the wind 'lashing' (*verberat*) our bodies foregrounds the use of *percussit* at 1.923 (cf. *percurrens* at 1.273). Both the blow of the wind and that inflicted by a supernatural entity (in the form of Dionysiac frenzy) are conceived as external, and potentially lethal, forces: the turmoil caused by *ventus* is characterized as 'fierce' (*acri*, 1.275; cf. 1.922–3: *acri thyrso*),[52] so much so that it leads to a form of cosmic madness (*perfurit*; 1.275). *Furor* is not mentioned explicitly in 1.921–28, but it is clearly suggested by *acri thyrso* and the implication of inspired 'possession' in these lines. The wind-passage contains a scene full of ruins (*ruit, turbine, sternit* etc.) which is felt by our bodies but it is manifested also in the physical environment that surrounds us; the same script is enacted in 1.921–28, although this time it is pointedly located in the poet's chest.

Spes occupies a central place in 1.921–28. Lucretius' reference to it becomes all the more salient if we consider that, syntactically, it is the subject which holds the thyrsus (*sed acri / percussit thyrso laudis spes magna meum cor*). Clearly, *spes* in this case is a force that can drive one mad (and this ties up well with what we have noted above regarding the link between *spes* and *furor* in Latin literature);[53] as such, it is distinctly contrasted with the sober reasoning, *ratio*, which defines the poem's didactic agenda. One may say that the close alignment of *spes* with *thyrso* in this case makes sense only if we assume that 'hoping' is predominantly affective. As for the reasons why Lucretius' poem contains so few references to *spes*, it seems plausible that his stance as a devoted Epicurean makes him treat

---

[52] See Segal 1990, 54 on *DRN* 3.252–3 (*dolor... potest penetrare neque acre / permanere malum*): "the more general metaphors of 'pain' that 'penetrates' us or of the 'bitter woe' that 'flows through us' also reminds us that the mortal body is not just a value-neutral physical barrier, but a living tissue full of sense and feeling. The addition of the otherwise gratuitous adjective *acre*, 'bitter', in particular seems to acknowledge the subjective dimension of the process of dying. It is the adjective that Lucretius chooses for his own passionate desire for poetic glory (*acri percussit thyrso*, 1.922–3)".

[53] With reference to 1.922–3 Segal 1988, 198 argues that although "Lucretius assimilates the literary tradition of poetic immortality, he holds back from laying claim to its ultimate gift"; this should explain why "he asserts the hope (*spes*) rather than the possession of immortality." However, a close look at 1.921–8 in light of 1.271–6 as well as the suggested connection with the 'erotic' framing of deluding hope in 4.1086–90 (cf. 1.924: *et simul incussit suavem mi in pectus amorem*) indicate that Lucretius' *spes* for immortality is not as innocent as it may seem at first sight; the poet seems to be carried away (although temporarily) by an enthusiasm which is not typical of what we find in the rest of the poem.

hope as essentially meaningless. In stating that *elpis* is part of the *orge*-script, Aristotle mentions that expectation (for revenge) is intimately linked with what looks feasible —in other words, anticipation is formed with reference to things that we consider to be 'up to us'. This is precisely the concept that makes hope redundant: in the Epicurean universe, (the causes of) things take place either by necessity (*ananke*) or chance (*tukhe*). In his letter to Menoeceus (133–4), Epicurus mentions a third possibility: by insisting that certain things are 'up to us' he allows that human agency, human rationality and moral development are real.[54] If we were to follow Aristotle, one would claim that it is precisely in this conceptual space delineated between feasibility and the knowledge that we can act for ourselves where hope can be nourished. However, considering that for the Epicureans human agency is intrinsically linked to rationality and the minimization of our desires (i.e. of the things we wish and hope for) it becomes clear that *elpis/spes* will turn out in that case to be a distraction rather than a viable option. Unlike Lucan's suggestion that hope can help us find our way in a universe governed by chance, Lucretius' silencing of the concept suggests that in a determinist world dominated by randomness and necessity it is meaningless to hope for anything; the best thing we can do is contain ourselves to the things over which we have control, but this is a process that relies precisely on the curtailing of our desires and hopes.[55] Additionally, the Epicureans seem to think that it is appropriate to distance oneself from intentional states projected into the future, since they can always be canceled by the reality of death.[56] Finally, even in cases where anticipation and hope are said to add to our happiness (e.g. in Philodemus, *De elect.* xxiii.7–13), they can do so only so long as they are of the right kind; in this context, nurturing a good hope for the future would mean, for instance, that one wishes to remain healthy or recover from disease, rather than aim for intense feelings of joy and pleasure.[57]

The philosophical background of *spes* is essential since it informs some of the concept's most important discussions in Latin literature (Lucretius, Cicero, Seneca, Lucan). The fact that in both Stoicism and Epicureanism *spes* is outlined

---

54 See O' Keefe 2005, 90; cf. Gill 2009, 135–6 and O' Keefe 2009.
55 Plutarch, *Non posse* 1107C attacks Epicurus precisely because, in addition to curtailing our desires as humans, he has also removed all 'hope of help and favours from the gods': τοιαύτην χώραν ἡδονῶν τοσούτων Ἐπίκουρος ἐκτέμνεται, καὶ ἐπὶ ταῖς ἐκ θεῶν ἐλπίσιν, ὥσπερ εἴρηται, καὶ χάρισιν ἀναιρεθείσαις τοῦ θεωρητικοῦ τὸ φιλομαθὲς καὶ τοῦ πρακτικοῦ τὸ φιλότιμον ἀποτυφλώσας εἰς στενόν τι κομιδῇ καὶ οὐδὲ καθαρὸν τὸ ἐπὶ τῇ σαρκὶ τῆς ψυχῆς χαῖρον συνέστειλε καὶ κατέβαλε τὴν φύσιν, ὡς μεῖζον ἀγαθὸν τοῦ τὸ κακὸν φεύγειν οὐδὲν ἐχούσαν.
56 See Warren 2001.
57 See Tsouna 2009, 261.

as a 'negative' concept,[58] however, by no means entails that Roman culture did not invest in hope —in various contexts and for the sake of serving different purposes. For one thing, it is extremely important to bear in mind that, unlike the limited evidence we have for the divine qualities of Greek *elpis*,[59] Roman *Spes* was worshipped as a goddess.[60] The earliest temple, devoted to *Spes Vetus* ('old Hope'), was located on the Esquiline, at the highest point on the east side of the city (Frontinus, *de aquis* 1.5)[61] and it is dated as early as 477 BC (Liv. 2.51.2–3; Dion. Hal. *Ant. Rom*. 9.24.3–4). The name avoided confusion with another temple of *Spes* built, at a later stage, by A. Atilius Calatinus during the first Punic war in the mid-3rd cent. BC. (Cicero, *De legibus* 2.28).

In *De natura deorum* 3.14, Cicero makes use of Cotta's Academic scepticism in order to cast doubt on the extent to which emotions or virtues (among which *spes* is counted as one) can indeed be conceived as abstract deities:[62]

> Quodsi tales dei sunt, ut rebus humanis intersint, Natio quoque dea putanda est, cui, cum fana circumimus in agro Ardeati, rem divinam facere solemus; quae quia partus matronarum tueatur, a nascentibus Natio nominata est. Ea si dea est, di omnes illi, qui commemorabantur a te, Honos, Fides, Mens, Concordia, ergo etiam **Spes**, Moneta omniaque, quae cogitatione nobismet ipsis possumus fingere. Quod si verisimile non est, ne illud quidem est, haec unde fluxerunt.

> If, moreover, it is characteristic of the gods to take part in human affairs, Natio, to whom, when we go the round of the shrines in the Æduan territory, we are accustomed to make sacrifice, must also be considered divine; she was so named from the offspring that is born (nascentibus), because, it was supposed, she aids the delivery of matrons. If she is divine, so are all those whom you were mentioning, Honour, Faith, Mind, and Concord, and

---

58 Momigliano 1987, 280, "Neither Stoics nor Epicureans gave importance to Hope in their systems. 'Prinzip Hoffnung' did not really find its Ernst Bloch in Greek thought".
59 See e.g. Theognis 1135–1150 with Cairns 2016, 27–28. As Cairns points out (2016, 28), however, *elpis*' "apotheosis as the only remaining power that can protect us against injustice emphasizes the poet's point about the precariousness of trust in circumstances of moral decline. Passages which present hope as at least potentially positive, as an antidote to despair, seem typically to carry this implication of its limitations" (on the limitations of *elpis*, see also pp. 9–10 above); cf. Calame 2005, 203 n.46. See also Momigliano 1987, 280: "I do not know of any official cult of Hope in Greek cities, though we find her as a goddess together with Nemesis and weeping Eros on the Chigi crater, and later by herself on coins of various cities (for instance of Alexandria)."
60 For a detailed discussion of the evidence, see Clark 1983.
61 See Claridge 2010, 379.
62 See Fears 1981 and Clark 2007.

therefore also Hope, and Memory, and everything that we can conceive by imagination in our own minds. If this is not probable, neither is the position which leads to these results.[63]

Later in the text (3.61), *spes*' divine qualities are criticized from a Stoic perspective: "Why, we see that mind, faith, hope, virtue, honour, victory, safety, concord, and everything else of that kind are in their nature abstractions, and not divinities (*vim habere videmus, non deorum*); for they are either resident in ourselves (*in nobismet insunt*), as is the case with mind, hope, faith, virtue, and concord, or they are things to be desired by us (*aut optandae nobis sunt*), as honour, safety, and victory. I see their usefulness, and also their images which have been consecrated, but why they have the force of divinities I shall not understand until I am informed". (*quarum rerum utilitatem video, video etiam consecrate simulacra; quare autem in iis vis deorum insit, tum intellegam, cum ex te cognovero*).

However, Cicero's philosophically inclined speakers do not tell the whole story about *spes* and the various beliefs which circulated in Rome at the time about hope's divine qualities. In fact, one can find instances even in Cicero's work which point to a different perspective. In *De legibus* 2.28, Marcus notes that the consecration of virtues (such as Piety, Virtue etc.) is a good thing, as long as "people who have those qualities —and all good people have them— should think that they have actual gods located in their minds". The same applies to the names of 'desirable things', such as Safety, Honor, Resource, and Victory; "and since the mind is aroused by the expectation of good things, it was right for Calatinus to consecrate Hope", (*quoniamque exspectatione rerum bonarum erigitur animus, recte etiam Spes a Calatino consecrata est*). Aulus Atilius is presented by various sources (Cicero, *de natura deorum* 2.23.61; Tacitus, *Ann.* 2.49) as the one who consecrated a large temple to *Hope* during the first Punic War (about the middle of the third century BC). The fact that during the 2nd century BC —and in the context of a largely popular genre— Plautus has several of his characters invoke *Spes* as a goddess (e.g. *Mercator* 866–7; *Mostellaria* 350; *Pseudolus* 709) can be taken as an indication that, as long as political turbulence and external wars persisted, Hope retained its importance as a divinity.[64] As Laurel Fulkerson's contribution in this volume shows, the appearance of *spes* in the socially versatile and eventful world of Plautine comedy is not simply attached to the personal wishes of individual characters (an *adulescens* who hopes to obtain the girl he is in love with, a slave who hopes to improve his life conditions, and so on) but, on a wider scale,

---

63 Translation in Brooks 1896.
64 For a sensitive reading of Roman comedy in light of contemporary historical developments, see Leigh 2004.

it is indicative of the fact that hope "is beginning to be felt as a problem in the context of the vicissitudes of almost-incessant war". Seen in this light, "perhaps contemporary temple foundations and cult offerings to *Spes* are best understood as an attempt to control the arbitrary goddess".

By the time we reach Augustan Rome, religious belief in hope becomes increasingly ingrained in popular and cultic morality: in his hymn to Fortuna of Antium (*Odes* 1.35), Horace introduces various personifications by her side, among which we find *Spes* and *Fides*.[65] The appearance of hope in this context could be connected with Augustus' rebuilding of the temple in the Forum Holitorium, following damage of the fire in 31 BC (see Tacitus, *Ann.* 2.49).[66] Whether or not the allusion is to an actual restoration, Horace's evidence is indicative of the importance of *Spes* in the ideology of the early Principate. In line with the long tradition which associated particular (often youthful) leaders of the late Republic and Triumviral period with *spes*,[67] Augustan ideology —as reflected, among others, in Horace— seems to have invested a lot on the divinity of *Spes*, in order to maintain the dawn of a new era. This is further confirmed by the fact that Augustus' successors and protégées were similarly preoccupied with connecting their public persona to the discourse of hope, often in religious contexts. To cite just one example, in *Ann.* 2.49 Tacitus mentions that the temple of Hope, originally built by Calatinus, was finally restored and dedicated in 17 CE by Germanicus (*Spei aedes a Germanico sacratur: hanc A. Atilius voverat eodem bello*). As Andrew Stiles argues in his chapter, "the cult of *Spes* had been revitalized in order to use it as an additional support during the first experiment in transitioning power within the *domus Augusta*".

The fact that the regime promoted a 'hopeful' discourse does not mean, of course, that imperial historiography reserved an optimistic and uncritical stance towards *spes*: on the contrary, just as Statius' *Thebaid* exploits (dashed) hopes "as a means to further the cycle of violence that is bound to be repeated by the sons of Oedipus" (Anthony Augoustakis, in this volume), so does Tacitus' opening episode in *Hist.* 1.1–49 —according to Sophia Papaioannou's essay— invests on the "gradual shattering of hope for the future" and presents Galba as a short-timed emperor precisely because he fails to meet the expectations of different groups of people across the social strata of Rome.

---

65 See Feeney 1988, 89.
66 See Andrew Stiles in this volume; cf. Cooley 2009, 43, 194–5.
67 See Clark 1983.

Overall, the distinction between *Spes* as a divinity and *spes* as an ideological construct is not clear-cut. Because 'religion' and 'politics' are interfaced,[68] it is natural to assume that a temple that would have been dedicated to hope could have been reflecting popular religion and beliefs, while at the same time serving to sustain a certain political agenda. In its political and ideological manifestations, *spes* was exploited by the Romans to a considerable degree; such exploitation, alongside the emphasis placed on its divine qualities, indicates that, in contrast with the philosophical scepticism which surrounds the concept, the Romans did think of 'hope' also in a positive way. The related evidence is abundant, so let us contain our discussion to two significant examples. Cicero —who goes so far as to make *spes* a Stoic *pathos* equivalent to *epithumia*— repeatedly embraces the power of hope in the political sphere. In one of his letters dated in 44 BC, he phrases his great expectations for the future of Octavian in precisely those terms (*ad Fam.* 12.23.2): *magna spes est in eo: nihil est, quod non existimetur laudis et gloriae causa facturus.*[69] Significantly, what makes Cicero 'hopeful' —in the sense that he has valid reasons to believe and *expect* that Octavian will make a great leader— is the fact that the latter is full of desires: "there is nothing that he won't do for the sake of praise and glory". There seems to be an intriguing interplay at this point between two different senses of *spes*: on the one hand, we have Cicero's hope in the form of calculated expectation based on observation; on the other hand, we have Augustus' high hopes, in the desiderative, passionate sense. Both *laus* and *gloria* are words with a potentially negative meaning (*spes laudis*, as we have seen above, is what compromises Lucretian *ratio*), and they are typically identified as objects of *epithumia*. What comes out as the result of this underlying contrast is the realization that Octavian is a person that one can hope with; despite the fact (or, rather, precisely because) *spes* can lead someone to be absorbed by his desires, it can accordingly be exploited as a powerful tool in the arena of Roman politics.

Finally, *spes* can be seen to dominate Virgil's foundational epic at crucial points in the narrative (and, like Cicero, there is a good chance that Virgil has Augustus in mind).[70] When Mercury in book 4 urges Aeneas to leave Carthage, he reminds him that being a leader means that one should not disregard the hopes of his people: "if the glory of such great prospect does not move you at all, then look to growing Ascanius and the hopes of your heir Iulus (*spes heredis Iuli*), to whom the kingdom of Italy and the Roman land is owed" (4.273–6). Unlike the

---

68 See Clark 2007.
69 Cf. *ad Fam.* 11.28.6: *optimae spei adulescens*.
70 For hope in Virgil, see Fulkerson 2017.

young Octavian in Cicero's letter above, Aeneas in Carthage becomes increasingly uninterested in *gloria rerum*, because of his growing infatuation with Dido. Desire, in this case, is focused on a specific erotic object and puts at risk the collective hopes and expectations of the people who rely on Aeneas. As in 4.273–6, the rhetoric of hope throughout the *Aeneid* is systematically linked to Aeneas' son, Ascanius.[71] When in book 5 the Trojan women are driven mad and burn their ships, the one who intervenes and calls them back to order is Ascanius, using the following words: *quis furor iste novus? Quo nunc, quo tenditis …/ heu, miserae cives? Non hostem inimicaque castra / Argivum, vestras spes uritis. En, ego, vester / Ascanius!* (5.570–3). Several scholars have pointed out the connection between *vestras* and *vester* in line 573: at the climax of his address, Aeneas' son reminds the women of their civic duty (*cives*) and presents himself as the very embodiment of their hopes for a better future in Italy. As Michael Paschalis points out in his chapter, "this is the one and only time Ascanius displays awareness of the future", and the role he will play in it; while "the burden of founding the Roman race is placed on the shoulders of Aeneas, the *hope* for the fulfillment of this mission… is specifically associated with his son". Finally, in 12.168 Ascanius appears side by side with his father to make a truce with Latinus, being called *magnae spes altera Romae*. Although subordinate to his father (hence *altera*), Ascanius' role at this point is emphasized by the proleptic use of *Roma*: the city does not yet exist, however the hope which Ascanius embodies is a promise for the future which will be fulfilled eventually. Virgil thus seems to set right the bitter reference to hope in book 2: in that case, it was Aeneas who, while Troy is burning, addresses, curiously, the ghost of Hector as *spes … fidissima Teucrum* (2.281). As we move to the epic's final book, another city, which is not yet visible, turns up in the narrative, but this time through a hopeful projection of *spes* into the future.

Virgil was of course aware that *spes* can play some grave tricks with people's minds, but he reserves its negative side (mostly) for Aeneas' enemies. In contrast with the calculated expectations of the Trojans, *spes* fuels the desires of Turnus to the point of driving him mad. A first glimpse is offered in 11.491, where Turnus eagerly prepares to meet Aeneas' attack: *exultat … animis et spe iam praecipit hostem*. What appears here as a feeling of elation turns in book 12 —the one in which Turnus meets his death— to frenzy.[72] When seeing that Aeneas has been injured in 12.325, Turnus 'burns, aflame with sudden hope' (*subita spe fervidus ardet*). The allusion here must be to Sophocles' *Ajax* who at the point of his bitter

---

71 See Rogerson 2017, 23ff.
72 See Tarrant 2012, 170.

disillusionment, and moments before his death, speaks the following words (475–8):

τί γὰρ παρ' ἦμαρ ἡμέρα τέρπειν ἔχει
προσθεῖσα κἀναθεῖσα τοῦ γε κατθανεῖν;
οὐκ ἂν πριαίμην οὐδενὸς λόγου βροτὸν
ὅστις κεναῖσιν **ἐλπίσιν θερμαίνεται**.

What joy is there in day following day, now advancing us towards, now drawing us back from the verge of death? I would not buy at any price the man who feels the glow of empty hopes.[73]

By that point in the narrative, Ajax has recovered from his insanity and, disappointed by his dashed hopes for revenge, ponders on the futility of a life without dignity and honour. In Virgil's hands, the 'empty hopes' transform into a sign of incipient madness, in accordance with the Roman connection between *spes* and *furor*. For Aeneas' calculated expectations to be fulfilled, his enemies' deluded, passionate hopes must be crashed before.

George Kazantzidis – Dimos Spatharas

Bibliography

Acosta-Hughes, B./S.A. Stephens. 2012. *Callimachus in Context: From Plato to the Augustan Poets*, Cambridge.

Aspinwall, L.G./S.L. Leaf 2002. "In Search of the Unique Aspects of Hope: Pinning our Hopes on Positive Emotions, Future-oriented Thinking, Hard Times, and Other People," in: *Psychological Inquiry* 13, 276–88.

Averill, J.R. 1975. "A Semantic Atlas of Emotional Concepts," in: JSAS *Catalog of Selected Documents in Psychology* 5, 330 [Ms. No. 421].

Barney, R/T. Brennan/C. Brittain (eds.). 2012. *Plato and the Divided Self*, Cambridge.

Braund, S.H. 1992. *Lucan: Civil War*, Oxford.

Brooks, F. 1896. *M. T. Ciceronis de natura deorum*, London.

Brown, R.D. 2007. "Lucretius and Callimachus," in: M. Gale (ed.), *Oxford Readings in Lucretius*, Oxford, 328–50.

Bruininks, P./B.F. Malle 2015. "Distinguishing Hope from Optimism and Related Affective States," in: *Motivation and Emotion* 29.4, 327–355.

Cairns, D.L. 2008. "Look Both Ways: Studying Emotion in Ancient Greek," in: *Critical Quarterly* 50, 43–62.

—— 2016. "Metaphors for Hope in Archaic and Classical Greek Poetry," in: R.R. Caston/R.A. Kaster (eds.), *Hope, Joy and Affection in the Classical World*, Oxford/New York, 13–44.

---

73 For these lines, see Finglass 2011, 277.

Cairns, D.L./L.Fulkerson. 2015. "Introduction," in: D. Cairns/L. Fulkerson (eds.), *Emotions Between Greece and Rome*, London, 1–22.
Calame, C. 2005. *Masks of Authority: Fiction and Pragmatics in Ancient Greek Poetics* (transl. P.M. Burk), Ithaca.
Claridge, A. 2010. *Rome: An Oxford Archaeological Guide*, Oxford.
Clark, A.J. 2007. *Divine Qualities: Cult and Community in Republican Rome*, Oxford.
Clark, M.E. 1983. "*Spes* in the Early Imperial Cult: 'The Hope of Augustus'," in: *Numen* 30, 80–105.
Cooley, A.E. 2009. *Res Gestae Divi Augusti: Text, Translation, Commentary*, Cambridge.
Damon, C. 2003. *Tacitus: Histories, Book 1*, Cambridge.
De Raeve, L. 1997. "Positive Thinking and Moral Oppression in Cancer Care," in: *European Journal of Cancer Care* 6, 249–256.
Dixon, T. 2003. *From Passions to Emotions: The Creation of a Secular Psychological Category*, Cambridge.
Fantuzzi, M./R. Hunter. 2002. *Tradition and Innovation in Hellenistic Poetry*, Cambridge.
Fears, J.R. 1981. "The Cult of Virtues and Roman Imperial Ideology," in: *ANRW* 17.2, 827–948.
Feeney, D. 1991. *The Gods in Epic: Poets and Critics of the Classical Tradition*, Oxford.
—— 1998. *Literature and Religion at Rome: Cultures, Contrasts and Beliefs*, Cambridge.
Finglass, P. 2011. *Sophocles: Ajax*, Cambridge.
Fowler, D. 2000. *Roman Constructions: Readings in Postmodern Latin*, Oxford.
Fulkerson, L. 2017. "The Vagaries of Hope in Vergil and Ovid," in: D. Cairns/D. Nelis (eds.), *Emotions in the Classical World: Methods, Approaches and Directions*, Stuttgart, 207–30.
Gale, M. 2000. *Virgil on the Nature of Things: The Georgics*, Cambridge.
—— 2007. "Lucretius and Previous Poetic Traditions," in: S. Gillespie/P. Hardie (eds.), *The Cambridge Companion to Lucretius*, Cambridge, 59–75.
Gill, C. 1997. "Passions as Madness in Roman Poetry," in: S.M. Braund/C. Gill (eds.), *The Passions in Roman Thought and Literature*, Cambridge, 213–41.
—— 2009. "Psychology," in: J. Warren (ed.), *The Cambridge Companion to Epicureanism*, Cambridge, 125–41.
Graver, M. 1999. "Philo of Alexandria and the Origins of Stoic *Propatheiai*," in: *Apeiron* 44, 300–25.
—— 2002. *Cicero on the Emotions: Tusculan Disputations 3 and 4*, Chicago.
Gravlee, Scott G. 2000. "Aristotle on Hope," in: *Journal of the History of Philosophy* 38, 461–477.
Hardie, P. 2002. *Ovid's Poetics of Illusion*, Cambridge.
—— 2009. *Lucretian Receptions: History, the Sublime, Knowledge*, Cambridge.
Haynes, H. 2003. *The History of Make Believe: Tacitus on Imperial Rome*, Berkeley.
Hobsbawm, E. 1999. *Uncommon People: Resistance, Rebellion and Jazz*, London.
Inwood, B. 1985. *Ethics and Human Action in Early Stoicism*, Oxford.
—— 1993. "Seneca and Psychological Dualism," in: J. Brunschwig/M. Nussbaum (eds.), *Passions and Perceptions: Studies in Hellenistic Philosophy of Mind*, Cambridge, 150–83.
—— 2005. *Reading Seneca: Stoic Philosophy at Rome*, Oxford.
Kazantzidis, G. 2013. "Quem nos furorem, μελαγχολίαν illi vocant: Cicero on Melancholy," in: W.V. Harris (ed.), *Mental Disorders in the Classical World*, Leiden, 245–64.
Kenney, E.J. 2007. "Doctus Lucretius," in: M. Gale (ed.), *Oxford Readings in Lucretius*, Oxford, 300–327.
Konstan, D. 2003. "Aristotle on Anger and the Emotions: The Strategies of Status," in: G.W. Most/S. Braund (eds.), *Ancient Anger: Perspectives from Homer to Galen*, Cambridge, 92–120.
Kövecses, Z. 2000. *Metaphor and Emotion: Language, Culture, and Body in Human Feeling*, Cambridge.

Lateiner, D./D. Spatharas (eds.) 2017. *The Ancient Emotion of Disgust*, Oxford.
Lazarus, R.S. 1999. "Hope: An Emotion and a Vital Coping Resource against Despair," in: *Social Research* 66, 653–78.
Leigh, M. 1997. *Lucan: Spectacle and Engagement*, Oxford.
—— 2004. *Comedy and the Rise of Rome*, Oxford.
Long, A.G. 2017. "Plato, Chrysippus, and Posidonius' Theory of Emotions," in: T. Engberg-Pedersen (ed.), *From Stoicism to Platonism: The Development of Philosophy, 100 BCE–100 CE*, Cambridge, 27–46.
Miceli, M./C. Castelfranchi 2015. *Expectancy and Emotion*, Oxford.
Momigliano, A. 1987. *Ottavo Contributo Alla Storia Degli Studi Classici e del Monto Antico*, Roma.
Moore, C.H. 1925. *Tacitus: The Histories, Books I-III,* Loeb Classical Library, Cambridge, Mass.
Musäus, I. 2004. *Der Pandoramythos bei Hesiod und seine Rezeption bis Erasmus von Rotterdam*. Hypomnemata 151, Göttingen.
O' Keefe, T. 2005. *Epicurus on Freedom*, Cambridge.
—— 2009. "Action and Responsibility," in: J. Warren (ed.), *The Cambridge Companion to Epicureanism*, Cambridge, 142–53.
Pearson, G. 2012. *Aristotle on Desire*, Cambridge.
Rimmel, V. 2015. *The Closure of Space in Roman Poetics: Empire's Inward Turn*, Cambridge.
Rogerson, A. 2017. *Virgil's Ascanius: Imagining the Future in the Aeneid*, Cambridge.
Russell, J.A. 2012. "Introduction to Special Section: On Defining Emotion," in: *Emotion Review* 4, 337.
Segal, C. 1988. "Poetic Immortality and the Fear of Death," in: *HSCP* 92, 193–212.
—— 1990. *Lucretius on Death and Anxiety: Poetry and Philosophy in De Rerum Natura*, Princeton, NJ.
Smith, M.F. 1992. *Lucretius: De Rerum Natura* (revised 2nd edition), Loeb Classical Library, Cambridge, Mass.
Snyder, C.R. 1989. "Reality Negotiation: From Excuses to Hope and Beyond," in: *Journal of Social and Clinical Psychology* 8, 130–57.
—— 1994. *The Psychology of Hope: You Can Get Here from There*, New York.
—— 2002. "Hope Theory: Rainbows in the Mind," in: *Psychological Inquiry* 13, 249–75.
Tarrant, R. 2012. *Virgil: Aeneid, Book 12*, Cambridge.
Theodoropoulou, M. 2012. "The Emotion Seeks to Be Expressed: Thoughts from a Linguist's Point of View," in: A. Chaniotis (ed.), *Unveiling Emotions: Sources and Methods for the Study of Emotions in the Greek World*, Stuttgart, 433–468.
Tiger, L. 1999. "Hope Springs Internal," in: *Social Research* 66, 611–623.
Tsouna, V. 2009. "Epicurean Therapeutic Strategies," in: J. Warren (ed.), *The Cambridge Companion to Epicureanism*, Cambridge, 249–65.
Volk, K. 2002. *The Poetics of Latin Didactic: Lucretius, Vergil, Ovid, Manilius*, Oxford.
Warren, J. 2001. "Epicurus and the Pleasures of the Future," in: *OSAP* 21, 135–79.
Welling, H. 2003. "An Evolutionary Function of the Depressive Reaction: The Cognitive Map Hypothesis," in: *New Ideas in Psychology* 21, 147–156.

Part I: *Elpis*. 'Hope' in Greek Literature

Alexandre Johnston
"Poet of Hope": *Elpis* in Pindar

In a recent monograph on God and eternity, the theologian George Pattison, following the late Michael Theunissen, calls Pindar "poet of hope".[1] Although my own chapter differs greatly in scope and approach from their two works, it shares with them the broad premise that hope is a central aspect of Pindar's poetry, and one that is given a highly sophisticated treatment. The vast majority of Pindar's extant poetry consists of victory odes or "epinicians", composed and performed to commemorate athletic success in the Panhellenic games.[2] These are poems fundamentally concerned with the possibility and tangible reality of exceptional human achievement, and as such, they celebrate hope as a positive and necessary drive to action, victory, and prosperity. Yet at the same time, like much archaic and classical Greek literature, they also emphasise the volatile and dangerous nature of hope, given the epistemic deficiencies which characterise humans and the unpredictability of the future. The word most frequently used for hope, *elpis*, encompasses a range of phenomena including expectation, supposition, and illusion;[3] in some contexts, it seems very close semantically to terms such as *erōs*, desire, and *pothos*, longing or yearning. These words can all carry broadly positive connotations, as (for instance) vehicles through which the poet, his patrons, and his mythical characters are able to visualise and entertain the possibility of success; yet they are also frequently associated with excess, suffering, and destruction. This ambiguity will be the focus of the first and second sections of the chapter, in which I explore the ethical, religious, and poetic contexts in which Pindaric hope operates. In the third and final part, I analyse the ways in which hope is conceptualised as affecting the human mind and body, in an attempt to delineate some of the contours of its elusive phenomenology. In this

---

[1] Pattison 2015, 212–46; see Theunissen 2002, 346: "Pindars Denken ist im Grunde und im Ganzen Hoffnungsdenken".
[2] On the victory ode, see most recently Agócs/Carey/Rawles 2012. As with most ancient genres, it is difficult (if not impossible) to provide a fixed, normative definition of epinician; on the genre's indeterminacy, see e.g. Currie 2005, 21–4 and Cairns 2010, 8–9, 19.
[3] As Cairns 2016, 22 notes, "Greek *elpis* is not coextensive with the English-language concept of hope". Different aspects of *elpis* may be emphasised in different contexts, and its precise connotations may depend on grammatical form (noun *elpis* or verb *elpomai*; singular or plural). See Theunissen 2002, 307–52 and Cairns 2016, 16–22.

way, I hope to suggest that Pindar's poetry can provide some historical perspective on the vexed question of whether or not hope is an emotion.[4]

1 *Nemean* 11: Positive and negative Hope?

The first poem with which I am concerned, *Nemean* 11, is not properly an epinician in that it did not arise from an athletic success, but it does celebrate a particular achievement, and in doing so it deploys many of the themes and techniques familiar from other victory odes.[5] The poem was composed to celebrate the installation of a man named Aristagoras as *prytanis* on the island of Tenedos.[6] Following an exhortation to praise the new magistrate and a catalogue of his successes in local athletic contests (17–21), the poetic speaker takes the unusual[7] step of blaming his parents for their "too hesitant" or "fearful" hopes or expectations (ἐλπίδες ὀκνηρότεραι, 22), which stopped their son from fulfilling his athletic potential at Delphi and Olympia. Had they had more ambitious *elpides* for Aristagoras, he would have had a glorious career in the Panhellenic games (24–9), bringing to fruition the inborn potential which he inherited from his ancestors (33–7).[8] In this context, *elpis* appears to be a stimulus to action, enabling the individual to project her-/himself into the future and to entertain the possibility of success. It is a necessary step in the coming into being of one's *aretē* and the achievement of glory. One might say that the poetic speaker himself demonstrates the very *elpis* which Aristagoras' parents lacked as he narrates the young man's imagined victories in a contra-factual conditional (24–6, "for I swear that, in my judgement, had he gone to Castalia ..."):[9] in implicit contrast to the overly hesitant hopes of verse 22, the speaker boldly visualises a brilliant career for Aristagoras, culminating in a victory *kōmos* at Olympia (27–8).

---

4 On this question in the context of an analysis of Greek poetry, see most recently Cairns 2016, 15–16 and *passim*, with some bibliography. For further discussion of what constitutes an emotion (with a focus on the ancient world), see also e.g. Cairns/Fulkerson 2015.
5 See Currie 2011, 295 and Fearn 2009, 31: in *Nem.* 11, Pindar applies an "enkomiastic paradigm concerning athletics" to what is in fact a political event.
6 On the poem's political and performative contexts, see Hornblower 2004, 143, Fearn 2009, 29–33, Currie 2011, 293–5.
7 Lefkowitz 1979, 53.
8 On inherited excellence in Pindar, see e.g. Boeke 2007, 111–13.
9 Text and translation are taken (with some modifications) from Race 1997.

The imaginary celebrations are suddenly interrupted by a passage which associates hope with boasting and arrogance (29–32):

ἀλλὰ βροτῶν τὸν μὲν κενεόφρονες αὖχαι
ἐξ ἀγαθῶν ἔβαλον· τὸν δ' αὖ καταμεμφθέντ' ἄγαν
ἰσχὺν οἰκείων παρέσφαλεν καλῶν
χειρὸς ἕλκων ὀπίσσω θυμὸς ἄτολμος ἐών.

But the empty-minded boasts of mortals cast one man from success, while a timid spirit, holding back by the hand another man too distrustful of his own strength, deprives him of achievements that belong to him.

These lines are obviously directed to the poem's addressee: although excessive restraint and overly hesitant *elpides* thwarted the development of his inborn excellence, he should avoid the opposite extreme, arrogant confidence, and find a balance between the two. Yet the passage also displays the poetic speaker's consciousness that his own *elpis* for Aristagoras, functioning as a surrogate for his parents' 'timid spirit' (θυμὸς ἄτολμος), is at risk of straying too far into fantasy as he visualises a glorious but now unrealisable career for his addressee. He thus checks himself before overstepping the mark, acknowledging that excessive hope and confidence may be dangerous for a singer as well as for an athlete, and of course, a magistrate. As in the Third *Pythian*, where the poet raises the prospect of eternal life for his patron before vehemently denying that such a thing is possible, the speaker of *Nemean* 11 sings a contra-factual "epinician" celebrating his addressee's imaginary Panhellenic victories, before reminding himself that these did not, and never will, happen. Restraint is necessary in the singer's praise as well as in Aristagoras' ambitions.

In the first half of the third triad (33–42), the speaker situates Aristagoras' family history and achievements in the context of a principle of alternation governing the natural and human worlds. Inborn excellence, such as that possessed by Aristagoras and his relatives, does not produce success in every generation; rather, like the fields and trees, it flowers at changing times and yields fruit of varying worth (37–42). By gaining success in the local games, Aristagoras revived his family's 'ancient virtues' (ἀρχαῖαι ἀρεταί, 37), which had lain dormant like a fallow field; yet his failure to compete in the Panhellenic festivals suggests that in his case, too, the family's inborn excellence has not blossomed to its full potential. The reason for this, as we have seen, was the excessive timidity of his parent's *elpides*, yet this explanation is now complemented with a broader one: human success and failure follow a movement of alternation, and it is Moira,

Fate, who allocates the good and bad gifts sent by Zeus (τὸ δ' ἐκ Διός, 43);[10] humans cannot know in advance whether they will receive one or the other (42–4). In this context of instability and human ignorance, the projection into the future required by the mental act of hoping becomes fraught with uncertainty, and Aristagoras' parents cannot therefore be blamed for the timidity of their aspirations —rather, the speaker suggests that Aristagoras did extremely well given the difficulties involved in human striving.

In the poem's final stanza, the theme of the potential risks of *elpis* reaches its climax. At verse 44, there is a shift in focalisation from the poet's point of view to that of a collective "we" (44–8):

> ἀλλ' ἔμπαν μεγαλανορίαις ἐμβαίνομεν,
> ἔργα τε πολλὰ μενοινῶντες· δέδεται γὰρ ἀναιδεῖ
> ἐλπίδι γυῖα, προμαθείας δ' ἀπόκεινται ῥοαί.
> κερδέων δὲ χρὴ μέτρον θηρευέμεν·
> ἀπροσίκτων δ' ἐρώτων ὀξύτεραι μανίαι.

> And yet we embark on ambitious projects, yearning for many accomplishments. For our limbs are bound to shameless hope, and the streams of forethought lie far off. One must seek due measure of gains; too sharp is the madness of unattainable desires.

Earlier, the speaker had relied on the benefit of hindsight and an elevated poetic perspective to imply, albeit cautiously, that bold *elpides* are a necessary step towards great achievements. Following his emphasis on alternation and humans' lack of foresight at verses 41–4, he now adopts a broader perspective —which we may understand variously as encompassing himself, the chorus, the audience, and/or humanity as a whole—[11] to demonstrate that the "self-confident ambitions"[12] upon which we "embark", "bound" by "shameless" hope, can easily become excessive and lead to painful madness. Without the retrospective knowledge possessed by the speaker at verse 22, it seems impossible to discern whether *elpis* is a positive stimulus to action or, on the contrary, an aimless and potentially destructive projection into an inaccessible future.[13]

---

10 So e.g. Boeke 2007, 35.
11 On the Pindaric first person plural, see most recently Currie 2013, 244 n.7, Maslov 2015, 102, and in more detail, Neumann-Hartmann 2005. At 157–8, she includes *Nem.* 11.43–5 in a list of passages in which the first person plural refers to the collective of humans as defined by their mortality (the 'mortal tribe', θνατὸν ἔθνος, of *Nem.* 11.42). As she notes, the clearest example of this is *Nem.* 6.1–7.
12 Verdenius 1988, 113.
13 As for instance in *Ol.* 12, where human hopes, instead of following a stable course towards their outcome, 'roll' up and down (πόλλ' ἄνω, τὰ δ' αὖ κάτω ... κυλίνδοντ' ἐλπίδες, 6–6a) and

One is reminded here of the pivotal moment in Solon's *Elegy to the Muses* (fragment 13 West) where the poetic speaker's authoritative analysis of divine justice suddenly moves into a depiction of apparently arbitrary suffering from the perspective of a generalising "we".[14] In this passage, too, the collective of humankind is characterised by a propensity to hope (Sol. 13.33–6W):

θνητοὶ δ' ὧδε νοέομεν ὁμῶς ἀγαθός τε κακός τε,
†ἐν δηνην† αὐτὸς δόξαν ἕκαστος ἔχει,
πρίν τι παθεῖν· τότε δ' αὖτις ὀδύρεται· ἄχρι δὲ τούτου
χάσκοντες κούφαις ἐλπίσι τερπόμεθα.

And thus we mortals, whatever our estate, think that the expectation which each one has [is progressing well?] until he suffers some mishap, and then afterwards he wails. But until then we take eager delight in light hopes.[15]

Here as in *Nem.* 11, there is a close correlation between the negative evaluation of hope and humans' lack of foresight, which is emphasised by the shift in perspective from "I" to "we". For Solon, our hopes are "light" or insubstantial because they bear no necessary relation to the way events will turn out in reality. In *Nem.* 11.45–6, the epithet used to qualify *elpis*, 'shameless' (ἀναιδής), points to a slightly different connotation.[16] As in verse 22, where hopes were "too hesitant", there is an emphasis on proportion: in both passages, the *elpis* depicted by the speaker is one that fails to attain a certain pragmatic and moral measure. An ἀναιδὴς ἐλπίς is literally without shame (*aidōs*), and thus without measure or restraint.[17] As Verdenius and others have seen, the fact that *elpis* binds our limbs need not "imply paralysis, [...] but only inescapable compulsion, [which] may refer to a holding as well as to a moving force".[18] Thus *elpis* is a force which can give

---

easily yield to 'vain lies' (ψεύδη μεταμώνια, 6a). In this poem, however, the benevolent intervention of 'saviour Fortune' (σώτειρα Τύχα, 2) ensures an unexpectedly good outcome. On *elpis* and Tychē in *Ol.* 12, see Strohm 1944, 12–23, Nisetich 1977, 240–3, Theunissen 2002, 372–8, Gentili *et al.* 2013, 584–5.
14 See e.g. Nesselrath 1992 and Gagné 2013, 234–6.
15 Tr. after Gerber 1999.
16 On the significance of the epithets used of hope here and at v.22, and the asymmetry between them, see Theunissen 2002, 360–1 and Adorjáni 2011, 162.
17 Theunissen 2002, 360: "ohne αἰδώς, Scheu [...] und damit ohne Maβ"; see also Šćepanović 2016, 24.
18 Verdenius 1988, 113–14; see also Theunissen 2002, 363–4, followed by Cairns 2016, 36 n.87. On these lines, see also Liberman 2003 and Adorjáni 2011, 163–4; I return to the passage in section 3 below.

rise to excessive and unrestrained ambitions, which in turn may lead to painful madness, as the gap between expectations and outcomes continuously widens.

As Theunissen has shown, however, the poem's final stanza may also imply that the potentially destructive consequences of unrestrained hope can be avoided under certain conditions.[19] The words κερδέων δὲ χρὴ μέτρον θηρευέμεν ('one must seek a measure of gains', 47), suggest the possibility of an *elpis* with measure and *aidōs*, and by implication, some form of grounding in reality. This is provided by *promatheia* ('forethought'), something that is said to be lacking in the case of a shameless hope. The 'streams of forethought' (προμαθείας ... ῥοαί, 46) lie far off, but they are not technically beyond our reach:[20] *promatheia* does not denote the absolute knowledge of the future which is reserved to the gods; rather, it is a kind of intelligence, stemming from learning (*mathēsis*) or experience, which provides us with a limited insight into the outcome of our actions.[21] An *elpis* which strikes the balance between overly hesitant and shameless hope is one that is guided, so to speak, by a combination of *aidōs* and *promatheia*. The relationship between the two concepts is somewhat uncertain,[22] but if Theunissen's analysis is correct, then *elpis*, when experienced by someone who possesses (and makes use of) *promatheia* and observes due *aidōs*, may be seen as a limited but possible avenue into an otherwise impenetrable future. Looking back at the overly hesitant hopes of *Nem.* 11.22, one may speculate that Aristagoras' parents displayed requisite (or perhaps excessive) *aidōs*, but did not have the *promatheia* which would have enabled them to project themselves into the future and to consider a different, more ambitious course of action for their son.[23] By contrast, the

---

19 Theunissen 2002, 364–5.
20 See Verdenius 1988, 115, Theunissen 2002, 364–5, and Šćepanović 2016, 27: "there are several Pindaric passages in which the poet praises those who successfully exercise μέτρον, προμάθεια, and αἰδώς".
21 Cairns 1993, 177: *promatheia* is "[t]he intelligence [...] which enables one to foresee the consequences of one's actions and properly to characterize one's conduct"; see also Theunissen 2002, 353.
22 See *Ol.* 7.43–4, where *aidōs* has been understood e.g. as "possessed by", or "directed to" someone who is προμηθής, or as "born of Prometheus". See Cairns 1993, 176 n.107, Theunissen 2002, 355–6, Moore 2015, 392–5, and Šćepanović 2016, 31–4 for differing interpretations.
23 In contrast to *Nem.* 11, see *Isthm.* 1, where the victor's father Asopodorus is said to have acquired *promatheia* from his past misfortunes (36–40) and, it is implied, used it to encourage his son Herodotus' athletic endeavour (41–2). The latter's effort was received favourably by Poseidon (52–4) and allows him to entertain further hopes of success (64–7): he is "lifted on the splendid wings" of the Muses, which recall the flight of hope in *Pythian* 8.90 or the "winged hope" of Bacchyl. 3.75 — see section 3 below. On *promatheia* in *Isthm.* 1, see e.g. Instone 1996, 182–3, Theunissen 2002, 357–8, Moore 2015, 389–92, and Šćepanović 2016, 28–30.

poem's speaker displays both *promatheia* and *aidōs*: with the benefit of hindsight, he is able to imagine the successes that Aristagoras could have gained, but he also checks himself before going too far into fantasy. Yet this poetic stance seems far removed from the reality of human striving. The fact that the speaker's short "epinician" for Aristagoras celebrates victories which did not, and cannot happen, emphasises the gulf which separates human ambitions from their outcomes. Although the poem does seem to imply the possibility of a hope which drives mortals to push their existential limits and attain the heights of human achievement, the audience are not told how to reach the "streams of forethought". Instead, *Nem.* 11 ends on the bleak picture of the collective "we" of humanity utterly dominated by uncontrollable emotion and the sharp pain which it brings.

2 *Elpis, erōs*, and the gods

In the closing lines of *Nem.* 11, shameless *elpis* is associated with *erōs*, "desire": if we do not manage to attain a "measure of gains", then we may experience the 'too sharp madness of unattainable desires' (ἀπροσίκτων δ' ἐρώτων ὀξύτεραι μανίαι, 48). The combination of *elpis* and *erōs* in a process of gradual mental deterioration recalls a passage of Diodotus' speech in Thucydides 3.45.5: humans are, by nature, encouraged to take risks by a sequence of desire and hope, "the first leading and the second following; the first thinking out the plan and the second suggesting that fortune will be kind".[24] Yet the clearest parallel is to be found in the second *stasimon* of Sophocles' *Antigone*, where both concepts occur in a context of human blindness and *atē*, the process combining disaster and the god-sent delusion leading to it (615–17):[25]

ἁ γὰρ δὴ πολύπλαγκτος ἐλ –
πὶς πολλοῖς μὲν ὄνησις ἀνδρῶν,

---

[24] I translate following Hornblower 1991, 437. It is interesting that in Thucydides, *erōs* is followed by *elpis* rather than the other way around (see also 4.108.4). As Stahl 2003, 120–1 puts it, "desire dictates the goal of the action and *only then* does hope of success command the intellect to look for reasons that also make the undertaking seem practicable in respect to supposedly objective facts." (his italics). In Pindar, the sequence is never as clearly defined, but *elpis* can certainly function autonomously (without *erōs*) and as the initial stimulus of an action.

[25] See e.g. Hornblower 2004, 71–2, discussing *elpis* in Pindar, Sophocles, and Thucydides. On *elpis* in Thucydides, see Lateiner and Tsoumpra (this volume) and below. On human blindness and *atē* see *Ant.* 614 and 618–25 with e.g. Easterling 1978 and Cairns 2013.

πολλοῖς δ' ἀπάτα κουφονόων ἐρώτων.

For roaming hope is a benefit to many men, but to many a deception consisting of light-minded desires.[26]

Hope can itself be a positive thing, but it is volatile, and prone to become the "deception of light-minded desires". This negative evaluation of *elpis* has reminded some commentators of the passage from *Ol.* 12 mentioned above.[27] Most interesting, however, is the depiction of *elpis* as a kind of trap behind which lurk desires. Here we may perhaps detect the same process as in *Nem.* 11: as hope becomes unrestrained or shameless, so human desires lose all proportion, seeking the "unattainable". A similar association of excessive hope and desire occurs in the myth of Coronis in *Pythian* 3.19–25:

> ἀλλά τοι
> ἤρατο τῶν ἀπεόντων· οἷα καὶ πολλοὶ πάθον.
> ἔστι δὲ φῦλον ἐν ἀνθρώποισι ματαιότατον,
> ὅστις αἰσχύνων ἐπιχώρια παπταίνει τὰ πόρσω,
> μεταμώνια θηρεύων ἀκράντοις ἐλπίσιν.
> ἔσχε τοι ταύταν μεγάλαν ἀυάταν
> καλλιπέπλου λῆμα Κορωνίδος.

> No, [Coronis] was in love with things remote — such longings as many others have suffered, for there is among mankind a very foolish race, who scorns what is at hand and peers at things far away, chasing the impossible with hopes unfulfilled.[28]

Here again, excessive *erōs* and *elpis* have their roots in the weakness of the human intellect.[29] As in the second *stasimon* of *Antigone*, they are associated with *atē* (24), which makes humans blind to the dangerous desires hiding behind an attractive but empty *elpis*. Under compulsion from her "desire for things far away", Coronis loses control of her mind.[30] She yields to errors (ἀμπλακίαισι, 13),[31] which lead her to scorn what is close at hand (Apollo) in order to pursue (θηρεύων, see *Nem.* 11.47) what is far away — she sleeps with a stranger from

---

26 Tr. Easterling 1978.
27 See e.g. Easterling 1978, 153 and Hornblower 2004, 71.
28 On ἄκραντος see Theunissen 2002, 367. The word, from κραίνω, 'accomplish', 'come to pass', may perhaps be understood as suggesting that Coronis' hopes were in a sense destined to remain unfulfilled; compare e.g. Aesch. *Ag.* 249.
29 This vision of human perception is contrasted with Apollo's omniscient mind; see *Pyth.* 3.27–31.
30 Theunissen 2002, 368.
31 Compare Bacchyl. 3.75 and 9.18, *elpis* "undoes" or "steals away" humans' "thought" (νόημα).

Arcadia (25–6).³² Later in the poem, the audience is told the story of her son Asclepius: 'bound by gain' (κέρδει ... σοφία δέδεται, 54), he attempted to bring a corpse back to life —the "vain goal of empty hopes", Pindar says elsewhere (*Nemean* 8.44–5)— and was brought down by Zeus. Similarly, Coronis is destroyed by a combination of unrestrained desires and impossible hopes.

Yet there is another side to the poem's presentation of *elpis*. Towards the end, a different hope is voiced by the speaker (110–11):

εἰ δέ μοι πλοῦτον θεὸς ἁβρὸν ὀρέξαι,
ἐλπίδ' ἔχω κλέος εὑρέσθαι κεν ὑψηλὸν πρόσω.

But if the god should grant me luxurious wealth, I have hope that in the future I may acquire lofty fame.

In an emphatic first-person singular,³³ the speaker openly expresses *elpis* that his ambitious desire for lofty *kleos* —often understood as the poetic immortality bestowed by the poem itself— be fulfilled.³⁴ Whereas it was deluded of Coronis to long for absent things and to "gaze at what is distant" (22), Pindar introduces an *elpis* that enables one to look far into the future (πρόσω) to the realisation of desire. In contrast to Coronis, who scorned Apollo's attentions and attempted to elude his gaze (27), the speaker combines his expression of hope with a mention of the god in a conditional, placing fulfilment in his hands.³⁵ The role of the divine is primarily to grant wealth and success; yet by appealing to the god, the speaker also acknowledges that human prosperity depends on him, and thereby

---

32 Compare *Pyth.* 3.59–60. On the near-far polarity in Pindar and its association with transgression and desire, see Hubbard 1985, 11–27, with 24 and Young 1968, 35–6 on Coronis specifically. As Young notes, the object of Coronis' desire (τῶν ἀπεόντων) is ambiguous: the word may be both a neuter ("distant things") and a masculine ("absent men"). This passage finds a striking parallel in Thuc. 6.13–24. Nicias, in his attempt to dissuade the Athenians to undertake the Sicilian expedition, calls them δυσέρωτας ... τῶν ἀπόντων (6.13.1), yet he ultimately fails to rid them of their desire (ἐπιθυμία, 6.24.2) for it. Instead, an *erōs* to sail fell upon them (6.24.3), partly consisting of (and/or encouraged by) a yearning for distant sights (τῆς ... ἀπούσης πόθῳ ὄψεως καὶ θεωρίας) and hope that they would be safe (they are εὐέλπιδες ... σωθήσεσθαι). On the "Pindaric theme" (Hornblower 2008, 362) in Thuc. 6, see Young 1968, 117, 120 n.18 and Hornblower 2004, 72–3 and 2008, 335–6, 360–3 (with further parallels and bibliography).
33 On the "first-person indefinite" and the relevance of these words to Hieron and beyond, see e.g. Burton 1962, 88–9, Young 1968, 60–1. On the long-standing (and still ongoing) debate about the nature of the Pindaric first person; see most recently Currie 2013 and Lattmann 2016, with bibliography.
34 Poetic immortality: Young 1968, 60–3 and 68, Robbins 1990, 317, Gentili *et al.* 2006, 80.
35 Theunissen 2002, 370–1.

legitimises his own and his patron's far-reaching *elpis*. In this way, it is hoped, their striving will be kept on a stable, divinely sanctioned course, avoiding the pitfalls of illusion and false desires.

The essential role of divine favour in the fulfilment of human hopes and desires is again evident in *Olympian* 13. The poem's myth recalls how Bellerophon longed to yoke Pegasus (63–4), and was decisively helped in this task by Athena's gift of a bridle which allowed him to obtain the object of his desire (65–86).[36] The story leads the speaker to reflect on the gods' superior abilities (83):

τελεῖ δὲ θεῶν δύναμις καὶ τὰν παρ' ὅρκον καὶ παρὰ ἐλπίδα κούφαν κτίσιν.

The gods' power easily brings into being even what one would swear impossible and beyond hope.

The gods can achieve anything easily,[37] while humans' epistemic limits are such that anything bestowed upon them by the divine comes "beyond hope" or "expectation".[38] Bellerophon's acquisition of Athena's bridle illustrates the wondrous results of the convergence of human striving and divine help, a theme which returns at the end of the poem (104–6):

νῦν δ' ἔλπομαι μέν, ἐν θεῷ γε μὰν
τέλος· εἰ δὲ δαίμων γενέθλιος ἕρποι,
Δὶ τοῦτ' Ἐνυαλίῳ τ' ἐκδώσομεν πράσσειν.

At this point I am hopeful, but with the god is the outcome. But if [the Oligaethidae's] family fortune should continue, we will leave it to Zeus and Enyalius to accomplish.

---

[36] On *Ol.* 13.63-4, see section 3 below.
[37] Compare *Pyth.* 2.49–51: θεὸς ἅπαν ἐπὶ ἐλπίδεσσι τέκμαρ ἀνύεται, / θεός, ὃ καὶ πτερόεντ' αἰετὸν κίχε, καὶ θαλασσαῖον παραμείβεται / δελφῖνα, καὶ ὑψιφρόνων τιν' ἔκαμψε βροτῶν, 'The god accomplishes every purpose just as he wishes, the god, who overtakes the winged eagle and surpasses the seagoing dolphin, and bows down many a haughty mortal'.
[38] The idea of events happening "contrary to" or "beyond" hopes, expectations, or thoughts is common in archaic and classical Greek poetry and drama: see e.g. Archil. 105 & 122W, Thgn. 639–40, Sim. 529*PMG*, *Ol.* 12.10–12a, *Pyth.* 12.28–32, Bacchyl. 3.57–8, Aesch. *Pers.* 1027, Soph. *Aj.* 646–9, 715, *Ant.* 330, 392, Eur. *Hipp.* 1120–1, *Hec.* 680, *Hel.* 1137–43, *Or.* 977–8. On drama, see Fisher and Slater (this volume).

As in *Pyth.* 3.110–11, the speaker projects his *elpis* far into the future, expressing his patron's desire for further success (101–3), yet he recognises that the outcome depends on the gods, thereby placing his hope on a divinely sanctioned course.[39]

A similar dialectic is visible in the Tenth *Nemean*, but in this case it is desire rather than hope that is envisaged as a positive form of striving: after a reminder of the victor Theaius' labours (24) and a catalogue of his victories, the speaker prays to Zeus (29–33):

> Ζεῦ πάτερ, τῶν μὰν ἔραται φρενί, σιγᾷ οἱ στόμα· πᾶν δὲ τέλος
> ἐν τὶν ἔργων· οὐδ' ἀμόχθῳ καρδίᾳ προσφέρων τόλμαν παραιτεῖται χάριν.
> γνῶτ' ἀείδω θεῷ τε καὶ ὅστις ἀμιλλᾶται περὶ
> ἐσχάτων ἀέθλων κορυφαῖς· ὕπατον δ' ἔσχεν Πίσα
> Ἡρακλέος τεθμόν.
>
> Father Zeus, what [Theaius] desires in his heart, his mouth keeps silent. The outcome of everything lies with you. But as he asks for a favour, he offers courage with a heart not unused to pain. The god knows of what I sing, and whoever strives for the peaks of the highest games. Pisa holds the highest ordinances of Heracles.

Here the victor's *erōs* acquires a fully positive value. Like the ideal *elpis* implied but never realised in *Nem.* 11, it is sanctioned both by the victor's experience of victory (24–8) and toil (24, 30), and by the *aidōs* which he displays in repressing the urge to voice (29) his desire for an Olympic victory (31–3). Instead, he turns to the poet as an intermediary to pray for his success (30), acknowledging that fulfilment will come from Zeus, and putting his fate in the god's hands. Theaius' desire, like the speaker's *elpis* at the end of *Pyth.* 3 and *Ol.* 13, is one that is sanctioned by its grounding in the divine. In these three passages, the cloud of uncertainty which shrouded the depictions of hope and desire in *Nem.* 11 is cleared by the stabilising presence of the gods.

3 *Elpis* and *erōs*: Mind and emotion

In this final section, I look briefly at Pindar's depictions of the ways in which hope affects humans physically and/or mentally and attempt, with the help of parallel

---

[39] For a similar "victory wish" involving a far-reaching and ambitious *elpis* dependent on the divine, see *Ol.* 1.106–11: the speaker hopes (ἔλπομαι, 109) to celebrate an even sweeter success for Hieron unless his 'guardian god' (θεὸς ἐπίτροπος, 106) should abandon him. Other such victory wishes may be taken to imply the presence of hope: see e.g. *Pyth.* 5.122–4 and other passages listed and analysed by Hubbard 1995; see also Boeke 2007, 136–7.

passages, to offer some suggestions towards outlining what one might call a Pindaric phenomenology of hope. Indications of the psychosomatic effects of hope are few and far between in his extant poetry, but certain passages provide fascinating glimpses, particularly those where *elpis* is associated or equated with *erōs*. As in Homer and much archaic and classical poetry, *elpis* is connected with the mental or psychic organs, as at *Isthm.* 2.43, where 'envious hopes' (φθονεραί ... ἐλπίδες) are said to hang about the *phrenes* of mortals, or in fragment 214, where hope fosters a man's 'heart' (*kardia*).[40] In this sense, hope is comparable to *erōs*, which Pindar also links to the *phrenes* or the *thumos* (as at *Nem.* 10.29, quoted above, and *Pyth.* 10.59–60).[41] Pindar's poems rarely tell us how *elpis* affects the mind or the body, but one exception is *Pythian* 8.88–94:

> ὁ δὲ καλόν τι νέον λαχών
> ἁβρότατος ἔπι μεγάλας
> ἐξ ἐλπίδος πέταται
> ὑποπτέροις ἀνορέαις, ἔχων
> κρέσσονα πλούτου μέριμναν. ἐν δ' ὀλίγῳ βροτῶν
> τὸ τερπνὸν αὔξεται· οὕτω δὲ καὶ πίτνει χαμαί,
> ἀποτρόπῳ γνώμᾳ σεσεισμένον.

He who has been allotted a new success, at a time of great splendour, takes flight out of hope on the wings of manly deeds, having aspirations superior to wealth. In a short time the delight of mortals burgeons, but so too does it fall to the ground, when shaken by a hostile purpose.

Here, *elpis* grounded in the attainment of athletic achievement is presented as the starting point from which one "takes flight",[42] leading to a short-lived but intense joy (τερπνός). That joy and flying here should be considered as part of the same metaphorical complex as hope is suggested by a number of passages which

---

[40] For *elpis* associated with *phrēn* and/or *kardia* (or *kēr/kear*), see e.g. Hom. *Il.* 21.583, *Od.* 21.157, Bacchyl. 1.160–5, fr. 20b.8, Aesch. *Pers.* 744–50, *Ag.* 11, 992–7, and 1030–4, Soph. *El.* 809–10, Eur. *HF* 746, *Tro.* 681–3, Ar. *Thesm.* 869–70, and see below on *Nem.* 11. In Homer and elsewhere, hope is also frequently associated with other mental organs such as *noos* and *thumos*; see e.g. the discussion in Cairns 2016, 20–2. On mental or psychic organs in general, see Jahn 1987, Schmitt 1990, and Pelliccia 1995 and 2011.

[41] See also *Nem.* 3.26–31, where the poetic speaker addresses his *thumos* because it is experiencing desires for 'foreign things' (ἀλλοτρίων ἔρωτες, 30) which recall Coronis' ἔρως ἀπεόντων in *Pyth.* 3.20. On the *Nem.* 3 passage and other addresses to the mental organs in Pindar, see Pelliccia 1995, 282–306.

[42] See Kirkwood 1982, 213 and Gentili *et al.* 2006, 584: "[l]a preposizione ἐξ indica la causa efficiente [...] e il verbo πέταται acquista un senso quasi passivo, come se fosse 'viene levato in volo'".

use a similar nexus of concepts. One is reminded notably of Bacchylides 13.121–63, where the Trojans, upon learning that Achilles would not be fighting them, are 'inspired with great hopes' (μεγάλαισιν ἐλπίσιν / [πνεί]οντες, 157–8) accompanied by intense joy and relief (121–40).[43] The association of hope with a pleasurable mental or physical state appears again in two passages, *Pythian* 4.201 and fragment 214 (mentioned above), where *elpis* is qualified as "sweet".[44]

Besides these few examples, most of the Pindaric passages analysing the psychosomatic effects of hope occur in contexts where *elpis* is associated with *erōs* or *pothos*. In such cases, hope is usually associated with pain rather than pleasure, and it is set in explicit contrast to reason and rational thinking. In Pindar, desire is generally depicted as more explicitly irruptive than hope; this is clear from the passages quoted above (*Nem.* 3.26–31 and *Pyth.* 10.59–60, where *erōs* "stirs" or "provokes" the minds of young men)[45] as well as from a fragment (123) classified as an encomium, where erotic desire is expressed using metaphors of flooding (4) and melting (10–11). That hope may somehow be emotionalised by desire is suggested by a fragment of Bacchylides (fr. 20b), where *elpis*, in conjunction with erotic desire and wine, is said to make men's hearts 'flutter' (ἐλπ[ὶς <δι>αιθύσσῃ φρέ]νας, 8).[46] All three elements combine together to send their thoughts on high (ὑψο[τάτω πέμπει] μερίμν[ας, 10), just as hope does in *Pyth.*

---

[43] Other relevant passages include Sol. 13.36W, [Aesch.] *PV* 537–8, Eur. *Heracl.* 433–4 (*elpis* and τερπνός or εὐφροσύνη); Aesch. fr. 154a.19–21 and Soph. *El.* 1460–1 (hope as something that 'lifts' or 'raises up' (ἐξαίρω)); Bacchyl. 3.74 (*elpis* as winged); see also *Isthm.* 1.64–8 (n.23 above) where the idea of being lifted on wings (πτερύγεσσιν ἀερθέντ' ἀγλααῖς, 64) may imply the presence of hope. For hope as an emotion prompted by the achievement of great or unusual success, see e.g. Thuc. 4.17.4.
[44] See also *Pyth.* 4.184–5, where Hera "lights up" "sweet longing" for the Argo in the Argonauts (γλυκὺν ... πόθον ἔνδαιεν Ἥρα, 184). Compare e.g. Eur. *Med.* 1035–6 (sweet *elpis*); Bacchyl. 1.163–5, Aesch. *Cho.* 194, Ar. *Thesm.* 869–70 (*elpis* as flattering, caressing, or tickling the heart); *Hom. Hymn Dem.* 37, Soph. *Aj.* 478–9 (*elpis* as warming). On these and other passages, see Cairns 2016, 30–1; on fragment 214 and its context in Plato's *Republic*, see Cannatà Fera 1990, 213–19. For a wonderful modern parallel to the "flutter" of hope, see the following passage of Jane Austen's *Sense and Sensibility*: "Elinor, conning every injunction of distrust, told herself likewise not to hope. But it was too late. Hope had already entered, and feeling all its anxious flutter, she bent over to watch — she hardly knew for what."
[45] The verb used at *Pyth.* 10.60, κνίζω, is used elsewhere of that most irruptive of emotions, anger (ὀργή: *Nem.* 5.32; χόλος: *Pyth.* 11.23), but also, interestingly, of *elpis* at *Isthm.* 5.56–8, on which see Adorjáni 2011, 140–71.
[46] On this passage, see Cairns 2016, 37–8, who comments (38) that "[t]his is perhaps the closest we get to an image of *elpis* as a sudden, irruptive, phenomenologically passive experience of the sort that is figured by the metaphors used of more prototypical emotions". See also Maehler 2004, 248.

8.88–94.⁴⁷ In Pindar, hope and desire are linked in three poems, all of which I have already discussed above. In the myth of Bellerophon in *Ol.* 13, *elpis* is not mentioned explicitly, but παρὰ ἐλπίδα at v.83 may be taken to suggest that hope was also involved in the hero's attempts to acquire Pegasus. Bellerophon's consuming desire is expressed in what almost looks like a pun, emphasising the closeness of longing and suffering: πόλλ' ... ποθέων ἔπαθεν (63–4), 'he suffered much in his yearning'.⁴⁸ Yet Bellerophon's pain, caused by the inability to acquire the object of his desire, ends through the sudden intervention of Athena. This does not happen in the case of Coronis, who is said to have suffered like many before her (οἷα καὶ πολλοὶ πάθον) in her desire for the distant and her unfulfilled hopes. The mention of Coronis' suffering looks forward to her death, which is the result of her delusion; yet it might also be said to refer to the embodied experience of excessive hoping or desiring, which the speaker relates to the *phrenes* (Coronis was seized by 'errors of the mind', ἀμπλακίαισι φρενῶν, 13).

The last relevant poem is *Nemean* 11, where hope, as we have seen, is given a strikingly physical depiction as 'binding' the limbs (γυῖα) of humans. In a way that recalls other, perhaps more prototypical emotions, *elpis* is conceptualised as the active force controlling the passive human subject, leading her/him to act in ways that s/he might not want to. As scholars have noted, the passage is unusual, because hope is normally depicted as affecting the mental organs rather than the limbs.⁴⁹ One explanation, suggested but not developed by Liberman, may be that Pindar is engaging with the traditional Homeric conception of sleep or death as "limb-loosening" or "loosening cares", expressed by the epithet λυσιμελής and formulae such as γυῖα λέλυνται.⁵⁰ Unlike sleep, unrestrained hope does not afford any respite or lead to a collapsing of the body; instead, it keeps us awake in a crazed frenzy as we constantly attempt to close the gap separating us from the object of our desire. Release is provided only by death, which had been mentioned earlier in the poem in connection with 'mortal limbs' (θνατὰ μέλη, 15–16). Λυσιμελής is also used of *erōs* and *pothos* in the *Odyssey* (18.212) and in lyric

---

47 For μέριμνα as 'ambition', 'aspiration' (a positive aspect of the more common meaning 'anxiety', 'care'), see e.g. (besides Bacchyl. 20b10 and *Pyth.* 8.92) *Ol.* 1.108, *Nem.* 3.69 with Thummer 1969, 130–1 and Day 1991, 57–9.
48 See Dickson 1986, 127–8, who notes (128) that "[p]athos and its cognates [...] are generally reserved in Pindar to denote extreme suffering".
49 See e.g. Liberman 2003, 94–5 with n.24.
50 Liberman 2003, 97. On λυσιμελής and its etymology (involving μέλος, limb, but also, already in antiquity, μέλω, to care or be cared for), see Rawles 2015, 134–5. On λυσιμελής in Homer see also e.g. Russo/Fernández-Galiano/Heubeck 1992, 63, 111–12 and Segal 1994, 71.

poetry;⁵¹ thus, if Pindar is indeed alluding to this tradition, he might simultaneously be turning it on its head by suggesting that hope and desire bind rather than loosen the limbs. In any case, one might speculate that this depiction of *elpis* as an embodied experience has to do, once again, with its proximity to *erōs*:⁵² the compulsion of hope on the human body is such that as long as it remains unfulfilled, the sharp pain of desire and the madness to which it gives rise get progressively worse (48).

One might detect a parallel between the poem's final verse ("too sharp is the madness of unattainable desires") and the speaker's earlier prayer that Aristagoras (or "the whole Council")⁵³ 'complete his/their twelve-month term in glory and with heart unwounded' (ἀλλὰ σὺν δόξᾳ τέλος / δωδεκάμηνον περᾶσαι νιν ἀτρώτῳ κραδίᾳ, 9–10). If we accept that these words look forward to the poem's last stanza, then we may perhaps read ἀτρώτῳ κραδίᾳ as referring to the hopes, desires, and ambitions which could "wound" the magistrates by giving rise to pain in their *kradia*. It would make sense, in a poem celebrating an election to political office, to warn against the unrestrained and potentially dangerous ambitions which may lurk behind attractive hopes. If this is accepted, then *Nem.* 11.9–10 provides another small insight into the phenomenology of hope and desire in Pindar. One final observation before closing. As Lefkowitz notes, the speaker of *Nem.* 11 has twice before referred to the human body:⁵⁴ first at v.12, where he praised Aristagoras' 'wonderful body' (θαητὸν δέμας), and then (as I mentioned above) in a warning to the latter to remember that "the limbs he clothes are mortal and that earth is the last garment of all he will wear" (15–16). The reminder that despite his exceptional stock and physical appearance, Aristagoras' 'limbs' (μέλη) will end up being covered in earth underlines the universality of death; in much the same way, the speaker's assertion that our limbs are bound to shameful *elpis* suggests that the process whereby humans succumb to excessive hopes and desires is, to paraphrase Thucydides, one that is inherent to 'human nature' (ἀνθρωπεία φύσις).⁵⁵

---

51 See e.g. Archil. 196W, Sapph. 130L–P, Alcm. 3.61 *PMG*, with Schlesier 1986/7.
52 One interesting passage in this connection is *Il.* 24.514, where the 'desire' (ἵμερος) to weep is conceptualised as something that can enter and then leave the heart and limbs (ἀπὸ πραπίδων ἦλθ' … ἠδ' ἀπὸ γυίων). See the short discussion of Liberman 2003, 96–7.
53 Verdenius 1988, 100, reading the infinitive περᾶσαι rather than the optative περάσαι (which is preferred e.g. by Henry 2005, 124).
54 Lefkowitz 1979, 55.
55 Thuc. 3.45.3–7. Compare 3.45.3, πεφύκασί τε ἅπαντες καὶ ἰδίᾳ καὶ δημοσίᾳ ἁμαρτάνειν ('all men are by nature prone to err, both in private and in public life') and 5, ἥ τε ἐλπὶς καὶ ὁ ἔρως ἐπὶ παντί κτλ. ('then, too, hope and desire are everywhere' etc., tr. Forster Smith) to the

In conclusion, I hope to have shed some light on the rich and variegated representations of hope and desire found in Pindar. In his poems, and particularly the victory odes, *elpis* is inseparable from the ethical, religious, and existential framework which forms the background of human action and deliberation. Because humans are defined by their epistemic limits and have little or no control over the outcome of their actions in a world dominated by the divine, hope is volatile and potentially illusory and dangerous. It can lead to excess, and in some extreme cases, to suffering and destruction. In this sense, Pindar's depictions of hope are similar to those found, for instance, in other archaic and classical poets. Yet his poetry also offers a positive conception of *elpis* as a necessary and desirable drive to action, a means for the individual to conceive, visualise and grasp the possibility of achievement. Although this remains merely a theoretical possibility in *Nemean* 11, a poem dominated by the instability and uncertainty of all human endeavour, a number of victory odes do provide concrete guidance in that direction. In all spheres of life, human action is dependent on divine intervention. It is only by trusting in, and turning to a god who has access to objective reality that humans can stand a chance of avoiding the pitfalls associated with hope and desire, and perhaps be crowned with success. This suggests that in some sense, unrestrained and illusory *elpis* and *erōs* are partly caused by a failure to acknowledge the gods and ask for their favour. In poems such as *Pythian* 3, *Olympian* 13, and *Nemean* 10, Pindar envisages both hope and desire as part of a positive, divinely sanctioned drive for achievement which may, under certain conditions, function as a necessary and even transcendent movement upwards to the very boundaries of the human sphere.

The ambiguity of Pindaric *elpis* is reflected in its phenomenology, of which I have attempted to provide a broad, but necessarily fragmentary sketch. Towards the close of *Pythian* 8, Pindar paints an enthralling depiction of a young man soaring on the wings of hope, suggesting that the experience of divine hope can be a short-lived but intensely joyful one, akin perhaps to the gentle life, the μείλιχος αἰών, which rests with humans when the gods send their brightness upon them (*Pyth.* 8.96–7). Yet the sweetness of hope has its dark obverse, which is linked once again with short-sightedness, excess, and *erōs*: when the human mind yields to unrestrained hope, then we may suffer as we become ever more fixated upon attaining the object of our desire. Particularly when it merges with a bitter and painful *erōs*, *elpis* may bind, hurt, or wound the mental organs and

---

observation of a scholiast commenting on *Nem.* 11.45–6 (Σ 59a Drachmann): δέδεται γὰρ ἀναιδεῖ ἐλπίδι γυῖα· τουτέστιν ἐμπέφυκεν ἡμῖν ἐλπίς ("'our limbs are bound to shameless hope': that is, hope is planted by nature within us").

the body. Although such phenomenological metaphors of *elpis* are few and far between, they do suggest that for Pindar and his audiences, hope could certainly be conceived of as what we would call an emotion.

Bibliography

Adorjáni, Z. 2011. *Auge und Sehen in Pindars Dichtung*, Hildesheim.
Agócs, P./C. Carey/R. Rawles. 2012. *Reading the Victory Ode*, Cambridge.
Boeke, H. 2007. *The Value of Victory in Pindar's Odes: Gnomai, Cosmology and the Role of the Poet*, Leiden.
Burnett, A.P. 2005. *Pindar's Songs for Young Athletes of Aigina*, Oxford.
Burton, R.W.B. 1962. *Pindar's Pythian Odes*, Oxford.
Cairns, D.L. 1993. *Aidōs: The Psychology and Ethics of Honour and Shame in Ancient Greek Literature*, Oxford.
—— 2010. *Bacchylides: Five Epinician Odes*, Cambridge.
—— 2013. "Introduction: Archaic Greek Thought and Tragic Interpretation," in: D. Cairns (ed.), *Tragedy and Archaic Greek Thought*, Swansea, ix–liv.
—— 2016. "Metaphors for Hope in Early Greek Poetry," in: R. Caston/R. Kaster (eds.), *Hope, Joy, and Affection in the Classical World*, Oxford/New York, 13–44.
Cairns, D.L./L. Fulkerson. 2015. "Introduction," in: D. Cairns/L. Fulkerson (eds.), *Emotions Between Greece and Rome*, London, 1–22.
Cannatà Fera, M. 1990. *Pindarus Threnorum Fragmenta*, Rome.
Currie, B.G.F.C. 2005. *Pindar and the Cult of Heroes*, Oxford.
—— 2011. "Epinician *Choregia*: Funding a Pindaric Chorus," in: L. Athanassaki/E. Bowie (eds.), *Archaic and Classical Choral Song*, Berlin/New York, 269–310.
—— 2013. "The Pindaric First Person in Flux," in: *Classical Antiquity* 32, 243–82.
Day, J.W. 1991. "The Poet's Elpis and the Opening of Isthmian 8," in: *TAPA* 121, 47–61.
Dickson, K.M. 1986. "Damasiphrōn Khrusos: Act, Implement and Tekhnē in Pindar," in: *Ramus* 15, 122–42.
Easterling, P.E. 1978. "The Second Stasimon of Antigone," in: R. Dawe/J. Diggle/P. Easterling (eds.), *Dionysiaca: Nine Studies in Greek Poetry by Former Pupils Presented to Sir Denys Page on his Seventieth Birthday*, Cambridge, 141–58.
Fearn, D. 2009. "Oligarchic Hestia: Bacchylides 14B and Pindar, Nemean 11," in: *JHS* 129, 23–38.
Gagné, R. 2013. *Ancestral Fault in Ancient Greece*, Cambridge.
Gentili, B. *et al.* 2006[4]. *Pindaro: Le Pitiche*, Milan.
—— *et al.* 2013. *Pindaro: Le Olimpiche*, Milan.
Gerber, D.E. 1999. *Greek Elegiac Poetry*, Cambridge, Mass.
Henry, W.B. 2005. *Pindar's Nemeans: A Selection*, Munich/Leipzig.
Hornblower, S. 1991. *A Commentary on Thucydides*. Volume I, Oxford.
—— 2004. *Thucydides and Pindar: Historical Narrative and the World of Epinician Poetry*, Oxford.
—— 2008. *A Commentary on Thucydides*. Volume III, Oxford.
Hubbard, T.K. 1985. *The Pindaric Mind*, Leiden.
—— 1995. "On Implied Wishes for Victory in Pindar," in: *ICS* 20, 35–56.
Instone, S. 1996. *Pindar: Selected Odes*, Warminster.
Jahn, T. 1987. *Zum Wortfeld* Seele-Geist *in der Sprache Homers*, Munich.

Kirkwood, G. 1982. *Selections from Pindar*, Chico.
Lattmann, C. 2016. "Pindar's Voice(s): The Epinician Persona Reconsidered," in: N.W. Slater (ed.), *Voice and Voices in Antiquity*, Leiden, 123–148.
Lefkowitz, M. 1979. "Pindar's *Nemean* XI," in: *JHS* 99, 49–56.
Liberman, G. 2003. "La XIe *Néméenne* de Pindare, un vers de la dernière épode et le sens de ΓΥΙΑ," in: J. Jouanna/J. Leclant (eds.), *La poésie grecque antique*, Paris, 89–102.
Maehler, H. 2004. *Bacchylides: A Selection*, Cambridge.
Maslov, B. 2015. *Pindar and the Emergence of Literature*, Cambridge.
Moore, C. 2015. "*Promētheia* ('Forethought') Until Plato," in: *AJP* 136, 381–420.
Nesselrath, H.-G. 1992. "Göttliche Gerechtigkeit und das Schicksal des Menschen in Solons Musenelegie," in: *Museum Helveticum* 49, 91–104.
Neumann-Hartmann, A. 2005. "Wenn Pindar 'Wir' sagt: Überlegungen zur 1. Person Plural bei Pindar," in: *Aevum Antiquum* 5, 145–62.
Nisetich, F.J. 1977. "The Leaves of Triumph and Mortality: Transformation of a Traditional Image in Pindar's *Olympian* 12," in: *TAPA* 107, 235–64.
Pattison, G. 2015. *Eternal God, Saving Time*, Oxford.
Pelliccia, H. 1995. *Mind, Body, and Speech in Homer and Pindar*, Göttingen.
–– 2011. "Mental Organs," in: M. Finkelberg (ed.), *The Homer Encyclopedia*, Volume II, London, 509–10.
Péron, J. 1974. *Les images maritimes de Pindare*, Paris.
Pfeijffer, I.L. 1999. *Three Aeginetan Odes of Pindar: A Commentary on Nemean V, Nemean III, & Pythian VIII*, Leiden.
Race, W.H. 1997. *Pindar*, Volumes I & II, Cambridge, Mass.
Rawles, R.R. 2015. "Lysimeleia (Thucydides 7.53, Theocritus 16.84): What Thucydides does not tell us about the Sicilian Expedition," in: *JHS* 135, 132–46.
Robbins, E. 1990. "The Gifts of the Gods: Pindar's Third *Pythian*," in: *CQ* 40, 307–18.
Russo, J./M. Fernández-Galiano/A. Heubeck 1992. *A Commentary on Homer's Odyssey*, Volume II, Oxford.
Šćepanović, S. 2016. "Wisdom and Human Temporality in Pindar's Victory Odes," in: *Antike und Abendland* 62, 18–37.
Schlesier, R. 1986/7. "Der bittersüsse Eros: Ein Beitrag zur Geschichte und Kritik des Metapherbegriffs," in: *Archiv für Begriffsgeschichte* 30, 70–83.
Schmitt, A. 1990. *Selbständigkeit und Abhängigkeit menschlichen Handelns bei Homer. Hermeneutische Untersuchungen zur Psychologie Homers (Abhandlungen der geistes- und sozialwissenschaftlichen Klasse)*, Mainz/Stuttgart.
Segal, C.P. 1994. *Singers, Heroes, and Gods in the Odyssey*, Ithaca.
Stahl, H.-P. 2003. *Thucydides: Man's Place in History*, Swansea.
Strohm, H. 1944. *Tyche: Zur Schicksalsauffassung bei Pindar und den frühgriechischen Dichtern*, Stuttgart.
Theunissen, M. 2002². *Pindar: Menschenlos und Wende der Zeit*, Munich.
Thummer, E. 1969. *Pindar: Die Isthmischen Gedichte*. Band II, Heidelberg.
Verdenius, W.J. 1988. *Commentaries on Pindar*, Volume II, Leiden.
Young, D.C. 1968. *Three Odes of Pindar: A Literary Study of Pythian 11, Pythian 3 and Olympian 7*, Leiden.

Nick Fisher
Hope and Hopelessness in Euripides

> "Hope" is the thing with feathers
> That perches in the soul
> And sings the tune without the words
> And never stops — at all
> And sweetest — in the Gale — is heard
> And sore must be the storm
> That could abash the little Bird
> That kept so many warm.
> Emily Dickinson
>
> Woody Allen, *Without Feathers,* (New York, 1975)

1 Introduction

This chapter focuses on the representation, in three of Euripides' most 'tragic' plays, of such "sore storms" which so "abash" Emily Dickinson's little song bird that they silence her and produce reactions which chime more with the attitude encapsulated in the title of Woody Allen's 1975 early collection of comic pieces. It will be concerned with *elpis* as hope for better in bad times, not with *elpis* as expectation, negative as well as positive; it will focus on how beliefs, well grounded or not, about the future produce, or are produced by, positive or negative feelings; the impact on such emotions of beliefs about the justice or reciprocity of men or gods; and the actions and reactions which these feelings and beliefs lead to.[1] More particularly, I shall consider hopelessness, an emotional response of despair based on the cognition of desperate situations, in *Hecuba*, *Troades* (briefly) and *Heracles*.[2] In the first, probably performed in the later 420s, the central character, rendered desperate and furious by cumulative disasters, especially the killings of Polyxena and Polydorus, seizes the chance for revenge for one of these deaths, with no hope of gain beyond the immediate pleasure of a revenge and a chance to gloat. The debate will concern how far her despair and the absence of any prospect of help from gods or men may be felt to justify her act, or

---

[1] So there will be little attention to the fear that positive *elpis* may be a dangerous temptation leading to miscalculation. See Introduction and Lateiner's chapter in this volume.
[2] For comedy's awareness of Euripides' treatement of hope and hopelessness, cf. Slater, this volume.

whether her inhuman revenge removes some or all of the audience's sympathy. Next it will look briefly at a second play set at the end of the Trojan War, *Troades* of 415, arguably the play with the greatest amount of despair at the final destruction of a whole community, with no hope for any amelioration at the end. And finally, it will consider the *Heracles* (composed at much the same time as *Troades*), whose distinctive structure sees the most violent switches of emotional temperature in any surviving tragedy, from well-grounded despair and an intense debate on the rationality of hope in extremis, to an unexpected salvation and new hope, to an even more unexpected and terrible disaster directly imposed by gods; this leads finally into a decision to resist suicide and live on, in response to a generous display of friendship, but with no hope for a less miserable life.

2 Hecuba

William Arrowsmith's introduction to the Chicago translation of the play stated:

> [The gods'] justice is so alien, so slow, so indifferent, as to make it impossible even the hope of communication or understanding. But man continues to demand justice and an order with which he can live, and it is the nobility of this demand, maintained against the whole tenor of his experience, in the teeth of the universal indifference and the inconstancy of fortune, that in Euripides makes man tragic. His suffering is limited only by his hope; take away his hope, as Hecuba's was taken, and he forfeits his humanity, destroyed by the hideous gap between his illusion and the intolerable reality.
>
> (Arrowsmith 1958, 6)

Arrowsmith thus identified a central conceptual connection between the removal of hope from Hecuba and her inhuman revenge. To assess this, I shall start by looking at the explicit uses of *elpis*-words and related terms, in order to trace the progressive removal of all hope. In the first scene between Hecuba and the chorus, she struggles to stay upright,[3] and is tormented by grief and fear of a further catastrophe, hinted at in her dreams,[4] and soon confirmed by the chorus' report of the Greek debate; her lyric anapaests cover a full range of emotional deprivation and desperation in a series of remarkable staccato, repetitive phrases.

---

3 For most of the play, Hecuba stumbles lamely, lies prostrate, or humbles herself in multiple supplications: see Michelini 1987, 173–7, Zeitlin 1996, 207–11 on the uses of her body.

4 The dream-visions of Polyxena's sacrifice (90–97, also 74–5) are probably later actors' interpolations: cf. Diggle's and Kovacs' texts, and Collard *ad loc.*

> τίς ἀμύνει μοι; ποία γενεά,
> ποία δὲ πόλις; φροῦδος πρέσβυς,
> φροῦδοι παῖδες.
> ποίαν ἢ ταύταν ἢ κείναν
> στείχω; ποῖ δὴ σωθῶ; ποῦ τις
> θεῶν ἢ δαίμων ἐπαρωγός;
> ὦ κάκ' ἐνεγκοῦσαι
> Τρωιάδες, ὦ κάκ' ἐνεγκοῦσαι
> πήματ', ἀπωλέσατ' ὠλέσατ'· οὐκέτι μοι βίος
> ἀγαστὸς ἐν φάει.
>
> Who is protecting me? What family,
> what city? Gone is the old man,
> gone the children. What path can I take, here,
> or there: Where will I be safe? Where is there
> god or power to bring help?
> Endurers of pain,
> Trojan women, endurers of pain,
> you've brought full ruin, ruin; I have life no more,
> no joy in the daylight. (153–68).

Second, early in Polyxena's *rhesis* expressing her readiness for self-sacrifice, her absence of any hope justifies her longing for death: at 349–66, she contrasts the high hopes (ἐλπίδων καλῶν ὕπο) of a good marriage at her upbringing with her only prospect now: a life as a maltreated slave of drudgery and forced sex with a low-born fellow slave.[5] In a way comparable to Megara's position in *Heracles* (cf. below), she asks Odysseus:

> ἄγ' οὖν μ', Ὀδυσσεῦ, καὶ διέργασαί μ' ἄγων·
> οὔτ' ἐλπίδος γὰρ οὔτε του δόξης ὁρῶ
> θάρσος παρ' ἡμῖν ὥς ποτ' εὖ πρᾶξαί με χρή.
>
> Come then, Odysseus, take me away and finish me off.
> For I see no confidence in my position, grounds
> for hope or belief that I should ever be happy. (369–72)

Third, Hecuba, having heard of Polyxena's noble death, is unexpectedly presented with a fresh corpse: not Polyxena, nor Cassandra as she then suspects, but Polydorus. The *therapaina* tells her:

> ζῶσαν λέλακας, τὸν θανόντα δ' οὐ στένεις
> τόνδ'· ἀλλ' ἄθρησον σῶμα γυμνωθὲν νεκροῦ,

---

5 Cf. Lloyd 2013, 211.

εἴ σοι φανεῖται θαῦμα καὶ παρ' ἐλπίδας.

> She you speak of is living, but you're not mourning
> this dead one: look now at the naked body of this corpse,
> see, it will astonish you, against your hopes. (678–80)

Hecuba's response to this further blow to her hopes conveys her incomprehension and desolation, in further staccato, broken, language: she is "destroyed", "I no longer live", "unbelievable, unbelievable", "new evils after evils"; "no day without grief, tears" (689–720). She is especially shocked by the atrocity of Polymestor's act, shamelessly butchering a boy in his charge, a crime against his close *xenoi*, for greed and political advantage: a breakdown of the most fundamental trust. Her language of dislocation, of the unspeakable, reflects her moral horror at the end of justice, reciprocity or law (*xenia, dike, nomos*).[6]

Correspondingly, Hecuba is repeatedly described as the most miserable or most unfortunate of women, by the *therapaina* (658), the chorus (721–2) and by Agamemnon (785). Her response to Agamemnon's comment is striking:

> Αγ. φεῦ φεῦ· τίς οὕτω δυστυχὴς ἔφυ γυνή;
> Εκ. οὐκ ἔστιν, εἰ μὴ τὴν Τύχην αὐτὴν λέγοις

> Ag. 'What woman was ever so unfortunate (*dystuches*)?',
> Hec. 'There is no one, unless you would mention Tuche herself'

She appears to identify herself as the equivalent of the personification of *Tuche*, a prime exemplar of the patterns of randomly imposed and inexplicable misfortunes in the world.[7] Thus her sense of a justified hopelessness is acknowledged as reasonable even by her enemy and master.

In this state of complete absence of hope, her strength of character is immediately reasserted. As soon as Agamemnon appears, she plans how to achieve

---

6 Cf. especially Nussbaum 1986, 408.
7 Cf. on *tuche* in the play, especially Talthybios at 487–91; Reckford 1985, 121–3, Nussbaum 1986, 408–9, Mossman 1995, 111. In this sense, *tuche* is fully compatible with necessity (*anagke*): events which seem inevitable when they have happened may remain incomprehensible to human understanding: cf. Guthrie 1965, 159–67, 414–9, on chance and necessity in Empedocles and the Atomists, and Williams 1993, 103–5 noting expressions such as 'necessary Chance', *anagkaia tuche*, e.g. Soph. *Ajax* 485, 803, *El.* 48, Eur. *I.A.* 511. On *anagke* in the play, see also Mossman 1995, 83.

revenge,⁸ and on his arrival she determines to attempt a supplication to aid that purpose. A commitment to revenge by any means may be hinted at even earlier, in her frantic appeal to her dead son:

ὦ τέκνον τέκνον,
αἰαῖ, κατάρχομαι νόμον
βακχεῖον, ἐξ ἀλάστορος
ἀρτιμαθὴς κακῶν

O child, child,
alas I start up the bacchic tune/law (*nomos*),
learning late of the evils
from an avenging spirit (*alastor*)   (684–7)

This may suggest no more than that she will begin a wild bacchic-song (*nomos*= 'tune'), having just learnt of the latest blow sent by the avenging curse (*alastor*) on all Trojans; this is how the chorus' response ("you realise then your son's *ate*", 688) seems to take it (cf. Mossman 1995, 167). But it may contain an additional, more sinister, implication, as Nussbaum (1986, 409) and Burnett (1998, 164) suspect: *nomos* there may also hint at the idea of a 'law', which is derived from an *alastor*, a spirit of vengeance: thus she may be already thinking of her revenge, rather than merely recognising that her family and city are still cursed;⁹ if so, the 'bacchic' song/law hints at the wild Dionysiac frenzy of collective female violence which will follow.¹⁰ There is no doubt, however, that Hecuba's drive for revenge above everything else becomes explicit in the scene with Agamemnon, first in her aside at 749–51 ("I would not be able to achieve revenge for my children without him"), carried on at 756–7 ("Having avenged myself on evil men, I am willing to be a slave for the rest of my life"),¹¹ and then again at 786–92 ("you [Agamemnon] be the avenger for me on that man"). Mossman (1995, 180–1) argues that the "indirect and almost casual" introduction of the revenge-plan, with no internal debate,¹² suggests that the audience would find her drive for revenge readily

---

8 As the editors remind me, in Aristotle's discussion of anger in the *Rhetoric* 'on every form of anger there [necessarily] follows pleasure derived from the hope for revenge' (καὶ πάσῃ ὀργῇ ἕπεσθαί τινα ἡδονήν, τὴν ἀπὸ τῆς ἐλπίδος τοῦ τιμωρήσασθαι) (Arist. *Rh*. 1378b1–4).
9 At 708–805 she appeals explicitly to the 'Law' (*nomos*) even more powerful than the gods, which would insist on retaliatory justice, without which nothing is safe.
10 Cf. especially 1075–8 with Segal 1993, 179–81, and on the Thracian Dionysos in the play as a whole, Zeitlin 1996, 172–216.
11 If these lines can be retained, with some transpositions, see Collard *ad loc*. Cf. Reckford 1985, 123.
12 She contrasts the case of Medea, but her revenge plan includes the killing of her own children as well as that of an innocent princess.

comprehensible and unproblematic. At this stage, it is not clear what form her revenge will take, and it might seem possible that she might achieve it through the agency of what passed for order at that time and place, the 'military law' of Agamemnon and the Greek army.[13] I would agree that all or most observers in the theatre would find her desire for revenge appropriate; but it does not follow that they would all remain content with the achievement of her revenge by any means whatsoever.

Fourth, Hecuba uses *elpizein* in her increasingly passionate and desperate supplication speech to Agamemnon. When she feels it is not going well, as Agamemnon seeks to break away from the physical contact of supplication,[14] she comments bitterly that in general through inadequate rhetorical training people are the less able to persuade others to do what they want; but she then corrects any implication this may give that she might have hopes for a better life:

τί οὖν ἔτ' ἄν τις ἐλπίσαι πράξειν καλῶς;
οἱ μὲν γὰρ ὄντες παῖδες οὐκέτ' εἰσί μοι,
αὐτὴ δ' ἐπ' αἰσχροῖς αἰχμάλωτος οἴχομαι,
καπνὸν δὲ πόλεως τόνδ' ὑπερθρώισκονθ' ὁρῶ.

But how could one hope yet to do well?
The children I had are no more alive,
I myself am gone, a slave-prisoner on shameful terms,
and I see the smoke here leaping over the city.   (820–3)

What she wants goes no further than her revenge; everything else in her life is without hope. She has no children left, only a life as a slave, and the city is ablaze. Hence any adverse consequences of an attempt at revenge could not make anything worse.

Fifth and finally, a very short choral song predicts death and despair for Polymestor, as he has entered the tent with Hecuba.

---

13 If, as seems probable, the story of Polymestor's murder of Polydorus was a Euripidean invention, they would have had no advance awarenesss of the nature of her revenge: cf. e.g. Collard 1991, 32–4.

14 Gould (2000, 41–2, n. 55) held that Hecuba does not complete the physical rite of supplication at 753–4, but the references to knees, chin and hand are still only 'figurative'; she approaches his knees again at 787–9, but Agamemnon evidently moves away at 812, and formal supplication is not completed until 841–51. But the scene may be read differently, so that she does make physical contact at 753, is still in contact with the knees at 787, but Agamermnon does not respond, but is seen to try to evade the commitment at 812; as she increases her rhetorical efforts and gets more desperate in her pleas, Agamemnon accepts it at 851 as he offers his cautious and limited assistance. Cf. Michelini 1987, 174–6.

οὔπω δέδωκας ἀλλ' ἴσως δώσεις δίκην·
ἀλίμενόν τις ὡς ἐς ἄντλον πεσὼν
λέχριος ἐκπεσῆι φίλας καρδίας,
ἀμέρσας βίον. τὸ γὰρ ὑπέγγυον
Δίκαι καὶ θεοῖσιν οὐ ξυμπίτνει,
ὀλέθριον ὀλέθριον κακόν.
ψεύσει σ' ὁδοῦ τῆσδ' ἐλπὶς ἥ σ' ἐπήγαγεν
θανάσιμον πρὸς Ἀίδαν, ὦ τάλας,
ἀπολέμωι δὲ χειρὶ λείψεις βίον.

You have not yet paid the penalty, but perhaps you will;
like someone falling into the bilge far from harbour
you will fall sideways from your heart's aim,
having removed a life. For where liability
to Justice and the gods fall together,
a destructive, destructive evil results.
The hope which brought you on this road will cheat you
down to deadly Hades, wretched man,
and you will leave your life by an unwarlike hand.   (1024–34)

Like a shipwrecked sailor, Polymestor, they suppose (inaccurately), will go to his just death at the hands of 'unwarlike' women. Unlike Hecuba, he arrived on this scene full of the greedy and foolish hope that he could trust Hecuba's promise of entrusting more Trojan wealth to him.[15] When he next appears, blinded and in great pain and grief, his first desire is for death (1099–1106), and later, like Hecuba, he lives only to insult and pain his tormentor and to look for revenge. So as Hecuba has herself successively lost all hope, and has suppressed all emotions beneath the single desire for revenge, her act has correspondingly denied Polymestor all his hopes.

So now in the light of this representation of cumulatively dashed hopes, we may consider the moral acceptability of Hecuba's revenge and the development of her character. Much of the debate focuses on elements of the final encounter between the two.

Εκ. ἀλγεῖς; τί δ'; ἦ 'μὲ παιδὸς οὐκ ἀλγεῖν δοκεῖς;
Πο. χαίρεις ὑβρίζουσ' εἰς ἔμ', ὦ πανοῦργε σύ.
Εκ. οὐ γάρ με χαίρειν χρή σε τιμωρουμένην;
Πο. ἀλλ' οὐ τάχ', ἡνίκ' ἄν σε ποντία νοτίς ...
Εκ. μῶν ναυστολήσηι γῆς ὅρους Ἑλληνίδος;

---

15 Collard (*ad loc.*) well compares Eur. *Suppl.* 479, fr. 650 for deceitful hope. Zeitlin (1996, 184–5) observes that the nautical image of falling at sea also foreshadows the fate he predicts for Hecuba.

Πο. κρύψηι μὲν οὖν πεσοῦσαν ἐκ καρχησίων.
Εκ. πρὸς τοῦ βιαίων τυγχάνουσαν ἁλμάτων;
Πο. αὐτὴ πρὸς ἱστὸν ναὸς ἀμβήσηι ποδί.
Εκ. ὑποπτέροις νώτοισιν ἢ ποίωι τρόπωι;
Πο. κύων γενήσηι πύρσ' ἔχουσα δέργματα.
Εκ. πῶς δ' οἶσθα μορφῆς τῆς ἐμῆς μετάστασιν;
Πο. ὁ Θρηιξὶ μάντις εἶπε Διόνυσος τάδε.
Εκ. σοὶ δ' οὐκ ἔχρησεν οὐδὲν ὧν ἔχεις κακῶν;
Πο. οὐ γάρ ποτ' ἂν σύ μ' εἷλες ὧδε σὺν δόλωι.
Εκ. θανοῦσα δ' ἢ ζῶσ' ἐνθάδ' ἐκπλήσω †βιον†;
Πο. θανοῦσα· τύμβωι δ' ὄνομα σῶι κεκλήσεται ...
Εκ. μορφῆς ἐπωιδὸν μή τι τῆς ἐμῆς ἐρεῖς;
Πο. κυνὸς ταλαίνης σῆμα, ναυτίλοις τέκμαρ.
Εκ. οὐδὲν μέλει μοι, σοῦ γέ μοι δόντος δίκην.

Hec. You feel pain? Well? Don't you think I feel pain for my son?
Pol. You rejoice in insulting me, you villain?
Hec. Shouldn't I rejoice in taking revenge on you?
Pol. Soon you won't, when the sea-waters...
Hec. Won't they carry me by ship to Greece's borders?
Pol. Will hide you when you fall from the masthead
Hec. Compelled to a jump by whose violence?
Pol. You'll climb yourself on foot up the ship's mast
Hec. With wings of my back or by what means?
Pol. You'll become a bitch with a blood-shot glare.
Hec. How do you know of this change in my shape?
Pol. The Thracian prophet Dionysos said this
Hec. Did he not foretell to you any of the evils you have?
Pol. No, or you would not have taken me with your tricks
Hec. Dying or living here shall I complete my <?fate>?
Pol. Dying; a name will be given over your tomb
Hec. You don't mean a name sung from my shape?
Pol. The sign of the wretched bitch, a mark for sailors.
Hec. I don't care, now you have given me justice. (1256–74)

Many scholars see the extent of the revenge as excessive with its butchery of innocent children and blinding of their father; in support of this interpretation it is observed how many elements in its imagery match in horror the original pain inflicted on Hecuba by Polymestor's slaughter of Polydorus, itself a culmination of so many earlier sufferings.[16] Both are child-killers,[17] both enter stumbling or crawling from Agamemnon's tent (53–4, 59–67; 1049–50, 1056–8),[18] both (and Hecuba's assistants) become (like) beasts/dogs or monsters, (1058–9, 1069–74, 1075–7, 1173–5).[19] Polymestor jointed up Polydorus' flesh and abandoned him on the shore, and fears his children's corpses will similarly be jointed and thrown out to the dogs on the mountain (714–20, 1077–8). Polymestor is blinded and Hecuba becomes a fiery-eyed dog (1035, 1049–50, 1066–8, 1265);[20] Polymestor goes to his death like a sailor (1024–6, cf. 1079–82), Hecuba becomes a sailor's mark (1071–4). On this view the prophecy of her transformation into a nameless bitch with fiery eyes and her lasting memorial as the "wretched bitch's sign for sailors", are fitting symbols of her horrific revenge and the degradation and brutalization that the war and its aftermath have worked in her. But there are not a few scholars who argue that in terms of contemporary Athenian values, her revenge would be seen as direct, albeit rough, justice, all that was available to the victim, given Agamemnon's refusal to offer anything more than tacit assistance.[21] Some observe that a female dog can be seen as positive, as a maternal protector,[22] and that Hecuba's canine transformation was the legend, comparable to the transformation of Cadmus and Harmonia into snakes at the end of *Bacchae*.[23] These points seem to me not to exclude the unpleasant associations of bitches, nor the impact of the loss of name and acquisition of bloodshot eyes.[24] In the context of Polymestor's

---

16 See e.g. Arrowsmith 1958, 6, Michelini 1987, 170–80, Segal 1993, 179–90, Rabinowitz 1993, 122–3, Zeitlin, 1996, 177–8, 183-91, 213–6, Nussbaum 1986, 409–18, Sourvinou-Inwood 2003, 341–5, Wohl 2015, 58–62.
17 Polymestor killed one son, Hecuba two; but she may be imagined as in some ways getting revenge for the killing of Polyxena as well: cf. Zeitlin 1996, 188–94, Mastronade 2010, 72, Wohl 2015, 57–61.
18 On their body —and foot— movements, see Zeitlin 1996, 209.
19 E.g. Michelini 1987, 171, Zeitlin 1996, 180–3.
20 Though not a barking or howling dog as has been claimed, see Burnett 1998, 173–4, Zeitlin 1996, 185–6.
21 Meridor 1978, Burnett, 1998, 157–68, Gregory 1999, xxxii-vi. More balanced, ambivalent readings are offered by Mossman 2013, 164–203, Heath 2003, Mastronade 2010, 72–3, 202–5, 229–34.
22 Best is Gregory 1999, xxxv-vi, who cites Hom. *Od.* 20. 14–15, Antipater, *Anth. Pal.* 7. 425.3–4; Burnett 1998, 175–6.
23 Cf. Meridor 1978, 34; Burnett, 1998, 173–6, who adds that the innovative Euripidean identification of Hecuba-dog with the Kynossema (Kilit Bahir, opposite Çannakale), a dog-shaped promontory with beacons warning sailors of danger makes her a useful feature and the beacons account for the 'red glare', but this need not rule out an effect of making the revenge bestial.
24 Cf. also Polymestor's anticipatory description of all the women as 'murderous bitches' (τὰς μιαιφόνους κύνας, 1173); cf. Zeitlin 1996, 181–3.

hate-filled prediction, the canine associations seem primarily hostile, and the transformation continues the matching of Hecuba with Polymestor as comparably bestial and inhumane.[25] The excessive cruelty of the children-butchery and the blinding, reasonably called *hubris* by its victim (1257),[26] constitute a significantly more horrific revenge than a swift death (cf. 1121).[27] The multiple blows inflicted on Hecuba have taken away all hope, and any sense of a just world or just gods;[28] she is prepared for death, and left only with the desire for an appropriate revenge, in which she feels justified in rejoicing (1258). When Polymestor seeks to hurt her with the bitch prophecy she responds that she does not care, now that he has given her 'justice' (*dike*, 1274, cf. 1050–3).

Hecuba is a victim of repeated traumas, and it may help to apply some results of explorations into the intensity of emotions and behaviour among those diagnosed with Combat Trauma, especially Vietnam War veterans both during and after the war. Here, as others have, one may use the pioneering applications made by Jonathan Shay, who has worked extensively with many sufferers, to the Homeric representation of Achilles and Odysseus.[29] Rather than offer a precise diagnosis of combat trauma, one may suggest that the powerful emotions and actions which result from the repeated shocks have interesting parallels in changes of character and emotional states identified in Shay's accounts of traumatised veterans.[30] Three may be mentioned. First, warriors who 'lose it' or go 'berserk' may feel like 'animals or, like 'gods', may act without restraint, are devoid of fear or concern for their safety, and are focused above all on achieving revenge for their comrades. Second, among the many traumatising stimuli, Shay includes deaths of children or the destruction of the community. Third, the elements of 'anti-social personality change' identified after such catastrophic experiences include a

---

25 Cf. also Mastronade 2010, 72–3.
26 Cf. Fisher 1992, 430–2.
27 Meridor (1978, 30–1) thinks it significant that in Polymestor's narrative of the revenge it is the collective of women who stabbed the boys and blinded him, and Hecuba is not mentioned specifically (1161–71); cf. also Burnett 1998, 171, seeing it as a "communal punishment". This does not, however, affect her responsibility as the leader, nor her own claim to have herself killed the boys (along with "the noblest Trojan women") and imposed a just penalty on their father (1051–4), nor Polymestor's earlier statement that Hecuba, with the other "murderous bitches", has destroyed —or more than destroyed— him (1120–1).
28 Cf. Reckford 1985, 124–8.
29 Shay 1995, 2002.
30 See especially Rabinowitz 2014, offering such an approach to the impact of wars on women in tragedy, also Konstan 2014, 9–10.

hostile attitude toward the world, social withdrawal, feelings of emptiness and hopelessness, and feelings of being on the edge, and of estrangement.[31]

So, while Hecuba had indeed every reason to seek revenge on the cynical and brutal Thracian king, and many Greeks would sympathise with her decision to use supplication and rhetorical manipulation followed by direct violence to achieve it, it seems to me that the extremity of her revenge and her delight in it are presented as excessive and horrific, and that an application of aspects of a Combat Trauma model is helpful. Her representation displays a traumatised, brutalised, disorder, an isolation from pity or decency, and, in the absence of any hope, a ruthless concentration on a single act of horror balancing as exactly as possible the horrors done to her and to Troy.[32] This may then well at least to reduce in many spectators or readers an acceptability of her revenge, and replace it with a sense of horror as well as pity. Her humanity, as Arrowsmith put it, is thus seriously undermined by her traumas and her sense of utter hopelessness and its concomitant longing for extreme revenge.

3 Trojan Women

This play unusually shows no change in fortunes, only the steady and remorseless ratcheting up of disasters and levels of hopelessness for the Trojans. The victims talk repeatedly of the destruction of their former hopes; as any remaining hopes are brutally crushed, so concomitantly is any sense that help might be forthcoming from the gods, despite the previously good reciprocal relations between Olympians and Trojans.[33]

At the start of the Cassandra scene, Talthybius fears that the women inside may be burning the place down or burning themselves to death:

κάρτα τοι τοὐλεύθερον
ἐν τοῖς τοιούτοις δυσλόφως φέρει κακά

---

31 Shay 1995, 32–5, 77–90, 165–81.
32 See Rabinowitz 2014, 200–2. It may be right to suspect that the delay caused by the adverse winds (898–901), which enabled the revenge, indicates that the gods approved the punishment of Polymestor, but that does not entail that one then has to approve the methods chosen by Hecuba (e.g. Mastronade 2010, 203–4).
33 See e.g. Conacher 1961, 139, "a faint, rhythmic pattern of hope revived and then betrayed again", and Mastronade 2010, 161–2 on the play's "dialectic of hope and despair, and how the growth of despair is matched by increasing criticism of the gods".

> After all free spirits
> in such misfortunes find ills hard to bear   (298–305).

Thus an unusually sympathetic Greek can recognize that the despair of the Trojan women makes their suicide plausible.[34]

In the first three uses of *elpis*, Hecuba is found expressing her growing sense of hopelessness. First she comments on Cassandra's first 'bacchic' song celebrating her 'marriage', in language comparable to Polyxena's speech in *Hecuba* (349–53):

> Ἥφαιστε, δαιδουχεῖς μὲν ἐν γάμοις βροτῶν,
> ἀτὰρ λυγράν γε τήνδ' ἀναιθύσσεις φλόγα
> ἔξω τε μεγάλων ἐλπίδων. οἴμοι, τέκνον,
> ὡς οὐχ ὑπ' αἰχμῆς σ' οὐδ' ὑπ' Ἀργείου δορὸς
> γάμους γαμεῖσθαι τούσδ' ἐδόξαζόν ποτε.
>
> Hephaistos, you're the torch-bearer at mortals' weddings,
> but this torch you're firing up is painful,
> far from my great hopes. Alas, my child,
> I never thought you would ever enter a marriage
> at spear-point or under the Argive weapon   (343–7)

After Cassandra has been taken away, Hecuba's next lament, delivered prostrate on the ground (463–5), contains two denials of hope; first, after a confessedly futile call on the gods, she comments that

> ἃς δ' ἔθρεψα παρθένους
> ἐς ἀξίωμα νυμφίων ἐξαίρετον,
> ἄλλοισι θρέψασ' ἐκ χερῶν ἀφῃρέθην·
> κοὔτ' ἐξ ἐκείνων ἐλπὶς ὡς ὀφθήσομαι
> αὐτή τ' ἐκείνας οὐκέτ' ὄψομαί ποτε.
> τὸ λοίσθιον δέ, θριγκὸς ἀθλίων κακῶν,
> δούλη γυνὴ γραῦς Ἑλλάδ' εἰσαφίξομαι.
>
> The girls I had brought up
> with a view to the select good repute of bridegrooms
> I brought up for others and I had them taken from my hands.
> And there is no hope that I shall be seen again by them
> nor will I myself be any longer see them.
> Finally, the coping stone of my wretched miseries,
> I shall come to Greece old woman and a slave.   (484–90)

---

34 On the theme of the slave-free polarity, and Talthybius' place in it, cf. Croally, 1994, 97–103.

And a little later, having mentioned two of these children, she rejects her attendants' help, as there is no hope, and prefers to lie in degradation and 'destroy' herself in extravagant grief, using the powerful image of a wool-carder for the laceration of her face by scratching and tears:

τί δῆτά μ' ὀρθοῦτ'; ἐλπίδων ποίων ὕπο;
ἄγετε τὸν ἁβρὸν δή ποτ' ἐν Τροίαι πόδα,
νῦν δ' ὄντα δοῦλον, στιβάδα πρὸς χαμαιπετῆ
πέτρινά τε κρήδεμν', ὡς πεσοῦσ' ἀποφθαρῶ
δακρύοις καταξανθεῖσα. τῶν δ' εὐδαιμόνων
μηδένα νομίζετ' εὐτυχεῖν, πρὶν ἂν θάνηι.

So why lift me up? In what sort of hope?
Guide my foot, once so delicate in Troy,
but now enslaved, to the straw pallet on the ground
and the stone head pillow, so I may fall and destroy myself
carding with tears. Of prosperous people
think none fortunate until they are dead.   (505–10)

There follow faint flickerings of hope, swiftly to be dashed. In the next scene, with Andromache, Hecuba displays contradictory emotions. Even though she says she now believes that the gods operate by randomly turning everything upside down (613-4), and hears from Andromache the latest dismal news of Polyxena's sacrifice, nonetheless, faced with Andromache's clear-sighted preference for death, she counters with a recommendation for a limited belief in hope:

οὐ ταὐτόν, ὦ παῖ, τῶι βλέπειν τὸ κατθανεῖν·
τὸ μὲν γὰρ οὐδέν, τῶι δ' ἔνεισιν ἐλπίδες.

It is not the same, my child, dying and living:
one is nothing, in the other are hopes.   (632–3)

Andromache delivers a lengthy speech to rebut this, with a prolonged comparison between her successful and happy marriage and the coming yoke of slavery. The conclusion emphasises the extremity of her despair:

ἐμοὶ γὰρ οὐδ' ὃ πᾶσι λείπεται βροτοῖς
ξύνεστιν ἐλπίς, οὐδὲ κλέπτομαι φρένας
πράξειν τι κεδνόν· ἡδὺ δ' ἐστὶ καὶ δοκεῖν.

For me there remains not even what is left for all
mortals, that is hope, nor am I deceived in my mind
that I might do well in anything; however sweet it is to suppose that.   (680–3)

Hecuba tries even so to persuade her daughter that, while she herself has run out of words to express the multitude of her woes, Andromache should stop mourning Hector and accommodate herself to her new husband, for the sake of her grandson Astyanax and his descendants,[35] now seen as the last hope for a new 'Troy' (701–7). Hecuba's attempts to defend even a faint 'hope' and offer advice to her daughter may suggest that a mother never ceases to seek to prepare a child to cope with the worst that can happen, and a queen will keep alive as long as possible hopes for the rebirth of her state. They provoke Andromache's detailed response, and lead with compelling irony into the scene where Talthybius, reluctantly, tells them that this last hope will be dashed when the grandson present on stage will be flung off the walls like a discus (cf. 1121–2).

The second *stasimon* (the 'Ganymede Ode') focuses on more remote sources of hope for Trojans which are now seen to have been equally futile. The second *strophe* and *antistrophe* recall two of Troy's most beautiful and luxurious young men, Ganymede and Tithonus, sons of Laomedon and brothers of Priam. They attained immortality by attracting the desire of Zeus and Eos, and were carried off to a care-free life with their lovers.[36] These two stanzas build on the stark contrast between the operations of *eros* and *charis*, the reciprocal pleasures and luxuries of the lovers' lives on Olympus, and the absence of any *charis* to those living in Troy burning below, facing death or slavery. The second *strophe* ends with the image of Ganymede's youthful, 'fair and serene' face with its charms and pleasures (*charites*) being nourished by Zeus' throne, contrasted with the shores groaning with dead and mourners, the land destroyed by the Greek spear:[37]

> τὰ δὲ σὰ δροσόεντα λουτρὰ
> γυμνασίων τε δρόμοι
> βεβᾶσι, σὺ δὲ πρόσωπα νεα-
> ρὰ χάρισι παρὰ Διὸς θρόνοις
> καλλιγάλανα τρέφεις.
> Πριάμοιο δὲ γαῖαν Ἑλλὰς ὤλεσ' αἰχμά.

---

35 At 703–5, I would favour accepting P's ἐξ οὗ for V's ἐκ σοῦ (V) and Nauck's εἶναι for the mss's ἵν' οἵ, so that the reference would be to putative sons of a grown-up Astyanax, rather than to sons Andromache might have by Neoptolemus, which gives a more plausible scenario. Cf. Barlow *ad loc.*
36 Scodel 1980, 134–5 on the theme of the failure of divine *charis*. The appearance of the irrepressibly beautiful Helen in the next scene, and the conviction at its end that despite Menelaus' promises she will escape punishment, present her as a compelling parallel on earth to Ganymede's serene existence on Olympus, cf. Wohl 2015, 44–7.
37 Ganymede's *charites* here combine his ever-youthful beauty and grace with the erotic pleasures and reciprocal obligations he shares with Zeus. The common motif that Tithonus lost his youth is not mentioned here (Burnett 1977, 304).

> Your dew-drenched baths
> and races at the gym
> are gone, but by Zeus' throne you keep your face
> fresh, fair and serene with its charms.
> But the Greek spear has destroyed Priam's land. (838–40)

Then the last stanza shows us a contrast between the glamour of the marriage and hopes (for Troy) of Eos and Tithonus, and the ending of any reciprocal kinship or friendship bonds between gods and the city:[38]

> ὃν ἀστέρων τέθριππος ἔλα-
> βε χρύσεος ὄχος ἀναρπάσας,
> ἐλπίδα γᾶι πατρίαι μεγάλαν.
> τὰ θεῶν δὲ φίλτρα φροῦδα Τροίαι.
>
> He whom a four-horse golden chariot
> from the stars snatched up and
> carried away to be a great hope for
> our native land. The love
> of the gods is gone for Troy (833–7)

So the chorus share with Hecuba and Andromache their despair and bitterness at the gods' betrayal and complete abandonment of Troy;[39] they expand on this in their next song, asking anxiously whether Zeus knows or cares that the fires of pious sacrifices are being replaced by the flames destroying the city (1060–80).[40]

Finally, the play ends with the laments of the women as they watch the city burning and themselves dragged off to the ships. Just before they see the torches, the chorus address the Astyanax' mangled corpse being prepared for burial, after Hecuba has once more commented bitterly that the gods did nothing for them, except make them subjects for sad songs (1241–45):

> ἰὼ ἰώ· μελέα μῆτερ, ἣ τὰς μεγάλας
> ἐλπίδας ἐν σοὶ κατέκναψε βίου·
> μέγα δ' ὀλβισθεὶς ὡς ἐκ πατέρων
> ἀγαθῶν ἐγένου

---

38 Burnett's view (1977) that the chorus-women here reveal despite themselves the moral errors, luxuries and impieties of Laomedon and his sons in the past and descendants in the present underplays the emotional power of their despair and sense of abandonment (nor did Athena and Poseidon make these points in the prologue). For a more balanced assessment of the gods' *charis* in this play, Scodel 1980, 133–7.
39 Cf. Mastronade 2010, 138–9, 171.
40 Cf. Yunis 1988, 81–9, Wohl 2015, 44–7.

δεινῶι θανάτωι διόλωλας.

Io, io,
wretched mother *(i.e. Andromache)*, who carded
to ruin the great hopes in you for life *(i.e. Astyanax)*;
though you were born with great wealth
from noble fathers,
you have been destroyed in a terrible death.   (1251–59)

This last reference to the 'carding' of hopes for Troy's proud and noble families repeats the brutal image used at 509, and neatly sums up what happens to all Trojan hopes and trust in the gods through the play.[41] Hecuba, who has struggled throughout the play to express the depths of her suffering while yet looking for survival, providing hope for her daughter, and seeking, against the odds, a just punishment for Helen, gives up at the end; after a final recrimination against the traitorous gods (1280–1) she leads the women into a mass suicide-attempt in the flames (1282–3). Prevented by Talthybius, they collapse again to the ground (cf. 98–100, 463–5),[42] and are led off by the soldiers, uttering final staccato phrases on fire, the destruction of Troy,[43] grief and appeals to the dead (1289–1332). This bleakest of endings offers the simplest, pared-down language of horror, loss and hopelessness, in a way comparable to the ending of *Hecuba*.[44]

4 Heracles

This play notoriously has many dramatic reversals and changes of fortune, most notably the most startling of all transformations in Greek tragedy half-way

---

41 The audience knows from the prologue, of course, that the gods will punish the Greeks on their journey home, but also that Athena's new hostility to the Greeks, and hence the divine decision to send the Greeks a tough homecoming, derives from the offence of Ajax son of Oileus against her image; they may reflect that this is too late to 'cheer Trojans up' as Athena hoped (65–6); contrast Lefkowitz 2003, 116–7.
42 Cf. Dunn 1997, 111–2.
43 On this, see Croally 1994, 192–4.
44 On the sudden ending, see Dunn 1997, 102–3, pointing out the absence of any concluding anapaests or tetrameters, any aitiology or a god from the machine: gods were restricted to the prologue, and Hecuba emphasises that none will help them (1279–81). For comparable bleakness and plain language one might think also of the end of King Lear.

through, with the appearance on the roof of Lyssa and Iris.[45] One of the themes which help to bring the disparate parts together is the issue on how to react to desperate situations: hope or despair, resisting or embracing death.[46] The situations are not identical. In the first main section of the play, Megara and Amphitryon, faced with the threats from the tyrant Lycus, debate whether to endure bravely what appears to be certain death and to make it less shameful, if they may be permitted the dignity of funeral dress, or to cling to hope and the supposed protection of the altar, and risk being burnt to death there. In the final part, the issue is Heracles' decision whether or not to end his life, after the madness-induced murder of his family. None of the characters has an opportunity to seek revenge, as did Hecuba; Heracles' dependants have no power and can see no help to deal with Lycus, while Heracles cannot touch the gods who drove him mad. Nor are they in the situation of the women in the *Troades*, all hopes gone, but no possibility of any action, even suicide, to avert bereavement and humiliating enslavement. They have choices, but only desperate and miserable ones.

The debate on hope and bravery starts early in the Prologue. Megara is convinced that the situation is hopeless (there are good reasons to suppose Heracles dead, they have no allies or friends, and a ruthless and irreligious opponent);[47] so she demands to know what if any hope or means for safety Amphitryon has to offer:

νῦν οὖν τίν' ἐλπίδ' ἢ πόρον σωτηρίας
ἐξευμαρίζηι, πρέσβυ; πρὸς σὲ γὰρ βλέπω.
ὡς οὔτε γαίας ὅρι' ἂν ἐκβαῖμεν λάθραι
(φυλακαὶ γὰρ ἡμῶν κρείσσονες κατ' ἐξόδους)
οὔτ' ἐν φίλοισιν ἐλπίδες σωτηρίας
ἔτ' εἰσὶν ἡμῖν. ἥντιν' οὖν γνώμην ἔχεις
λέγ' ἐς τὸ κοινόν, μὴ θανεῖν ἕτοιμον ἦι.

Well now, what hope or means of safety
do you have ready to hand, old man? I look to you.
For we cannot cross the land's borders in secret
(there are guards stronger than us at the exits)
nor are there any hopes for safety in the friends
we may yet have. Tell us openly
what view you have, that our death may not be certain.   (85–94)

---

45 On the structural dislocation as central to the play's power and strategy, cf. Barlow 1982; Riley 2008, 14–24.
46 On this 'dialectic', cf. again Mastronade 2010, 167–9.
47 53–9, 80–4, 430, 550–60, which adds that Eurystheus' heralds kept reporting his death.

Amphitryon has no plan, but believes they should play for time even from their position of weakness; charged with being too attached to life, he agrees

> Me. λύπης τι προσδεῖς ἢ φιλεῖς οὕτω φάος;
> Amph. καὶ τῶιδε χαίρω καὶ φιλῶ τὰς ἐλπίδας.
>
> Me. Do you yet need more grief? Or do you so love the light?
> Amph. I do like life and am fond of hopes. (90–1)

and he still thinks delay may yet produce a result. Megara finds the pain unbearable.[48] At this point Amphitryon has the last word: his son may yet come, human affairs are ever changing, and

> οὗτος δ' ἀνὴρ ἄριστος ὅστις ἐλπίσιν
> πέποιθεν αἰεί· τὸ δ' ἀπορεῖν ἀνδρὸς κακοῦ.
>
> The best man is the one who always puts his trust
> in hopes; to despair is the act of a bad man. (105–6)

Megara has strong arguments in terms of the apparent hopelessness of their chances of salvation and the miseries they are enduring; yet at this point, apparently facing a slow death by starvation, Amphitryon seems to have the better case, that as long as there is any hope for the return, holding on is the right thing.[49] He puts it in terms of what a good man would do, i.e where *arete* lies in such a case: for him, trusting in hope it is the mark of the best sort of man, and giving up the act of a coward.

Chalk (1962) saw this argument as a conflict between two conceptions, or even definitions, of *arete*, as also at the end of the play. Megara holds that the good man should have the courage to choose the more honourable death when there is no reasonable grounds for hope, but for Amphitryon clinging to hope is the brave act. Both views are clearly possible; both involve courage or *arete*, though neither is exactly 'redefining' *arete*.[50] Some argue that Megara's view would seem the more plausible, because it is characteristic of Greek ideas to take a less positive view of hope in general: hope, though emotionally appealing,

---

48 I accept, as most do, the transposition of l. 87. Dunn (1997, 85) is unduly dismissive on Amphitryon's "abject faith in hope", which "he paradoxically describes as a virtue".
49 As argued strongly by Yoshitake 1994, 136–7.
50 Adkins' insistance (1966, 209–14) that Amphitryon is not giving a "(re)definition" of *arete* is fair in that it is only a statement of what a good man would do in these very limited and difficult circumstances; but his view that brave but powerless people who cling to hope cannot be called 'good' or display *arete* at all is over-rigid in its application of such value terms.

leads people astray into rash decisions and ends in failure, as with the herald at Eur. *Suppl.* 479 (cf. Collard *ad loc.*), and in many Thucydidean passages (especially 3.45.5, 5.102–3).[51] It is certainly the case that Christian thought and values, in contrast to Greek, have a greater tendency to elevate Hope into a virtue, necessary for salvation, and closely linked to Faith and the expectation of an after-life based on divine judgment. But Greek ideas of hope are none the less complex and ambivalent, and one has to be precise about the contexts in every case. As Thucydides' Athenians at Melos observe (5.103), there is a significant difference between trusting to hope when 'sufficient resources' (*periousia*) ensure that failure will not be disastrous, and risking everything on one last, hopeless, throw; the second is what they say the Melians are contemplating, and the Melians —foolishly— take the hopeful gamble in the romantic but foolish belief that to surrender is to lose 'everything' anyway. But the choice facing Megara and Amphitryon is not quite that which the Melians faced; for the play's characters to give up hope and leave the altar is to meet a swifter and more dignified death than the alternative, not to survive with dishonour. On the other hand Amphitryon turned out to be right to cling to hope, as Heracles returned.[52] In fact they both have a reasonable case; and Amphitryon's view, ironically, that it takes courage to resist despair and a quick death, to hold on to life, will connect to a comparable, but significantly different, decision at the end: enduring life may be the brave thing to do even if that life is full of shame and without hope.

Lycus then changes the balance of the choice, threatening the immediate and impious burning of the sanctuary, heightening the idea that clinging to hope is pointless (143–50). So Megara returns to the charge against Amphitryon's 'hope', as the choice has changed to dying with semblances of freedom and dignity, leaving the altar and dressing the boys for death, or the immediate pain and humiliation of being burnt alive.[53]

σκέψαι δὲ τὴν σὴν ἐλπίδ' ἧι λογίζομαι·
ἥξειν νομίζεις παῖδα σὸν γαίας ὕπο;
καὶ τίς θανόντων ἦλθεν ἐξ Ἅιδου πάλιν;
ἀλλ' ὡς λόγοισι τόνδε μαλθάξαιμεν ἄν;
ἥκιστα.

---

51 See especially Bond on 105f. and see also Tsoumpra, this volume, 11–19.
52 Also, as appears later (1063–71), Theseus was on his way with a force.
53 On the combination of despair and disgrace as twin drivers for, and for some justifications for, suicide, see Yoshitake 1994, 138–9.

> See now the way I calculate about your grounds for hope.
> You think your son will come back from beneath the earth?
> Well, which of the dead has ever returned from Hades?
> Or perhaps you think that we may soften this man by arguments?
> There's no chance.   (295–7)

> τόλμα μεθ' ἡμῶν θάνατον, ὃς μένει σ' ὅμως.
> προκαλούμεθ' εὐγένειαν, ὦ γέρον, σέθεν·
> τὰς τῶν θεῶν γὰρ ὅστις ἐκμοχθεῖ τύχας
> πρόθυμός ἐστιν, ἡ προθυμία δ' ἄφρων·
> ὃ χρὴ γὰρ οὐδεὶς μὴ χρεὼν θήσει ποτέ.

> Endure with us bravely the death which waits for you anyway.
> We appeal to your nobility, old friend.
> A man who struggles through the fortune sent by the gods
> is determined, but it's a foolish determination.
> What is inevitable no one will ever evade.   (307–11)

The change makes Amphitryon give in.[54] Still insisting that it is not cowardice (*to deilon*) or longing for life, but the wish to save the children that holds him back from death, he admits this is now to be 'in love pointlessly with the impossible', and he is ready for death.

> οὔτοι τὸ δειλὸν οὐδὲ τοῦ βίου πόθος
> θανεῖν ἐρύκει μ', ἀλλὰ παιδὶ βούλομαι
> σῶσαι τέκν'· ἄλλως δ' ἀδυνάτων ἔοικ' ἐρᾶν.

> It's not cowardice nor longing for life
> that keeps me from dying, but I wish to save the children
> for my son. But it seems I'm pointlessly in love with the impossible.   (316–8)

So they win two concessions from Lycus, a death before that of the children, and the limited honour of wearing their chosen clothes.

These shifting decisions interact closely with changing attitudes to the gods and their reciprocity. Amphitryon ends this scene with an embittered reproach to Zeus, the third person in his marriage. He has found that Zeus is less than the friend he seemed, and so he, a mortal, outdoes Zeus, a great god, in *arete*; Zeus may be good at adultery but he is not good at saving his *philoi*, either from stupidity or from natural injustice (339–47).[55] Giving up his last drop of hope of a future goes along with despair at any idea of trust in the gods, and particularly in

---

54 Cf. Yunis 1988, 141, Yoshitake 1994, 137–8.
55 On the interpretation of line 347, see Bond *ad loc.*, Yunis 1988, 144.

Zeus; there is no sign of any reciprocity from Zeus to his friends.⁵⁶ Whether clinging to hope, or giving it up and facing immediate death, Amphitryon believes his *arete*, his moral principles, are secure.

The last instances of *elpis*-words in this context of facing Lycus come in the next scene as the wife and father-in-law prepare to die first. Megara's farewell to her sons contrasts at length the high hopes she had for them with their humiliating fate.⁵⁷

ἦ πολύ γε δόξης ἐξέπεσον εὐέλπιδος,
ἣν πατρὸς ὑμῶν ἐκ λόγων ποτ' ἤλπισα.

Oh, how far have I fallen from that expectation of good hope,
which I hoped for once from the words of your father. (458–61)

For his part, Amphitryon suggests all one can do in this miserable and brief life ruled by an uncaring Zeus is to 'get through it' (διαπεράσατε) as pleasantly as possible (503–5) and give up on hope, since 'time' makes hope pointless:

θανεῖν γάρ, ὡς ἔοικ', ἀναγκαίως ἔχει.
ἀλλ', ὦ γέροντες, σμικρὰ μὲν τὰ τοῦ βίου,
τοῦτον δ' ὅπως ἥδιστα διαπεράσατε
ἐξ ἡμέρας ἐς νύκτα μὴ λυπούμενοι.
ὡς ἐλπίδας μὲν ὁ χρόνος οὐκ ἐπίσταται
σώιζειν, τὸ δ' αὑτοῦ σπουδάσας διέπτατο.

Dying, it seems, has inevitably to happen.
but, old friends, the affairs of life are brief
so work through it as pleasantly as possible
getting from day to night without pain.
Time has no knowledge of how to preserve
our hopes, but pursuing its own business it flies off. (503–7)

The last two lines seem to mean both that 'time' is always likely to prevent the fulfillment of any one's hopes, and, further, that because it can always do this, it takes away any point of retaining hope.⁵⁸

---

56 See Yunis 1988, 141–5. On the relation of these cases of morally based scepticism in this play to contemporary philosophical speculation, see recently Whitmarsh 2016, 107–9.
57 Cf. the comparable cases in *Hecuba* 349–54 and *Trojan Women* 342–7, 484–90.
58 It is probably right to see both these two meanings here which Bond (*ad loc.*) suggests may be present, though he doubts the second, on the grounds that hope always "springs eternal"; but the point here is precisely that experience should teach that hope should not so spring: cf. Yunis 1988, 144–5.

In these scenes dramatising desperate decisions, many ideas of how to face up to the adversities or misfortunes sent by the gods, compatible with displays of of *arete*, are explored and described in a series of related verbs such as 'work out', 'work though', 'endure', or 'push through' (and such ideas recur differently later). These terms seem often obscure or ambiguous. So in this scene Megara challenged Amphitryon to "endure (*tolman*) death with us, which waits for us anyway" and display his nobility (*eugeneia*); on the other hand it is a "foolish enthusiasm" 'to try to work right (*ekmochthein*) through the fortunes of the gods"; apparently indicating the advice to cut through the endless waiting for renewed blows and die immediately (307–11).[59] The chorus, not sure how Amphitryon will respond, says that as they are powerless, it is up to him to decide how to 'push through (*diōsein*) these fortunes' (315) —perhaps deliberately leaving both alternatives open.[60]

The first startling reversal, Heracles' return, leads the chorus to proclaim three times the return of their hopes and the power to hope, against expectations,[61] as they hear with joy the death cries of Lycus. With the revival of hope come the reassertions that the gods do after all care for justice and punish villains, and that Zeus must indeed have shared Alcmene's bed and parenthood, as he now protects his son. Thus the chorus in effect now opposes Amphitryon's skepticism (757–60), and happily turn to enjoy the ritual forms which celebrate human reciprocity with the gods, song-dances and feasts.[62]

χοροὶ χοροὶ καὶ θαλίαι μέλουσι Θή-
βας ἱερὸν κατ' ἄστυ.
μεταλλαγαὶ γὰρ δακρύων,
μεταλλαγαὶ συντυχίας
< ?νέας > ἔτεκον ἀοιδάς.
βέβακ' ἄναξ ὁ καινός, ὁ δὲ παλαίτερος
κρατεῖ, λιμένα λιπών γε τὸν Ἀχερόντιον.
δοκημάτων ἐκτὸς ἦλθεν ἐλπίς.
θεοὶ θεοὶ τῶν ἀδίκων μέλουσι καὶ
τῶν ὁσίων ἐπάιειν.

---

59 On *ekmochthein* here, see Bond *ad loc.*
60 See also below (81–4) on Heracles' decision to "endure to go on living" (1351).
61 At 745–6 the chorus welcome the return of the king of their land "which before I had never expected (ἤλπισ' ἄν) to experience".
62 See Yunis 1988, 147. On the way self-referential mentions of choral dancing and song reflect the sudden mood transformations of this central section of the play, from despair, to joy and dancing, to the horrifically Dionysian aulos-music of madness (871–2, 877–9), see Wilson 1999–2000, 434–7.

> Dances, dances and feasts are the concern
> in the sacred city of Thebes.
> Changes from tears,
> changes in fortune
> have given birth to <?new?> songs.
> The recent king has gone, and the older one
> rules, leaving the Acherontian harbour.
> Hope has returned against expectations.
> Gods, gods do care to listen to
> the unjust and the pious. (763–73)

Time, after all, does not remove hope, but has revealed Heracles' brilliance against expectation.

Chorus
ὡς πιστόν μοι τὸ παλαιὸν ἤ
 δη λέχος, ὦ Ζεῦ, σὸν ἐπ' οὐκ ἐλπίδι φάνθη.
λαμπρὰν δ' ἔδειξ' ὁ χρόνος
τὰν Ἡρακλέος ἀλκάν·[63]

Now, Zeus, your old marriage-bed has been shown
to be true against expectation. Time has revealed
Heracles' strength to be brilliant. (801–6)

The final destruction of such hopes and any belief in caring gods descends immediately and startlingly with the arrival on the roof of Lyssa and Iris, charged by Hera with forcing Heracles in a state of sudden madness to carry out the appalling killing of his children and wife. One debated issue, relevant to Heracles' reactions, is whether the madness is to be seen as solely and entirely external, reflecting the Hera's heartless malevolence and jealousy and the indifference or powerlessness of Zeus who shares her throne (as Amphitryon bitterly puts it, 1127),[64] or whether divine hatred works along with weaknesses in Heracles' character, perhaps as a consequence of his remarkably violent career: this might suggest that he too could in part be seen as subject to a form of combat trauma.[65] The impression of Hera's malevolence is remarkably strong, and I would resist any

---

63 The text of 803–4 is problematic, but whether one reads σὸν ἐπ' οὐκ ἐλπίδι or (with Bond) τὸ σὸν ἐπ' οὐκ εὐέλπιδι the idea that Zeus' sharing of the marriage-bed and paternity has been confirmed contrary to their expectation is certain.
64 See Michelini 1987, 270.
65 See the full and excellent analysis of the complex interplay of divine assault and human personality in the presentation of the 'polysemy' of Heracles' symptoms, Holmes 2010, 242–46, 265–74.

modification of it by supposing that any human behaviour provoked the goddess to act, whether one adduces Heracles' general 'megalomania' and violent career,[66] or a specific offence by him or others.[67] The strongest element in Heracles' character in these scenes is the extent to which he sees it as his primary duty to protect his family (despite his prolonged absences, which he admits were regrettable), both before and after their killing (575–82, 629–35, 1147–50, 1237, 1279–80, 1367–70, etc).[68] But a taste for extreme violence and revenge is also present, in his bloodthirsty and comprehensive plans to kill Lycus and clean up Thebes (565–73), and in the delivery of the plan: the plurals at 940 and 965–7 suggests he killed some or all of Lycus' men, and perhaps even sought out some more distant Theban supporters, as he had threatened.[69] This relish is present equally in the deluded killings. The possibility of a form of trauma from his homicidal career contributing to this outburst of violence against his nearest kin is in effect raised by Amphitryon's reported question in the Messenger's narrative, before he realized the role of Hera:

Ὦ παῖ, τί πάσχεις; τίς ὁ τρόπος ξενώσεως
τῆσδ'; οὔ τί που φόνος σ' ἐβάκχευσεν νεκρῶν
οὓς ἄρτι καίνεις;

My son, what is happening to you? What type of alienation (*xenosis*)
is this? Has the killing of those you have just been slaying
really driven you to bacchic madness   (965–7)?[70]

Further, Heracles' belief when mad that he is killing Eurystheus' children, not just Eurystheus, may suggest that a ruthless preparedness to extend revenge to

---

66 Wilamowitz' formulation was influential, that Heracles' kin-killings had roots in his excessive ideal of manhood or *arete* as based on force (1959, 2.127–29); against e.g. Chalk, 1962, 12–16; Yunis, 1988, 151; Riley, 2008, 18, 28–30.
67 E.g. Burnett's idea that Amphitryon's and Megara's decision to abandon suppliant-status at the altar to seek a more honourable death has angered the gods (Burnett, 1971, 159–68). Her arguments that they show religious "scepticism", and would be seen as acting "against the rules of the suppliant plot", seem not to recognise that Lycus, an impious tyrant, has changed the rules, and that they have good reason not to believe divine help will arrive. See also Knox 1972, 276–9; Michelini 1987, 38–45; Riley 2008, 18–19.
68 Cf. Riley 2008, 28–30.
69 Cf. Papadopoulou 2005, 41–5; Kosak 2004, 168–70.
70 On the perverted musical and Dionysiac imagery in descriptions of his madness, see also 925–6, 1119, 1142; Wilson 1999–2000, 433–9; Papadopoulou 2005, 48–54; Riley 2008, 34–6; Holmes 2010, 244–5, 270–1.

children preceded his derangement.⁷¹ The horrific details of the actual murders display a wild brutality reminiscent of a combat trauma berserker.⁷² So while this idea is not to be seen as in any way an alternative explanation, letting the goddesses off the hook, it may lead one to reflect on the effects on warriors as well as on victims of constant killings and savagery. The goddesses may yet be working with elements of his character.⁷³ His ruthlessness and speed of action may also cause us to reflect, with Silk (1985), on the interstitial, ambivalent position between human and divine held uniquely by Heracles. Nevertheless, far overriding this, are the innumerable expressions of the extremity of undeserved suffering the gods have suddenly imposed on Heracles and his family, and his generally noble and tender behaviour in the scene just before the external onset of madness (e.g. 1087–8, 1127, 1303–12, 1392).⁷⁴

Invitations to reflect further on 'combat trauma' are not offered in the last third of the play, and Heracles' decision to prefer a new life in Athens to suicide. As Silk put it, his semi-divine powers, his kinship with the gods, and his brutality, are 'burned off' by the madness and kin-killings,⁷⁵ and, having been brought by

---

71 Cf. Stafford 2012, 90–1; Konstan 2014, 6. Kosak (2004, 151–62) suggests as well that that the *stasis* and *taragmos* that had affected Thebes and permitted Lycus' coup has somehow become internalized in the mental turmoil and disorder in Heracles, whose descriptions have parallels in medical texts.

72 The symptoms of his madness may also seem compatible with an epileptic fit (as implied by [Arist.] *Probl.* 953a11): see e.g. Wilamowitz 1959, 2. 91–3; Riley 2008, 31, 96–7. Crowley (2014) argues against identifying tendencies towards combat trauma among Athenian hoplites, in contrast to American GI's. But his account of cultural differences exaggerates the extent to which Christian values among GIs in practice problematize the use of violence and homicide; as Shay pointed out, Biblical models among Christian soldiers (appealing to the YAHWEH of the *Old Testament*), and the pioneering spirit that still resists any form of gun control, encourage contempt for and dehumanization of the 'enemy'. Conversely Crowley understates the ambivalence of Athenian values to warfare, and the horrors and brutality of Greek warfare and its treatment of non-combatants.

73 So Chalk 1962, 17, Rabinowitz 2014, 196, Barlow 1982, 122; on the multiple combinations of divine and human causes and symptoms, above all, Holmes 2010, 242–46, 265–74. Konstan 2014, 6–8 is cautious on the idea of combat trauma; Riley 2008, 37–8 and esp. n 87 opposes the idea, arguing that 966–7 is the only place suggesting such an idea, and that the implication is ruled out by the emphatic central epiphany. For ways in which combat trauma has informed many recent treatments of the family-killing theme, see Riley 2008, chs. 9 and 10.

74 Cf. Meridor 1984, 206, Riley 2008, 34–8.

75 A reversal of the idea that his 'burning' on the pyre burnt off his mortal state and rendered him suitable for admission to Olympus (Silk 1985). Occasional allusions to 'second youth' in the second stasimon (655–62, and suicide by fire (1151–2, may hint at the alternative version of his

his father to realise what he has done, he faces the choice of life or death as a calm and humane mortal, albeit crushed and shamed. Here there are no more *elpis* words, and no other indications that any hope for a better outcome might be possible for him. Why Heracles decided he would live remains problematic, as do the relation to this decision of his developing attitudes to the gods, to his family, his weapons and to friendship, and the type, if any, of 'closure' provided by the play's ending.

Heracles' initial reaction is to decide on suicide, to "drive off the dishonour of his life which remains" (1146–52); he fears, when he sees Theseus, that his arrival may delay this; and he veils his head in shame and in fear of pollution (see esp. 1197–1202).[76] Amphitryon supplicates him and begs him to unveil. Theseus argues that he cares nothing for the risk of pollution from his friend and benefactor; his *charis* counts for more, and he helps him to unveil his head and stand up (1229–31). Theseus' initial attempts to discourage the suicide present it as the act of a man determined foolishly to challenge the gods (1242–5);[77] an act of an 'ordinary' man (1248), and a piece of stupidity which Greeks who revere his benefactions would not 'tolerate' (1254).[78]

Heracles' first speech responds by mounting a powerful case for the hopelessness of continuing to live. After reviewing miserably his confused parenthood, rejecting his supposed divine father, and finding his labours totally devalued, he argues that he has no prospects: he cannot stay in Thebes, cannot return to Argos, nor settle anywhere else as a polluted and deeply shamed figure who would be hounded out. Hence he has no hope of a useful life or access to society and ritual, and nurtures deep and bitter distrust of the gods ("let Zeus' wife dance in triumph", who has destroyed the best man in Greece from jealousy, 1303–5). Theseus' opening points in reply are lost in the lacuna before 1313, though it seems the opening sentence accepted that living would mean a life of dreadful suffering (*paschein kakōs*). He then responds (rather unconvincingly) to the criticisms of the gods, seeing them oddly as victims of their own offences of adultery and kin-killing, and more practically offers Heracles a purification ritual, and gifts of the *temene* the polis had given him for saving the fourteen children from the Minotaur, to be named *Herakleia* in his lifetime, with the honours

---

deification, but not to the extent that offers it as any sort of consolatory possibility at the end (contra Meridor, 1984, 207).
76 See Bond *ad loc.*, Cairns 2002, 75. On the debate here on the relation of pollution and shame, see also Osborne 2011, 178–80.
77 A couplet following line 1241 seems lost: see Bond *ad loc.*
78 If Bond's transposition of lines 1410–17 to this context is right, Theseus further presents this as a womanly act, not great as he had been in the past. See below 83.

of sacrifices and monuments after his death.⁷⁹ He ends by emphasizing that this gift is his *charis* to Heracles for being saved, because now it is Heracles who needs friends.

Heracles' reply presents a new decision to reject suicide, centred on the crucial statement: 'I shall endure to go on living' — (ἐγκαρτερήσω βίοτον), 1351.⁸⁰

> ἐσκεψάμην δὲ καίπερ ἐν κακοῖσιν ὢν
> μὴ δειλίαν ὄφλω τιν' ἐκλιπὼν φάος·
> ταῖς συμφοραῖς γὰρ ὅστις οὐχ ὑφίσταται
> οὐδ' ἀνδρὸς ἂν δύναιθ' ὑποστῆναι βέλος.
> ἐγκαρτερήσω βίοτον· εἶμι δ' ἐς πόλιν
> τὴν σήν, χάριν τε μυρίαν δώρων ἔχω.
> ἀτὰρ πόνων δὴ μυρίων ἐγευσάμην,
> ὧν οὔτ' ἀπεῖπον οὐδέν' οὔτ' ἀπ' ὀμμάτων
> ἔσταξα πηγάς, οὐδ' ἂν ᾠόμην ποτὲ
> ἐς τοῦθ' ἱκέσθαι, δάκρυ' ἀπ' ὀμμάτων βαλεῖν.
> νῦν δ', ὡς ἔοικε, τῆι τύχηι δουλευτέον.

> Even when in my troubles I reflected
> that I should incur the charge of cowardice if I left the light.
> For one who would not stand up to misfortunes
> would be unable to stand up to a man's weapon.
> I shall endure to go on living, and go to your
> city, and I own a thousand thanks for your gifts.
> Yet a thousand labours have I tasted
> and I refused none of them, nor did I shed
> streams from my eyes, nor did I ever think
> that I would come to this, to shed tears from my eyes.
> Now it seems, I must be enslaved to fortune. (1347–1357)

But there is no sense at all of any pleasure in this life he will find the courage to endure. His explicit reason is avoid a charge of cowardice (*deilia*) made by

---

79 On the cults and monuments envisaged here, see Bond *ad loc.*, Stafford 2005, 399–1, arguing they should be seen as appropriate to the mortal hero he will remain, not to a god. Despite Adkins 1966, 219, as Bond observes, Heracles retains his general claim to be a 'good man' (*esthlos*).
80 Like most I accept Wecklein's βίοτον in place of θάνατον; it gives the right sense, and as (e.g.) Bond *ad loc.* argued, it is difficult to take ἐγκαρτερήσω with θάνατον to mean 'have the courage to resist death', rather than 'face death' as at *Andr.* 262 (despite de Romilly 2003, 289–94). Gibert's ingenious reading (1997) 'I will fight against Death by living' (Thanaton personified) is better, but it too does not connect so well with the persistent motif of 'working through' words (see above p.70–4), nor give as strong a sense that he will endure over time the continuance of life. Kovacs' acceptance of Kirchhoff's ἐγκαρτερήσας, added to the end of previous sentence, deprives the text of the needed statement that he is committing to the difficult choice of life.

Theseus (more insistently if Bond's transposition of 1410–7 is right); this courage is comparable to withstanding weapons in battle. Hence it is legitimate to see this as an appropriate, revised and limited, form of *arete* for a crushed man —one who has lost his basic independence, who feels (as was Hecuba) "compelled to be enslaved to Tuche" (1357).[81] But he remains shamed, confused, and resigned. Dunn's deconstruction of any sense of a coherent, let alone a positive, ending, may go too far, but he is right to stress Heracles' confusion and lack of any positivity. He accepts graciously Theseus' offers of purification, *temene*, and post-mortem cults and monuments,[82] offering 'a thousand-fold thanks' as he accepts that they are genuine and freely offered.[83] But he regards them as irrelevant (πάρεργα) to his life and its problems, as he rejects Theseus' arguments about the gods, and he never returns to them.[84] He hesitates on whether to keep his famous weapons, but decides he must, to avoid a shameful death from his enemies; they will be a vivid reminder of his noble exploits but more of his kin-killings (1377–86). Thus they will be used only for self-defence, not glory, and kept but only

---

81 Cf. Stinton 1990, 182–3, responding to the debate between Chalk (1962) and Adkins (1966); Adkins was mistaken in denying any change in *arete*; Chalk went too far in finding a complete new *arete* in itself, rather than the discovery of new, limited, possibilities for brave and moral action, in hugely humiliating conditions. Cf. also Papadopoulou 2005, 176–7, Riley 2008, 40–2. On enslavement to *Tuche* here, subjection to a compelling power which lacks comprehension, cf. above p.58 on *Hec*. 785–6.
82 Whether we read Wakefield's μυρίαν or L's μυρίων, a thousand thanks or thousands of gifts, makes little difference as the reciprocity of charis leads one to suggest the other. Dunn (1997, 102–6) argues that their value should be doubted, because Theseus lacks political authority and the offers are hopelessly vague. The promises to purify and honour mention no purifying god and do not specify any cults; such a hypercritical attitude to the positive representation of Theseus in the play seems unjustified, and in the context details of the offers and credentials are not required.
83 The claim that 'all' Theseus' cults became Herakleia is no doubt a Euripidean exaggeration, but it is disputed whether some of the Heracleia in Attica were already seen as having been transferred from Theseus to Heracles, as Plutarch attests, quoting Philochorus — 'all but four' (Plut. *Thes*. 35 = Philoch. *FGH* 328 F 18, with Jacoby's commentary), or whether this is all an aitiology invented by Euripides, as argued by Dunn (1997). Dunn's scepticism is supported by Scullion, 1999/2000, but doubted by Parker, 2005, 142–3; Stafford 2005, 400–1; cf. also on cults of Heracles in Attica, Kearns 1989, 35–6, 166, 168–9, Stafford 2012, 176–80.
84 At 1340 "All these points are irrelevant to my troubles" probably refers both to Theseus' arguments about the crimes of the gods and to his offers of honours (see Bond *ad loc.*); the gods, for Heracles, in so far as they affect human events, are represented above all by Hera and her hen-pecked husband, who destroyed his family (1393–4); on his view expressed at 1341–5, they are not to be thought of as 'properly gods', ὀρθῶς θεοί.

'miserably' (*athliōs*).⁸⁵ His "thousand-fold thanks" for Theseus' gifts (1352), are repeated, when he accepts the 'friendly yoke' as he is led away, an 'ill-fated' man (*dustuches*) and he praises Theseus as the best sort of friend (1403–4). These phrases emphasize the theme of emotional and practical friendship as the primary positive left, but also, like the earlier recognition that he must accept enslavement to fortune (1357), and the final image of himself as a small boat in tow to Theseus (*epholkides*, 1425),⁸⁶ they also convey the idea of a lasting loss of independence, virtual enslavement, and wretched memories. Any optimism is further diminished by his anxieties about burying his wife and children, as he instructs Amphitryon to do it, and promises he will bury him when the time comes (1360–4, 1419–20), and getting Theseus' help in taking Cerberus to Argos (his reduced state means he recognises he can no longer expect to win battles on his own and will need an ally, 1386–8), and finally, indulging his grief with lingering looks at and kisses for the bodies of his family (1374–7). If the disputed lines 1410–17 should remain in their place, Theseus' replies here enhance the sense of misery and shame, insisting that he should not extend his gazing at his sons and embracing his father in a womanly way, and accept that his choice to live is indeed humiliating, as he, in his illness, is no more the famous Heracles of old (1413–14).⁸⁷ His final words, after the small boat image, stress the value of friendship, far more important than wealth or power, which is matched by the chorus mourning the loss of their greatest friend (1425–8); what is left to the greatest hero is endurance of shame and suffering with his friend and his refuge, in a world of unfriendly and unfair gods (or of none). It is right, I believe, to see a deeply humanized ending, with a Heracles stripped of divine elements and sympathies who has to learn to live with a new, restricted, ideal of *arete* and a need for friendship.⁸⁸ Euripides gives no hint of the traditional stories of Heracles' death and admission of Olympus, beyond the cults at Athens which seem to mean nothing

---

85 E.g. Michelini 1987, 266; de Romilly 2003, 286; Riley 2008, 42–3, against Dunn's belittling of the 'self-defense' point (1996, 123).
86 All the more pointed as it reverses the earlier image of his towing the children as his *epholkides* (629–36).
87 Bond's case that lines 1410–17 work better in the earlier debate when Heracles still clings to the idea of suicide is well-countered by Barlow 1996 *ad loc.* and Holmes 2010, 270. Heracles' reminder that Theseus had been low in spirits in Hades (1415) is perhaps the beginning of a slight recovery.
88 Cf. Papadopoulou 2005, 187–94, Mastronade 2010, 70, 214–5, Riley 2008, 40–45 (and see her telling comparisons of this ending with those of King Lear and Pericles, Prince of Tyre, 2008, 140–46).

to him.[89] While then there may be some hope for others, for this hero the ending remains deeply pessimistic; Heracles' future seems to be filled with grief, pain and duty, mitigated by friendship but lacking hope.

5 Conclusion

These three powerfully tragic plays present three different ways in which the central characters respond to the multiple disasters and suffering inflicted on them by murderous or ruthless male commanders, aided by indifferent or hostile gods, or achieved by a divine imposition of homicidal madness producing a family massacre. In *Hecuba*, the primary victim's horrific response to the last outrage (Polymestor's) stems from her traumatised disorder and isolation, and her hopelessness and despair feeds her all-embracing passion for an act of revenge which matches as exactly as possible the horrors done to her. The female victims of the *Trojan Women*, when all their hopes have been progressively 'carded' into shreds, once their mass suicide attempt has been thwarted, can only lament Troy's rule and rail against unjust men and gods. Finally Heracles chose a new form of 'goodness' (*arete*), following the destruction of his career and reputation as a semi-divine hero, to endure to live on in grief and shame, with nothing but the support of Theseus' friendship to sustain an irredeemably bleak existence 'without feathers'.[90]

Bibliography

Adkins, A.W.H. 1966. "Basic Greek Values in Euripides' *Hecuba* and *Hercules Furens*," in: *CQ* 16, 193–219.
Arrowsmith, W. 1958. "Introduction to Heracles," in: *The Complete Greek Tragedies: Euripides* Vol. III, Chicago.
Barlow, S. 1982. "Structure and Dramatic Realism in Euripides' *Heracles*," in: *Greece & Rome* 29, 115–25.

---

[89] Naturally, too, there is nowhere in the final scene any hint of Heracles' death or post-mortem elevation to the company of the Olympian gods. Theseus suggests that Heracles will go to Hades after death (1331; Stafford 2012, 92) and that for the Athenians Heracles' name and past glories make him still a good (*esthlos*) man and they will gain honour for helping him. This means nothing to him. Cf. Gregory 1977, 274–5.
[90] Warmest thanks to Dimos Spatharas and George Kazantzides and all involved in the splendid Rethymno conference and its hospitality, and to Dimos and George for comments on my draft.

—— 1986. *Euripides: Trojan Women*, Warminster.
—— 1996. *Euripides: Heracles*, Warminster.
Bond, G.W. 1981. *Euripides' Heracles*, Oxford.
Burnett, A.P. 1971. *Catastrophe Survived: Euripides' Plays of Mixed Reversal*, Oxford.
—— 1977. "Trojan Women and the Ganymede Ode," in: *Yale Classical Studies: Greek Tragedy* 25, 291–316.
—— 1998. *Revenge in Attic and Later Tragedy*, California.
Cairns, D.L. 2002. "The Meaning of the Veil in Ancient Greek Culture," in: L. Llewellyn-Jones (ed.), *Women's Dress in the Ancient Greek World*, London/Swansea, 73–93.
Chalk, H. 1962. "Arete and Bia in Euripides' Heracles," in: *JHS* 82, 7–18.
Collard, C. 1991. *Euripides' Hecuba*, Warminster.
Conacher, D.J. 1967. *Euripidean Drama: Myth, Theme and Structure*, Toronto.
Croally, N. 1994, *Euripidean Polemic: The Trojan Women and the Function of Tragedy*, Cambridge.
Crowley, J. 2014. "Beyond the Universal Soldier: Combat Trauma in Classical Antiquity," in: P. Meineck/D. Konstan (eds.), *Combat Trauma and the Ancient Greeks*, New York, 105–30.
Dunn, F.M. 1996. *Tragedy's End: Closure and Innovation in Euripidean Drama*, Oxford.
—— 1997. "Ends and Means in Euripides' Heracles," in: D.H. Roberts/F.M Dunn/D. Fowler (eds.), *Classical Closure: Reading the End in Greek and Latin Literature*, Princeton, 83–111.
Fisher, N.R.E. 1992. *Hybris*, Warminster.
Foley, H. 1975. *Ritual Irony: Poetry and Sacrifice in Euripides*, Ithaca/New York.
Gibert, J.C. 1997, "Euripides' *Heracles* 1351 and the Hero's Encounter with Death," in: *CPh* 92, 247–58.
Gould, J. 2001. *Myth, Ritual, Memory and Exchange: Essays in Greek Literature and Culture*, Oxford.
Gregory, J. 1977. "Euripides' Heracles," in: *Yale Classical Studies: Greek Tragedy* 25, 259–75.
—— 1999. *Euripides' Hecuba: Introduction, Text and Commentary*, Atlanta.
Guthrie, W.K.C. 1965. *A History of Greek Philosophy Vol. III: The Presocratic Tradition from Parmenides to Democritus*, Cambridge.
Heath, M. 2003. "'Iure Principem Locum Tenet': Euripides' *Hecuba*," in: J. Mossman (ed.), *Euripides: Oxford Readings in Classical Studies*, Oxford, 218–60 (= *BICS* 34 (1978) 40–68).
Holmes, B. (2010). *The Sympton and the Subject: The Emergence of the Physical Body in Ancient Greece*, Princeton.
Kearns, E. 1989. *Heroes of Attica*, BICS Suppl. 57, London.
Knox, B.M.W. 1972. "Review article: New Perspectives in Euripidean Criticism," in: *CPh* 67, 270–79.
Konstan, D. 2014. "Introduction: Combat Trauma: The Missing Diagnosis in Ancient Greece," in: P. Meineck/D. Konstan (eds.), *Combat Trauma and the Ancient Greeks*, New York, 1–14.
Kosak, J.C. 2004. *Heroic Measures: Hippocratice Medicine in the Making of Euripidean Tragedy*, Leiden.
Lefkowitz, M.R. 2003. "'Atheism' and 'Impiety' in Euripides' Dramas," in: J. Mossman (ed.), *Euripides: Oxford Readings in Classical Studies*, Oxford, 102–21.
Lloyd, M. 2013. "The Mutability of Fortune in Euripides," in: D.L. Cairns (ed.), *Tragedy and Archaic Greek Thought*, Swansea, 205–26.
Mastronade, D. 2010. *The Art of Euripides: Dramatic Technique and Social Context*, Cambridge.
Meridor, R. 1978. "Hecuba's Revenge: Some Observations on Euripides' *Hecuba*," in: *AJP* 99, 28–35.
—— 1984. "Plot & Myth in Euripides' *Heracles* and *Troades*," in: *Phoenix* 38, 205–15.
Michelini, A. 1987. *Euripides and the Tragic Tradition*, Madison, Wisc.
Mossman, J. 1995. *Wild Justice: A Study of Euripides' Hecuba*, Oxford.
—— (ed.). 2003. *Euripides: Oxford Readings in Classical Studies*, Oxford.

Nussbaum, M.C. 1986. *The Fragility of Goodness: Luck and Ethics in Greek Tragedy and Philosophy*, Cambridge.
Osborne, R. 2011. *The History Written on the Classical Body*, Cambridge.
Papadopoulou, T. 2005. *Heracles and Euripidean Tragedy*, Cambridge.
Parker, R. 2005. *Polytheism and Society at Athens*, Oxford.
Rabinowitz, N.S. 1993. *Anxiety Veiled: Euripides and the Traffic in Women*, Ithaca, NY.
—— 2014. "Women and War in Tragedy," in: P. Meineck/D. Konstan (eds.), *Combat Trauma and the Ancient Greeks*, New York, 185–206.
Reckford, K. 1985. "Concepts of Demoralization in the *Hecuba*," in: P. Burian (ed.), *Directions in Euripidean Criticism*, Durham, NC, 112–128.
Riley, K. 2008. *The Reception and Performance of Euripides' Heracles*, Oxford.
Romilly, J. de. 2003. "The Rejection of Suicide in *Heracles*," in: J. Mossman (ed.), *Euripides: Oxford Readings in Classical Studies*, Oxford, 285–94.
Scodel, R. 1980. *The Trojan Trilogy of Euripides*, Gottingen.
Scullion, S. 1999/2000. "Tradition and Innovation in Euripidean Aitiology," in: M. Cropp/K. Lee/D. Sansone (eds.) *Euripides and Tragic Theatre in the Late Fifth Century* (= *ICS* 24–5), 217–33.
Segal, C. 1993. *Euripides and the Poetics of Sorrow: Art, Gender, and Commemoration in Alcestis, Hippolytus, and Hecuba*, Durham, NC.
Shay, J. 1995. *Achilles in Vietnam: Combat Trauma and the Undoing of Character*, New York.
—— 2002. *Odysseus in America: Combat Trauma and the Trials of Homecoming*, New York.
Silk, M. 1985. "Heracles and Greek Tragedy," in: *Greece & Rome* 32, 1–22.
Sourvinou-Inwood, C. 2003. *Tragedy and Athenian Religion*, Lanham, MD.
Stafford, E. 2005. "Héraklès : encore et toujours le problème du heros-theos," in: *Kernos*, 18, 391–406.
—— 2012. *Herakles*, London/New York.
Stinton, T.C.W. 1990. *Collected Papers on Greek Tragedy*, Oxford.
Whitmarsh, T. 2016. *Battling the Gods: Atheism in the Ancient World*, London.
Wilamowitz-Moellendorff, U. von. 1959. *Euripides Herakles Vols 1–3*. Reprint of 2nd ed. (Berlin, 1895), Darmstadt.
Williams, B. 1993. *Shame and Necessity*, Berkeley/Los Angeles/Oxford.
Wilson, P. 1999–2000. "Euripides' Tragic Muse," in: M.J. Cropp/K. Lee/ D. Sansone (eds.), *Euripides and Tragic Theatre in the Late Fifth Century* (= *Illinois Classical Studies* 24/25), 427–49.
Wohl, V. 2015. *Euripides and the Politics of Form*, Princeton.
Yoshitake, S. 1994. "Disgrace, Grief and Other Ills: Heracles' rejection of suicide," in: *JHS* 114, 135–53.
Yunis, H. 1988. *A New Creed: Fundamental Religious Beliefs in the Athenian Polis and Euripidean Drams*, Gottingen.
Zeitlin, F. 1996. *Playing the Other: Gender and Society in Greek Literature*, Chicago.

Niall W. Slater
Up from Tragicomedy: The Growth of Hope in Greek Comedy

"Hope" is the thing with feathers -
That perches in the soul -
And sings the tune without the words -
And never stops — at all —
Emily Dickinson

How wrong Emily Dickinson was! Hope is not "the thing with feathers." The thing with feathers has turned out to be my nephew. I must take him to a specialist in Zurich.

Woody Allen, *Without Feathers*, "Selections from the Allen Notebooks" (1975)

For much of its history the discourse of hope in Greek comedy is deeply entangled with that in Greek tragedy. It is an intriguing question as to whether this appearance is a function of the Athenocentric nature of our evidence or even more specifically of the profound interest that our two main witnesses, Aristophanes and Menander, took in the rival genre of tragedy. The nature of Menander's views of hope may prove more multifaceted, however, even as they bleed over into other, sometimes anonymous, but much more hopeful views of hope in the age of New Comedy.

Our first fleeting glimpse of hope in Greek comedy lies far to the west of Athens and earlier than any Athenian evidence but is tantalizingly minimal. Later Greeks remembered Epicharmus in Sicily as an important innovator in comedy.[1] Aeschylus apparently knew his work, perhaps from his own sojourn in Sicily, when Epicharmus was nearing the end of his very long career. Among Epicharmus' known plays and represented by seven surviving fragments is a work with a double title, Ἐλπὶς ἢ Πλοῦτος. This is one of at most three plays by Epicharmus recorded with a double title, attested by Athenaeus, Herodian, and the Antiatticist.[2] We can leave aside the play called in a couple sources *Pyrrha or Prometheus*;

---

1 Good brief discussion with all the important testimonia in Rusten *et al.* 2011, 59–62, followed by translations of the major fragments.
2 Athenaeus 6. 235E with fr. 31 K–A., Ἐπίχαρμος ἐν Ἐλπίδι ἢ Πλούτῳ (although Athenaeus 4. 139B with fr. 34 K–A. refers only to Ἐπίχαρμος γοῦν ἐν Ἐλπίδι); Herodian II, p. 927.12 L with fr. 35 K–A., Ἐπίχαρμος ἐν Ἐλπίδι <ἢ> Πλούτῳ, Antiatt. λ 2 (Valente 2015, 207) with fr. 37 K–A., Ἐπίχαρμος Ἐλπίδι ἢ Πλούτῳ.

Kassel and Austin opt for the title *Pyrrha and Prometheus*.[3] His *Komasts or Hephaestos* looks like a pattern familiar from Attic comedy, where one title may refer to the chorus, the other to a title character, although there is general agreement that Epicharmus's plays did not have choruses. Nonetheless we can easily imagine a plot or setting in which the *komasts* and Hephaestos were very closely associated. For *Hope or Wealth* therefore, the natural inference is that the two elements of the title were closely related in the author's and therefore the audience's mind, not polar opposites. The scenario included a drinking party and one or more parasites, and although one of the parasites complains about the dangers of walking home after dinner, undoubtedly the play offered a generally desirable picture of comic revelry. No one in the world of comedy thinks wealth in and of itself a bad thing. When *Hope* is the alternative title to *Wealth*, hope must therefore be a good thing too, although we can scarcely say any more than that.

Aristophanes is our sole witness for the depiction and understanding of hope in Old Comedy. His *Thesmophoriazusae* with its multiple tragic parodies has the greatest number of explicit references to hope, but it is striking how often even the earlier scattered references occur in close relation to other instances of parody. *Knights, Clouds, Wasps,* and *Peace* each provide one explicit mention of hope where the tragic or grandiloquent overtones suggest that hope is at best a doubtful thing and at worst highly deceptive.

The first occurrence is in *Knights*, as Paphlagon discovers how dangerously close the background of his opponent the Sausage Seller lies to his own career and skills. In his fear he appeals to Apollo for protection:

ΠΑΦΛΑΓΩΝ
ὦ Φοῖβ' Ἄπολλον Λύκιε, τί ποτέ μ' ἐργάσει;
τέχνην δὲ τίνα ποτ' εἶχες ἐξανδρούμενος;
ΑΛΛΑΝΤΟΠΩΛΗΣ
ἠλλαντοπώλουν καί τι καὶ βινεσκόμην.
ΠΑΦΛΑΓΩΝ
οἴμοι κακοδαίμων· οὐκέτ' οὐδέν εἰμ' ἐγώ.
λεπτή τις ἐλπίς ἐστ' ἐφ' ἧς ὀχούμεθα.[4] (*Knights* 1240–44)

Paphlagon
"Phoebus Apollo of Lycia, what do you mean to do to me?"
And when you were becoming a man, what sort of trade did you follow?

---

3   Also known as Deucalion or Leucarion. See Kassel and Austin for details.
4   The texts of Aristophanes throughout, and the translations unless otherwise noted, are from Henderson.

Sausage Seller
I sold sausages, and now and then I also sold my arse.
Paphlagon
Oh, I'm damned! This is the absolute end of me!
There's but a splinter of hope keeping me afloat. (trans. Henderson)

The first line here quotes Euripides' *Telephus* (fr. 700), a play Aristophanes returned to again and again as a source of humor, and probably spoken by Telephus himself after his exposure in the Greek camp. Paphlagon clearly knows he is in trouble. The notion that the adjective λεπτή, combined with a verb often used for sailing vessels (ὀχούμεθα), here indicates that hope is a flotation device, as it were, goes back to Casaubon.[5] The lightness of hope here therefore has utilitarian advantages but also carries a connotation of insubstantiality.[6] Nauck considered line 1244 a tragic quotation as well (adespota fr. 55 K–S), although it may already have been proverbial.[7]

The concept of light or slender (λεπτή) hope recurs a couple decades later in Aristophanes' *Gerytades*, a play that apparently anticipated *Frogs* in sending a delegation to Hades, in this case representatives of the poets:

(A.) καὶ τίνες ἂν εἶεν;
(B.) πρῶτα μὲν Σαννυρίων
ἀπὸ τῶν τρυγῳδῶν, ἀπὸ δὲ τῶν τραγικῶν χορῶν
Μέλητος, ἀπὸ δὲ τῶν κυκλίων Κινησίας.
 (A.) ὡς σφόδρ' ἐπὶ λεπτῶν ἐλπίδων ὠχεῖσθ' ἄρα.
τούτους γάρ, ἢν πολλῷ ξυνέλθῃ ξυλλαβὼν
ὁ τῆς διαρροίας ποταμὸς οἰχήσεται.   (Gerytades 156. 7–12 K–A.)

(A) And who might they be?
(B) First, Sannyrion
represents the trygic choruses, and the tragic ones
Meletus, and the dithyrambic ones Cinesias.
(A) How very slender the hopes you're riding on!
For the diarrhoea river, if it's in spate,
will take these fellows and carry them away.

---

5   Quoted by Neil 1905, 163 ad. 1244. Hope has or gives wings in some tragic usages (e.g., Sophocles, *OT* 487–488, Euripides *Auge* fr. 271.1) and Bacchylides 3.75 (references I owe to Cairns 2016, 35 n.85), but Paphlagon's transport here does not seem to be winged.
6   The very near synonym κούφη, when applied to hope, clearly indicates insubstantial or illusory hopes, as in Solon 13. 36; cf. Cairns 2016, 23, n.85 and 40–41.
7   Rau 1967, 171 says „daß das Sprichwort einer Tragödie entstammt, ist möglich (bei Nauck Fr. adesp. 55), aber nicht sicher."

Line 10 here is essentially the same thought as *Knights* 1244, made plural. The sources that preserve this fragment tell us that key to the joke is the fact that Sannyrion was unnaturally thin (and persistent bowel trouble — in some way linked to the river of diarrhoea in the Underworld? — might account for that thinness). Slender hopes apparently go with slender verse, and we are long before the Hellenistic idealization of λεπτότης as a good poetic quality.[8]

Following Aristophanes' notable success with *Knights*, he clearly had great hopes for his topical satire of Socrates in *Clouds* — hopes that were shockingly disappointed by its third-place finish. In the revised but never produced second version of the play surviving to us there is again exactly one mention of hope. While Strepsiades clearly had in the opening of the play what we would call hopes for escaping his debts and improving his son, it is intriguing that those desires are never expressed in the language of hope.[9] For what it is worth, the

---

[8] Socrates' 'subtlety' (λεπτότητος) is the ironic object of Strepsiades' admiration in *Clouds* 153 and leads to the discussion of the discussion of the gnat bugling from its 'narrow' (λεπτοῦ, 161) gut. The voice of the Clouds makes Strepsiades want to speak in subtleties (λεπτολογεῖν, 320), and the *Cloud* chorus in turn dubs Socrates a priest of the subtlest nonsense (λεπτοτάτων λήρων ἱερεῦ, 359). Despite some fascinating new subtleties about Hellenistic theories of subtlety in Porter 2011, the Aristophanic examples are not enough to recover a larger fifth century theory of λεπτότης. The ironies here do suggest that metaphorical thinness / subtlety is no virtue either.

[9] The language of desire is all over the *Clouds*, particularly in the mouth of Strepsiades or others describing his wishes. We find hortatory subjunctives (11, 289, 300), εἴθε (24, 41) and ἵνα clauses, and various grander verbs (ἀντιβολῶ, 110, 314; χρῄζεις, 359, 891) including the *Cloud* chorus's recognition of Strepsiades' yearning (ἐπιθυμήσας, 412), but commonest of course are forms of βούλομαι. Socrates and the Clouds repeatedly quiz Strepsiades on what he desires (636, 737, and *passim*). Strepsiades turns himself over to the *Clouds* to do whatever they want with him (439, 454), and they in turn promise Strepsiades that others will come to him, once he has learned, to fulfill their own desires (470). Only as the play nears the end does the chorus suggest that Strepsiades' desire for the unjust logos has become more of an eros (οἷον τὸ πραγμάτων ἐρᾶν ... ἀποστερῆσαι βούλεται, 1303, 1305; "How momentous it is to lust for villainous business ... he wants to avoid repaying") and warns that he may wish his son were mute (βουλήσεται / κἄφωνον αὐτὸν εἶναι, 1319–1320) rather than a master of the unjust logos.

Intriguing modern psychological approaches attempt to differentiate desires and wishes, e.g. Miceli and Castelfranchi 2015, 6: "Whereas wishes are goals whose attainment is either (logically) impossible or possible, *desires* typically refer to goals whose attainment is viewed as not impossible" (emphasis original). This however may be a function of English and other modern languages. Aristophanic βούλομαι does not distinguish based on logical possibility. The *Clouds* offer to negotiate an exchange of desires with the audience: they want to win the prize (βουλόμεσθ', 1116), and the audience wants rain for their crops (βούλησθ', 1117), both certainly possible, but the *Clouds* predict that if a judge votes against them, said judge will wish (βουλήσεται, 1129) he were living in Egypt, rather than suffering the *Clouds*' stormy wrath. See

scholarly consensus tends to see little revision in this part of the play. Hypothesis I tells us explicitly that the ending, along with the *parabasis* and the *agon*, was revised for the second version.[10] Certainty is impossible, but it seems likely that the one mention of hope in the ending is an addition for the revised version and once again a parody of the style of tragedy, visual as well as verbal. Strepsiades has mounted to the top of the *skenê* and begun chopping holes in the roof of the Thinkery in order to set it on fire. One of the fleeing students asks him if he wants to destroy them all, and his answer is explicit:

τοῦτ' αὐτὸ γὰρ καὶ βούλομαι,
ἢν ἡ σμινύη μοι μὴ προδῷ τὰς ἐλπίδας
ἢ 'γὼ πρότερόν πως ἐκτραχηλισθῶ πεσών. (*Clouds* 1499 – 1501)

That's precisely my intention,
if this hatchet doesn't betray my hopes
or I fall first and break my neck!

Socrates entered the play on the crane, 'treading the air' (ἀεροβατῶ, 225) like a *deus ex machina*; Strepsiades now usurps his place aloft and his language, for when the fleeing Socrates demands to know what he is doing, Strepsiades answers in the very same words (ἀεροβατῶ καὶ περιφρονῶ τὸν ἥλιον, 1502; 'I tread the air and scrutinize the sun'). In this fantastic and possibly unstageable as well as never staged version of the ending, the axe does not betray Strepsiades' hopes. He displaces Socrates as ruler of this (stage) universe in order to tear it down.[11] Would it be too much psychologizing to suggest, however, that the audience and the judges at the first performance had indeed betrayed Aristophanes' hopes? His bitterness over the play's third-place finish certainly shows through in comments in the *parabasis* of *Wasps* the next year and even *Peace* thereafter.

---

also below on the problematics of the concept of 'beyond hopes' (παρ' ἐλπίδας) in Aristophanes and tragedy.
10 καὶ τελευταῖον ὅπου καίεται ἡ διατριβὴ Σωκράτους.
11 Whether tragic parody here is more systematic than opportunistic is open to question. One of the editors points me to Gregory Dobrov's analysis of the *Peace* as a comic "contrafact" of Euripides' *Bellerophon* (Dobrov 1999, 89–104): where the tragic hero mounts to the heavens to prove there are no gods and is cast down for his hubris, the comic hero Trygaeus shows the gods have indeed decamped—but brings back Peace anyway. There may be a distant adumbration here: Socrates has dethroned Zeus in favor of "Whirl" (Δῖνος, 379, 828), but Strepsiades implicitly if violently restores divine justice. Someone, probably the chorus, does try to comfort Bellerophon in Euripides' play with the prospect of unhoped for/unexpected reversals of fortune ἀέλπτους ... ἀναστροφάς, fr. 301.1), but no other language of hope survives from that work.

The one explicit mention of hope in *Wasps* comes from one of the boys accompanying the old wasp jurors in their *eisodos*. These impoverished men rely on their jury pay for daily sustenance, as their sons know well. One of the boys asks:

ἄγε νυν, ὦ πάτερ, ἢν μὴ
τὸ δικαστήριον ἄρχων
καθίσῃ νῦν, πόθεν ὠνη-
σόμεθ' ἄριστον; ἔχεις ἐλ-
πίδα χρηστήν τινα νῷν ἢ
πόρον Ἕλλας ἱερόν; (*Wasps* 303–08)

Tell me then, father, if the archon
doesn't call the court into session today,
how can we buy lunch? Do you have
any firm hope for us,
any "holy way to Helle"?

The last three words are parodic quotation from Pindar (fr. 189), although their use may represent quite an interesting innovation on Aristophanes' part: πόρος here is a passage, a crossing, the strait of the Hellespont (implicitly of course dangerous and uncertain, the very opposite of "firm"), and that metaphor for hope is unknown previously.[12] In the hardscrabble world of these jurors and their sons, firm hope (ἐλπίδα χρηστήν) even for their next meal is as difficult as swimming the Hellespont.

Wasps in turn betrayed the poet's hopes for a comeback victory after the stinging defeat of *Clouds*. While we cannot be sure precisely what Aristophanes thought was so special about the dance contest he staged between old Philocleon and the explicitly billed sons of Carcinus in the play's finale, apparently it was not the success with the audience or the judges that he was looking for.[13] He certainly complains about it in the *parabasis* of *Peace*. Aristophanes' chorus tells the audience that they should never entrust anything to the sons of Carcinus but rather should:

---

12 As Cairns 2016 demonstrates, metaphors for hope in Greek literature before comedy are not numerous. Pindar gives us one example of hopes as vehicles, specifically ships tossed on the seas, at *Ol.* 12. 6a, τάμνοισαι κυλίνδοντ' ἐλπίδες, but nothing resembles this bridge or passage metaphor.

13 A much disputed scene. MacDowell 1971, 326–327 *ad Wasps* 1501 believes Aristophanes actually hired the sons of Carcinus to appear. Olson 1998, 226 *ad Peace* 782-4 suggests other performers played these historical individuals.

ἀλλὰ νόμιζε πάντας
ὄρτυγας οἰκογενεῖς, γυλιαύχενας ὀρχηστὰς
νανοφυεῖς, σφυράδων ἀποκνίσματα, μηχανοδίφας.
καὶ γὰρ ἔφασχ' ὁ πατὴρ ὃ παρ' ἐλπίδας
εἶχε τὸ δρᾶμα γαλῆν τῆς
ἑσπέρας ἀπάγξαι.   (*Peace* 787–796)

But consider them all
home-bred quails, hump-necked dancers
of dwarfish build, demi-dungballs, caper-chasers.
For their father once insisted that the play
he'd got booked beyond all hope
was throttled one night by the weasel. (trans. Henderson, modified)

Details here are rather obscure, but Aristophanes' resentment is not. This looks like classic displacement. There are at least three layers to his mockery of Carcinus's failure. The humiliation of Carcinus's failure is clear in itself, but Aristophanes suggests that Carcinus then offered a completely ridiculous excuse for it. Just what the 'weasel' (γαλῆν) is doing in the story remains unclear: is this the ancient Greek equivalent of "the dog ate my homework"?[14] The almost offhand mockery of the third element is perhaps the most telling: the fact that Carcinus obtained a performance slot from the archon at all was a matter "beyond hope" (παρ' ἐλπίδας).

This phrase has a pedigree in lyric and tragedy. In Euripides παρ' ἐλπίδας may indeed more often mean expectation. After the chorus sees Hippolytus sent away by his father, they call this result something beyond all expectation:

οὐκέτι γὰρ καθαρὰν φρέν' ἔχω, παρὰ δ' ἐλπίδ'
ἃ λεύσσω.[15]   (*Hippolytus* 1120–21)

For my mind is no longer untroubled: beyond all expectation are the things I behold. (trans. Kovacs)

---

14   Against previous opinion that the reference is to the failure of one of Carcinus's plays during the festival performance, Halliwell 1980, 164 suggests "blaming something on the γαλῆ might have been practically proverbial for giving a thin excuse for a suspicious disappearance" and theorizes that Aristophanes mocks Carcinus for failing to produce a script in time when offered a slot by the archon. Carcinus may have gained a spot based on previous reputation, and we should not assume that he offered the archon a scenario, let alone had a full script already written. Kaimio and Nykopp 1997, 34–35 and n. 63 defend the idea that his drama failed at the festival and suggest that a weasel was itself "a sign of bad luck."
15   Texts and translations are from Kovacs, unless otherwise noted.

When the servant reveals to Hecuba the body of her son, this too is something totally unexpected:

> θαῦμα καὶ παρ' ἐλπίδας   (*Hecuba* 680)
>
> an astonishing sight, one you had not looked for

After the messenger reports Orestes' failure to persuade the assembly, the chorus laments his and Electra's impending fate:

> λεύσσεθ' ὡς παρ' ἐλπίδας / μοῖρα βαίνει   (*Orestes* 977–78)
>
> see how fate defeats your expectations!

None of these events in Euripides are what the speakers or their hearers would have hoped for. Yet earlier, Pindar in describing the deeds of Bellerophon suggests that hopes and expectations are not so easily distinguished:

> τελεῖ δὲ θεῶν δύναμις καὶ τὰν παρ' ὅρκον καὶ παρὰ ἐλπίδα κούφαν κτίσιν.   (*Olympian* 13. 83)
>
> The gods' power easily brings into being even what one would swear impossible and beyond hope.[16]   (trans. Race)

The notion that even obtaining the chance for performance should have been παρ' ἐλπίδας for Carcinus undoubtedly is meant to say more about Carcinus than the nature of hope. At the risk of being exceedingly pedantic, however, I must note that here in Aristophanes it cannot mean "beyond rational expectation." As the advertisements for the lottery say, you can't win if you don't play. The only way Carcinus could have been awarded a slot at the festival was to seek one. Obtaining one of the slots therefore cannot have been something unimaginable, but rather beyond the hopes of Carcinus in particular. The phrasing leaves open the implication that others (and here Aristophanes would undoubtedly include himself) *were* entitled to hope, perhaps even expect that the archon would give them a slot at the festival—worth stressing, because this use of ἐλπίς in surviving Aristophanes seems least tied to tragedy or paratragedy and thus may reflect

---

16 Barrett 1964, 372 in commenting on *Hippolytus* 1120 asserts that παρ' ἐλπίδα is used of "things that one was confident would not happen" and cites this passage of Pindar but translates it "achieves lightly even the accomplishment *that one would* have sworn and *have believed impossible*" (emphasis original). Cf. Alexandre Johnston's discussion of hope and the gods in Pindar in this volume.

categories of popular usage, in which some hopes were ridiculous but others might be legitimate.

For hope is rather consistently ridiculed in the many games of Aristophanes' *Thesmophoriazusae*. The play's first instance may be the one most open to dispute. Euripides and his old relative have come to Agathon for help in finding out what the women of Athens are plotting. Agathon refuses to get involved in Euripides' problems with the following speech:

ΑΓΑΘΩΝ
μή νυν ἐλπίσῃς τὸ σὸν κακὸν
ἡμᾶς ὑφέξειν. καὶ γὰρ ἂν μαινοίμεθ' ἄν.   (*Thesmophoriazusae* 195–196)

Agathon
Then don't expect us to shoulder
your misfortune. We'd have to be crazy!

Henderson's translation opts for the more intellectual and less emotive "don't expect" for Aristophanes' μή ... ἐλπίσῃς. Undoubtedly the verb can refer to a purely rational calculation. When the servant asks his master in Euripides' *Hippolytus* whether the gods themselves also attempt to charm each other:

ἦ κἀν θεοῖσι ταὐτὸν ἐλπίζεις τόδε;   (*Hippolytus* 197)

Do you think the same is true among the gods?   (trans. Kovacs)

the question clearly concerns expectation based on mental calculation. He is not asking if he *hopes* this to be true. On the other hand when Menelaus talks about why they brought Ajax to take part in the war in Sophocles' *Ajax*:

ὁθούνεκ' αὐτὸν ἐλπίσαντες οἴκοθεν   (*Ajax* 1052)

when we had hoped we were bringing Ajax from home to be an ally   (trans. Jebb)

It seems impossible to separate desire from calculation. If we return to the point of contention between Euripides and Agathon, it seems clear that Agathon's rejection of Euripides' request tends more toward the emotional rather than the rational end of the spectrum of meaning for ἐλπίζω. Agathon is warning against hope rather than expectation.[17]

---

[17] Here also modern cognitive approaches to hope may mislead about the Greek mind. Miceli and Castelfranchi 2015, 161 suggest: "The basic cognitive ingredients of hope are in our view very simple: a belief that an event *p* is possible and the goal that *p* occurs." Euripides certainly

In the theatre on the day of the single performance of this play in 411, the performance and intonation of the actor playing Agathon will have done more to determine the connotation of μὴ νυν ἐλπίσῃς than any conscious ratiocination by the members of the audience sitting in the Theatre of Dionysus about the possible meanings of the verb. Let us note, however, that the often paratragic mockery of subsequent hopes in play reinforces such a reading here.

As the plot progresses, Euripides ends up shaving and disguising his old relative as a woman in order to send him to spy on the women's gathering, where the unfortunate old man is ultimately exposed and bound to the plank in the most humiliating circumstances. The old man longs for Euripides to come and rescue him, whereupon the language of hope reappears. At line 869 it is first given voice:

> ΚΗΔΕΣΤΗΣ
> ἀλλ' ὥσπερ αἰκάλλει τι καρδίαν ἐμήν·
> μὴ ψεῦσον, ὦ Ζεῦ, τῆς ἐπιούσης ἐλπίδος.   (*Thesmophoriazusae* 869–70)
>
> Kinsman
> Yet something, as it were, tickles at my heart:
> deceive me not, o Zeus, in my nascent hope!

This fawning metaphor (αἰκάλλω is especially used of dogs fawning on humans or wagging their tails) may be a further development by Aristophanes;[18] while an indefinite τι is strictly the subject, it seems to be identical with oncoming hope. Euripides himself does come on stage (imperfectly embodying ἐπιούσης ἐλπίδος?), but his first attempt at tragic role-playing is a complete failure, and the old relative plunges into despair. He is particularly humiliated that he has been left in his female costume as part of his punishment:

> ΚΗΔΕΣΤΗΣ
> ἰατταταιάξ. ὦ κροκώθ', οἷ' εἴργασαι.
> κοὐκ ἔστ' ἔτ' ἐλπὶς οὐδεμία σωτηρίας.   (*Thesmophoriazusae* 945–46)
>
> Kinsman
> Aieee! O dresses, what ye have wrought!
> There's no hope I'll be saved now!   (trans. Henderson, modified)

---

believes that persuading Agathon is possible and has that goal in mind, but Agathon's response is not a rational recalibration of probability but an emotional directive to abandon the feeling of hope.

18 Already used of Paphlagon fawning on Demos like a dog in *Knights* 47–48, ὑποπεσὼν τὸν δεσπότην / ᾔκαλλ'; cf. Plato Comicus fr. 248.

Once again tragic parody is closely linked to a despairing discourse about hope.[19] Here the old relative apostrophizes the dresses he is wearing, and this direct address to an object parallels some famous tragic examples.[20] Compare a famous instance from Aristophanes' second favorite source in the number of known quotations and parodies in his own plays, Euripides' *Alcestis*. From the servant's speech preceding her arrival on stage we learn how Alcestis bade farewell to her marriage bed:

Ὦ λέκτρον, ἔνθα παρθένει' ἔλυσ' ἐγὼ
κορεύματ' ἐκ τοῦδ' ἀνδρός, οὗ θνῄσκω πάρος.   (*Alcestis* 177–78)

O marriage bed, where I yielded up my virginity to my husband,
the man for whose sake I am now dying

The old relative's accusation that the dresses are responsible for the terrible things happening to him can be paralleled by Phaedra's accusation against her Nurse, who has failed to win Hippolytus over:

ὦ παγκακίστη καὶ φίλων διαφθορεῦ,
οἷ' εἰργάσω με.   (*Hippolytus* 682–83)

Vile destroyer of your friends, see
what you have done to me!

The old relative's claim that all hope of safety/rescue has vanished echoes Iolaus's fears for the children in the *Children of Heracles* of perhaps 430 BC:[21]

οὐχ ἅπασα γὰρ
πέφευγεν ἐλπὶς τῶνδέ μοι σωτηρίας.   (*Heracleidae* 451–52)

for I have not completely
lost hope for the safety of the children

Indeed, ἐλπίς and σωτηρίας appear in exactly the same metrical positions in the line in both *Thesmophoriazusae* and *Heracleidae*. οὐκ and οὐδεμία may be a bit

---

19   See also Fisher, this volume.
20   Noted by Austin and Olson 2004 *ad loc.* with further examples.
21   On hope as a fleeing figure in this passage of *Heracleidae*, see Cairns 2016, 39 and n.94. For reviews of the question of the play's date, see Wilkins 1993, xxxiii–xxxv and Allan 2001, 54–56, who supports Zuntz's view that the play's reference to the protection of Eurystheus's tomb could not have been made after the full-scale Spartan invasion in the summer of 430.

of overkill in Aristophanes' version, but the tragic pretensions of his line cannot be in doubt.

The old relative's hopes revive when Euripides trots out his final scheme, the dancing girl named Fawn, who finally distracts the Scythian guard long enough for Euripides to release the old man from the plank and lead him away. The old man greets this final appearance thus:

ΚΗΔΕΣΤΗΣ
ταυτὶ τὰ βέλτιστ' ἀπολέλαυκ' Εὐριπίδου.
ἔα· θεοί, Ζεῦ σῶτερ, εἰσὶν ἐλπίδες.
ἀνὴρ ἔοικεν οὐ προδώσειν.[22]   (*Thesmophoriazusae* 1009–10)

Kinsman
This is the reward I get for befriending Euripides!
Ah! Ye gods and Savior Zeus, there's still hope!
It seems the man won't give up on me …

In the end, is there consistent picture of hope in *Thesmophoriazusae*? It seems fair to say that Agathon ridicules Euripides' hopes, while the old relative prays to Zeus to protect his hopes, rejects all hope, and then allows hope to revive. In the end, he escapes, and Euripides negotiates a peace treaty or at least an armistice with the women of Athens. Despite all the jokes then, hope turns out not to be an inherently ridiculous emotion for these nonetheless ridiculous characters.

Whether accepted as a representative of Middle Comedy or not,[23] much about Aristophanes' final play *Wealth* certainly feels different from his earlier work. Perhaps there is some distant connection to the ethos and therefore the kind of hope that animated Epicharmus' play with which it shared a title. The plot of the play, a plan to cure the god Wealth of his blindness so that he may bestow his favors on the truly deserving, is explicitly driven by hope — as Chremylus announces when he emerges from Apollo's shrine at Delphi:

ΧΡΕΜΥΛΟΣ
ἔχω τιν' ἀγαθὴν ἐλπίδ' ἐξ ὧν εἶπέ μοι
ὁ Φοῖβος αὐτὸς Πυθικὴν σείσας δάφνην.   (*Wealth* 212–13)

---

22 Is there an implicit identification again of Euripides himself with ἐλπίδες? Note the linkage of betrayal and hopes back in *Clouds* 1500, μὴ προδῷ τὰς ἐλπίδας.
23 For problems with the classification, see Csapo 2000 and (briefly) Hanink 2014, 270–271.

> I have high hopes, after what Phoebus told me,
> "when he personally shook the Pythian laurel bough."[24]

The echo of tragedy lingers, but not in a way that seems to mock the notion of hope. Chremylus quotes an unknown tragedian to reinforce Apollo's endorsement of his plan to cure Wealth. The plot of the play will demonstrate the effectiveness of the plan, and Chremylus' divinely endorsed hope will be fulfilled. Is this view of hope new in the world of the 4th century, or has it always been available but just not well represented in the tragic parodies of hope in earlier Aristophanic comedy?

The two other witnesses that can be firmly located in the age of Middle Comedy seem to look back to earlier tragic and therefore more pessimistic views of hope. Eubulus wrote many mythological burlesques, among them his *Antiope*. The play seems to have ended with a send-up of the *deus ex machina*. A god (Hermes in Euripides, but unclear whether the same in Eubulus's play) appeared on high to announce the fates of Antiope's two sons, Zethus and Amphion.

> Ζῆθον μὲν ἐλθόνθ' ἁγνὸν ἐς Θήβης πέδον
> οἰκεῖν κελεύει, καὶ γὰρ ἀξιωτέρους
> πωλοῦσιν, ὡς ἔοικε, τοὺς ἄρτους ἐκεῖ·
> σὺ[25] δ' ὀξύπεινος. τὸν δὲ μουσικώτατον
> κλεινὰς Ἀθήνας ἐκπερᾶν Ἀμφίονα
> οὗ ῥᾷστ' ἀεὶ πεινῶσι Κεκροπιδῶν κόροι
> κάπτοντες αὔρας, ἐλπίδας σιτούμενοι.[26]   (*Antiope* *9 K–A)

He orders Zethus to go to the sacred plain of Thebes to make his home; because it seems that they sell their bread cheaper there. And you ARE ravenous. But he orders the musical Amphion to make his way to famous Athens; Cecrops' sons always starve easily there, gulping down the breezes and eating hopes.

(trans. Olson, modified to match the text of K–A. and Hunter)

---

24 trag. adesp. 61c; cf. Sommerstein *ad loc.*
25 For σὺ as the "comically effective" reading, see Hunter *ad loc.* On the page it is confusing for the divine speaker to shift from 3rd person to 2nd and back, but performance could make it perfectly clear.
26 Cf. Aegisthus in Aeschylus, *Agamemnon* 1668, οἶδ' ἐγὼ φεύγοντας ἄνδρας ἐλπίδας σιτουμένους; and Jocasta in Euripides, *Phoenissae* 396: αἱ δ' ἐλπίδες βόσκουσι φυγάδας, ὡς λόγος.

Eubulus here picks up one of the most common metaphors for hope, something that nourishes and sustains,[27] but then bathetically subverts it. The mockery of Athens' citizens "eating hopes" plays off famous tragic descriptions of exiles. Aegisthus in Aeschylus's *Agamemnon* says, "I know exiles are men feeding on hopes" (1668, οἶδ' ἐγὼ φεύγοντας ἄνδρας ἐλπίδας σιτουμένους), while Jocasta in Euripides' *Phoenissae* says, "Hopes nourish exiles, as the story goes" (396, αἱ δ' ἐλπίδες βόσκουσι φυγάδας, ὡς λόγος). In Eubulus's version then, the painful lives of exiles turn into the vain but everyday hopes of ordinary Athenians.

Another poet of Middle Comedy, Antiphanes, locates his doubtful view of hope very much in the situations of ordinary life. In his *Fuller*, someone, perhaps the title character, describes the life of an artisan in contrast to the unskilled man who gambled his life as a mercenary soldier:

> ὅστις τέχνην πρῶτος κατέδειξε τῶν θεῶν,
> οὗτος μέγιστον εὗρεν ἀνθρώποις κακόν.
> ὅταν γὰρ ἀπορῆταί τις, ἂν μὲν ἀργὸς ᾖ,
> ἐλθὼν ἀπεκινδύνευσεν ἡμέραν μίαν,
> ὥστ' ἢ γεγονέναι λαμπρὸς ἢ τεθνηκέναι.
> ἡμεῖς δ' ἔχοντες ἀρραβῶνα τὴν τέχνην
> τοῦ ζῆν, ἀεὶ πεινῶμεν ἐπὶ ταῖς ἐλπίσιν,
> ἐξόν τε μικρὸν διαπορηθῆναι χρόνον,
> τὸν βίον ἅπαντα τοῦτο δρᾶν αἰρούμεθα.   (*The Fuller*, 121 K–A.)

> The god who first revealed our trades
> he invented the greatest of human evils.
> When someone is unskilled and has no way out,
> he goes and risks his life on a single day,
> to turn into either a hero or a corpse.
> But we, who possess a skill to guarantee
> staying alive, we always make a poor living on our hopes.
> Although we might be desperate for a brief time
> we prefer to do so our whole life long.   (trans. Rusten)

Perhaps Antiphanes is consciously innovating on that tragic theme of exiles feeding themselves on hope. His artisans too subsist on hopes, but it is a starvation diet.

Hope finally grows more hopeful in the age of New Comedy, though even here it does not succeed in freeing itself completely from tragic associations and therefore potentially tragic meanings. The most sustained treatment of hope in Menander is a constellation of usages in the unfortunately quite fragmentary

---

27   See Cairns 2016, 29–33.

Sicyonians.²⁸ The unusually complicated plot involves a soldier, Stratophanes, raised as a foster son by now deceased Sicyonian parents but unexpectedly revealed to be an Athenian,²⁹ who is as usual in love with a girl, Philoumene, initially enslaved but eventually recognized as free herself. His competition is his biological brother Moschion, and once his own real parentage is discovered, Moschion gives way so that Stratophanes can marry the girl. Part way through the play Philoumene takes refuge at Eleusis, and Stratophanes pursues her there. All these events were reported in a very lengthy speech by a character named Eleusinios. The speech contains a number of paratragic reminisces of the messenger speech about Orestes' trial in Euripides' *Orestes*, as Eleusinios tells how Stratophanes appealed to the crowd at the sanctuary to take care of Philoumene until he can find her real Athenian father and ask for her hand. Eleusinios quotes Stratophanes directly:

> τὴν ἐλπίδα
> μήπω μ' ἀφέλησθ', ἀλλ', ἂν φανῶ τῆς παρθένου
> κἀγὼ πολίτης, ἣν ἔσῳσα τῷ πατρί,
> ἐάσατ' αἰτῆσαί με τοῦτον καὶ λαβεῖν.30   (*Sicyonioi* 251–54)

> Don't dash
> My hopes now, but if I as well am shown
> To share my citizenship with this girl,
> Whom I protected for her father, let me ask
> Him for her hand in marriage.   (trans. Arnott)

As the events of the play will show, Stratophanes' hopes are not only admirable but will be fulfilled.

Nor are his the only hopes in the play. A recognition scene follows in which the old Athenian Smicrines and his wife recognize and identify the birth tokens that prove Stratophanes is their son.³¹ Smicrines says to Stratophanes:

---

28 For the question of whether the title was singular or plural, see Arnott 1997, 3 and Arnott 2000, 196–198.
29 The slave Pyrrhias reporting the foster mother's deathbed revelations describes them as 'things quite unexpected' (ἀνελπίστοις τισίν, *Sik.* 127), so the ἐλπισ- root continues to mean 'expectation' as well in Menander; compare the 'unexpected disaster' (τῆς ἀνελπίστου τύχης, 18) of the apparent death of the hero announced at the beginning of Menander's *Aspis*.
30 Texts and translations of Menander are from Arnott, where available. Other fragments are quoted from Kassel and Austin, with translations by the author, except as noted.
31 Arnott 265 *ad loc.* notes of this scene: "the rhythms and style approximate closely to those of tragedy, just as in the recognition scene of *Perikeiromene*."

ἤ]δη καὐτὸς ἐμβλέπω σε, παῖ,
]ηται καιρὸς ὡς παρ' ἐλπίδας.   (*Sicyonioi* 286–87)

] now I myself look at you, son
] opportunity has [ ] beyond our hopes.

Since the messenger speech preceding this scene echoed so much of Euripides' *Orestes*, it may be possible that a very alert spectator might hear a specific echo in παρ' ἐλπίδας of the same phrase at line end in *Orestes* 977, where that play's chorus lamented the imminent disaster looming over Orestes and Electra. Here however the καιρός with its tragic associations nonetheless suggests the right or fated time that brings everything to fulfillment has come, and the tonality is the opposite of despairing.[32] The father rejoices at recovering the son he had to give up through poverty, and it looks like his wife remembers her own hopes in the same scene as well, although the text is very fragmentary:

] ἐλπίσασά[33] τε
]ν ἡ τύχη   (*Sicyonioi* 293–94)

] having hoped
] fortune

Moreover this play may also have contained an anticipation of Terence's duality plots. Near the end a second couple seems to be getting married, Malthake and Theron. Much is very uncertain here, but it may be Theron speaking of himself when he refers to (416):

ἄνθρωπον ἐλπίσαντα δεο[

a man with hopes

Despite multiple tragic associations then, the hopes expressed in *Sicyonioi* are consistently estimable and fulfilled.

The one preserved reference to hope in *Epitrepontes* also designates a hope destined to be fulfilled. The slaves Syros and Daos are disputing possession of the tokens abandoned with the child in this play, and Syros insists that they belong with the child:

---

32 Compare the guard who returns with the captured Antigone and expresses his ἡ γὰρ εὐκτὸς καὶ παρ' ἐλπίδας χαρά (Soph., *Antigone* 392, "delight that one has prayed for beyond hope," trans. Lloyd-Jones).
33 Arnott gives ἐλπίσασα to Stratophanes' mother.

οὐ δὴ καλῶ[ς ἔχ]ει τ[ὸ] μὲν σῶμ' ἐκτρέφειν
ἐμὲ τοῦτο, [τὴ]ν [δὲ] τοῦδε τῆς σωτηρίας
ἐλπίδα λαβόντα Δᾶον ἀφανίσαι, πάτερ. (*Epitrepontes* 338–340)

It's not fair that I should tend
This infant's body, sir, while Daos grabs
His prospect of escape, and smashes it!

Syros wins the immediate dispute, and child and parents are eventually reunited, so hope here is also warranted both morally and in action.[34]

In sharp contrast, in Menander's *Aspis* deceptive hope is a tool that the sympathetic characters can use to manipulate and frustrate the chief villain of the piece, coincidentally also named Smicrines. This play opens with the return of the slave Daos, bringing the spoils won in war by his master Cleostratos, believed to be dead in his last battle. This being a comedy, Cleostratos will eventually turn up alive. In the meantime however, the prospect of gaining his deceased nephew's wealth tempts Smicrines to claim the right to marry Cleostratos's sister in accordance with the Athenian law on heiresses. To save the girl from this fate, Daos comes up with a plan to convince Smicrines that his own younger brother Chairestratos is dying and will leave his daughter as an even richer heiress. If Smicrines can be persuaded to renounce his claim to the first girl officially, she will be safe. The section outlining the plot is much damaged, but undoubtedly the plan is specifically to offer:

αὐτῶι τιν' ἐλπίδ[(*Aspis* 322)

some hope to him

To convince Smicrines, the plotters also hire a fake doctor to pretend to examine Chairestratos in his house. On the street thereafter discussing the patient's likely fate, Smicrines asks the fake doctor:

μανθάνω. τί οὖν;
οὐκ ἔστ]ιν ἐλπὶς οὐδεμία σωτηρίας. (*Aspis* 446–47)

---

34 Someone speaks of 'hopes' in Menander's *Kolax* (fr. 57 Austin, B56 Arnott,]α ἐλπίδων), but the context is so fragmentary that we can have no way to know whether such hopes are justified. Arnott thinks Gnathon may be speaking.

I see. What happens then?
[Is there] no hope of his recovery?[35]

Hope in this play then is necessarily false but used to a good end.

A number of other Menander fragments, mostly from unknown plays, suggest contradictory assessments of hope. Sometimes hope is the consolation or even the salvation of the righteous:

ὅταν τι πράττῃς ὅσιον, ἀγαθὴν ἐλπίδα
πρόβαλλε σαυτῷ, τοῦτο γινώσκων ὅτι
τόλμῃ δικαίᾳ καὶ θεὸς συλλαμβάνει.   (fr. 717 K–A. [494 Koerte])

Whenever you're doing something right, propound
a good hope for yourself, knowing this, that
the god also aids righteous daring.

In previous literature, hope may itself be the container, or a person may be the container in which hope is placed,[36] but the notion that a man may take control of hope and use it as a tool seems innovative.[37] Menander's final line here clearly echoes Euripides *Temenus* fr. 746a (τῷ γὰρ πονοῦντι καὶ θεὸς συλλαμβάνει, "for the god also aids the sufferer") but suggests far more specifically that righteousness justifies hope. On the other hand, a one-line fragment (and the only one of Menander's *Sententiae* that Kassel and Austin accept as a genuine play fragment):

---

35 Speaker attribution is uncertain here. Austin assigns line 447 to the doctor, making it is a statement, rather than a question. Note also that ἐλπὶς οὐδεμία σωτηρίας is the exact same line ending as the old relative's at *Thesmophoriazusae* 946. Gomme and Sandbach 1973, 100 *ad loc.* hasten to assure us that "Menander may have easily invented the line afresh" and also quote a passage in Thucydides to suggest it may be a "stock phrase." I wonder if we should be so brisk in our assurance that Menander did not know Aristophanes or, if he did, would have no interest in quoting him.
36 See Cairns 2016, 33–35 on the "container metaphor" for hope.
37 The verb προβάλλω is originally physical, as in raising one's shield in combat, and *LSJ s.v.* cites this passage as a metaphorical variation of the physical usage. The action here seems to me more akin to verbal or mental activities. In Aristophanes Socrates already throws a hypothetical problem at Strepsiades as a test (σοι προβαλῶ τι δεξιόν, *Clouds* 757), while in Menander's own time, Demosthenes in the *Third Philippic* charges Philip with using the (false) name of peace as a propaganda weapon against the Greeks (τοὔνομα μὲν τὸ τῆς εἰρήνης ὑμῖν προβάλλει, 9.8). It is of course useful to remember that the hoplite shield in the *othismos* was as much an aggressive weapon as a defensive one.

> ἄνθρωπος ἀτυχῶν σῴζεθ' ὑπὸ τῆς ἐλπίδος. (fr. 859 K–A. [636 Koerte])
>
> An ill-fated man is saved by hope.

tells us nothing about whether this man deserved his fate.

Someone discussing a farmer's life suggests hope is a very poor consolation indeed:

> ὁ τῶν γεωργῶν ἡδονὴν ἔχει βίος,
> ταῖς ἐλπίσιν τἀλγεινὰ παραμυθούμενος. (fr. 782 K–A. [559 Koerte])
>
> The farmers' life has this pleasure:
> it consoles miseries with hopes.

Much the same view of the workingman's life is expressed in Antiphanes fr. 121 K–A. (above), though a little more positively. Someone else, possibly the title character in Menander's *Naucleros* or *Shipowner*, claims hope is a positive evil:

> ὦ Ζεῦ πολυτίμηθ', οἷόν ἐστ' ἐλπὶς κακόν. (fr. 249 K–A. [289 Koerte])
>
> O most honored Zeus, what an evil is hope!

As Menander is the only other known comic author of a play entitled *Dardanus*, it is possible that a line preserved from Caecilius's play of that title might reflect an originally Menandrean notion:

> Nihil spei ego credo: omnis res spissas facit. (fr. 22 Ribbeck [1 Guardi][38])
>
> I put no trust in hope; she makes everything tardy.

The idea that one might place something into hope or entrust it is not new, but hope as something capable of tripping up or slowing down progress is.

Philemon is the only other New Comedy author with more than one fragment dealing with hope. His plays depict a more decisive move toward regarding hope as a good thing. A fragment from his *Pancratiast* (of course preserved by Stobaeus because he was collecting edifying sentiments) suggests hope cooperates with fortune (τύχη):

> καὐτόν τι πράττειν· οὐ μόνον τὰς ἐλπίδας
> ἐπὶ τῇ τύχῃ ⟨χρή⟩, παιδίον, πάντως ἔχειν

---

38 Nonius, 392, 15 M. (628 L.).

ὧν βούλεταί τις, ἀλλὰ καὐτὸν τῇ τύχῃ
συλλαμβάνεσθαι· ῥᾷον ἡ τύχη πονεῖ,
ἐὰν μεθ' ἑτέρου τοῦτο, μὴ μόνη, ποιῇ. (fr. 56 K–A.)

and (for) him to do something; not only is it necessary to have hopes
for good fortune, child, for what one altogether
wishes, but for him to cooperate
with fortune; for fortune works easily,
if it does this with another, not alone.

Again we cannot tell if this is a view expressed by the title character; only one other, quite unilluminating fragment survives from this play, so we have no idea of its plot. Still, it would not be a bad philosophy for a sportsman.

Another unattributed fragment is no more than a pious nicety, and Kassel and Austin list it among the "dubia":[39]

οἱ γὰρ θεὸν σέβοντες ἐλπίδας καλὰς
ἔχουσιν εἰς σωτηρίαν. (fr. 197 K–A.)

Those honoring the god have good hopes of safety.

Particularly intriguing, however, is Philemon's view that hope is a stage in the development toward love:

ὁρῶσι πάντες πρῶτον, εἶτ' ἐθαύμασαν,
ἔπειτ' ἐπεθεώρησαν, εἶτ' εἰς ἐλπίδα
ἐνέπεσον· οὕτω γίνετ' ἐκ τούτων ἔρως.[40] (fr. 126 K–A.)

First they all see, then they marvel,
then they gaze intently, then fall into hope;
so love arises by these stages.

Clement of Alexandria preserves these lines to support a view of love that he explicitly attributes to Plato, though it appears nowhere in our texts of the philosopher:

Πλάτωνος εἰπόντος 'ἡμεῖς δὲ τοῦτο δείξομεν ἴσως οὐκ ἀτόπως, ὅτι ἀρχὴ μὲν ἔρωτος ὅρασις,
αὔξει δὲ τὸ πάθος ἐλπίς, τρέφει δὲ μνήμη, τηρεῖ δὲ συνήθεια' (*Stromata* 6.2.23)

---

39 Meineke earlier rejected it as a "pious fraud." Kock also attributed verses preserved in the *Comparison of Menander and Philistion* 47–48 (see appendix I, below) to Philemon as fr. 233K.
40 Preserved by Clement of Alexandria, *Stromata* 6.2.23.

Plato says, "We shall show, perhaps not paradoxically, that seeing is the beginning of love, and hope increases the feeling, memory nourishes it, and intimacy protects it."

Even if Clement's citation of a Platonic aetiology of love is a post-Platonic fabrication,[41] that probably does not undermine the authenticity of the passage from Philemon. There is, however, no indication of who speaks these lines in the play. The unknown speaker implies that one travels from initial vision to full-blown love — but then is hope a stumble or even pitfall along the way? Love is often described as a disease, and the verb Philemon uses, ἐμπίπτω, often applies to both emotions and diseases falling upon the victim.[42] Here, perhaps in an unusual variation on the container metaphor, the lover himself falls into hope (ἐνέπεσον),[43] like a distracted Thales into the well. Such a description of hope as something that lovers fall into makes them more accident victims than agents, so perhaps this is a father or another older character, less than sympathetic to the travails of young lovers. Philemon's rising tricolon of verbs of vision (ὁρῶσι ... ἐθαύμασαν ... ἐπεθεώρησαν) implies an increasingly willful gaze that eventually blocks out any other sight, perhaps thus leading to the fall into hope. In any case, the notion that hope is a way station on the road to love represents an intriguing development.

Perhaps the latest comic witness to hope[44] is also one of the most intriguing as well as mysterious. A fragment of New Comedy found in 1929 has sometimes been attributed to Menander, but opinion now seems to suggest an unknown

---

41 Though perhaps elaborating on originally Platonic views. Cairns 2011 offers a fascinating review of the role competing haptic theories of vision in antiquity (intromissive or extramissive) play in showing how the lover falls victim to the vision of the beloved. Cairns 2013 then studies Plato's portrayal of this erotic process of vision in the *Phaedrus*, where the function of the memory of the Forms in transforming a common *eros* into a philosophic one is key. Hope, however, does not seem to play a significant role in the process in the *Phaedrus*, so where Clement found the version he cites remains unknown.

42 Cf. Homer, *Iliad* 14. 207, χόλος ἔμπεσε θυμῷ.

43 Is this also an innovation from earlier tragic notions? In Aeschylus Zeus flings mortals down from their 'towering hopes' (ἐλπίδων ἀφ' ὑψιπύργων, *Supplices* 96–97), and in Euripides tyrants fall out of their hopes and end up flat on their backs (ἐξ ἐλπίδων πίπτοντας ὑπτίους ὁρῶ, *Ino* fr. 420. 4–5 K). Cf. Cairns 2016, 35. Dimos Spatharas (pers. comm.) points out to me "Uncontrollability is a characteristic of more prototypical emotions, such as anger or *eros*. Hence, one would normally expect the subject of *empipto* to be *eros* rather than *elpis*." Yet hope is not simply being equated with *eros*.

44 Apart from Adespota 1093.101 K–A.,]νυν εἰ μὲν ἐλπίς ἐστί τις, where the context is so fragmentary we can really say nothing.

writer.⁴⁵ The first part of the preserved scene portrays the speaker trying to work up his courage to tackle a difficult task. If he is indeed a slave, his name Megas is unique in the comic record.⁴⁶

> νῦν ἀνὴρ γενοῦ, Μέγα.
> μὴ ἐγκ]αταλίπης Μοσχίωνα. βούλομαι, νὴ τοὺς θεούς,
> βούλομ',] ἀλλ' ἀπροσδοκήτως εἰς κλύδωνα πραγμάτων⁴⁷   5
> ἐμπε]σὼν ἠγωνίακα καὶ πάλαι ταράττομαι
> μή πο]θ' ἡ τύχη λάβῃ μου τὴν ἐναντίαν κρίσιν.
> δειλὸ]ς εἶ, νὴ τὴν Ἀθηνᾶν, δειλὸς εἶ· βλέπω· σύ γε
> τὸν π]όνον φεύγων προσάπτεις τῇ τύχῃ τὴν αἰτίαν.
> τοῖς π]λέουσιν — οὐ θεωρεῖς; — πολλάκις τὰ δυσχερῆ   10
> ἀντίκει]ται πάντα· χειμών, πνεῦμ', ὕδωρ, τρικυμία,
> ἀστραπ]αί, χάλαζα, βρονταί, ναυτίαι, σύναγ[μα,]⁴⁸ νύξ.
> ἀλλ' ὅμω]ς ἕκαστος αὐτῶν προσμένει τὴν ἐλπίδα
> καὶ τὸ μέ]λλον οὐκ ἀπέγνω.   (1063 K–A. 3–14 [CGFPR 255])

> Be a man now, Megas!
> Don't] abandon Moschion. I wish—by the gods—
> I wish] —but unexpectedly falling into a sea of troubles
> I have struggled and I'm long since thrown into confusion
> Lest fate take a judgement against me.
> You're a coward, by Athena—a coward! I see; you in fact
> run away from suffering and fasten the blame on fate.
> For most men—don't you see? — often all difficulties
> lie in opposition; storm, wind, rain, mighty waves,
> lightning, hail, thunder, seasickness, wreckage, night.
> And yet every one of them awaits the gleam of Hope
> and despairs not of the future.

Megas here looks and sounds like the forerunner of plotting slaves in Roman comedy.⁴⁹ We have no idea whether what he is resolving on succeeds or fails, but in a

---

45 Vitelli 1929. Excellent summary of both the contents of the papyrus and the state of the authorship question is found in Arnott 1998, 54–57.
46 „ein seltsamer Name, aber ein Sklave konnte wohl so heissen" (Wilamovitz in a letter to Vitelli: Pintaudi and Römer 1981, 380).
47 Cf. Aeschylus *Persae* 599, κλύδων κακῶν; Sophocles, *OT* 1527, κλύδωνα δεινῆς συμφορᾶς.
48 σύναγμα is very rare, and no meaning in *LSJ* fits the context. K–A. seem to accept Morel's view in the original publication of *PSI* 1176 that it should derive from συνάγω, comparing Poseidon rousing the storm in *Od.* 5.291: ὣς εἰπὼν σύναγεν νεφέλας, ἐτάραξε δὲ πόντον. Thus in this context it might indicate a gathering of clouds, stormheads. Arnott 1998, 55–56 insists it must derive from συνάγνυμι and therefore mean wreckage.
49 Compare particularly Epidicus in Plautus's play of that name.

sense it does not matter. He appeals to a universality of hope, which seems to endorse his efforts, whether they succeeded in the context of his play or not.

Do we have enough points to draw any meaningful trend lines in summary? While our Old Comic evidence is solely Aristophanes, the gravitational pull of tragic views of hope seems powerful throughout his career.[50] In the early plays hope is mostly mocked, and the only protagonist who expresses his own hope is Strepsiades in his efforts to destroy the Phrontisterion. If the old relative is the protagonist of *Thesmophoriazusae*, his hopes, however ridiculous they seem in the course of the play, do ultimately lead to his rescue. The last surviving Aristophanic hero, Chremylus in *Wealth*, is the only protagonist both to express hope that seems legitimate and to achieve his hoped-for ends. In Middle Comedy, Eubulus looks back to tragic mockery of hope, while the hopes expressed in Antiphanes, though starved ones, belong legitimately to the ordinary person and are preferable to the life or death gambles of the soldier's life. In Menander, parents and child alike hope for the family reunion they receive in *Sicyonioi*. While unplaced fragments offer contradictory views of hope, the *Aspis* shows us how hope can deceive, but there in the interests of justice. Philemon shows us hope favoring the deserving and aiding in the growth of love. Before the poets of Greek New Comedy fall silent, one portrays hope as a universal encouragement toward daring. While there is no explicit reference to fear in this passage, the references to confusion (ταράττομαι) and cowardice (δειλὸς εἶ) suggest we are moving ever closer to a linkage between hope and fear that would popularize itself in later philosophy.[51]

As the comic torch passes to Rome, the expectations of hope in Greek comedy are looking up.

Appendix I: Menander, *Sententiae*[52]

There seem to be good reasons to doubt that many of the sayings attributed to Menander in antiquity are actually quotations from his plays and may well simply

---

50   See also Fisher, this volume.
51   See for example Seneca *Ep.* 5. 7: *apud Hecatonem nostrum inveni cupiditatium finem etiam ad timoris remedia proficere.* "*Desines,*" *inquit,* "*timere, si sperare desieris*" ... *spem metus sequitur* ("In Hecaton I've found that the end of desires also provides remedies for fear. 'You'll cease to fear, if you cease to hope' ... Fear follows hope."). Cf. Boethius, *Consolation* 1. 7. 26–27: *pelle timorem / spemque fugato* ("cast out fear and flee hope").
52   Texts and numbering after Jaeckel 1964, supplemented by Pernigotti 2008.

have been edifying thoughts foisted onto his name. I nonetheless collect those referring to hope here for easy reference.

Ἄνθρωπος ἀτυχῶν σῴζεθ' ὑπὸ τῆς ἐλπίδος.⁵³ (30)
An unfortunate man is saved by hope.

Αἱ δ' ἐλπίδες βόσκουσι τοὺς κενοὺς βροτῶν. (51)
Hopes feed the empty-handed⁵⁴ among mortals.

Ἔλπιζε τιμῶν τοὺς θεοὺς πράξειν καλῶς.⁵⁵ (213)
By honoring the gods hope to do well.

Ἔλπιζε πάντα μέχρι γήρως θνητὸς ὤν. (254)
Although mortal, keep hoping until old age.

Ἐλπὶς γὰρ ἡ βόσκουσα τοὺς πολλοὺς βροτῶν.⁵⁶
(appendix 1. 12 / *897 Pernigotti)
Hope feeds many among men.

Ἀλλ' ἐκ πονηρῶν μὴ πορί[ζε τ]ὸν βί[ον
....ε πονηρᾶς προ[φά]σεώ[ς] εἰσ' [ἐ]λπίδες.
(Pap. V 1–2)
Don't get your livelihood from wickedness,
... [from?] a wicked pretence there are hopes.

Γράμματα †μάνθανε [καὶ] ἐλπίδας ἔξε<ι>ς καλάς.
(Pap. XIV 20 / *897 Pernigotti)
Learn literature, and have good hopes.

ὀργῆς χάριν τὰ κρυπτὰ μὴ ἐκφάνῃς φίλου·
†ἔλπιζε γὰρ αὐτὸν πάλιν γενέσθαι φίλον.†⁵⁷
(Comp. Men. Philistionis 47–48)
Don't betray a friend's secrets because of anger;
hope rather that he will become a friend again.

---

53 K–A. accept this as fr. 859. It is transmitted by Stobaeus 4. 46 as well as *P. Oxy.* 3006. 26. The sentiment is very generic, however: cf. Romans 8, 24, τῇ γὰρ ἐλπίδι ἐσώθημεν; and Publilius Syrus 672: *spes inopem, res avarum, mors miserum levat* (noted by Liapis 2002, 354 *ad loc.*).
54 Or perhaps "empty-headed." Liapis 2003, 261 *ad loc.* (numbering this fragment 48) suggests κενός here means ἀνόητος and cites *LSJ* s.v. II.2.b. The usage seems to be a transfer of epithet from "empty hopes" (Aeschines 1. 171 accuses Demosthenes of filling Aristarchus with empty hopes, ἐλπίδων κενῶν ἐμπλήσας) to the empty individuals.
55 Cf. *213a Pernigotti: Ἔλπιζε τιμῶν τοὺς γονεῖς πράξειν καλῶς.
56 Also transmitted as Sophocles, fr. 948N. For hopes nourishing mortals, cf. Simonides fr. 1.5–6 West: ἐλπὶς δὲ πάντας κἀπιπειθείη τρέφει / ἄπρηκτον ὁρμαίνοντας (and cf. Liapis 2003, 261–263 *ad loc.*).
57 Kock attributed these verses to Philemon as fr. 233K.

Bibliography

Allan, W. 2001. *Euripides: The Children of Heracles*, Warminster.
Arnott, W.G. 1979, 1996, 2000. *Menander*. 3 vols., Cambridge, Mass.
—— 1997. "First Notes on Menander's Sikyonioi," in: *ZPE* 116, 1–10.
—— 1998. "Menander's Fabula Incerta," in: *ZPE* 123, 49–58.
Austin, C./S.D. Olson 2004. *Thesmophoriazusae*, Oxford/New York.
Barrett, W.S. 1964. *Hippolytos*, Oxford.
Borthwick, E.K. 1968. "The Dances of Philocleon and the Sons of Carcinus in Aristophanes' *Wasps*," in: *CQ* 18, 44–51.
Cairns, D. 2011. "Looks of Love and Loathing: Cultural Models of Vision and Emotion in Ancient Greek Culture," in: *Mètis* 9, 37–50.
—— 2013. "The Imagery of Erôs in Plato's *Phaedrus*," in: E. Sanders/C. Thumiger/C. Carey/N. Lowe (eds.), *Erôs in Ancient Greece*, Oxford, 233–250.
—— 2016. "Metaphors for Hope in Archaic and Classical Greek Poetry," in: R.R. Caston/R.A. Kaster (eds.), *Hope, Joy, and Affection in the Classical World: Emotions of the Past*, Oxford/New York, 13–44.
Chaniotis, A. 2012. "Moving Stones: The Study of Emotions in Greek Inscriptions," in: A. Chaniotis (ed.), *Unveiling Emotions: Sources and Methods for the Study of Emotions in the Greek World*, Stuttgart, 91–129.
Csapo, E. 2000. "From Aristophanes to Menander?" in: M. Depew/D. Obbink (eds.), *Matrices of Genre*, Cambridge, Mass., 115–33.
Dobrov, G. 1999. *Figures of Play Greek Drama and Metafictional Poetics*, New York.
Gomme, A.W./F.H. Sandbach. 1973. *Menander: A Commentary*, London.
Halliwell, F.S. 1980. *Personal Jokes in Aristophanes*, diss. Oxford University.
http,//ora.ox.ac.uk/objects/uuid,e189bcb9-ba9c-421f-a9e6-25125997ddf2/datastreams/ATTACHMENT1
Hanink, J. 2014. "Crossing Genres: Comedy, Tragedy, and Satyr Play," in: M. Fontaine/A. Scafuro (eds.), *The Oxford Handbook of Greek and Roman Comedy*, Oxford/New York, 258–77.
Henderson, J. 1998. *Aristophanes*, 5 vols, Cambridge, Mass.
Jaeckel, S.H. 1964. *Sententiae: Comparatio Menandri et Philistionis*, Leipzig.
Kaimio, M./N. Nykopp. 1997. "Bad Poets Society: Censure of the Style of Minor Tragedians in Old Comedy," in: J. Vaahtera /R. Vainio (eds.), *Utriusque linguae peritus: studia in honorem Toivo Viljamaa*, Turku, 23–37.
Liapis, V. 2002. *Menandrou Gnōmai Monostichoi*, Athens.
MacDowell, D.M. 1971. Aristophanes: *Wasps*, Oxford.
Miceli, M./C. Castelfranchi. 2015. *Expectancy and Emotion*. Series in Affective Science, Oxford.
Olson, S.D. 1998. *Aristophanes' Peace*, Oxford.
—— 2006. *Athenaeus: The Learned Banqueters*, 8 vols., Cambridge, Mass.
Pernigotti, C. 2008. *Menandri sententiae*. Studi e testi per il corpus dei papiri filosofici greci e latini 15, Florence.
Pintaudi, R./C. Römer. 1981. "Le lettere di Wilamowitz a Vitelli," in: *Annali della Scuola Normale Superiore di Pisa* 11, 363–392 [379–383].
Porter, J. 2011. "Against λεπτότης: Rethinking Hellenistic Aesthetics," in: A. Erskine/L. Llewellyn-Jones/E.D. Carney (eds.), *Creating a Hellenistic World,* Swansea, 271–312.
Rau, P. 1967. *Paratragodia: Untersuchung einer komischen Form des Aristophanes*, Munich.

Rusten, J.S., *et al.* 2011. *The Birth of Comedy: Texts, Documents, and Art from Athenian Comic Competitions*, 486–280. Baltimore.
Valente, S. 2015. *The Antiatticist.* Sammlung Griechischer und Lateinischer Grammatiker, Vol. 16. Berlin.
Vitelli, G. 1929. *SIFC* 8, 235–242.
Wilkins, J. 1993. *Euripides: Heraclidae*, Oxford.

Natalia Tsoumpra
The Politics of Hopelessness: Thucydides and Aristophanes' *Knights*

Hope has always played an important role in political thinking and has often been appropriated by various political movements and theorists throughout the years. Marxist and other socialist movements were hope-mobilized and hope-driven: in advocating the transformative power of political action by the working class they expressed a secularized hope that was formerly embodied in religion.[1] The classic understanding of hope in the Marxist conception is articulated by Ernst Bloch (1986):[2] the act of hoping is able to provide a response to adverse circumstances, sustain the process of changing the world and create a better future. In the 21st century the discourse of hope persists across what has often been described as a 'left-wing' or 'progressive' agenda. Various politicians in Europe and the US have appropriated and capitalized on the discourse of hope in order to signal a new age of politics and gain the favour of their audience: Barack Obama appealed to his voters through a rhetoric of hope;[3] Alexis Tsipras' political campaign before the Greek elections of January 2015, and the referendum held in July 2015, was inspired by the idea of a hopeful resistance against the political crisis; Jeremy Corbyn's campaign for the Labour party leadership in the UK also promoted the idea of hopeful politics against the conservative and austerity-oriented agenda of the Torries.[4] Although the rhetoric of hope and the political agenda it involves have been thought by their advocates to inaugurate a new era of politics and a return to an ideological purity, for their critics they represent nothing more than a groundless illusion with no ground in reality. One should be cautious, it seems, as to what kind of hope they seek to cultivate: Bloch points out that hope and reason should go hand in hand,[5] and that a hope-charged act should be realistic and 'fully attuned ... to the objectively real possibility ... and consequently to the properties of reality which are themselves utopian, i.e. contain future'.[6]

---

1   See Aronson 1999, 472.
2   See especially Ch. 55 in Volume 3 entitled *Karl Marx and Humanity: The Stuff of Hope*.
3   See Atwater 2007. Obama's book *The Audacity of Hope* (2006) can be defined as the blueprint of his political career.
4   In September 2015, the independent radical left magazine *Red Pepper* ran a cover with Corbyn pictured in the style of the famous 2008 Barack Obama 'Hope' poster.
5   He distinguishes between 'fraudulent' and 'genuine' or 'knowing-concrete' hope (1986, 5).
6   Bloch 1986, 145. See also Mittleman 2009, 260 "Democracy cannot survive without hope but neither can it survive by stimulating hopes beyond its capacity to fulfil them. There is danger on

Bloch refers to fear as the competing emotion of hope.[7] This is hardly surprising: both hope and fear involve an estimation of good and bad outcomes, but they differ in what they consider important in the pictured future.[8] In fact, the political theorists who caution against a (delusional) hopeful political model most commonly exploit fear, an emotion which supposedly dictates a more careful and reasonable consideration of the political situation at hand.[9]

What I would like to argue in this chapter is that these strategic uses of the emotions of hope and fear in political discourse are not a new, or even recent, phenomenon. I will set out to examine the place of hope in political discourse and decision-making in two contemporary writers, Thucydides and Aristophanes, with the aim of assessing their political outlook. In particular, I will look at the use of the emotion of hope in both authors as a foil to fear, as well as the association of hope with erotic passion and religious superstition. Both Thucydides and Aristophanes' *Knights* appear to present an argument against hope-fuelled politics which is viewed as dangerous and self-destructive when intertwined with erotic desire and superstitious beliefs. In Thucydides' narrative, hope accompanied by strong emotions is considered as a bad basis for political decisions, because it indicates delusional political thinking, which distorts the perception of reality and, finally, leads those who nurture it to their demise. Aristophanes seems to share the pessimistic realism of Thucydides. His plays often revolve around a 'great idea', which is typical of the comic genre: the comic hero, dissatisfied with the contemporary political situation, conceives a plan to alter, rectify or totally subvert it. Contrary to what one might expect, the word 'hope' and its cognates very rarely appear in this context. The vocabulary of hope is not linked to the formulation and the execution of the great plan or the new world which arises (in *Birds*, for instance, once the construction of the new city is

---

either side." For the significance of hope in contemporary politics, see Lear 2006; Westbrook 2005; Delbanco 1999.
7   Bloch 1986, 4, 5, 12.
8   Nussbaum 2001, 28.
9   The contemporary political examples are numerous: the referendum for Scotland's independence in 2014 quickly evolved into a contest between hope and fear (see Cairns 2016, 14–5 and S. Carrell, N. Watt, and P. Wintour, "The Real Story of the Scottish Referendum: Britain on the Brink," part 1, The Guardian, December 15, 2014); After Corbyn's election as the new Labour leader in September 2015, the leader of the UK's conservative party and former Prime Minister, David Cameron characterized the Labour Party in the social media as a "threat to our national security, our economic security and your family's security"; in Greece, during the elections of January 2015 and before the referendum in July 2015, a climate of fear and terror was systematically and persistently cultivated with the aim of presenting the left-wing party Syriza as an anti-European force who would put Greece's EU and euro membership in danger.

completed, Euelpides, Mr Good Hope, quite suggestively disappears).[10] In the *Knights*, which will be the focus of this study, hope appears just once, right at the turn of the old to the new world, and, as I will show, proves to be deceptive. Does this mean that the new world which emerges holds no hope?

Sommerstein argues for a progressive development of Aristophanes' political outlook: in the plays preceding *Birds* "a youthful Aristophanes, eager for combat with the likes of Kleon and willing to run considerable risks in the process, and confident in (or at least hopeful of) the support of his public if he can only persuade it, gives place to a mature and more disillusioned poet who sees the Athenian people as being beyond persuasion and suspects they can be saved only against their will".[11] I believe that this is not an accurate evaluation. As I will argue, Aristophanes endorses a pessimistic political model as early as the *Knights*, which very much resembles the overarching tone of pessimistic realism in Thucydides. I will conclude my analysis by putting forward the tentative argument that the picture of hope which emerges from both writers as an unreliable and precarious emotion[12] in the political arena may not be very dissimilar to the attitude of the right-wing politicians and political theorists towards hope in modern times.

In Thucydides, the political and military practices of the Athenians are initially connected with a seemingly positive kind of hope that defies obstacles and leads to great success, as opposed to the fearful practices of their Spartan opponents.[13] In Book 1, the Corinthians, seeking to persuade the Spartans to unite with them against the Athenians claim that the Athenians live in constant hope and do not hesitate to leap forward, since they can achieve anything they hope for (1.70.3 καὶ παρὰ δύναμιν τολμηταὶ καὶ παρὰ γνώμην κινδυνευταὶ καὶ ἐν τοῖς δεινοῖς εὐέλπιδες, "they are bold even beyond their strength and risk-takers beyond their judgement and hopeful amidst dangers").[14] By contrast, the Spartans procrastinate since they fear to endanger what they have left behind (1.70.5 ὑμεῖς δὲ [οἴεσθε] τῷ ἐξελθεῖν καὶ τὰ ἑτοῖμα ἂν βλάψαι, "you [believe] that by making any move you will damage even your present assets"). Indeed, the truest cause of the Peloponnesian war according to Thucydides was the fear which the Spartans felt on the account of the growing power of Athens (1.23.6). This analysis is repeated

---

10   See Bowie 1993, 171–2.
11   Sommerstein 2009, 217.
12   The ambiguity of hope is stressed throughout Greek literature. For general remarks about the position of hope in Greek thought and literature, see Cairns 2016 and Fulkerson 2016. See also Strauss-Clay 2003, 102–4 on Hesiod and hope, and Segal 1993, 137–53 on Euripides and hope.
13   See Petersend and Liaras 2006; Luginbill 1999, 65–81.
14   All translations of Thucydides are those of Lattimore 1998, slightly modified.

after the debates in Sparta: Thucydides writes that the Spartans voted for war "not so much by the influence of the speeches of their allies, as by fear (φοβούμενοι) of the Athenians, lest they become too powerful" (1.88; cf. 1.118.2).

While at the beginning of the *History* hope seems to be a better strategy than fear, it soon becomes obvious that hope cannot be compatible with reason and thus gradually loses any positive aspects as a guide in political deliberations. By contrast, fear is associated with rationality and reflection.[15] While the negative portrayal of hope peaks with the Melian dialogue and the Sicilian Expedition, the problematization of hope appears earlier: it is pronounced by Diodotus in the Mytilenian Debate.

> ἥ τε ἐλπὶς καὶ ὁ ἔρως ἐπὶ παντί, ὁ μὲν ἡγούμενος, ἡ δ' ἐφεπομένη, καὶ ὁ μὲν τὴν ἐπιβουλὴν ἐκφροντίζων, ἡ δὲ τὴν εὐπορίαν τῆς τύχης ὑποτιθεῖσα πλεῖστα βλάπτουσι, καὶ ὄντα ἀφανῆ κρείσσω ἐστὶ τῶν ὁρωμένων δεινῶν.
>
> And in every case, hope and desire – the one leading while the other follows, the one thinking up the scheme while the other holds out the full assistance of fortune – do the greatest damage, and although invisible, they have power over perils that can be seen.
>
> Thucydides, 3.45.5–6

The appearance of *eros* is important here as it serves to emphasize the pathology of hope. Hope becomes delusional when coupled with erotic pathos.[16] *Eros* conceives the attempt, inflaming hope with erotic energy, and hope leads, making success seem easy, when it is not. The futility of hope becomes even more evident through the contrast between the invisibility of hope and *eros* (ἀφανῆ), and the visibility of the dangers (ὁρωμένων): hope becomes a mirage, a false expectation, the result of discrepancy between perception and reality. Hope and desire are dangerous exactly because (and not despite the fact that)[17] they are invisible.[18]

---

15 Cf. Aristotle's remarks on fear (*Rhetoric* 1382a21–25) which as an emotion depends essentially on reasoning and evaluation: in order to be afraid of something, one must have already evaluated this object as being harmful. Failure to experience fear testifies to a cognitive deficit. ἀφοβία, then, lack of fear, characterizes a person who is either mad or insensible. Moreover, far from being irrational, as Aristotle puts it, fear makes people deliberative; believing themselves in danger, men desire safety and engage in practical deliberations. See also Konstan's analysis of Aristotle (2006, 134–5).
16 For hope and *eros* as opposed to pragmatism and moderation in Thucydides, see Rahe 1995.
17 See Gomme 1956 *ad loc.*
18 One may compare the invisible banes to the silent diseases that escape from Pandora's jar in Hesiod's *Works and Days*. All the sicknesses were deprived of voice by Zeus, so that they come

That hope when imbued with erotic passion leads to demise becomes painfully obvious in the Sicilian expedition. The Sicilian expedition was a love-child of the Athenians, conceived in moments of great erotic passion[19] and accompanied by vast hopes for things which were far-off sight:[20]

καὶ **ἔρως** ἐνέπεσε τοῖς πᾶσιν ὁμοίως ἐκπλεῦσαι· [...] τοῖς δ' ἐν τῇ ἡλικίᾳ τῆς τε **ἀπούσης πόθῳ ὄψεως** καὶ **θεωρίας**, καὶ **εὐέλπιδες** ὄντες σωθήσεσθαι

and a passion for the expedition afflicted everyone alike [...] others with the longing of youth for faraway sights and experiences and confident of surviving.

Thucydides 6.24.3

This passage suggestively links (lack of clear) vision, erotic passion and hope. *Eros*, it is suggested, falls upon the Athenians like a veil which hinders their vision,[21] and leads them to irrational and ill-fated decisions. While there is a great emphasis on ὄψις in the description of the preparation and the setting off of the military expedition,[22] sight, in this context, is not equated with reality. The narrative creates a very vivid visual perception of the splendour and grandeur of the armament, but this image is qualified –or rather fundamentally undermined– by the statement that the launching of the expedition was more a display of wealth and power rather than a serious business[23] (6.31.4 ἐπίδειξιν [...] τῆς δυνάμεως καὶ ἐξουσίας ἢ ἐπὶ πολεμίους παρασκευήν, "an exhibition of might and wealth [...] rather than an army directed against enemies"). Indeed, the preparation was inadequate for the undertaking (6.31.3 ἀλλὰ ἐπί τε βραχεῖ πλῷ ὡρμήθησαν καὶ

---

unannounced and allow mankind to hope for tomorrow. Viewed more positively, hope becomes the necessary illusion that informs human life and makes it bearable. See Strauss-Clay 2003, 102–4.
19   The metaphor of *eros* is often taken as Thucydides' commentary on the nature of Athenian imperialism and has been studied systematically with reference to the Sicilian expedition: see de Romilly 1963, 77–79; Arrowsmith 1973; Hunter 1973, 124; Connor 1984, 178; Loraux 1986, 15–21; Scanlon 1987; Forde 1989, 31–7, 39, 50, 66, 119; Wohl 2002, 171–214.
20   Cf. Alcibiades' encouragement of the Athenians for the conquest of Sicily in Plutarch, *Alcibiades* 17. 1–4, where the language of hope coupled with erotic passion features prominently.
21   Or as a disease, as is frequently the case with πίπτω compounds. For *eros* as a disease attacking its victims cf., for example, Eur. *Hipp.* 38; Winkler 1990, 82–93; Faraone 1999, 43–9. For the medical imagery of love and its association with the body politic see, among others, Wohl 2002, *passim* and esp. 188–214; Brock 2013, 69–82.
22   See Kallet 2001, 21–3. On the prominence of the preparation see also Allison 1989, 66–120.
23   For the 'glittering façade' of the Sicilian expedition as concealing its weakness, see Jordan 2000. Walter (1993) discusses the connection between visual perception and emotional subjectivity in Thucydides and notes that "in the Piraeus scene ... the visual perception works to restore confidence in the decision [the Athenians] had made the day before" (356).

παρασκευῇ φαύλῃ, "but it set out for a short voyage with limited equipment"). The beginning of the description (6.30.2–31.1) is packed with words denoting 'sight' and 'seeing',[24] which aim to highlight the element of wasteful display and the false impression of power, and climaxes with the distinction between the future (vain) hopes and the present circumstances, thus underlining the divergence between conception and actuality (6.31.6 ἐπὶ μεγίστῃ ἐλπίδι τῶν μελλόντων πρὸς τὰ ὑπάρχοντα ἐπεχειρήθη, "[the expedition] was attempted with the highest hopes for the future compared with the actual circumstances").[25] The discrepancy between present certainty and future impressions, perception and reality is also emphasized in book four, which foreshadows the vanity of the undertaking: the extraordinary success of the Athenians in the recent past and present (4.65.4 οὕτω τῇ [τε] παρούσῃ εὐτυχίᾳ χρώμενοι ἠξίουν σφίσι μηδὲν ἐναντιοῦσθαι, "so extreme, in the midst of their current good fortune was their conviction that nothing would stand in their way") led them to confuse their strengths with their hopes (4.65.4 αἰτία δ' ἦν ἡ παρὰ λόγον τῶν πλεόνων εὐπραγία αὐτοῖς ὑποτιθεῖσα ἰσχὺν τῆς ἐλπίδος, "the cause was their extraordinary success in most respects, lending strength to their hopes"). Thus, they formed delusive hopes about an uncertain future based on a success due to mere good fortune.[26] In book 6, hope is tellingly mixed with lamentation (6.30.2 καὶ μετ' ἐλπίδος τε ἅμα ἰόντες καὶ ὀλοφυρμῶν, "combining hope with lamentations as they were going down"). All in all, the Athenian παρασκευή was a big show inflated to grand proportions by erotic desire. The Sicilian expedition begins and, as we shall see later ends with (vain) hope.

A rather different picture emerges in Pericles' *Funeral Oration*.[27] Hope appears again coupled with *eros*, but in this speech Pericles presents a hopeful democracy, in which the citizens of the *polis* have reasons to fight because they have

---

24 6.30.2 ἑώρων, ὄψει, θέαν, 6.31.6 ὄψεως. See Kallet 2001, 49–50.
25 See Parry 1981, 74–5 "ὑπάρχοντα are the real things that are, and are at hand, now; μέλλοντα are things one plans, hopes to get, things that exist only in conception". Parry links this antithesis to the opposition between λόγος and ἔργον which he also traces in the Melian dialogue.
26 Cf. 4.17.4–19, where the Spartans point out that the Athenians unwisely refuse to make peace with them because they base their optimism on present good luck (εὐτυχίαν τὴν παροῦσαν) and immoderate hope (ἀεὶ γὰρ τοῦ πλέονος ἐλπίδι ὀρέγονται διὰ τὸ καὶ τὰ παρόντα ἀδοκήτως εὐτυχῆσαι). Again, hope is linked to desire. See de Romilly 1963, 173–5. Disillusionment of that hope follows in 5.14.1.
27 See Kallet (2001, 21) who claims that "the Sicilian narrative takes Pericles' comment in the *Funeral oration*, 'we use wealth more for action than for show' (2.40.1), which implies criticism for those who do the opposite, and turns it on its head".

invested their hopes in the city. In this eroticized speech, Athens becomes the ideal for all of Greece, a model to imitate and an object to love.[28] The Athenians should gaze on the city and its power, and become her lover[29] (2.43.1 μᾶλλον τὴν τῆς πόλεως δύναμιν καθ' ἡμέραν ἔργῳ θεωμένους καὶ ἐραστὰς γιγνομένους αὐτῆς, "wondering at the city's power as you actually see it each day and becoming her lovers"). Sight, *eros*, and hope, the familiar by now triplet, crops up again, but takes on a positive angle because it is grounded in the endurance of the *demos* as a whole and the empirical reality of the *polis*. Citizens can (and should) commit to hope the uncertainty of the final success and die for Athens because Athens will outlive them. Hope is again coupled with invisibility and is juxtaposed to factuality, action, and visible danger (2.42.4 ἐλπίδι μὲν τὸ ἀφανὲς τοῦ κατορθώσειν ἐπιτρέψαντες, ἔργῳ δὲ περὶ τοῦ ἤδη ὁρωμένου σφίσιν αὐτοῖς ἀξιοῦντες πεποιθέναι, "leaving to hope the uncertainty of prospering in the future but resolving to rely on their actions in what confronted them now"). Kallet notes that the connotations are positive here, because Pericles is instructing the Athenians to experience an emotion which enhances feelings of empowerment and leads to sober deliberation.[30] Thus, passions are mastered, harnessed and applied to constructive use (i.e. to the service of the state), in sharp contrast to the post-Periclean period, where, as we saw, passion and deluded hope led men astray. Yet, it is hard not to read this hopeful democratic *eros* as an ironic comment: in the narrative of the *History*, the funeral speech is followed by the description of the advent of the plague which sweeps all hopes away.[31] Faced with despair after the invasions of Attica and the plague, the Athenians' confidence is ruined. Once more hope manifests its power of deception: it promises but all too rarely delivers.

What happens if the limits between metaphor and reality are blurred even more, and the love the Athenians are encouraged to feel for their city and their leaders is taken a bit too literally? The implications of the Periclean hopeful democracy in which the Athenians are urged to become the lovers of their *polis* and its power are shown in Aristophanes' *Knights*. As Victoria Wohl has shown,[32]

---

28 Wohl 2002, 53.
29 αὐτῆς most probably refers back to πόλεως and not δύναμιν. See Hornblower 1991, 311.
30 See Kallet 2001, 46–7.
31 Hopelessness and vain hope prevail (2.51.4 ἀνέλπιστον, 2.51.6 ἐλπίδος [...] κουφῆς).
32 Wohl 2002, 73–123 and *passim*. See also Scholtz (1997 and 2004) who describes the political practices employed by the two rivals in *Knights* as a comic progression from φιλία to κολακεία and finally παιδεραστία; Yates (2005) focuses on the role of the two rivals as ἀντερασταί, whose perpetual competition for Demos sustains democracy. Worman (2008, 62–92) sees the Sausage-seller as the effeminized type of politician who is characterized by his open anus, by contrast to Paphlagon, who is mostly the politician of the open mouth.

Knights constitutes a parodic revision of the erotic relationship between the people and their leaders in the post-Periclean era. All signs of a hopeful democracy and the practice of a healthy democratic sexuality, as conceived by Pericles in Thucydides, have vanished in the comic play. Prostitution is here the model for a debased politics with Demos, the people personified, being a *kinaidos*, and Paphlagon/Cleon and the Sausage-seller his corrupt lovers, who rival for his attention.[33] Pericles' instigation to fall in love with the beautiful city is "brought down to the basest corporeal terms and the courtship is imagined in all its sordid detail."[34]

When the Sausage Seller faces Paphlagon and contests with him in front of the Knights, he claims that his trick of stealing meat by hiding it in his buttocks and then lying about it caused an orator to say that he would one day become a guardian of the people (422–3). That this practice is a sure sign of future leadership is also confirmed by Demosthenes (424–5). We are then presented with a distorted notion of politics which merits prostitution or passivity in sex[35] as qualities which render a leader successful. The contest for leadership in *Knights* becomes a race for depravation of the anus, which further confirms the immorality and baseness of character the leader should exhibit.

If *Knights* directly echoes Thucydides' erotic diction in the *Funeral oration Speech*, Pericles' hopeful democracy becomes, in Cleon's debased enactment, political prostitution, while Demos becomes the unattractive *eromenos*, who promises himself to the politician who offers the greatest gifts (1007–9). No wonder why hope is missing from this picture —both in linguist terms ('hope' and its cognates do not appear) and as a theme (a hopeful vision of the future).

There is only one instance where the vocabulary of hope appears in the *Knights*. This brings me to the second part of my study which concerns the relation between hope and religious sentiments. Apart from the erotic passion, hope may also be inspired by superstition, religious prophecies and beliefs,[36] which impair judgement and show that hope is contrary to logic and pragmatism. This

---

33 Ar. *Eq.* 730–40, 1162–3, 1340–3.
34 Wohl 2002, 87.
35 Cf. 167 ἐν πρυτανείῳ λαικάσει ("you will suck cocks in the prytaneum"), 719–21 ΠΑ.: καὶ νὴ Δί' ὑπό γε δεξιότητος τῆς ἐμῆς / δύναμαι ποιεῖν τὸν δῆμον εὐρὺν καὶ στενόν. /ΑΛ.: χὠ πρωκτὸς οὑμὸς τουτογὶ σοφίζεται ("PA: and what is more, by Zeus, with my wizardry I can make Demos expand and contract at my pleasure. S.S.: even my arsehole knows that trick"). That pathics are dominating the political scene is a recurrent idea in Aristophanes. cf. McGlew 1996, 355 and Henderson 1991, 68.
36 According to Cornford (1965) hope in Thucydides appears as a supernatural entity, a living agency which affects people's decisions.

can be demonstrated both in Thucydides and in the *Knights*. I shall first revisit the Sicilian expedition in Thucydides and show how ungrounded hopes and religion are linked in its tragic ending, and then move on to discuss the relationship between unfounded hopes and superstition in the *Knights*.

In Book 8 we find out that when the news of the disaster in Sicily reached Athens, the people grew angry at those who encouraged their hopes by means of oracles and divination (8.1.1 ὠργίζοντο δὲ καὶ τοῖς χρησμολόγοις τε καὶ μάντεσι καὶ ὁπόσοι τι τότε αὐτοὺς θειάσαντες ἐπήλπισαν ὡς λήψονται Σικελίαν, "they were furious at the oracle-mongers, seers, and anyone whose divinations had made them hope that they would capture Sicily"). After irrational passion then, what incited the Athenian hopes for Sicily was divination and oracle-mongering,[37] practices about which Thucydides often phrases his scepticism, and whose interpretation cannot be relied upon.[38] That superstition is not a reliable guide for hope is painfully evident in the case of Nicias too throughout the Sicilian expedition.

Let us observe the reactions of the Athenians to a series of defeats, and to Gylippus' capture of one of their main supply forts. Demosthenes asked Nicias to return home while the army and the navy were still intact (7.47.3–5). Nicias initially opposed this view, as he thought there was still hope (7.48.2 ἐλπίδος τι ἔτι παρεῖχε). The narrative repeatedly stresses, however, that this is the kind of hope which is grounded on empirical facts and reality, as Nicias based his decision on accurate knowledge and information (7.48.2 ἀφ' ὧν ἐπὶ πλέον ἢ οἱ ἄλλοι ᾐσθάνετο αὐτῶν, "according to the information he possessed more abundantly than anyone else", 7.48.3 ἐπιστάμενος, "knowing very well", 7.49.1 ἰσχυρίζετο, "said this with firmness", αἰσθόμενος ἀκριβῶς, "since he had accurate information", ἐθάρσει, "he had confidence", 7.49.4 ὑπόνοια μή τι καὶ πλέον εἰδὼς ὁ Νικίας ἰσχυρίζηται, "there was the apprehension that Nicias was being firm because he had some extra knowledge"). Later on he concedes to the move, but at this point the eclipse takes place, and Nicias changes his mind — and seals the doom of the expedition. There now appears this superstitious side of Nicias' character, which will become even more prominent later. As the reality progressively becomes worse, Nicias, who initially seemed reluctant to rely upon hope, becomes a fervent advocate of it. Due to his superstition, he is classed among those who are

---

37 On χρησμολόγοι and μάντεις see Bowden 2003 and Dillery 2005. See also Hornblower's note (2008) pp. 750–1.
38 *Pace* Marinatos (1981), who claims that Thucydides' criticism focuses on the interpretation of the oracles rather than their content. But see de Romilly 1963, 292, Oost 1975, and Bowden 2003, 74–5, who stress Thucydides' general scepticism about oracles and divination.

irrationally clinging on hopes, which are not supported by factual information and knowledge, but are desperate and invisible.

Fear is also prominent here. In his address to the army before the final naval battle (7.61–4), Nicias asks the Athenians not to let their hopes be tainted by fear and thus be (mis)led to equate their present situation with a calamity (7.61.2 ἀθυμεῖν δὲ οὐ χρὴ οὐδὲ πάσχειν ὅπερ οἱ ἀπειρότατοι τῶν ἀνθρώπων, οἳ τοῖς πρώτοις ἀγῶσι σφαλέντες ἔπειτα διὰ παντὸς τὴν ἐλπίδα τοῦ φόβου ὁμοίαν ταῖς ξυμφοραῖς ἔχουσιν). While Nicias suggests that the fear of the Athenians might be clouding their judgement, making them forget about positive past experiences and, all in all, getting in the way of them being hopeful (note how 'fear' governs 'hope' in this dense passage), ironically, the way the Athenians feel (ἀθυμεῖν, 'disheartened') corresponds to the reality they have to face and accurately reflects their dire situation. Although hope is strategically employed by Nicias and 'served' to the army as a counter-emotion to fear that should dictate the Athenians' thinking,[39] it becomes obvious that it is hope, not fear that impairs and distorts their mental faculties. Hope, pitted against fear, creates a feeling of foreboding.[40]

In the rest of the speech Nicias consistently "retreats from qualified but real confidence in a great army, to a catalog of futile cliches about chance and hope".[41] Although he does mention Athenian preparedness and skill,[42] he appeals to hopefulness on the grounds that luck may contribute to success (7.61.3 καὶ τὸ τῆς τύχης κἂν μεθ' ἡμῶν ἐλπίσαντες στῆναι, "hoping that the element of fortune may stand by us"). Hope keeps cropping up frequently in the following passages and its frequency gives a warning (and worrying) signal for the Athenians: after another Syracusan naval victory the army prepares to move in a terrible condition

---

39 See Petersend and Liaras 2006, 322 and 327 on hope employed as a strategy to effectively counter terror's effects.
40 One can compare here the use of fear in the speeches of the Syracusan leader Hermocrates in two instances in books 4 and 6: fear of the Athenians in both cases is treated as an emotion grounded on reality, which should prompt, on the one hand, the Sicilian cities to form an alliance (4.59–64), and, on the other hand, his compatriots to prepare adequately for a fight (6.33–4). Note also Nicias' failed attempt to dissuade the Athenians from launching the Sicilian expedition (6.20–6) by instilling fear for the numbers they are going up against (6.23.3 φοβούμενος). Even though the information given is messy and confusing (see Kallet 2001, 42–5), the threat posed by the Greek cities of Sicily was very much real and should not have been underestimated.
41 Lateiner 1985, 202.
42 Edmunds (1975, 135) notes that the appeal to the superiority of the Athenian skill is meaningless, "since the Athenians have been forced to fight a land battle on ships in the old-fashioned style, in which episteme and techne have no scope". Thus, the emphasis remains on the themes of uncertain hope and general inadequacy.

which is in sharp contrast with the big hopes they had been nurturing (7.75.2 ἀντὶ μεγάλης ἐλπίδος καὶ αὐτοὶ καὶ ἡ πόλις κινδυνεύοντες, "amid dangers for both themselves and their city after their great hopes"). The phrase ἀντί μεγάλης ἐλπίδος purposefully evokes the hopes with which the expedition was launched in 415. The contrast becomes even more obvious in the description of the sight the retreat presented, which was painful to the eye (7.75.2 τῇ τε ὄψει ἑκάστῳ ἀλγεινά, "things that were painful to see"): nothing could be further from the description of the preparation and the launching of the armament in book 6. The Athenians now are not only apprehensive of their present miseries, but also of those which are invisible and yet to come (7.75.4 τὰ δὲ περὶ τῶν ἐν ἀφανεῖ δεδιότας μὴ πάθωσιν, "while fearing what unknown suffering might lie ahead"). Again, the contrast between visibility and invisibility harkens back to the unreliability of sight encountered earlier on during the launching stages, and shows fear once more as a justified and more reliable emotion than hope.

In the next speech that Nicias gives in order to encourage and comfort the army the discourse of hope proliferates. The Athenians should not lose hope because "men have found salvation from worse plights than this" (7.77.1 καὶ ἐκ τῶν παρόντων, ὦ Ἀθηναῖοι καὶ ξύμμαχοι, ἐλπίδα χρὴ ἔχειν (ἤδη τινὲς καὶ ἐκ δεινοτέρων ἢ τοιῶνδε ἐσώθησαν), "even in the present circumstances, Athenians and allies, you must still have hope (there are men who have been saved before now from even more terrible situations that this). The recommendation to "hope for better luck" is nothing more than a platitude and, therefore, immensely unconvincing.[43] This explicitly groundless hope is a far cry from Nicias' earlier caution and foreshadows the impending disaster. Nicias goes on to argue for a theodicy on the basis of which he believes the Athenians should hold out hope. However, his argument seems to preclude any possibility of hope.[44] The logic runs as follows (7.77.3): a) I have always been pious, b) nevertheless, the gods have not favoured me, c) but, even so, I still have bold (*thraseia*) hope, d) and, therefore, you should not lose hope either. Thus, while Nicias appeals to the gods, it is clear that his hope in divine help is groundless. He goes on to envisage a different theodicy which has to do with the gods' retributive justice (7.77.3–4): if the gods wanted to punish us, we have surely suffered enough and deserve their

---

43 See Lateiner 1985, 202 who notes a similar decline in Nicias' speech in 7.61–4: "In his last three exhortations, Nicias retreats from qualified but real confidence in a great army, to a catalog of futile clichés about chance and hope"; see also Lateiner in this volume.
44 See Edmunds 1975, 136–7.

pity, and so the gods will now be more benevolent to us. This expectation of a sudden change from bad to good luck is nothing more than wishful thinking.[45]

Hope is therefore inextricably linked with superstition and a naïve, groundless belief in the divine. As such, it is once more strongly opposed to reason: by impairing rationality, hope affects one's ability to make accurate judgements and decisions. Nicias becomes a fervent proponent of hope, only when everything else has failed and the situation is hopeless. It is worth noting that Nicias' (indirect) speech in 7.69.2 has been thought to contain allusions to Pericles' Funeral Oration.[46] However, unlike Nicias, Pericles foregoes any reference to the gods. This serves to emphasize how 'inept' and 'pathetic' Nicias' exhortation is.[47]

Before moving on to Aristophanes, I wish to make a brief comment on a passage which no treatment of hope in Thucydides could afford to ignore: the Melian dialogue. This is probably the most famous manifestation of ἐλπίς in Thucydides, and it sums up nicely our findings on hope so far. The Athenians give to the Melians a sermon on hope, the 'danger's comforter' (5.103 ἐλπίς δέ κινδύνῳ παραμύθιον οὖσα). They make the point that hope may not be fully disastrous to those who find themselves in dire straits but have other resources to fight, yet it is definitely harmful to those who have nothing but hope to rely on. The contrast between visible and invisible hopes, present reality and future probability reappears, and is linked once more with the divine: the Athenians reproach the Melians for trusting in future hopes, while their present resources are too light. This is not what men who rely on human action rather than on divine intervention (we are supposed to understand) are expected to do (5.111 ἐνθυμούμεθα δὲ ὅτι φήσαντες περὶ σωτηρίας βουλεύσειν οὐδὲν ἐν τοσούτῳ λόγῳ εἰρήκατε ᾧ ἄνθρωποι ἂν πιστεύσαντες νομίσειαν σωθήσεσθαι, ἀλλ' ὑμῶν τὰ μὲν ἰσχυρότατα ἐλπιζόμενα μέλλεται, τὰ δ' ὑπάρχοντα βραχέα πρὸς τὰ ἤδη ἀντιτεταγμένα περιγίγνεσθαι, "but we reflect that you, who asserted that you would give thought to your survival, have said a great deal without mentioning anything that would give human beings the confidence to think that they will be saved, but in your case the main source of strength is what you hope lies in the future"). They warn the Melians that blind hopes, based on precarious religious sentiments —divination, oracles, and the like— bring ruin (5.103.2 ἐπειδὰν πιεζομένους αὐτοὺς ἐπιλίπωσιν αἱ φανεραὶ ἐλπίδες, ἐπὶ τὰς ἀφανεῖς καθίστανται μαντικήν τε καὶ

---

[45] See Lateiner 1985, 207 "The speech [...] is saturated with the religious and other delusions of a desperate man". See also Connor 1984, 202: "these naïve and old-fashioned arguments are grounded in a theology and a view of history that has nowhere else been affirmed in the *Histories*".
[46] See Rawlings 1981, 156–7.
[47] Lateiner 1985, 206.

χρησμοὺς καὶ ὅσα τοιαῦτα μετ' ἐλπίδων λυμαίνεται, "[don't emulate the common run of men], who when human means of saving themselves are still available, in times when tangible hopes desert them in their afflictions turn to intangible ones, to prophecy, oracles, and whatever else of this sort combines with hope to bring ruin"). As de Romilly notes (1963, 292) "it is obvious that the idea of divine providence helping the pious through the medium of chance is quite foreign to his [Thucydides'] very realistic attitude".

I will now move on to the *Knights* and the final part of my contribution in order to show that the single appearance of the word 'hope' right at the turn from the old to the new world is connected with a series of arbitrary and futile interpretations of oracles. As I will argue, this connection indicates that the new political model which Agorakritos establishes inspires no hope for change in the community, but, on the contrary, has damaging effects for it.

The play begins with the two slaves of Demos, who represent Demosthenes and Nicias, commiserating on their misfortune to have the vile Paphlagonian, or Cleon, presiding over them and over the house of Demos as his steward. They contemplate a way out of the hopeless situation. After the usual comic routine which involves jokes about Euripides and masturbation, one of the two slaves suggests seeking the gods' help. This passage has been considered to evoke the opening chorus from Aeschylus' *Seven Against Thebes* (95–9),[48] where the Theban girls are terrified at the clash of arms. Eteocles manages to dispel the chorus' fears effectively only by reasoning with them, laying out his strategy against the enemy and proving that he is equal to the challenge.[49] In the comic context, however, the desperation of the two slaves does not lead to logical deliberation, but to wine drinking, libations, and oracle consultation. The solution that Demosthenes comes up with is the product of 'divine inspiration' (85–6) —or simply of having one too many— and relies on his reading of an oracle. This reminds us of Nicias' superstition in Thucydides (and the *Knights* does allude to Nicias' religious reputation and piety),[50] which as already noted, was not a good guide to his decision-making. The oracle and its interpretation decide the fate of Paphlagon, and, consequently, of the house of Demos: if it is not fulfilled, Paphlagon has one (and slim) hope to prevail upon the Sausage-seller (1244 λεπτή τις ἐλπίς ἐστ' ἐφ'

---

48 See Sommerstein 1981, 146.
49 See Konstan 2006, 144–8 who notes that this is an effective strategy as fear, according to Aristotle, involves sophisticated social judgement about a potential harm, which often derives from the impression that someone is in a superior position than you.
50 Cf. l. 30–4. Sommerstein (1980) believes that the slave Nicias stands for the politician; contrast Dover (1975).

ἧς ὀχούμεθα, "there is a slim hope that keeps us yet afloat");[51] otherwise, the Sausage Seller will emerge as his successor. It soon becomes obvious that, according to the oracles,[52] the Sausage-seller bears all the credits[53] and is the one destined to beat Paphlagon, who finally relinquishes his position in a paratragic fashion (1248–9). Paphlagon's hope is failed: does this mean that the future now holds out hope for the house of Demos, as the slaves had thought when they happened upon the oracle?

The scene from line 997 onwards, which leads to the appointment of the Sausage seller as Demos' new steward, suggests otherwise. This phase of the competition between Paphlagon and the Sausage Seller is structured around oracles and their interpretation, misinterpretation, and counter-interpretation and provides us with the framework for a sober reading of the supposed hopefulness of the oracle. As Paphlagon and the Sausage-Seller strive to cap each other's efforts to keep control of or win over Demos, they prove to be masters of improvisation, invention, and manipulation, by reciting and interpreting their very own made-up oracles. As Ian Ruffell has shown, although the referent of the oracle cited each time seems clear, it is constantly negotiated and manipulated by the rival so that a final or stable interpretation becomes impossible.[54] One example will suffice: Paphlagon recites an oracle, which bids the Demos to preserve the 'holy jagtoothed dog' which barks for him (1015–20). According to Paphlagon's interpretation, the dog stands for him as the guardian of Demos (1023–4). The Sausage-Seller, however, refutes this interpretation (1025 οὐ τοῦτό φησ' ὁ χρησμός, "that's not what the oracle says"): he spins the metaphor around and, in the place of the dog as a guard, introduces the idea of a dog as a thief, and then proceeds to recite the "correct" version of the oracle (1027 ἐμοὶ γάρ ἐστ' ὀρθῶς περὶ τούτου τοῦ κυνός, "I've got the right version about this dog").

The systematic re-interpretation of the oracles continues in the same fashion throughout the scene and reflects their fluidity and unreliability: the meaning is constantly destabilized, and, therefore, a final and correct reading is rendered impossible. Although Demos seems to be persuaded by the Sausage-seller's "correct" interpretations –and it is finally the oracle which determines the outcome

---

51 All translations of Aristophanes are those of Sommerstein 1981.
52 l. 1233 τοῦ θεοῦ τοῖς θεσφάτοις, 1237 ὥς μου χρησμὸς ἅπτεται φρενῶν, 1240 ὦ Φοῖβ' Ἄπολλον Λύκιε τί ποτέ μ' ἐργάσει; culminating in l. 1248 (οἴμοι πέπρακται τοῦ θεοῦ τὸ θέσφατον) and the Sausage-seller's prayer to Zeus at l. 1253 (Ἑλλάνιε Ζεῦ σὸν τὸ νικητήριον).
53 Those are being raised in the singeing pits (i.e. not receiving a proper education), stealing and perjuring, engaging in male prostitution, and doing business at the gates, a disreputable location (1236–46).
54 Ruffell 2011, 69–70.

of the contest between the two rivals– the audience knows better than that and is asked to be distrustful of the supposed hopefulness of the oracles.

The Sausage seller reveals his true identity as Agorakritos right after the fulfilment of the oracle and Paphlagon's tragic exodus. Thus, the most seminal moment of the play, the moment which signals the turn of the Old to the New world, is marked by a slender hope, a hope relying on an oracle, which proves to be equally futile for both Paphlagon and the people of Athens: they are still gaping morons, and most importantly, are still treated by Agorakritos as such (1262–3). Agorakritos does not differ at all from Paphlagon or every other man who will act as the political advisor of Demos; he has done nothing more than deepen the process of manipulation he inherited from Cleon. Earlier in the play, Demos provides a justification of his political motives and boasts about his political tactics. He claims that he has everything under control and is being intentionally stupid, as he fattens, like animals, all the politicians who wish to control him, and then sacrifices them and consumes them at the appropriate time (1121–30). Demos seems to believe that this diet works for him and that he has the last laugh over the politicians (1141–4). It is clear, however, that he employs a delusional positive thinking which sustains false visions of having his desires met indefinitely in the future through a never-ending alteration of political advisors. As with Paphlagon, disillusionment is always destined to follow hope while Demos will never be able to break free from this vicious circle. Demos himself express his weariness of the politicians' services (1156–1157), but remains in his inertia and indolence without taking any action to dispose of them. His appearance after his miraculous transformation (1331–2 ὅδ' ἐκεῖνος ὁρᾶν τεττιγοφόρας, ἀρχαίῳ σχήματι λαμπρός, / οὐ χοιρινῶν ὄζων ἀλλὰ σπονδῶν, σμύρνῃ κατάλειπτος, "behold the man, wearing a golden cicada, resplendent in antique costume, / smelling not of mussel-shells but of peace libations, and anointed with myrrh") recalls an oracle cited earlier by the Sausage-seller (967–9):

ΑΛ.: οὑμοὶ δέ γ' αὖ λέγουσιν ὡς ἁλουργίδα
ἔχων κατάπαστον καὶ στεφάνην ἐφ' ἅρματος
χρυσοῦ διώξεις Σμικύθην καὶ κύριον.

S.S. And mine say that, wearing a spangled
purple robe and a diadem, riding a golden chariot
you will pursue ... Smicythe (and husband) through the courts.

The purple robe, the crown and the golden chariot point to a king but are immediately converted to an image of litigation, and Demos, instead of a king, is promised to become a prosecutor against a man noted for his effeminate vices.[55] Yet, at the end of the play, in one more twist of the oracle, Demos is hailed as a king and a monarch (1330 μόναρχον, 1333 βασιλεῦ), who smells off libations and not voting-pebbles (1332), while the function of the courts is suspended (1317).[56]

The addressing of Demos as a monarch of Greece is deeply ironic since he looks more like a rich Ionian ready to join a symposium and he appears to have but a dim memory of his past actions.[57] It is the Sausage-seller who reminds him of the stupid things he used to do, asks for his future measures, and finally rewards him with a παῖδα ἐνόρχην (1385) and a bunch of girls embodying the σπονδαί (1388–91). This is another twist of the oracles: earlier on Paphlagon had warned Demos that if he followed the Sausage-seller's oracles he would become a μολγός (963), that is a pathic.[58] The Sausage-seller responded that by listening to Paphlagon's oracles Demos would acquire a hard-on and become an aggressive pederast (964 ψωλὸν γενέσθαι δεῖ σε μέχρι τοῦ μυρρίνου, "you are destined to end up with a cock skinned back to the root"),[59] which is precisely what happens at the end of the play, despite the fact that Paphlagon is now banished. The image is rather distasteful: Demos, whom we knew as a peevish old man (42–3), now appears to have both male and female lovers.

The new political model inspires no hope for change in the community, but, on the contrary, has damaging effects on it. Demos' transformation is not substantial, as he remains as stupid as he used to be, and perhaps even more, since he is under the impression that he has undergone a change. This fake transformation might have been visible on stage: Demos could show up after his rejuvenation wearing the same mask as before, so that while the chorus would marvel at his supposed transformation, the audience would be able to see through it. Moreover, the *phallos* would not be erect, but dangling, thus highlighting the fact that Demos' sexual potency was not actually restored. At the end of the play the Sausage seller takes his place in the Prytaneum, where he had accused Paphlagon of enjoying himself improperly (280–281). The oracle about the succession

---

55 See Sommerstein 1981, 195–6.
56 Contra Sommerstein (1981, 216) who believes that the courts will continue to function, but jury service was normally taken up by old men, and Demos is not one anymore.
57 τί δ' ἔδρων πρὸ τοῦ, κάτειπε, καὶ ποῖός τις ἦ, 339 ("Tell me, how did I used to act, and what was I like?"); τί φῄς; ταυτί μ' ἔδρων, ἐγὼ δὲ τοῦτ' οὐκ ᾐσθόμην, 1346 ("You don't say! They did that to me, and I didn't catch on?"); οὕτως ἀνόητος ἐγεγενήμην καὶ γέρων, 1349 ("Was I that mindless and senile?").
58 For this interpretation, see Henderson 1991, 68–9, 212.
59 Henderson 1991, 218.

of politicians has been fulfilled, but the hope it was supposed to bring has failed. Nothing has changed: Demos remains in the grip of demagogues.

Through this comparative reading of Thucydides' and Aristophanes' respective models of hope I tried to show that a pessimistic political message emerges regarding the predominance of blind illusion over reality in the politics of the time, and the limited ability of the people to predict and control the future. But what does this negative portrayal of hope suggest for the political outlook of both authors? It is true that, apart from their scepticism about hope, both Thucydides and Aristophanes also share a distrust for those politicians who can be labelled as upstart over those labelled as upper-class.[60] Their pessimistic realism regarding the use of hope in political discourse and hope-fuelled decisions at the very least provides one more clue about their political agenda which leans rather towards pragmatism and Realpolitik than progressivism. And yet, both Aristophanes and Thucydides may write their works in the hope[61] that their critique of the narratives of the Athenian democratic culture may inform judgment and diminish the persistence of delusional politikal thinking.

Bibliography

Allison, J.W. 1989. *Power and Preparedness in Thucydides*, Baltimore.
Aronson, R. 1999. "Hope after Hope?," in: *Social Research* 66.2, 471–94.
Arrowsmith, W. 1973. "Aristophanes' *Birds*: The Fantasy Politics of Eros," in: *Arion* 1, 119–67.
Atwater, D.F. 2007. "The Rhetoric of Hope and the American Dream," in: *Journal of Black Studies* 38.2, 121–129.
Bloch, E. 1986. *The Principle of Hope* (translated by N. Plaice, S. Plaice and P. Knight), Oxford.
Bowden, H. 2003. "Oracles for Sale," in: P. Derow/R. Parker (eds.), *Herodotus and His World: Essays from a Conference in Memory of George Forrest*, Oxford, 256–74.
Bowie, A.M. 1993. *Aristophanes: Myth, Ritual and Comedy*, Cambridge.
Brock, R. 2013. *Greek Political Imagery from Homer to Aristotle*, London.
Cairns, D. 2016 "Metaphors for Hope in Archaic and Classical Greek Poetry," in: R.R. Caston/R.A. Kaster (eds.), *Hope, Joy, and Affection in the Classical World*, Oxford/New York, 13–44.
Connor, W.R. 1984. *Thucydides*, Princeton.
Cornford, F.M. 1965. *Thucydides Mythistoricus*, London.
Delbanco, A. 1999. *The Real American Dream: A Meditation on Hope*, Cambridge, Mass.
De Romilly, J. 1963. *Thucydides and Athenian imperialism* (translated by P. Thody), New York.
Dillery, J. 2005. "Chresmologues and Manteis: Independent Diviners and the Problem of Authority," in: S.I. Johnston/P. Struck (eds.), *Mantikê: Studies in Ancient Divination*, Leiden, 167–231.

---

60 See Rhodes 2004.
61 Cf. Thucydides' use of ἐλπίζειν in the first lines of his historical account (1.1), which shows that the *History* offers itself as a way of thinking about the hopes it chronicles in its narrative.

Dover, K.J. 1975. "Portrait-masks in Aristophanes," in: H.J. Newiger (ed.), *Aristophanes und die alte Komödie*, Darmstadt, 155–69.
Edmunds, L. 1975. *Chance and Intelligence in Thucydides*, Cambridge, Mass.
Faraone, C. 1999. *Ancient Greek Love Magic*, Cambridge, Mass.
Forde, S. 1989. *The Ambition to Rule: Alcibiades and the Politics of Imperialism in Thucydides*, Ithaca.
Fulkerson, L. 2016 "Torn between Hope and Despair," in: R.R. Caston/R.A. Kaster (eds.), *Hope, Joy, and Affection in the Classical World*, Oxford/New York, 75–92.
Gomme, A.W./A. Andrewes/K.J. Dover. 1945–1981. *A Historical Commentary on Thucydides*, Oxford.
Henderson, J. 1991. *The Maculate Muse: Obscene Language in Attic Comedy*, New Haven/London.
Hornblower, S. 1991. *A Commentary on Thucydides* (vol. 1), Oxford.
–– 2008. *A Commentary on Thucydides* (vol. 3), Oxford.
Hunter, V. 1973. *Thucydides the Artful Reporter*, Toronto.
Jordan, B. 2000. "The Sicilian Expedition Was a Potemkin Fleet," in: *CQ* 50, 63–79.
Kallet, L. 2001. *Money and the Corrosion of Power in Thucydides: The Sicilian Expedition and Its Aftermath*, Berkeley/London.
Konstan, D. 2006. *The Emotions of the Ancient Greeks: Studies in Aristotle and Classical Literature*, Toronto.
Lateiner, D. 1985. "Nicias' Inadequate Encouragement (Thucydides 7. 69. 2)," in: *CPh* 80.3, 201–213.
Lattimore, S. 1998. *Thucydides,* The Peloponnesian War*: Translated with Introduction, Notes, and Glossary*, Indianapolis/Cambridge, Mass.
Lear, J. 2006. *Radical Hope: Ethics in the Face of Cultural Devastation*, Cambridge, Mass.
Loraux, N. 1986. *The Invention of Athens: The Funeral Oration in the Classical City* (translated by A. Sheridan), Cambridge, Mass./London.
Luginbill, R.D. 1999. *Thucydides on War and National Character*, Boulder, CO.
Marinatos, N. 1981. "Thucydides and Oracles," in: *The JHS* 101, 138–140.
McGlew, J. 1996. "Everybody Wants to Make a Speech: Cleon and Aristophanes on Politics and Fantasy," in: *Arethusa* 29, 339–361.
Mittleman, A. 2009. *Hope in a Democratic Age: Philosophy, Religion, and Political Theory*, Oxford.
Nussbaum, M.C. 2001. *Upheavals of Thought: The Intelligence of Emotions*, Cambridge.
Oost, S.I. 1975. "Thucydides and the Irrational: Sundry Passages," in: *CPh* 70.3, 186–96.
Parry, A.M. 1981. *Logos and Ergon in Thucydides*, New York.
Petersend, R./E. Liaras. 2006. "Countering Fear in War: The Strategic Use of Emotion," in: *Journal of Military Ethics* 5.4, 317–33.
Rahe, P.A. 1995. "Thucydides' Critique of *Realpolitik*," in: *Security Studies* 5.2, 105–41.
Rawlings, H.R. 1981. *The Structure of Thucydides' History*, Princeton.
Rhodes, P.J. 2004. "Aristophanes and the Athenian Assembly," in: D.L. Cairns/R.A. Knox (eds.), *Law, Rhetoric and Comedy in Classical Athens: Essays in Honour of Douglas M. MacDowell*, Swansea, 223–38.
Ruffell, I.A. 2011. *Politics and Anti-realism in Athenian Old Comedy: The Art of the Impossible*, Oxford.
Scanlon, T.F. 1987. "Thucydides and Tyranny," in: *Classical Antiquity* 6, 286–301.
Scholtz, A. 1997. "*Erastēs tou dēmou*: Erotic Imagery in Political Contexts in Thucydides and Aristophanes", Yale University Diss. thesis.
–– 2004. "Friends, Lovers, Flatterers: Demophilic Courtship in Aristophanes' *Knights*," in: *Transactions of the American Philological Association* 134, 263–93.

Segal, C. 1993. *Euripides and the Poetics of Sorrow: Art, Gender, and Commemoration in Alcestis, Hippolytus, and Hecuba*, Durham, N.C./London.
Sommerstein, A. H. 1980. "Notes on Aristophanes': *Knights*," in: *The CQ* 30.1, 46–56.
—— 1981. *Aristophanes:* Knights, Warminster.
—— 2009. *Talking about Laughter and Other Studies in Greek Comedy*, Oxford.
Strauss-Clay, J. 2003. *Hesiod's Cosmos*, Cambridge.
Walker, A.D. 1993 "Enargeia and the Spectator in Greek Historiography," in: *TAPA* 123, 353–77.
Westbrook, R. 2005. *Democratic Hope: Pragmatism and the Politics of Truth*, Ithaca, NY.
Winkler, J.J. 1990. *The Constraints of Desire: The Anthropology of Sex and Gender in Ancient Greece*, New York/London.
Wohl, V. 2002. *Love Among the Ruins: The Erotics of Democracy in Classical Athens*, Princeton.
Worman, N. 2008. *Abusive Mouths in Classical Athens*, Cambridge.
Yates, V.L. 2005. "*Anterastai*: Competition in *Eros* and Politics in Classical Athens," in: *Arethusa* 38, 33–47.

Donald Lateiner
Elpis as Emotion and Reason (Hope and Expectation) in Fifth-century Greek Historians

Introduction

Hope or *elpis* is a real experience, one product of our primitive neuro-bath of chemical secretions such as endorphins and serotonin. *Hope* is necessary for individual and social action —a vital force necessary to overcome cognition's discouraging predictions for any action. Human beings developed *hopes* that energize them for hunting fat, protein, and sugars, for sexual selection and reproduction.[1] Emotions and cognitive capacities derive from survival and reproductive instincts. *Hope* combines these mental processes. But, hope also can disable prudent calculations when success is unlikely. Early historians record wars and other adventures in which men both tamp down hope, or stimulate this two-edged emotion to a bad end.

Hope is classified by current psychologists as a positive emotion. Goal-oriented humans wish to enhance good circumstances in their lives and repair or reverse bad. Psychologists assert that hope produces better coping mechanisms and success for, e.g., athletes and entrepreneurs. Like fear, hope arises from predictions. "Affective cognition" denotes interpretations of phenomena in line with positive or negative expectations. So, success leads to hope and hope leads to success, a feedback loop that Thucydides' angry but perceptive Korinthians acknowledge. "Hope theory" suggests that optimism in persons—hope—leads to beneficial outcomes (Cheavens and Ritschel 2014, 396-405). Herodotos (3.39.4) and Thucydides (4.65.4), however, argue that success, *eutychia*, in states and individuals encourages *elpis*, and *elpis* leads to bad outcomes, since others' good fortune and consequent hopes arouse fear, envy, alliances, and other preventive, protective reactions (Thuc. 1.23.6; Connor 1984, 125).

Psychologists and philosophers continue to contest the nature of "emotions" themselves. Greek *elpis* is doubly contested. It has at least two distinct meanings as well as translations into other languages: e.g., Latin *spes* and *exspectatio*, English hope and rational supposition —past, present, or future. All lexica recognize

---

[1] Tiger 1999 develops the evolutionary anthropological perspective on moderated optimism in a social science periodical's special issue on "Hope and Despair."

this duality, but a conceptual coherence, a small "family of scripts," underlies the diversity.[2] Therefore, lack of "univocity" demands close investigation, not despair, or *anelpistia* (this noun first in Asklepiodoros' *Taktika* 5.2; cf. Thucydides polyphonic *to anelpiston:* 3.83, 6.33*, etc.). The generally negative valence of hopefulness in Classical writers has been obscured by the influential early Christian inversion and then stimulation of the emotion among its once oppressed adherents. Recent managers and promoters of hope —ambitious men engaged in politics, business, and religion– contribute to the encouragement of public conceptions and distortions of what past investigators of the dangers of hope realized.[3] Herodotos, Thucydides, and Xenophon (in *Hellenica*) follow Homer in distinguishing hopeful but reasoned expectations from wishful thinking, and both these predicting procedures from their execution in council and battle.

They follow Hesiod (and Homer) in recognizing that *hope is not a strategy*. The more rational meaning of *elpis*, "expect"-data-crunching *elpis*[4] —usually cedes to the more emotional "*hopes* for"— empty *hopes*, dithering in wait for vain *hopes* (cf. *Op.* 498-501).[5] Conventional epithets for Greek *elpis*, hope, are *kenos*, empty or *typhlos*, blind—undesirable characteristics.[6] Hesiod's prelapsarian, misogynistic Pan-Dora story accounting for the genesis of Woman[7] maintains *elpis*

---

[2] Cairns and Fulkerson's "Introduction" (2015, esp. 14) explores definitional (lack of "univocity") and translational problems into English and other languages and cultures for emotions in general. See also this volume's Introduction.

[3] Paul's notorious triad, "faith, hope, and charity" (1 *Cor.* 13), became watchwords for virgin saints and martyrs as well as the name of a Tampa, Florida, disco band. For one theology of hope, consider Greer's discussion (2001, 3, 9) of Christian hope informing both this life and the next.

[4] Myres 1949, 46 is brief but comprehensive on *elpis* in its rational and positive senses.

[5] Martin West (*ad loc.*) believes that Pandora's hope nourishes us; a solace that comforts us in present ills and has not been lost. West openly addresses the problem of why one good quality of life would come immersed in a package of evils and diseases. The futility and fatuity of hope is a Hellenic commonplace, but historians track actual misapprehensions.

[6] Verdenius (1971 and 1985) discusses Hope's remaining in the pithos as "prison and/or pantry." Is it a negative force that cannot be expelled or a positive force that enables humans to continue? Myres oddly ignores reactions ex post facto to other men's delusive and inappropriate hopes, as for example those politicians and mediums who encouraged the Sicilian expedition: fortune-tellers, oracle-mongers, and other men claiming access to divine will (Thuc. 8.1.1: ὁπόσοι τι τότε αὐτοὺς θειάσαντες ἐπήλπισαν ὡς λήψονται Σικελίαν).

[7] Elpidologists recognize that Hebrew and subsequent Christian thought inflected Greek concepts: identifying a Messiah to come and a better next world for the observant. Myres (1949, 46) finds both rational belief and "assurance of a better life after death" in NT texts (e.g., *Eph.* 2,12).

inside the *pithos,* symbiotic with humans, appropriately good and bad —but worse than the escaped κακά for its oblique ambivalence.⁸

ἐσκέδασ'·ἀνθρώποισι δ'ἐμήσατο κήδεα λυγρὰ.
μούνη δ'αὐτόθι Ἐλπὶς ἐν ἀρρήκτοισι δόμοισιν
ἔνδον ἔμιμνε πίθου ὑπὸ χείλεσιν, οὐδὲ θύραζε
ἐξέπτη·πρόσθεν γὰρ ἐπέμβαλε πῶμα πίθοιο...

She [Pandora] devised anxious miseries for men.
Hope alone remained in the unbreakable prison-house,
within the great jar, under the lip, and did not
fly out the opening. Before that, Pandora set on it a lid ...

Historians "play a double game:" they provide an "objective" investigation and narrative, and they variously authorize their accounts exhibiting intrusive (Herodotos) or recessive (Thucydides) *personae.* Herodotos argues with, even cajoles his readers, produces polemics and questions alternative accounts and explanations.⁹ Thucydides' readers are present only as a vague τις, but he makes his views felt indirectly, often alerting his reader through repeated themes such as Athenian resilience or harmful individualism.¹⁰ A category of unexpected outcomes includes intended (military surprise) attacks and unexpected "natural" or inconceivable outcomes (τὸ παράλογον).¹¹ Frequently *hope* or expectation crashes into improbable eventualities, one frequent theme brilliantly explored by Stahl. Men and cities, despite warnings, persist in *hoping* or *expecting* favorable

---

8   Personified *Elpis* remains near to humans the pithos (*Op.* 95–98); cf. "empty *elpis*" 498–501: κενεὴν ἐπὶ ἐλπίδα μίμνων, Theog. 570–616. Like African "dilemma tales," Hesiod's story promotes audience discussion of this tricky emotion rather than providing a clear answer as to Hope's nature.

9   Herodotos asks thirteen rhetorical questions (Lateiner 1989, 72–3), Thucydides only two. Dewald (2012, 267–90; cf. Dewald 2011) discusses Herodotos' authorial persona, neutral 'information', and the rhetoric of his investigative techniques, polemic, and criticism. Gribble (1998, 43) supplied the 'double game' metaphor for authorial interventions. He also addresses the later historian's impress throughout the text, a writer who does not dispense "nuggets" of opinion (45, 47, 53, 62, 67).

10 Micro habits such as superlative adjectives, counterfactual hypotheses, firsts or other uniquenesses also interrupt the steady chronological flow, e.g., value-laden accounts of paradigmatic events such as the plague at Athens, stasis in Kerkyra, massacre at Mykalessos, and other unexpected twists.

11 The unexpected, expressed commonly by ἀδόκητον, draws Thucydides' attention, as at Mykalessos: οὐδεμιᾶς ἥσσων μᾶλλον ἑτέρας ἀδόκητος. Cf. 4.17.4, 6.34.6–8*, 7.43.6 and Bosworth (1999, 43).

outcomes that never come out. Human nature, hard-wired and hard to change, only later comes to regret optimistic strategies.

Herodotos' characters express few *hopes* by *elpis* words.[12] His forty-nine examples of the verbs and fourteen of the noun voice mostly dubious, expected calculations, not wild *hopes*. That is, these hopes *exspectare*, not *sperare*. Herodotos *in propria persona* evaluates specific *elpides* as mostly foolish. For the past's present and future events, the ambivalent sense of English 'reckon' or 'suppose' well fits most uses of the noun and verb. Themistokles' strategic advice to Spartan Eurybiades before the battle of Salamis unusually *anticipates* the result correctly (τὰ ἐγὼ ἐλπίζω), and he pleads for a reasoned strategy, οἰκότα βουλεύματα (8.60γ*).

Amestris supposed —wrongly— that the wife of Masistes was behind her daughter Artaynte's adultery with Xerxes, her husband. Therefore, she horrifically tortured and misguidedly destroyed the mother (1.110.1). Scyth commanders supposed—wrongly, from animal sounds heard and fires seen burning in the night—that the Persian invaders had remained in place, when, in fact, employing this deluding stratagem, the army had turned tail and retreated towards the Ister (4.135). *Elpis* here again, as often, is perfectly rational but entirely wrong. *Elpis* remains a mental construct, one that reality dissolves. Past results not only do not guarantee future performance but for Herodotos, *elpis* —hope or expectation— can be exploited to misdirect competitors or enemies. For example, Kroisos' ancestor Alyattes, comes a cropper. Alyattes reasonably thought Miletos *would* suffer famine and surrender after eleven years of war and siege. The Milesians were starving, but Thrasyboulos, their tyrant, created a ruse of constant feasting. The pretense fooled a visiting enemy delegation and led the deceived Lydian aggressor to treat for peace. The stratagem deluded his rational strategy (1.17–22).

Prospective *elpides*, based on past facts, may be calculated and reasonable in themselves (*oikota*: 1.27.4, 1.77, 8.10) but, even so, Herodotos mentions them mostly when they fail. When these suppositions describe past expectations and reckoning, they nearly always prove to have been erroneous.[13] Kroisos is Herodotos' "poster boy" for *elpis*, a paradigm of hoping gone bad, and repeatedly shot down for it. Herodotos associates *elpis* vocabulary with Kroisos more than with anyone else. His story illustrates *in nuce* and *ab initio* the frequent historical futility of confusing desire for power with reality. Although he has "lucked into"

---

12 Perhaps the relative frequencies reflect the fact that the παραίνησις, one favorite locus of *elpis*, the Battle-Speech exhortation, had yet to be incorporated into Greek historiography. Thucydides 5.69.1, 2, etc., cf. Luschnat 1942 *Feldherrnrede*.
13 Powell 1938 and Myres 1949.

material happiness, soon he will be S.O.L., "shit out of luck." I summarize his seven *elpi-* incidents. Kroisos, in colloquy with Bias of mainland Priene (1.27.4*),[14] is induced to face the hypothetical issue of Hellenic islanders attacking him on land, the element where he is strong. He could only *hope* [1] they would be so foolish. But, Bias springs the trap of his argument: that foolish is Kroisos at that very moment in his *hoping* to defeat the Greeks at sea, the element where they are strong.

Herodotos' Kroisos is repeatedly afflicted by *elpis*, mistaken *hopes* and suppositions even before [2] he expected that Solon would deem him *olbiôtatos* (1.30.3: ἐλπίζων εἶναι ἀνθρώπων ὀλβιώτατος). Kroisos *hoped* to acquire [3] Apollo's goodwill by offerings (1.50.1). He interpreted the Pythia's puzzling oracle about a Median mule coming to rule that nation to mean "never," falsely *supposing* [4] that outcome to be an *adynaton* (1.56.1). So, most famously, he *supposes* [5] that he understands Delphi's oracle about crossing a river to guarantee Lydia's victory and overjoyed, he attacks Kyros' realm (1.54.1, 71.1, 75.2). In the ensuing battle at Pterea, his *hope* [6] is destroyed.[15] Finally, Kroisos, after fighting at Pterea to a draw, never *expects* [7] or imagines that Kyros would attack Sardis directly (οὐδαμὰ ἐλπίσας, 1.77.4). Consequently, he disbanded his mercenary army and plans to fight another spring. Wrong again! His *elpis*, while it is rational expectation, does not anticipate Kyros' superior plan, itself constructed from his enemy's sanguine expectation. Kroisos suffers defeat; and the royal POW is consigned to Kyros' Persian pyre.

Herodotos also employs *elpis* words for his own rational but unprovable speculations and calculations (such as geological hypotheses about the Nile: 2.11.4, 26.2), or for reasonable but erroneous suppositions held by others about the past. Xerxes defends Demaratos' honest expression of *expected* outcomes (7.237.1*), even if he deemed them unlikely. Ἐλπίζω, however, usually implies Herodotos' present judgment assigning error for some party's past calculations (1.22: Alyattes for Miletos; 3.62: Cambyses concerning Smerdis; 6.5.1: Histiaios for subduing Sardis).

Herodotos disvalues any supposer's present or future "high *hopes*": Polykrates' for Ionian thalassocracy, the oligarchic Naxian exiles' "high *hopes*," and feckless Histiaios and Aristagoras' "high *hopes*" for Ionian dominion (3.122; 5.30, 35, 36: πολλὰς ἐλπίδας). Herodotos' idioms ἐλπίδος ψεύσασθαι or

---

14 Following Powell's useful *Lexicon* precedent, asterisked references indicate *oratio recta*.
15 1.80.5: the noun is rare (2x) in Herodotos and here it appears in emphatic final sentence position: when his horses smell and see the Persian camels, they fled, and διέφθαρτό τε τῷ Κροίσῳ ἡ ἐλπίς.

ἀποσφαλῆναι mark men "deceived by *hope*," namely Kyros' fable of the piper and the fish, an Egyptian prophecy for the Hellenes, and Pausanias' negative prayer at Plataiai (1.141.2*, 2.13.3, 9.61.3; cf. 6.9.1). Rarely is *elpis*, when mentioned, fulfilled in Herodotos' pages.[16]

Mardonios, for example, "expected in full confidence" easily to rule the sea and Hellas, if he won over the Athenians to the Persian cause (8.136.3: κατήλπιζε (hapax) εὐπετέως ...κρατήσειν, τά περ ἂν καὶ ἦν...; cf. 8.10.2).[17] Herodotos even endorses the General's reasoning (ἐλογίζετο) and expectation of conquest, τὰ πὲρ ἂν καὶ ἦν.[18] His agent, the Macedonian Alexander, declared that the Athenians had no reasonable *elpis* for victory–if they calculated intelligently (8.140α3*): τοῦ [νικῆσαι] περ ὑμῖν οὐδεμία ἐλπὶς, εἴ περ εὖ φρονέετε. But Mardonios' own *elpis* proves inadequate. *Elpis* describes either inadequate supposition or a fallback, deceptive comfort, when events deviate from human plans, control, and conceivable efforts. Herodotos observes that results almost always discomfit human calculations.[19] Thucydides invents a name for this distressing but common sequence in which outcome contradicts rational expectation: τὸ παράλογον (Stahl 1966/2003).

Thucydides employs *elpis* words more than twice as frequently as Herodotos, approximately 150 occurrences against 63.[20] He speculates about the emotions of his agents, and his speakers attribute various impulses to others. The Athenian general's obsession with the dynamics of political policy-making and reversals accounts for the ubiquity of *elpis*.[21] The events that he selects *typically* turn out contrary to human *expectation*. Human outcomes proceed παρὰ λόγον or ἀμαθῶς, as Perikles once recognizes (e.g., 1.140.1*). Thucydides spotlights, for

---

[16] Dareios' podiatric cure provides one trivial exception (3.130.3: οὐδαμὰ ἔτι ἐλπίζοντα ἀρτίπουν ἔσεσθαι).

[17] Crane (1998, 46–57) develops parallels between the "Realist" Persian arguments after Salamis and the "Realist" Athenian arguments at Melos, the position of the Athenians having been inverted from once attacked to attackers.

[18] Herodotos unexpectedly adds that perhaps the oracles counselled this strategy of alliance/surrender.

[19] American World War II military slang created an acronym: SNAFU—i.e., Situation Normal: All Fucked Up.

[20] Huart (1968, 141–52) discusses *elpis* vocabulary, positive and negative. His collection and analyses of the vocabulary of emotions in Thucydides underlies these studies. Connor (1984, 57) emphasizes the fragile insecurity of those experiencing *elpis*. Luginbill (1999, 65–81) and Desmond (2006, 359) emphasize fear as the omnipresent emotion in Thucydides, but the former critic sees *elpis* as equally important.

[21] Related motivational terms (with corresponding verbs) for Thucydides include *epithumia* (6.13.3*, 24.4), *orexis* (6.10.5*, 16.6*), and *eros* (6.24.3), emotions of desire signposting trouble.

five brief examples, the Akhaian chiefs *expected* to obtain supplies easily at Troy (1.11.1); Xerxes *hoped* Themistokles would enable him to subdue all Hellas (1.138.2); the Athenians and Spartans *expected* the Persians quickly to aid their respective causes (2.7.1); Harmodios and Aristogeiton *expected* disaffected Athenians to join them in attacking the tyrants (6.56.3); and the contemporary Athenian expeditionary army still *hoped* for Sikel supporters when it was already in full retreat (7.80.5). Every one proved wrong.

Elpides can be soundly formed on fact but still wrong, such as Archidamos' at Plataiai (2.75.1, 77.5). Or they can be unfounded such as the the Peloponnesians', the Athenians', the Mytileneans', the Melians', possibly the Kamarinans' (1.81.6*, 2.21.1, 3.39.3*, 5.103*, 6.78.2*). Most fantastical are Alkibiades' professed *hopes* for Mediterranean conquest and personal restoration (6.15.2*, 6.90.3*, 8.81.2, 8.89.2). Most pathetic are *hopes* placed in sheer luck or desperation like Demosthenes' or the Melians': τῇ τύχῃ ἐλπίσας, αἱ ἀφανεῖς ἐλπίδες (3.97.2, 5.103.2*, cf. 3.45.5*).[22] Nikias, even before he was pushed to desperation, exemplifies improbable, indeed pathetic, *hopes* of other decent but deluded men—like the Mytileneans and Melians: men fail to rightly calculate their situation, especially in tight corners (7.61.2*, 77.4*; cf. Diodotos, 3.46.1*, Stahl 2003, 164–9).

The Korinthians early in Book I attribute *elpis* to the Athenians, their enemies, grudgingly admiring an energy that they contrast to scorn for Spartan political torpidity (1.70.4*). They also condemn Attic over-confidence and overreaching—a weakness but also a threat to *their* national security. Athenian *elpides* incline them to innovate and dare, indeed they are "daring and venturesome beyond good judgment and hopeful against adversities" (1.70.3*): τολμηταὶ καὶ παρὰ γνώμην κινδυνευταὶ καὶ ἐν τοῖς δεινοῖς εὐέλπιδες. The Korinthians highlight Athenian—could it be Periclean?—restless and constant *expectations*. Even when they fail, to compensate they simply "redirect their *hopes* to other spheres" (1.70.7*).[23] "Only Athenians [in their swiftness] can call a thing *hoped* for, a thing got."[24]

---

22 Hermokrates warns other Sicilians to avoid these dangerous hopes, 6.78.2*.
23 Natalia Tsoumpra made this point at the 2015 Rethymno conference. ἀντελπίζω (1.70.7*) is *hapax* in Greek until Libanius (*Decl.* 26.28). The unprecedented word directed listeners to the singularly audacious hope.
24 The Athenians surpass all other polities in expectations. Successes "carry the Athenians away." The fatal conjunction of hope and desire for far-off things (6.24.3) afflicts them as much as the rebel Lesbians (3.45.5*). ἐπαίρεσθαι: Nikias 6.11.6*, cf. prudent men: 1.120.3–4*, 4.18.4*, and the Spartans' contrary self-image of patient strategizing [according to Archidamos]: 1.84.2*.

Perikles himself, however, marshals *elpis*, if only in its 'rational expectations' sense (cf. 2.62.5*, imprudent *hope*), since a statesman must provide a prognosis and persuade his constituents of his vision.²⁵ He must respond to the need to restore spirit, to console or cheer up his fellow citizens (2.59.3), and so he expresses good *hopes* for Athenian victory in the war. Before war commences, he states that he has many reasons to <u>hope for</u> /<u>expect</u> success, provided the Athenians do not try to extend their empire (1.144.1*): πολλὰ δὲ καὶ ἄλλα ἔχω ἐς ἐλπίδα τοῦ περιέσεσθαι. The dead Athenians that he eulogizes at the end of the year put their trust in *hopes* of success, but boldly combatted their enemies and died in that (erroneous but battle-suited) *hope* of survival (2.42.4*; cf. 2.44.3*). He praises the Athenian war dead for dying with a shared *hope* of success rather than with the blame of cowardice (43.5-6*: κοινῆς ἐλπίδος). His vision, nevertheless encourages the Athenians to imagine their dominion to be potentially as wide as the sea (2.62.2*: ἐφ' ὅσον τε νῦν νέμεσθε καὶ ἢν ἐπὶ πλέον βουληθῆτε). The restraint need only be temporary (Orwin 1994, 28).

Elpis colors many of Thucydides' other speakers. His speakers attribute empty *elpis* to their desperate, cornered enemies, or to unreasonably elated (*epairesthai*)²⁶ fellow citizens or opponents. Individuals and polities can be "carried away" by *hopes* and fears, and other emotions. Good commanders and good politicians can stimulate *hope* when their citizens and soldiers need morale-boosting. Thucydides praises Perikles' first-man government (ὑπὸ τοῦ πρώτου ἀνδρὸς ἀρχή), lauding his πρόνοια, προγνοὺς τὴν δύναμιν (2.65.5–6, 9). "Whenever Perikles perceived his citizens emboldened by excessive confidence contrary to the situation, he struck fear in them by speech, and when again he saw them stuck in an irrational state of fear, he contrariwise brought them back to boldness" (2.65.9: ὁπότε γοῦν αἴσθοιτό τι αὐτοὺς παρὰ καιρὸν ὕβρει <u>θαρσοῦντας</u>, λέγων <u>κατέπλησσεν</u> ἐπὶ τὸ <u>φοβεῖσθαι</u>, καὶ <u>δεδιότας</u> αὖ ἀλόγως ἀντικαθίστη πάλιν ἐπὶ τὸ <u>θάρσειν</u>).

Thucydides' Korinthians analyze the aggressive Athenians as Herodotos had Kroisos, Astyages, and Xerxes. Herodotos' psychological recreations had

---

25 Over-confident Perikles alleged, before he fell ill, that only the plague escaped his expectations (2.64.1*): πρᾶγμα μόνον δὴ τῶν πάντων ἐλπίδος κρεῖσσον γεγενημένον. The boast either condemns him in Thucydides' eyes or both strategists in ours. While de Romilly (1963, 235) believed that Thucydides thought Pericles did no wrong, recent investigators, e.g., Foster, see more critique in his account, although others (e.g., Badian (1993, 158–62), Luginbill (2015, 361–7)) consider him an apologist for Perikles' errors.
26 See Huart (1968, 390 n.4) and Lugenbill (1999, 77 n.20). Human nature aroused to desire acquisitions beyond rational calculation: e.g., 1.81.6* & 83.2* Archidamos, 3.38.2* Kleon, 3.45.1* Diodotos, 7.41.3 Syracusan ship crews, etc.

attributed *elpis* to powerful individuals, especially to imperial-minded autocrats with a climaxing sequence of Lydian, Median, and Persian imperial expansionists. The result repeated over-confident, over-extended expansion ending in setback or deposition.[27]

Thucydides applies Herodotos' *elpis* paradigm to his agents, mostly *poleis* and not persons.[28] He concentrates on how emotional forces pervade and often dominate political groups' political life, at least in wartime. He analyzes *elpis* emotions in crowds, city-states, and alliances more than in individuals. Thucydides' repeated attributions of cities' delusional *hopes* and *unexpected* outcomes likewise devalue *elpis* (and related optimistic emotions, like θρασεῖα). He extends the paradigm. Greater focus on the communal power of *elpis* constitutes one transformation of Herodotus' invention, perhaps not for the better, but an attempt at an historical sociology.

Thucydides' Atheno-Peloponnesian War offers a pathology of national psychologies (cf. Crane 1998, Luginbill 1999). Their mistaken calculations derive from (3.82.3) contagious emotional inclinations. *Elpis* impelled all sides, both over-confident assemblies and Athenian subjects, to pursue unviable options and *expect* success after a short war. Thucydides, in retrospect, judges as unjustified expectation what Hellenic communities in prospect once judged reasonable strategies (5.14.1, 8.1.1–2). *Elpis* can be a resource in war, but only when statesmen properly evaluate other capacities and the immediate situation. Thucydides only invokes *anthrōpeia physis* for its ugliest and least admirable traits. *Elpis* adds a pathetic facet to that brutal nature.[29]

When especially sardonic, Thucydides modifies the *elpi-* verb or noun *expectation* with ῥαδίως or βέβαιον—Demosthenes' *hopes* before the Delian catastrophe in Boiotia, many Athenians' *hopes* to conquer all Greece before the Sicilian campaign, according to Alkibiades in Sparta (4.76.5, 6.90.3*). Likewise, the Spartans *expect* easily to seize the Athenians' Pylos fort, but the *elpis* proves false (4.8.4). The former Athenian subjects in the north confidently *expected* adequate Spartan aid for their rebellions on the basis of Brasidas' qualities (4.81.3). *Hopes* placed on Spartans and their assistance repeatedly fail: the Korinthians

---

27 Thucydides extends the analogy of imprudent over-hopefulness to the imperial Athenians, but only by implication. Fornara (1971), arguing that he wrote and "published" in the period 440–420 BCE, initiated awareness of Herodotos' oblique references to the Peloponnesian War context.

28 Hermokrates' bouleutic address concentrates *elpi-* terminology (6.33.4*, 33.6*, 34.2*) but space prohibits their analysis.

29 Desmond (1999, 343) observes that Thucydides invokes *anthropeia physis* for war, plague, stasis, atrocities, and when ruthless speakers explore facets of *Machtpolitik*.

generalize this fact, the Potidaians experience it, as do the Mytileneans soon after, and later the Melians (1.69.5, 1.65.1; 3.14.1*, 5.113.1* —*elpis* no better than chance, *tychē*). The Plataians no sooner call the Spartans "their only *hope*" than they dismiss the idea, fearing the Spartans will prove untrustworthy—as they do (3.57.4: ὑμεῖς τε... ἡ μόνη ἐλπίς, δέδιμεν μὴ οὐ βέβαιοι ἦτε). Brasidas' Thraceward allies had the *hope* or expectation that other Spartans in the field would resemble the effective and generous Brasidas (4.81.3), the first "liberator" that they had met. The retrospective remark conveys Thucydides' ironic judgment of their naiveté. Their *hopes* fatally misread a mendacious General jockeying for rebel pawns that Sparta could later trade for Spartiate captives.[30]

The Spartan delegates come to Athens after their defeat, surrender, and capture on Pylos to offer reasonable terms for ending the war, for peace. Nevertheless, in their elegant, unlaconic development of the proposals, they warn the Athenian assembly against excessive *hopes* of total victory in the Ten Year War. If they blindly and madly overestimate the significance of their *unexpected* and unexpectable success at Pylos (4.17)—a rapid victory that has rendered them over-confident—they may find that good luck turns bad (4.17.4): αἰεὶ γὰρ τοῦ πλέονος ἐλπίδι ὀρέγονται διὰ τὸ καὶ παρόντα ἀδοκήτως εὐτυχῆσαι.

Anelpiston situations in civil and military affairs (both unexpected events and feelings of hopelessness) gain Thucydides' attention. The plague deprived the Athenians of all *hope* for the future (2.51.4). The absence of *hope* in plague-stricken Athens or civil-war-torn Kerkyra (3.83.2) provides a symptom of social pathology, the collapse of morale and trust. Alkibiades in Athens, to persuade the Athenian assembly to invade Sicily, alleges increased *hopelessness* among the Spartan citizens, a further loss of will to fight overseas campaigns (6.17.8*). The Spartan polity had *not anticipated* their Pylos catastrophe and the capture of fellow Spartiates —and this loss affected their will to fight (4.55.1). The Athenian *demos* remaining at home later felt even more *hope*less, when news of the catastrophe arrived, since they had been deceived by the *hopes* spawned for the expedition by politicians, soothsayers, and such (8.1.1: ἐπήλπισαν). Less globally, surprise (unexpected) attacks seriously debilitate defense forces' military capacities, as Teutiaplos correctly but ineffectively explains to dilatory Alkidas, a Spartan admiral (3.30.2*). Similar to the Spartans' Pylos setback, Athenian troop morale was reduced by their *unanticipated losses* on land in Sicily (7.4.4: ἀνελπιστότερα). When Athenian troops perceive the Syracusans' successful resistance, they lose all *hope*, dispirited by their diseased condition and marshy position (7.47.2: ὅτι ἀνελπιστότατα, Reiske). When the ships are lost, Thucydides

---

[30] Connor 1984, 135; cf. 112n.9 on *elpi-* words anticipating error.

explicitly parallels the Athenian military collapse at Syracuse to the Spartans' at Pylos; no *hope* of salvation lest some inexplicable miracle arise (7.71.7: ἀν<u>έλπισ</u>τον ἦν... σωθήσεσθαι, ἢν μή τι παρὰ λόγον γίγνηται). Thucydides, emphasizing earlier lack of forethought, highlights present *hope*lessness.

Elpides are fragile when the Athenian *demos* faces military defeats and oligarchy (5.14.1, 8.54.1). Thucydides portrays Athenians and their forces as quick to *hope* and quick to despair (6.24.3, 8.1.1; *athumia*). An emotional wave may afflict sailors and troops before battle or while in political assembly (Naupaktos 2.88.3, Pylos 4.26.4, Samos, 8.76.3). Such loss of confidence and despair thickens when the Athenians suffer a cascade of Sicilian setbacks (7.24.3, 55.1, 60.5, 76.1, 79.3).[31] Only once does Thucydides ascribe *athymia* to the Spartans, when they experience their first failure in the Ionian War (8.11.3).[32] Only once does he describe the Spartans as eu<u>elpides</u>, and that at a moment when the Athenians are *anelpistoi* (8.2.4, 8.1.2).

Three extended Thucydidean incidents of risk-taking that engender fanciful *hopes* demand further attention: the Mytilenean debate at Athens, the Melian conference, and the Sicilian expedition.

A. In the debate about proper punishment for rebel Mytileneans, Kleon first condemns the islanders for yielding to *hope*. Then, he insists that the Athenians, as tyrants, grant them and other rebels no *hope* of forgiveness or survival, if they revolt (3.39.3*, 40.1*). "Make examples of them". His opponent Diodotos invokes *elpis* three times in his response to the violent demagogue. *Hope* leads all men to take risks, *eros* for goods or freedom leading in the conception, *elpis* following with expectations of success. Both impulses are irresistible and invisible (3. 45.5– 7*, Diodotos on Mytileneans: ἥ τε <u>ἐλπὶς</u> καὶ ὁ ἔρως ἐπὶ παντί, ὁ μὲν ἡγούμενος, <u>ἡ δ'</u> ἐφεπομένη, καὶ ὁ μὲν τὴν ἐπιβουλὴν ἐκφροντίζων, <u>ἡ δὲ</u> τὴν εὐπορίαν τῆς τύχης ὑποτιθεῖσα, <u>πλεῖστα βλάπτουσι</u>, καὶ ὄντα <u>ἀφανῆ</u> ... ἐς τὸ <u>ἐπαιρεῖν</u> ... ἀδοκήτως ... περὶ τῶν μεγίστων τε, ἐλευθερίας ἢ ἄλλων ἀρχῆς, ... ἀλογίστως ...). *Elpides* are ἀφανῆ and stronger than phenomena that can be seen (3.45.5*). Since this eager *hope*fulness (cf. 3.45.6: <u>τῇ ἐλπίδι ἐπαιρόμενοι</u>... , 1.76.3*, 3.64.4*, 3.82.2, 5.105*) identifies an element of human nature, it is naïve for politicians to expect laws or any threats to prevent rebellions (3.45.7*: ἁπλῶς τε ἀδύνατον καὶ πολλῆς εὐηθείας ... ἀποτροπήν τινα ἔχειν). Therefore, Athenians must not render all

---

31 The despondent Athenians come to regret that former *eutychia* that had led them to reject Spartan peace proposals and now to fear that their imperial "allies" would revolt (5.14.1–2). Diodotos predicted this damaging syndrome of success arousing hopes and desire.
32 The Korinthians demand that the Spartans attack Athens, or they threaten that the Peloponnesians will seek another ally in their *athymia* caused by Spartan lethargy (1.71.4*).

future rebels *hopeless* about obtaining mercy (3.46.1*: οὔτε ἀν<u>έλπισ</u>τον καταστῆσαι τοῖς ἀποστᾶσιν), if they choose to surrender. That is, he recognizes that foolish *hope* is ineradicable, but imperial Athens can turn that weakness to its own advantage. (3.46.1*). Diodotos' anatomy of delusional *elpis* and *tyche* (3.45.5*: πλεῖστα βλάπτουσι) agrees with Thucydides' analyses (3.3.1 Athenians' fantasies about the revolt: μεῖζον μέρος νέμοντες τῷ μὴ βουλέσθαι ἀληθῆ εἶναι).[33] Thucydides' glum purpose was to identify self-damaging regularities[34] such as the misbegotten *elpides* of men and states (1.22.4).[35]

Elpides are repeatedly dashed on both sides and for other parties caught in-between. Kerkyreans[36] and Spartans[37] lose hope (6.104.1, Gylippos τῆς μὲν Σικελίας οὐκέτι <u>ἐλπίδα</u> οὐδεμίαν εἶχεν...).[38] Athens' early successes contrary to

---

[33] Cf. Saar 1953, 83–5. He notes (81 n.4) negative descriptions for *elpis* in tragedy such as: Aesch. *PV* 250: τυφλὰς ἐν αὐτοῖς ἐλπίδας; paronomastic Eur. *Suppl.* 479: ἐλπίς ἄπιστον. Cairns in Caston/Kaster (2016, 31, 33, 38) discusses these and many other tragic metaphors for *elpis*.

[34] Collingwood (1946, 24) criticized Thucydides for precisely this aspect of his work so beloved of political philosophers: "Herodotos may be the father of history, but Thucydides is the father of psychological history. Now what is psychological history? It is not history at all, but natural science of a special kind." A tension affects the historian's particulars of there-and-then and the normative features of individual and state behaviors now-and-always. Huart's thorough study of Thucydides' "psychological vocabulary" considers *elpis* to provide *espoirs peu fondés le plus souvent, contraire a la logique, dangereux* (141–52). He also dissects its emotional opposite, ἀθυμία.

[35] The dynamics of Thucydides' impenetrable mind to get his "mere" facts right and to observe behavioral universals cannot be unified in one or another modern discipline (history or sociology/anthropology), but their tension remains suspended in solution. One rarely can verify facts or determine intentional omissions.

[36] 3.83.2 Kerkyraians' hopelessness in any trust because of the *stasis*: λογισμῷ ἐς τὸ ἀνέλπιστον τοῦ βεβαίου. Fault lies in *anthrōpeia physis*, human nature.

[37] Spartans' morale: 4.8.4, 4.13.1, 4.17.4* [neg.] 4.34.3, 4.55.1 (Pylos/Sphakteria), 6.17.8* [Alkibiades], 7.18.2–3 (post-Pylos), 8.2.3–4 εὐέλπιδες, with 8.11.3 ἀθυμήσαντες, 8.71.1, 8.94.2 [Agesandridas].

[38] Stahl (1966/2003) shows that Thucydides' unrelenting pessimism about mass and individual wishful thinking applies to all sides. The Mytileneans and nearly all Lesbos defect from the Athenian "League" or Empire, confident of Peloponnesian support for their premature decision. Meanwhile, the stubborn Athenians disbelieve reliable reports describing the real progress of the Lesbian revolt (3.1–3). Desires dictate goals and expectations, and then hopes of success direct the intellect to discover reasons that validate false expectations (Thuc. 3.3.1; Stahl 2003, 120–1): μεῖζον μέρος νέμοντες τῷ μὴ βουλέσθαι ἀληθῆ εἶναι. The Athenians hoped to attack the Mytileneans by surprise, but word reached the rebels (3.3.3–6). Kleon criticizes the Mytileneans for having *hopes* beyond their powers (3.39.3*), and his opponent Diodotos criticizes the rebel cities' for their *hope* led by *eros* that "supplied an easy road to success" (3.45.5: τὴν εὐπορίαν τῆς

logic strengthen their *expectations and hopes* (4.65.4. cf. Hornblower *ad loc.*): ἡ παρὰ λόγον ... εὐπραγία αὐτοῖς ὑποτιθεῖσα ἰσχὺν τῆς ἐλπίδος. Εὐτυχία convinced them that they were unstoppable: σφίσι μηδὲν ἐναντιοῦσθαι. Later, Thucydides similarly generalizes about *hope*ful thought processes in the rebel cities of the Thraceward region (424/3 at 4.108.4): "the [former allies] based their judgment more on unclear wishing than safe forethought, accustomed as men are to entrust their desires to *unexamined hope*" (ἐλπίδι ἀπερισκέπτῳ) and to reject with sovereign reason (λογισμῷ αὐτοκράτορι) what they do not want" (cf. the rebel Lesbians: 3.2–3 and below).[39] This was folly in Thucydides' long view of both the rebels' and Athenian imperial strategy. Before long, both sides will come to regret their errors. Thucydides describes plummeting Athenian morale (5.14.1–2) and changed-mind readiness to consider peace: πληγέντες ἐπί τε τῷ Δηλίῳ καὶ δι' ὀλίγου αὖθις ἐν Ἀμφιπόλει, καὶ οὐκ ἔχοντες τὴν ἐλπίδα τῆς ῥώμης πιστὴν ἔτι,... δοκοῦντες τῇ παρούσῃ εὐτυχίᾳ καθυπέρτεροι γενήσεσθαι ... μετεμέλοντό τε ὅτι μετὰ τὰ ἐν Πύλῳ καλῶς παρασχὸν οὐ ξυνέβησαν.

B. The besieged and overmatched Melian authorities delegate fellow oligarchs to parlay. The delegates of the Athenian army attacking Melos chastise their opponents' wild *hopes*.[40] The ever *hope*ful and ambitious Athenians[41] are here the moment's "realists." A depressing irony arises, since elsewhere it is the Athenians who act on farfetched *hopes*, before and after the six years' truce and the hiatus in warfare. The Athenian representatives demolish Melian *hopes* of help from Sparta (5.102*, 104*, 113*), or of assistance from divine justice (5.104*, 113* τὰ δὲ ἀφανῆ τῷ βούλεσθαι ὡς γίγνομενα ἤδη θεᾶσθε, καὶ Λακεδαιμονίοις καὶ τύχῃ καὶ ἐλπίσι πλεῖστον δὴ παραβεβλημένοι καὶ πιστεύσαντες πλεῖστον καὶ σφαλήσεσθε). They skewer any Melian gamble on the ultimate reserve of hope – *tychē* (5.112.2*: τῇ τε μέχρι τοῦδε σῳζούσῃ τύχῃ ἐκ τοῦ θείου). These Melians sophistically contrast hope in self-defense to hopeless surrender (5.102*: καὶ ἡμῖν τὸ μὲν εἶξαι εὐθὺς ἀνέλπιστον, μετὰ δὲ τοῦ δρωμένου ἔτι καὶ στῆναι ἐλπὶς ὀρθῶς).[42] These Athenians posit that *elpis* constitutes one encouragement

---

τύχης ὑποτιθεῖσα). When Gylippos loses hope for saving Sicily from the Athenians, he is mistaken, but the moment marks a prudent connection to military realities.
39   Rood (1998, 74–75) analyzes the temporal displacement ("proleptic") of this comment and the forces that crippled Brasidas' ambitions. "Anachronies" commonly offer Thucydides' perspective.
40   5.111.2, 113: τὰ μὲν ἰσχυρότατα ἐλπιζόμενα μέλλεται, τὰ δ' ὑπάρχοντα βραχέα ... πολλὴν ἀλογίαν τῆς διανοίας παρέχετε ... καὶ τύχῃ καὶ ἐλπίσι πλεῖστον δὴ παραβεβλημένοι.
41   Perikles and Alkibiades had full confidence in Athenian success, if their advice were followed.
42   Schlosser imprudently claims that this example is a "constructive" hope, but his examples are few. Furthermore, he ignores the preponderance of counter-examples, especially Perikles' prudent pessimism. On the contrary, future events work out *amathos* and *para logon* (both in

(παραμύθιον) allowable only to powerful parties who can survive occasional missteps (5.103.1*: Ἐλπὶς δὲ κινδύνῳ παράμυθιον οὖσα, τοὺς μὲν ἀπὸ περιουσίας χρωμένους αὐτῇ, κ' ἂν βλάψῃ, οὐ καθεῖλεν). Prodigal by nature (δάπανος φύσει), *elpis* appears in "plentiful supply" for desperate men just before disaster strikes (litotic οὐκ ἐλλείπει). The Melians' limited present resources do not match their very strong <u>future</u> hopes to prevail against enemy forces already in place (5.111.2*: ἀλλ' ὑμῶν τὰ μὲν ἰσχυρότατα <u>ἐλπιζόμενα</u> μέλλεται, τὰ δ' ὑπάρχοντα βραχέα πρὸς τὰ ἤδη ἀντιτεταγμένα).⁴³ In other words, here and in the Mytilenean debate (3.45.9*), Thucydides' speakers distinguish visible and invisible grounds for hope, rational and unreliable, and the results bear out his speakers' analyses.⁴⁴ Athenians correctly evaluate the dangers of *elpis* when they do not need it themselves.

C. Immediately after the isolated Melians imprudently *hope* when *hope* has little to offer, at the pinnacle of Athenian success and imperial power, Thucydides presents in slow-motion the Athenians' decision-making process for invading Sicily. They *hope for* (6.30.2: μετ' ἐλπίδος), indeed expect, success and endless riches (6.24.3: ἀργύριον οἴσειν ... ἀΐδιον μισθοφοράν).⁴⁵ The assembly rejects failure as a possibility for their pleonectic aggression. *Hopes* infect the emotions and expectations of individuals, groups, and the sovereign *ekklesia*. Athenian successes from 424 on and during the uneasy peace have clouded Athenian judgment. Alkibiades *expects/hopes* to conquer Sicily and Carthage (6.15.2; his selfish motives condemned), and he seduces the Athenian assembly into sharing those *hopes* (6.30.2, 31.6). Later, Alkibiades speaking in Sparta reveals his own and his

---

1.140.1*: ἀμαθῶς χωρῆσαι, ... ὅσα ἂν παρὰ λόγον ξυμβῇ). Perikles elsewhere scorns hope (2.42–43*; 2.62.5*). The Athenians, when they hold the upper hand, as at Melos or Kamarina, mock hope as foolish, the strategy of weak parties (5.103*; 6.86* perhaps). Hope is comforting or inciting (παραμύθιον); prodigal or extravagant (δάπανος [*hapax*]); and never-ceasing (οὐκ ἐλλείπει), but hope is not reliable. Thucydides structures the "cat and mouse" discussion (cf. the Plataians' appeal to Spartan judges!) to evoke sympathy for the Melians' situation, but not for their reasoning. Their stance compounds pseudo-Thermopylaean bravery and foolish fantasies (as the "hanging judge" Athenians point out). The stubborn Melian oligarchs' stand ignominiously ends, when they suspect excluded Melian citizens of betrayal (προδοσία τις, 5.116.3).

43 Hornblower (2008) notes that this "now—someday in the future" antithesis already appeared in 5.87.

44 A fortiori, reliance on diviners, oracles, eclipses, and dream interpreters, hope-predators, is absurd: 2. 47 & 54, 5.26 & 103*, 7.50, 8.1 (χρησμολόγοι τε καὶ μάντεις, καὶ ὁπόσοι τι τότε αὐτοὺς θειάσαντες ἐπήλπισαν ὡς λήψονται Σικελίαν).

45 Avery (1973, 1–6) identifies *elpis* as one of three leading themes of Books VI and VII. The other two are daring and colonization. Hope and daring migrate from Athenians to Syracusans in the course of this two-book drama.

city's bloated post-Peace Athenian *"hopes"* to conquer and control the entire Greek world and beyond (6.90.2–4*: ῥᾳδίως ἠλπίζομεν καταπολεμήσειν ...καὶ τοῦ ξύμπαντος Ἑλληνικοῦ ἄρξειν). When the lavishly decorated triremes and many thousands of troops sailing on supply-ships depart the Peiraeus, the expedition draws circumspect Thucydides' climactic, anticipatory judgment. He critiques the greatest fleet's greatest *hope* for the future –disproportionate (like the Melians') to current resources (6.31.6): καὶ ὅτι μέγιστος ἤδη διάπλους καὶ ἐπὶ μεγίστῃ ἐλπίδι τῶν μελλόντων πρὸς τὰ ὑπάρχοντα ἐπεχειρήθη).⁴⁶ Athenians again ignore essential reality-checks.⁴⁷

After the Syracusans repeatedly defeat them, during the Athenians' retreat, "instead of [their initial] great *hope*," disaster confronts them and their city: their warships have been destroyed, and they and their city face extreme peril (7.75.2): καὶ ἀντὶ μεγάλης ἐλπίδος καὶ αὐτοὶ καὶ ἡ πόλις κινδυνεύοντες). Later, addressing his troops, the reluctant commander Nikias tries to cheer up (ἐθάρσυνε) his discouraged (*athumia*) men. They must have *hope*, and he himself doubles down with a "bold *hope*" for the future (7.77.1, 3*: καὶ ἐκ τῶν παρόντων... ἐλπίδα χρὴ ἔχειν... ἀνθ' ὧν ἡ μὲν ἐλπὶς ὁμῶς θρασεῖα τοῦ μέλλοντος). Stunned Nikias alleges that the Athenian invaders have suffered punishment enough (ἀποχρώντως ἤδη τετιμωρήμεθα). Like the Melians, they may now *expect* gentler treatment from the god above (7.77.4*: καὶ ἡμᾶς εἰκὸς νῦν τά τε ἀπὸ τοῦ θεοῦ ἐλπίζειν ἠπιώτερα ἕξειν). Nikias jams three *elpis* words into half a paragraph, his internal delusion corresponding to the Korinthians' external emphasis on Athenian character.⁴⁸ Thucydides connects a network of *elpis* passages. Nikias above all, and increasingly as his situation worsens,⁴⁹ falls prey to the mistakes about hope that the Athenians have pointed out to others, when they operate beyond their resources (Fulkerson, unpubl.).

---

46 Hornblower (2008) vigorously annotates this passage, discussing λαμπρότης, θάμβος, and the Athenians' other emotional responses.
47 The Syracusans Hermokrates and Athenagoras debate the likelihood of an Athenian fleet and army's approach, at the time of the Athenian debates (6.32–41). Hermokrates is "not unhopeful" of success (6.33.4, 6*; litotes).
48 Nikias the prudent politician tried to stifle or temper hopes before the *ekklesia* approved the expedition. When his men and resources were exhausted, Nikias the general felt compelled to encourage groundless hope.
49 In two consecutive sentences, Nikias deploys *elpis* as expectation and hope (7.61*): "Don't have expectation arising from fear and do have hope for good fortune," σφαλέντες τὴν ἐλπίδα τοῦ φόβου ὁμοίαν ταῖς ξυμφοραῖς ... τὸ τῆς τύχης κἂν μεθ' ἡμῶν ἐλπίσαντες στῆναι.

Conclusions

Hope lends itself to literary dramatization, the suspenseful, temporal interval between expectation and unexpected outcome, often arresting because of subsequent disjunctions.[50] Thucydides' Themistokles is supreme in prediction, but Thucydides assigns him no *elpis* words (1.135–38, esp. 138.3). The Spartan King Archidamos, like Perikles, tries to dampen inappropriate and hasty *elpides*, but fails (1.81.6*, 84.4*). Sthenelaidas, the Spartan Kleon, successfully promotes immediate action based on imprudent hopes (1.86*: ἐν τάχει; cf. 1.84.6). Nikias, *in extremis*, employs the most *elpis* words.[51] Thucydides nearly personifies *elpis* as a villain or a disease —a mood contagion. The *eros* of the Athenian *demos*,[52] their *pleonexia*,[53] and Nikias' *theiasmos* (7.50) name three other crowd and personal urges that afflict men and motivate human action. These impulses feed imprudent forms of *hope* and thus derail more prudent policies of the sort that Archidamos always and Perikles sometimes recommend (1.81*, 84*, 2.62*).[54] Thucydides presents *hope* as another self-destructive emotion amalgamating with *eros* (6.24.3; cf. 3.45.5). Thucydides, thus, like Herodotos, cues the reader to

---

[50] Historians and biographers, too, track their subjects' limited predictive powers (Fulkerson 2015, 69, 72, 85–6). Fulkerson acutely notes and charts the fact that Plutarch's *elpis* is concentrated in disapproving portraits and are rarely found in his admired "favourites." Plutarch's Nikias is δύσελπις—not hopeful but despondent—before adversity turns him into an unwilling optimist (if his *paraineseis* reflect his true thoughts). Meanwhile Crassus "has delusive hopes from the beginning" (78 n.56). *Dyselpis* describes another, later Archidamos appealing in vain to Agesilaus, his father (Xen. *HG* 5.4.31).

[51] Nikias poorly predicts events and repeatedly falls victim to his own under-appreciated foresight, e.g., in the debates before attacking Pylos and Syracuse. His most catastrophic hope, costing thousands of lives, was his alleged inside information that the Syracusans would either starve because of the Athenian blockade or rebel against their government. The rumor was either planted as disinformation, or the uprising was squelched, or it was hopeful thinking. This unnecessary delay blocked the Athenians' last chance to retreat before harm engulfed them (7.48.2). As a failed commander himself, Thucydides has sympathy for Nikias *in extremis*, but the mitigating modifiers of his epitaph (7.86.5) do not cancel out his superstitious inclinations and delay in attack and retreat.

[52] Cornford's *Thucydides Mythistoricus* (1907), however wrong in its main thesis, encouraged study of his narratological patterns. He discovered significant tragic elements in this historiographer, but these seem less important than epic ones for conceptual habits.

[53] *Pleonexia* becomes ever more fiercely pejorative in Thucydides who would have invented the concept for the Athenians' imperial expansion (4.61.5*), had not Herodotos already done so for the Spartans' (7.149, *hapax*).

[54] Foster (2010, 138) shows how *elpis* undermines the intransigent Athenian *demos*. Perikles too believes that the Athenians can rise above the need for hope.

expect foolish or desperate responses (cf. Stahl 1966/2003, Crane 1998). The two first historians select such incidents in order to highlight human incapacities and inclinations. The Athenians who had hoped for conquest refused to believe (8.1: ἠπίστουν) plain and lucid reports of their well-equipped expedition's total destruction.

Community spirits are malleable.[55] Effective speakers direct crowd moods for better (as rational Perikles can do) and for worse (as angry Kleon does). *Elpis* must be promoted in soldiers facing battle and death. Thucydides was the first to record such battle exhortations, as he was also first to analyze *elpis* in assemblies of Spartans, Athenians, and their allies. Hope promotes resilience, a desirable quality for soldiers facing death, not so desirable when assemblies or generals make fateful strategic choices — first baby-steps towards disaster.

Thucydides counts, when he can or when he wishes to, men mustered, ships dispatched, or walls destroyed, but his emphasis on human nature brought him to report equally major factors, namely the political emotions, *hope* and fear, also greed and anger. These ineradicable, generally negative passions drive polities to self-defeating decisions. Hope and fear, opposing but complementary emotions about the future, lead to political and military mistakes. Thucydides features more *hope* than Herodotos did, precisely because his contemporaries fancied themselves more rational and well-informed than their grandfathers, but their terrible *kinesis* proved all sides wrong. For Herodotos and Thucydides, *elpis* brings men, rulers, and their cities, alliances, and empires to unexamined, unwise, indeed calamitous, decisions. Hope—ἐλπίς—brings them harm.[56]

Appendix

Xenophon in the *Hellenika* employs the word *elpis* least (15x) of the three historians. When his assembly speakers and generals form or express expectations, they too usually fail of fulfillment. For example, Agesilaus' *hopes* of conquering the Persian King vanish when he is recalled to Sparta. The Spartan had great *hopes* of conquest (*Hell.* 3.5.1): ἐλπίδας ἔχοντα μεγάλας αἱρήσειν βασιλέα, but his hopes are yanked away (4.2.3): οἵων ἐλπίδων ἀπεστερεῖτο. The Argives and Arcadians *hope* to starve the Phliasians but are routed (7.2.10). The Athenians *hope and*

---

55 Athenian crowd sentiments: 4.28, 5.14.1–2, 8.1–2; Spartan: 4.55.1, 7.18.2–3, 8. 2 and 11.
56 I thank Dimos Spatharas and George Kazantzides, and the University of Crete at Rethymno for inviting me to the December 2015 Rethymno Hope Conference and for Cretan hospitality.

expect to decimate the Thebans (6.3.20, 6.5.35). The Spartan ambassador seeking military cooperation from the Athenians (6.5.43) certainly encourages their *suppositions* of success (*elpis*). Xenophon's discouraged ending (7.5.26–7) does not specify frustrated *elpides*, but he writes that all Greeks' *expectations* were stymied, all predictions confounded (τοὐναντίον ἐγεγένετο οὗ ἐνόμισαν πάντες... οὐδεὶς ἦν ὅστις οὐκ ᾤετο...). After the indecisive battle of Mantineia (362 BCE), Xenophon ends his narrative in the middle of hopeless political chaos.

Bibliography

Avery, H. 1973. "Themes in Thucydides' Account of the Sicilian expedition," in: *Hermes* 101, 1–13.
Badian, E. 1993. *From Plataea to Potidaea*, Baltimore/London.
Bétant, E.-A. 1843. *Lexicon Thucydideum*, Geneva.
Bosworth, A.B. 1993. "The Humanitarian Aspect of the Melian Dialogue," in: *JHS* 113, 30–44.
Cairns, D. 2016. "Metaphors for Hope in Archaic and Classical Greek Poetry," in: R.R. Caston/R.A Kaster (eds.), *Hope, Joy, and Affection in the Classical World*, Oxford/New York, 13–44.
Cairns, D./L. Fulkerson (eds.). 2015. *Emotions between Greece and Rome*, London.
Cheavens, J.S./L. Ritschel. 2014. *"Hope* Theory," in: M. Tigade/M. Shida/L.D. Kirby (eds.), *Handbook of Positive Emotions*, New York/London, 396–410.
Collingwood, R.G. 1946. *The Idea of History*, Oxford.
Connor, W.R. 1984. *Thucydides*, Princeton.
Corcella, A. 1984/5. "Ελπίς," in: *Annali della Facoltà di Lettere e Filosofia a Bari* 27/28, 41–100. [non vidi].
Cornford, F.M. 1907. *Thucydides Mythistoricus*, London.
Crane, G. 1998. *Thucydides and the Ancient Simplicity: The Limits of Political Realism*, Berkeley/Los Angeles.
Cunliffe, M. 1924. *A Lexicon to the Homeric Dialect*, Edinburgh.
Desmond, W. 2006. "Lessons of Fear: A Reading of Thucydides," in: *CPh* 101, 359–79.
Dewald, C. 2011. "Happiness in Herodotus," in: *SO* 85, 18–39.
—— 2012. "'I didn't give my own genealogy.' Herodotus and the Authorial Persona," in: E.J. Bakker/I. de Jong/H. van Wees (eds.), *Brill's Companion to Herodotus*, Leiden, 267–90.
Fornara, Ch. 1971. *Herodotus: An Interpretative Essay*, Oxford.
Foster, E. 2010. *Thucydides, Pericles, and Periclean Imperialism*, Cambridge.
Fulkerson, L. 2015. "Plutarch and the Ambiguities of ΕΛΠΙΣ," in: Cairns/Fulkerson, 67–86.
—— 2015. Unpublished. "The Dangerous Qualities of Hope in Thucydides."
Greer, R.A. 2001. *Christian Life and Christian Hope: Raids on the Inarticulate*, New York.
Gribble, D. 1998. "Narrator Interventions in Thucydides," in: *JHS* 118, 41–67.
Hornblower, S. 1991–2008. *A Commentary on Thucydides*, 3 vols., Oxford.
Huart, P. 1968. *Le vocabulaire de l'analyse psychologique dans l'oeuvre de Thucydide*, Paris.
Lateiner, D. 1975. "The Speech of Teutiaplus," in: *GRBS* 16, 175–84.
—— 1985. "Nikias' Inadequate Encouragement," in: *CPh* 80, 201–13.
—— 1989. *The Historical Method of Herodotus*, Toronto.
Luginbill, R.E. 1999/2015 (2nd ed.). *Thucydides on War and National Character*, Boulder.

Luschnat, O. 1942. *Die Feldherrnreden im Geschichtswerk des Thukydides*. Philologus Suppl. 34.2, Leipzig.
Myres, J.L. 1949. "ἔλπις, ἐλπίζω, ἔλπομαι," in: *CR* 63, 46.
Orwin, C. 1997. *The Humanity of Thucydides*, Princeton.
Powell, A. 1938. *A Lexicon to Herodotus*, Cambridge.
Proctor, D. 1980. *The Experience of Thucydides*, Warminster.
Romilly, J. de. 1963. *Thucydides and Athenian Imperialism*, (translated by Ph. Thody), Oxford.
Rood, T. 1998. *Thucydides: Narrative and Explanation*, Oxford.
Rusten, J. 1989. [Commentary on] *Thucydides: The Peloponnesian War*. Book II, Cambridge.
Saar, H.G. 1953. *Die Reden des Kleon und Diodotos und ihre Stellung im Gesamtwerk des Thukydides*, Diss. Hamburg.
Schlosser, J.A. 2013. "'Hope, Danger's Comforter': Thucydides, Hope, Politics," in: *The Journal of Politics* 75.1, 169–82.
Schneider, Chr. 1974. *Information und Absicht bei Thukydides*. Hypomnemata 41, Göttingen.
Stahl, H.-P. 2003. *Thucydides: Man's Place in History*, Swansea (Original German ed., 1966).
Tamiolaki, M. 2013. "Ascribing Motivation in Thucydides: Between Historical Research and Literary Representation," in: A. Tsakmakis/M. Tamiolaki (eds.), *Thucydides between History and Literature*, Berlin, 41–72.
Tiger, L. 1999. "Hope Springs Internal," in: *Social Research* 66.2, 611–23.
Verdenius, W.J. 1971. "A 'Hopeless' Line in Hesiod: Works and Days 96," in: *Mnemosyne* 24, 225–31.
—— 1985. *A Commentary on Hesiod: Works and Days, Vv. 1-382*, Leiden/New York.
West, M.L. 1978. *Hesiod, Works and Days*, Oxford.

Part II: *Spes*. 'Hope' in Latin Literature

Laurel Fulkerson
Deos speravi (*Miles* 1209): Hope and the Gods in Roman Comedy

What kind of people hope, and how, if at all, do they act to realize their hopes? Is hoping a spur to acting, or is it rather a crutch, preventing those who hope from acting to improve their circumstances? This chapter tackles these grand questions in a small way, but one with larger implications, by examining the emotion of hope[1] as it intersects with the divine in Roman comic texts. In keeping with an increased scholarly interest in context-based studies of emotions, which in the modern world try to take into account the lived circumstances of those who felt them, but in the ancient world often resort to emotion "scripts,"[2] I focus on the class, status, and gender of the emotion of *spes* as it occurs in Roman comedy. More particularly, I explore the nexus of status, plot-development, and Roman religion via prayers to the gods for the realization of individual hopes, and also personifications of the goddess *Spes*, showing the ways in which Roman comedy is both like and unlike other genres in its understanding of the emotion of *spes*.

But first, a brief overview of some of the most common ways *spes* functions in Roman comedy, where it is an emotion felt by a number of different kinds of characters in different situations. The regular occurrence of *spes* in the plays of Plautus and Terence — just over 100 examples in Plautus and about 75 in Terence — should occasion little surprise, given the genre's standard plots, prominent among which are an *adulescens* who hopes to obtain the girl of his dreams but who has no money,[3] and subplots including slaves who hope to avoid

---

Very many thanks to Dimos Spatharas and George Kazantzidis, organizers of the Hope conference, and to the attendees at that conference for their stimulating papers and helpful comments on my own work. Thanks too to Jessica Clark, Trevor Luke, Dan-el Padilla Peralta, and Niall Slater for bibliographic suggestions, encouragement, and sage advice.

1 The question of whether hope, or its ancient equivalents, is genuinely an emotion is a complicated one; see Cairns 2016 and Fulkerson 2015, 2016, and 2017 (the first three on ἐλπίς, the last on *spes*). The end of this chapter suggests that there may be both emotional and non-emotional varieties of hope, without an always-clear distinction between them.
2 For recent work on emotional "scripts" within the classical world, see Kaster 2005, Cairns 2008, and Sanders 2014.
3 For the hopes of *adulescentes*, see e.g. Philolaches, who gives himself over to Tranio in *Most.* 406: *In tuam custodelam meque et meas spes trado*, Tranio ("I put myself and my hope in your keeping"). Stratippocles, the adulescens of the Epidicus, seeks help from his friend Chaeribulus, in the form of a loan of money. Chaeribulus, himself strapped for cash, cannot oblige, but urges Stratippocles to keep hoping: *alicunde ab aliqui aliqua tibi spes est fore meliorem fortúnam* (*Epid.*

punishment for their misbehavior.⁴ In the majority of literary genres in Greco-Roman antiquity, expressed hopes are often frustrated (as when, e.g. the general of the soon-to-be-losing side hopes for the best because he is inadequately prepared), but in comedy, progatonists' hopes tend to be fulfilled.⁵ This feature relates to comedy's festive spirit and positive outcomes for its low-status characters, two aspects of the genre which also permit the hopes of certain secondary characters to come to fruition, even when they are incapable of bringing about their desires through action. So, for instance, both lost children and their parents hope for reunion, and although parents are sometimes in a position to find — or at least look for — their children, the children must normally wait to be found.⁶ Given the optimistic nature of comedy, such hopes are mentioned only when they will be fulfilled. And parasites, men who flatter wealthy patrons in the hopes of getting a meal, sometimes have their wishes come true (but they are more often disappointed).⁷ There are, however, limits to the efficacy of hope: in keeping with the Saturnalian atmosphere of reversal, fathers who hope to steal the girl from

---

332, "somehow, someway, there's some hope for you of better luck"). Most adulescentes seek money or help in gaining money, and so their hopes are centered around this topic.

4 For the kinds of things slaves hope for, see e.g. Epidicus, being threatened with beatings, who notes: *Salva res est: bene promittit, spero servabit fidem* (*Epid.* 124, "The situation is saved: he's promised well and good, and I expect he will keep faith"). The irony of Epidicus' "hopes" —for something he does not in fact want— serve to emphasize the fact that, outside the world of the play, slaves could and did expect to be beaten whether they deserved it or not; inside the play, such punishment is always deferred to a time when the show is over (see Parker 1989). This brief throwaway statement provides a small clue to the lives, and the hopes of slaves, which may well always have been less grandiose than those of their masters. The boy-slave Paegnium in the Persa expects to be free (this is likely to be in part because of his attractiveness), and assures the slave Sagaristio that he has no hopes of freedom (*nam ego me confido liberum fore, tu te numquam speras*, "I'm confident I will be free, and you can't even hope for it," *Persa* 286). On hope and Greek slavery, see Vlassopoulos in this volume.

5 See Fulkerson 2016 on the hopes of protagonists in the Greek novel, another key exception to this general rule.

6 See, e.g., the adult woman Philippa, who has been searching for her lost daughter to no avail, and who complains *neque ubi meas spes collocem habeo usquam munitum locum* (*Epid.* 531, "I have no safe place anywhere to put my hopes in"). Here we see an ironic/foreshadowing use of hope, insofar as Philippa is just about to run into the man she is seeking, and will soon be reunited with her daughter.

7 Among several examples of parasitic hopes, the best is surely Ergisilaus at *Capt.* 496 *nunc ibo ad portum hinc: est illic mi una spes cenatica* ("I'm off to the harbor, where is my last dinnerish hope").

their sons — despite their significantly superior wealth and position — never succeed:[8] the *adulescens* always gets the girl.

By way of expanding upon this summary, I offer sustained treatment of all of the occurrences of *spes* in Plautus' *Rudens*, a play which has the dual advantages of covering nearly all of the situations in which hope happens in Roman comedy as a whole, and of containing by far the most instances of *spes* of any Roman comedy, 24 of them.[9] First, an *adulescens* goes to an island rendezvous where the pimp was supposed to bring the *meretrix* he had put money down on; the effort is substantial, but he does not want to give up his hope because of laziness (92). His level of activity is unusual for an *adulescens*, although the ineffectiveness of his behaviour is typical of them.

In the meantime, the pimp had planned to escape; he had decided to abscond with the down-payment and sell his two *meretrices* (the one already purchased by the *adulescens*, and another, his own slave) elsewhere. But —thanks to the god Arcturus, who explains to us in the prologue that he is looking out for justice in the world— they have all been shipwrecked, along with a friend of the pimp. Palaestra, the *meretrix*-who-will-turn-out-to-be-freeborn, feels hopeless (*nunc quam spem aut opem aut consili quid capessam,* "now what hope or what help or what plan should I adopt?" 204; *quae mihi est spes qua me vivere velim,* "what hope is there for me by which I would want to stay alive?" 209), as does Ampelisca, the *meretrix*-who-is-really-a-slave (*perdidi spem qua me oblectabam,* "I've lost the hope which I used to rejoice in," 222). Upon hearing her voice (the two women are each isolated onstage), Palaestra becomes frightened and prays to the goddess Hope (*Spes bona, opsecro, subventa mihi,* "Good Hope, I beg, help me," 231 — see below).[10] But it turns out that the voice she heard was not a malefactor but Ampelisca. The two women are reunited, and Ampelisca calls Palaestra her hope (*opsecro, amplectere, spes mea* "I beg you, hug me, my hope," 246–7). The *meretrices* then ask for help from a priestess of Venus, since they are unsure of their hopes (*quae in locis nesciis nescia spe sumus,* "we who are in unknown places with unknown hope" 275).

---

8 For the disappointed, because inappropriate, hopes of the *senex*, see e.g. Lysidamus in the *Casina* (53, 312, 346, 973 —the only occurrences of *spes* in that play). See further Fulkerson 2013, 114–32 on status-based emotions in Roman comedy.
9 *Fortuna* is similarly well-represented in the play; see Champeaux 1981–1982.
10 My orthography capitalizes where Latin would leave the matter ambiguous; often in discussions of such abstract concepts as hope which also receive cult, the question is precisely one of whether the characteristic is personified or not.

In the following scene, a group of fishermen express their reliance upon hope for their livelihood (*atque ut nunc valide fluctuat mare, nulla nobis spes est*, "and now that the sea is seething so strongly, there is no hope for us," 303; the point is that they cannot go out and fish), and note that false hope will surely be the death of them ([*perii*] *ut piscatorem aequom est, fame sitique speque falsa* "[I am dying] in the probable manner for a fisherman, from hunger and thirst and false hope," 312). Later, the male slave who is working on behalf of the *adulescens* expresses the opinion that good things sometimes happen beyond hope (*nam multa praeter spem scio multis bona evenisse* "for I know that many good things happen to many people beyond their hope," 400); to him a more realistic (but in this case, wrong) female slave replies that hope does not benefit hopers (*at ego etiam, qui speraverint spem decepisse multos* "and I know that hope has deceived many who have hoped," 401).

The pimp who has lost his *meretrices* hopes to recover them (*saltem si mihi/ mulierculae essent salvae, spes aliquae forent* "if at least my little women were safe, there would be some hopes," 552–3); his friend notes that Neptune has "hoped" to settle their stomachs by filling them with salt water (*itaque alvom prodi speravit nobis salsis poculis* "and so he hoped that our bellies would be freed by salted cups," 589). A slave asks a favor of the *senex*, begging by the hope the *senex* has of making money (*si speras tibi hoc anno multum futurum sirpe et laserpicium* "if you hope that this year you'll have much silphium and resin," 629–30), and the *senex* urges him to get to the point, ironically invoking the slave's "hope" of receiving a beating (*at ego te per crura et talos tergumque optestor tuom,/ ut tibi ulmeam uberem esse speras virgidemiam/ et tibi eventuram hoc anno uberem messem mali* "and I beg you by your shins and ankles and back, just as you hope for a rich elm-rod crop of beatings, and that there will come to you a rich harvest of evil this year," 635–7). Palaestra refers to the clever slave of the *adulescens* as her "hope of safety" (*o salutis meae spes*, 680). In the meantime another slave has found a treasure-chest, which he swears nobody can hope to take from him (*hunc homo ferret a me nemo, ne tu te speres potis* "this no man will take from me, and don't you hope that you can," 968); the clever slave asserts that the slave who has found the treasure has no hope of deceiving him (*nil agis, dare verba speras mihi posse, furcifer* "you're not accomplishing anything, you hope to be able to fool me, gallows-bird," 996). The chest turns out to belong to Palaestra and contains, as she observes, all her hopes of parental recognition (*huc opesque spesque vostrum cognoscendum condidi* "here I have hidden away my means and hopes of recognizing you," 1145). In an economy of persons typical for comedy, the *senex* who has been asked to adjudicate the ownership of the chest begins to suspect that Palaestra may be his lost daughter; he calls upon the gods to confirm his hope (*di immortales, ubi loci sunt spes meae* "immortal gods, where are my hopes?" 1161). When the two are reunited Palaestra asserts that she never hoped for this (*salve, mi pater insperate* "greetings, my unhoped-for father," 1175), and the *senex* echoes the sentiment (*ego hodie <qui> nec speravi nec credidi, is improviso filiam inveni tamen* "I who never hoped for it or believed in it, nonetheless unexpectedly found my daughter today," 1195). The slave who has been deprived of his treasure is told, in an echo of his own denial of the hopes of others, to have no further hopes (*nihil hercle hic tibi est, ne tu speres* "there is certainly nothing here for you, and don't hope that there is," 1414), but he is in fact freed. And all live happily ever after.

This survey of all of the occurrences of *spes* in the *Rudens* offers a picture that is in many ways typical, although it displays a few differences from the comic norm. The focus in this play on the hope of young women is uncharacteristic, but the lack of control which they have over their fates is a standard feature of comedy, and presumably also an (exaggerated?) version of real life; comic young women tend to focus their hopes around love, and secondarily on finding their true parents —and sometimes, as in this play, they get both. Another uncharacteristic aspect of hope in the *Rudens* is that slaves regularly have hope in comedy, but only very rarely do they express hopes of freedom; comedy tends to promulgate a benevolent picture of slavery, and to presume that slaves are, for the most part, content to remain so.[11] Finally, it is not clear why this play has such a concentration of hope, but it may derive from the fact that it is multiply focalized (two *meretrices*, two different slaves, an *adulescens*, and a *senex*); this diffuse structure allows more characters than usual the opportunity to express their hopes.

In the *Rudens*, and indeed in Roman comedy as a whole, those without the status or means to bring about what they wish are more likely to express hopes for it than those with that status or means. This finding —that hope is not normally related to action— is in keeping with a larger trend in both Greek and Roman sources, with only a few exceptions, whereby ancient texts attribute hope to those who are both without resources and without forethought. That is, hope is recognizably a fallback emotion, and it is thus especially apt for those with limited options (whether these limitations are status-based or represent more personal failures).[12]

---

[11] For helpful discussion of the complex issue of slaves and slavery in Roman comedy, see McCarthy 2000, Fitzgerald 2000, and Stewart 2012. See too n. 5 for the kinds of hopes slaves (in the minds of comic playwrights) admit to.

[12] My sense, from surveying the literature, is that this aspect of hope is more Greek than Roman, and it also seems to be more prevalent in earlier literature than late. So too, hope seems to cluster

Thus far I have attempted both to situate the reader within Roman comedy and to offer a conception of hope as an emotion of last resort. My more particular subject is the divine aspects of *spes* in comedy, and also in contemporary Roman Republican society, insofar as we have access to it. Interestingly, the phenomenon in which I am interested does not appear at all in Terence, so my study is confined to Plautine comedy (see once again the examples in nn. 3–4). For many years now one of the primary strands of Plautine scholarship has revolved around distinguishing the *Plautinisches* from the Greek substratum.[13] In different periods this practice has had different aims, and there has recently been an outpouring of sophisticated work on early Republican Latin authors which has called into question the fundamental assumptions behind such Quellenforschung.[14] Putting the somewhat fruitless debate about "originality" aside, one of the areas in which scholars have always seen genuinely Roman elements in Roman comedy has been religion: Plautus especially describes and alludes to a wide variety of religious practices and technical language in a way that makes clear their essential Romanness.

Religion in Plautus is a vast topic, and fairly under-studied;[15] here I will use a small piece of that puzzle to explore a few of the ramifications of the connections the playwright draws between hope and divinity, in two distinct ways, one focusing on hope as an object for prayer, the other on hope as an addressee *of*

---

around incidents in which there is a great deal of chance (that is, in the neat phrasing of the editors of this volume, "in cases where agents' anticipatory representations revolve around possibilities rather than probabilities").

13 The phrase is from Fraenkel 2007, on whose centrality see Goldberg 2011, 206–7. Other (very different) recent studies of the sophistication of Plautine language include Fontaine 2010 and Sharrock 2009. ἐλπίς appears in Menander, to take the Greek new comic playwright for whom we have the most (still exiguous) fragments, twelve times in the identifiable fragments (thrice in the standard phrases παρ' ἐλπίδα and ἀνελπίστως), and eleven times in the scraps that come to us from later quotations. Without context it is difficult to say much about these fragments, except that they run the gamut; one refers to hope as bad (Kock Fr 351.1, *FCG* vol. 4 Nau fr. 5.1), one stereotypically thinks of hopes as "empty" (κενούς, *Sententiae e codicibus Byzantinis* 51, *Sent. Mono.* 42), and one suggests that hope can save the unlucky (ἄνθρωπος ἀτυχῶν σῴζεθ' ὑπὸ τῆς ἐλπίδος, Kock Fr 813.1, *Sententiae e codicibus Byzantinis* 30).

14 See e.g. Elliott 2013 and Goldschmidt 2013 on the importance of the fragmentary contexts in which Ennius appears to us.

15 See Gulick 1896, Hanson 1959, and Dunsch 2009, usefully revisited by Slater 2011 (see especially pp. 303–7 on characters' aspirations to divinity or identification as divine personifications) and Rey 2015. For the religious (and political) nature of the ludi at which comedies were performed, see Bernstein 1998, Morgan 1990, and Gruen 1992, 183–222 (the latter following the mostly Terentian evidence); for discussion of the religious role of Republican tragedy, Freyburger 2000; for the physical performance context, see Goldberg 1998.

prayer. Specifically, I first discuss the places where hope is explicitly stated to be a matter for the gods or a particular god; second, places where the divinity of *Spes* herself is mentioned.[16] Along the way, we will necessarily touch upon some key topics in mid-Republican history and religion.

The ancient notion of hope, as I've already suggested, is often implicitly connected to things beyond one's own control[17] (which is part of why, as the other essays in this volume so richly show, it so often comes under suspicion in the ancient world). And this is amply demonstrated in Plautus: hoping regularly means not being able to act, is a replacement for the action you would like to be able to take if only you could. This area of things desired-but-not-able-to-be-acted-upon is also the realm of the gods, so it is perhaps no surprise to find that sometimes Plautine characters talk about the things they hope for as potentially or ideally matters of divine concern.

Ten examples constitute the total of Plautine passages in which hope is connected to the gods. In the first, in the *Bacchides*, the *adulescens* Pistoclerus observes that the heart hopes,[18] but how things turn out is in the gods' hands (*Sperat quidem animus: quo evenat dis in manust, Bacch.* 144). In this instance, matters are in his slave Chrysalus' hands, and the slave proves perfectly capable of taking care of things on his own; in comedy, it often happens that any desiderated divine interest is also given a boost by human action. Interestingly, however, in sharp distinction from the modern conception of the divine as "helping those who help themselves," there is usually a distinction in comedy between the one who hopes and the one who acts. An example from the *Miles* offers a similar twinning of human and divine potential agency: *Deos sperabo teque* ("I hope in the gods and you," *Miles* 1209). Here the statement is ironically expressed: Pyrgopolynices is in the process of falling into the trap which Palaestrio has set for him, and the latter assures the former that he trusts him. The undermining of the statement suggests just how conventional it is: Palaestrio (falsely) expresses the hope that the gods will take an action which is directly contrary to what he himself is working to bring about.

The principle that hoping tends to preclude doing holds true for most of our remaining examples as well. In the *Casina*, two slaves, proxies for their respective

---

16 This chapter treats neither divine appearances in comedy (on which see Slater 2014, who is interested in the differences between divine comic and tragic epiphanies), nor instances where the gods speak prologues; it is concerned with abstract rather than manifest divinities.
17 See Introduction, this volume and Cairns 2016 on how the metaphors used of ἐλπίς reflect this suspicion.
18 See Cairns 2016 on bodily metaphors for hope.

masters, father and son, will draw lots for marriage with the soon-to-be-found-freeborn Casina. Lysidamus, the *senex*, speaks to his slave ally about the result of the lot, expressing hopes that the gods will give him what he wants: *Dis sum fretus, deos sperabimus* ("I trust to the gods; we'll put our hopes in the gods," *Cas.* 346). His slave, Olympio, is less sanguine about relying upon chance: *nam omnes mortales dis sunt freti, sed tamen/ vidi ego dis fretos saepe multos decipi* ("For all men trust in the gods, but still I have often seen those trusting in the gods get deceived," *Cas.* 348–9). His sentiment, similar to that expressed by Ampelisca at *Rud.* 401, seems to be a reflex reaction on the part of slaves to the expression of hopes. (Indeed, if Romans are to continue to believe in their gods, they had better not expect them to fulfill all hopes, and this is probably truer the further down the social scale we look.) Lysidamus' situation, as noted above, is an interesting one that occurs sometimes in comedy: his role is that of a powerful older man, and so he ought not to need hope that he will get the girl. But the rules of the genre, and his own lascivious nature, doom him to hoping and fruitless plotting (see above, n. 8): the play ends in his near-complete humiliation.

In the *Cistellaria*, Phanostrata, mother of a long-lost but soon-to-be-discovered daughter, beseeches her slave Lampadio to take further action, telling him *Deos teque spero* ("I hope from the gods and you," 596); he replies *eosdem ego ... uti abeas domum* ("I do too, that you'll go home," 597). Here again the pious message of one character is undermined by that of another, who wants Phanostrata to get out of his way and allow him to act to achieve her hopes.

In the *Persa*, on the other hand, the slave Sagaristio utters a prayer of thanks to Jupiter *Iovi opulento, incluto,/ Ope gnato, supremo, valido, viripotenti/ opes, spes bonas, copias commodanti* ("wealthy and glorious Jupiter, born to wealth, the supreme, strong, powerful, who provides wealth, happy hopes, and resources," *Persa* 251–3). His hopes (of being able to assist a friend) have been fulfilled, so he is naturally more sanguine about the role the gods play in assisting the worthy. But here as well there is a slight disjunction between wanting or hoping for a thing and being able to make it happen; without Jupiter, Sagaristio suggests that he would have no resources.

In the *Poenulus*, in the midst of a prayer to Jupiter, Hanno calls him the one *per quem vivimus vitalem aevom,/ quem penes spes vitae sunt hominum omnium* ("through whom we live our living lives, in whom are the hopes of life of all men," *Poen.* 1187–8). Anterastilis, one of two enslaved sisters, has heard from a soothsayer that both girls will receive their freedom, but remains unconvinced: *id ego nisi quid di aut parentes faxint, qui sperem hau scio* ("I don't know how to hope for freedom, unless the gods or our parents do it," *Poen.* 1208). Both hopes are expressed shortly before they are fulfilled: the girls turn out to be the daughters of Hanno, and the reunion takes place within a hundred lines. As usual, the gods are invoked but the second example also emphasizes the usefulness of human action, and this is, again, a trope familiar in comedy. Even here, though, acting and hoping are done by two distinct groups: Anterastilis does not herself expect to take any action to bring about what she hopes for.

So too, when the *senex* Daemones believes that he may have found his lost daughter, he exclaims *Di immortales, ubi loci sunt spes meae?* ("Good gods! Where are these hopes of mine?" *Rudens* 1161) — but it is clear that the gods need not do anything further to bring about the happy reunion. And in the *Menaechmi*, the slave Messenio intervenes in an argument between twin brothers, who are just about to discover their relationship: *Di immortales, spem insperatam date mihi quam suspicor* (*Men.* 1081) "Gods, fulfill the unhoped for hope I think I see before me." Here, interestingly, the slave's hope, expressed aloud to the gods, is precisely the action that brings about the recognition, as he goes on to explain that the two men share a birthplace and a father.

Finally, Roman comedy contains a single reference to the hope of a god: *itaque alvom prodi speravit nobis salsis poculis* ("and so [Neptune] hoped that our bellies would be freed by salted cups," *Rudens* 588–9). The comment here is an ironic one, but it is still unparalleled; we might speculate that the informality of the genre allows for such anthropomorphic speculation, but also that Charmides, by his blasphemous words, confirms his own and the pimp Labrax's disreputable natures, and so retrospectively justifies the punishment they have suffered.[19]

Another key feature of Plautine comedy is that *Spes* is specifically invoked as a divine being. (Here again, Terence has nothing to say on the matter, though his plays do include a number of other personifications.) I offer some historical context about the contemporary worship of *Spes* before treating these Plautine instances. She, along with *Fides*, is vowed a new temple in (probably)[20] 258 BCE, both by the general Atilius Caiatinus or Calatinus. The two temples are built in the Forum Holitorium and dedicated 1 August (also the dedication day for the temple of Victory, which makes even more obvious than does the year that this is

---

19 As Slater 2000 notes, this play offers a variety of impious portraits of the god Neptune, most of them eventually revised (352–3; see e.g. *Rudens* 359–62, 371–2). See too Sharrock 2009, 216–8 on the larger plot implications of this (among other things, the repetitive Neptune-jokes connect the play, she suggests, to the *Odyssey*).
20 See Weigel 1998, 126–7 for a plausible reconstruction of the circumstances of dedication; 136–42 on the principles that seem to have guided dedications during the early and middle Republic.

a very specific, martially-based kind of hope).²¹ This temple seems to have replaced an earlier temple, built in 477, and which retroactively comes to be known as *Spes Vetus* (though it is not clear whether that temple remained in use or not).²² The mid-third century is a period when temple dedications and buildings increase noticeably; scholars of Roman religion differ about whether to take this as a sign of religious decay or vitality, despair or self-assurance.²³ So too, the dedication of a temple is a complex decision, which relies upon religious feelings (perhaps of enlisted soldiers as well as of generals) and also senatorial politics, in this period as in much better-attested ones, making it impossible to disentangle personal or political motives from religious ones. What we can say with confidence is that the majority of mid-century temple foundations are personifications, some adopted from the Greek world but some uniquely Roman; that these foundations focus on Roman militaristic values; that they tend to be built in areas of political import, especially along the triumphal procession route (as the Forum Holitorium was); and that they are certain to have added to the prestige of the generals who vowed them and to those who dedicated them (given the amount of time

---

21 Forum Holitorium: Cic. *Leg.* 2.11.28, Liv. 21.62.4, 25.7.6, 24.47.16, Tac. *Ann.* 2.49, Dio 50.10.3. See too Axtell 1907, 18–20. Platner-Ashby 1929, 493–4; *LTUR* 336–7; Ziolkowski 1992, 152–4. Pietilä-Castrén 1987, 38–44 suggests that the temple might have been vowed during the siege of Mytistraton or the ambush on the way to Camarina. There were also a Diocletianic(?) temple (*LTUR* 337) and there were a number of non-Roman temples (cf. e.g. τύχη εὔελπις, Plut. *QR* 281e; *Fort. Rom.* 323a; see too temples at Ostia (*CIL* VIX.375) and Capua (*ILLRP* 707, *CIL* I² 674; X.3775) and dedications at Minturnae (*ILLRP* 730, 734, 740; *CIL* I²2689, 2698, 2700) and Genzano (*ILLRP* 58; *CIL* I² 46; XIV 2158), on all of which see Clark 2007). On some of the implications of temple 'anniversaries', see Padilla Peralta 2014, 165–71. See too Weigel 1998, 127 for the suggestion that the temples of Spes and Fides were built and dedicated in 247, during Calatinus/Caiatinus' censorship.
22 *Spes Vetus*, built 477: Platner-Ashby 1929, 494 and *LTUR* 337, with ancient citations. The temple remains puzzling: it might have been a private cult site, or might be a public religious foundation. As Axtell (1907, 18–19) notes, is it by no means clear that the goddess originally had an agricultural purview, although this is sometimes assumed.
23 See Orlin 1997 and Weigel 1998, with bibliography, for discussion of some of the major issues surrounding temple foundation in this period, particularly in political terms. Padilla Peralta 2014 offers in the first three chapters a helpful discussion of the mechanics of and ideologies behind mid-Republican temple building. A number of the new temples were for divinities already worshipped, especially in the Greek-speaking world; on Roman religious programs as "an exceptionally efficacious form of generating and cementing a type of civic consensus" (Padilla Peralta 2014, 6); see Padilla Peralta 2014, 89–97. See too Orlin 2010, *passim*, on some of the political implications of the Roman openness to foreign cults.

required, not always the same individual or even family).²⁴ It is less clear to what extent temple-building programs reflect the interests of the Senate in conjunction with, or as opposed to, individual generals. So while we cannot attribute beliefs to particular individuals (e.g. by concluding that Calatinus/Caiatinus was especially hopeful), we can probably conclude that the gods selected for temple worship are those that appeal to the Roman people as a whole, or at least to the elite. Temples, then, are certainly political as well as religious events, but they need not represent the specific political program of any individual or group.

In addition to *Spes*, the goddesses *Salus*, *Fortuna*, and *Fides* are also important during this period, and are regularly connected to *Spes*, both physically, in that their temples are sometimes found in proximity to one another, and literarily, in the sense that they are often joined with her in our literary sources (see below). Our evidence for such personifications does not usually allow us to determine if they are recent imports or re-foundations of already extant temples.²⁵

The dating of Plautine plays is profoundly insecure, but his *floruit* is generally agreed to be about 200, i.e. near the end and just after the second Punic War (218–201). This war itself might well have seemed to contemporaries like a repeat of the first Punic War (264–241), with the potential of Roman disaster at every turn – and indeed, the second Punic War appeared at many periods bleaker for the Romans than the first. At the same time, since the Romans eventually won the earlier war, there are also good reasons to imagine contemporary interest in the gods of the previous generation, including perhaps the personifications whose temples were founded or re-founded during it. We have much less information about religious practices and even temple foundations during the lifetime of Plautus than we do for (some) earlier or later periods. So in what follows, *faute de mieux*, I assume that the religious and political spirits that animated public worship and practices of the Second Punic War were relatively similar to those in the First, when temple foundations flourished.²⁶

---

24 See too Fears 1981 and Clark 1983 for a history of Imperial *spes*, Weigel 1998 for how vows and dedication might have been related, and Aberson 1994: on the primary funding sources for temples.
25 But note that the connection between these goddesses continues to be an obvious one in later periods, as at e.g. Horace *Od*. 1.35.21–2, where *Spes* and *Fides* are the companions of *Fortuna*, with Nisbet and Hubbard 1970 *ad loc*. See too Champeaux 1987, 208–13 on *Spes* and *Fides* as ancillary divinities, brought in to help disambiguate *Fortuna* in the middle Republic.
26 On temple foundations in the fourth and third centuries, see Padilla Peralta 2014 (with the charts on p. 38 showing building programs in twenty-five year intervals and on p. 39 showing that sacred building was more common than other types during the Middle Republic). On the

There are, depending upon how you count, at least six Plautine passages in which *Spes* is treated as a goddess of some sort. In each of the first three, a case can be made that *Spes* is invoked as a personified goddess, although the point is less clear than with my next three instances. We start with Charinus in the *Mercator*: about to leave home because his girlfriend is lost to him, he is summoned back by his friend Eutychus (*Merc.* 866–7):

> Ch: Qui me revocat?
> Eut: Spes, Salus, Victoria
>
> "Who calls me back?"
> "Hope, Safety, Victory...."

Here three interrelated goddesses, of recent historical import, are invoked. This is an inert case, so a good place to start: all that needs to happen for the joke to work is for an audience to recognize that the nouns are, or could be, female characters as well as abstract nouns.

Very similar is the *Mostellaria* passage (350), in which Tranio personifies two figures:

> occidit Spes nostra, nusquam stabulum est Confidentiae
>
> "Hope is dead, Confidence has nowhere to stand".

Once again the nouns may represent goddesses (there is no evidence for worship of *Confidentia*), but need only be recognized as personifications of abstractions for the lines to have point.

More interesting for our purposes is Calidorus in the *Pseudolus*, who, discovering that Pseudolus has solved his problem, addresses him with what look like cult-titles (*Pseud.* 709):

> Dic utrum Spemne an Salutem te salutem, Pseudole?
>
> "Shall I greet you as Hope or Salvation, Pseudolus?"

---

worship of the related goddess Salus, see Winkler 1995, and on *Fortuna*, Champeaux 1982 and 1987, with the latter, 1–35 on worship of *Fortuna* during the Second Punic War.

Here I think we have a recognition that Roman gods proliferate, and also that already-extant gods can accrue new titles.[27] We might push Calidorus' statement a bit farther and speculate that it reflects a genuine confusion among Romans; here the comic point is enhanced by the extension of worship titles even to a slave.[28]

Three further passages allow for more extensive comment. First, Chrysalus, in *Bacchides* 892–4, who, in the context of swearing an (untrue) oath about his young master's whereabouts, brings to bear what looks like every god he can think of:

> Ita me Iuppiter Iuno Ceres
> Minerva Lato Spes Opis Virtus Venus
> Castor Polluces Mars Mercurius Hercules
> Summanus Sol Saturnus dique omnes ament
>
> So help me Jupiter Juno Ceres Minerva Latona Hope Wealth Virtue Venus Castor Pollux Mars Mercury Hercules the Highest Sun Saturn and may all the gods love me...

As Fisher notes, Plautus' language here is paralleled by the Ennian list of the canonical twelve gods, jammed into two lines of hexameter,[29] and Plautus' own listing, in Fisher's words, "has a distinctive italic coloring" (2014, 14). The sheer number of gods is comical — Chrysalus "caps" the epic list by extending it — but so is their nonhierarchical order, the untraditional membership of the list, and the final, summative item. As with *Pseudolus* 709, it is not unreasonable to take these lines — and those like them[30] — as reflecting the perception, exaggerated

---

27 Spes Pseudolus, by analogy to, e.g., the much-later Jupiter Julius? Pseudolus' name extends the joke further: "tricksy hope" and "tricksy safety" are hardly gods worthy of worship, even under the broadest conception of divinity.

28 The slave being beseeched by his master is elsewhere in comedy called a *patronus*.

29 *Iuno Vesta Minerva Ceres Diana Venus Mars/ Mercurius Iovis Neptunus Vulcanus Apollo* (Enn. *Ann.* 60–1 ("Juno, Vesta, Minerva, Ceres, Diana, Venus, Mars, Mercury, Jupiter, Neptune, Vulcan, Apollo").

30 See Fisher (2014, 17) for the idea that the Plautine passage responds to the Ennian. Plautine comedy thrives on repetition (especially nouns; see Sharrock 2009, 172–3, who discusses a number of passages), and gods are multiplied also at *Bacchides* 115–16: to the question of who lives in his girlfriend's house, Pistoclerus replies with the divine personifications *Amor, Voluptas, Venus, Venustas, Gaudium,/ Iocus, Ludus, Sermo, Suavisaviatio* ("Love, Pleasure, Venus, Venery, Joy, Pleasantry, Play, Talking, Sweetkissing"). The "good" slave Lydus explicitly clarifies that these are *dis damnosissumis* ("the most damnable gods," but the phrase contains a pun on the monetary loss they entail), and the lines introduce a discussion on whether *Suavisaviatio* is genuinely a god or not. See too e.g. *cor meum, spes mea,/ mel meum, suavitudo, cibus, gaudium* ("My

for comic effect, that new gods were popping up all over the place, such that it could be difficult to keep track of them all.

We move to *Cistellaria* 670, where Phanostrata, thinking she may have discovered evidence that her lost daughter is still alive, invokes the assistance of hope: *Spes mihi sancta subveni* ("Sacred Hope, come to my aid!"). Here, interestingly, Hope appears on her own, with a clarifying epithet, as a regular goddess, who could be prayed to and who might intervene to one's advantage. And finally, at *Rudens* 231, as noted above, the freeborn Palaestra uses nearly the same words in asking for help in recovering from a shipwreck, *Spes bona, opsecro, subventa mihi* ("Good hope, I beg you, save me").

***

By way of conclusion, I focus on an ambiguity in the ancient treatment of hope which I think deserves attention, as it points to one of the primary aspects in which Greek and Roman sources differ from modern Western understandings of hope. In a world in which a variety of gods interest themselves in many aspects of humans' lives, many events which seem to moderns like chance occurrence were presumed to have supernatural causes: so, for instance, the belief that illness was sometimes divinely ordained — but the gods also sometimes intervened to make someone fall in love, fail in business, lose money on a chariot race, trip over a rock, and any number of other things. That is, it seems to be in precisely those moments when it looks like the other gods have let you down that you might want to turn to Hope. So this "last-chance" goddess might ironically share features with certain other personifications, such as Robigo, the goddess of wheat-rust, who might avoid your crops if you appease her.[31] Indeed, this might explain the cult or quasi-cult titles *sancta* and *bona*, applied to *Spes* in some of the personifications just treated: not all *Spes* is positive, but by specifying the "good" kind, suppliants may seek to separate themselves out from the ordinary run of mortals who hope fruitlessly, unwittingly attracting the attentions of the "bad" kind of hope.[32]

---

heart, my hope, my honey, my sweetness, food, delight," *Bacch.* 17–18, Non. 173M), which uses hope in a similarly exaggerated, but probably not personified, list of nouns. Feeney 1998, 87–92 discusses the problem of personification in Roman religion (88–90 with Plautine examples, including those cited above); as he notes, the difficulties are as old as Latin literature. See too Clark 2007, 73–116 on literary personifications, mostly Plautine (she focuses on *Salus* and *Fortuna*).
31 Ov. *Fas.* 4.905–42 for details of her worship.
32 See e.g. Augustine's complaint about the similar goddess *Fortuna*, that she is both good and bad, and his suggestion that she is either random (in which case there is no point worshipping her) or not (in which case she is not fortuitous) (*CD* 4.18), with the invocation of *Malam Fortunam*

Finally, although this is much more speculative, I suspect that some of the difficulty scholars have in understanding the spate of temple foundations during the First Punic War is connected to the ambiguity of emotions like hope in this period, as is evidenced not only by the epithets *sancta* and *bona*, but also by Polybius' roughly contemporary, very nuanced treatment of *elpis*.[33] For the historian, *elpis* comes into play primarily in his treatment of the *metabolai tuches*, the changes of fortune which inhere in war and history, but which are especially prevalent in the Punic war narratives. On the one hand, Polybius makes clear that the best generals will always leave as little room as possible for the changes of fortune, thus suggesting a distrust of the emotion of hope, or at least, a wariness about being in a circumstance where hope is your best option (and of course Polybius is not alone in this belief). On the other hand, Polybius also recognizes, as I have suggested above, that there is a kind of hope which is more rational than emotive. Or so I would explain his use of compounds of *elpis* (*euelpis*, *duselpis*, and the like), which seem to indicate a desire to securely distinguish between two kinds of hope. One is reasonable and well-grounded, and is what a general might feel after he has taken many precautions, trained the troops, reconnoitered the terrain to select a promising spot, delivered a rousing speech to the men, and slept well. But Greek and Latin normally[34] use the very same word, *elpis/spes*, to denote a general who has been outmaneuvered into marching all night and who finds himself forced to fight in an unfavorable location without preparation and without time for the men to eat. Such imprecision in terminology (or attitude) is frustrating, and imprecision relating to the gods can be positively dangerous.

The increased attention to *spes* and the increase in descriptive adjectives in the Middle Republic suggest that the ambiguity which had always been inherent in *spes* is beginning to be felt as a problem in the context of the vicissitudes of almost-incessant war. Perhaps contemporary temple foundations and cult offerings to *Spes* are best understood as an attempt to control the arbitrary goddess; like *Fortuna*, but unlike the much-touted Roman *Fides*, *Spes* is, and remains, unpredictable.

---

at Plaut. *Rud.* 501. Note too the later application of *sancta* to *fides* at Cat. 76.3, Cic. *Verr.* 2.3.6, Verg. *Aen.* 7.365, etc.; *sancta* does not catch on as an epithet of *spes*, which may indicate its more ambiguous status.
33 What follows is an abbreviated version of a larger treatment of *elpis* in Polybius, which will form part of a monograph on hope in Greco-Roman antiquity.
34 Polybius, and a few other authors, do not obey this general stricture.

Bibliography

Aberson, M. 1994. *Temples votifs et butin de guerre dans la Rome républicaine*, Rome.
Axtell, H.L. 1907. *The Deification of Abstract Ideas and Roman Literature and Inscriptions*, Chicago.
Bernstein, F. 1998. *Ludi publici: Untersuchungen zur Entstehung und Entwicklung der öffentlichen Spiele im republikanischen Rom*, Historia Enzelschriften 119, Stuttgart.
Cairns, D. 2008. "Look Both Ways: Studying Emotion in Ancient Greek," in: *Critical Quarterly* 50.4, 43–62.
—— 2016. "Metaphors for Hope in Archaic and Classical Greek Poetry," in: R.R. Caston/B. Kaster (eds.), *Hope, Joy, and Affection in the Classical World*, Oxford/New York, 13–44.
Champeaux, J. 1981–2. "*Fortuna* et le vocabulaire de la famille de *fortuna*," in: *Revue Philologique* 55–6, 285–307; 57–71.
—— 1982. *Fortuna: recherches sur le culte de la Fortune à Rome et dans le monde romain: des origines à la mort de César*, Rome.
—— 1987. *Fortuna: le culte de la fortune dans le monde romain: les transformations de Fortuna sous la République*, Rome.
Clark, A.J. 2007. *Divine Qualities: Cult and Community in Republican Rome*, Oxford.
Clark, M. 1983. "*Spes* in the Early Imperial Cult: 'The Hope of Augustus'," in: *Numen* 30.1, 80–105.
Delbrück, R. 1903. *Die drei Tempel am Forum holitorium in Rom*, Rome.
Duckworth, G.E. 1952. *The Nature of Roman Comedy: A Study in Popular Entertainment*, Princeton, NJ.
Dunsch, B. 2009. "Religion in der römischen Komödie: Einige programmatische Überlegungen," in: A. Bendlin/J. Rüpke (eds.), *Römische Religion im historischen Wandel: Diskursentwicklung von Plautus bis Ovid*, Stuttgart, 17–56.
Elliott, J. 2013. *Ennius and the Architecture of the* Annales, Cambridge.
Fears, J.R. 1981. "The Cult of Virtues and Roman Imperial Ideology," in: *ANRW* II.17.2, Berlin, 827–948.
Feeney, D. 1998. *Literature and Religion at Rome: Cultures, Contexts, and Beliefs*, Cambridge.
Fisher, J. 2014. *The Annals of Quintus Ennius and the Italic Tradition*, Baltimore, MD.
Fitzgerald, W. 2000. *Slavery and the Roman Literary Imagination*, Cambridge.
Fontaine, M. 2010. *Funny Words in Plautine Comedy*, Oxford.
Fraenkel, E. 2007. *Plautine Elements in Plautus*, (translated by F. Muecke and T. Drevikovsky), Oxford.
Freyburger, G. 2000. "Der religiöse Charakter der frühromischen Tragödie," in: G. Manuwald (ed.), *Identität und Alterität in der frühromischen Tragödie*, Würzburg, 37–48.
Fulkerson, L. 2013. *No Regrets: Remorse in Classical Antiquity*, Oxford.
—— 2015. "Plutarch and the Ambiguities of ΕΛΠΙΣ," in: D.L. Cairns/L. Fulkerson (eds.), *Emotions Between Greece and Rome*, London, 67–86.
—— 2016. "'Torn between Hope and Despair': Narrative Foreshadowing and Suspense in the Greek Novel," in: R.R. Caston/R.A. Kaster (eds.), *Hope, Joy, and Affection in the Classical World*, Oxford/New York, 75–91.
—— 2017. "The Vagaries of Hope in Vergil and Ovid," in: D.L. Cairns/D. Nelis (eds.), *Emotions in the Classical World: Methods, Approaches, and Directions*, Stuttgart, 207–30.
Goldberg, S.M. 1998. "Plautus on the Palatine," in: *JRS* 88, 1–20.
—— 2011. "Roman Comedy Gets Back to Basics," in: *JRS* 101, 206–221.
Goldschmidt, N. 2013. *Shaggy Crowns: Ennius'* Annales *and Virgil's* Aeneid, Oxford.
Gruen, E.S. 1992. *Culture and National Identity in Republican Rome*, Ithaca, NY.

Gulick, C.B. 1896. "Omens and Augury in Plautus," in: *HSCPh* 7, 235–47.
Hanson, J.A. 1959. "Plautus as a Sourcebook for Roman Religion," in: *TAPA* 90, 48–101.
Kaster, R.A. 2005. *Emotion, Restraint, and Community in Ancient Rome*, Oxford.
Leigh, M. 2004. *Comedy and the Rise of Rome*, Oxford.
McCarthy, K. 2000. *Slaves, Masters, and the Art of Authority in Plautine Comedy*, Princeton, NJ.
Morgan, M.G. 1990. "Politics, Religion and the Games in Rome, 200–150 B.C," in: *Philologus* 134, 14–36.
Nisbet, R.G.M./M. Hubbard. 1970. *A Commentary on Horace*, Odes book 1, Oxford.
Orlin, E.M. 1997. *Temples, Religion and Politics in the Roman Republic*, Mnemosyne Suppl. 164, Leiden.
—— 2010. *Foreign Cults in Rome: Creating a Roman Empire*, Oxford.
Padilla Peralta, Dan-El. 2014. Divine Institutions: Religious Practice, Economic Development, and Social Transformation in Mid-Republican Rome, Diss. Stanford.
Parker, H.N. 1989. "Crucially Funny or Tranio on the Couch: the *Servus Callidus* and Jokes about Torture," in: *TAPA* 119, 233–46.
Pietilä-Castrén, L. 1987. *Magnificentia Publica: Victory Monuments of the Roman Generals in the Era of the Punic Wars*, Helsinki.
Platner, S.B./T. Ashby. 1929. *A Topographical Dictionary of Ancient Rome*, Oxford.
Rey, S. 2015. "Aperçus sur la religion romaine de l'époque républicaine, à travers les comedies de Plaute," in: *Archiv für Religionsgeschichte* 16, 311–336.
Sanders, E. 2014. *Envy and Jealousy in Classical Athens: A Socio-Psychological Approach*, Oxford.
Segal, E. 1987. *Roman Laughter: The Comedy of Plautus*, 2nd ed., Oxford.
Sharrock, A. 2009. *Reading Roman Comedy: Poetics and Playfulness in Plautus and Terence*, Cambridge.
Slater, N. 2000. "The Market in Sooth," in: E. Stärk/G. Vogt-Spira (eds.), *Dramatische Wäldchen: Festschrift für Eckard Lefèvre*, Spoudasmata 80, Hildesheim, 345–61.
—— 2011. "Plautus the Theologian," in: A. Lardinois/J.H. Blok/M.G. van der Poel (eds.), *Sacred Words: Orality, Literacy and Religion*, Mnemosyne Suppl. 332, Leiden, 297–310.
—— 2014. "Gods on High, Gods Down Low: Romanizing Epiphany," in: I.N. Perysinakis/E. Karakasis (eds.), *Plautine Trends*, Berlin, 105–26.
Steinby, E.M. 1993–2000. *Lexicon Topographicum Urbis Romae*, Rome.
Stewart. R. 2012. *Plautus and Roman Slavery*, Oxford.
Weigel, R.D. 1998. "Roman Generals and the Vowing of Temples, 500–100 BC," in: *Classica et Mediaevalia* 49, 119–42.
Winkler, L. 1995. *Salus: Vom Staatskult zur politischen Idee: eine archäologische Untersuchung*, Heidelberg.
Ziolkowski, A. 1992. *The Temples of Mid-Republican Rome and their Historical and Topographical Context*, Rome.

Michael Paschalis
uestras spes uritis: Hope and Empire in Virgil's *Aeneid*

The concept of hope and related Greek and Latin terms are usually excluded from studies of ancient emotions. They are not found in relevant bibliographies and are absent from mainstream books like *The Emotions of the Ancient Greeks* by David Konstan and *The Passions in Roman Thought and Literature* by Susanna Braund and Christopher Gill. It is only quite recently that hope attracted scholarly attention and was treated in two edited volumes on ancient emotions.[1] Hope occupied an ambiguous space in ancient thought. Aristotle understood hope (*elpis*) as a neutral term indicating expectation or anticipation and hopefulness as a state of being rather than an emotion.[2] As far as Rome is concerned, it should be kept in mind that *Spes* was worshipped as a goddess in Republican times and beginning with Augustus it became a monopoly of the emperor as an imperial virtue. The *Spes Augusta* represented the promise of prosperity for the Roman people and the capacity of the emperor to ensure it.[3] Cicero included *spes* in his list of Stoic emotions (*Tusc.* 4.37.80) labelling it "an expectation of good" (*expectatio boni*) as opposed to fear which would represent "an expectation of bad" (*expectatio mali*). According to Francesca Tataranni Roman *spes* was an essentially positive concept (as a divinity she was often called *bona Spes*), unlike its Greek counterpart *elpis* that had an ambivalent nature. Despite occasional negative depictions the Romans viewed *spes* as "an overall virtuous quality, a benevolent goddess and a benign force operating in their personal life and community."[4]

In Virgil's *Aeneid* there are 46 occurrences of *spes* and 14 of *spero*,[5] figures indicative of their prominent role in the narrative. Yet studies of the epic treating hope, optimism, and pessimism, major Virgilian topics, have systematically ignored the Latin terms and their significance.[6] Rudolph Rieks' monograph *Affekte und Strukturen. Pathos als ein Form- und Wirkprinzip von Vergils Aeneis*, which is the most comprehensive study of emotions in the *Aeneid*, discusses *spes* and *spero* only in connection with desire (*amor*) in the story of Dido and Aeneas. In

---
1 See Douglas Cairns, Damien Nelis, and Laurel Fulkerson, in Caston/Kaster 2016; Fulkerson 2017.
2 Gravlee 2000.
3 Tataranni 2013, 67; see also Axtell 1907, 18–20; Fears 1981, 861–3 and *passim*; Clark 1983.
4 Tataranni 2013, 65–67.
5 Rieks 1989, 164. For Ovid, Lucan and Statius the occurrences are respectively the following: 42/15, 36/24, 29/18.
6 Cf. Parry 1963; Johnson 1976; Jenkyns 1985; O'Hara 1990.

his view "*amor* is one of various manifestations of *spes* and as a matter of fact it is the most important".[7] In restricting the emotional aspect of *spes* to this context only, Rieks seems to have had in mind Stoic views on emotions.[8] A broader assessment of the Latin terms for hope was very recently given by Laurel Fulkerson: departing from the standpoint that "hope is similar enough to an emotion, if it is not actually one", Fulkerson surveyed many instances of *spes* and *sperare* in the *Aeneid*, among them Trojan hopes fated to be realized and the misplaced and frustrated hopes of major characters like Dido and Turnus.[9]

In the *Aeneid* there is a direct and strong link between *spes* and Trojan future, settlement in Italy, establishment of the Roman race and growth of the Roman empire till the Augustan Age. In this sense *spes* possesses a deeply political aspect. As made clear very early in the epic, however, the task of establishing the Roman nation was an immense and laborious undertaking (1.33 *tantae molis erat Romanam condere gentem*) immersed in public and private emotions. These include the relentless wrath of Juno and her persecution of the Trojans who are tried and suffer by land and sea; Aeneas' painful and traumatic experience of losing his homeland, his tumultuous amorous engagement with the tragic queen of Carthage, his rage following the death of young Pallas that is vented into indiscriminate massacre, and last but not least his terrible and furious wrath that drives him to kill the wounded and suppliant Turnus at the very end of the *Aeneid*.

The question if *spes* is an emotion in itself may be less important vis-à-vis the context of violent passions in which it is sometimes placed in Virgil's epic. Most readers are, for instance, familiar with Dido's furious first reaction to Aeneas' secret preparations for departure in obedience to Jupiter's command to abandon Carthage and resume his mission:

dissimulare etiam sperasti, perfide, tantum
posse nefas tacitusque mea decedere terra?
[...]   (*Aeneid* 4.305–6)

Was it your hope to *disguise*, you perfidious cheat, such a monstrous
Wrong, to get out, *with no word said*, from this land that I govern?
[...][10]

---

7 Rieks 1989, 162–175 (168).
8 69 note 6: "Vergils Unterscheidung zwischen bona spes und mala spes paßt demnach besser zur stoischen als zur epikureischen Lehre."
9 Fulkerson 2017.
10 The text of the *Aeneid* is quoted from Mynors 1969 and the translation from Ahl 2007.

In *Aeneid* 5 there is an emblematic episode in the voyage towards Italy which thematizes the clash within the Trojan camp in Sicily of extreme desperation with the hope of reaching the promised land, that is of private with public pursuits. It is the episode of the burning of the ships by the Trojan women in 5.604–99.[11] Because of its conceptual comprehensiveness, its dramatic and highly emotional features and its potentially disastrous outcome regarding the fulfilment of Aeneas' mission, I have chosen this episode to be the focus and guiding event in the following brief study of the topic of "Hope and Empire in the *Aeneid*".

Here is an outline of the episode. While the Trojans are conducting funeral games on the anniversary of Anchises' death, Juno sends Iris down from heaven. Her mission is to incite the Trojan women, who are gathered on the shore weeping over the loss of Anchises and their endless wanderings, to burn the ships that would take them to Italy, their fated destination:

> at procul in sola secretae Troades acta
> amissum Anchisen flebant, cunctaeque profundum
> pontum aspectabant flentes. heu tot uada fessis
> et tantum superesse maris, uox omnibus una;
> urbem orant, taedet pelagi perferre laborem.   (*Aeneid* 5.613–7)

> But, far off, on a lonely beach, in seclusion, the Trojan
> Wives are lamenting the loss of Anchises. They all, while lamenting,
> Stare at the deep sea's surge: 'We're exhausted, yet so many seaways,
> So much water is still to be crossed!' Many voices sing one song.
> Tired of enduring the high seas' hardships, they pray for a city.

Since the beginning of the *Aeneid* Juno has directed all her efforts towards thwarting Trojan arrival in Italy and, if the ships were burned, they would be unable to resume their journey. Iris disguises herself as one of the women named Beroe and proceeds to accomplish her mission by means of a skillfully constructed speech which exploits their fatigue and unanimous feelings in favor of settling in Sicily.

Beroe begins by portraying in vivid colors the *utter futility* of their voyage; it has been seven years of endless wanderings with no prospect of ever reaching Italy:

> septima post Troiae excidium iam uertitur aestas,
> cum freta, cum terras omnis, tot inhospita saxa
> sideraque emensae ferimur, dum per mare magnum
> Italiam sequimur fugientem et uoluimur undis.   (*Aeneid* 5.626–9)

---

11 See West 1975, 168–74; Paschalis 1997, 197–200; Fletcher 2014, 176–185.

> Summers have passed, almost seven by now, since Troy was demolished.
> We, though, are still mapping all lands, seas, cruel reefs, constellations
> Far beyond count, we're shipped over the vast deep, rolled by the heaving
> Waves, chasing Italy — which, in turn, tries hard to escape us.

Iris-Beroe proposes a deceitful remedy for their desperate situation consisting in the hope of immediate and assured settlement: nobody can stop them, she argues, from founding a new Troy in the hospitable land tracing its name to Eryx, Aeneas' half-brother, and ruled by hospitable Acestes; so let them burn the accursed ships:

> hic Erycis fines fraterni atque hospes Acestes :
> quis prohibet muros iacere et dare ciuibus urbem?
> o patria et rapti nequiquam ex hoste penates,
> nullane iam Troiae dicentur moenia? nusquam
> Hectoreos anmis, Xanthum et Simoenta, uidebo?
> quin agite et mecum infaustas exurite puppis.   (*Aeneid* 5.630–5)
>
> Here we have brotherly Eryx's land; and a host in Acestes.
> Who says we *can't* put up walls and give *citizens* something: a city?
> Homeland and household gods! What a waste! You were saved from the foeman,
> But will there never be walls to make Troy's name real? Will I never
> See Hector's rivers, the Xanthus and Simoïs, redefined somewhere?
> Come then — why don't you? — and join me in burning these miserable galleys!

Iris-Beroe adds that the previous night she dreamed of the prophetess Cassandra giving her burning torches and advising her as follows: "Seek Troy here: here is your home" (637–8 "*hic quaerite Troiam; / hic domus est*"). She further cunningly suggests that the four burning altars dedicated to Neptune are a sign that the god himself provides the firebrands and the courage needed to perform the action. Having said this she seizes herself a brand from one of the altars and hurls it against the ships.

The women are startled and stunned. Then an elderly woman and nurse to Priam's sons named Pyrgo points out one by one the divine features of the woman that has just spoken to them and reveals that she has just seen with her very own eyes the true Beroe lying sick in bed and very much regretting that she could not pay the offerings due to Anchises (644–52).

Having heard the two speeches the Trojan women are torn between two contrasting feelings (hopelessness and hope) and two diametrically opposed courses of action: the desire to settle in Italy and the obligation to proceed towards their destination ordained by the *fata*:

at matres primo ancipites oculisque malignis
ambiguae spectare rates miserum inter amorem
praesentis terrae fatisque uocantia regna, [...]   (*Aeneid* 5.654–6)

Well, as the ladies, at first, were in two minds (yet casting an evil
Eye on the ships), hearts torn between pitiful love for this real,
Tangible land, and the call of the powerful realms that fate promised,
[...]

The women are driven to action only when the goddess flies off to the sky tracing a rainbow and thus revealing her divine identity (657–8). The supernatural sign confirms the authority of the first speaker and instills the spirit of Juno into their hearts. Stunned at the miraculous sight (*attonitae*) they are next seized by frenzy (*actaeque furore*) and set the ships aflame with brands taken from Neptune's altars (659–63).

When the news of the fire raging among the ships reaches the Trojan males, they are engaged in the final event of the funeral games consisting in an equestrian display by the younger generation of Trojans commonly known as *lusus Troiae*. *Aeneid* 5.548–603 is our main mythological source for this event, which in historical times is first mentioned in the period of Sulla; it was revived by Julius Caesar and established under Augustus as a regular event performed by boys of noble and respected families.[12] On this occasion the display is led by Ascanius, Aeneas' son, and his participation constitutes an important stage in the course of his *Bildung*.[13] It is precisely Ascanius who first responds to the news of the burning ships. His lightning reaction combines the impetuosity of youth with a sense of the gravity of the situation befitting an adult leader:

primus et Ascanius, cursus ut laetus equestris
ducebat, sic acer equo turbata petiuit
castra, nec exanimes possunt retinere magistri.
'quis furor iste nouus? quo nunc, quo tenditis' inquit
'heu miserae ciues? non hostem inimicaque castra
Argiuum, uestras spes uritis. en, ego uester
Ascanius !'—galeam ante pedes proiecit inanem,
qua ludo indutus belli simulacra ciebat.   (*Aeneid* 5.667–74)

First to respond is Ascanius, as piqued now as he'd been delighted
Earlier, leading the cavalry show. And he gallops his stallion

---

12 On the *lusus Troiae*, see Mehl 1956; Heinze 1994, 128–9; Scheid and Svenbro 1995; Kürvers/Niedermeier 2005.
13 On Iulus-Ascanius, see Ross 1977; Petrini 1997; Paschalis 1997, 61–63; Rogerson 2017.

Into the rioting camp. Though his trainers try hard, they can't stop him.
'What is this new form of madness?' he asks. 'What's your goal or your purpose,
Citizens, pitiful creatures? For shame! We're not foemen! You're torching
Your own hopes, not an Argive attack-force. It's me, your Ascanius,
Look!' And he tore off and flung at their feet the toy helmet he'd sported
During the games, when they'd staged mock versions of combat and warfare.

During the equestrian display, which represents the hopes placed in the younger generation, the Trojans are delighted in gazing at the boys whose names and faces evoke the older generations (5.576 *ueterumque [...] ora parentum*).[14] Ascanius himself who is in charge of the display (548–50) links Trojan past with Roman and Augustan future in more than one ways.[15] By telling the women that it is madness to burn the ships because they are actually "torching their own hopes" (*uestras spes uritis*) he condemns their action as hopeless and implies that all their hopes are placed in the continuation of their voyage. The gesture of pointing to himself (*en, ego uester / Ascanius!*) and flinging his helmet to the ground in front of his feet can only mean that he views himself as embodying hopes for the future (as implied by *uestras spes*) and that by their reckless action they are destroying those hopes as well, which he only just now displayed in the mock-battle equestrian maneuvers.

Through his brief speech and dramatic gesture Ascanius manages to bring the women to the realization of their crime. They scatter in fear along the shore and hide in the woods; they deeply regret their action; they recover their senses and, as the narrator puts it, "Juno is driven from their hearts" (679 *excussaque pectore Iuno est*). Eventually the flames are put out but only thanks to the intervention of Jupiter who responds to Aeneas' prayer by sending a thunderstorm. His intervention confirms in action the promise that Aeneas will arrive in Italy and his destiny will be fulfilled. All the ships are saved except for four. It is eventually decided that those unable or unwilling to proceed may stay behind and settle in the city of Acesta (Segesta), named after king Acestes, while the rest will resume their voyage to Italy.

Against Juno who strives to change the fated course of history and the divine messenger who undertakes to carry out her plan Virgil has set not Aeneas himself but Ascanius, his son, heir and successor. Ascanius comes victorious out of this peculiar *impar pugna*, the battle of a boy against cosmic forces (the reader may compare at this point the opening episode of the epic where Aeneas is caught in

---

14 Cf. Sullivan 2009.
15 According to Virgil (5.596–603) he introduced the equestrian display to Alba Longa and from there it was handed on to Rome and called the *lusus Troiae*.

the storm raised by Juno's agent Aeolus). Trojan-Roman future spans a time of over a thousand years beyond the end of the epic. Ascanius is the character destined to found Alba Longa, the city that will bridge the gap between Troy and Rome. I quote the relevant passage from Jupiter's prophecy to Venus in *Aeneid* 1.267–77:

> at puer Ascanius, cui nunc cognomen Iulo
> additur (Ilus erat, dum res stetit Ilia regno),
> triginta magnos uoluendis mensibus orbis
> imperio explebit, regnumque ab sede Lauini
> transferet, et Longam multa ui muniet Albam.
> hic iam ter centum totos regnabitur annos
> gente sub Hectorea, donec regina sacerdos
> Marte grauis geminam partu dabit Ilia prolem.
> inde lupae fuluo nutricis tegmine laetus
> Romulus excipiet gentem et Mauortia condet
> moenia Romanosque suo de nomine dicet.

> Youthful Ascanius, who'll now be known by a new name, "Iulus", —
> "Ilus" it was while the Ilian state still ruled in the Troad —
> *He* will go on to complete full thirty cycles of rolling
> Months in command. Then he'll transfer the centre of power from Lavinium
> And, with a huge show of force, make Alba Longa his fortress.
> Over the next three centuries, then, this will be the command post
> Ruled by the people of Hector, until such time as a royal
> Priestess named Ilia, pregnant by Mars, gives birth to her twin boys.
> Romulus, happy to wear the tan hide from the she-wolf who nursed him,
> Then will inherit the line. And, in Mars' honour, he'll found a city,
> Giving its people a name he derives from his own name: the Romans.

By his other name Aeneas' son is also the divine ancestor of the Julian family and the emperor Augustus. This is how the god Apollo hails his victory over Numanus Remulus in 9.641–4, alluding to the *gens Iulia* and the *pax Augusta*:

> 'macte noua uirtute, puer, sic itur ad astra,
> dis genite et geniture deos. iure omnia bella
> gente sub Assaraci fato uentura resident,
> nec te Troia capit.'

> 'Blessings on your new manhood, my boy. That's the pathway to heaven,
> You, who are born of a god, and will some day beget gods! For all wars
> Fated to come will subside when Assaracus' people is ruling
> Justly. And Troy doesn't set its restrictions on you.'

Therefore though the burden of founding the Roman race is placed on the shoulders of Aeneas, the *hope* for the fulfilment of this mission and the Augustan future of Rome is specifically associated with his son. Elsewhere in the *Aeneid* this kind of hope is conveyed through stock phrases combining the word *spes* most commonly with the name Iulus: *spes Iuli, spes heredis Iuli, spes surgentis Iuli*. That Iulus embodies hope for the future is portrayed as a universal understanding and expectation. It is placed in the mouth of Trojans and aliens as well as of divine characters: Trojan Ilioneus addressing Dido in 1.556; Mercury addressing Aeneas on behalf of Jupiter in 4.274; Trojan Palinurus addressing Aeneas in the Underworld in 6.364; the Rutulian Mago pleading to Aeneas for his life on the battlefield in 10.524; and the narrator himself in 12.168. I quote two of these references where the content of *spes Iuli* is specified. In *Aeneid* 4 Jupiter sends Mercury to Aeneas who has settled at Carthage at the side of Dido and has devoted himself to the Carthaginian cause in order to remind him of his mission and the destiny of his son, heir and successor:

> 'tu nunc Karthaginis altae
> fundamenta locas pulchramque uxorius urbem
> exstruis? heu, regni rerumque oblite tuarum!
> ipse deum tibi me claro demittit Olympo
> regnator, caelum et terras qui numine torquet,
> ipse haec ferre iubet celeris mandata per auras:
> quid struis? aut qua spe Libycis teris otia terris?
> si te nulla mouet tantarum gloria rerum
> [nec super ipse tua moliris laude laborem,]
> Ascanium surgentem et spes heredis Iuli
> respice, cui regnum Italiae Romanaque tellus
> debetur.' (*Aeneid* 4.265–76)

> '*You*, laying foundations for mighty
> Carthage!' he said. 'Obsessed with your wife, you're now building a lovely
> City for her. You've forgotten your own obligations and kingdom!
> Heaven's own king, who spins both the sky and the earth with his power,
> Sends me to you himself, directly from gleaming Olympus,
> Tells me himself to convey these instructions through swift-moving breezes:
> What do you hope you can build, you deserter, in Libya's deserts?
> If, in fact, glory from such great deeds doesn't fire up your spirit,
> Being indifferent yourself to the plaudits earned by this hard work,
> Think of the growing Ascanius, the dreams for Iulus to cherish.
> He is your heir. Thus Rome's fine earth and Italy's kingship
> Stand as his due.

In *Aeneid* 12.166–8 father and son appear side by side. It is a most solemn occasion for Latins and Trojans: a treaty is about to be concluded and their differences will be resolved through a duel between Aeneas and Turnus. First a sacrifice is conducted and next king Latinus and Aeneas take public oaths accepting the conditions of the treaty and promising to preserve peace. In introducing Aeneas and Ascanius the narrator calls the former "the root-stock of Roman growth" (*Romanae stirpis origo*) and the latter "the second hope for the greatness of Rome" (*magnae spes altera Romae*):

> hinc pater Aeneas, Romanae stirpis origo,
> sidereo flagrans clipeo et caelestibus armis
> et iuxta Ascanius, magnae spes altera Romae.
>
> Then, on this side, Aeneas, the father, the root-stock of Roman
> Growth, sets forth from the camp with his star-bright shield and celestial
> Armour: a vision of fire. At his side is Ascanius, the second
> Hope for the greatness of Rome.

Calling Ascanius *spes altera Romae* may imply that Aeneas himself embodies the "[first] hope" for Rome (*spes una*). But since *spes* is consistently associated not with Aeneas but with his son, I would assume that *Romanae stirpis origo* and *spes altera Romae* probably represent an order of succession.[16]

A more important question concerns the youth's *awareness* of his destiny as "hope for the greatness of Rome." It is the omniscient narrator who knows about the Roman future of the Trojans and of course the gods. When other characters refer to the *spes Iuli* their knowledge cannot extend beyond Trojan arrival and settlement in Italy. Towards the end of the epic Aeneas invites his son "to learn from him courage and true labor" ('*disce, puer, uirtutem ex me uerumque laborem, / fortunam ex aliis* [...]') and be inspired by his own example and the example of his uncle Hector (12.435–40). This is the only conversation between father and son recorded in the epic and in it Aeneas tells his son about the Trojan past and present but nothing about Troy's Alban and Roman future; this is most probably because Aeneas himself remains *rerum ignarus*, though he heard about them from his father's lips in the Underworld and was later given by his mother a shield representing scenes of Roman history. The Trojan past and present figures prominently also in the so-called *aristeia* of Ascanius in 9.590–671. Numanus Remulus derides the beleaguered Trojans for being effeminate Phrygians twice conquered

---

16 According to Servius *auctus* Aeneas represents the *spes una* of Rome and Ascanius the *spes altera*, an interpretation accepted by most commentators. According to Tarrant (2012, *ad loc.*) *altera* suggests "Ascanius' position vis-à-vis Aeneas, parallel to the place of Turnus in relation to Latinus in 12.161–5."

in the past[17] and Ascanius shoots an arrow through his head uttering the following sarcastic reply (634–5):

> 'i, uerbis uirtutem inlude superbis!
> bis capti Phryges haec Rutulis responsa remittunt.'

> 'Go on! Mock bravery now with your arrogant speeches!
> Here's the retort twice-captured Phrygians send in dispatches!'

The one and only time Ascanius displays awareness of the future is in the much earlier episode of the burning of the ships and it is specifically and prominently associated with *spes*. By speedily reacting to the women's action and shouting to them that the ships they are burning represent Trojan hopes for the future (*uestras spes uritis*) he displays awareness of the significance and vital importance of continuing the voyage to Italy and of course leadership pointing towards the future. By implying through word and gesture that it is himself who embodies Trojan hopes for the future (*en, ego uester Ascanius*), he shows consciousness of his role as an heir and successor to Aeneas. Despite the fact that we are unable to say how much he had been told and how much he was expected to know, his attitude in *Aeneid* 5 suggests a precocious maturity (his intervention strongly reminds of Laocoon's in *Aeneid* 2)[18] and therefore the course of his *Bildung* in the *Aeneid* does not seem to be a straightforward one. One may compare in this respect the immaturity he displays in 9.257–80, where he praises without any reservation the night expedition of Nisus and Euryalus and promises rich rewards. As regards his *aristeia* in the same book it is not certain that it marks the transition from boyhood to manhood;[19] and though it carries long-term political and ideological significance in the eyes of Apollo, all Ascanius does is defend the Trojans against the charge that they are effeminate Orientals by shooting an arrow from within the safety of the Trojan camp.

Hope is associated with the Trojan future elsewhere in the epic as well especially in connection with prophecies uttered by Anchises: when he directs the Trojans towards Crete by erroneously interpreting the Delian oracle (3.103 *spes*

---

17 On his speech see especially Dickie 1985.
18 There are conspicuous formal reminiscences of Laocoon's speech, especially as regards the opening address (5.670–1 '*quis furor iste nouus? quo nunc, quo tenditis*' inquit / '*heu miserae ciues?* [...]': 2.42 '*O miseri, quae tanta insania, ciues?* [...]') and the gesture that accompanies and concludes his speech (helmet-flinging: spear-hurling).
19 Hardie (1994, 16) argues this point on the basis of the juxtaposition of *noua uirtute* and *puer* in 641. Yet in 12.435 Ascanius is still a *puer* in his father's eyes and expected to learn from him the true meaning of *uirtus*.

discite uestras); when he predicts not only war but also peace for the Trojans upon their first sight of Italy and the view of grazing horses (3.543 *spes et pacis*); when his prophecy of the eating of tables signifying arrival at the promised land is fulfilled (7.126 *tum sperare domos defessus*). But the first of these predictions is mistaken while the other two offer a partial view of the future. By contrast the *spes Iuli* is far-reaching, Roman, imperial and, through Iulus' name and lineage, prominently Augustan. Does this aspect of hope anticipate in some way *Spes* as an imperial virtue? It is hard to say.

Evander in *Aeneid* 8 and Amata in *Aeneid* 12 place their hope for the future respectively in his son Pallas (8.514 *spes et solacia nostri*) and her aspiring son-in-law Turnus (10.56 *spes tu nunc una, senectae*). But Pallas and Turnus are both slain on the battlefield (cf. Evander in 11.49), in a chain of killings where Turnus slays Pallas in an *impar pugna* (10.426–509) and Aeneas avenges the death of Pallas on Turnus at the end of the *Aeneid* (12.887–952). By contrast the *spes surgentis Iuli*, the hope for the future which Aeneas' growing son embodies, is unshakable; because it is so that the *fata* have ordained, Jupiter has promised, and Apollo has predicted; because he is the grandson of Venus and ancestor of the Julian family, and stands for future Roman grandeur and Augustan Rome.

The *spes* invested in Aeneas' son is deeply political but at the same time, as noted at the beginning, it is immersed in emotions. In the episode of the burning of the ships on which I have focused hopes private and public, divine and human clash fiercely against a background of weariness, desperation, and reckless action. Ascanius' impetuous ride towards the burning ships, his passionate speech to the women, the telling gesture of flinging his helmet to the ground create a highly emotional context for the message he wants to convey: by burning the ships the women are burning their hopes to reach Italy and casting away the hope he embodies as son, heir and successor to Aeneas: *uestras spes uritis. En, ego uester Ascanius.*

Bibliography

Ahl, F. 2007. *Virgil: Aeneid, Translated with Notes*, Oxford.
Axtell, H.L. 1907. *The Deification of Abstract Ideas in Roman Literature and Inscriptions*, Chicago.
Morton Braund, S./C. Gill (eds.) 1997. *The Passions in Roman Thought and Literature*, Cambridge.
Caston, R.R./R.A. Kaster (eds.) 2016. *Hope, Joy, and Affection in the Classical World*, Oxford/New York.
Clark, M.E. 1983. "*Spes* in the Early Imperial Cult: 'The Hope of Augustus'," in: *Numen* 30, 80–105.
Dickie, M. 1985. "The Speech of Numanus Remulus (*Aeneid* 9,598-620)," in: *PLLS* 5, 165–221.
Fears, J.R. 1981. "The Cult of Virtues and Roman Imperial Ideology," in: *ANRW* II.17.2, 827–948.
Fletcher, K.F.B. 2014. *Finding Italy: Travel, Nation and Colonization in Vergil's Aeneid*, Ann Arbor.

Fulkerson, L. 2017. "The Vagaries of Hope in Vergil and Ovid," in: D.L. Cairns/D. Nelis (eds.), *Emotions in the Classical World: Methods, Approaches, and Directions*, Stuttgart, 207–30.
Gravlee, S.G. 2000. "Aristotle on Hope," in: *Journal of the History of Philosophy* 38, 461–477.
Hardie, P. 1994. *Virgil: Aeneid, Book IX*, Cambridge.
Heinze, R. 1994. *Virgil's Epic Technique*, Berkeley/Los Angeles/Oxford.
Jenkyns, R. 1985. "Pathos, Tragedy and Hope in the *Aeneid*," in: *JRS* 75, 60–77.
Johnson, W.R. 1976. *Darkness Visible: A Study of Vergil's Aeneid*, Berkeley/Los Angeles/London.
Kermode, F. (ed.) 1975. *Selected Prose of T.S. Eliot*, New York.
Konstan, D. 2006. *The Emotions of the Ancient Greeks: Studies in Aristotle and Classical Literature*, Toronto.
Kürvers, K./M. Niedermeier 2005. "Wunderkreis, Labyrinth und Troiaspiel: Rekonstruktion und Deutung des 'lusus troiae'," in: *Kritische Berichte* 33, 5–25.
Mehl, E. 1956. "Troiaspiel," in: *RE Suppl. VIII*, 888–905.
Mynors, R.A.B. (ed.) 1969. *P. Vergili Maronis Opera*, Oxford.
Parry, A. 1963. "The Two Voices of Virgil's *Aeneid*," in: *Arion* 2, 66–80.
Paschalis, M. 1997. *Virgil's Aeneid: Semantic Relations and Proper Names*, Oxford.
Petrini, M. 1997. *The Child and the Hero: Coming of Age in Catullus and Vergil*, Ann Arbor.
Rieks, R. 1989. *Affekte und Strukturen: Pathos als sein Form- und Wirkprinzip von Vergils Aeneis*, Zetemata vol. 86, Munich.
Rogerson, A. 2017. *Virgil's Ascanius: Imagining the Future in the Aeneid*, Cambridge/New York.
Ross, M.M.W. 1977. The Role of Ascanius in the Aeneid, Diss. Vanderbilt University.
Scheid, J./J. Svenbro 1995. *The Craft of Zeus: Myths of Weaving and Fabric*, (translated by C. Volk), Harvard.
Sullivan, T.M. 2009. "Death *ante ora parentum* in Virgil's *Aeneid*," in: *TAPA* 139, 447–486.
Tarrant, R. 2012. *Virgil: Aeneid, Book XII*, Cambridge.
Tataranni, F. 2013. "Hope and Leadership in Ancient Rome," in: *Teoria* 33, 65–78.
West, G.S. 1975. Women in Vergil's Aeneid, Diss. University of California.

Andreas N. Michalopoulos
Hope Dies Last at Tomis

In 8 A.D.[1] Ovid was banished by the Emperor Augustus to Tomis on the Black Sea.[2] Leaving behind the comfortable life of the capital, he was forced to move to a hostile place, inhabited by (semi)barbarian people —or at least this is what he wanted his readers to believe in the verse letters, the *Tristia* and the *Epistulae ex Ponto*, which he kept sending from exile. The prospects of Ovid's life at Tomis certainly did not look bright, at least according to his own testimony in his poems.

My aim in this paper is to discuss the role of hope[3] in Ovid's exile poetry. I will address the following issues: what can Ovid realistically hope for at Tomis? Who/what are the agents and givers of Ovid's hope? Who/what is Ovid's hope affected by? Does Ovid conceive of hope as a positive sentiment or rather as a treacherous emotion which makes his life at Tomis miserable and difficult? How does hope affect the dynamics of Ovid's exile poetics and his perception of reality? Does Ovid's hope have any religious connotations? Is it associated with any other emotions?[4]

Let me first make two necessary preliminary considerations:

1. I take it as a fact that Ovid's exile was real and not fictional, not invented by the poet. The theory about Ovid's fictional exile is imaginative, yet unconvincing.[5]

2. What *is* truly fictional in Ovid's exile poetry is his *persona* as an exiled poet. One should always bear in mind the necessary distinction between Ovid as a historical person, whose emotions are unknown to us, and Ovid as a literary *persona* who manipulates emotions. Ovid's exile poetry is certainly not to be taken as the

---

[1] For the dating of Ovid's exile, see Green 1994, xviii.
[2] Ovid was supposedly banished on account of the provocative erotic content of his *Ars Amatoria*, and of an unspecified error. For various attempts to clarify this thorny issue, see Thibault 1964, 125–129, Holleman 1976, Ford 1977, Syme 1978, 215–216, Green 1982, Goold 1983, Claassen 1986 sect. 3.2.3, Claassen 1987, Verdière 1992, Hexter 2007, 212–214, Ingleheart 2010 on Ov. *Tr.* 2.103–110.
[3] Hope has existed across time, cultures, and ethnic groups. For a concise summary of views on hope throughout history, see Snyder 2000, 3–5. For contemporary definitions of hope, see Snyder 2000, 8f.
[4] For the study of emotions in ancient Greece and Rome, see among others the seminal studies of Kaster 2005, Konstan 2006, Cairns 2008, Chaniotis 2012, Caston/Kaster 2016.
[5] In a 1985 paper Fitton Brown suggested that Ovid's exile was simply an invention of the poet, a theory which has been convincingly refuted, among others, by Helzle 1988, Ehlers 1988, and Green 1994, xvii.

DOI 10.1515/9783110598254-011

historical record of the poet's life in Tomis. Ovid's exilic poems serve a specific goal, namely to achieve the poet's recall to Rome. The depiction of Tomis as an inhospitable, cold, hostile, and uncivilized environment may be part of the poet's strategy. Therefore, Ovid's exilic poetry should be read with caution: the actual circumstances of his life in exile may have been –or rather, must have been– different from those depicted in his poetry.[6]

I begin my discussion with statistics: in Ovid's pre-exilic works the noun *spes* and the verb *sperare*, the main terms related with hope (and/or expectation, anticipation, prospect, promise) in Latin,[7] feature 7x in the *Amores*, 38x in the *Heroides*, 12x in the *Ars amatoria*, 2x in the *Remedia amoris*, 53x in the *Metamorphoses*, 11x in the *Fasti*. In his exilic poetry the situation is as follows: 20x in the *Tristia*, 25x in the *Epistulae ex Ponto*. The numbers are indicative: taking into account the size of the works, hope is much more frequent in the *Heroides*, the *Tristia*, and the *Epistulae ex Ponto*, because in these works the poet or the letter-writers are separated from their loved ones and face dire straits. Hope is naturally born in such trying circumstances and caters for people's psychological need to believe that the conditions of their life will ameliorate; hope is based on positive expectations for goal attainment. In an odd and cruel twist of fate, the banished Ovid found himself in a situation similar to that of his mythological heroines in the *Heroides*. He could look for themes and motifs for his exile poetry in his own elegiac epistolographic work.

For methodological reasons, my treatment of Ovid's hope in his exilic poetry is divided into the following sections: 1) the power of hope, 2) *spes* and *timor*, 3) *spes*, *consolatio*, and a god, 4) deceiving *spes* / frustrated *spes*.

1 The power of hope

Ovid's exile lasted for nearly a decade. In all these years he never stopped writing poetry, which was perhaps the only intellectual occupation he had at Tomis and his steady companion in exile. Together with poetry, Ovid depicts hope as his other permanent companion in exile. Ovid highlights the power and importance

---

6 See Williams 1994, ch. 1, *idem* 2002a, 235, Green 1994, xxiii–xxvi. For an overview of the topic, with bibliography, see Williams 2002b, 340–349. For the complex issue of the conflict between 'historical truth' and 'poetic truth', see Claassen 1988.
7 See *OLD* s.v. *spes* and *spero*.

of hope in his *apologia* to Augustus (*Tr.* 2.145–8): *ipse licet sperare*[8] *vetes, / sperabimus usque; / hoc unum fieri te prohibente potest. /* spes *mihi magna subit, cum te, mitissime princeps, /* spes *mihi, respicio cum mea facta, cadit* ("Though you yourself forbid hope, I'll still hope: this is the only thing that can be done even though you forbid it. Great hope fills me, gazing at you, most merciful prince, and fails me when I gaze at what I've done"). This is arguably Ovid's most defying declaration as regards Augustus and hope. The word *spes* is emphatically placed at the beginning of both the hexameter and the pentameter. Ovid links his hope with the *princeps*,[9] but this time he claims that hope lies beyond his jurisdiction and that Augustus does not have the power to prevent and prohibit it. Hope seems like the only form of 'revolution' available to Ovid in exile.[10] Ovid counts on the fact that Augustus is *mitissimus*, but he seems to despair when he recalls the reason of his punishment[11] and he feels remorse (cf. *Pont.* 4.6.15f. below).[12] Of course the sincerity of Ovid's praise of the emperor's *clementia* is questionable.[13]

By far Ovid's most enthusiastic exilic account on hope is *Pont.* 1.6.27–44, written after five years of exile and while the poet's return to Rome was nowhere in sight. This is an Ovidian hymn to the goddess *Spes*[14] illustrating her might.[15]

---

8 The verb *sperare* is here used as intransitive, without object. See Luck 1977, *ad loc.*, Ciccarelli 2003 on *Tr.* 2.143–8.
9 For the association of Augustus with hope on the political field, see Ingleheart 2010 on *Tr.* 2.145–54 and section iii below.
10 Ciccarelli 2003 on *Tr.* 2.143–8.
11 In contrast, at *Tr.* 3.5.43f. Ovid justifies his hope for deliverance by claiming that his error is not heavy, since it does not involve bloodshed (*Tr.* 3.5.43f.): *denique non possum nullam sperare salutem, / cum poenae non sit causa cruenta meae* ("So it's impossible for me not to hope of salvation, since the cause of my punishment's not stained with blood"). Ovid elaborates on the famous Vergilian line (*Aen.* 2.354) *una salus victis nullam sperare salutem* and gives it an optimistic twist, see Luck 1977 on *Tr.* 3.5.43f.
12 Fulkerson 2013b, 17f. suggests that just as hope is often the quality possessed by those who have not planned properly and usually fail, so too remorse is the natural after-effect of one's failures. For Ovid's handling of remorse towards Augustus in his exile poetry, see Fulkerson 2013b, ch. 6.
13 For Ovid's praises of Augustus in his exilic poetry, see Michalopoulos 2014.
14 In contrast to the Greeks, the Romans considered *Spes* a much more benevolent goddess, her typical modifier being *bona*. For the cult of *Spes* in Rome, see Walsh 1974, Clark 1981 and 1983, Armstrong 1998, ch. 1 section c. On the iconography of *Spes*, see Fullerton 1990, 103–126 and Perassi 1991.
15 This hymn is modeled on Theogn. 1135–6 and Tib. 2.6.19–28, which belong to a long tradition going back to Hesiod (*Works* 96). See Helzle 2003, 178 with n. 2, Gaertner 2005 on *Pont.* 1.6.29–40, and Tissol 2014 on *Pont.* 1.2.29–30.

Ovid begins by stating that he still nourishes the hope that Augustus may be placated (*Pont.* 1.6.27f.): *spes igitur menti poenae, Graecine, levandae / non est ex toto nulla relicta meae* ("Graecinus, all hope of seeing my sentence reduced, therefore, hasn't completely left me"). Then, using a list of examples (a worker in the fields (31f.), a shipwrecked sailor (33f.), a man whose heart has stopped beating (35f.), those who are in prison (37), a man who is crucified (38),[16] people who have decided to commit suicide (39f.)), Ovid stresses that nobody ever gives up hope even in the most adverse circumstances, even when death is imminent. Hope is much better than a doctor, or rather hope is in fact *the* best doctor and never abandons a patient, even when one stands on the threshold of death. Ovid's mention of death is surely significant, given the *topos* 'exile = death' which dominates his exilic poetry.[17] In fact, Ovid claims that at a certain point he had decided to kill himself,[18] but hope stopped him in the last minute, promising that Augustus' rage would be softened by his tears of entreaty (41–4): *me quoque conantem gladio finire dolorem / arguit iniecta continuitque manu: / 'quid' que 'facis? lacrimis opus est, non sanguine', dixit, / 'saepe per has flecti principis ira solet'* ("She reproved me too, and checked me with her hand, / as I was trying to end my sorrows with a sword, / saying: 'What are you doing? Tears not blood are needed, / often a prince's anger can be turned aside by weeping'").

But what can Ovid really hope for at Tomis and how does he formulate his hope? Unsurprisingly, his main goal and hope is to return to Rome. He is, however, very cautious and discreet when it comes to voicing his wish, because he does not want to provoke Augustus' anger[19] any more than he already has. In two characteristic passages from the *Tristia* Ovid clearly associates his hope of return with the *princeps* (*Tr.* 3.5.53f.): *spes igitur superest, ut molliat ipse, futurum / mutati poenam condicione loci* ("So hope remains that he might bring himself to

---

16 Ovid's remark about those who still hope while hanging on the cross is a precursor to the brilliant, bitingly sarcastic final scene of Monty Pythons' *Life of Brian*, when all the crucified sing merrily "Always look on the bright side of life".
17 'Exile = death' is a commonplace in Ovid's exile poetry: *Tr.* 1.2.65–66, 1.2.71–72, 1.3.21–24, 1.3.89–98, 1.4.28, 3.3, 5.9.19, *Pont.* 1.8.27, 1.9.17, 4.9.74, 4.16.51. See Owen 1902, 99 on *Tr.* 1.2.72, Wistrand 1968, 6–26, Nagle 1980, 22–35, Doblhofer 1987, 166–178, Helzle 1988, 78, Williams 1994, 12f., Claassen 1996, 576–585, *idem* 1999, 239–241 with n. 37, *idem* 2008, 44, 196–199, Gaertner 2005 on *Pont.* 1.5.86, *idem* 2007, 160 with n. 26. See also Gaertner 2007, 159 with n. 24 for the wordplay *exilium-exitium* in Ennius and for the possibility that the association of exile and death is of Latin origin.
18 For Ovid's references to suicide throughout his exilic poetry, see McGowan 2009, 151 n. 63.
19 For Augustus' *ira* see more recently Fulkerson 2013b, 139 n. 21. For Ovid's depiction of Augustus in his exile poetry, see Drucker 1977, *passim* and Videau-Delibes 1991, 233–64.

ease my punishment by changing the terms of its location")[20] and (*Tr.* 4.9.13f.): *et patriam, modo sit sospes, speramus ab illo: / saepe Iovis telo quercus adusta viret* ("My country: I even hope for that from him, if only he lives: the oak blasted by Jove's lightning often grows green again").[21] Since everything depends on Augustus' *clementia*,[22] Ovid can only hope for a change of the emperor's mood towards him, no matter how likely this may be. Ovid depicts himself in a state of utter destruction, caused by the emperor; even so, this does not lead him, at least for the time being, to hopelessness and despair. He is resilient, he struggles for survival, and he has the proper antidote to despair. Hope is still alive and keeps him going. In essence, hope provides Ovid with the necessary weaponry to fight against Augustus' autocratic power.[23]

This kind of approach is typical in the *Epistulae ex Ponto* too, composed at around 13 AD, after five years in exile,[24] at a time when Ovid should have realized that the possibility of his return to Rome was becoming more remote by the day (*Pont.* 2.7.79f.): *spes quoque posse mora mitescere principis iram / vivere ne nolim*

---

20 All *Tristia* and *Epistulae ex Ponto* translations are taken from A.S. Kline (with slight modifications), available at: <http,//www.poetryintranslation.com/PITBR/Latin/Ovidexilehome.htm> (last accessed February 4, 2018).
21 On metaphorical uses of hope in Greek poetry, see Cairns 2016. Ovid expresses similar thoughts throughout his exilic poetry: *nec fore perpetuam sperat sibi numinis iram, / conscius in culpa non scelus esse sua*, "He hopes the god's anger won't last forever conscious there was no evil in his offence" (*Tr.* 5.4.17f.); *neve tamen tota capias fera gaudia mente, / non est placandi spes mihi nulla dei*, "Still, so cruel joy might not grip your soul complete, my hope of placating the god's not wholly dead" (*Tr.* 5.8.21f.); *dum faciles aditus praebet venerabile templum, / sperandum est nostras posse valere preces*, "while the sacred powers offer an easy approach, it's to be hoped our prayers might have some worth" (*Pont.* 3.3.91f.).
22 See Aug. *RG* 3: *victor omnibus superstitibus peperci. externas gentes quibus tuto ignosci potuit conservare quam excidere malui*. For *clementia* as a key element of political behavior and Augustan propaganda, see Bux 1948, Adam 1970, Weinstock 1971, 228–243, Hoben 1978, 4–6, Syme 1978, 159f., Gaertner 2005, 9–12. *Clementia, virtus, iustitia,* and *pietas* were Augustus' four cardinal virtues inscribed on the *clupeus virtutis* awarded to him by the Senate. On Ovid's trust in Augustus' *clementia* in his exilic poetry, see Luck 1977 on *Tr.* 5.4.17f. and on 5.8.25ff.
23 For the struggle between poetry and political power, Ovid and the princeps, which is a staple theme of Ovid's exile poetry, see among others Evans 1983, 17–19 and 182 n. 20 with bibliography, Williams 2002a, 240, Boyle 2003, 11, McGowan 2009, 203ff. It has contributed significantly to Ovid becoming the embodiment of the conflict between art and authoritarian regimes, see Michalopoulos 2011, 280 with n. 20.
24 According to Syme 1978, 37–47 the dates of publication of Ovid's works in exile are as follows: *Tristia* (5 books) 9–12 AD, *Epistulae ex Ponto* (Books 1–3 in 13 AD, Book 4 perhaps posthumously). Claassen 1986, Section 4.1 too investigates the dating of composition and publication of Ovid's exile poetry, and she summarizes her findings in Claassen 1987, 32. On the dating of the *Epistulae ex Ponto*, see Galasso 2009, 195f.

deficiamque cavet ("The hope too that time might soften the prince's wrath, warns me against aversion to life, losing heart"). Augustus is depicted as the sole provider of Ovid's hope. The poet is entirely dependent on the emperor, and so are his emotions and his psychological mood. Despite the difficult circumstances, it is his hope for a change of the emperor's decision that practically keeps the poet alive and prevents him from giving up. Hope is life-saving for Ovid, at least temporarily. As it turned out, Ovid's hope died with him on the solitary shore of Tomis.

2 *Spes* and *timor*

Hope (ἐλπίς, *spes*)[25] and fear (φόβος, *timor-metus*) form an inseparable pair and an interchangeable continuum in both Greek and Latin literature.[26] Hope may give way to fear, it may replace fear, and so on and so forth. Hope and fear frequently go hand in hand in Ovid's pre-exilic poetry regarding mythological characters and elegiac lovers.[27] Ironically, hope and fear keep on featuring together in his exile, only this time they concern the poet himself. Fear typically threatens to obliterate hope. Very tellingly, the two emotions are associated, vying with each other, already in the first, programmatic elegy from exile (*Tr.* 1.1.102f.): *tantum ne noceas, dum vis prodesse, videto – / nam spes est animi nostra timore minor* ("Only see you don't do harm, while you have power to help – since my hope is less than my fear"). For the time being, at the early stages of his exile, Ovid considers hope as a positive emotion which struggles against fear and is in

---

25 Fulkerson 2013a, 67 rightly notes that the Greek ἐλπίς (and its cognate verb ἐλπίζω) does not map precisely onto English hope or Latin *spes*, and that its semantic range covers a number of thoughts and emotions, such as 'hope', 'expect', 'fear', 'think'.
26 On hope and fear see Day 1970 and 1998, Aronson 1999, Nussbaum 2001, 28, 87, Lear 2006, Mittleman 2009, Schlosser 2013, Fulkerson 2013a, 68, Cairns 2016, 13–15, 23–27. At *Tusc.* 4.80 Cicero considers *spes* "the expectation of good" and distinguishes it from *metus*, which he calls "the expectation of evil": *si spes est expectatio boni, mali expectationem esse necesse est metum.* Seneca (*Ep.* 5.7) emphasizes hope's close relation to fear depicting them as a prisoner and the escort he is handcuffed to marching in unison: *quemadmodum eadem catena et custodiam et militem copulat, sic ista quae tam dissimilia sunt pariter incedunt: spem metus sequitur.*
27 Cf. e.g. the hopes and fears of Deianeira (*Her.* 9.42) and Laodamia (*Her.* 13.124), see Luck 1977 on *Tr.* 4.3.11f. Pichon 1966, 267 writes on the close association of *spes* and *timor* in love elegy: *Saepius sperare est confidere aut se amatum iri aut amantem rediturum, et ita spes timori frequenter opponitur.*

no case to be excised.²⁸ As is often the case, fear regularly proves stronger than hope, especially as time goes by and Ovid's longed-for return to Rome or transfer to another place is not achieved. Ovid expresses his concerns again at a significant position of his exilic poetry, the second elegy of the *Epistulae ex Ponto* (*Pont.* 1.2.61–4): *cum video quam sint mea fata tenacia, frangor / spesque levis magno victa timore cadit, / nec tamen ulterius quicquam sperove precorve / quam male mutato posse carere loco*²⁹ ("When I see the enduring nature of my fate, I weaken, and slight hope subsides, conquered by great fear. Yet I neither hope nor pray for anything other than, by exchange of ills, to be free to leave this place").

In overall, in Ovid's exilic poems fear dominates his hopes. Fear is able both to fuel and to destroy hope. This is most emphatically stated in *Tristia* 2, Ovid's famous 'apology' to Augustus for his poetry. The poet's hope to appease the emperor both stems from fear and can be frustrated by fear (*Tr.* 2.153–4): *sic abeunt redeuntque mei variantque timores, / et spem placandi dantque negantque tui.* ("So my fears vanish, change, return, give, or deny me hope of pleasing you"). The association of fear and hope³⁰ acquires particular importance later on in the same elegy, when Ovid, using similar diction, addresses the emperor and asks him not to forget about him (*Tr.* 2.181f.): *parce, pater patriae, nec nominis immemor huius / olim placandi spem mihi tolle tui!* ("Spare me, father of the country, don't take away all hope of placating you, forgetful of my name!"). On the basis of Ovid's words some thirty lines above, Ovid essentially identifies Augustus with fear, since both threaten to crush his hopes.

3 *Spes*, *consolatio*, and a god

As seen above, hope is under the constant threat of fear. On the other hand, consolation in such adverse circumstances is beneficial to hope and actually

---

28 In contrast, the Stoics claimed that if one could free oneself from the passions of hope, despair, fear, and anger, then it would become possible to confront the trials and misfortunes of life without any great concern. Cf. Zeno *SVF* 1.51, fr.211, 3.92, fr.378; Cic. *Tusc.* 4.15, 3.24, *Fin.* 3.35.
29 Tissol 2014 on *Pont.* 1.2.61–2 notices the similarities of the language and content of 1.2.59–62 with *Tr.* 2.147–8.
30 For the mixing of hope and fear see also *Tr.* 4.3.11f.: *ei mihi, cur nimium quae sunt manifesta, requiro? / cur iacet ambiguo spes mea mixta metu?* ("Ah, why should I fear? I seek what is clearly known. Why should my hope be mixed with anxious dread?"). See further Luck 1977 on *Tr.* 1.1.101f., Helzle 2003, 178 and on *Pont.* 1.2.61–2, Ingleheart 2010 on *Tr.* 2.153.

nourishes it[31] (*Pont.* 1.3.3f.):[32] *reddita confusae nuper solacia menti / auxilium nostris spemque tulere malis* ("The solace you've lately granted my troubled mind brought help and hope to my ills"). By the same token, the consolation that Ovid gets from the letter of a loyal friend, Cotta Maximus, enables him to hope that the wrath of Augustus, the insulted god, will soften (*Pont.* 2.3.67f.):[33] *tum tua me primum solari littera coepit / et laesum flecti spem dare posse deum* ("Then your letters began to bring me comfort, bringing hope that the wounded god might be softened"). Although Ovid's hope here does not seem to have any religious connotations whatsoever, in the sense that he does not address or refer to the deified *Spes*, Ovid's hope is associated with Augustus, who is constantly portrayed as a god, Jupiter, in both the *Tristia* and the *Epistulae ex Ponto*.[34] All Ovid hopes for is to appease a god. His appeal to a deified figure arguably raises divine implications, especially in the light of the significance of hope in the social, religious, and political sphere of Rome. During the Republican age *spes* was mainly associated with military leadership, however during the imperial times *spes* became closely associated with the (deified) *princeps* and his qualities as the leader of the empire. Beginning with Augustus, hope was transformed into an extension of the personality of the emperor and stood for the promise of prosperity for the Roman people embodied by a charismatic leader.[35] Hence, it is only natural for Ovid to depict Augustus as the divine sponsor of hope.

---

31 Giving hope is the goal of every proper Consolatio, see Helzle 2003 on *Pont.* 2.3.67–8 and 1.3.3–4, and cf. e.g. Cic. *Tusc.* 3.33. For hope as encouragement and consolation (*spei solacium*) see most recently Cairns 2016, 25, 43 with n. 110.
32 Martin 2004, 111 n. 375 notices the medical imagery and terminology of lines 1.3.3–30. See also Gaertner 2005 on *Pont.* 1.3.5–6.
33 Ov. *Pont.* 4.12.41f.: *effice constanti profugum pietate tuendo, / ne sperata meam deserat aura ratem* ("See that the winds of hope don't desert my boat, protect the exile, with your endless devotion").
34 See e.g. *Tr.* 1.1.20, 1.2.3–4, 12, 1.3.37–40, 1.5.77–78, 2.37–40. See Owen 1924, 79–81, Scott 1930, 52–58, Green 1994, xxxii–xxxiii and on *Tr.* 4.3.63–70, Claassen 1999, 227, *idem* 2001, 36–39, *idem* 2008, 29–33, 125f., 177–183, Ciccarelli 2003 on *Tr.* 2.33–8, Gaertner 2005, 14, McGowan 2009, ch. 3, Ingleheart 2010 ad *Tr.* 2.33–42. Warde Fowler 1915 discusses the development in time and the changes in Augustus' presentation as Jupiter in Ovid's exile poetry. For Augustus as a *laesus deus* in Ovid's exile poetry, see Helzle 2003 on *Pont.* 1.4.43–4.
35 See Fears 1981, 882, Tataranni 2013, 67.

4 Deceiving *spes* / frustrated *spes*

In Hesiod's famous version of the tale of Pandora, hope was the only evil not to escape from Pandora's jar (*Works* 96–99):[36] μούνη δ' αὐτόθι Ἐλπὶς ἐν ἀρρήκτοισι δόμοισιν / ἔνδον ἔμεινε πίθου ὑπὸ χείλεσιν οὐδὲ θύραζε / ἐξέπτη· πρόσθεν γὰρ ἐπέμβαλε πῶμα πίθοιο / αἰγιόχου βουλῇσι Διὸς νεφεληγερέταο. Hope can be either good or bad: on the one hand, hope can be someone's only support and comfort in life, it can be the only thing that keeps them going; on the other hand, hope can be futile, deceiving, delusive, and frustrating, it may lead to error, overconfidence, and failure, both moral and practical.[37] Accordingly, Ovid does not always perceive hope as a positive sentiment. There are instances in which he takes it as a treacherous emotion[38] which makes his life at Tomis miserable and difficult, especially when he deals with the antithesis between *spes* and *res*[39] (*Pont.* 2.8.71f.), *aut ego me fallo nimioque cupidine ludor / aut spes exilii commodioris adest* ("Either I am deceiving myself, mocked by excess of longing, or hope of a more appropriate exile is here"). Hope involves desire for something and also some estimation of probability;[40] yearning and desire are essential

---

36 See Verdenius 1985, 66 on the competing interpretations of why hope remained in Pandora's jar.
37 On the dual nature of hope, see West 1978 on Hes. *Works* 96; Clay 2003, 103. For a thorough review of the question, posed by the Pandora tale, whether hope is good or bad for men, see Komornicka 1990.
38 In pseudo-Seneca's elegiac poem *De spe*, *Spes* is depicted as a deceiver, a sweet evil, and the sum of all evils (*De Spe* 1): *Spes fallax, Spes dulce malum, Spes summa malorum*. On this poem see Armstrong 1998.
39 Based on the contrast between *spes* and *res* Lucretius famously attacks the lovers' illusions and the *spes erotica* at *DRN* 4.1086–90. On the assonant and proverbial antithesis between *spes* and *res*, which is more cultivated in oratory than poetry, see Hardie 2002, 11f. Leander picks up this antithesis in his love letter to Hero (Ov. *Her.* 18.178): *et res non semper, spes mihi semper adest*. See Kenney 1996, *ad loc.*
40 In Schopenhauer's words: "Hope is to confuse the desire that something should occur with the probability that it will. Perhaps no man is free from this folly of the heart, which deranges the intellect's correct estimation of probability to such a degree as to make him think the event quite possible, even if the chances are only a thousand to one. And still, an unexpected misfortune is like a speedy death-stroke; while a hope that is always frustrated, and yet springs into life again, is like death by slow torture" [Essays of Schopenhauer, tr. by Mrs Rudolf Dircks, London: Walter Scott, 1897, p. 131]. In the Oxford English Dictionary hope is defined as "expectation of something desired, a feeling of expectation and desire combined". Lazarus 1999, 653 claims that "to hope is to believe that something positive, which does not presently apply to one's life, could still materialize, and so we yearn for it". Capps 2001, 53 similarly associates hope with desire: "Hoping is the perception that what one wants to happen will happen, a perception that is fueled by desire and in response to felt deprivation".

features of it.⁴¹ Very sensibly, Ovid seems to be aware of the fact that his burning desire to return to Rome or move to a better place may be distorting his perception of reality.

Ovid seems to be conscious of the dual and dubious influence of hope again at *Pont.* 3.7.21f.: *spem iuvat amplecti, quae non iuvat inrita semper, / et, fieri cupias si qua, futura putes* ("It helps to embrace hope — that's no help, being always in vain — and think that what you wish to occur, will happen"). Ovid realizes that hope is futile and illusory and he acknowledges its power to deceive and make someone believe that they can actually materialize their wishes. Such thoughts are also expressed when he voices his disappointment in his friends, upon whom he had placed his hopes, all in vain (*Pont.* 3.7.9f.): *quod bene de vobis speravi, ignoscite, amici: / talia peccandi iam mihi finis erit* ("Forgive me, friends: I hoped so much from you: let there be an end for me to such mistakes"). In this case, Ovid also touches upon the theme of *amicitia*, a relationship of trust which entails certain expectations from others.⁴² Hope can be an aid to friendship, it can be a cause of friendship, it can sustain friendship, it can also ward off the destructive social impact of despair.⁴³ Carried away by his hopes Ovid seems to have overestimated the care and loyalty of his friends.

The frustration of the hope Ovid had invested in his friends is combined with the frustration of his hope of appeasing the emperor, which appears in the later books of his exile poetry (*Pont.* 3.7.31f.): *cur aliquid de me speravi lenius umquam? / an fortuna mihi sic mea nota fuit* ("Why did I ever hope for any leniency in my case? Surely my fate was clear enough to me"). Already in *Tristia* 4 Ovid seems to have accepted the fact that he is going to die in exile (4.6.49f.): *una tamen spes est quae me soletur in istis, / haec fore morte mea non diuturna mala* ("There's only one hope that comforts me in all this; these troubles will not outlast my death"). This is truly a bitter realization. Ovid no longer seems to hope to return to Rome

---

41 See Cairns 2016, 16–19. Walsh 1974, 35 rightly notes that desiring (*cupere*) has a more derogatory sense that hoping (*sperare*) and that the Romans were slow to identify the two. Seneca (*Ben.* 7.17 and *Const. Sap.* 9.2) employed *spes* in the sense of "acquisitive aspiration towards worldly things" and eventually *spes* acquired the status of a vicious emotion to be excised by the wise men together with *aegritudo, metus,* and *laetitia*. Boethius' famous moral exhortations are characteristic (*Consol.* 1.7): *gaudia pelle, / pelle timorem, / spemque fugato / nec dolor adsit.*
42 For a scenario of deceived hopes in connection with power dynamics, cf. Juv. 9.125–34.
43 Cf. Cic. *Amic.* 23: *Cumque plurimas et maximas commoditates amicitia contineat, tum illa nimirum praestat omnibus, quod bonam spem praelucet in posterum nec debilitari animos aut cadere patitur.* See also Schwartz 2007, 122 and Schulz 2010, 131–136 on Aquinas' views on hope, trust, and friendship.

or move to some place closer. All he can now hope for is that his sufferings may last only a lifetime and not remain after his death. So far, as discussed above, Ovid has been nurturing hope for a move away from Tomis, but as the years go by and his situation remains unchanged Ovid's hope gives place to despair.[44] Disappointment and despair is a natural negative response when perceived goals cannot be achieved,[45] and Ovid's response is no exception to the rule. Judging by the way he depicts himself at *Tr.* 4.6.49f., it appears that Ovid's exilic *persona* has gone through the psychological stages which someone can go when they endure no progress against the constraints of their goal blockages: from hope to rage, from rage to despair, and from despair to apathy,[46] except of course that for obvious reasons Ovid cannot openly express his rage against the omnipotent emperor.

Things get even worse for Ovid after Augustus' death. The death of the *princeps* automatically signaled the death of Ovid's hope for return. He points that out very clearly with a striking *syllepsis*,[47] joining Augustus' life and his own hope (*Pont.* 4.6.15f.): *coeperat Augustus deceptae ignoscere culpae, / spem nostram terras deseruitque simul* ("Augustus was beginning to forgive my mindless error: he left the world, and my hopes, bereft together"). Ovid's loss of hope for return to Rome earns him the pity of his readers, who become emotionally involved in his sufferings.

To sum up: Ovid's exilic 'death'[48] would normally leave no room for hope, still hope, the *spes salutis*, springs eternal on the icy coast of the Black sea and is the poet's most reliable companion and unfailing partner, along with love and nostalgia for his friends and family back in Rome. The banished Ovid finds himself in a very difficult situation and is totally unable to influence the course of events. His sole provider of hope, the only person that can bring Ovid back to Rome, is Augustus, the offended god who is thousands of miles away and whose priority is certainly not Ovid's recall from exile. On the one hand, Ovid's exilic *persona* derives pleasure from his hopes, which arise from the idea that his return to Rome may be achieved with a little help from his friends; on the other hand,

---

[44] On hope and despair, see e.g. Lazarus 1999, Nesse 1999. For a clear distinction between hope and despair, see Meirav 2009, 222–227. For Greek terms about despair and for the opposition between despair (negative) and hope (positive), see Cairns 2016, 42f.
[45] Repeated and profound goal blockages result in negative emotional responses, see Snyder *et al.* 1996.
[46] These stages of course are not limited to any particular pattern for all people, see Rodriguez-Hanley & Snyder 2000, 41.
[47] See Akrigg 2006, *ad loc.*
[48] For exile as death, see n. 17.

his hopes are always mixed with fear and pain arising from the awareness that the satisfaction of his burning desire is still out of reach. Either mixed with fear or strengthened by the comfort of his loved ones, Ovid's hope in exile is not illusory: hope may occasionally deceive and mislead him, however it does not distort his overall perception of reality. In the end, Ovid's hope receives a serious blow when Augustus dies and then vanishes unfulfilled when the poet himself dies on the inhospitable shore of the Black sea.

Bibliography

Adam, T. 1970. *Clementia Principis*, Stuttgart.
Akrigg, M.B. 2006. *The Last Poems of Ovid: A New Edition, with Commentary, of the Fourth Book of the Epistulae ex Ponto* [ebook: Original unpublished edition 1985. First published edition, corrected and augmented 2006].
Armstrong, M.S. 1998. *"Hope the Deceiver": Pseudo-Seneca De Spe (Anth. Lat. 415 Riese)*, Hildesheim/Zurich/New York.
Aronson, R. 1999. "Hope after Hope?," in: *Social Research* 66.2, 471–94.
Boyle, A.J. 2003. *Ovid and the Monuments: A Poet's Rome*, Bendigo.
Bux, E. 1948. "*Clementia Romana:* Ihr Wesen und ihre Bedeutung für die Politik des römischen Reiches," in: *WJA* 3, 210–31.
Cairns, D.L. 2008. "Look Both ways: Studying Emotion in Ancient Greek," in: *Critical Quarterly* 50, 43–63.
—— 2016. "Metaphors for Hope in Archaic and Classical Greek Poetry," in: R.R. Caston/R.A. Kaster (eds.), *Hope, Joy, and Affection in the Classical World. Emotions of the Past*, Oxford/New York, 13–44.
Capps, D. 2001. *Agents of Hope: A Pastoral Psychology*, Eugene, Oregon.
Caston, R.R./R.A. Kaster (eds.). 2016 *Hope, Joy, and Affection in the Classical World: Emotions of the past*, Oxford/New York.
Chaniotis, A. 2012. "Unveiling Emotions in the Greek World: Introduction," in: A. Chaniotis (ed.), *Unveiling Emotions: Sources and Methods for the Study of Emotions in the Greek World*, Stuttgart, 11–31.
Ciccarelli, I. 2003. *Commento al II libro dei Tristia di Ovidio*, Bari.
Claassen, J.-M. 1986. Poeta, Exsul, Vates: A Stylistic and Literary Analysis of Ovid's Tristia and Epistulae ex Ponto, Diss. Stellenbosch.
—— 1987. "*Error* and the Imperial Household: An Angry God and the Exiled Ovid's Fate," in: *AClass* 30, 31–47.
—— 1988. "Ovid's Poems from Exile. The Creation of a Myth and the Triumph of Poetry," in: *A&A* 34, 158–169.
—— 1996. "Exile, Death and Immortality: Voices from the Grave," in: *Latomus* 55, 571–590.
—— 1999. *Displaced Persons: The Literature of Exile: From Cicero to Boethius*, Madison/London.
—— 2001. "The Singular Myth: Ovid's Use of Myth in the Exilic Poetry," in: *Hermathena* 170, 11–64.
—— 2008. *Ovid Revisited: The Poet in Exile*, London.
Clark, M.E. 1981. The Evidence for Spes as an Early Imperial Idea, Diss. Indiana University, Bloomington.
—— 1983. "*Spes* in the Early Imperial Cult: The Hope of Augustus," in: *Numen* 30.1, 80–105.
Clay, J.S. 2003. *Hesiod's Cosmos*, Cambridge.

Day, J.P. 1970. "The Anatomy of Hope and Fear," in: *Mind* 79, 369–384.
—— 1998. "More About Hope and Fear," in: *Ethical Theory and Moral Practice* 1, 121–123.
Doblhofer, E. 1987. *Exil und Emigration: Zum Erlebnis der Heimatferne in der römischen Literatur*, Darmstadt.
Drucker, M. 1977. *Der verbannte Dichter und der Kaiser-Gott: Studien zu Ovids späten Elegien*. Diss. Leipzig.
Ehlers, W.W. 1988. "Poet und Exil: Zum Verständnis der Exildichtung Ovids," in: *A&A* 34, 144–157.
Evans, H.B. 1983. *Publica carmina: Ovid's Books from Exile*, Lincoln/London.
Fears, J.R. 1981. "The Cult of Virtues and Roman Imperial Ideology," in: *ANRW* 17.2, 827–948.
Fitton Brown, A.D. 1985. "The Unreality of Ovid's Tomitan Exile," in: *LCM* 10.2, 18–22.
Ford, B.B. 1977. *Tristia II: Ovid's Opposition to Augustus*, Diss. Rutgers University.
Fulkerson, L. 2013a. "Plutarch and the Ambiguities of ἐλπίς," in: D.L. Cairns/L. Fulkerson (eds.), *Emotions between Greece and Rome*, BICS Supplement 125, London, 67–84.
—— 2013b. *No Regrets: Remorse in Classical Antiquity*, Oxford/New York.
Fullerton, M.D. 1990. *The Archaistic Style in Roman Statuary*, Leiden.
Gaertner, J.F. 2005. *Ovid Epistulae ex Ponto, Book 1*. Edited with Introduction, Translation, and Commentary, Oxford.
—— 2007. "Ovid and the 'Poetics of Exile': How Exilic is Ovid's Exile Poetry?," in: J.F. Gaertner (ed.), *Writing Exile: The Discourse of Displacement in Greco-Roman Antiquity and Beyond*, Leiden/Boston, 155–72.
Galasso, L. 2009. "Epistulae ex Ponto," in P.E. Knox (ed.), *A Companion to Ovid*, Chichester/Malden, MA, 194–206.
Goold, G.P. 1983. "The Cause of Ovid's Exile," in: *ICS* 8, 94-107.
Green, P. 1994. *Ovid: The Poems of Exile*, London.
Green, R. 1982. "*Carmen et Error*: πρόφασις and αἰτία in the Matter of Ovid's Exile," in: *ClAnt* 1, 202–220.
Hardie, Ph. 2002. *Ovid's Poetics of Illusion*, Cambridge.
Helzle, M. 1988. "Ovid's Poetics of Exile," in: *ICS* 13, 73–83.
—— 2003. *Ovids Epistulae ex Ponto*. Buch I-II. Kommentar, Heidelberg.
Hexter, R.J. 2007. "Ovid and the Medieval Exilic Imaginary," in: J.F. Gaertner (ed.), *Writing Exile: The Discourse of Displacement in Greco-Roman Antiquity and Beyond*, Leiden/Boston, 209–236.
Hoben, W. 1978. "Caesar-Nachfolge und Caesar-Abkehr in den Res gestae divi Augusti," in: *Gymnasium* 85, 1–19.
Holleman, A.W.J. 1976. "*Femina virtus*: Some New Thoughts on the Conflict between Augustus and Ovid," in: N. Barbu/E. Dobroiu/M. Nasta (eds.), *Ovidianum. Acta Conventus Omnium Gentium Ovidianis Studiis Fovendis*, Bucharest, 341–355.
Ingleheart, J. 2010. *A Commentary on Ovid, Tristia Book 2*, Oxford.
Kaster, R.A. 2005. *Emotion, Restraint, and Community in Ancient Rome*, Oxford.
Kenney, E.J. (ed.) 1996. *Ovid: Heroides XVI–XXI*, Cambridge.
Komornicka, A.M. 1990. "L'*elpis* hésiodique dans la Jarre de Pandore," in: *Eos* 78, 63–77.
Konstan, D. 2006. *The Emotions of the Ancient Greeks: Studies in Aristotle and Classical Literature*, Toronto.
Lazarus, R.S. 1999. "Hope: An Emotion and a Vital Coping Resource against Despair," in: *Social Research* 66, 653–78.
Lear, J. 2006. *Radical Hope: Ethics in the Face of Cultural Devastation*, Cambridge, Mass.
Luck, G. 1967–1977. *P. Ovidius Naso: Tristia*, 2 vols. (Vol. 1 Text and Translation / Vol. 2. Commentary), Heidelberg.

Martin, J.A. 2004. *Was ist Exil? Ovids Tristia und Epistulae ex Ponto*, Hildesheim/Zurich/New York.
McGowan, M.M. 2009. *Ovid in Exile. Power and Poetic Redress in the Tristia and Epistulae ex Ponto*, Leiden/Boston.
Meirav, A. 2009. "The Nature of Hope," in: *Ratio* n.s. 22, 216–233.
Michalopoulos, A.N. 2011. "Ovid's Last Wor(l)d," in: J. Ingleheart (ed.), *Two Thousand Years of Solitude. Exile after Ovid*, Oxford, 275–88.
—— 2014. "*Laudatio Tomitana*: Praising the Emperor from the Black Sea," in: S. Tzounakas (ed.), *Praises of Roman Leaders in Latin Literature*, Nicosia, 140–53.
Mittleman, A. 2009. *Hope in a Democratic Age: Philosophy, Religion, and Political Theory*, Oxford.
Nagle, B.R. 1980. *The Poetics of Exile: Program and Polemic in the "Tristia" and "Epistulae ex Ponto" of Ovid*, Brussels.
Nesse, R.M. 1999. "The Evolution of Hope and Despair," in: *Social Research* 66.2, 429–469.
Nussbaum, M.C. 2001. *Upheavals of Thought: The Intelligence of Emotions*, Cambridge.
Owen, S.G. 1902. *Ovid's* Tristia *Book 1*. 3rd ed. (1st ed. 1885), Oxford.
—— 1924. *P. Ovidi Nasonis Tristium Liber Secundus*, Oxford (repr. Amsterdam 1967).
Perassi, C. 1991. *Spes: Iconografia, Simbologia, Ideologia nella Moneta Romana (I–III sec.)*, Milan.
Pichon, R. 1966. *Index verborum amatoriorum*, Hildesheim.
Rodriguez-Hanley, A./C.R. Snyder 2000. "The Demise of Hope: On Losing Positive Thinking," in: C.R. Snyder (ed.), *Handbook of Hope: Theory, Measures, and Applications*, San Diego, CA, 39–54.
Schlosser, J.A. 2013. "'Hope, Danger's Comforter': Thucydides, Hope, Politics," in: *Journal of Politics* 75, 169–82.
Schulz, J.W. 2010. Friendship and Fidelity: An Historical and Critical Examination, Diss. Marquette University.
Schwartz, D. 2007. *Aquinas on Friendship*, Oxford.
Scott, K. 1930. "Emperor Worship in Ovid," in: *TAPA* 61, 43–69.
Snyder, C.R. 2000. *Handbook of Hope: Theory, Measures, and Applications*, San Diego, CA.
Snyder, C.R./S.C. Sympson/F.C. Ybasco/T.F. Borders/M.A. Babyak/R.L. Higgins. 1996. "Development and Validation of the State Hope Scale," in: *Journal of Personality and Social Psychology* 70, 321–335.
Syme, R. 1978. *History in Ovid*, Oxford.
Tataranni, F. 2013. "Hope and Leadership in Ancient Rome," in: *Teoria* 33, 65–78.
Thibault, J.C. 1964. *The Mystery of Ovid's Exile*, Berkeley/Los Angeles.
Tissol, G. 2014. *Ovid: Epistulae ex Ponto, Book I*, Cambridge.
Verdenius, W.J. 1985. *A Commentary on Hesiod's Works and Days 1–382*, Leiden.
Verdière, R. 1992. *Le Secret du voltigeur d'amour ou le mystère de la relégation d'Ovide*, Brussels.
Videau-Delibes, A. 1991. *Les Tristes d'Ovide et l'élégie romaine: une poétique de la rupture*, Paris.
Walsh, P.G. 1974. "Spes Romana, Spes Christiana," in: *Prudentia* 6, 33–42.
Warde Fowler, W. 1915. "Note on Ovid, *Tristia* III.6.8 (Augustus et Juppiter)," in: *CR* 29, 46–47.
Weinstock, S. 1971. *Divus Iulius*, Oxford.
West, M.L. 1978. *Hesiod's Works and Days: Edited with Prolegomena and Commentary*, Oxford.
Williams, G.D. 1994. *Banished Voices: Readings in Ovid's Exile Poetry*, Cambridge.
—— 2002a. "Ovid's Exile Poetry: *Tristia, Epistulae ex Ponto* and *Ibis*," in: P. Hardie (ed.), *The Cambridge Companion to Ovid*, Cambridge, 233–245.
—— 2002b. "Ovid's Exilic Poetry: Worlds Apart," in: B.W. Boyd (ed.), *Brill's Companion to Ovid*, Leiden, 337–81.
Wistrand, E. 1968. *Sallust on Judicial Murders in Rome: A Philological and Historical Study*, Studia Graeca et Latina Gothoburgensia XXIV, Gothenburg.

Antony Augoustakis
Quaenam spes hominum? Dashed Hopes in Statius' *Thebaid*

After Lucan's historical epic on the civil war between Caesar and Pompey, composed under Nero, and after Valerius Flaccus' return to mythological epic and the Argonautic saga in the early Flavian period,[1] Statius chooses the Theban cycle for his *Thebaid*, a poem about civil strife and fratricide in the house of Oedipus, followed by the subsequent war between Creon of Thebes and Theseus of Athens.[2] To be sure, Statius returns to a topic in mythological epic that has deep roots in Rome's own foundational past, Aeneas the wanderer, Remus and Romulus. The epic poem unfolds in twelve books, in an attempt to restore the Virgilian ktistic epic model,[3] after the Ovidian experimentation in the fifteen books of the *Metamorphoses*.[4] Unfortunately we do not know how many books Lucan intended for the *De bello civili* or Valerius for his *Argonautica*, but we do know of Statius' Flavian competitor, Silius Italicus, who dedicates seventeen books to the *Punica*. Statius draws on a variety of sources; the Theban tradition was rich and across many genres: we ought to remember that Statius' Neapolitan father, Statius the grammarian, had offered his son a profoundly wealthy education in the Greek tradition, not just epic and tragedy, but poets like Stesichorus, Pindar, and Corinna (Stat. *Silu*. 5.3. 149–58). The relevant Greek tragedies are fully exploited by Statius as he recounts Polynices' trip to Argos, his alliance with king Adrastus, the march of the Seven against Thebes, their stop in Nemea and encounter with Hypsipyle, former queen of Lemnos, and her nursling, the baby Opheltes/Archemorus, the war in Thebes with the ensuing fratricide, and finally the suppliants' trip to Athens to seek Theseus' intervention for the cremation of the Argive dead.[5] The epic ends with Creon's death in the hands of Theseus and the burial of the Argive soldiers by the women, as Statius swiftly brings his epic to an end:

---

1 I follow Stover 2008 and 2012 for an early dating of the Argonautica before the end of the 70s CE.
2 For the most recent overview and survey of poem with up-to-date bibliography, see Augoustakis 2016b, 7–11.
3 Ganiban 2007 offers an extensive discussion of Statius' exploitation and transformation of Virgil's *Aeneid*.
4 For Statius' Ovidianisms in the Theban narrative, see most recently Keith 2014.
5 On Statius' use of Greek tragedy, see Bessone 2011, Hulls 2014, and Marinis 2015.

> non ego, centena si quis mea pectora laxet
> uoce deus, tot busta simul uulgique ducumque,
> tot pariter gemitus dignis conatibus aequem:
> turbine quo sese caris instrauerit audax
> ignibus Euadne fulmenque in pectore magno
> quaesierit; quo more iacens super oscula saeui
> corporis infelix excuset Tydea coniunx;
> ut saeuos narret uigiles Argia sorori;
> Arcada, quo planctu genetrix Erymanthia clamet,
> Arcada, consumpto seruantem sanguine uultus,
> Arcada, quem geminae pariter fleuere cohortes.
> uix nouus ista furor ueniensque implesset Apollo,
> et mea iam longo meruit ratis aequore portum.   (Stat. *Theb.* 12.797–809)[6]

> Were some god to loose my breast in hundred voices I could not in worthy effort do justice to so many pyres of captains and common folk alike, such a chorus of groaning: telling how Evadne boldly strewed herself on beloved flames, seeking the thunderbolt in the mighty breast; in what fashion Tydeus' hapless wife excuses him as she lies over the savage corpse's kisses; how Argia tells her sister of the cruel sentinels; with what lamentation the Erymanthian mother bewails the Arcadian, for whom both armies wept alike. Hardly would a new frenzy and Apollo's coming have discharged the task; and my bark in the wide ocean has already earned her harbor.

Scholars often point out that lament here constitutes a means of resolution, an outlet for emotion and closure in this otherwise dark epic of *nefas*.[7] At the same time, other recent readings of the poem have sought to analyze this closural gesture as one that privileges lack of resolution, the silencing of women's voice, of female lament; as Statius trespasses into the territory of elegy, he has to rebuild and reimpose epic boundaries; Statius' *ratis*, boat, has to find its destined harbor as soon as possible; to recount the many voices of lament and the power of grief proves too much of a burden for the epic poet to bear.[8] In this chapter, I would like to discuss the role of *spes* in the poem, as I demonstrate how the use of the term punctuates the narrative in important turning points. Here I follow a line of inquiry that will allow me to allign myself with those who opt for a pessimistic reading of the poem, namely that a disastrous future is foreshadowed as a continuation and repetition of the gloomy present.

---

6   Texts and translations used are as follows: for Statius, Hill 1996 and Shackleton Bailey 2003; for Lucan, Shackleton Bailey 1997 and Braund 1992; for Seneca, Gummere 1917.
7   E.g., Ripoll 1998; Braund 1996 and 2006; Franchet d'Espèrey 1999; Bessone 2011; Putnam 2016.
8   E.g., Dietrich 1999; Keith 2000; Ganiban 2007; Coffee 2009; Augoustakis 2010; Lovatt 2013 and 2016.

First, I would like to look at some passages from Seneca and Lucan, especially with an emphasis on the Stoic treatment of hope in Statius' predecessors. After Caesar's crossing of the Rubicon and the desperation and consternation it caused Italy and the city of Rome in particular, Lucan prefaces the second book of the *De bello civili* with a sharp criticism levelled against the divine, whatever we can call 'divine'. By apostrophising Jupiter, the poet is asking a fundamental question in this programmatic preface to the second book of the poem: why has the king of the gods apprised mortals of upcoming disasters by means of omens and thus imposed on them such an anxiety (*curam*, 5) of the coming civil war. The aetiological explanation blends Stoic and Epicurean philosophical elements to provide a world view that is important for our understanding of hope in the context of civil war:

> siue parens rerum, cum primum informia regna
> materiamque rudem flamma cedente recepit,
> fixit in aeternum causas, qua cuncta coercet
> se quoque lege tenens, et saecula iussa ferentem
> fatorum immoto diuisit limite mundum,
> siue nihil positum est, sed fors incerta uagatur
> fertque refertque uices et habet mortalia casus,
> sit subitum quodcumque paras; sit caeca futuri
> mens hominum fati; <u>liceat sperare timenti</u>.   (Luc. 2.7–15)

> Perhaps when the Creator first took up his shapeless realm of raw matter after the conflagration had died down, he fixed causes for eternity, binding himself too by his all-controlling law, and with the immovable boundary of destiny arranged the universe to introduce prescribed ages. Or perhaps nothing is ordained, but Chance at random wanders bringing change after change, and accident is master of mortal affairs. Whatever you intend, let it be sudden; let men's minds be blind to future disaster; <u>let the fearful have hope!</u>

Lucan expresses deep anxiety as to whether one ought to follow the Stoic vision of a benevolent deity obedient to fate or the Epicurean attribution of events to random chance.[9] According to Stoic doctrine, hope and fear are harmful emotions that disturb the soul. The last phrase in the poet's apostrophe *liceat sperare timenti* constitutes a strong statement that even if man is afraid, he should be spared foreknowledge and be left with hope as a medicine for the unknown. This is a radically different view of hope, in my opinion, since it unexpectedly promotes *spes* to same level as fear, *timor*: when you fear, one would think, there is no hope. But Lucan keeps both feelings in this last statement in a (vain) effort to

---

[9] See Feeney 1991, 279–80 and Fantham 1992, 82. As Leibniz once claimed, Stoicism is a philosophy of patience rather than hope; see Rutherford 2003.

offer a solution, a way out of the grim present of civil war strife. Neither emotion will ultimately be of much help.

This conjunction of hope and fear is also found in Seneca's fifth epistle, a text evoked by Lucan in the passage above. Seneca includes instructions on how to focus on the present:

> apud Hecatonem nostrum inueni cupiditatium finem etiam ad timoris remedia proficere. 'Desines', inquit, 'timere, si sperare desieris'. Dices: 'Quomodo ista tam diuersa pariter eunt?' Ita est, mi Lucili: cum uideantur dissidere, coniuncta sunt. Quemadmodum eadem catena et custodiam et militem copulat, sic ista, quae tam dissimilia sunt, pariter incedunt; spem metus sequitur. Nec miror ista sic ire; utrumque pendentis animi est, utrumque futuri exspectatione solliciti. Maxima autem utriusque causa est, quod non ad praesentia aptamur, sed cogitationes in longinqua praemittimus. Itaque prouidentia, maximum bonum condicionis humanae, in malum uersa est. Ferae pericula, quae uident, fugiunt; cum effugere, securae sunt; nos et uenturo torquemur et praeterito. (Sen. *Ep.* 5.7–9)
>
> I find in the writings of our Hecato that the limiting of desires helps also to cure fears: "Cease to hope," he says, "and you will cease to fear." "But how," you will reply, "can things so different go side by side?" In this way, my dear Lucilius: though they do seem at variance, yet they are really united. Just as the same chain fastens the prisoner and the soldier who guards him, so hope and fear, dissimilar as they are, keep step together; fear follows hope. I am not surprised that they proceed in this way; each alike belongs to a mind that is in suspense, a mind that is fretted by looking forward to the future. But the chief cause of both these ills is that we do not adapt ourselves to the present, but send our thoughts a long way ahead. And so foresight, the noblest blessing of the human race, becomes perverted. Beasts avoid the dangers which they see, and when they have escaped them are free from care; but we men torment ourselves over that which is to come as well as over that which is past.

The adoption of Hecato's pithy statement, *desines timere, si sperare desieris*, encapsulates the Senecan alternative medicine to fear, abandonment of hope: hope constitutes a dangerous emotion for the Stoic philosopher, one that feeds on constant anguish and therefore urges him on to forsake tranquility.[10] As Seneca advises, *providentia* can be perverted, precisely because humans look ahead. In this literary landscape, Statius' *Thebaid*, as we shall see, offers little improvement compared to Lucan's dark, pessimistic outlook at both the present and (less certain) future, while Statian characters do not follow the Senecan path either. And before we look at particular instances of *spes/sperare* in Statius' epic, I would like to clarify here that I am not attempting to connect Statius with any particular philosophical school, since Latin poets are highly eclectic and elude easy categorization —and Statius himself draws on a variety of sources.

---

10 Cf. *Ep.* 98.6, *Dial.* 9.2.7–9, *Tro.* 425; see Edwards 2014, 329 and the Introduction to this volume.

In *Thebaid* 1, the first mention of hope is intriguing: Jupiter calls a council of the gods to declare that Argos and Thebes ought to be punished for their many offenses against gods and humankind. Jove responds to Oedipus' curse on his sons, with which the book opens, by confirming that Oedipus' ill-wish deserves to be fulfilled:[11]

> iam iam rata uota tulisti,
> dire senex. meruere tuae, meruere tenebrae
> ultorem sperare Iouem. noua sontibus arma
> iniciam regnis, totumque a stirpe reuellam
> exitiale genus. belli mihi semina sunto
> Adrastus socer et superis adiuncta sinistris
> conubia. hanc etiam poenis incessere gentem
> decretum; neque enim arcano de pectore fallax
> Tantalus et saeuae periit iniuria mensae.   (Stat. *Theb.* 1.239–47)

Now, now your prayers are answered, dire ancient. Your darkness has deserved, ay truly, to hope for Jove as its avenger. I shall bring new warfare on the guilty reigns and tear the whole deadly stock out from the root. Let Adrastus' gift of his daughter in a marriage unblessed of heaven be my seed of battle. This line also I have resolved to assail and punish, for false Tantalus and the outrage of the cruel banquet have not vanished from my secret heart.

The collocation *ultorem sperare* sets the tone quickly: the reader is informed that this is going to be an epic of vengeance (even uncontrolled vengeance and unleashed violence), as hope is tightly connected with revenge. Moreover, *ultio* and *spes* are here associated with the gods. Jupiter insists on Tantalus' deception, as he sows the seeds of war with an emphatic future imperative *sunto*, locating the *belli semina* in the fatal alliance between Adrastus and the two exiles, Tydeus and Polynices. Note here that marriage offers the illusory hope, expectation of posterity, as in the following passage, where we hear about Adrastus' daughters, Argia and Deipyle and their suitors:

> geminae mihi namque, nepotum
> laeta fides, aequo pubescunt sidere natae.
> quantus honos, quantusque pudor (ne credite patri)
> et super hesternas licuit cognoscere mensas.
> has tumidi solio et late dominantibus armis
> optauere uiri (longum enumerare Pheraeos
> Oebaliosque duces) et Achaea per oppida matres,

---

11 On the complex characterization of Jupiter in the *Thebaid*, see Criado 2000 and 2013; on this scene, see Ganiban 2007, 50–5.

spem generis, nec plura tuus despexerat Oeneus
foedera Pisaeisque socer metuendus habenis.   (Stat. *Theb*. 2.158–66)

For I have two daughters growing into womanhood under an equal star, happy pledge of grandchildren. Their grace and modesty (credit not their father) you could even judge at yesterday's feast. Men proud in throne and far-dominating arms (it'd be long to list the Pheraean and Oebalian chieftains), and mothers throughout the towns of Achaea have desired them, hope of posterity; nor did your Oeneus despise more matches or that other father feared for his Pisaean bridle.

The emphasis here is placed on the people's desire (*optauere*) to see offspring from these royal maidens.[12] I would like to return to the notion of *spes generis* when I discuss the role of the Epigoni in the poem, the descendants of the Seven.

In the first books of the *Thebaid*, Statius associates future hope with the exiled Polynices, while the possibilities afforded by such hope are only temporarily realized, in particular as soon as the Argive expedition begins. Immediately after Jupiter's proclamation in the first book, we find the exiled brother, Polynices, facing a *spes anxia*:

spes anxia mentem
extrahit et longo consumit gaudia uoto.
tunc sedet Inachias urbes Danaëiaque arua
et caligantes abrupto sole Mycenas
ferre iter impauidum, seu praeuia ducit Erinys,
seu fors illa uiae, siue hac inmota uocabat
Atropos.   (Stat. *Theb*. 1.322–8)

Torturing hope drags out his soul and in prolonged desire exhausts his joy. Then he decides to take his way boldly to the cities of Inachus and Danaë's fields and Mycenae darkened with sun cut short. Does a guiding Fury lead him on, or is it the chance of the road, or was inexorable Atropos summoning him that way?

It is either an Erinys or pure chance, *fors*, that guides the steps of Polynices, as we imagine him making his way south to the Peloponnese; compare, for instance, how a few lines later, *spes* is exploited again to indicate the swift passage of Oedipus' son through glades and valleys on his way to Argos: *spe concitus omni* ("urged on by all his hope," 1.382).[13]

---

12   On fateful marriage in the poem, see now Newlands 2016.
13   The tragic intertext of has been identified in Euripides' *Phoenissae*, when Polynices attacks his brother, Eteocles, claiming that the ever-watchful ἐλπίδες are his driving force that will eventually compel him to kill his brother and regain the throne: ἐλπίδες δ' οὔπω καθεύδουσ', αἷς πέποιθα σὺν θεοῖς / τόνδ' ἀποκτείνας κρατήσειν τῆσδε Θηβαίας χθονός ("but hope never sleeps,

Immediately after his wedding to Argia, Polynices can no longer rest; the memory of his haunting past urges him on to seek Thebes again, to seek revenge:

namque una soror producere tristes
exulis ausa uias; etiam hanc in limine primo
liquerat et magna lacrimas incluserat ira.
tunc quos excedens hilares (quis cultus iniqui
praecipuus ducis) et profugo quos ipse notarat
ingemuisse sibi per noctem ac luce sub omni
digerit; exedere animum dolor iraque demens
et, qua non grauior mortalibus addita curis,
spes, ubi longa uenit. talem sub pectore nubem
consilii uoluens Dircen Cadmique negatas
apparat ire domos.   (Stat. Theb. 2.313–23)

Only his sister dared bear the exile company on his sad way. Even her he had left on the threshold, stifling his tears in mighty rage. Every night and day he makes the count; whom had he himself marked rejoicing as he left, who paid particular court to the unrighteous ruler, and who had a tear for the fugitive? Grief and mad wrath devoured his soul, and hope, heaviest of mortal cares when long deferred. Revolving such a cloud of counsel in his breast, he makes ready to go to Dirce and the forbidden home of Cadmus.

As Kyle Gervais notes, *spes longa* echoes passages in Ovid's *Heroides*, where *spes longa* applies to erotic desire: it is therefore ironic that "Polynices' political *spes* even now is overcoming his erotic interest in Argia."[14] But one ought to consider how Polynices' hope springs from the past, as he is traumatized and perpetually stuck to the moment of his exile, looking back, overcome by *dolor* and *ira demens*— *ira* is repeated from 315, *incluserat ira*, when he stifles his tears in anger, as if enclosing this anger in a box to bring with him, a companion to his exile. Polynices wavers between present and past, between Antigone and Argia, love of Thebes and power vs. love of wife and his new family. In book 4, Polynices' entry in the catalogue of the Argive forces joining the expedition is described in the following manner:

---

hope which makes me confident that with the gods' help I will kill this man and rule Thebes," Eur. *Phoen.* 634–5). The lines recall Jocasta's earlier statement about the role of ἐλπίδες in exile: αἱ δ' ἐλπίδες βόσκουσι φυγάδας, ὡς λόγος ("exiles, they say, live on hopes," Eur. *Phoen.* 3). On hope and exile, see Michalopoulos in this volume.

14 See Gervais 2017, 187 with Ov. *Ep.* 16.105, 17.74, 18.175–6; cf. also Sen. *Ep.* 101.4: *quam stultum est aetatem disponere ne crastini quidem dominum! O quanta dementia est spes longas inchoantium* ("But how foolish it is to set out one's life, when one is not even owner of the morrow! Oh, what madness it is to plot out far-reaching hopes!").

> iam regnum matrisque sinus fidasque sorores
> spe uotisque tenet, tamen et de turre suprema
> attonitam totoque extantem corpore longe
> respicit Argian; haec mentem oculosque reducit
> coniugis et dulces auertit pectore Thebas.   (Stat. *Theb.* 4.88–92)

> Already in hope and prayer he possesses his realm and his mother's bosom and his faithful sisters, yet looks far back to Argia as she stands out with all her body from a turret-edge distraught. She calls back her husband's mind and eyes and turns sweet Thebes from his heart.

Polynices looks forward in hope and prayer that he returns home, as he looks back to Argia, just as he remembers Antigone in book 2.[15] The exiled brother is torn between past, present, and future, a future, however, that encapsulates his past, with a startling allusion to incest: *iam regnum matrisque <u>sinus</u> fidasque sorores / tenet.*[16] And even Argia participates in this back and forth between past, present, and future, when she asks her father Adrastus at the end of the previous book, book 3 that is, to allow the expedition to go forward:

>   da bella, pater, generique iacentis
> aspice res humiles, atque hanc, pater, aspice prolem
> exulis ...
> non equidem has umquam culparim, nata, querelas;
> pone metus, laudanda rogas nec digna negari.
> sed mihi multa dei (nec tu sperare quod urgues
> desine), multa metus regnique uolubile pondus
> subiciunt animo.   (Stat. *Theb.* 3.696–8 and 712–16)

> Give war, father; regard the lowly fortunes of your fallen son-in-law and this child of an exile. One day he will be ashamed of his birth ...
> Never, daughter, should I blame these plaints. Lay fears aside; what you ask is praiseworthy nor meet to be denied. But the gods (nay, cease not to hope for what you urge) and my qualms, and the ever shifting burden of ruling give me many a thought.

Argia sets the expedition in motion by making use of her son, Thersander, in her appeal to Adrastus, a son who one day will be ashamed of his father, if there is no vindication.[17] Adrastus cannot grant her wish immediately but assuages her fears by urging her not to stop hoping (*nec tu sperare quod urgues / desine*). The

---

15   See Parkes 2012, 91 for further intertexts and bibliography.
16   See Hershkowitz 1998, 278 on the sexual overtones.
17   For a discussion of the scene's contrast between uxorilocal residence in Argos and virilocal residence in Thebes, see Bernstein 2008, 96–7. On the various intertexts, see Hershkowitz 2016, 136–9.

expedition is to be fatal, and in the opening of book 4, immediately after Argia's request to her father, the seer, Amphiaraus, pretends to hope,[18] even though the sacrifices are telling:

> dicta dies aderat. cadit ingens rite Tonanti
> Gradiuoque pecus, nullisque secundus in extis
> pallet et armatis simulat sperare sacerdos.   (Stat. *Theb.* 4.13–15)

> The appointed day arrives. A huge number of beasts fall in ritual sacrifice to the Thunderer and Gradivus, and the priest, finding no good in the entrails, feigns hope to the men in arms.

As the poem progresses, the reader comes across several manifestations of dashed hopes, and the next two instances are associated with kinsmen. The first occurs during the chariot race in honor of the dead baby, Opheltes, in Nemea. Here one of the participants, Polynices, has an accident as he falls off the chariot and is almost run over by the others:

> ruit ilicet exul
> Aonius nexusque diu per terga uolutus
> exuit: abripitur longe moderamine liber
> currus; at hunc putri praeter tellure iacentem
> Taenarii currus et Thessalus axis et heros
> Lemnius obliqua, quantum uitare dabatur,
> transabiere fuga. tandem caligine mersum
> erigit accursu comitum caput aegraque tollit
> membra solo, et socero redit haud speratus Adrasto.   (Stat. *Theb.* 6.504–12)

> The Aonian exile straightway plunges and sprawls for a space on his back, till he frees himself from the ties; the chariot, released from guidance, is swept afar. As for him, as he lies on the sandy earth the Taenarian car and the wheels of Thessaly and the Lemnian hero fly past him, swerving to avoid him as best they could. At last his companions run up, he raises his head, sunk in darkness, and lifts his injured limbs from the ground, and returns unhoped-for to Adrastus his wife's father.

His return to his father-in-law Adrastus is unexpected, unhoped for, *haud speratus*, an opportunity for the poet to compose a quasi-epitaph for the exile, who, had he died on the spot, would have been celebrated in a hero-cult, greater than Archemorus':

---

18   See Parkes 2012, 54 on the repetition of the phrase from Virgil and Lucan.

> quis mortis, Thebane, locus, nisi dura negasset
> Tisiphone, quantum poteras dimittere bellum!
> te Thebe fraterque palam, te plangeret Argos,
> te Nemea, tibi Lerna comas Larisaque supplex
> poneret, Archemori maior colerere sepulcro. (Stat. *Theb.* 6.513–17)

> "What a chance to die, Theban, had not harsh Tisiphone denied! What a war you could have banished! Thebes and your brother would have mourned you in public, and Argos and Nemea; for you Lerna and Larisa would prayerfully have sacrificed their hair. Your grave would have had more worship than Archemorus".

As the baby's death rehearses the events that will soon take place in Thebes, Statius exploits the counterfactual scenario to underscore the unreliability of hope in Polynices' pursuits; from the perspective of the poet and Adrastus, it would have been much better if Polynices had died in Nemea, not in the hands of his brother, Eteocles.[19] And finally, this frustration of Polynices' hopes and investment in the future comes to an abrupt end with the death of Tydeus, who in the last minute manages to lose the gift of immortality/*athanasia* that Pallas Minerva brings to him in book 8: he eats the brains of his opponent Melanippus as he dies on the battlefield, having given into madness, *furor* and *ira*.[20] Polynices laments the loss of Tydeus as a *spes suprema* in the opening of the following book:

> hasne tibi, armorum spes o suprema meorum,
> Oenide, grates, haec praemia digna rependi,
> funus ut inuisa Cadmi tellure iaceres
> sospite me? nunc exul ego aeternumque fugatus,
> quando alius misero ac melior mihi frater ademptus. (Stat. *Theb.* 9.49–53)

> Is this the thanks, last hope of my arms, son of Oeneus, this the worthy reward I have rendered you, that you lie a corpse on the hated earth of Cadmus while I survive? Now indeed I am an exile, banished forever, since my other and better brother has been taken from me.

Tydeus' demise reinforces the feeling and intensity of Polynices' exiled status: *nunc exul ego aeternumque fugatus*, especially since Tydeus and Polynices were brothers, a bond stronger than the one uniting Polynices to his own blood brother, Eteocles.[21]

As has become clear from my foregoing analysis, in an epic that 'celebrates' the nefarious murder of brothers there can be no hope for the future of

---

19 See Nagel 1999 on the counterfactual scenario played here.
20 See Augoustakis 2016a.
21 On Tydeus as Polynices' *melior frater*, see Korneeva 2011, 99–103.

humankind. In fact, before the fratricide, Capaneus, the theomach who fights Jupiter himself, is struck down by the king of the Olympians at the end of book 10.[22] As Capaneus climbs up to the towers of Thebes and threatens heaven and earth, Jupiter laughs at the madman's audacity:

> ingemuit dictis superum dolor; ipse furentem
> risit et incussa sanctarum mole comarum,
> 'quaenam spes hominum tumidae post proelia Phlegrae?
> tune etiam feriendus?' ait.   (Stat. *Theb.* 10.907–10)

> At his words the High Ones grieved and groaned. Himself laughed at the madman, and shaking the mass of his sacred hair "What hope," says he, "do men have after the battles of presumptious Phlegra? Must I strike you down too?"

And yet, it is not easy to kill this born-again Titan/Giant: as we expect him to drop dead, when he catches on fire, *stat tamen*:

> stat tamen, extremumque in sidera uersus anhelat,
> pectoraque inuisis obicit fumantia muris;
> nec caderet, sed membra uirum terrena relinquunt,
> exuiturque animus; paulum si tardius artus
> cessissent, potuit fulmen sperare secundum.   (Stat. *Theb.* 10.935–9)

> But still he stands and breathes his last against the stars, leaning his smoking breast against the hated walls. Nor would he have fallen; but his earthly limbs desert him and his spirit is set free. If his body had yielded a little later, he might have hoped for a second bolt.

In defiance, the poet creates a counterfactual scenario, imagining Capaneus welcoming an encore of Jupiter's performance: had his body yielded a little later, *potuit fulmen sperare secundum* (with an emphatic indicative *potuit*). But Jupiter is weary, when asking: *tune etiam feriendus?* He reaffirms that human *spes* cannot exist in a post-Phlegra world, while of course the reality of the situation easily serves to counter this argument: yes, this is a post-Phlegra world where Gigantomachy still exists and can wreak havoc!

As Statius explains after the fratricide, the hopes of the two brothers were cheated by a personified *Fortuna*:

> et iam laeta ducum spes elusisse duorum
> res Amphionias alio sceptrumque maligna
> transtulerat Fortuna manu, Cadmique tenebat
> iura Creon. miser heu bellorum terminus! …

---

[22] On the theomach, see McNelis 2007, 140–5 and Chaudhuri 2014, 256–97.

>   scandit fatale tyrannis
> flebilis Aoniae solium: pro blanda potestas
> et sceptri malesuadus amor! numquamne priorum
> haerebunt documenta nouis?   (Stat. *Theb.* 11.648–51, 654–7)

> And now Fortune, happy to have cheated the hopes of the two chieftains, had in her malice transferred Amphion's realm and scepter to another: Creon held Cadmus' power. Alas, a sorry end to the war! … Weep for him, he mounts Aonia's throne, fatal to tyrants. Ah, cozening power, ill-counseling love of the scepter! Will newcomers never keep in mind the examples of their predecessors?

Random chance controls the fates of the Thebans as well as the Argives, and in this case, Creon wins the throne, albeit temporarily, a *fatale solium*. As Randall Ganiban notes, "Creon's actions … show the futility of the poem's hope about the power of history to prevent future tyranny."[23] Creon exiles Oedipus, sarcastically apostrophizing him with references to *spes* and *uota*:

> 'procul', inquit, 'abi, uictoribus omen
> inuisum, et Furias auerte ac moenia lustra
> discessu Thebana tuo. spes longa peracta est:
> uade, iacent nati. quae iam tibi uota supersunt?'   (Stat. *Theb.* 11.669–72)

> "Get you far," he says, "hateful omen to victors. Turn away your Furies and purge the walls of Thebes by your departure. Your long-cherished hope is accomplished. Go, your sons lie low. What now is left you to pray for?"

Oedipus' curse has been fulfilled, he can now go, mission accomplished. Creon's reference to the *spes longa* may look back to Polynices' *spes longa* in book 2. Oedipus' wish is equated to his son's wish to return and claim the throne, but Creon in poignant irony is now in possession of the *fatale solium*.

It is this last passage also that provides a final connection for our investigation of the semantics of *spes* in the *Thebaid*. In the final book of the poem, as Argia and the Argive women travel to Thebes and Athens respectively with a view towards burying their loved ones, *spes* becomes exclusively tied to women's efforts and goals.[24] Argia dares to travel to Thebes, while the suppliant women make their way to Athens to seek Theseus' help. Argia is fearless and stubborn:

> hic non femineae subitum uirtutis amorem
> colligit Argia, sexuque inmane relicto

---

23 Ganiban 2007, 199.
24 On the connections between the two sisters-in-law, see Augoustakis 2010; Korneeva 2011; Keith 2016; and Manioti 2016.

> tractat opus: placet (egregii spes dura pericli)
> comminus infandi leges accedere regni ...   (Stat. Theb. 12.177–80)

Here Argia conceives a sudden passion for unwomanly courage and engages in monstrous work, abandoning her sex. She resolves (stubborn hope of noble peril) to confront head on the laws of the impious monarchy ...

Argia goes out on the battlefield at night, and she locates Polynices' corpse:

> ... peracta
> spes longinqua uiae: totos inuenimus artus ...
> sed nec te flammis inopem tua terra uidebit:
> ardebis lacrimasque feres quas ferre negatum
> regibus, aeternumque tuo famulata sepulcro
> durabit deserta fides, <u>testis</u>que dolorum
> natus erit, paruoque torum Polynice fouebo.   (Stat. Theb. 12.339–40, 344–8)

... The distant hope of my journey is accomplished. I have found his body whole. But you too your land shall not see destitute of flame. You shall burn, and win tears not to be won by kings. Forsaken loyalty shall forever endure, serving your tomb. Our son shall be witness to my sorrows; with a little Polynices I shall warm my bed.

The phrase *peracta spes longinqua uiae* echoes Creon's apostrophe to Oedipus in book 11, which, as we saw above, in turn echoes Polynices' *spes longa* in book 2: here Argia's repetition allows Statius to triangulate this relationship between Oedipus, Polynices, and Argia in terms of hope, *spes*. We have here then another journey, Argia's, whose goal comes to completion. But as Argia's mission and Oedipus' curse become linked, one wonders how Argia's burial of Polynices brings the poem to a desired closure. In distress, she unleashes her own fury and seeks vengeance on Eteocles' body: she promises to foster in her own bed a small 'Polynices', her son Thersander, who will return to Thebes for revenge.[25] In this regard, Argia's hope for the future aligns her also with Hippolyte, queen of the Amazons, who is brought to Athens by Theseus when he returns from the Amazonomachy; actually the suppliant women arrive in Athens as Theseus is portrayed to have just returned from his campaign. Hippolyte would have followed him to Thebes in the war against Creon, but she is pregnant with Hippolytus:

> isset et Arctoas Cadmea ad moenia ducens
> Hippolyte turmas: retinet iam certa tumentis

---

[25] See Pollmann 2004, 170 on the ironical foreshadowing of the *Epigoni*.

> spes uteri, coniunxque rogat dimittere curas
> Martis et emeritas thalamo sacrare pharetras.   (Stat. *Theb.* 12.635–8)

> Hippolyte would have gone, leading Arctic squadrons against Cadmus' walls, but the hope of her swelling womb, now assured, keeps her back and her husband asks her to dismiss thoughts of war and dedicate her quiver, its service done, in the marriage chamber.

spes uteri in this case underscores the sinister connotations of the word: a captive Hippolyte is brought to Athens pregnant with Hippolytus; the disastrous future is foreshadowed as a continuation and repetition of the gloomy present.[26]

Argia is promising revenge, in a way contracting the *ira* and *dementia* that has plagued her husband in book 2 (*iraque demens*, 319). In the final occurrence of *spes* in the poem, the noun acquires further sinister overtones. Argia locates Polynices at the moment when Antigone, also defying Creon's orders, comes to the battlefield at night with the goal of burying her brother and thus finally having her Sophoclean moment. The two sisters (sister and sister-in-law) get to know each other, bestow final rites, and are caught by Creon's guards. In this final passage, the two women fight over agency: who first buried Polynices and therefore is to blame:

> ambitur saeua de morte animosaque leti
> spes furit: haec fratris rapuisse, haec coniugis artus
> contendunt uicibusque probant: 'ego corpus', 'ego ignes',
> 'me pietas', 'me duxit amor'. deposcere saeua
> supplicia et dextras iuuat insertare catenis.
> nusquam illa alternis modo quae reuerentia uerbis,
> iram odiumque putes; tantus discordat utrimque
> clamor, et ad regem qui deprendere trahuntur.   (Stat. *Theb.* 12.456–63)

> They are ambitious of a cruel end, courageous hope for death maddens within them. Against each other they claim to have stolen the body, she her brother's, she her husband's, and win credence in turn. "I took the body": "I lit the fire." "Affection made me": "Me love." They demand cruel punishment and rejoice to put their hands in chains. Gone the mutual respect in their exchanges, you might think it anger and hate, so loudly they both shout at each other and drag their captors to the king.

The narrator intervenes with the striking *iram odiumque putes*, a further explanation to the *animosaque leti / spes furit*.[27] In Statius' epic, we have moved from the hope of future power and kingdom to the hope of death. Just before the end, as

---

26 See further Augoustakis 2010, 79–80.
27 On hope and *furor*, see Pollmann 2004, 194–5.

Antigone and Argia are dragged to Creon to be put to death, Statius describes them at 12.679 as *mortis amore superbae*, "arrogant in their love of death." And to return to the opening passage of this chapter, as the women lament and bury their husbands, there only Argia constitutes a dissonant voice: Evadne jumps onto the pyre, Deipyle kisses the cannibal Tydeus, Atalanta laments her son Parthenopaeus, but Argia is busy narrating to Deipyle, her sister, the story of her capture by the sentinels.

In this overview, I have looked at those instances of *spes/spero* that affirm my reading of the poem as a cycle of violence that is bound to be repeated not only by the sons of Oedipus but also by the Epigoni, whose presence looms large over the narrative but lies outside the perimeter of the poem. *Quaenam spes hominum?* one may ask. Hope is associated with the darkest side of human predisposition towards despotism, while the future is foreshadowed as a continuation and repetition of a disastrous present.

Bibliography

Augoustakis, A. 2010. *Motherhood and the Other: Fashioning Female Power in Flavian Epic*, Oxford.
—— 2016a. *Statius, Thebaid 8: Edited with Text, Translation, and Commentary*, Oxford.
—— 2016b. "Introduction: Flavian Epic Renaissance," in: A. Augoustakis (ed.), *Oxford Readings in Flavian Epic*, Oxford, 1–14.
Bernstein, N. 2008. *In the Image of the Ancestors: Narratives of Kinship in Flavian Epic*, Toronto.
Bessone, F. 2011. *La Tebaide di Stazio: Epica e potere*, Pisa.
Braund, S.H. 1992. *Lucan: Civil War*, Oxford.
—— 1996. "Ending Epic: Statius, Theseus and a Merciful Release," in: *PCPhS* 42, 1–23.
—— 2006. "A Tale of Two Cities: Statius, Thebes, and Rome," in: *Phoenix* 60, 259–73.
Brown, J. 2016. "*lacrimabile nomen Archemorus*: The Babe in the Woods in Statius' *Thebaid* 4-6," in: A. Augoustakis (ed.), *Oxford Readings in Flavian Epic*, Oxford, 195–233.
Chaudhuri, P. 2014. *The War with God: Theomachy in Roman Imperial Poetry*, New York.
Coffee, N. 2009. *The Commerce of War: Exchange and Social Order in Latin Epic*, Chicago.
Criado, C. 2000. *La teologia de la Tebaida Estaciana: El anti-virgilianismo de un clasicista*, Hildesheim.
—— 2013. "The Contradictions of Valerius' and Statius' Jupiter: Power and Weakness of the Supreme God in the Epic and Tragic Tradition," in: G. Manuwald/A. Voigt (eds.), *Flavian Epic Interactions*, Berlin, 195–214.
Dietrich, J.S. 1999. "*Thebaid*'s Feminine Ending," in: *Ramus* 28, 40–53.
Edwards, C. 2014. "Ethics V: Death and Time," in: G. Damschen/A. Heil (eds.), *Brill's Companion to Seneca*, Leiden, 323–41.
Fantham, E. 1992. *Lucan, De bello civili Book II*, Cambridge.
Feeney, D. 1991. *The Gods in Epic: Poets and Critics of the Classical Tradition*, Oxford.
Franchet d'Espèrey, S. 1999. *Conflit, Violence et Non-Violence dans la Thébaïde de Stace*, Paris.
Hershkowitz, D. 1998. *The Madness of Epic: Reading Insanity from Homer to Statius*, Oxford.
—— 2016. "*parce metu, Cytherea*: 'Failed' Intertext Repetition in Statius' *Thebaid*, or, Don't Stop Me If You've Heard This One Before," in: A. Augoustakis (ed.), *Oxford Readings in Flavian Epic*, Oxford, 129–48.
Hill, D.E.P. 1996. *P. Papini Stati Thebaidos Libri XII*, 2nd edn., Leiden.

Hulls, J.-M. 2014. "Greek Author, Greek Past: Statius, Athens, and the Tragic Self," in: A. Augoustakis (ed.), *Flavian Poetry and its Greek Past*, Leiden, 193–213.
Ganiban, R. 2007. *Statius and Virgil: The Thebaid and the Reinterpretation of the Aeneid*, Cambridge.
Gervais, K. 2017. *Statius, Thebaid 2*, Oxford.
Gummere, R. M. 1917. *Seneca, Epistles*, 2 vols., Cambridge, Mass.
Keith, A. 2000. *Engendering Rome: Women in Latin Epic*, Cambridge.
—— 2014. "Ovid's Theban Narrative in Statius' *Thebaid*," in: A. Augoustakis (ed.), *Oxford Readings in Flavian Epic*, Oxford, 149–69.
—— 2016. "Sisters and their Secrets in Flavian Epic," in: N. Manioti (ed.), *Family in Flavian Epic*, Leiden, 248–75.
Korneeva, T. 2011. *Alter et ipse: Identità e duplicità nel sistema dei personaggi della Tebaide di Stazio*, Pisa.
Lovatt, H. 2013. *The Epic Gaze: Vision, Gender and Narrative in Ancient Epic*, Cambridge.
—— 2016. "Competing Ending: Re-reading the End of Statius' *Thebaid* through Lucan," in: A. Augoustakis (ed.), *Oxford Readings in Flavian Epic*, Oxford, 262–91.
Manioti, N. 2016. "Becoming Sisters: Antigone and Argia in Statius' *Thebaid*," in: N. Manioti (ed.), *Family in Flavian Epic*, Leiden, 122–42.
Marinis, A. 2015. "Statius' *Thebaid* and Greek Tragedy: The Legacy of Thebes," in: W.J. Dominik/C.E. Newlands/K. Gervais (eds.), *Brill's Companion to Statius*, Leiden, 343–61.
McAuley, M. 2016. *Reproducing Rome: Motherhood in Virgil, Ovid, Seneca, and Statius*, Oxford.
McNelis, C. 2007. *Statius' Thebaid and the Poetics of Civil War*, Cambridge.
Nagel, R. 1999. "Polynices the Charioteer: Statius, *Thebaid* 6.296-549," in: *EMC* 18, 381–96.
Newlands, C. 2016. "Fatal Unions: Marriage at Thebes," in: N. Manioti (ed.), *Family in Flavian Epic*, Leiden, 143–73.
Parkes, R. 2012. *Statius,* Thebaid 4: *Edited with Text, Translation, and Commentary*, Oxford.
Pollmann, K. 2004. *Statius, Thebaid 12: Introduction, Text, Commentary*, Paderborn.
Putnam, M.C.J. 2016. "The Sense of Two Endings: How Virgil and Statius conclude," in: *ICS* 41, 85–149.
Ripoll, F. 1998. *La morale héroïque dans les épopées latines d'époque flavienne: Tradition et innovation*, Leuven.
Rutherford, D. 2003. "*Patience sans Espérance*: Leibniz's Critique of Stoicism," in: J. Miller/B. Inwood (eds.), *Hellenistic and Early Modern Philosophy*, Cambridge, 62–89.
Shackleton Bailey, D.R. 1997. *Lucanus, De bello ciuili*, 2nd edn., Stuttgart.
—— 2003. *Statius*, 3 vols, Cambridge, Mass.
Stover, T. 2008. "The Date of Valerius Flaccus' *Argonautica*," in: *PLLS* 13, 211–29.
—— 2012. *Epic and Empire in Vespasianic Rome: A New Reading of Valerius Flaccus' Argonautica*. Oxford.
Walter, A. 2014. *Erzählen und Gesang im flavischen Epos*, Berlin.

Sophia Papaioannou
'A Historian Utterly Without Hope': Literary Artistry and Narratives of Decline in Tacitus' *Historiae* I

The progressive course of moral decline, which is accompanied by rising corruption and civil discord, is not just commonplace but a raison-d'-être for Roman historiography. In all major surviving Roman historians this course of decline is natural. And yet, just because pessimism is not the same as hopelessness, despite the gloom of their narratives, Roman historians do admit, more or less overtly, that this decline is not irreversible. Livy in his preface clearly held out hope for a remedy. For Livy, the leading causes of decline were *avaritia* and *luxuria* (Livy, *AUC Praefatio* 11), but the damage they caused can be repaired, because Rome always gives birth to leaders who transcend these vices, thus founding Rome anew.[1] Even Sallust, who adopted an outright pessimistic view of Roman history (cf. his analysis of the decline of Roman morals in the *Bellum Catilinae* 5.9–13.5) and blamed Rome's troubles on the absence of *metus hostilis* and unchecked *ambitio*, chose to write about the particular incidents of the recent past not only because they illustrated the sinking morality of the times and universal wickedness of his own day but also because they show that exemplary individuals may emerge even in the darkest moments of Rome's history, for the regeneration of the Republic. The portrayals of Caesar and Cato in the *Bellum Catilinae* emphasize that the two heroes gained equal glory because they were both excellent even though their characters were completely different (*BC* 54.2–3). Thus, like Livy (*AUC Praefatio* 10) Sallust has faith in the power of *exempla* to uplift morals and the state.

Tacitus does not seem to believe that his age can nurture exemplary statesmen. His works, especially the *Histories*, are full of acts of violence, betrayal and injustice. His *exempla* though not absent are principally individuals who exemplify the virtues of Stoicism,[2] and therefore may primarily offer moral instruction.[3]

---

1   On the potential reversal of decline in Livy see Woodman 1988, 136–137; also 146: "Livy came to adopt an optimistic view of Roman History which he reinforced by writing in the style that Cicero had recommended". On Livy's prefacing his work by expressing hope for a remedy to Rome's decline (in opposition to Sallust), see Levene 1992, 69.
2   A comprehensive study of Tacitus' use of *exempla* is still a desideratum; the most important study is Salmon 1989; see also Feldherr 1998, 218–21.
3   On Stoic exempla in Tacitus, see Turpin 2008.

And yet, this unfulfilled hope for the rise of an exemplary leader becomes in his hands a tool for building a fascinating narrative and contributing to the characterization of the agents and the dramatization of the events.[4] Focusing presently on the account of Galba's reign in *Histories* 1.1–49,[5] I shall explore the diverse ways in which hope is experienced by the Roman people in the aftermath of Nero's death, and I shall show how the employment of the vocabulary of hope in key moments of the narrative tightens structure and facilitates plot-development, thus interpreting Tacitus' pessimistic perspective as a literary technique.

A second point my analysis will illustrate is the impact of the popular memory of Galba, either individual or collective, upon hope. Galba's regime was seriously impeded by his conduct in the past as a general, which elicited painful memories. These memories of yesteryear, which Galba failed to take into account to the detriment of his success, doomed his chances with crucial parties, especially the army of Upper Germany, once the initial enthusiasm following Nero's death faded away. Similarly, Galba's decision to proceed to the adoption of his successor, which was directed by his memory partly of an idealized Republic, partly of Augustus, failed to overcome Otho's populism. Galba strove to reverse Nero's paradigm and, in imitation of Augustus, offered the Romans a ruler with a traditional, republican-like, way of thinking and acting. Unlike the Romans of the Augustan era, however, the Romans of Galba's day do not really wish for a return to the Republic (which they know only in theory), but rather for a new emperor—ideally an improved version of Nero.

'Hope' (lat. *spes*), and its derivatives, verbal or nominal forms (*spero* and the opposite *despero, prosper, desperatio,* and possibly *asper*[6]) are employed with notable frequency in Tacitus' corpus. As far as the *Histories* is concerned, in Book 1 'hope'-related vocabulary occurs 26 times —14 in the Galba episode— the positive

---

4 Considering Tacitus' systematic engagement with tragic modes, his perception of hope that is not to be fulfilled is situated within a wider tragic vision. For Syme 1958, 545 Tacitus is a poet and a dramatist; a number of critical studies since explore the poetic and the dramatic in Tacitus' works. See e.g, Lauletta 1998; and Foucher 2000; L'Hoir 2006. On Tacitus' theatrical presentation of the events under Nero, see Woodman 1993, 104–28; and Bartsch 1994, Chapters 1 and 2. L'Hoir 2006, 71–108 discusses Tacitus' dialogue with Aristotle's *Poetics* in the *Annals*.
5 The text of the *Histories* is taken from Damon 2003; the translation is Moore 1925, with revisions.
6 Though the adjective *asper* is said to be of dubious etymology, L–S s.v. I, records an etymological suggestion by Corssen from 'spes': "Corssen, Ausspr. II. p. 593, regards *asper* (i.e. *ab spe*) as the proper opposite of *prosper* (i.e. *pro spe*); thus *asper* originally meant 'hopeless', 'desperate'; v. also *id. ib.* II. p. 870; cf. the use of *res asperae* as the opposite of *res prosperae*".

terms *spes* and *prosper* accounting for all but three of the total number.⁷ Hope is an important concept for Tacitus' historical narrative because it is the leading motivation for the Romans. Tacitus' approach to hope is phenomenological: he identifies hope through how it is perceived by the actors in various situations. Also, he points out that the way hope is perceived is usually different from the way hope exists outside of these actors (and is perceived by us, Tacitus' readers). To this end, Tacitus' rampant pessimism should be reconsidered and offered a new definition that excludes identification with hopelessness. The quotation of the first half of my title slightly paraphrases a phrase from Lionel Trilling's essay, "Tacitus Now", published in his book *The Liberal Imagination*, where, on p. 199, Tacitus is declared to be "one of the few great writers who are utterly without hope".⁸ Trilling's assessment of Tacitus in this short (barely six-page-long essay) has been extremely influential, despite the fact that it was coming from someone who was not a Classicist, because Trilling was among the first literary theorists who read the classical texts in light of contemporary cultural and social experiences and preoccupations.⁹ In fact, the main theme of *The Liberal Imagination* is the moral and political character of literary criticism, and Tacitus' "deep pessimism" is introduced by Trilling as an example of a historian who did not let his own personal beliefs determine the character of his narrative, and so he never imposed his hopelessness upon the reader. After a careful study of Trilling's article, one cannot help but notice the author's eagerness to dismiss Tacitus' historical acumen as myopic: "Tacitus has no notions of historical development to comfort him; nor did he feel it his duty to look at present danger and pain with the remote eyes of posterity" (Trilling, p. 201). Several important studies on Tacitus in the last few decades have shown otherwise,¹⁰ cautioning against sweeping conclusions on the basis of isolated evidence.

The proposed phenomenological approach of hope encourages a reconsideration of the traditional view of Tacitus' pessimism. Tacitus, it will be shown, is not an inherently dark author, who believes that the narrative of Rome is a course

---

7 *Spes* is a favorite word of Tacitus; in the other books of the *Histories*, *spes*-related vocabulary features 36 times in Book 2, also 36 in Book 3, 41 in Book 4 and 6 in the 26 surviving chapters of Book 5. In the *Annales*, *spes* runs like a watchword throughout all sixteen books; see Gerber and Greef, *s.v. spes*.
8 Trilling 2012 [1950]. "Tacitus Now" is a short essay that covers pp. 198–204.
9 The popularity of Trilling's short paper is attested also by the fact that it has made it into the *Oxford Readings in Tacitus* [= Ash 2012] (it closes the collection of 18 most influential papers on Tacitus in the last century).
10 Most recently Damon 2016. Also Damon 2003, 5–6; Joseph 2012, 157; Kraus and Woodman 1997, 100–1.

of progressive and irreversible decline, but rather is concerned to illustrate that human disillusionment is to be responsible for this course of progressive decline. Upon hearing of Nero's death, the Romans largely approach the rise of Galba as illusionists: they absolutize it. The illusion they exhibit freezes their capacity for critical, unprejudiced thinking, as they exclude from their mind the possibility of an alternative reality—that things will turn out differently than they themselves hope. They have placed their trust in Galba, and when they discover that Galba is not what they were hoping for, they readily become disillusioned and react contrary to reason. This reaction is at the core of Tacitus' pessimism. Tacitus describes the catastrophic consequences tied to the unreasonable acts of individuals who cannot control their reaction when their hope is inoperative, either because it fails to rise or because it is disappointed. Further, because Roman expectations are repeatedly disappointed, Tacitus' pessimism may be approached as a literary technique, not a personal conviction. His negative assessment of the actions of his heroes on account of the grim consequences following them, do not constitute a confession of despair, but an admission against setting expectations and nurturing hope with predetermined positive results. Tacitus the author is a pessimist, but he is not hopeless. Pessimism is not contrary to hope. In pessimism things are just going to turn out badly. One may make a statement about the reality of things independently of a ground of hope or the negation of a ground of hope. Tacitus can hope that a new emperor will reverse the course of Roman decline, and be pessimistic that this new emperor will succeed in light of the serial failures of rulers in his lifetime so far. In this respect, Tacitus' narrative is bereft of both hopelessness and despair. In hopelessness an event (just *one* event) is impossible both now and ever. Despair lacks completely the ground of hope; it is the experience of ultimate and decisive abandonment.[11]

Failed hope, however, fuels action which in turn generates history. Tacitus' *Histories* construct rather than record history in the aftermath of the Julio-Claudians. The great detail in which the historian notes down the repeated failures of the Empire during that year to benefit from the end of the Julio-Claudian imperial line means to point out that in the face of habitual failure there is hope for political recovery, and attests to the extensive corruption of all Roman institutions and the citizen body —a corruption that reaches all the way to Tacitus' day. The irreparably wounded state of Rome is given with graphic detail very early in the narrative:

---

[11] For a succinct, recent investigation of the experience of hope by focusing on experiences that seem to rival hope, namely, disappointment, desperation, panic, hopelessness, and despair, and on their definitions, see Steinbock 2007.

Hist. 1.2: Opus adgredior opimum casibus, atrox proeliis, discors seditionibus, ipsa etiam pace saevum. quattuor principes ferro interempti: trina bella civilia, plura externa ac plerumque permixta [...] iam vero Italia novis cladibus vel post longam saeculorum seriem repetitis adflicta. haustae aut obrutae urbes, fecundissima Campaniae ora; et urbs incendiis vastata, consumptis, antiquissimis delubris, ipso Capitolio civium manibus incenso. pollutae caerimoniae, magna adulteria: plenum exilii mare, infecti caedibus scopuli. atrocius in urbe saevitum: nobilitas, opes, omissi gestique honores pro crimine et ob virtutes certissimum exitium. [...]

The history on which I am entering is that of a period rich in disasters, terrible with battles, torn by civil struggles, horrible even in peace. Four emperors were slain by the sword; there were three civil wars, more foreign wars, and often both at the same time. [...] Italy was distressed by disasters unknown before or returning after the lapse of ages. Towns on the rich fertile shores of Campania were swallowed up by the earth or overwhelmed; Rome was devastated by fires, in which her most ancient shrines were destroyed and the very Capitol fired by citizens' hands. Sacred rites were defiled; there were adulteries in high places. The sea swarmed with exiles, its cliffs made foul with the bodies of the dead. Worse cruelty reigned in the city. High birth, wealth, the refusal or acceptance of office – all gave ground for accusations, and virtues caused the surest ruin. [...]

Like a delayed prologue in a dramatic performance,[12] Tacitus produces an informative summary of his work as he sets out a) to arrest the attention of his reading audience by promising a narrative fast-paced, and full of excitement, gore and death; but also, b) to forewarn that the content of his work is a concatenation of calamities that leave little room for hope. The style adopted, of successive brief clauses strung together in sequential asyndeta, communicates the rapidness, endlessness and ubiquity of disaster, both human-caused and god-sent. The same sense of comprehensive devastation is enhanced by the way Tacitus manipulates the geography and time of his serial historical tragedies. As Ash (2006, 66) has noted, regarding space, the historian follows "a centripetal momentum, moving briskly from events around the empire, to a sweeping view of trouble within Italy, and culminating in devastation at the centre of Rome itself. The sheer pace of the narrative style is extraordinary, with items placed paratactically (side-by-side without subordinate clauses or connectives". Regarding time, the proposed narrative spreads over a full thirty-year period, from Nero's murder, the three successive civil wars and the murders of three emperors, all in less than a year, to the destruction of Pompeii and Herculaneum ten years later, and to the wrong accusation for profanity of the Vestal Cornelia under Domitian and her execution. Destruction is total, and is underscored by means of employing vocabulary of

---

12 Kraus and Woodman 1997, 89: "The paragraph as a whole [sc. *Hist.* 1.2–3] constitutes a foretaste of, or 'blurb' for, all the gripping events which Tacitus will describe in his work".

desecration and defiling ("Sacred rites were defiled; ... cliffs made foul with the bodies of the dead"), as if to suggest that it is predestined and therefore irreversible by divine mandate —thus hopelessly corrupt. Reversal of all that is proper and good stresses the feeling of hopelessness: virtues lead to destruction; vices guarantee success.[13]

Chapter two features the first occurrence of 'hope', in its cognate *prospera* ('successful'): *prosperae in Oriente, adversae in Occidente res: turbatum Illyricum, Galliae nutantes, perdomita Britannia et statim omissa: coortae in nos Sarmatarum ac Sueborum gentes, nobilitatus cladibus mutuis Dacus, mota prope etiam Parthorum arma falsi Neronis ludibrio* ("There were successes in the East, disaster in the West, disturbance in Illyricum, the Gallic provinces were wavering; Britain was conquered and immediately given up; the Sarmatian and Suebic tribes rose against us; the Dacians won fame by defeats inflicted and suffered; and a pretender claiming to be Nero almost deluded the Parthians also into declaring war"). The term is conspicuously placed at the opening of a long sentence which trails with cinematic glance the political situation in the four corners of the empire at the time of Nero's death, and is part of a *para prosdokian* structure: it begins optimistically and describes a positive situation (the affairs in the East are going well), but a retrospective assessment at the end of the period reveals that the opening successes were an exception —the only rosy spot in an otherwise completely dark political situation of failures and disasters.

Structured along the lines of this dichotomy isolated hope/general disaster, the narrative of chapter three, next, gives the impression that there are exceptions to the rule of universal corruption, but these positive examples are isolated. They cannot lead to the restoration of traditional virtues and signal a new era, but instead are dishonoured and ultimately driven to extermination because the Roman *populus* is corrupt through and through. The impossibility of recovery is underscored by the negative attitude of the gods towards Rome:

> *Hist.* 1.3: Non tamen adeo virtutum sterile saeculum ut non et bona exempla prodiderit. comitatae profugos liberos matres, secutae maritos in exilia coniuges: propinqui audentes, constantes generi, contumax etiam adversus tormenta servorum fides; supremae clarorum virorum necessitates fortiter toleratae et laudatis antiquorum mortibus pares exitus. praeter multiplicis rerum humanarum casus caelo terraque prodigia et fulminum monitus et futurorum praesagia, laeta tristia, ambigua manifesta; nec enim umquam atrocioribus populi Romani cladibus magisve iustis indiciis adprobatum est non esse curae deis securitatem nostram, esse ultionem.

---

13 See the full argument in Ash 2006, 66–7.

> Yet this age was not so barren of virtue that it did not display noble examples. Mothers accompanied their children in flight; wives followed their husbands into exile; relatives displayed courage, sons-in-law firmness, slaves a fidelity which defied even torture. Eminent men met the last necessity with fortitude, rivalling in their end the glorious deaths of antiquity. Besides the manifold misfortunes that befell mankind, there were prodigies in the sky and on the earth, warnings given by thunderbolts, and prophecies of the future, both joyful and gloomy, uncertain and clear. For never was it more fully proved by awful disasters of the Roman people or by indubitable signs that the gods care not for our safety, but for our punishment.

This grim introduction to the reign of Galba directs both the pace of the narrative and the readers' expectations. Chapters 1–11 offer an overview of the situation in the armies across the empire at the time of Nero's death and Galba's rise. In the opening part of the unit which serves as the prologue to the whole work, Tacitus describes the hope Nero's death inspired to the Romans throughout the empire, and underscores its programmatic function for the *Histories*. Chapters 12–20 centre on Galba's effort to inspire hope by choosing a successor —and, at the same time, introducing a new pattern for imperial succession: appointment by choice instead of inheritance. Chapters 21–49 describe the conspiracy of Otho and the fall of Galba. Tacitus' Otho succeeds because he can sense what the people wish —corrupt himself, he thinks exactly like the corrupted audience that has lost the ability to judge correctly.[14]

The self-containment of the opening unit is made clear by the fact that it begins and ends in nearly identical diction: *Hist.* 1.1.1: <u>Initium</u> mihi operis **Servius Galba iterum Titus Vinius consules** erunt ("The beginning of my work will be the consulship of Servius Galba, for the second time, and Titus Vinius") ~ *Hist.* 1.11.3: *hic fuit rerum Romanarum status, cum* **Servius Galba iterum Titus Vinius consules** <u>inchoavere</u> annum sibi <u>ultimum</u>, rei publicae prope <u>supremum</u> ("Such was the state of the Roman world when Servius Galba, consul for the second time, and Titus Vinius his colleague, inaugurated the year which was their last, and almost the last for the Commonwealth of Rome"). The section opens self-

---

14 On the division of the Galba section into two units, an opening unit comprising chapters 1.1–11, and a large second unit that includes the remaining 38 chapters, and its structure as paradigmatic for the entire narrative of the year of the four emperors; cf. Devillers 2012, 162–5; Keitel 2006, 244. I side with those critics who consider chapters 12–20 to be a second unit for it treats Galba's one and only major political initiative to introduce a new pattern of succession politics through adoption. On the complex structure of *Histories* I, see Damon 2003, 20–2. Damon also notes that chapters 12–20 form a clearly defined unit, to which she gives the subtitle 'Galba's acta' (p. 125) The most convincing argument for the independent standing of this unit is Morgan 1993, 567–86.

consciously with the word *initium*, 'beginning',[15] also denoting that this is the opening, of the first unit and the entire *Histories* opus, and also of the post-Julio-Claudian era, and closes with the word *supremum*, 'last', enhanced by its synonym, *ultimum*, set only two words prior. The concept of 'beginnings' recurs in the closing phrase in the use of *inchoavere*, 'began',[16] while it is additionally stressed by the fact that the beginning of Tacitus' narrative time is set on New Year's Day, January 1st, of the year 69, and is amplified by the mention of the two new consuls, traditionally set to assume their duties on that very day.[17] Further, the first day of AD 69 is also the beginning of a new era for Rome: Galba is a new emperor (and the first individual to be named), while 69 is the first year in living memory without a Julio-Claudian at the helm of Roman government.[18] And yet, the optimism that this amplitude of new beginnings should inspire is beset by the adverb *iterum*, 'for a second time', footnoting that, what is so emphatically advertised as new, is actually quite old. As Mary Beard has noted, the mention that Galba's consulship was his second, should make Tacitus' readers wonder when the new emperor first served in the same office. This happened in AD 33, under Emperor Tiberius, over thirty-five years earlier, and in this respect Galba is hardly the leader to embody the new and the hopeful —even though for many of the people living through the events of 69 the events of 33 were ancient history, perhaps too far back to remember and even beyond their lifetimes.[19] What we are about to read, in other words, is not a fresh start for Roman historical time but one that is informed by the past. Tacitus' readers are challenged to review Galba's first consulship and subsequently Galba's past —a review that would illuminate and justify certain crucial decisions of the new emperor, and also explain his failure to gain the support of part of the Roman army.

---

15 On the significant placement of initium in *Hist.* 1.1, and the several beginnings implied by it, see Kraus and Woodman 1997, 88–9; also Kraus and Woodman 1997, 88–97 on the studied way in which Tacitus opens and closes his works, and crafts beginnings and endings more broadly.

16 Kraus and Woodman 1997, 90 on *Hist.* 1.11.3 as both an ending and a beginning on account of featuring the three terms, *supremum, ultimum, inchoavere* in a single phrase.

17 Ironically, Tacitus begins the narrative of the new phase in the history of Rome in a strongly traditional way, with a consular date (in the pattern of Sallust) and by marking the beginning of the new year with the names of the two new consuls (following after Livy); Damon 2003, 78. On the opening dates of Tacitus' historical works, see also Shotter 1967.

18 The conspicuous self-containment of the first unit by means of the implementation of a ring-composition figure based on the names of the two consuls of 69 has been repeatedly observed; see e.g. Martin 1981, 68; Cole 1992, 243; Geiser 2007, 173; Feeney 2009, 147; Devillers 2012, 162.

19 Beard 2013, 168.

The opening eleven chapters comprise a 'script' or 'mini-narrative' that contextualizes Galba's ultimate failure in terms of his past life and actions. Chapter four, which contains an account of the actual beginning of the historical narrative proper, describes the conditions that host and determine the first occurrence of *spes*:[20]

> *Hist.* 1.4.1–3: finis Neronis ut laetus primo gaudentium impetus fuerat, ita varios motus animorum non modo in urbe apud patres aut populum aut urbanum militem, sed omnis legiones ducesque conciverat, e vulgato imperii arcano posse principem alibi quam Romae fieri. Sed patres laeti, usurpata statim libertate licentius ut erga principem novum et absentem; primores equitum proximi gaudio patrum; pars populi integra et magnis domibus adnexa, clientes libertique damnatorum et exulum in spem erecti.
>
> Although Nero's death had at first been welcomed with outbursts of joy, it roused varying emotions, not only in the city among the senators and people and the city soldiery, but also among all the legions and generals; for the secret of the empire was now revealed, that an emperor could be made elsewhere than at Rome. The senators rejoiced and immediately made full use of their liberty, as was natural, for they had to do with a new emperor who was still absent. The leading members of the equestrian class were nearly as elated as the senators. The respectable part of the common people who were attached to the great houses, the clients and freedmen of those who had been condemned and driven into exile, were all roused to hope.

Hope in the aftermath of Nero's death distinguishes the reactions of senators, *equites*, and the righteous members of the citizen body (*integra pars*)—these classes, Tacitus wishes us to believe, appreciated the situation from the standpoint of the impartial observer and saw in the death of Nero the beginning of a better era, even though they had not experienced the new regime yet. On the contrary, the hopes of the worthless plebs (1.4.3) and, most notably, the military (1.5) were less concerned with the welfare of the Commonwealth and more with their own personal interests. The case of the military deserves special discussion, for their hope was shaped from corrupt habit and not least from their collective memory. On the basis of Tacitus' assessment of the Roman military in the capital at the time of Galba's rise (alike the praetorian guard and the legions that happened to be stationed there at the time; cf. Damon 2003, 104 *ad* 5.1), a series of motives for their less than warm support for the new emperor stands out. Firstly, the army is

---

20 On the importance of contexts ('scripts' or 'mini-narratives') for a full understanding of emotion labels in Classical literature, see the Introduction to Kaster 2005; also Cairns 2008, 46, "A script is a mini-narrative that will usually encompass (at least) the conditions in which emotion X occurs, the perceptions and appraisals of those conditions, and the responses (whether symptomatic, expressive, or pragmatic) that result".

traditionally prone to show allegiance to the emperor, and in AD 69 the Roman army, even though restless due to a long period of inactivity, remained loyal to Nero. Galba had to try hard in order to win their favour (cf. *Hist.* 1.5.1). He seems to have attempted so initially by promising gifts and money —a promise he retracted once he entered Rome and decided that the army posed no threat to him. Secondly, Galba not only backed down on his promise of great financial rewards to the army but chose to dismiss publicly what had been an age-long established practice, namely the habit to maintain the army's loyalty with monetary rewards and bribes, by uttering the famous phrase —*anceps*, 'double-edged', Tacitus characterizes it— "I chose my soldiers; I do not buy them" (1.5.2, *legi a se militem, non emi*; cf. also Plutarch, *Galba* 18.2; Suetonius, *Galba* 16.1; Dio 64.3.3). The retraction of the bribes angered the army (1.5.1) who proffered their own interpretation of Galba's alleged incorruptible self-portrayal, by publicly reinterpreting the new emperor's parsimony as meanness and greed (1.5.2 *nec deerant sermones senium atque avaritiam Galbae increpantium,* "and some could be heard berating Galba's senility and avarice").

Thirdly and most importantly, the collective memory of the Roman legions of the North was hardly favouring Galba, who had served as commander of the Roman legions of Upper Germany from AD 39 to 41: he had been appointed by Caligula in order to restore discipline in the army there in the aftermath of a conspiracy that led to the execution of Lentulus Gaetulicus. Even though nearly thirty years later few of the soldiers and officers serving in Upper Germany in AD 39 would still be in active duty, the lore or collective memory of Galba's severity must have been standing and circulated widely, especially among the four legions that had been subjected to Galba's severe rule in 39, and which by 69 had been dispersed in different parts of Europe carrying their long-term memory of Galba with them.[21] In short, whatever hope Galba's rise might have generated, a good part of the army could not relate to it.[22]

Next to the bad reputation that austerity had garnered for the new emperor among those who knew him (or had heard of him), Galba's failure to meet up the standards of physical appearance and populism raised by Nero doomed his hope to win over the lower classes, as well:

---

[21] On Galba's unpopularity among the legions of Northern Italy and the Rhine, and the impact of their long-term memory on the downfall of the emperor, see Morgan 2006, 26–30.
[22] This probably explains why Galba who had based his rhetoric of rule on the *mos maiorum* was so unpopular with the army. Tacitus and Suetonius opine that Galba's traditionalism and his *severitas* was unpopular and outdated (*Hist.* 1.18; Suet. *Galba* 12, 14, 15), but they fail to provide a better explanation for this unpopularity.

Hist. 1.7.3 Ipsa aetas Galbae in risui ac fastidio erat adsuetis iuventae Neronis et imperatores forma ac decore corporis, ut est mos vulgi, comparantibus.

Even Galba's age aroused ridicule and scorn among those who were accustomed to Nero's youth and compared emperors, as vulgar people are accustomed to do, by their looks and personal attraction.

Galba's old age and physical infirmity, accompanied by weakness of character, is another strongly pronounced leitmotif throughout the episode, as if to prove that the new beginning Galba supposedly promises is just another manifestation of deceptive hope. To contain ourselves only inside the first unit: in *Hist.* 1.6.1, Galba is called old and weak (*invalidum senem*)[23], a characterization which encourages the supposition that he also might have been subject to manipulation by corrupt aids; in *Hist.* 1.7 his variable character is mentioned once (1.7.2, *mobilitate ingenii*) and his old age twice, the first time to justify the powerlessness of Galba to control his household (1.7.3, *venalia cuncta, praepotentes liberti, servorum manus subitis avidae et tamquam apud senem festinantes,* "Everything was for sale; his freedmen were all-powerful, his slaves were eager to capitalize on their unexpected fortune, and with so elderly an emperor were losing no time"), the second as the cause for ridicule by those who were still longing for Nero (7.3, *imperatores forma ac decore corporis... comparantes,* "those who compared emperors ... in point of looks and personal attraction"); and in *Hist.* 1.9.1, the mention of the general Hordeonius Flaccus' inability to impose discipline over his soldiers in Upper Germany on account of his advanced age and infirmity of body recalls Galba's comparable situation—especially since Flaccus was appointed commander of the troops in Upper Germany by Galba himself.[24]

Besides his old age (in 69 Galba was 73 years old), two additional traits to be added to the reasons that inhibited Galba's popularity were his unattractive

---

23 According to Miller 1987, 92–3, the phrase likely evokes the invalid old men of Lavinium in *Aen.* 12.132 (*invalidique senes*), who personify the doomed fate of their city. Vergil's subtext may be detected behind the description of Galba's death, as well: the weak old man, wearing an armour that he can hardly bear is murdered and decapitated, in striking reminiscence of the circumstances of Old Priam's death as described in *Aeneid* 2. The parallels are many and have been noted by several critics, among others, Benario 1972; Miller 1987, 99–100; Ash 1999, 79–83; Pagan 2006, 208–9; Keitel 2010, 346–50; Damon 2010, 382–3; and Joseph 2012, 79–112, esp. 79–88.
24 Damon 2003, 118–9, briefly records the disastrous leadership of Flaccus, who was responsible for the revolt of Civilis, an unprecedented, most dangerous, and difficult to suppress, uprising that combined elements of a foreign and a civil war. Tacitus is our principal source for the Batavian revolt; the entire episode is described in the *Histories* (4.1–37, 54–79; 5.14–26); thorough narratives of the affair are offered in Wellesley 2000, esp. pp. 168ff. and Lendering and Bosman 2012.

appearance and his old-fashioned habits and discipline. According to Suetonius, *Galba* 21, the emperor "was very bald... with a hooked nose, and hands and feet so crippled by arthritis that he could not endure wearing shoes for long, nor could he unroll books or even hold them. On his right side, too, his flesh had grown out and hung down [sc. he had a hernia] so far that it could hardly be kept in place by a bandage" (... *capite praecalvo ... adunco naso, manibus pedibusque articulari morbo distortissimis, ut neque calceum perpeti nec libellos evolvere aut tenere omnino valeret. Excreverat etiam in dexteriore latere eius caro praependebatque adeo ut aegre fascia substringeretur*).[25] This was in stark contrast with the physical appearance and the youth of Nero, who at the time of his death was just over 30 years old, a dandy who paid particular attention to his appearance.[26] Galba also embraced old-fashioned Republican values —partly because he was a traditionalist himself (his unattractive appearance enhanced his austere profile as it reminded of the severe-looking naturalistic busts of the Republican political leaders of the past), partly because he embraced the paradigm of Augustus and the latter's political rhetoric of the 'restituted republic'.[27] As noted above, this old-fashioned discipline— a taste thereof the army had always kept in their collective memory, and had no desire to experience again— alienated the Roman army from Galba's imperial claim.

If the military failed Galba because of their negative memory of his earlier leadership performance, the new emperor alienated the *vulgus*, both civil and military, because *he was not Nero*. This paradox underscores the pathological, indeed incurable, corruption of the Roman state at large: the oblivious plebs measured Nero's successor by Nero's standards. Filtered through the distorted prism of a military accustomed to bribes and inactivity, and a senseless mob, Galba's positive qualities were distorted. Aptly, then, Tacitus compares adulation, the prime motivation of the Roman majority for bestowing their support on their preferred imperial candidate, to 'foolish hope':[28]

---

25 Transl. Edwards 2000.

26 Seneca in *Apocolocynthosis* 4.1 compares Nero's talent in singing and physical appearance to that of Apollo. The praise is ironic yet inspired by the young emperor's obsession with his image and artistic profile.

27 On Galba's republicanism, including his embrace of key Augustan initiatives that likewise appealed to Republican ideology, see Wilkinson 2012, 77–80; Gowing 2005, 102–4; Zehnacher 1987, 340; Hammond 1963, 101; Shotter 1997, 80 (all discussing how Galba issued coins in the name of the SPQR and *Libertas PR Restituta*, while he modelled the iconography of his coins on the iconography of Brutus' coins); also Wilkinson 2012, 3, 78.

28 False hope and adulation govern Roman decision making also in *Hist*. 1.57.2 and 1.88.3; see Devillers 2012, 174.

> *Hist.* 1.12.3: paucis iudicium aut rei publicae amor: multi stulta spe, prout quis amicus vel cliens, hunc vel illum ambitiosis rumoribus destinabant.

> Few were guided by sound judgment or real patriotism; the majority, prompted by foolish hope, named in their selfish gossip this man or that whose clients or friends they were.

The military was the first who deserted Galba, when the option of an alternative candidate was presented in Otho who not only promised generous bonus payments, but also was young and looked like Nero. Tacitus actually enhances Otho's appeal to the military masses by emphasizing his resemblance to Nero, both in physical appearance and in overall character—a resemblance diligently pursued by Otho himself:[29]

> *Hist.* 1.13.3: credo et reipublicae curam subisse, frustra a Nerone translatae si apud Othonem relinqueretur. Namque Otho pueritiam incuriose, adulescentiam petulanter egerat, gratus Neroni aemulatione luxus. ... faventibus plerisque militum, prona in eum aula Neronis ut similem.

> Galba, one may suppose, felt some concern for his country, too. Why take the throne from Nero, if it was to be left to Otho? Otho had spent his boyhood in heedlessness, his early manhood under no restraint. He had found favour in Nero's eyes by imitating his extravagance... The majority of the soldiers favoured him, and Nero's court was inclined to him because he was like Nero.

Otho had been proposed as a potential heir to Galba when the elderly emperor decided to make a statement towards stabilizing his rule by adopting his successor. Tacitus notes that Otho himself hoped to be that successor. In fact, the third occurrence of *spes* in the Galba episode refers to Otho's emotions, when the emperor starts thinking about his succession:

> *Hist.* 1.13.4 donec bellum fuit, inter praesentis splendidissimus, spem adoptionis statim conceptam acrius in dies rapiebat.

> Being the most distinguished of Galba's officers in the war, he had instantly conceived <u>the hope of being adopted</u> by Galba, and with each passing day he grasped at it more eagerly.

When Galba surprised him and adopted Piso Licinianus instead, Otho re-directed his hopes and began ingratiating himself with the army masses, the very community Galba's parsimonious policy and hard discipline had alienated:

---

29   Also in more detail, *Hist.* 1.22; on Otho's resemblance to Nero and his studied effort to win over the military by avoiding to break with the Neronian era, see Haynes 2003, 54–7; Ash 1999, 86.

Hist. 1.23: Sed sceleris cogitatio incertum an repens: studia militum iam pridem spe successionis aut paratu facinoris adfectaverat, in itinere, in agmine, in stationibus vetustissimum quemque militum nomine vocans ac memoria Neroniani comitatus contubernalis appellando; alios agnoscere, quosdam requirere et pecunia aut gratia iuvare, inserendo saepius querelas et ambiguos de Galba sermones quaeque alia turbamenta vulgi. labores itinerum, inopia commeatuum, duritia imperii atrocius accipiebantur, cum Campaniae lacus et Achaiae urbes classibus adire soliti Pyrenaeum et Alpes et immensa viarum spatia aegre sub armis eniterentur.

Yet it is uncertain whether the idea of committing a crime came suddenly to Otho; he had long been trying to win popularity with the soldiers because he hoped for the succession or was preparing some bold step. On the march, at review, or in camp he addressed all the oldest soldiers by name, and, reminding them that they had attended Nero together, he called them messmates. Others he recognized, some he asked after and helped with money or influence; oftentimes he let drop words of complaint and remarks of a double meaning concerning Galba, and did other things that tended to disturb the common soldiery. For they were grumbling seriously over the toilsome marches, the lack of supplies, and the hard discipline. The men who had been in the habit of going by ship to the lakes of Campania and the cities of Achaia found it hard to climb the Pyrenees and the Alps under arms and to cover endless marches along the high roads.

Galba's decision to pass over Otho, even though the latter was the first provincial governor (legate of Lusitania) to endorse him as emperor, and choose for his successor the young aristocrat Lucius Calpurnius Piso Licinianus, is the occasion for the first major speech in the *Histories* (chapters 15–16). This lengthy speech is not recorded in any of the other sources on Galba —it is likely an invention of Tacitus after the pattern of the Thucydidean *demegoriae* which allegedly captured the spirit of what the speaker could or would have said at the time. In this speech the new emperor expresses his regret that the restoration of Republican government (or *libertas*, a core idea of the traditional Republican constitution, broadly understood as the constitution which enables the *civitas* to be domination-free, and decision-making to be directed only by the *auctoritas* of the Senate) is no longer an option.[30] What can replace *libertas* is adoption, the emperor's decision to choose wisely as his successor the best man (and not leave state leadership to the vicissitudes of hereditary succession). This is Galba's idea of the new regime, a different political scheme proposed *in loco libertatis*.[31] By embracing this idea Galba

---

30 The classic study on Republican libertas is Wirszubski 1960; other important and more concise treatments include Hammond 1963; Brunt 1988; and more recently Kennedy 2014.
31 Tacitus opens the *Annales*, too, by associating *libertas* and hope, and in similar fashion: *spes* is transferred to the people's hopes for *libertas*, which are destined to prove abortive (*Ann.* 1.4.2).

sets himself against Augustus, in order to prove that he emulated the great *princeps*: like Augustus, Galba was a traditionalist who propagandized avidly his desire to restore the Republic, yet, unlike Augustus, who declared that his regime was not a monarchy but rather the restitution of the Republic (*Res Gestae* 1.1), Galba bravely admits that the ancestral Republic is not possible to be revived, and that the best one might hope for is a comparable constitution *in loco libertatis*. Then, the new emperor shares with the attending crowd his decision to adopt his successor, just as Augustus had done; but unlike the first emperor who selected his heirs from relatives related to him by blood or marriage, Galba distances himself from his model and adopts his heir on the basis of merit. In this respect, Galba introduces a ground-breaking change to the political structure, as he introduces an imperial heir who was made, not born. Succinctly, Galba's effort to inspire in his reign the hope generated by Augustus' rhetoric for the restitution of the Republic is also an effort to move beyond Augustus' paradigm and avoid the pessimism of the decline and corruption that hereditary succession brought in the aftermath of Augustus' death.[32]

Identifying the power of hope as a rhetorical device aiming at persuasion — the persuasion of one's own self—, Averill and Sundararajan have argued that hope must be creative if it is to be effective. Effectiveness means that an action or episode that is considered to generate hope has to combine novelty (whether it offers new approaches or solutions to a problem) and authenticity (whether it reflects desires of the self). The former is expressed by actions, which are taken to change a situation, while the latter is expressed by wishes, whose fulfilment depend on the success of the actions.[33] Galba's adoption of Piso seemingly combines novelty and authenticity. The emperor does offer a solution to a problem by

---

32 It is worth noting that under Augustus *Spes* is deified and tied to the emperor: each year the Romans offered a *supplicatio* to the deified *Spes* on the anniversary of Augustus' manhood ceremony (*Feriale Cumanum* = ILS 108; cf. Severy 2004, 130). This focus on the emperor identified hope as both private and public (all the more so, given that Augustus was the *Pater Patriae* —the leader who broke the borders between public and private, starting with the architecture of his own house; cf. Carettoni 1983). Clark (1982, 41) notes: "We should imagine here the virtue as proceeding from the hope of a great name to the hope of the Empire and down to the expectations of all Romans. The emanation of *spes* was a single process, for the hope of the imperial family was also the personal hope of private citizens". Clark shows that this concept was picked up and used by later emperors, who likewise wished to convey the idea of succeeding Augustus and perpetuating Augustus' leadership paradigm. The special personal connection to *Spes Augusta* in the context of strengthening their leadership profile is used as late as the Flavian era; see Seelentag 2009.

33 On hope as rhetorical device articulated as a creative emotional experience, which may be evaluated in terms of novelty and authenticity, see Averill and Sundararajan 2005.

means of a novel, unprecedented solution, that is adoption, and his act is authentic, sensible and in accordance with his own desires. But, the narrative of Piso's adoption proves ineffective because the particular successor is not the right one: Galba fails to appreciate properly the situation at hand; he projects his own hope on that of the majority of his people, who, once again (cf. 1.12.3 *multi*), contrary to him, are reported to nurture hope only for their own private interests and care nothing for the State (*Hist.* 1.19.1: *Inde apud senatum non comptior Galbae, non longior quam apud militem sermo: Pisonis comis oratio. et patrum favor aderat: multi voluntate, effusius qui noluerant, medii ac plurimi obvio obsequio, privatas spes agitantes sine publica cura*, "Galba's speech to the senate was as bold and brief as his address to the soldiers. Piso spoke with grace; and the senators showed their approval. Many did this from good-will, those who had opposed the adoption with more effusion, the indifferent — and they were the most numerous — with ready servility, for they had their private hopes in mind and cared nothing for the state"). Thus, what is introduced as a great hope and a great political cure by the emperor, in the end brings about yet another civil war.

To readers with strong memories and solid knowledge of politics, Piso's candidacy is a mixed blessing. The details surrounding Piso's biography reveal that in adopting Piso, Galba chooses a younger version of himself. In his explanation of the reasons for his choice, Galba points out that Piso has a glorious lineage stretching back into the 'free' Republic and Pompey the Great; Galba himself was a descendent of another glorious aristocratic family, the Sulpicii, whose line allegedly went as far back as Greek myth and Jupiter (Suet. *Galba* 2). Further, for Galba, Piso was an outsider to court politics and had a blameless record of political conduct under Nero, since during the latter's reign he was in exile. Galba's long stay in remote Spain likewise may be considered a kind of exile. Finally, just like Galba, Piso was a traditionalist and childless.

Ironically, all these credentials appear impressive only when considered from Galba's optimistic perspective. In truth, Piso had a blameless political record only because he had not held prior to that date political office in Rome and hardly had a chance to test his abilities; once he acquired his first leading office, that of the emperor's heir, he died in less than five days. His noble family was one of the families most severely struck in recent memory: his cousin was Gaius Calurnius Piso, the conspirator against Nero in AD 65. Both his parents, Marcus Licinius Crassus Frugi and Scribonia (direct descendant of Pompeia, the daughter of Pompey the Great), were murdered by the Emperor Claudius (for unknown reasons). Likewise, his older brother who bore the name Gnaeus Pompeus Magnus and was married to Claudia Antonia, a daughter of Claudius, was executed in 46 at the instigation of the empress Messalina.³⁴ Another brother, Marcus Licinius Crassus Frugi, was killed by Nero, between 66 and 68, because of information brought against him. A third one, older than Piso, was killed at a later date.³⁵ Even the childlessness detail, which in Galba's political rhetoric astutely acquired a new meaning (a childless leader is free to choose the best for his successor), in reality serves Galba's undisclosed vainglorious aspiration to clone himself —to institute not just a new dynasty, but to perpetuate the leadership model of the Roman state after himself.

The futility of Galba's utopian fixation with traditionalism Tacitus dismisses in a sarcastic statement that conveys the popular feeling of betrayal of hope. This sentence epigraphically wraps up Galba's career:

> *Hist.* 1.49.4: maior privato visus dum privatus fuit, et omnium consensu capax imperii nisi imperasset.
>
> When he was a commoner he seemed too great to be a commoner: and all would have agreed that he had the qualifications to be an emperor—if only he had not become one.

A few lines earlier in the same paragraph, Tacitus repeats the paradox that underscored Galba's imperial prospects (*Hist.* 1.49.2: *hunc exitum habuit Servius Galba, tribus et septuaginta annis quinque principes prospera fortuna emensus et alieno imperio felicior quam suo*, "This was the end of Servius Galba. He had lived seventy-three years, through the reigns of five emperors, with good fortune, and he was happier under the rule of others than in his own"), and by this anadiplosis underscores the juxtaposition between hope and reality.

In conclusion, Galba's brief imperial tenure offers a mini-narrative of failed hope on several levels. Nero's reign caused an identity crisis in many respects, as roles were shifting and power relations changed. The death of Nero generated hope, not only for a better future but also for the existence of a future, a different next phase in the history of the *Respublica*, and Galba became its first embodiment. In theory, Galba's rule invigorated the body politic for it offered the opportunity to imagine that the present would change for the better. He tried to give concrete shape to the hopes of the Romans, by offering them a) a new regime that

---

34 Cassius Dio (Epitome of Book 61, ch.29.6) states that Messalina ordered Gnaeus Pompeius's death because "of his family and his relationship to the emperor"; evidently she feared that he would be a rival to Messalina and Claudius' son Britannicus.

35 *Hist.* 1.48; about this elder brother and his death after Piso Tacitus notes: "Piso had at least this advantage over his elder brother, that the latter was to be killed first" (*ad hoc tantum maiori fratri praelatus est ut prior occideretur*). On Piso's family and career, see Damon 2003, 135 (*ad* 14.1) and 138 (*ad* 15.2).

would revive many features of the idealized *Respublica* (the political version of the Golden Age for Rome); b) a leader who abided by the *mos maiorum*; c) a concrete vision for the future, in the adoption of Piso and in the detailed presentation of the rationale that determined his decision to adopt Piso. Galba's vision never materialized because it circumvented Otho, who saw his own hopes being crushed when Galba chose Piso instead as his successor. To Otho, failed hope brought about drastic reaction.

The opening episode of the *Histories* is determined by hope and memory, two interrelated themes. Galba's rise is expedited by the fact that hope, which overwhelmed the Roman people and their individual leaders in the aftermath of Nero's death, is a fuzzy concept, realized in the desire to experience a different situation, better than the one just concluded. 'Better', however, is not defined in the *Histories*, and it could not possibly be so: Tacitus energizes his heroes (individual leaders or groups of people with common interests) by offering them motives, plans, and visions through which their rush of excitement and the prospects of operative hope may acquire shape and morph into expectations. The formation of these expectations is directed by memory —in the case at hand, by the way the Romans remembered Galba or related to him in the past, either individually or collectively. This importance of memory in determining hope is brought to the fore already in the opening line of the *Histories*, when Tacitus instructs his readers to recourse to their memory (personal or literary) and revisit Galba's past. The readers' memory of Galba is directed to blend with the memory of the aspiring emperor in the Roman historical memory, which is rather negative. Originally, the general elation in the early days following Nero's death and Galba's retirement in the periphery of the empire blurs the actual memory of his leadership and stirs up hopes that the new emperor will be better than his predecessor. When memory returns and personal desire overshadows public interest, Tacitus' pessimistic prism makes a successful turnout of his imperial prospects seem unlikely.

Bibliography

Ash, R. 1999. *Ordering Anarchy: Armies and Leaders in Tacitus' Histories*, London.
— — 2006. *Tacitus* (Ancients in Action), Bristol.
— — 2012. *Oxford Readings in Tacitus*, Oxford.
Averill, J.R./L. Sundararajan. 2005. "Hope as Rhetoric: Cultural Narratives of Wishing and Coping," in: J.A. Eliott (ed.), *Interdisciplinary Perspectives on Hope*, New York, 133–166.
Bartsch, S. 1994. *Actors in the Audience: Theatricality and Doublespeak from Nero to Hadrian*, Cambridge, Mass.
Beard, M. 2013. *Confronting the Classics: Traditions, Adventures, and Innovations*, New York.
Benario, H.W. 1972. "*Imperium* and *Capaces imperii* in Tacitus," in: *AJP* 93, 14–26.

Brunt, P.A. 1988. "Libertas in the Republic," in: P.A. Brunt (ed.), *Fall of the Roman Republic and Related Essays*, Oxford, 281–350.
Cairns, D.L. 2008. "Look Both Ways: Studying Emotion in Ancient Greek," in: *Critical Quarterly* 50.4, 43–62.
Carettoni, G. 1983. *Das Haus des Augustus auf dem Palatin*, Mainz.
Clark, M.E. 1982. "Images and Concepts of Hope in the Early Imperial Cult," in: K.H. Richards (ed.), *Society of Biblical Literature: Seminar Papers*, Chico, CA, 39–44.
Cole, T. 1992. "Initium mihi operis Servius Galba iterum T. Vinius consules," in: *YCS* 29, 231–45.
Damon, C. 2003. *Tacitus: Histories Book 1*, Cambridge.
—— 2010. "Déjà vu or déjà lu? History as Intertext," in: *PLLS* 14, 375–88.
—— 2017. "Writing with Posterity in Mind: Thucydides and Tacitus on Secession," in: S. Forsdyke/E. Foster/R. Balot (eds.), *Oxford Handbook on Thucydides*, Oxford, 677–89.
Devillers, O. 2012. "The Concentration of Power and Writing History: Forms of Historical Persuasion in the *Histories* (1.1–49)," in: V.E. Pagan (ed.), *A Companion to Tacitus*, Malden, MA, 162–88.
Edwards, C. 2000. *Suetonius: Lives of the Caesars. A New Translation*, Oxford.
Feeney, D. 2009. "Time," in: A. Feldherr (ed.), *The Cambridge Companion to the Roman Historians*, Cambridge, 139–51.
Foucher, A. 2000. *Historia proxima poetis: L'influence de la poésie épique sur le style des historiens latins de Salluste à Ammien Marcellin*, Bruxelles.
Geiser M. 2007. *Personendarstellung bei Tacitus am Beispiel von Cn. Domitius Corbulo und Ser. Sulpicius Galba*, Remscheid.
Gerber, A./A. Greef (eds.). 1903. *Lexicon Taciteum*. U et V litteras confecit C. John, Leipzig.
Gowing, A. 2005. *Empire and Memory: The Representation of the Roman Republic in Imperial Culture*, Cambridge.
Hammond, H. 1963. "*Res olim dissociablies-Principatus ac libertas*: Liberty under the Early Roman Empire," in: *HSCP* 67, 93–113.
Haynes, H. 2003. *The History of Make-Believe: Tacitus on Imperial Rome*, Berkeley.
Joseph, T.A. 2012. *Tacitus the Epic Successor: Virgil, Lucan, and the Narrative of Civil War in the Histories*, Leiden.
Kaster, R.A. 2005. *Emotion, Restraint, and Community in Ancient Rome*, Oxford.
Keitel, E. 2006. "*Sententia* and Structure in Tacitus, *Histories* 1.12–49," in: *Arethusa* 39, 219–44.
—— 2010. "The Art of Losing: Tacitus and the Disaster Narrative," in: C.S. Kraus/J. Marincola/C. Pelling (eds.), *Ancient Historiography and Its Contexts: Studies in Honour of A.J. Woodman*, Oxford, 331–52.
Kennedy, G. 2014. "Cicero, Roman Republicanism and the Contested Meaning of *Libertas*," in: *Political Studies* 63.2, 488–501.
Kraus, C.S./A.J. Woodman. 1997. *Latin Historians* (Greece and Rome. Surveys in the Classics 27), Oxford.
Lauletta, M. 1998. *L'intreccio degli stili in Tacito: intertestualità prosa-poesia nella letteratura*, Napoli.
Lendering, J. 2011. "The Batavian Revolt," in: *Ancient History Encyclopedia*. Last modified November 28, 2011. http://www.ancient.eu /article/286/.
Lendering, J./A. Bosman. 2012. *Edge of Empire: Rome's Frontier on the Rhine*, Rotterdam.
Levene, D.S. 1992. "Sallust's Jugurtha: An 'Historical Fragment," in: *JRS* 82, 53–70.
L'Hoir, F.S. 2006. *Tragedy, Rhetoric, and the Historiography of Tacitus' Annales*, Ann Arbor.
Martin, R.H. 1981. *Tacitus*, Berkeley.

Miller, N.P. 1987. "Virgil and Tacitus Again," in: *PVS* 18, 87–106.
Moore, C.H. tr. 1923. *Tacitus: Histories. Books 1–3* (Tacitus vol. II). Loeb Classical Texts, Cambridge, Mass.
Morgan, M.G. 1993. "The Unity of Tacitus, *Histories* 1.12–20," in: *Athenaeum* 81, 567–86.
—— 2006. *69 AD. The Year of the Four Emperors*, Oxford.
Pagan, V.E. 2006. "Shadows and Assassinations: Forms of Time in Tacitus and Appian," in: *Arethusa* 39, 193–218.
Seelentag, G. 2009. "*Spes Augusta*: Titus und Domitian in der Herrschaftsdartstellung Vespasians," in: *Latomus* 69, 83–100.
Severy, B. 2004. *Augustus and the Family at the Birth of the Roman Empire*, London.
Shotter, D.C.A. 1967. "The Starting-Dates of Tacitus' Historical Works," in: *CQ* 17, 158–63.
—— 1997. *Nero*. New York/London.
Steinbock, A.J. 2007. "The Phenomenology of Despair," in: *International Journal of Philosophical Studies* 15.3, 435–51.
Syme, R. 1958. *Tacitus*, Oxford.
Trilling, L. 2012 [1950] "Tacitus Now," in: L. Trilling (ed.) *The Liberal Imagination: Essays on Literature and Society* (with an introduction by L. Menand), 2nd edn., New York, (1st edn. 1950): 198–204 (repr. in Ash 2012, 435–39).
Turpin, W. 2008. "Tacitus, Stoic 'Exempla', and The *Praecipuum Munus Annalium*," in: *CA* 27.2, 359–404.
Wilkinson, S. 2012. *Republicanism in the Early Roman Empire*, London/New York.
Wirszubski, C. 1960. *Libertas as a Political Idea at Rome during the Late Republic and Early Principate*, Cambridge, Mass.
Wellesley, K. 2000. *The Year of the Four Emperors*, 3rd edn., with an Introduction by B. Levick, London/New York.
Woodman, A.J. 1988. *Rhetoric in Classical Historiography*, London/Sydney.
—— 1993. "Amateur Dramatics at the Court of Nero: *Annals* 15.48–74," in: T.J. Luce/A.J. Woodman (eds.), *Tacitus and the Tacitean Tradition*, Princeton, 104–28.
Zehnacher, H. 1987. "Tensions et contradictions dans l'Empire au Ier siècle. Les témoignages numismatiques," in: A. Giovanni/D. van Bercham (eds.), *Opposition et résistances à l'Empire d'Auguste à Trajan*, Entretiens Fondation Hardt 33, Geneva, 321–57.

Part III: **Scripts of 'Hope' in History, Art, and Inscriptions**

Kostas Vlassopoulos
Hope and Slavery

What is the relationship between hope and slavery? The answer to this question depends on the assumptions one makes regarding slavery. A very influential approach starts from Orlando Patterson's famous definition of slavery as social death: "the permanent, violent domination of natally alienated and generally dishonoured persons".[1] If slavery is tantamount to social death, then it is a truly hopeless situation. The only hope a slave might entertain is to reverse the 'day of slavery', gain his freedom and, within this new condition, entertain the full range of hopes that those who are socially alive can dream of. Nobody would deny that the concept of social death captures an essential aspect of the experience of slavery. Equally, the hope for freedom is undoubtedly a particularly strong emotion for most slaves across time and space. I shall have more to say about this in the latter part of this essay; but before this, I think it is quite essential to situate the link between hope and slavery within an alternative, and much wider framework, than the one that reduces slavery to a form of social death.

What is problematic about approaches like that of social death is their essentialist quest. Such approaches, shaped by the methodology of the social sciences, aimed to pinpoint the 'essence' of the diverse forms of slavery across space and time. This sociological tradition of studying slavery is characterized by its top-down and unilateralist perspective; slavery is seen as a relationship of domination and exploitation unilaterally defined by the masters. In this perspective, slaves are merely passive objects of exploitation and domination: their agency is shaped by the fact that their status is unilaterally defined by others, and that they exist instrumentally, in order to serve the aims and purposes of others.[2] Aristotle has provided an excellent illustration of this perception of slavery:[3]

> τὸ δὲ κτῆμα λέγεται ὥσπερ καὶ τὸ μόριον. τό τε γὰρ μόριον οὐ μόνον ἄλλου ἐστὶ μόριον, ἀλλὰ καὶ ὅλως ἄλλου· ὁμοίως δὲ καὶ τὸ κτῆμα. διὸ ὁ μὲν δεσπότης τοῦ δούλου δεσπότης μόνον, ἐκείνου δ' οὐκ ἔστιν· ὁ δὲ δοῦλος οὐ μόνον δεσπότου δοῦλός ἐστιν, ἀλλὰ καὶ ὅλως ἐκείνου.[4]

---

1 Patterson 1982, 13.
2 For a critique of such approaches, see Vlassopoulos 2016.
3 The reasons why Aristotle has proved so useful for modern essentialist approaches to slavery, and the extent to which Aristotle's approach differed from most Greek approaches to slavery is explored in Vlassopoulos 2011a.
4 Aristotle *Politics*, 1254a9–13.

> And the term piece of property is used in the same way as the term part: a thing that is a part is not only a part of another thing, but absolutely belongs to another thing, and so also does a piece of property. Hence, whereas the master is merely the slave's master and does not belong to [the slave], the slave is not merely the slave of the master but wholly belongs to the master.

In other words, a master is not defined exclusively by the fact that he is master of a slave: he also has other identities (father, citizen, architect, Greek), and, accordingly, he is the sum of all those identities and the aims, hopes and disappointments connected with them. But in the case of the slave, Aristotle argues, this does not apply: a slave is exclusively defined by his instrumental existence for other people's aims and wishes.

If we want to situate the link between hope and slavery within a wider framework, we need to challenge this pervasive assumption. And one can think of few means that are more apt for such a purpose than Artemidorus' marvellous handbook *Oneirocritica* (*The Interpretation of Dreams*). It is true of course that Artemidorus makes a clear distinction between two kinds of dreams: the *enypnion*, the dream that expresses the hopes and fears of individuals, and the *oneiros*, the predictive dream, which strictly speaking constitutes the sole subject of Artemidorus' work.[5] Nevertheless, the reason that people would consult the dream interpreter who would be armed with Artemidorus' handbook is precisely in order to find out how the predictive power of dreams would relate with their hopes and fears about the future.

Apart from its links with hope, what makes Artemidorus' book particularly useful is the multiplex framework he employs in the act of interpretation. The same dream can have very different meanings depending on the identity of the dreamer and the life context for which the dream stands as a metaphor.[6] Slaves are present in Artemidorus' handbook both as dreamers and as elements in the dream repertoire. But it is crucial that slaves do not appear as a single category with identifiable features; instead, the identity and the features of the slaves as a category can change significantly, depending on the point of view from which Artemidorus approaches them.[7]

I will now offer a few examples that illustrate this point, and tease out their implications. My first example is a neat illustration of the instrumental view of slavery presented by Aristotle above:

---

5 Artemidorus, *Oneirocritica*, 4, preface.
6 Pomeroy 1991; Hahn 1992.
7 For slaves and slavery in Artemidorus, see Annequin 1987, 2005, 2008; Klees 1990.

ἅμα τοῖς ἄλλοις ἀποτελέσμασιν οἱ δοῦλοι καὶ πρὸς τὸ σῶμα τῶν δεσποτῶν τὴν ἀναφορὰν ἔχουσιν. ὁ γοῦν δόξας τὸν οἰκέτην πυρέσσοντα ἰδεῖν εἰκότως αὐτὸς ἐνόσησεν· ὃν γὰρ ἔχει λόγον ὁ οἰκέτης πρὸς τὸν ὁρῶντα, τὸν αὐτὸν καὶ τὸ σῶμα πρὸς τὴν ψυχήν.[8]

Together with their other outcomes, slaves also have a certain correlation with the bodies of their masters. Indeed someone who had imagined that he observed his slave having a fever fittingly fell ill himself; for the connection that a slave has in relation to the dream-observer, the body has in relation to the soul.

In this case a slave's dream does not even refer to the future of the slave; because the slave only exists for the sake of his master, the slave's dream actually predicts something concerning the master. A rather different perception of slavery appears in the next passage:

τὸ δὲ δοκεῖν καιομένους ἰδεῖν τοὺς πόδας πᾶσιν ἐπίσης κακὸν καὶ σημαίνει ἀποβολὴν καὶ διαφθορὰν <τῶν> ὑπαρχόντων, ναὶ μὴν καὶ παίδων καὶ δούλων· ἐπίσης γὰρ τοῖς θεράπουσιν οἱ παῖδες ὑπηρετοῦσί τε τοῖς γονεῦσι καὶ θεραπεύουσιν αὐτοὺς ὥσπερ οἰκέται. ὅπερ τοὺς πολλοὺς ἔλαθε τῶν ὀνειροκριτῶν ἡγουμένους ὅτι οἱ πόδες μόνους οἰκέτας σημαίνουσι.[9]

And imagining that one sees one's feet on fire is bad for all alike and signifies the loss and destruction of one's belongings, yes, even of one's children and slaves. For children, like attendants, minister to their parents and attend to them just as slaves do. This has escaped the notice of the interpreters, who think that feet signify the slaves alone.

In this example, Artemidorus brings together children and slaves as belonging in a single category, from the point of view of the father and master. The feet stand as a metaphor for service, and in this respect, children and slaves should be considered together, as Artemidorus insists.[10] A rather different perspective emerges from the juxtaposition offered in the next passage:

Λέοντα ἰδεῖν ἥμερον μὲν καὶ σαίνοντα καὶ προσιόντα ἀβλαβῶς ἀγαθὸν ἂν εἴη καὶ φέρον ὠφελείας στρατιώτῃ μὲν ἀπὸ βασιλέως... δημότῃ δὲ ἀπὸ ἄρχοντος καὶ δούλῳ ἀπὸ δεσπότου· τούτοις γὰρ [καὶ] τὸ ζῷον ἔοικε διὰ τὸ δυνατὸν καὶ ἰσχυρόν.[11]

---

8 Artemidorus, *Oneirocritica*, 4.30.
9 Artemidorus, *Oneirocritica*, 1.48.
10 In Roman households children and slaves were both under the full power of the *pater familias*, even if duties and expectations between fathers and children and masters and slaves could diverge significantly: Saller 1994, 102–53.
11 Artemidorus, *Oneirocritica*, 2.12.

> To observe a lion that is tame and simpering and approaches harmlessly is good and delivers assistance to a soldier from a king... to a citizen from the magistrate and to a slave from his master; for this animal resembles these people due to its power and strength.

In this case, the lion stands as a metaphor for relations of power: slaves are juxtaposed with soldiers and citizens, as people who have the subordinate position in relations of power with masters, kings and magistrates. Slavery is conceptualised as a relationship of domination, in which two asymmetrical sides negotiate power. The fourth example shifts from domination and power to adversity:

> ὄμβρος δὲ καὶ λαῖλαψ καὶ χειμὼν κινδύνους καὶ ζημίας ἐπάγουσι, μόνοις δὲ δούλοις καὶ πένησι καὶ τοῖς ἔν τινι περιστάσει οὖσιν ἀπαλλαγὴν τῶν ἐν ποσὶ κακῶν προαγορεύουσι· μετὰ γὰρ τοὺς μεγάλους χειμῶνας εὐδία γίνεται.[12]

> And a thunderstorm and hurricane and winter storm bring about dangers and losses. But alone for slaves and poor people and those who are in a difficult position they foretell a release from their present ills; for following great storms good weather arises.

Slaves are individuals who face difficult circumstances, and this brings them together with the poor; slavery is considered as an extreme form of bad luck, which with perseverance and good fortune one could see through.[13] Our next passage moves in a very different direction:

> τὸ κεραυνοῦσθαι... δούλων μὲν τοὺς μὴ ἐν πίστει ὄντας ἐλευθεροῖ, τοὺς δὲ ἐν πίστει ὄντας ἢ τιμῇ παρὰ τοῖς δεσπόταις ἢ πολλὰ κτήματα ἔχοντας ἀφαιρεῖ τῆς πίστεως καὶ τῆς τιμῆς καὶ τῶν κτημάτων.[14]

> To be struck by a thunderbolt...frees those slaves who are not trusted. But those who are trusted or honoured by their masters, or who possess much property, it removes from this trust and honour and property.

The thunderbolt is a symbol of radical reversals of circumstances for diverse groups of people. Having delineated various categories among free people, Artemidorus moves on to explore the differential meaning of the thunderbolt by distinguishing two categories among slaves: slaves without favour and trust, and slaves who are trusted and honoured by their masters and enjoy material benefits of property as a result. This focus on trust and honour as aspects that differentiate certain slaves from others points towards an alternative conceptualisation of

---

12 Artemidorus, *Oneirocritica*, 2.8.
13 For ancient views of slavery as a form of bad luck, see Williams 1993, 116–24.
14 Artemidorus, *Oneirocritica*, 2.9.

slavery. Slaves who enjoy trust, honour and property from their masters have clearly earned them as a result of their behaviour and actions. From this point of view, slavery is not only an instrumental relationship in which slaves merely exist in order to serve the needs of their masters; it is rather a reciprocal relationship of mutual benefaction and reward between masters and slaves, in which both benefit from it, even if in widely asymmetrical ways. Equally significant is the reference to honoured slaves: it is one example among many why Patterson's essentialist understanding of slavery as a state of dishonour can be quite misleading. That symbols can be used in mixed ways is illustrated by the next example:

> εἴ τις δόξειε γεννᾶσθαι ὑπὸ γυναικὸς ἡστινοσοῦν.... δούλῳ δὲ σημαίνει τὸ φιλεῖσθαι παρὰ τοῦ δεσπότου κἂν ἁμάρτῃ συγγνώμης ἀξιοῦσθαι, ἐλευθερωθῆναι δὲ οὐδέπω· καὶ γὰρ οὐδὲ τὰ βρέφη ἑαυτῶν ἄρχει, κἂν ἐλεύθερα ᾖ.[15]

> To imagine to be born from any woman... for the slave signifies being held dear by his master and that, even if he makes a mistake, he will be worthy of forgiveness, but will not yet be freed; for babies also do not rule themselves, even if they are free.

In this case the metaphor of the baby symbolises both the intimate relationship between master and slave, as well as the power hierarchy that subordinates a slave to his master. This link between intimacy and power is well explored in another passage:

> λεκάνη οἰκέτην σημαίνει καὶ θεράπαιναν πιστούς. πίνειν δὲ ἐκ λεκάνης ἐρασθῆναι θεραπαίνης σημαίνει, τὸ δ' αὐτὸ καὶ εἴ τις ἐσθίοι ἐν λεκάνῃ. λεκάνην χρυσέαν ἢ ἀργυρέαν ἔχειν ἤτοι θεράπαιναν ἀπελευθερώσαντα γῆμαι σημαίνει ἢ ἀπηλευθερωμένῃ συνοικῆσαι... λεκάνῃ ἐγκατοπτρίζεσθαι τεκνῶσαι ἀπὸ θεραπαίνης σημαίνει.[16]

> The pot signifies a trusted male or female slave. To drink from a pot signifies to fall in love with a maid, and the same if one eats from a pot. To have a golden or silver pot signifies either that he will liberate and marry his female slave, or that he will live together with his freedwoman... To see one's reflection on a pot signifies having children from the maid.

A major context for intimacy and power between masters and slaves is that of sexual relationships.[17] The passage envisions the possibilities of falling in love with a slave, having children from a slave, and, finally, manumitting and marrying a slave. The significance of the sexual lives of slaves for the link between sex

---

15 Artemidorus, *Oneirocritica*, 1.13.
16 Artemidorus, *Oneirocritica*, 3.30.
17 See Klees 1998, 155–75; Harper 2011, 249–325; Green 2015.

and hope will emerge in the course of this chapter. A final passage turns our attention away from relations between masters and slaves:

> οἷον ἔδοξέ τις ὑπὸ τοῦ δεσπότου πεφονεῦσθαι. ἠλευθερώθη ὑπὸ τοῦ φονεύοντος, ἐπειδὴ ὁ θάνατος τοῦτο ἐσήμαινεν· ὁ δὲ τοῦ θανάτου αἴτιος καὶ τῆς ἐλευθερίας ἦν αἴτιος· ἐδύνατο γάρ. ὁ δὲ ὑπὸ τοῦ συνδούλου δόξας φονεύεσθαι ἐλεύθερος μὲν οὐκ ἐγένετο (οὐ γὰρ οἷός τε ἦν ὁ σύνδουλος αὐτὸν ἐλευθεροῦν), εἰς ἔχθραν δὲ κατέστη αὐτῷ· οὐ γὰρ φίλοι οἱ φονεύοντες τοῖς ἀναιρουμένοις.[18]
>
> Someone dreamed that he was killed by his master; he was freed by the killer, because this is what the murder signified, and the cause of his murder was the cause of his freedom, since this was possible. Someone else who dreamed that he was killed by a fellow slave was not liberated (for the fellow slave could not liberate him), but they became enemies, since murderers are not friends of their victims.

While relations between masters and slaves were clearly important, we should never forget that relationships among slaves, as in the passage above, and relationships between slaves and other free people apart from their master had a significance of their own: many slave hopes revolved around such relationships, and such relationships often proved crucial for the fulfilment of many slave hopes, an issue we will examine in detail below.

It is time to tease out the implications of the passages above. Slavery is an instrumental relationship in which slaves exist for the purpose of serving the needs and wishes of their masters; but instrumentality was not the only means of conceiving and employing slavery.[19] Slavery could be seen as an asymmetrical negotiation of power between masters and slaves: a relationship not unilaterally defined from above, but the outcome of struggle, negotiation, compromise and failure.[20] From this point of view, slave hopes would focus on limiting the power of masters and putting forward their own agenda of aims to the extent of the possible.[21] Slavery could also be envisaged as an asymmetrical relationship of benefaction and reward; masters could opt to see slave labour as loyal service and choose to reward deserving slaves with trust, honour and material benefits; slaves could see their service as the foundation for claims to just rewards. From

---

18 Artemidorus, *Oneirocritica*, 4.64.
19 For the concept of the variable modalities of slavery, see Vlassopoulos forthcoming.
20 For such an approach, see Genovese 1974; Glassman 1991; Berlin 1998.
21 For an impressive, if rare in its clarity and visibility, example from eighteenth-century Brazil, see Schwartz 1977.

this point of view, slave hopes would focus on eliciting master goodwill and the various rewards that came with it.[22]

The above observations show the limits of the instrumental and unilateral approach to slavery. The extent to which masters instrumentalized slavery to cover every aspect of slaves' lives, or only employed it for certain aspects and purposes varied greatly in space and time and for different masters. Masters might attempt to enforce this tool on the full range of slave life, or they might apply it to only certain facets; slaves could try to define aspects of their lives by means of other tools, given that there were other ways of conceptualising slavery that slaves and masters could employ in certain contexts and for certain purposes. Finally, we must take into account that slaves should not be seen exclusively from the point of view of the relationship with their masters. Slaves also formed relationships with other free people apart from their masters; they created slave families; they created communities and networks on the basis of ethnicity, kinship, profession, residence or religion.

Slaves did not merely react to a relationship which was set by others. They also tried to change the rules of the game by creating a world of their own, next, below, and against the world of their masters. They constantly tried to turn slavery into something different than what it claimed to be. Slaves did not lack the drive to create a family, to belong, to achieve recognition and respect, to dream. Their hopes to create families, to enhance their economic condition, to create community, to achieve recognition in the eyes of other people, even to become independent, continuously challenged and modified slavery as a relationship in any given society.[23] Slaves were historical agents, because they constantly strove to make themselves other things apart from being solely slaves, and to redefine the relationship of slavery in their own terms and for their own benefit. Of course, given the enormous asymmetry of power, slaves never achieved their aims completely or permanently; but the battles they won, or did not lose, are historically important.

To sum up: slave hopes have to be situated in the context of slaves aiming to run their lives on lines different than the instrumental aims they were supposed to serve. But the nexus of slavery meant that their hopes and their fulfilment often led to paths significantly different or significantly more complicated than those of free people. This also applies to the most distinctive slave hope: that of annulling the day of slavery and winning their freedom.

---

22 Zelnick-Abramovitz 2005, 6–7.
23 Vlassopoulos 2011b.

Exploring slave hopes under slavery

Let us start with a relatively direct source on slave hopes and fears: that of oracles. Ancient societies had a very wide spectrum of divination practices. We have already encountered the tradition of dream interpretation in the handbook of Artemidorus; other examples include the questions and responses addressed to institutional oracles, like Delphi and Dodona, and sortition oracles, on which I shall focus.[24] Sortition oracles depend on an apparently random and therefore divine link between the enquirer's question and a list of possible answers. While dice oracles were common in many parts of the Mediterranean world, for our purposes of particular interest are the written collections of sortition oracles. The earliest version known to us is the so-called *Sortes Astrampsychi*, a collection composed in the early imperial period, but preserved in two late-antique recensions;[25] the *Sortes Sangallenses* is a late-antique Latin derivative of the *Sortes Astrampsychi*.[26]

The enquirer would select his question among a list of 92 numbered questions; he was then invited to choose randomly a number from 1–10 and add this number to the number of the chosen question. Enquirers would then consult a table in which the added sum (e.g. 68+7=75) would correspond with a particular decade (a collection of ten numbered answers) among a list of 103 decades. The enquirer would then consult within that decade the numbered answer that corresponded to the number from 1–10 he had randomly chosen (i.e. answer 7 of decade 75) — and, lo and behold, he would find an answer that corresponded exactly to the question he had asked. In other words, for every question there was a set of ten possible answers.

Among the list of 92 questions, there are two slave-related questions asked by masters concerning fugitive slaves (36: 'will I find the fugitive?'; 89: 'will the fugitive escape my detection?'), while another one might be construed as the same question asked from the point of view of the fugitive slave ('will my flight be undetected?').[27] But there also exist three questions that were clearly asked by the slaves themselves: number 32 asked 'will I be freed from servitude?'; number

---

[24] For an approach to oracles in terms of dealing with risk, see Eidinow 2007; for slave hopes in the institutional oracles, see Eidinow 2012.
[25] Browne 1983–2001; translated in Hansen 1998, 285–324.
[26] Dold and Meister 1948–51.
[27] On the interpretative issues surrounding this question, see Eidinow 2012, 247, n. 14.

46 'will I come to terms with my master?', and number 74 'am I going to be sold?'.[28]

I shall examine slave hopes for freedom in the final section, so I postpone examining those answers for that section. Let us start by presenting the list of answers for the question concerning relations between masters and slaves:

> 'You won't come to terms with your masters' (33.1)
> 'You won't come to terms with your masters now' (5.2, 39.6, 11.7)
> 'You won't come to terms with your masters just yet' (49.10)
> 'You won't come to terms with your masters. It's not to your advantage' (100.4)
> 'You will come to terms with your masters after a while' (41.5)
> 'With effort you will come to terms with your masters' (10.9)
> 'You will come to terms with your masters and benefit' (45.3)
> 'You will come to terms with your masters and be treated with affection' (74.8)

The answers can be divided along three axes: the first on the basis of whether the reconciliation will take place (6) or not (4); the second concerns the manner of the reconciliation, and whether it will be immediate (2), postponed (5) or achieved after some effort (1); the third concerns the outcome of the reconciliation, with two answers focusing on the particular benefits that the slave will derive out of it; the presumed negative effects of the lack of reconciliation are not specified. Perhaps a good idea of what it meant for a slave to be on bad terms with his master, and how a slave hoped to improve his condition under those circumstances, comes from a fourth-century lead letter from Athens:

> Λῆσις{ις} ἐπιστέλλει Ξενοκλεῖ καὶ τῆι μητρὶ μηδαμῶς περιιδεῖν αὐτὸν ἀπολόμενον ἐν τῶι χαλκείωι, ἀλλὰ πρὸς τὸς δεσπότας αὐτõ ἐλθεῖν καὶ ἐνευρέσθαι τι βέλτιον αὐτῶι. Ἀνθρώπωι γὰρ παραδέδομαι πάνυ πονηρῶι μαστιγόμενος ἀπόλυμαι δέδεμαι προπηλακίζομαι μᾶλλον μᾶ[λ]λον.

> Lesis is sending (a letter) to Xenokles and his mother (asking) that they by no means overlook that he is perishing in the foundry, but that they come to his masters and that they have something better found for him. For I have been handed over to a thoroughly wicked man; I am perishing from being whipped; I am tied up; I am treated like dirt - more and more!

There are various interpretative issues with this letter, which there is no space to treat here in detail. A crucial issue is whether we should envisage the letter as

---

28 For the link between slaves, slavery and sortition oracles, see Kudlien 1991; Eidinow 2012. See also the comments on Kudlien's approach in McKeown 2007, 30–41.

being written by Lesis himself, or composed by somebody else on his behalf.[29] Whatever the answer, it is obvious from the letter's rhetoric, as expressed through its vocabulary, alliteration and asyndeton, that it describes a situation of despair, which offers particularly fertile ground for hope scripts. The most plausible interpretation is that Lesis is a young slave, apprenticed by his masters to a smith and working in a foundry, where he is maltreated and faces terrible conditions.[30] His hope for deliverance lies with Xenokles and his own mother, whom he requests to attend his masters and persuade them to take him out of the foundry and find another less oppressive placement for him. We can neither tell what exactly the relationship between Xenokles and Lesis is, nor what the relationship between Xenokles and Lesis' mother might have been. But whatever the case, this is a clear illustration why we should not reduce slavery to a binary relationship between masters and slaves; Lesis hopes that employing his wider network of kinship and support will succeed in convincing his masters to improve his lot. This shows why a significant part of slave hopes revolved around the creation and maintenance of such networks and communities of kinship and support, as we shall see below.[31]

Let us now move to the answers to the question concerning slave sale:

> 'You won't be sold. It won't benefit you. Stand fast' (55.5)
> 'You won't be sold just yet, but it won't benefit you' (30.6)
> 'You won't be sold to your benefit' (58.8)
> You won't be sold, but you will be set free with a bequest' (87.10)
> 'You will be sold, but not just yet' (60.1, 14.4)
> 'You will be sold and you will be sorry when you don't profit at all' (43.3)
> 'Where you will be purchased, you'll have regrets' (64.7)
> 'You will be purchased and it will go well for you with those to whom you're sold' (84.2)
> 'You will be sold and you will be set free' (85.9)

As with the previous question, the answers can be divided along three axes: the first is according to whether the slave will be sold (6) or not (4); the second in regard to whether the outcome will be positive (3), negative (5) or undefined (2); the third concerns the timescale, and whether the sale will be immediate (4) or postponed (3). Most of the answers that state that the slave will not be sold, predict that this will not be to the slave's benefit (30.6, 58.8), although one advises the slave to stand fast and not try to improve his luck by fleeing (55.5); equally,

---

29 For publication of this text and variant interpretations, see Jordan 2000; Harris 2004, whose interpretation I generally follow; Eidinow and Taylor 2010.
30 This letter is also discussed in Olympia Bobou's contribution to this volume.
31 For the significance of such networks and communities for ancient slaves, see Vlassopoulos 2011b.

two answers predict that the slave will be sold and will regret his new masters and surroundings (43.3, 64.7). On the other hand, it is predicted that the slave will not be sold, but rewarded with freedom and a bequest (87.10), that he will be sold and freed (85.9), or that he will be sold, but succeed with his new masters (84.2).

Sale constituted one of the most critical moments in a slave's life. As such, it was potent with both hope and fear. Hope concerned the possibility of gaining freedom, or of enhancing one's condition, as we have already examined. Fear obviously related to the unknown circumstances that awaited the slave in his new surroundings; 'better the devil that you know' was often an apt summary of how slaves thought about changing masters. But fear did not concern only the risk of the unknown: it also concerned the risk of dismantling existing networks and communities of kinship, emotion and support, in which the slave already participated. A telling example is the incident narrated in the *Life of Melania the Younger*, a late-antique scion of one of the richest senatorial families, who, along with her husband Pinianus, decided to divest themselves from their riches and follow an ascetic mode of life:

> καὶ ἅμα ταῦτα αὐτῶν βουλευομένων, μέγιστον αὐτοῖς πειρασμὸν ἐξήγειρεν ὁ ἐχθρὸς τῆς ἀληθείας διάβολος. φθονήσας γὰρ τῇ τοσαύτῃ κατὰ Θεὸν πυρώσει τῶν νέων, ὑπέβαλεν τῷ ἀδελφῷ τοῦ μακαρίου Πινιανοῦ Σευήρῳ καὶ ἀνέπεισεν τοὺς δούλους αὐτῶν εἰπεῖν ὅτι «ὅλως οὐ πιπρασκόμεθα· εἰ δὲ βιασθῶμεν ἐπὶ πλεῖον τοῦ πραθῆναι, ὁ ἀδελφός σου Σευῆρος δεσπότης ἡμῶν ἐστιν καὶ αὐτὸς ἡμᾶς ἀγοράζει». ἐθορυβήθησάν τε ἐκ τούτου σφοδρῶς ὁρῶντες τοὺς ἐν τοῖς προαστείοις Ῥώμης δούλους αὐτῶν στασιάζοντας.[32]
>
> While they were planning these things, the Devil, the enemy of truth, subjected them to an enormous test. Since he was jealous at the great zeal these young people showed for God, he prompted Severus, the brother of the blessed Pinianus, and he persuaded their slaves to say: 'we realize we haven't been sold yet, but if we are forced to be sold, rather than be put on the open market, we prefer to have your brother Severus as our master and have him buy us'. [Melania and Pinianus] were very upset by this turn of events, at seeing their slaves in the suburbs of Rome rising in rebellion.

The plan of Severus, Pinianus' brother, was to acquire his brother's property on the cheap; to achieve this aim, he incited the slaves in his brother's landholdings to revolt, in order to put pressure on Pinianus to sell the whole portfolio to him at a bargain price, rather than opt for the higher price he would acquire, if the properties were sold piecemeal to the highest bidders on the market. But the crucial question for our purposes is what made the slaves demand not to be sold, or if

---

32 Gerontius, *Life of Melania*, 10.

that were not possible, to be sold to a single master and the relative of their former owner. The answer is not explicitly provided in this particular passage, but can be plausibly supplied: it was caused by the slave's wish to preserve the families and communities that they had managed to create and the mode of life with its customs and accommodations to which they were used.

This reality of slave life and this form of slave hope is rather invisible in the oracular texts, partly of course because the relevant questions about health, love and prosperity would apply equally to free and slave alike; given that we have established beyond doubt, on the basis of the slave-related questions, that the slaves consulted such oracles, there should be little doubt that slaves would have consulted the oracles for matters that did not revolve exclusively on their slave status. But this is a negative conclusion, and we need to turn to alternative forms of sources in order to explore the issue in explicit ways.

Many of the examples to follow belong to the most common category of expressing prospective or fulfilled hopes in the epigraphic record: that of the votive inscription. Votive inscriptions record the enlisting of divine agencies in order to fulfil the hopes and avert the fears of their creators. My first example is a fourth-century BCE inscription originating from the mining region of Laureion in Attica:

> [Τυ]ράν[νωι Μηνὶ ἀν]έθ[εσα]ν ἐπ' εὐτυχίαις ἐρανισταὶ οἴδε: Κάδους, Μάνης, Καλλίας, "Αττας, Ἀρτεμίδωρος, Μάης, Σωσίας, Σαγγάριος, Ἑρμαῖος, Τίβειος, "Ερμος.[33]
>
> The following *eranistai* devoted [this] to [Lord Mên] for prosperity: Kadous; Manes; Kallias; Attas; Artemidoros; Maes; Sosias; Saggarios; Hermaios; Tibeios; Hermos.

The inscription records a dedication by an *eranos*, a group of contributors, which includes eleven unidentified persons. While some of their names are typically Greek (Kallias, Artemidoros, Hermaios, Sosias), others are foreign (Kadous, Manes, Attas, Tibeios), or names of foreign geographical places (Saggarios, Hermos). The combination of the foreign names and the find-spot in the mining region of Laureion makes it highly likely that this *eranos* consists of foreign slaves.[34] Their ex-voto expresses succinctly their desire: success and prosperity.

My next few examples are inscriptions originating from another place and time: the region of Lydia in Asia Minor during the early empire. The epigraphic habit of this particular area has a number of peculiar aspects that make slaves and their wishes and hopes particularly visible. The first and the third

---

33 *IG* II² 2940.
34 For this inscription, see Lauffer 1956, 185–94; for the implications of slave names, see Vlassopoulos 2010, 2015.

inscriptions belong to a form traditionally called 'confession inscription', which is commonly found in the regions of Lydia and Phrygia. Inscriptions record an offence or sin committed by the dedicators, who have faced divine punishment as a result of their transgression or failed vow, and hope to atone through its public confession.[35]

> Μηνὶ Ἀξιοττηνῷ καὶ τῇ δυνάμι αὐτοῦ· ἐπὶ Πρέπουσα ἀπελευθέρα τῆς ἱερείας εὔξετο ὑπὲρ υἱοῦ Φιλήμονος, εἰ ἔσται ὁλόκληρος καὶ ἰατροῖς μὴ ποσδαπανήσι, στηλλογραφῆσαι, καὶ γενομένης τῆς εὐχῆς οὐκ ἀπέδωκεν, νῦν ὁ θεὸς ἀπήτησε τὴν εὐχὴν καὶ ἐκόλασε τὸν πατέρα Φιλήμονα· καὶ ἀποδίδι τὴν εὐχὴν ὑπὲρ τοῦ υἱοῦ καὶ ἀπὸ νῦν εὐλογῖ.[36]

> To Men Axiottenos and his power: when Prepousa, the freedwoman of the priestess, made a vow on behalf of her son Philemon to raise an inscribed stele, if he would be unblemished and not spend money for doctors, and when the wish was fulfilled she did not render, now the god demanded the vow and punished Philemon the father; and she renders the vow on behalf of the son and from now on praises (the god).

In this case, the freedwoman Prepousa has made a vow to the god in regards to the health of her son: her hope was that her son would survive unblemished his illness and that speedy recovery would save the family from spending money for medical help. The same hope for health is expressed by another inscription from Lydia:

> Εὔτυχος Ἰουλίας Ταβίλλης δοῦλος πραγματευτὴς σὺν καὶ τῇ γυναικὶ Ἐπιγόνῃ εὐχὴν ὑπὲρ υἱοῦ Νεική[τ]ου Μηνὶ Ἀξιεττηνῷ διὰ τὸ σ<ω>θῆναι αὐτὸν ὑπὸ τοῦ θεοῦ ἀσθενοῦντα.[37]

> Eutychos, slave agent of Ioulia Tabille, along with his wife Epigone as a vow to Men Axiottenos on behalf of their son Neiketas, because he was saved by the god when he was ill.

In this case, a slave agent and his wife had hoped for the health and survival of their son. In both cases, we come across the families of slaves and former slaves and their concerns and hopes: there is no doubt that they express precisely the same concerns recorded by countless inscriptions erected by free families in the same area. The significance of slave family and slave community becomes clearly visible; the hopes of slaves were not determined by their instrumental role as tools for the fulfilment of the wishes of their masters: their hopes revolved around the concerns of the world beyond and below slavery that they actively tried to

---

35 Chaniotis 1995, 2009.
36 *SEG* XXXIX 1276.
37 *TAM* V,1 442.

create and maintain. Our final inscription from Lydia expresses similar concerns, but presents them in a new light:

> [Μην]ὶ Ἀξιοτηνῷ Ἐ[παφρόδ]ειτος οἰκο[νόμος Κλαυ]δίο[υ Στρατ]ονείκου εὐξά[με]νος ἐὰν λήψεται γυναῖκαν ἣν θέλω καὶ λαβὼν καὶ μὴ ἀποδὼν τὴν εὐχήν, κολασθεὶς ἀνέθηκεν καὶ ἀπὸ νῦν εὐλογεῖ μετὰ τῶν ἰδίων πάντων.[38]

> To Men Axiotenos. Epaphrodeitos, the manager of Klaudios Stratoneikos, having made a vow if he received the woman whom I want, and although receiving her did not fulfil the vow and was punished, made the dedication and from now on praises [the god] with all of his own.

The dedicator Epaphrodeitos describes himself as the manager of Klaudios Stratoneikos, which would imply his slave status. He records the making of a vow if his hope to receive the woman he wanted were to be fulfilled, and confesses that despite the realisation of his wish he did not actually fulfil the vow, and was accordingly punished by the deity. On the one hand, we get another example of the slave wish for family and emotional fulfilment, for the sort of hopes entertained by the free members of society;[39] on the other hand, his expression leaves tellingly open how exactly he realised his wish. What does "receiving the woman I want" means in this context? Does it mean that the relatives and guardians of the girl he wanted acceded to his request, as it would happen with respectable free people? Does it mean that he requested his master's permission to marry, if the woman was a slave who belonged to the same master? Or does it mean that he requested the permission of the master of the woman, if he was different from his own master?[40] We cannot answer these questions in this particular case; but the narrative of Longus' novel *Daphnis and Chloe* provides an excellent illustration of the issue. Daphnis and Chloe are two children who have grown up together in the countryside of Mytilene, tending the flocks of their families, and gradually falling in love as they grow up; but while Chloe is a foundling adopted by a free family, and therefore free, Daphnis is a foundling adopted by a slave family, and therefore slave. When the two adolescents decide to marry, Daphnis has to ask for the hand of Chloe from her father. But while he ultimately gets permission

---

[38] Lane 1971, no. 80.
[39] See question 55 in the Sortes Astrampsychi: 'will I get the woman I want?'
[40] For such different scenarios of courtship involving slaves, see Menander, *Hero*, 40-9; Plautus, *Casina*, 47–78; Diodorus, 36.2a; Galen, *How to detect malingerers*, 19.4–5; *Vita Aesopi*, G29; Basil the Great, *Epistles*, 199.18; Libanius, *Epistles*, 567; Aristaenetus, *Epistles*, 2.4.

from Chloe's father, Daphnis also needs to get permission for his marriage from his absentee master.[41]

The above discussion has, I hope, illustrated in sufficient detail the extent to which slave hopes under slavery often aimed to create a world of their own, with relationships defined by emotion, kinship, ethnicity and work, rather than the imposed identity of slavery. Slave hopes that focused on their relationship with their masters also show why slavery should not be treated solely as a unilateral and instrumental relationship: slave hopes express the slave attempt to shape this relationship as an asymmetrical negotiation of power or an asymmetrical exchange of mutual service and benefaction.

The slave hope for freedom

Notwithstanding these slave efforts to turn slavery into something different from a mere instrumental relationship, the fulfilment of such aims was always beyond the reach of many slaves, and success was always fragile. Escaping slavery, either by means of flight or through manumission, was commonly one of the defining hopes in the slave experience. The issue is illustrated evocatively in a passage from Phaedrus' *Fables*:

> Seruus profugiens dominum naturae asperae Aesopo occurrit, notus e uicinia. 'Quid tu confusus?' 'Dicam tibi clare, pater, hoc namque es dignus appellari nomine, tuto querela quia apud te deponitur. Plagae supersunt, desunt mihi cibaria. Subinde ad uillam mittor sine uiatico. Domi si cenat, totis persto noctibus; siue est uocatus, iaceo ad lucem in semita. Emerui libertatem, canus seruio. Vllius essem culpae mihi si conscius, aequo animo ferrem. Nunquam sum factus satur, et super infelix saeuum patior dominium. Has propter causas et quas longum est promere abire destinaui quo tulerint pedes'. 'Ergo' inquit 'audi: cum mali nil feceris, haec experieris, ut refers, incommoda; quid si peccaris? Quae te passurum putas?' Tali consilio est a fuga deterritus.[42]

> A slave who was running away from his cruel master happened to meet Aesop, who knew him as a neighbour. 'What's got you so excited?' asked Aesop. 'Father Aesop — a name you well deserve since you are like a father to me — I'm going to be perfectly frank, since you can be safely trusted with my troubles. There's plenty of whipping and not enough food. I'm constantly sent on errands out to the farm without any provisions for the journey. If the master dines at home, I have to wait on him all night long; if he is invited somewhere else, I have to lie outside in the gutter until dawn. I should have earned my freedom by now, but

---

41 Longus, *Daphnis and Chloe*, 29–31.
42 Phaedrus, *Fables*, Appendix 20.

my hairs have gone grey and I'm still slaving away. If I had done anything to deserve this, I would stop complaining and suffer my fate in silence. But the fact is that I never get enough to eat and my cruel master is always after me. For these reasons, along with others that it would take too long to tell you, I've decided to go wherever my feet will lead me'. 'Well', said Aesop, 'listen to what I say: if you must endure such hardship without having done anything wrong, as you say, then what is going to happen to you now that you really are guilty of something?' With these words of advice, Aesop scared the slave into giving up his plans of escape.

The fugitive slave presents eloquently his grievances: physical maltreatment, lack of adequate nourishment, the frustration and humiliation of serving others meekly, the lack of personal time and space. Escape from slavery would be the obvious solution to all these problems. But the hope for manumission has been frustrated so far and is likely to remain beyond reach: under the circumstances, flight seems the only way forward. It is only the fear of even worse conditions, should the attempt at flight fail, which convinces the slave to abandon his plans.[43] Particularly notable is the slave's complaint "that he should have earned his freedom by now": the conceptualisation of slavery as an asymmetrical relationship of mutual service and benefaction is crucial for the slave's understanding of his claim to freedom being the result of his faithful service.

The way in which this hope for freedom is represented in ancient literary texts tells us something significant about conceptions of slavery in antiquity. On the one hand, there is no doubt that one can find multiple examples of discourses that tried to naturalise slavery, by presenting slaves as inferior beings who were fit for that particular role, or deserved the fate of slavery.[44] From this point of view, the slave hope for freedom is something that could only be portrayed as monstrous, futile or perverse.[45] It is therefore remarkable that one can find numerous portrayals of the slave hope for freedom from a wholly sympathetic point of view. The following passage from Menander is a characteristic example:[46]

| (Ον) ἐκεῖνο δ' οὐ λέγεις, ὅτι ἐλευθέρα γίνηι σύ· τοῦ γὰρ παιδίου μητέρα σε νομίσας λύσετ' εὐθὺς δηλαδή.
(Ἁβρ) οὐκ οἶδα· βουλοίμην δ' ἄν. | **Onesimos:** There is only one thing you've not said, that you'll be freed. For if he thinks you're mother to the child, then obviously he'll buy your liberty.
Habrotonon: I don't know that. I'd like it. |

---

43 For slave flight in antiquity, see Bellen 1971.
44 This theme is well explored in Garnsey 1996.
45 The portrayal of the freedom effort of the Scythian slaves in Herodotus (4.1–4) is characteristic.
46 Menander, *Epitrepontes*, 538–66.

(Ον) οὐ γὰρ οἶσθα σύ; ἀλλ' [ἦ]
χάρις τις, Ἁβρότονον, τούτων
ἐμοί;
(Ἁβρ) νὴ τὼ θεώ, πάντων γ' ἐμαυ-
τῆι σ' αἴτιον ἡγήσομαι τούτων.
(Ον) ἐὰν δὲ μηκέτι
ζητῆις ἐκείνην ἐξεπίτηδες, ἀλλ'
ἐᾶις παρακρουσαμένη με, πῶς τὸ
τοιοῦθ' ἕξει;
(Ἁβρ) τάλαν, τίνος ἕνεκεν; παίδων
ἐπιθυμεῖν σοι δοκῶ; ἐλευθέρα
μόνον γενοίμην, ὦ θεοί. τοῦτον
λάβοιμι μισθὸν ἐκ τούτων.
(Ον) λάβοις.
(Ἁβρ) οὐκοῦν συναρέσκει σοι;
(Ον) συναρέσκει διαφόρως· ἂν γὰρ
κακοηθεύσηι, μαχοῦμαί σοι τότε·
δυνήσομαι γάρ. ἐν δὲ τῶι παρόντι
νῦν ἴδωμεν εἰ τοῦτ' ἐστίν.
(Ἁβρ) οὐκοῦν συνδοκεῖ;
(Ον) μάλιστα.
(Ἁβρ) τὸν δακτύλιον ἀποδίδου
ταχύ.
(Ον) λάμβανε.
(Ἁβρ) φίλη Πειθοῖ, παροῦσα σύμ-
μαχος πόει κατορθοῦν τοὺς λόγους
οὓς ἂν λέγω.
(Ον) τοπαστικὸν τὸ γύναιον. ὡς ἤι-
σθηθ' ὅτι κατὰ τὸν ἔρωτ' οὐκ ἔστ'
ἐλευθερίας τυχεῖν ἄλλως δ' ἀλύει,
τὴν ἑτέραν πορεύεται ὁδόν. ἀλλ'
ἐγὼ τὸν πάντα δουλεύσω χρόνον,
λέμφος, ἀπόπληκτος, οὐδαμῶς
προνοητικὸς τὰ τοιαῦτα. παρὰ
ταύτης δ' ἴσως τι λήψομαι, ἂν
ἐπιτύχηι· καὶ γὰρ δίκαιον. ὡς κενὰ
καὶ διαλογίζομ' ὁ κακοδαίμων,
προσδοκῶν χάριν κομιεῖσθαι παρὰ
γυναικός· μὴ μόνον κακόν τι προσ-
λάβοιμι.

O: Don't you know? But will I get some thanks for this myself, Habrotonon?
H: By both the goddesses, I shall consider you the cause of all my happiness.
O: Suppose you stop the search for her on purpose and you give it up and leave me in the lurch, what happens then?

H: My goodness, why should I? Do you think I long for children? Gods above, I only ask for freedom. That's the prize I want for this.
O: I hope you get it.
H: Well, do you like my plan?
O: I do, extremely. If you try to cheat, I'll fight you then. I'll find a way. But for the moment let us see if this is really true.
H: So you agree with me?
O: I do.
H: Then quickly hand the ring to me.

O: Here, take it.
H: Dear Persuasion, be my friend, be at my side and make the words I speak succeed.

O: The girl's a clever creature. When she found she couldn't get her liberty through love and was just wasting all her pains this way, she takes another road. But I shall stay a slave for ever, snotty, paralysed, incapable of making schemes like hers. Perhaps I shall get something from the girl, if she succeeds; that would be fair – poor fool, what empty hopes you have, if you expect to earn, from any woman, gratitude! I only hope my troubles don't increase.

The audience is presented with two slaves scheming to gain their freedom with a plan that will inadvertently lead to the happy ending of the plot. The slaves express on numerous occasions their hope for freedom, which is presented as a matter of fact, and without any negative connotations. This sympathetic portrayal of the slave hope for freedom makes evident the fact that in a society like classical Athens a variety of alternative conceptualisations of slavery co-existed. If slavery is an extreme form of bad luck, then the hope for freedom is an understandable attempt to mitigate adverse circumstances. If slavery is an asymmetrical relationship of mutual service, then the slave hope for freedom is a legitimate attempt to obtain a reward for faithful service.

Let us now return to the answers provided in the *Sortes Astrampsychi* to the question of whether a slave will gain his freedom:

> 'You won't be freed just yet' (3.1)
> 'You won't be freed just yet: don't expect it' (68.2, 4.6)
> 'You won't be freed just yet, but after a time' (50.4, 21.9)
> 'You will be freed, but not just yet' (76.3)
> 'You will be freed after some time, but don't be distressed' (96.7)
> 'You will be freed with an appeal once you've paid money (53.5)
> 'You will be freed with a good bequest' (40.8)
> 'You won't be freed. Be silent' (23.10)

As above, the answers can be analysed along three axes. The first axis concerns whether the manumission will take place or not; only one answer categorically denies that possibility. Another three focus on the fact that the hope for freedom will not be realised immediately, without explicitly denying that it could happen in the future. Another two predict that the manumission will not take place soon, but promise manumission at some time in the future, while another one makes the same promise, but stated in a more positive manner. The second axis concerns the circumstances of the manumission: one answer predicts that freedom will be gained by an appeal, after paying money, while the other predicts that manumission will be accompanied by a bequest from the master. Finally, the third axis concerns responses to the emotional state of the slave hoping for freedom: one answer asks the enquirer not to be distressed because the manumission will not happen for some time, while in another the bad news that the manumission will not happen is supplemented by the telling command: 'be silent!' Overall, the inclusion of the query on manumission in the list of questions is a telling indication of how normal the slave hope for freedom is considered.

If the slave hope for freedom is presented sympathetically, its realisation presents us with some of the most challenging questions in understanding slavery. Various ancient sources illustrate the terrible choices that slaves faced in attempting to materialise the hope of freedom. Studying these choices, and the problems they raised, is an excellent litmus test for figuring out what exactly the hope for freedom consisted of. Our best means for exploring this issue comes through the corpus of manumission inscriptions, one of the most common forms of the Greek epigraphic record. In some areas of the Greek world, like the two inscriptions from Delphi presented below, manumission inscriptions set out in detail the conditions under which slaves have gained or will gain their freedom. Our first example comes from the first century CE:

ἀπέδοτο Εὐ[πορία τῷ Ἀ]πόλλωνι τῷ Πυθίῳ σώματα δύο, οἷς ὀνόματα Ἐπι[φάνε]α καὶ Ἐπαφρώ, τειμᾶς ἀ[ργυ]ρίου μνᾶν ἕξ... ἐπὶ τοῖσδε ὥστε παραμείνωντι Εὐπορία πάν<τα> τὸν τᾶς ζ[ωᾶς] χρόνον ἀνενκλήτως, ποιοῦντα τὸ ἐπιτασσόμενον πᾶν. εἰ δὲ μὴ ποιέοισα<ν>, ἐξουσίαν ἐχέτω ἐπιτειμέουσα Εὐπορία τρόπῳ ᾧ κα θέλῃ. μετὰ δὲ τὰν [ἰδία]ν τελευτὰν δότω Ἐπαφρὼ τῷ ἐγγόνῳ μου Γλαυκίᾳ Λύσωνος βρ[έ]φη διετῆ τρία. ἐὰν δὲ μὴ ἔχῃ τὰ βρέφη, δότω δεινάρια διακόσια· καὶ Ἐπιφάνεα δότω τῷ υἱῷ μου Σ[ωστράτῳ] μετὰ ἔτη πέντε παιδίον τριετές, καὶ μετὰ ἔτη τρία κ[αὶ τῷ ἐγ]γόνῳ μου Γλαυκίᾳ παιδίον τριετές, καὶ ἔστωσαν ἐλεύθεραι Ἐπα[φρὼ καὶ] Ἐπιφάνεα.[47]

Euporia sold to Apollo Pythios two bodies, whose names are Epiphanea and Epaphro, for a price of six mnas...under these conditions: that they will remain [with Euporia] for the rest of her life, without reproach, doing everything that they have been ordered...and after her death, Epaphro shall give my grandson Glaukias, the son of Lyson, three babies of two years old. If she does not have the babies, she should give 200 denarii. And Epiphanea shall give my son Sostratos after five years a three-year old child, and after three years a three-year old child to my grandson Glaukias.

The inscription records the manumission of two female slaves, Epiphanea and Epaphro. The manumission includes various conditions. The first one is the condition of *paramone*, the obligation of the manumitted slaves to remain with their former owners and serve them for a period of time, commonly till the latter's death, as in here.[48] But the manumission also contains a second condition that will apply at the time of the manumittor's death: in order to gain their full freedom, the two slaves are obliged to surrender to her relatives a number of children over a span of time: three two-year old babies in the case of Epaphro, while in the case of Epiphanea the obligation is to surrender a three-year old child after five years, and a second three-year old child after another three years.

The obligation for female slaves to surrender one or more children in order to gain their full freedom is by no means rare in the ancient world.[49] From the master's point of view the aim of this condition is patently obvious: it would provide free of cost the new generation of slaves that would replace those who were manumitted. But from the slave's point of view the condition illustrates the difficult choices that the hope for freedom entailed. For the fulfilment of this condition

---
47 *FD* III, 6.38.
48 Zelnick-Abramovitz 2005, 222–48.
49 Zelnick-Abramovitz 2005, 229–31.

effectively meant that female slaves had to have sex in order to get pregnant and use their children as bargaining chips for gaining their own freedom. In a world of very high infant mortality, where one out of three children would die before their first birthday and half the children before the age of five, clearly attitudes towards children could not have been the same with contemporary societies with extremely low infant mortality.[50] And yet, it would be misleading to think that ancient people did not get emotionally involved with their children, or that slaves merely thought of babies as means to an end. The inscriptions we saw above, and the hope for recovery and health for slave children, document the extent to which slaves cared for their children. But this still lives our question unanswered. Slaves cared deeply about their children and their families, even under conditions of slavery, which made families fragile and the ability to protect loved ones limited. In what consisted the hope of freedom, if attaining it meant surrendering your new-born children as the new generation of slaves in exchange for your own freedom?

This kind of question becomes even more difficult to answer in the case of our next example, a first-century BCE inscription from Delphi:

> ἀπέδοτο Φίλαγρος Ἀρχύτα τῶι Ἀπόλλωνι τῶι Πυθίωι σῶμα γυναικεῖον ἆι ὄνομα Διόκλεα τὸ γένος οἰκογενές, τιμᾶς ἀργυρίου μνᾶν τριῶν... παραμεινατω δὲ Διόκλεια [παρ]ὰ Κλεοπάτραι τῆι ματρὶ Φιλάγρου ποιοῦσα [τὸ ἐ]πιτασσόμενον πᾶν τὸ δυνατόν, ἐξουσίαν δὲ ἐχέτω ἐπιτιμέουσα καὶ διδέουσα τρόπωι ὧι κα θέληι πλὰν μὴ πωλέουσα. ἐπεί κά τι πάθοι Κλεοπάτρα, ἐλευθέρα ἔστω Διόκλεα καὶ ὑπαγέτω πᾶι κα θέληι...εἰ δέ τι γένοιτο ἐγ Διοκλέας τέκνον ἐν τῶι τᾶς παραμονᾶς χρόνωι, εἴ κα μὲν θέληι ἀποπνεῖξαι Διόκλεα ἐξουσίαν ἐχέτω, εἰ δὲ θέλοι τρέφειν, ἔστω τὸ τρεφόμενον ἐλεύθερον· εἴ κα μὴ αὐτὸ θέληι, πωλῆσαι δὲ τὸ γενηθέν μὴ ἐχέτω ἐξουσίαν Διόκλεα μηδὲ ἄλλος μηθείς.[51]

> Philagros, son of Archytas, sold to Apollo Pythios a female body called Dioklea, born in the house, for a price of three mnas... Dioklea shall remain with Kleopatra, the mother of Philagros, obeying all orders to the extent of her ability; Kleopatra will have the power to punish her in any way she sees fit, except from selling her. And when something happens to Kleopatra, Dioklea will be free and she can go anywhere she wants... if Dioklea has a child in the time of paramone, she will have the right to choke it, if she wants; if she wants to raise it, it will be free, but if she does not want this, neither Dioklea nor anyone else will have the right to sell the child.

The manumission includes the usual condition of *paramone*; but its stipulations as regards children are quite different than those in the previous example. The manumission document gives Dioklea the right either to raise any child born

---

50 Saller 1994, 43–69.
51 *SGDI* 2171.

during the paramone as a free person, or to kill it. These conditions are easy to understand: effectively, the manumittors gives the former slave full rights over the child, both in surrendering to the slave the right to decide whether the child will be raised, and in surrendering any right to the slave's progeny. It is the final condition that becomes more difficult to understand: if the former master is happy to surrender his rights over the child, why does he then prohibit Dioklea from selling the child? A plausible interpretation has been suggested: Philagros wants to safeguard that Dioklea will remain with his old mother till her death. If Dioklea could sell her children, she could then use the money raised in order to buy up her time in *paramone*, a provision attested in many Delphic manumissions.[52] This is another example of how the hope for freedom could clash with a number of hopes that slaves entertained under slavery, and clearly also entertained once freed.

The frustration of the hope for freedom by the complexities of what life in freedom actually means is the subject of a famous exhortation by a former slave, the philosopher Epictetus:

ὁ δοῦλος εὐθὺς εὔχεται ἀφεθῆναι ἐλεύθερος. διὰ τί; δοκεῖτε, ὅτι τοῖς εἰκοστώναις ἐπιθυμεῖ δοῦναι ἀργύριον; οὔ· ἀλλ' ὅτι φαντάζεται μέχρι νῦν διὰ τὸ μὴ τετυχηκέναι τούτου ἐμποδίζεσθαι καὶ δυσροεῖν. «ἂν ἀφεθῶ», φησίν, «εὐθὺς πᾶσα εὔροια, οὐδενὸς ἐπιστρέφομαι, πᾶσιν ὡς ἴσος καὶ ὅμοιος λαλῶ, πορεύομαι ὅπου θέλω, ἔρχομαι ὅθεν θέλω καὶ ὅπου θέλω». εἶτα ἀπηλευθέρωται καὶ εὐθὺς μὲν οὐκ ἔχων, ποῖ φάγῃ, ζητεῖ, τίνα κολακεύσῃ, παρὰ τίνι δειπνήσῃ· εἶτα ἢ ἐργάζεται τῷ σώματι καὶ πάσχει τὰ δεινότατα κἂν σχῇ τινα φάτνην, ἐμπέπτωκεν εἰς δουλείαν πολὺ τῆς προτέρας χαλεπωτέραν ἢ καὶ εὐπορήσας ἄνθρωπος ἀπειρόκαλος πεφίληκε παιδισκάριον καὶ δυστυχῶν ἀνακλαίεται καὶ τὴν δουλείαν ποθεῖ. «τί γάρ μοι κακὸν ἦν; ἄλλος μ' ἐνέδυεν, ἄλλος μ' ὑπέδει, ἄλλος ἔτρεφεν, ἄλλος ἐνοσοκόμει, ὀλίγα αὐτῷ ὑπηρέτουν. νῦν δὲ τάλας οἷα πάσχω πλείοσι δουλεύων ἀνθ' ἑνός;»[53]

The slave wishes to be set free immediately. Why? Do you think that he wishes to pay money to the collectors of the 5% tax? No; but because he imagines that hitherto through not having obtained this, he is hindered and unfortunate. 'If I shall be set free, immediately it is all happiness, I care for no man, I speak to all as an equal and like to them, I go where I choose, I come from any place I choose, and go where I choose'. Then he is set free; and forthwith having no place where he can eat, he looks for some man to flatter, someone with whom he shall sup: then he either works with his body and endures the most dreadful things; and if he can obtain a manger, he falls into a slavery much worse than his former slavery; or even if he is become rich, being a man without any knowledge of what is good, he loves some little girl, and in his unhappiness laments and desires to be a slave again. He says: 'what evil did I suffer in my state of slavery? Another clothed me, another supplied me with shoes,

---

52 Zelnick-Abramovitz 2005, 229–30.
53 Epictetus, *Discourses*, 4.1.33–7.

another fed me, another looked after me in sickness; and I did only a few services for him. But now a wretched man, what things I suffer, being a slave to many instead of to one'.

Conclusion

This exploration of hope and slavery has tried to underline three issues. The first is that slave hopes provide an excellent litmus test for thinking carefully about the historical experience of slavery and the various conceptualisations of slavery in ancient societies. The exploration of slave hope gives the lie to the essentialist and instrumentalist approaches, which have exercised such a powerful influence on the study of slavery. Hope places slave agency at the forefront of our attention: and this requires us to think carefully about the relationship between slave agency and the various practices employing slaving for a variety of aims. This leads to my second point: instead of a top-down relationship unilaterally defined by the masters, the exploration of slave hopes has revealed a co-existence of different conceptualisations of slavery and a complex negotiation of power. A major aspect of this phenomenon was the extent to which masters attempted to employ the tool of slavery to shape the full extent of slave life, and slaves attempted to use other tools (kinship, religion, ethnicity, work, residence) in order to shape various aspects of their lives into a world that existed beyond and below slavery. As a result, a significant part of slave hopes concerned life within slavery, but a life that was affected by slavery as little as possible. Obviously, and this is my third point, the hope for freedom had an immense value for slaves. Exploring this hope has major implications, both for how slaves envisaged freedom, as well as the difficult choices they faced in the process of realising their hope.

Abbreviations

FD III   N. Valmin, *Fouilles de Delphes*, III. *Épigraphie*. Fascicule 6 : *Inscriptions du théâtre*, Paris, 1939.
SEG   *Supplementum Epigraphicum Graecum*.
SGDI   H. Collitz *et al.*, *Sammlung der griechischen Dialekt-Inschriften*, II. Epirus, Akarnanien, Aetolien, Göttingen, 1885–1899.
TAM V,1   P. Herrmann (ed.), *Tituli Asiae Minoris*, V. *Tituli Lydiae, linguis Graeca et Latina conscripti. I: Regio septentrionalis, ad orientem vergens*, Vienna, 1981.

Bibliography

Annequin, J. 1987. "Les esclaves rêvent aussi... Remarques sur 'La clé des songes' d'Artémidore," in: *Dialogues d'histoire ancienne* 13, 71–113.
—— 2005. "L'autre corps du maître: les représentations oniriques dans *l'Onirocriticon* d'Artémidore de Daldis," in: V.I. Anastasiadis/P.N. Doukellis (eds.), *Esclavage antique et discriminations socio-culturelles*, Bern, 305–313.
—— 2008. "Les esclaves et les signes oniriques de la liberté : *l'Onirocriticon* d'Artémidore," in: A. Gonzales (ed.), *La fin du statut servile? (affranchissement, libération, abolition). Hommage à Jacques Annequin* 1, Besançon, 89–93.
Bellen, H. 1971. *Studien zur Sklavenflucht im römischen Kaiserreich*, Stuttgart.
Berlin, I. 1998. *Many Thousands Gone: The First Two Centuries of Slavery in North America*, Cambridge, Mass.
Browne, G.M. 1983–2001. *Sortes Astrampsychi*, I–II, Leipzig/Munich.
Chaniotis, A. 1995. "Illness and Cures in the Greek Propitiatory Inscriptions and Dedications of Lydia and Phrygia," in: H.F. Horstmanshoff/P.J. van der Eijk/P.H. Schrijvers (eds.), *Ancient Medicine in its Socio-Cultural Context*, II, Amsterdam/Atlanta, GA, 323–44.
—— 2009. "Ritual Performances of Divine Justice: The Epigraphy of Confession, Atonement and Exaltation in Roman Asia Minor," in: H.M. Cotton/R.G. Hoyland/J.J. Price/D.J. Wasserstein (eds.), *From Hellenism to Islam: Cultural and Linguistic Change in the Roman Near East*, Cambridge, 115–53.
Dold, A./R. Meister (eds.). 1948–51. *Die Orakelsprüche im St. Galler Palimpsestcodex 908 (die sogenannten 'Sortes Sangallenses') auf Grund neuer Lesung und mit erweitertem Text nach Materien geordnet*, I–II, Vienna.
Eidinow, E. 2007. *Oracles, Curses and Risk among the Ancient Greeks*, Oxford.
—— 2012. "'What will happen to me if I leave?' Ancient Greek Oracles, Slaves and Slave Owners," in: S. Hodkinson/D. Geary (eds.), *Slaves and Religions in Graeco-Roman Antiquity and Modern Brazil*, Newcastle upon Tyne, 244–78.
Eidinow, E./C. Taylor. 2010. "Lead-letter Days: Writing, Communication and Crisis in the Ancient Greek World," in: *CQ* 60, 30–62.
Garnsey, P. 1996. *Ideas of Slavery from Aristotle to Augustine*, Cambridge.
Genovese, E.D. 1974. *Roll, Jordan, Roll: The World the Slaves Made*, New York.
Glassman, J. 1991. "The Bondsman's New Clothes: The Contradictory Consciousness of Slave Resistance on the Swahili Coast," in: *Journal of African History* 32, 277–312.
Green, F.M. 2015. "Witnesses and Participants in the Shadows: The Sexual Lives of Enslaved Women and Boys," in: *Helios* 42, 143–62.
Hahn, I. 1992. *Traumdeutung und gesellschaftliche Wirklichkeit: Artemidorus Daldianus als sozialgeschichtliche Quelle*, Konstanz.
Hansen, W. (ed.) 1998. *An Anthology of Ancient Greek Popular Literature*, Bloomington, IN.
Harper, K. 2011. *Slavery in the Late Roman World, AD 275–425*, Cambridge.
Harris, E.M. 2004. "Notes on a Lead Letter from the Athenian Agora," in: *HSCP* 102, 157–70.
Jordan, D. 2000. "A Personal Letter Found in the Athenian Agora," in: *Hesperia* 69, 91–103.
Klees, H. 1990. "Griechisches und Römisches in den Traumdeutungen Artemidors für Herren und Sklaven," in: C. Boerker/M. Donderer (eds.), *Das antike Rom und der Osten: Festschrift für K. Parlasca*, Erlangen, 53–75.
—— 1998. *Sklavenleben im klassischen Griechenland*, Stuttgart.
Kudlien, F. 1991. *Sklavenmentalität im Spiegel antiker Wahrsagerei*, Stuttgart.

Lane, E.N. 1971. *Corpus Monumentorum Religionis Dei Menis I*, Leiden.
Lauffer, S. 1956. *Die Bergwerkssklaven von Laureion*, I-II, Wiesbaden.
Lhôte, E. 2006. *Les lamelles oraculaires de Dodone*, Paris.
McKeown, N. 2007. *The Invention of Ancient Slavery?*, London.
Patterson, O. 1982. *Slavery and Social Death: A Comparative Study*, Cambridge, Mass.
Pomeroy, A.J. 1991 "Status and Status-concern in the Greco-Roman Dream-books," in: *Ancient Society* 22, 51–74.
Saller, R.P. 1994. *Patriarchy, Property and Death in the Roman Family*, Cambridge.
Schwartz, S.B. 1977. "Resistance and Accommodation in Eighteenth-century Brazil: The Slaves' View of Slavery," in: *Hispanic American Historical Review* 57, 69–81.
Vlassopoulos, K. 2010. "Athenian Slave Names and Athenian Social History," in: *ZPE* 175, 113–44.
—— 2011a. "Greek Slavery: From Domination to Property and Back Again," in: *JHS* 131, 115–30.
—— 2011b. "Two Images of Ancient Slavery: The 'Living Tool' and the '*koinônia*,'" in: E. Herrmann-Otto (ed.), *Sklaverei und Zwangsarbeit zwischen Akzeptanz und Widerstand*, Hildesheim/Zurich/New York, 467–77.
—— 2015. "Plotting Strategies, Networks and Communities in Classical Athens: The Evidence of Slave Names," in: C. Taylor/K. Vlassopoulos (eds.), *Communities and Networks in the Ancient Greek World*, Oxford, 101–27.
—— 2016. "Does Slavery Have a History? The Consequences of a Global Approach," in: *Journal of Global Slavery* 1, 5–27.
—— forthcoming. "Introduction: An Agenda for Studying Greek and Roman Slaveries," in: S. Hodkinson/M. Kleijwegt/K. Vlassopoulos, *The Oxford Handbook of Greek and Roman Slaveries*, Oxford.
Williams, B. 1993. *Shame and Necessity*, Berkeley/Oxford.
Zelnick-Abramovitz, R. 2005. *Not Wholly Free: The Concept of Manumission and the Status of Manumitted Slaves in the Ancient Greek World*, Leiden.

Andrew Stiles
Velleius Paterculus, the Adoptions of 4 CE, and the *Spes* Race

1 Introduction: Velleius on the return and adoption of Tiberius

The exceptional position of Augustus within the *res publica* was justified partly by playing on both hopes and fears, emotions oriented towards the future –hope for peace and prosperity after a lengthy period of civil war, fear that in his absence it might erupt once more, or that foreign enemies might threaten Rome. Rich has described this phenomenon as "making the emergency permanent".[1] The virtues of the *princeps* supposedly held everything together, and flowed down through the various social orders. Yet even for a *divi filius*, there remained the small problem of Augustus' mortality. Thus, a public role for his family emerged, with emphasis placed on prospective 'successors', who became a focal point for hopes transferred from the *princeps*, and who helped to secure his position in the present and his memory for later ages. The adoption arrangement in 4 CE, in which Augustus adopted Tiberius (and Agrippa Postumus), and compelled Tiberius to adopt Germanicus, was the final dynastic plan made before the death of Augustus, after a series of earlier potential candidates had died unexpectedly. The concept of *spes* played an important role in the promotion of successors from this point on, and this is reflected in the sources which cover the period. Velleius Paterculus is a useful springboard, since his account provides a unique insight into late Augustan and Tiberian political tensions.

When composing his brief *Historia Romana* in 29 CE, Velleius took every opportunity to present his former commander and *princeps*, Tiberius, in a positive light.[2] He is particularly enthusiastic in his account of Tiberius' return to Rome

---

[1] Many thanks to audiences in Rethymno, Sydney, and Oxford, and especially Josiah Osgood, Kathryn Welch, Stephen Heyworth, Anna Clark, Katherine Clarke, and Dimos Spatharas and George Kazantzidis, for their comments on an earlier version of this paper. All errors that remain are my own.
[2] Indeed, the work has been described as 'triumphal history' by de Monte, working seamlessly through the Republic and Triumviral period, and the dominance of Augustus, towards the *telos* of Tiberius' principate. See de Monte 1999.

from Rhodes in 2 CE, and his political resurrection in 4 CE following the deaths of the young preferred 'successors', Lucius Caesar on 20 August 2 CE, and Gaius Caesar on the 21 Feb. 4 CE (2.103):

> Sed fortuna, quae subduxerat **spem magni nominis**, iam tum rei publicae sua praesidia reddiderat: quippe ante utriusque horum obitum patre tuo P. Vinicio consule Ti. Nero reversus Rhodo incredibili laetitia patriam repleverat. Non est diu cunctatus Caesar Augustus; neque enim quaerendus erat quem legeret, sed legendus qui eminebat. Itaque quod post Lucii mortem adhuc Gaio vivo facere voluerat atque vehementer repugnante Nerone erat inhibitus, post utriusque adulescentium obitum facere perseveravit, ut et tribuniciae potestatis consortionem Neroni constitueret, multum quidem eo cum domi tum in senatu recusante, et eum Aelio Cato C. Sentio consulibus V. Kal. Iulias, post urbem conditam annis septingentis quinquaginta quattuor, abhinc annos septem et viginti adoptaret. Laetitiam illius diei concursumque civitatis et vota paene inserentium caelo manus **spemque conceptam perpetuae securitatis aeternitatisque Romani imperii vix in illo iusto opere abunde persequi poterimus,** nedum hic implere temptemus, contenti id unum dixisse quam ille omnibus faustus fuerit. **Tum refulsit certa spes liberorum parentibus, viris matrimoniorum, dominis patrimonii, omnibus hominibus salutis, quietis, pacis, tranquillitatis, adeo ut nec plus sperari potuerit nec spei responderi felicius.**

> But fortune, which had removed the hope of the great name [of Caesar], had already restored to the state her real protector; for the return of Tiberius Nero from Rhodes in the consulship of Publius Vinicius, your father, and before the death of either of these youths, had filled his country with joy. Caesar Augustus did not long hesitate, for he had no need to search for one to choose but merely to select the one who towered above the others. Accordingly, what he had wished to do after the death of Lucius but while Gaius was still living, and had been prevented from doing so by the strong opposition of Nero himself, he now insisted upon carrying out after the death of both young men, namely, to make Nero his associate in the tribunician power, in spite of his continued objection both in private and in the senate; and in the consulship of Gaius Sentius, on the twenty-seventh of June, he adopted him, seven hundred and fifty-four years after the founding of the city, and twenty-seven years ago. The rejoicing that day, the concourse of the citizens, their vows as they stretched their hands almost to the very heavens, and the hopes which they entertained for the perpetual security and the eternal existence of the Roman empire, I shall hardly be able to describe to the full even in my comprehensive work, much less try to do it justice here. I shall simply content myself with stating what a day of good omen it was for all. On that day there sprang up once more in parents a sure hope of children, in husbands of marriage, in masters of inheritance, and in all men the hope of safety, order, peace and tranquillity; indeed, it would have been hard to entertain larger hopes, or to have them more happily fulfilled.[3]

---

3 Translations taken from Loeb editions, and modified by me in places: Velleius, Shipley 1924; Tacitus' *Annals*, Moore and Jackson 1931; Suetonius' *Lives*, Rolfe 1913, rev. 1998, Cicero's *de Legibus*, Keyes 1928.

As Woodman has noted, this passage is interesting for the fact that it does not make a clear distinction between Tiberius' arrival in the city in 2 CE and his adoption, which occurred two years later.⁴ According to Suetonius, after repeated requests and Livia's intercession, Augustus had allowed Tiberius to return to Rome with the approval of Gaius: Tiberius had fallen out with Marcus Lollius, who had been his primary enemy in Gaius' entourage, but following Lollius' own disgrace after accusations of bribery, and death (possibly by suicide), no major obstacle for Tiberius' return remained.⁵ This was permitted on the condition that Tiberius would play no role in public affairs. Tiberius' arrival in Rome was a far cry from the spectacle in Velleius' account, and according to Suetonius, after introducing his son Drusus into public life, he retired to the Gardens of Maecenas and exercised no public functions.⁶

By conflating these two events —Tiberius' arrival and the adoption— Velleius avoided the awkwardness of dwelling upon his unspectacular return. Woodman notes that some of the *topoi* associated with the arrival of a great man at the city (the *adventus*) are applied to his adoption, and I would suggest this gives the amalgamated episode greater coherence and credibility.⁷ Woodman, Lobur and others have noted that *festinatio, brevitas*, and the appeal to a lengthier forthcoming history are characteristic features of Velleius' work; a useful way of skimming over awkward details, as well as selecting themes that displayed his control over his material.⁸

Furthermore, not only is it Tiberius who reluctantly agrees to be adopted, thereby empowering him instead of portraying him as Augustus' last resort, but directly following this, Velleius also notes Augustus' adoption of Agrippa Postumus, with no fanfare whatsoever.⁹ The disparity between the two adoptees is obvious, but more interesting is his deliberate omission, for immediately after this, he moves hastily onto Tiberius' departure for Germany. The elephant in the

---

4 Woodman 1983, 130.
5 Suet. *Tib.* 13.2.
6 Suet. *Tib.* 15; Levick has noted that it was very likely the younger Drusus' coming of age which brought Tiberius back to Rome, and that his return would have been a very modest affair. Levick 1976, 46.
7 Woodman 1983, 130–1.
8 Lobur 2007, 211–30.
9 Vell. Pat. 2.104: *Adoptatus eadem die etiam M. Agrippa, quem post mortem Agrippae Iulia enixa erat, sed in Neronis adoptione illud adiectum his ipsis Caesaris verbis: hoc, inquit, rei publicae causa facio.* "On the same day Marcus Agrippa, to whom Julia had given birth after the death of Agrippa, was also adopted by Augustus; but, in the case of Nero [i.e. Tiberius], an addition was made to the formula of adoption in Caesar's own words: 'This I do for reasons of state.'"

room, of course, is Germanicus Caesar. As a part of the succession arrangement in 4 CE, Tiberius had been compelled by Augustus to adopt Germanicus before being adopted himself, according to Suetonius, Tacitus, and Dio.[10] The allegedly uncontrollable Agrippa was easily dismissed from Velleius' narrative shortly afterwards, into exile (9 CE) and death (14 CE).[11] Germanicus was more difficult for Velleius to handle, and a far more sensitive topic, with continuing discussions about his death (allegedly due to poisoning), which of them would have made a better *princeps*, the fate of his wife and children, and so on. Thus in Velleius' history Germanicus' life and career remain deliberately muted but still positive; a loyal nephew, then son, who is a footnote to Tiberius' achievements. We shall return to this point below.

Perhaps the most important feature of Velleius' account of the adoption (2.103), aside from the chronological compression and Germanicus' absence, is the large number of instances of *spes* or *sperare*.[12] It is hope that ties together all of the blessings of the forthcoming age under Tiberius.[13] Aside from the five instances in this passage, the words *spes* or *sperare* occur nineteen other times in Velleius' work, and no other passage is infused with hope to the same extent.[14] Of these, the two others which refer to members of the *domus Augusta* occur at 2.75 and 2.94, both of which are concerned with Tiberius' *fortuna*, and in the latter, the *spes* that those around him placed in him while he was still a youth. The former (2.75) introduces Tiberius into the narrative and relates the story of Tiberius' narrow escape as a baby in Livia's arms, fleeing to Sicily during the civil wars – implying a disastrous counterfactual scenario in which Tiberius does not become *princeps*.[15] The latter (2.94) follows the account of Marcellus' death and Agrippa's return from the East, when Velleius turns to the promising nineteen year old Tiberius and his quaestorship.[16]

---

10 Suet. *Tib*.15, Tac. *Ann*.1.3, Dio 55.13.
11 Vell. Pat. 2.112.
12 An issue briefly noted by Woodman 1983, 135.
13 Also observed by Clark 1983, 98–9.
14 There are none in a similar cluster, and none referring to 'successors' – aside from the one reference (2.94.2) prefiguring Tiberius' greatness.
15 Woodman 1983, 183–4.
16 Vell. Pat. 2.94: *Hoc tractu temporum Ti. Claudius Nero, quo trimo, ut praediximus, Livia, Drusi Claudiani filia, despondente Ti. Nerone, cui ante nupta fuerat, Caesari nupserat, innutritus caelestium praeceptorum disciplinis, insignis genere, forma celsitudine corporis, optimis studiis maximamque ingenio instructissimus, qui protinus quantus est, sperari potuerat visuque praetulerat principem, quaestor undevicesimum annum agens capessere coepit rem publicam maximamque difficultatem annonae ac rei frumentariae inopiam ita Ostiae atque in urbe mandatu vitrici moderatus est, ut per id, quod agebat, quantus evasurus esset, eluceret.*

With the connection between Tiberius' fortune and hope established, returning to our original passage (2.103), we should consider why Velleius chose to emphasise hope so strongly at this point in his history. As *spes* is a 'forward-looking' emotion, the basic answer might be that Velleius is pointing us towards the climax of his work, when Tiberius assumes the role of his adoptive father and an abundance of blessings follow for the *res publica* (most prominently at 2.126). Yet Velleius, in 29 CE, was not the first to make the association between *spes* and potential successors to Augustus, and it is possible to propose an idea that makes more of Velleius' political context. With this in mind, we turn briefly to the cult of *Spes* in the period leading up to Velleius' composition.

2 Germanicus, the cult of *Spes*, and the temple rededication

Cicero briefly discussed *spes* in the *de Legibus* (2.11.28), providing us with at least one definition:

> bene vero, quod Mens, Pietas, Virtus, Fides consecratur manu; quarum omnium Romae dedicata publice templa sunt, ut, illa qui habeant (habeant autem omnes boni), deos ipsos in animis suis conlocatos putent... quoniam expectatione rerum bonarum erigitur animus, recte etiam Spes a Calatino consecrata est.

> It is a good thing also that Mens, Pietas, Virtus, and Fides should be deified; and in Rome temples have been dedicated to all these qualities, the purpose being that those who possess them (and all good men do) should believe that the gods themselves are established within their own souls... And since the mind is encouraged by the anticipation of good things, Calatinus was right in deifying Spes also.

The 'emotion' or 'concept' of *spes* was thus tied at some point (perhaps prior to the early fifth century BCE) to the activity of an eponymous goddess.[17] The origins

---

See Woodman 1977, 95–100. For *insignis* instead of *iuvenis*, see Harrison 2005.

17 This idea of these so-called 'abstract deities' or 'divine qualities' manifesting themselves in the emotions or virtues of individuals is discussed by Fears 1981, and Clark 2007. Elsewhere, Cicero casts some doubt upon the idea of *spes et al.* being divine, through the Academic scepticism he uses Cotta to present in the third book of *de Natura Deorum*. At 3.14 the tension between fatalism and *spes* is noted, and an argument advanced that *divinatio* —which could, if true, reveal a predestined future— would remove even "the last, and universal, consolation of *spes*". At 3.46–7 he argues that if some of these 'qualities' or 'concepts' are in fact deities, then *Natio* (and thus many others) must be as well (cf. Clark 2007, 134–5). *De Nat. Deor.* 3.61 (and 3.88–9,

of the Roman cult of *Spes* are obscure, and the goddess developed quite a different reputation and set of meanings from that of *Elpis*.[18] By contrast, the Roman conception was more often quite positive, and at worst ambivalent, depending on its focus.[19] The earliest temple on the outskirts of Rome was known in later periods as '*Spes Vetus*'. Sources suggest it existed by 477 BCE, and appears in Livy and Dionysius in connection with Horatius' victory over the Etruscans, prior to the Battle of the Colline Gate.[20] This is the temple which later gave its name to the area near the modern site of Porta Maggiore, known as *ad Spem Veterem*, and to the nearby *Horti Spei Veteris*.[21]

The establishment of a new temple in the Forum Holitorium, which was vowed by Aulus Atilius Calatinus probably in 258 BCE, marked the transition to a more significant cult, during the First Punic War.[22] Livy records that this temple burned down in 213 BCE and was restored the following year by a special

---

depending upon a textual emendation) calls into question whether *spes* (and other emotions or qualities that reside within man) can in fact be divinities, from a Stoic perspective. The broader question of how representative Cicero's ideas in his theological and philosophical works actually were remains (and indeed the different positions presented in *de Nat. Deor.* suggest it was contested among the elite). Nevertheless, it seems probable that *spes* continued to be seen as a goddess in society more generally (as *de Legibus* 2.11.28, and the rebuilding of her temple on more than one occasion, discussed below, would suggest). Clarifying the precise relationship of *spes* with human emotional states, other deities, fatalism, and divination, might not have been seen as such an urgent task in wider society —many such paradoxes and ambiguities remained unresolved in Roman theology and cult.

18 As well as Clark 1983, see the other contributions in this volume, especially by Johnston and Chaniotis.
19 Whether hope was considered a good thing was largely dependent upon its particular focus (usually attached in the genitive e.g. *spes victoriae*, *spes fugae*) and the literary context in which it appeared. See Clark 1983, 80–105; Clark lists a series of literary representations, cf. 86f.
20 Liv. 2.51.2–3; Dion. Hal. *Ant. Rom.* 9.24.3–4. See also Fulkerson, in this volume, on the Republican temples to *spes*.
21 Frontin. *Aq.*, 1.5, 19, 20, 2.65, 76, 87; H.A. *Elag.* 13. See *LTUR IV (P–S)*, 338.
22 cf. Ziolkowski, 1992, 29: "It is impossible to establish when Caiatinus, who apart from two consulates held imperium in Sicily as praetor in 257 and as dictator in 249, vowed this temple [to Fides in Capitolio], especially considering that he also built a temple to *Spes*. All that can be said is that, whereas during his second consulate he apparently did not achieve anything spectacular, in 258–257 he earned a triumph and in 249 primus dictator extra Italiam exercitum duxit. In the wake of the disasters suffered by the consuls of that year dedications both to *Fides* and *Spes* would have been quite à propos, though Zonaras explicitly states that the dictator and his master of horse did not achieve anything worth remembering." [Zon. 8.15.14] and 152: "It is impossible to ascertain the exact date of Caiatinus' vow, which may have taken place in 258–257, 254, or 249." *LTUR IV (P–S)*, 336–7.

commission. It also appears in Dio, being consumed by fire once more in 31 BCE.[23] The temple was again restored, as Tacitus notes (*Ann.* 2.49), and this time dedicated by Germanicus Caesar in 17 CE:

> Isdem temporibus deum aedis vetustate aut igni abolitas coeptasque ab Augusto dedicavit, Libero Liberaque et Cereri iuxta Circum Maximum, quam A. Postumius dictator voverat, eodemque in loco aedem Florae ab Lucio et Marco Publiciis aedilibus constitutam, et Iano templum, quod apud forum holitorium C. Duilius struxerat, qui primus rem Romanam prospere mari gessit triumphumque navalem de Poenis meruit. Spei aedes a Germanico sacratur: hanc A. Atilius voverat eodem bello.

> At the same time, he [Tiberius] consecrated the temples, ruined by age or fire, the restoration of which had been undertaken by Augustus. They included a temple to Liber, Libera, and Ceres, close to the Circus Maximus, and vowed by Aulus Postumius, the dictator; another, on the same site, to Flora, founded by Lucius and Marcus Publius in their aedileship, and a shrine of Janus, built in the Forum Holitorium by Gaius Duilius, who first carried the Roman cause to success on sea and earned a naval triumph over the Carthaginians. The temple of Hope, vowed by Aulus Atilius in the same war, was dedicated by Germanicus.

According to the most recent excavation reports, the temple is to be identified with the southernmost of the three which form the skeleton of San Nicola in Carcere in the Forum Holitorium, just a few metres down the road from the Theatre of Marcellus —a Doric peripteral hexastyle structure, with eleven columns of stuccoed travertine on each side.[24]

One of the most important studies of the temple of *spes* and successors is an article by Mark Edward Clark, which was the first lengthy discussion of the concept of *spes* in a political context.[25] Clark drew attention to the association between particular (often youthful) leaders of the late Republic and Triumviral period and *spes*, in a range of sources (such as Cicero's Pompey in *Pro lege Manilia*, or Octavian in the *Philippics*), before arriving at a discussion of its role in the ideology of the early Principate (including figures such as Virgil's Aeneas and particularly Ascanius, as well as imperial family members, such as the young Marcellus).[26]

While providing a useful survey of the evidence, the article presents a narrative with phases (often named after coin legends —*Spes Augusta*, *Spes Populi Romani* etc) that progress rather unproblematically from a 'civic' religious cult in the context of the Punic wars, to the hope invested in individual charismatic

---

23 Liv. 25.7.6; 24.47.15–6; fire, Dio 50.10.3.
24 Crozzoli Aite refers to the excavation reports from the 1960s; Crozzoli Aite 1981, 119.
25 Clark 1983, 80–105.
26 On *spes* in Virgil, see the contribution by Paschalis in this volume.

leaders with personal armies in the late Republic and Triumviral period, before finally arriving at the role it played in the formation of imperial 'propaganda' as a so-called 'virtue'.

Within the periods Clark has designated, there is little sense of political development – each period appears 'synchronic' in its own right. For example, *Spes Augusta*, which does not appear as a slogan until a coin of Claudius from 41 CE, characterises the entire Julio-Claudian period, without a close analysis of its gradual development and contested nature.[27] Clark writes: "While numismatic and literary evidence from the time of the later principate is helpful in showing the eventual development of *Spes* in the imperial cult, it does not shed much light upon the origin of the virtue and its transformation from a religious symbol of the republic into imperial propaganda."[28] As Anna Clark has shown, among others, the essentially modern division made between 'religion' and 'politics' did not exist in the same way for the Romans, and distinguishing between 'upper' and 'lower case' *spes* is problematic, and so to suggest it was taken from a murky religious sphere and transported into the political realm, is somewhat mistaken.[29] For example, were our sources more informative, the motivations behind Calatinus' vow of the original temple might turn out to be far more 'political' than it initially appears (perhaps competitive triumphal building); certainly, the 'religious' aspects of the cult later in the principate were not easily separated from the 'political.'

However, perhaps the most unusual aspect of Clark's article, for our purposes, is the fact that he places the rededication of the temple in 19 CE.[30] *Isdem temporibus* in *Annals* 2.49 refers to the previously narrated events of 17 CE, including the earthquake in Asia Minor, and Germanicus' triumph.[31] Tacitus is working largely within an annalistic framework that often places structures built in a given year together at the end of the chapter. What can be established from the Tacitean passage, is that firstly, Augustus had apparently begun restorations, following damage from the fire of 31 BCE —his death therefore, on August 19th, 14 CE, is the *terminus ante quem* for the start of renovations— but that secondly,

---

[27] Clark 1983, 83; A coin issued at Pella from 16 BCE does feature the legend *Spes Coloniae Pellensis*, which apparently refers to Augustus, and does seem to prefigure the later evidence, such as the *Feriale Cumanum*.
[28] Clark 1983, 84; in another section that seeks to establish the origins of the cult (86), a Hadrianic coin is used to illustrate the civic qualities associated with *spes* from an early age —a synchronic approach that obscures various sorts of changes (semantic, contextual etc).
[29] Clark 2007.
[30] Clark 1983, 96. This may simply be a typographical error.
[31] Tac. *Ann.* 2.47.

they were not finished until at least 17 CE. This seems rather a long time, even for the construction of an entirely new temple.³²

Why, then, was there such a delay? The political context provides a good explanation. After his consulship in 12 CE, Germanicus had been sent to the Rhine by Augustus in 13 CE, when Tiberius was recalled to Rome to assume equal power.³³ Following the death of Augustus, in the ensuing period of instability, with mutinies on the Rhine and Danube, Germanicus remained in command. His reckless campaigns against the Chatti and the Cherusci began with the purpose of bringing the mutinous legions under control, but eventually resulted in the recovery of standards lost in the *clades Variana* of 9 CE. Probably in 15 CE (or less likely, 16 CE), according to Tacitus, Tiberius was concerned with the extent of these campaigns, Germanicus' conduct and his popularity, and so a triumph was voted to him in order to bring the expeditions to a close.³⁴ Despite this, Germanicus continued the campaigns in 16 CE, and eventually, after a series of battles and shipwrecks, and letters from Tiberius recalling him, he decided to return for his triumph. This was eventually celebrated on May 26th, 17 CE.³⁵

It is well known that the Republican tradition of triumphal or manubial building continued throughout and after the civil wars. In an excellent article on Augustan *Iustitia*, Lott notes how the arrival of members of the *domus Augusta* in Rome, the *adventus*, was often celebrated with special attention being given to a

---

32 In the *Res Gestae*, written (or revised) sometime before his death in 14 CE, Augustus claimed (20.4) to have repaired all of the temples that needed restoration (in 28 BCE), despite the fact that *Spes* was dedicated in 17 CE —either Augustus counted the temple as having been restored once work had begun, Tacitus (or his source) incorrectly attributed the work to Augustus, Augustus is ignoring the structures he did not wish to rebuild (a point Ovid may make with regard to the Palatine cult of Juno Sospita, *Fasti* 2.55–66), or Augustus is not counting structures outside the pomerium. On the dating, Cooley 2009, 43, and on this passage, 194–5.
33 Tac. *Ann*. 1.3 collapses the chronology: *At hercle Germanicum, Druso ortum, octo apud Rhenum legionibus inposuit adscirique per adoptionem a Tiberio iussit*, "Yet, curiously enough, he placed Drusus' son Germanicus at the head of eight legions on the Rhine, and ordered Tiberius to adopt him..."; as does Suet. *Cal*. 1.1. However, it is clear from *Cal*. 8.3 that Germanicus was appointed to the command of the Gauls and Germany in 13 CE, immediately following his consulship, after Tiberius' return to Rome.
34 Tac. *Ann*. 1.55.
35 On the letters from Tiberius, Tac. *Ann*. 2.26. The triumph itself is noted by Tacitus (*Ann*. 2.41), Strabo (7.1.4), and (proleptically) Ovid (*Fasti* 1.285–6), and very briefly by Velleius in a passage discussed at greater length below (2.129).

new or old cult, including even occasions when triumphs were celebrated —*Fortuna Redux, Pax Augusta, Concordia Augusta* and so on.³⁶

With these comparanda in mind, it seems probable that Germanicus' triumph and *Spes* fall into a similar category. Various young family members had already been promoted as potential successors, and Augustus had been associating youth with hope, as the *Feriale Cumanum* demonstrates.³⁷ This sacrificial calendar from Cumae, probably drafted in the period between 4 and 14 CE, features a *supplicatio* to *Spes* and *Iuventas*, on October the 18th, to commemorate the day on which Augustus assumed the *toga virilis*. This might be seen as a part of a wider concern to buttress the succession arrangement through revitalising the cult of *Spes*, and connecting it with youth.³⁸ This is an explanation that fits well with the unusual chronology of the rebuilding in Tacitus, Germanicus' movements in those years, and other examples of cults being founded or rededicated at the time of a triumph or *adventus*. Though a contentious issue, according to most reconstructions, the temple was likely located on Germanicus' triumphal route in 17 CE.³⁹

---

36 "The arrival of the princeps or a member of his family was an event of great significance: The Adventus of Tiberius was itself deified before 14 [10?]; votive games were offered to Jupiter Optimus Maximus pro reditu Augusti in 8 and 7 B.C.; and other Augustan testimonia might be cited. But Augustus' policy after 19 B.C. of allowing infrequent triumphs made some other celebration when he or a member of his family returned from abroad necessary if the day were to be remembered. The declaration of a cult ensured a festive reception for the princeps and provided a means whereby an annual holiday might remark the day. Tiberius' declaration in 7 B.C. shows that even when a rare triumph was held, special attention might be paid to an old or new cult. We may suppose, then, that the cults of *Fortuna Redux, Pax Augusta* and *Concordia Augusta* were promoted when they were in order to provide an immediate ceremony which coincided with Augustus or Tiberius' arrival; the physical shrines for the new cults were dedicated later after their completion." Lott 1996, 265.
37 *CIL* 10.8375; the date of the *Feriale Cumanum* is deduced from the fact that the names of the adoptees have changed, whilst Augustus is not yet deified, giving us a *terminus ante quem*. So the connection between hope and youth was made in *supplicationes*, in the period in which Augustus was making what were to become his final dynastic arrangements, potentially at the same time as the temple in the Forum Holitorium was being rebuilt.
38 Tiberius could hardly be called a young man in 4 CE, but Germanicus certainly could.
39 cf. Beard 2007, 92–106.

3 Germanicus and *spes* in Tacitus

I would suggest then, that the rededication associated the cult of *spes* with Germanicus more than any other potential successor. Though much later, and employing the associations for its own purposes, Tacitus' *Annals* appear to be adapting an earlier tradition connecting Germanicus and hope.

For example, the troops during the mutinies in 14 CE have *magna spes* that Germanicus will march on Rome with the legions (*Ann.* 1.31); the same hopes and affection centre on the young Germanicus as they did on the elder Drusus, who allegedly had desired to give back *libertas* (*Ann.* 1.33); the nearer Germanicus stood to the highest hopes, the more energy he threw into the cause of Tiberius, writes Tacitus (*Ann.* 1.34); Piso is sent to Syria to constrain the hopes of Germanicus (*Ann.* 2.43); then there are two important instances worth closer attention. First, in Germanicus' deathbed speech (*Ann.* 2.71) Tacitus has him say:

> Si quos **spes meae**, si quos propinquus sanguis, etiam quos invidia erga viventem movebat, inlacrimabunt quondam florentem et tot bellorum susperstitem muliebri fraude cecidisse.

> If any were ever stirred by the hope I inspired [*or* hope of me], by kindred blood — even by envy of me while I lived — they must shed a tear to think that the once happy survivor of so many wars has fallen by female treachery.

And secondly, at Germanicus' funeral at the Mausoleum (*Ann.* 3.4):

> Dies quo reliquiae tumulo Augusti inferebantur modo per silentium vastus, modo ploratibus inquies; plena urbis itinera, conlucentes per campum Martis faces. Illic miles cum armis, sine insignibus magistratus, populus per tribus concidisse rem publicam, **nihil spei reliquum clamitabant**, promptius apertiusque quam ut meminisse imperitantium crederes.

> The day on which the remains were consigned to the mausoleum of Augustus was alternatively a desolation of silence and a turmoil of laments. The city streets were full, the Campus Martius alight with torches. There the soldier in harness, the magistrate lacking his insignia, the people in their tribes, iterated the cry that the "commonwealth had fallen, and no hope remained" too freely and too openly for it to be credible that they remembered their governors.

Even taking into account the fact that Tacitus has manipulated his material for dramatic effect, this suggests that an association between Germanicus and *spes* had existed in popular memory, and was likely incorporated into earlier historiography in some way (perhaps including, but not necessarily limited to, the memoirs of the younger Agrippina) —and moreover, that all of these developments occurred as a result of the political discourse of the 20s CE. Furthermore, there is some external support for this reading found in the *Senatus Consultum de Gnaeo Pisone Patre*. Discovered in Spain, the *SCPP* from the 10th December, 20 CE, illustrates another connection between *spes* and successors in imperial ideology. At line 126–130 it states:

> ut omnem curam, quam in duos quondam filios suos partitus erat, ad eum, quem haberet, converteret, sperareq(ue) senatum eum, qui supersit, tanto maiori curae dis immortalibus fore, quanto magis intellegerent, **omnem spem futuram paternae pro r(e) p(ublica) stationis in uno repositam.**

> that all the care he [Tiberius] had previously divided between his two sons he devote to the one he had; and that the senate hoped that the one who survives would be all the more an object of the immortal gods' concern insofar as they understood that all future hope of his father's guardianship of the state was now placed in one man.

Here we can see a senatorial expression of the future hope for the succession attached to the younger Drusus, with the implication that hope had formerly been placed in Germanicus as well. Yet despite the equality presented here, there was something particular about Germanicus.

At the height of his popularity, the designated successor and recent *triumphator* died in Antioch, two years after the rededication of the temple. It was this combination, perhaps more than anything else, that solidified his connection with hope. The situation in Rome was extremely volatile owing to the outpouring of grief for Germanicus, and there are numerous passages which highlight this fact.[40] Tiberius was accused by some of a conspiracy against Germanicus via his legate Gnaeus Calpurnius Piso. The *SCPP* presents a picture of widespread though controlled grief, but later sources have more effusive accounts of anguish and distress and even of riotous behaviour; or to use Versnel's term, *anomie*, the breakdown of social norms. This is seen for example in Suetonius (*Cal.* 5–6):

---

[40] Undoubtedly the most detailed analysis of the mourning for Germanicus, though it predates the discovery of the *SCPP*, is by Versnel 1980; Versnel's religious and anthropological approach highlights the different aspects of the popular grief recorded in the literary accounts, demonstrating that it was not an ordinary display of grief. When using *anomie* to describe this episode he follows Durkheim's definition, which was much broader than the Greek *anomia*. This grief was exacerbated owing to the amount of hope placed in an individual, he argues, brought about especially through the shift in allegiance from *patria* to *pater patriae* through *supplicationes*, *vota* etc. Germanicus in this sense came to embody hope for the future. In literature on the *SCPP*, this context of grief in Rome is perhaps most strongly emphasised by González 1999, especially 138–9; also Flower 1999, 108.

Tamen longe maiora et firmiora de eo iudicia in morte ac post mortem exstiterunt. Quo defunctus est die, lapidata sunt templa, subversae deum arae, Lares a quibusdam familiares in publicum abiecti, partus coniugum expositi. [...] Romae quidem, cum ad primam famam valitudinis attonita et maesta civitas sequentis nuntios opperiretur, et repente iam vesperi incertis auctoribus convaluisse tandem percrebruisset, passim cum luminibus et victimis in Capitolium concursum est ac paene revolsae templi fores, ne quid gestientis vota reddere moraretur, expergefactus e somno Tiberius gratulantium vocibus atque undique concinentium: Salva Roma, salva patria, salvus est Germanicus! Et ut demum fato functum palam factum est, non solaciis ullis, non edictis inhiberi luctus publicus potuit duravitque etiam per festos Decembris mensis dies. Auxit gloriam desideriumque defuncti et atrocitas insequentium temporum, cunctis nec temere opinantibus reverentia eius ac metu repressam Tiberi saevitiam, quae mox eruperit.

Yet far greater and stronger tokens of regard were shown at the time of his death and immediately afterwards. On the day when he passed away the temples were stoned and the altars of the gods thrown down, while some flung their household gods into the street and cast out their newly born children. [...] At Rome when the community, in grief and consternation at the first report of his illness, was awaiting further news, and suddenly after nightfall a report at last spread abroad, on doubtful authority, that he had recovered, a general rush was made from every side to the Capitol with torches and victims, and the temple gates were all but torn off, that nothing might hinder them in their eagerness to pay their vows. Tiberius was roused from sleep by the cries of the rejoicing throng, who all united in singing: Safe is Rome, safe the homeland, Germanicus is safe! But when it was at last made known that he was no more, the public grief could be checked neither by any consolation nor edict, and it continued even during the festal days of the month of December. The fame of the deceased and regret for his loss were increased by the horror of the times which followed, since all believed, and with good reason, that the cruelty of Tiberius, which soon burst forth, had been held in check through his respect and awe for Germanicus.

A similar report of the intense communal grief is found in Tacitus' account.[41] Furthermore, at the start of Book 3, beginning with the evocative scene of Agrippina's arrival at Brundisium bearing the ashes of Germanicus, lies the most famous account of this grief. It ends with his funeral, shortly after which we find that Tiberius issued an edict to try to put an end to the public unrest —perhaps the same one mentioned by Suetonius.[42]

---

41 Tac. *Ann.* 2.82.
42 Tac. *Ann.* 3.6: *utque premeret vulgi sermones, monuit edicto multos inlustri Romanorum ob rem publicam obisse, neminem tam flagranti desiderio celebratum. Idque et sibi et cunctis egregium, si modus adiceretur. Non enim eadem decora principibus viris et imperatori populo quae modicis domibus aut civitatibus. Convenisse recenti dolori luctum et ex maerore solacia; sed referendum iam animum ad firmitudinem, ut quondam divus Iulius amissa unica, ut divus Augustus ereptis nepotibus abstruserint tristitiam. Nil opus vetustioribus exemplis, quotiens populus Romanus cladis exercituum, interitum ducum, funditus amissas nobilis familias constanter tulerit. Principes*

Thus it seems, even taking into account the hyperbole of anti-Tiberian sources in Tacitus and Suetonius, grieving in Rome continued in some form at least from the first news of Germanicus' death on October 10th, 19 CE, right through December, and up until the official cessation sometime shortly before games of the Magna Mater on April 4th. Therefore, the reported events in Rome with displays of despair and anguish suggest that Germanicus had indeed been considered or promoted as the future hope of the state.

4 Conclusion: Velleius in context

We return then, to Velleius and the passage concerning the adoption (2.103) with which we began. Velleius had lived through the rise and sudden death of Germanicus, and the ensuing struggle to determine the nature of his reputation and memory, between Agrippina and her adherents, Tiberius' supporters, and eventually Sejanus. The conspicuous absence of Germanicus from the adoption passage has already been noted; another passage demonstrates how conscious Velleius is of the sensitivity surrounding Germanicus in 29. In his synopsis of Tiberius' principate, he writes (2.129.1–3):

> Quibus praeceptis instructum Germanicum suum imbutumque rudimentis militiae secum actae domitorem recepit Germaniae! Quibus iuventam eius exaggeravit honoribus, respondente cultu triumphi rerum, quas gesserat, magnitudini! Quotiens populum congiariis honoravit senatorumque censum, cum id senatu auctore facere potuit, quam libenter explevit, ut neque luxuriam invitaret neque honestam paupertatem pateretur dignitate destitui! Quanto cum honore Germanicum suum in transmarinas misit provincias!

---

mortales, rem publicam aeternam esse. Proin repeterent sollemnia, et quid ludorum Megalesium spectaculum suberat, etiam voluptates resumerent, "...and to repress the comments of the crowd, he reminded them in a manifesto that "many illustrious Romans had died for their country, but none had been honoured with such a fervour of regret: a compliment highly valued by himself and by all, if only moderation were observed. For the same conduct was not becoming to ordinary families or communities and to leaders of the state and to an imperial people. Mourning and the solace of tears had suited the first throes of their affliction; but now they must recall their minds to fortitude, as once the deified Julius at the loss of his only daughter, and the deified Augustus at the taking of his grandchildren, had thrust aside their anguish. There was no need to show by earlier instances how often the Roman people had borne unshaken the slaughter of armies, the death of generals, the complete annihilation of historic houses. Statesmen were mortal, the state eternal. Let them return, therefore, to their usual occupations and —as the Megalesian Games would soon be exhibited— resume even their pleasures!".

How well had Germanicus been trained under his instructions, having so thoroughly learned the rudiments of military science under him that he was later to welcome him home as conqueror of Germany! What honours did he heap upon him, young though he was, making the magnificence of his triumph to correspond to the greatness of his deeds! How often did he honour the people with largesses, and how gladly, whenever he could do so with the senate's sanction, did he raise to the required rating the fortunes of senators, but in such a way as not to encourage extravagant living, nor yet to allow senators to lose their rank because of honest poverty! With what honours did he send his beloved Germanicus to the provinces across the seas!

Velleius is pleading with his readers that Tiberius had caused Germanicus no harm and the accusations against him were unfounded.[43] Moreover, Germanicus' military achievements are credited to Tiberius. He is subordinated to the *princeps* even as he is being praised for his triumph, which sits within a compliment to Tiberius. The important point to note is that Germanicus was a difficult subject for Velleius. His image had been sanitised by Tiberius and his supporters after his death, through documents such as the *SCPP* that depict him as a loyal and subordinate son. Consequently, he was not denigrated by Velleius like Julia, Agrippa Postumus or Agrippina; but neither could he be praised, for that would play into the hands of Tiberius' detractors who promoted Germanicus as a superior *princeps*, now lost. As a result, we can have greater confidence that Velleius was writing the account of the adoption with one eye on Germanicus and his reputation.

The cult of *spes* had been revitalised in order to use it as an additional support during the first experiment in transitioning power within the *domus Augusta*. Following Germanicus' death, the anticipation which had built up around him was to become extremely problematic for Tiberius. It appears that Velleius decided to contribute to the defence of his former commander in a sophisticated way. He took the concept by now associated with young potential successors, and above all Germanicus owing to his triumph and cult dedication in 17 CE, and projected it back onto the amalgamated episode of Tiberius' own unspectacular arrival and eventual adoption. In this way, Velleius attempted to counteract the discourse of hope that had developed around the prince by placing his popularity before Germanicus' chronologically, at the same time as he silenced the alternative narratives of 'lost futures' propagated by Agrippina's family and supporters.

---

43 Further evidence in support of this reading of 2.192 is the way in which Velleius foregrounds the just manner in which Tiberius dealt with Rhascupolis, the slayer of his brother's son Cotys, who shared the throne with him —a strikingly similar scenario to the accusations against Tiberius preserved in Tacitus. His treatment of Drusus Libo immediately afterwards further underscores the idea that Tiberius' *iustitia* is a key virtue in this passage.

Bibliography

Beard, M. 2007. *The Roman Triumph*, Cambridge, Mass.
Clark, A.J. 2007. *Divine Qualities: Cult and Community in Republican Rome*, Oxford.
Clark, M.E. 1983. "*Spes* in the Early Imperial Cult: 'The Hope of Augustus'," in: *Numen* 30, 80–105.
Cooley, A.E. 2009. *Res Gestae Divi Augusti: Text, Translation, and Commentary*, Cambridge.
Cowan, E. (ed.) 2010. *Velleius Paterculus: Making History*, Swansea.
Crozzoli Aite, L. 1981. *I Tre Templi del Foro Holitorio*, in: Memorie: Atti della Pontificia Accademia Romana di Archeologia Serie 3, Vol. 13, Rome.
de Monte, J. 1999. "Velleius Paterculus and 'Triumphal' History," in: *AHB*, 13.4, 121–135.
Fears, J.R. 1981. "The Cult of Virtues and Roman Imperial Ideology," in: *ANRW* 17.2, 827–948.
Flower, H.I. 1999. "Piso in Chicago," in: *AJPh* 120.1, 99–115.
González, J. 1999. "Tacitus, Germanicus, Piso and the Tabula Siarensis," in: *AJPh* 120.1, 123–142.
Harrison, S.J. 2005. "Velleius on Tiberius: A Textual Problem at Velleius Paterculus 2.94.2," in: *SO* 80.1, 58–59.
Levick, B. 1976 (revised ed. 1999). *Tiberius the Politician*, London.
Lobur, J.A. 2007. "*Festinatio* (Haste), *Brevitas* (Concision), and the Generation of Imperial Ideology in Velleius Paterculus," in: *TAPA* 137, 211–30.
Lott, J.B. 1996. "An Augustan Sculpture of August Justice," in: *ZPE* 113, 263–70.
Palombi, A. 2006. *La Basilica di San Nicola in Carcere: Il Complesso Architettonico dei Tre Templi del Foro Olitorio*, Rome.
Rich, J. 2012. "Making the Emergency Permanent: *auctoritas*, *potestas*, and the Evolution of the Principate of Augustus," in: Y. Riviére (ed.), *Des réformes augustéenes*, Rome, 37–21.
Rowe, G. 2002. *Princes and Political Cultures: The New Tiberian Senatorial Decrees*, Ann Arbor.
Sumner, G.V. 1970. "The Truth about Velleius Paterculus: Prolegomena," in: *HSCPh* 74, 257–97.
Syme, R. 1978. "Mendacity in Velleius," in: *AJPh* 99.1, 45–63.
Versnel, H.S. 1980. "Destruction, *Devotio* and Despair in a Situation of Anomy: The Mourning for Germanicus in Triple Perspective," in: *Perennitas: Studi in onore di Angelo Brelich, Promossi della Cattedra di Religioni del mondo classico dell'Universitá degli Studi di Roma*, Rome, 541–618.
Woodman, A.J. 1977. *Velleius Paterculus: The Tiberian Narrative (2.94–131)*, Cambridge.
—— 1983. *Velleius Paterculus: The Caesarian and Augustan Narrative (2.41–93)*, Cambridge.
Woodman, A.J./R.H. Martin, 1996. *The Annals of Tacitus*, Book 3, Cambridge.
Ziolkowski, A. 1992. *The Temples of Mid-Republican Rome and their Historical and Topographical Context*, Rome.

Antti Lampinen
Against Hope? The Untimely *elpis* of Northern Barbarians

1 Introductory remarks

The motivations of strangers are generally felt to be harder for us to decipher than those of the members of our own ingroup. Moreover, when a culture or society surveys the frontiers —social, spatial, or cognitive— of its own system of values or identities, the motivations of the outsiders can loom much larger than when operating closer to its own epistemic centre.[1] Within the ingroup, the projection of emotions or mental states onto outgroups can be enacted over a broad array of textual registers, from invective and admonitory rhetoric to historical causation or epigraphy. Common to such projections of hope (or confident expectation) onto outgroups —especially those regarded as 'barbarians' by the Greek and Roman audiences— is that in almost all cases of ancient evidence they cannot be held to represent evidence for the real aspirations of said outgroups. Hope is a difficult mental state to extract from our ancient sources without succumbing to anachronism, but ἐλπίς tended to incorporate both an element of yearning and of expectation, though it could also convey an opinion without much motivational force.[2] Thus it seems best to opt for an open-ended and inclusive view of the desiderative emotions and aspirations that were thought to motivate the 'polemical outsiders'.

This paper will look at the portrayal of northern barbarians' aspirations from three interconnected angles: first, the hopes for a rebirth or an afterlife that certain northern peoples were supposed to harbour; then what seems like their yearning or greedy hope for plunder or land; and lastly their hope for a revenge or reversal. Finally, I will briefly look at how the Greeks and Romans imagined the hopes of the barbarians failing —the turning of hope into hopelessness— as well as the literary conventions and epistemic regimes that buttressed such

---
[1] See Parker Tapias *et al.* 2007 and Hackel *et al.* 2014 on how the ascription of emotions interacts with prejudice and social identity.
[2] Konstan 2006, 3–40 warns against anachronism. On 'hope' having both desiderative and propositional (expectative) dimension, see Cairns 2016, 16–20, 22–3; *elpis* focused on future good, but semantically it was less distinctive than our 'hope', its meaning balancing between an anticipation of a future good, and a longing for it: 24.

reversals. The sources used range from the Hellenistic to the Imperial era, but they are unified by their joint technique of projecting affectively or emotively formulated expectations onto the barbarian outgroups of Europe in order to explain their behaviour. By tying the ancient discourse on barbarian hopes and aspirations into the broader ethnographical register, I wish to contribute to the study of the Greek and Roman emotional responses to their encounters with outgroups, as well as to demonstrate how perceptions of intentionality could be elided, in such contexts, with the ascription of collective emotions to outgroups.

Studies on 'mindreading' within the framework of social identity theory have pointed out how outgroup mental states and aspirations are prone to be understood in starkly one-dimensional ways.[3] In literature, the corresponding operation of 'writing emotions' has clear linkages to the morally charged rhetoric of praise and blame, while the 'theories of mind' embedded in outgroup descriptions and perceptions tend to be fairly simplified.[4] The emotions of external peoples are seldom given the same range as those of the Greeks or Romans, and these descriptions are frequently 'ethnicised' through references to culturally distinctive practices.[5] The barbarians of ancient Greek and Roman thinking constitute typical examples of essentialisingly conceived outgroups: each barbarian individual of a given group tends to be portrayed according to a narrow set of stereotypes, and many barbarian groups are seen as largely similar to each other, or even interchangeable.[6] Despite this, we humans tend to allow even for very negatively viewed outgroups a certain internal logic in their actions: even when appearing irrational, they are granted to be acting according to their worldview. Their aspirations are admitted to guide their actions, even as these aspirations are often portrayed in terms inimical to the ingroup.[7]

---

[3] 'Theory of mind' (or 'mindreading') as the framework within which we attribute beliefs, knowledge, emotions and other mental processes to, and understand them in, individuals or outgroups: Barr and Keysar 2005, 271–4; Reeder and Trafimow 2005, 108–20. On the social identity theory's approach to ingroup favouritism, see Scaillet and Leyens 2000; Ros *et al.* 2000.

[4] The best example of 'theory of mind' approach applied to Classics is Scodel 2016. To my knowledge, no study has yet been devoted to 'theories of mind' for barbarians in the ancient literature, although Adler 2011 often has pertinent things to say, including about the textual 'mindreading' of both barbarians and Romans (and of Romans by barbarians, and vice versa): e.g. 172–3 generally, and 67–9 on Hannibal.

[5] Such as Boudicca's speech in Tacitus' *Ann.* 14.35: Adler 2011, 117–39. See also Todorov 2010, 15–18.

[6] On the 'impossibility of new barbarians', see Wolfram 1997, 37; cf. Murphy 2004, 82. On the essentialising tendencies in Greek anthropological thinking, Sassi 2001, esp. 140–60.

[7] Cf. Gutsell and Inzlicht 2012, 601–2.

In addition to being involved in emotively oriented causation, 'mindreading' the barbarians plays a natural role in emotionally charged ingroup communication. The Greek attitude towards barbarian threats frequently tended towards the strongly emotional at least since the Persian wars and the attack of the Galatae against Macedonia and Greece in the 270s BCE. In the case of the Romans, the most emotively laden episodes of collective memory seem to be those dealing with the semi-legendary Gallic attack, the Punic Wars, and the Cimbric wars (113–101 BCE).[8] The personifications *Spes* and *Victoria* had been conceptually linked in the Roman religion from early on, and it is easy to see how the contrary hopes of outgroups would thus be seen as oppositional to Rome's success.[9] The perceived moral insufficiencies of barbarian peoples and the theoretical underpinnings used to validate these perceptions are a wide subject, but one that needs to be carried along as we examine the evidence from the Greek and Roman literary tradition. The underdeveloped souls of the cultural outsiders were frequently seen as too easily swayed by sudden emotions and agitation. The barbarians' perceived lack of *ratio* or σωφροσύνη was used to explain their (hoped-for) lack of success in bringing their hopes to reality, but this simple epistemic basis could be put into a variety of uses, as will be seen.[10]

2 Hopes for an afterlife

Hope could be used to explain the stereotypical ferociousness of northerners. The long-lived Greco-Roman notion that hope for a rebirth or an afterlife was widespread among northern peoples has a Herodotean pedigree; in his *Histories*, it is the Thracians who are attributed this belief. The connection of the area with the doctrines of Orpheus might have made the association more salient in the Greek mind. The Getae are repeatedly said to 'profess a belief' in their own immortality.[11] Zalmoxis, a clever former slave of Pythagoras, had tricked the credulous Thracians by withdrawing into a subterranean chamber and returning from there after

---

8   On the effect of the Persian wars, see Rhodes 2007; on the Galatian invasions, Nachtergael 1977 and Mitchell 2003; on Roman fear of the given outgroups: Bellen 1985; Williams 2001; and Kerremans 2016. On high salience of negative associations (such as feeling threatened) leading to more explicit ingroup favouritism: Otten and Mummendey 2000, 43–7.
9   On *Spes* and *Victoria*, see Clark 1983, 81–2.
10 On the barbarian irrationality e.g. Isaac 2004, 189, 205; Boletsi 2013, 103; Ahonen 2014, 81–3, 91–2. As a related dynamic, one may point to the discourse on *kakia*: Fantham 2008, 319–20, 326.
11 Hdt. 4.93.1 (Γέτας τοὺς ἀθανατίζοντας); 4.94.1 (ἀθανατίζουσι).

three years: he taught the Thracians that after their deaths they could expect to come to a place where they will live for ever and have all good things.¹² In this case, a culturally inheritable hope must first be learned, even if from a charlatan. In Herodotus' view, the Thracians' poor mode of life and general simple-mindedness were the preconditions that made them susceptible to Zalmoxis' cult-peddling –living conditions could thus be implicated as a reason for barbarian hopes for afterlife. This contrasts with the later case of Tacitus' Fenni, examined below, whose poverty makes them impervious even to gods and hope. Herodotus also implies a connection between the barbarians' beliefs and their ἀνδρεία, by which the Getae put up a very spirited resistance to the Persians.¹³ Plato and Aristotle discussed the fearlessness of several barbarian peoples from a philosophical point of view: the explanation for their apparently mad disregard for danger tended towards seeing it as a result of their natural θυμός and hot-headedness – the latter an element linking this cultural reflection with the Greek humoral theory and climatic determinism.¹⁴ These uses of the theme are, however, entirely instrumental: they function as examples in a broader argument and were apparently well-known to the prospective audiences.

The idea of northerners' actions being motivated by a confident expectation —a mental state intermeshing with hope—¹⁵ for either *metempsychosis*, *anabiosis*, *palingenesis*, or some other form of life-after-death became more widely applied during the Hellenistic period, although it is difficult to conclusively point to any single writer who would have popularised the image.¹⁶ Alexander Polyhistor, a doxographically interested polymath of the Late Republic, may have been influential in introducing the theme to the Romans, and may well have formulated a direct link between Pythagoras and the northern barbarians' beliefs.¹⁷ The idea that the northern groups' proverbial fearlessness in war stemmed from their hope for rebirth had become relatively wide-spread by the Late Republic. Caesar attributed the teaching of immortality to the druids, who spread among the lower classes of Gauls the doctrine of souls passing to other bodies after death, so as to make them eager for war.¹⁸ He implies that by removing the druidic influence, Gauls can be made to conform with the practices of the rest of the humankind:

---

12 Hdt. 4.95.3.
13 For the Getic *andreia*, see Harrell 2003, 79–80. Outlandish hopes of foreigners could, certainly, partake in the thaumasiographic register of miracle-writing.
14 For climatic and other explanation models, see Romm 2010 and Woolf 2011, 32–58.
15 Cf. Pl. *Leg.* 1.644c-d, with ἐλπίς influenced by δόξα; Ar. *Rhet.* 1383a 17–18. See Cairns 2016, 23–4.
16 Also cf. Hellan. Lesb. *FGrH* 4 F 73 ap. Suda/Phot. *Lex. s.v.* Ζάμολξις.
17 Brunaux 2006, 173–88.
18 Caes. *BG* 6.14.5. Amm. Marc. 15.9.8 represents a more positive Late Antique take on the detail.

the outlandish parts of their religiosity are blamed on the druids, whose doctrine, besides, originated in Britain.[19]

Caesar came to be very influential for the further spread of the motif and we subsequently find references to the northerners' hope for rebirth or immortality applied enduringly but hazily to a variety of peoples, with the leap from Gauls to Germans particularly easy. Pomponius Mela attributes the belief both to Getae and the Gauls, while Appian points out that the Germans of Ariovistus are free from the fear of death "through the hope of a return to life" (δι' ἐλπίδα ἀναβιώσεως).[20] An inference of mental state, first formulated as a culturally relative projection onto an outgroup behaviour, was well on its way into becoming a literary trope. Lucan gives an eloquent and much emulated form to some popular conceptions about the northern peoples' bravery as he describes the Gallic area going back to its ancestral pursuits in the wake of Caesar's departure. The druids proclaim a creed that runs contrary to those of all the other peoples, one that liberates Gauls from fear of death through the hope for a 'return of a life that is lost'.[21] Lucan's section —which more properly forms an ethnographicising set piece, possibly even with parodic undertones— lifts the druidic doctrine of rebirth directly from Caesar (*BG* 6.14.5).

The physical, mental, and cultural qualities of the European barbarians were easily transferable from one group to another, and any group from among them could be chosen for salience when stereotypical motivations of barbarians were debated.[22] Valerius Maximus not only refers to the Gallic attitudes being avaricious (*avara et feneratoria Gallorum philosophia*), but attributes the belief in immortality to the Gauls in a close textual connection with the discussion of Cimbric and Celtiberian bravery.[23] The original group linked with this notion, the Thracian Getae, also continue being cited, as in Arrian's *Anabasis*.[24] Indeed, structurally speaking, any group who exhibited warlike attitude and an apparent lack of concern for their lives could attract this motif to themselves. Interestingly, in Tacitus, the scorn for death among the Jews is attributed to their belief that the souls of those among them who die in battle or by execution are immortal. It may be one of several instances in the work where Tacitus wants to construct symmetries between the eastern and western disturbances of the time.[25]

---

19 Caes. *BG* 6.13.18.
20 Mela, *De situ* 2.2, 3.19; App. *Celt.* 4.
21 Luc. *Bell. Civ*. 1.450–62.
22 See Lampinen 2012, esp. 222–29.
23 Val. Max. 2.6.10–11.
24 Arr. *Anab*. 1.3.2.
25 Tac. *Hist*. 5.5. On such mirroring techniques, see e.g. Yavetz 1998.

3 Hope for plunder or land

All enemies can, of course, be accused of hope for plunder, but due to the Greek conceptions regarding civilizational levels and luxury, the northerners were perceived to have a more logical reason to yearn for riches than the already-wealthy stereotypical easterners. It is only natural to expect that a yearning for plunder in war can be satisfied by looting; but what marks these barbarians as barbarous is how they choose their targets: the sanctuaries of the gods feature often.[26] Greed shapes the aspirations and motivations of the barbarians to such an extent that their ability to assess the risks involved —and hence modulate their expectations— becomes severely impaired. While this venality cannot be called 'hope' in the narrow sense, it contributes to our discussion of ascribing expectations to barbarians, if only because it demonstrates how deeply intertwined with moralising rhetoric the 'mindreading' of barbarians tended to be. A good example of this idea of loot as the sole barbarian aspiration is Pompeius Trogus' narrative of the motivations of Gauls for their attack on Delphi, transmitted through Justin's *Epitome*.[27]

While Trogus' account was Augustan (and Justin's context is even later) — and thus influenced by many of the later epistemic reinforcements for the theme of avaricious northerners yearning for the sacred treasures of the Mediterranean world— it seems justifiable to suppose that already the Hellenistic causations for the Gallic attack almost certainly referred to their hope for plunder or land in order to explain their sudden irruption into the Greek consciousness.[28] The Hellenistic historians had earlier literary *exampla* for this image, such as Thucydides' dramatic description of mercenary Thracians plundering Mycalessus; Thracians had been proverbially avaricious already at Thucydides' time.[29] As Iron-Age European subsistence and social patterns go, such causations are probably not very far off the mark, but we must recognise that for the Greeks, this motif had its own textual and ideological aptness quite irrespective of the actual motivations of the Galatae. The tragic fault of the northerners was their lack of understanding of the proper human-divine relationship:

---

[26] E.g. Hdt. 1.105.4; *OGIS* 765 (=*IvP* 17); Plb. 2.7.6–11 (see Berger 1992, 120–21). For pictorial conventions: Marszal 2000, 215–16.
[27] Just. *Epit.* 24.6.1.
[28] Polybius on the values and motivations of the Galatai invading and settling Etruscan North Italy: 2.17.3, 9–12. Trogus probably used Hellenistic sources, for instance Hieronymus of Cardia, for his Delphic episode, in which plunder is an important motivation: Hornblower 1981, 65–7.
[29] Mycalessus episode in Thuc. 7.29.3f.; cf. judgments of Thracian avarice 2.95.101, 97.4, 98.3.

> Then, as if the spoils of the mortals were too paltry for him, [Brennus] turned his thoughts (*animum convertit*) to the temples of the immortal gods, saying in profane jest that the gods, being rich, ought to be generous to men. He suddenly, therefore, directed his march (*iter vertit*) towards Delphi, motivated more by plunder than by religion, and valuing gold higher than an offense to the immortal gods, who he said did not need riches, being accustomed to bestow them on mortals.[30]

Brennus' impiety is illuminated by his misplaced jokiness, and the twinned expressions *animum convertit* and *iter vertit* emphasise the causal dependency of irreverent aspirations leading to impious deeds. A few sentences later, the correct Greek way of divine reverence and the fulfilled hopes of the pious are indicated through an emphasis on the sumptuous dedications at Delphi and the visual impact of these monuments.

> Hence many rich presents of kings and nations are to be seen there, which, by their magnificence, testify the grateful feelings of those that have paid their vows, and their belief in the oracles given by the deity.[31]

The implication seems to be that while the Greeks correctly read Apollo's treasures as evidence of the right way of going about with one's mortal hopes —seeking divine affirmation for them— the Gauls read the display in an entirely mistaken way, fixating on the physical, measurable weight and outward value of the treasures.

> Brennus, to rouse the courage of his men, pointed to the plentiful spoils in sight, declaring that the statues and four-horse chariots, visible at a distance in great numbers, were made of solid gold, and would prove greater prices when they came to be weighed than they were in appearance. The Gauls, animated by these assertions, and at the same time disordered after the previous day's wine-bibbing, rushed to battle without any concern for danger.[32]

Despite the anticipatory —almost lip-smacking— dwelling on the prize, the Gauls are ill-prepared for the attack, and fail to recognise their own crapulous inability (*hesterno mero saucii*).[33] The Greek projection of venal hopes to Gauls already gestures towards the ultimate lack of success for their sacrilegious endeavour, and the way in which they have already failed to recognise the correct moment

---

30 Just. *Epit.* 24.6.4–5. Translation adapted from J. Selby Watson's 1853 translation (London: Henry G. Bohn).
31 Just. *Epit.* 24.6.10. Transl. J. Selby Watson (1853 London: Henry G. Bohn).
32 Just. *Epit.* 24.7.9–8.1. Translation adapted from J. Selby Watson's 1853 translation (London: Henry G. Bohn).
33 Alcohol feeds the ἐλπίς of conquests already in Bacchyl. fr. 20 (Maehler): Cairns 2016, 37–8.

(καιρός) for their action. Theirs is an insolence of hope. This misguidedness — essentialised or reified into an indelible part of barbarian character through a set of theoretical underpinnings— is at the heart of the Greek and Roman image of why barbarian hopes turn to hopelessness. More on this below.

***

As for the hope for settling new lands, this aspiration seems also to have been affixed upon European barbarians —especially those fitting the trope of a *fugax gens*, a 'people on the move'.[34] Writers engaging with the ethnographical register sought to explain the wanderings of the northerners by having a recourse to a potent mixture of Herodotean elements and geographical and etymological reordering of knowledge. Here, the Greek shock reaction caused by the Galatian attacks of the early third century BCE was to prove particularly fertile ground for explanations. In terms of the stereotypical characteristics of European barbarian groups, their *mobilitas animi* or *levitas*, to use standard Latin terminology, was manifested both in their sudden greedy impulses and in their constant movement along the wide continental expanse. Their hopes, similarly restless, are implied to affix upon new areas all the time.

A relatively early, Hellenistic reflection on this thinking is revealed by an etymology quoted by several Byzantine lexicographers on the authority of Euphorion of Chalcis, a Hellenistic polymath. Stephanus of Byzantium's *Ethnica*, *Lexicon Zonarae*, and the *Etymologicum Magnum* all derive the Galatian group name Γαιζῆται from 'seeking land' (οἱ τὴν γῆν ζητοῦντες), and imply that this is another name for the Galatae as a whole.[35] An etymology such as Euphorion's would have helped to reify a gesture of epistemic essentialism whereby a barbarian people carried their most destructive urge as their very label, neatly ethnicising their salient characteristic.

The Cimbric Wars left a very durable trauma on the Romans, and their memory coloured many of the ethnographicising references to northerners until Caesar's *Gallic War* and even beyond. Even Posidonius of Apamea, the polymath whose description of Gauls had often been emphasised to stem from personal observations, uses the portrait of northerners constantly seeking to maximise their

---

[34] The term *fugax gens* is coined by Nenci 1990, 316. On the literary attestations of the theme, see Tomaschitz 2002.
[35] The Γαισάται or Gaesatae are also mentioned in Plb. 2.22–34 on the battle of Telamon between Celts and Romans.

plunder.³⁶ Posidonius' fragment 274 (Edelstein-Kidd), preserved by Strabo (7.2.2), tells a moralising story about how the previously peaceable and already very wealthy Helvetii, an Alpine population, were convinced by the even vaster collected spoils of the wandering Cimbri to join in with their excursion. It was easily conceivable to Posidonius, his Roman patrons, and his Roman and Greek audiences that even formerly peaceful groups of northerners could be incited (ἐπαρθῆναι) to war and pillage by the hope of magnifying even their already vast wealth.³⁷ For Livy, the Galatae of Anatolia had set off from their far-away homelands on account of their poverty, passed many inhospitable lands, and seized the rich lands of Galatia. It is a combination of originally Hellenistic causation and Late Republican Roman preoccupation with the reasons of northern peoples' movements.³⁸

Such stories do point towards a desiderative theory of mind for the northerners. But does greed for either gold, women, or lands to settle constitute hope in the narrow sense —a reasonable expectation of a favourable outcome? In its guise as a yearning for undeserved gain, hope practically elides into greed, and plays a significant part in the rhetoric of praise and blame. Both greed and impiety as stereotypical barbarian characteristics were understood in connection with their unrestrained *hubris*. Despite its conventionality as an attribute, this *hubris* could appear as logically justified within the generally deficient world-view of the barbarians.³⁹ It certainly causes the barbarians of the literature to confidently expect a favourable outcome: there is as little need to explain their hope for plunder as there is to state the ingroup members' hope for security. The implicit, 'naturalistic' expectation was that barbarians would be ruthless in satisfying their venality; the exception of a non-greedy northerner is worth of remark.⁴⁰ It is thus not surprising that the Hellenistic and Roman metaphors used for the marauding groups of barbarians often borrowed from the traditional stock imagery of the animal world. It was not just the externality of predators that was evoked; the analogy with lions or wolves was also partly prescriptive or diagnostic –very much in the way we see it used in physiognomical arguments: if someone fails to

---

36 Lampinen 2014, with bibliography and a review of the earlier scholarship on Posidonius' 'Gallic ethnography'.
37 Pos. *ap*. F 274 ap. Str. 7.2.2.
38 Livy 38.17.16–17.
39 Cf. Todorov 2010, 125: "To transgress human rules [...] makes you feel close to the gods." A similar corollary of the hubristic theory of mind devised for the ancient barbarians posited their fundamental aloofness from the humano-divine relationships as defined by every ingroup. See also Dauge 1981, 426–29, 540–41.
40 As in Parth. *Narr.* 8.5.

foresee what can be expected from such people, it is not for the lack of signs.[41] The perceptions of barbarian hopes and aspirations can, moreover, be studied in connection with Hellenistic conceptions of madness, mental disturbance, and extreme emotional states.[42]

4 Hope for a reversal or revenge

For Aristotle, hope for revenge had played an important part in defining anger, whereas barbarian anger itself formed a long-standing literary trope on its own.[43] In terms of narratology, revenge plots allowed writers to have their barbarians enact their barbarous character traits in ways which made immediate sense to their audiences: Livy's Hannibal is a good example of this. Some references, especially in the Roman context, were also clearly motivated by the unease that the insiders of any colonial or imperial system feel when contemplating the subaltern's possible hopes for revenge. Projections of the hope for a reversal in the power structure are easily identifiable in Cicero's treatment of provincial groups. *Pro Fonteio*, his speech defending Marcus Fonteius against the accusations of Gallic provincials, demonstrates that it was possible for an average Roman elite audience to believe that provincial groups, at least in Gaul, were simply waiting for the right time to pounce at their Roman rulers. In section 33 Cicero claims quite explicitly that the Gauls are holding grudge against the Romans as part of their very existence: they both entertain and enact deep-seated animosity (*insitas inimicitias ... et habeant et gerant*) towards the name of Rome.[44] Further on, in *Font.* 36, Cicero tells his audience that Romans should pose a very simple choice to the Narbonese Gallic provincials accusing Fonteius of financial malfeasance: either they should keep quiet and humble as befits the conquered, or if they chose to threaten the people of Rome with war, they should understand that this only meant offering Romans the hope of a new triumph (*non metum belli sed spem triumphi*). Like the theme of barbarians expecting to plunder riches and settle lands, the hope for revenge partly stems from the dynamics of cross-cultural (mis)understanding and reflection in antiquity. In the case of 'hope for reversal', the insecurities of the colonising or otherwise dominant social and cultural hegemony

---

[41] Barton 1994, e.g. 100.
[42] On the irrationality of the barbarians, see Ahonen 2014, 91–2, 165.
[43] Ar. *Rh.* 1378b–1379b; cf. *Top.* 156a, Sen. *Ira* 2.19.1–2, 4.15.1. See Harris 2001, 98, 171, 176, 194, 210.
[44] Cic. *Font.* 33. On the use of emotions in persuasion: Cic. *De orat.* 2.72; Quint. *I.O.* 6.2.4ff.

while looking at its subaltern are very much implicated in the endurance of the theme.⁴⁵

Some among Rome's provincial subjects were imagined to be particularly avidly hoping for the chance to turn the tables on their rulers. As Flavius Josephus writes about the Gallic and Germanic hopes for a reversal during the last stages of Nero's reign, he gives a wonderful glimpse into the ideas about what subjugated northerners want.⁴⁶ Importantly, ἐλπίς features prominently as a motivator for action. The Germani are by nature devoid of good counsel (ἡ φύσις οὖσα λογισμῶν ἔρημος ἀγαθῶν) and prone to throwing themselves after every small hope (μετὰ μικρᾶς ἐλπίδος ἑτοίμως ῥιψοκίνδυνος). This time, in a situation which to them seems exceptionally promising, they develop μεγάλας ἐλπίδας due to a variety of reasons: primarily, the leaders of the conspiracy think that the great misfortunes of the Romans had produced a καιρός, or opportune moment, for putting to action their deep aspirations (ὑπὸ τοῦ καιροῦ δὲ θαρσῆσαι προαχθέντες ... καιρὸν ᾠήθησαν παραδεδόσθαι). There is a textual display of 'mind reading' via the reference to the disasters of the rebels' 'enemies' (i.e. the Romans), but tension between the Roman and barbarian interpretations —the unease of any colonial hegemony— is forecast already: have the barbarians, though lacking in sound reasoning, still judged accurately what seems like a moment of weakness in the empire?

The politics of correctly recognising καιρός are also highlighted by certain passages in Tacitus, a contemporary of Josephus; he presents the Jews, Gauls, and Germani as peoples actively nourishing vengeance towards the Romans and biding their time.⁴⁷ The hopes of the northerners for a great reversal in their domination by Rome recur frequently and are handled with a flair for pathos. Their hopes are widely assumed to be knowable —consistent in their inconstancy— and amenable to be offset by firm action by the Romans. The best way for the Romans to dampen the rebellious spirits of northerners is to decisively demonstrate that they have misjudged their opportunity. In Book 2 of the *Annales*, the rumoured loss of the Roman navy fires the Germani *ad spem belli*.⁴⁸ Germanicus acts quickly, however, recovering one of the eagles lost by Varus, and causes by this feat a stupefied sense of resignation among the Germans, who start thinking that

---

45 On subalternity and the dynamics between the coloniser and the colonised, see Memmi 1974, 89–120. A telling case study of the colonisers' preoccupation with the minds of the colonised in another context: Pols 2007.
46 Jos. *BJ* 7.76 (7.4.2).
47 Syme 1958, I 458; Ash 2006, 76. Cf. also Yavetz 1998.
48 Tac. *Ann.* 2.25.

every catastrophe only strengthens the Romans. The reasoning of the Germans has been premature and faulty, and hence their hope entirely futile. The workings of an empire are impenetrable to them, Tacitus implies, which is also why they will never be able to accurately identify the right moment to overthrow it.

In other instances, however, Tacitus' retrospectively confidence-boosting narrative does introduce more insecurity to its description of resurgent barbarian hopes —largely in the name of heightening the drama. In writing about the Gallic disturbances during the Batavian rebellion of Civilis— the beginning of which Josephus refers to in the passage we already saw —Tacitus conjures up an image of Civilis tapping into sentiments already roused by the news of Capitolium being burnt down in the civil war:

> The Gauls' spirits had been uplifted by the belief that all our armies were everywhere in the same case, for the rumour had spread that our winter quarters in Moesia and Pannonia were being besieged by the Sarmatae and Dacians; similar stories were invented about Britain. But nothing had encouraged them to believe that the end of our rule was at hand more than the burning of the Capitol. Once, long ago, Rome was captured by the Gauls, but since Juppiter's home was unharmed, the Roman power stood firm: now this fated conflagration had given a proof from heaven of the divine wrath and presaged the passing of the sovereignty of the world to the Transalpine peoples. Such were the vain and superstitious prophecies of the Druids.[49]

Like the Gauls in Caesar's *Gallic war*, the rebels in Tacitus' *Histories* operate on the basis of rumours, and similarly to Josephus' account they base their hopes and courage upon *rationes* or λογισμοί that are either defective or made up. The hopes of the northern rebels again stem from faulty understanding and wishful misrepresentation. One may compare this with Tacitus' briefer and earlier description of the Boudiccan revolt in Britain, in which the Britons discuss the *mala servitutis*, compare the *iniuriae* heaped upon them by the Roman rulers, and aggravate these through their own interpretations (*interpretando accendere*).[50] When clouded by foolish hopes, the barbarian mind is not something that can formulate correct assessments. The fire of Capitolium convinces the rebels because they want to be convinced (*ut ... crederent, impulerat*), and the predictions of the druids stoke a *superstitio* about the supernatural symbolism and lack of divine favour. Tellingly, the geographical perspective denoted by the term *Transalpinae* looks from Italy outwards. Civil strife had for a long time tended to shake Roman belief in the supernatural protection of their empire. Such insecurities

---

49 Tac. *Hist.* 4.54. Translation adapted from C.H. Moore's 1931 translation (Cambridge, Mass.: Harvard University Press).
50 Tac. *Agr.* 15–16. See Adler 2011, 119–61.

would have lent plausibility to the supposed irredentist hopes projected onto the northerners, and the druids —by this time securely figures of the past— are brought along as a Caesarean, suitably ethnicising element which probably would have been by and large believable to Tacitus' audience.[51]

It is perhaps no wonder that the hope for a reversal, or even for a usurpation of the position occupied by the Romans, appears as a motif particularly in Tacitus and Josephus. Both are writers with agendas that occasionally embrace either overt or covert moral and cultural criticism towards Roman imperialism. At the end of Tacitus' *Germania*, we find a polemical negation of the theme of hope, as the text nears the limits of both Germania and reliable enquiry.

> Their only hope (*spes*) lies in their arrows, which, lacking iron, they tip (*asperant*) with bone. Both sexes support themselves by hunting; the women accompany the men everywhere and insist upon sharing the catch. The only way they have of protecting their infants against wild beasts or bad weather is to hide them under a makeshift covering of interlaced branches. Such is the shelter to which the young folk come back and in which the old must lie. Yet they regard themselves happier than those who groan over the tilling of fields, sweat over house-building, or risk the fortunes of themselves and others due to hope or fear. Unafraid of either men or gods, they have reached the most difficult of states: that they do not even feel the need to pray for anything.[52]

The 'astonishingly savage and disgustingly poor' Fenni, constructed as a conscious antithesis for the themes of luxury and slavery that permeate the work, are devoid of both, and with them, also hope: neither *avaritia* nor a desire for *libertas* moves them. Thus, the two primary hopes and motivators of the stereotypical northern barbarians are absent from this society which comes across as a conscious nod towards the tradition of primitivistic utopias.[53] The reversal of the cultural expectations may also be a comment upon the inherently ambiguous role of hope in an ethnographical description of a barbarian society. The ancient ethnographicising mode tended to prefer clear-cut categories, with human groups 'remaining themselves'. If the typical hopes of the barbarians were to succeed, their ethnographical description would be destabilized. Tacitus cannot let hope enter into the timeless and primeval lifestyle of the Fenni, as it would imply a capacity for change —and with change, time. It should further be noted that in

---

51 Cf. Wiśniewski 2007, 151–54. Another group of barbarians who attempt to seize the moment to cast aside the Roman yoke are the Usipi in Agricola, see Ash 2009.
52 Tac. *Germ*. 46. My translation.
53 Unlike Herodotus' Thracians, who are described largely through the prism of 'hard primitivism', Tacitus' Fenni inhabit a more ambiguous ground between the two types of 'hard' and 'soft' primitivism, of which see Lovejoy and Boas 1935.

addition to belonging to the tradition of philosophical writing, the pairing of fear and hope was a basic rhetorical juxtaposition that a learned writer would have been well acquainted with from their early *progymnasmata* onwards.[54] The impression of a rhetorical set-piece is also conveyed by Tacitus' clever arrangement of elements within the passage. These include the reduplication of *spes* with *asperant*, and the more wide-scale structural pattern whereby *Germania* –the boundaries of which are at the beginning of the work defined by a *metus* between barbarian groups— finishes at its outer extremity with a utopia where both fear and hope are unnecessary. *Spes*, one of the Roman imperial virtues —and the very one with which the continuation of the world-rule had become entangled— becomes unnecessary in a world of bone-tipped arrows and absent religion, a past that was a permanent present.[55] Without hope, the possibility of ethnographical change is negated.

5 From hope to hopelessness

To sum up the reflections and readings offered in this paper, the two crucial concepts of περιπέτεια and καιρός need to be brought to bear. A reversal (περιπέτεια) was of course a mainstay of Greek dramatic imagination and should probably be examined while keeping firmly in mind the traditions of 'pathetic' historiography and tragedy. The barbarians lack neither fervour nor a sense of grievance. They may even have internally justified expectations for attaining their hopes. But what they most often do lack in comparison with the Greeks and Romans is the knowledge that an unexpected reversal may take place. Polybius makes this one of his central points in reflecting upon Rome's success over the Celts:

> For there is no-one whom hosts of men or abundance of arms or vast resources could frighten into abandoning his last hope (ἄν τις ἀποσταίη τῆς τελευταίας ἐλπίδος), that is to fight to the end for his native land, if he kept before his eyes what part the unexpected played in those events, and bore in mind how many myriads of men, what determined

---

54 Fear is a 'negative' subtype of ἐλπίς in Pl. *Lg.* 1.644c–d, which presents φόβος as an expectation of a future pain just as the 'positive' bravery of θάρρος is an expectation of a positive outcome. Such a 'hope' seems to be misleading almost by definition, or at least contain a strong potential for it, as it cannot be certain of the outcome. Cf. Sen. *Ep. ad Lucil.* 5.7, quoting Hecato of Rhodes.

55 For the role of *Spes* in the Augustan empire, see Clark 1983. For Tacitus' *Germania* as reflection of Rome: O'Gorman 1993.

courage and what armaments were brought to nought by the resolve and power of those who faced the danger with intelligence and coolness.⁵⁶

As cultural critique and retrospective strategy assessment goes, this does not reach very far beyond the most stereotypical conception of Mediterranean insiders versus their outgroups. Even so, it points to the existential comfort which Greeks and Romans derived from such tenets. A contrary reversal is what breaks the barbarian resolve, but the crucial lack behind the barbarian hopes in the Greco-Roman imagination is their faulty estimate of καιρός, the opportune or correct moment for an action to take place. In Plutarch's *Life of Marius*, by this time almost proverbially, it is the correct judgment of the Romans which allows them to triumph over the passionate onrush of the Cimbri and Teutones in battle.⁵⁷

Rumour, another traditional literary device of the drama —but also a very real consideration for the Roman rule over their disparate empire— has been strongly implicated in some of our texts. If hope was a double-edged emotion for the Greeks, the lack of σωφροσύνη among the barbarians ensured that they were even more susceptible to its lures and liable to misjudge the καιρός for fulfilling their hopes. In our written sources, the barbarian hopes tend to turn to hopelessness with notable regularity. Without wanting to advance too structuralist an explanation, one could still suggest that this results from a combination of the Greco-Roman cultural assumption of barbarian insufficiency in any normative behaviour, and the epistemic comfort inherent in reflecting on their almost predestined defeat. Unlike the *Spes* delicately holding a flower in Roman imperial coinage, the barbarians tended to grasp the fragile thing with blind strength, crushing their own hope.⁵⁸

By the High Empire, it seems fair to say that the *topos* of barbarian hopes suffering a dramatic turn due to a wrongly judged opportunity had formed into a fully-fledged and conventional set-piece, with each new reiteration participating in a chain of utterances wherefrom it drew its communicative force.⁵⁹ In quoting from Herennius Dexippus' *Skythika*, the Porphyrogennetan *Excerpta de Legationibus* elucidates some of the ways in which the mid-third century perception of barbarian hopes turning into futility would still toe the earlier classical line, while admitting agency and reflection to the outsiders, too. Yet as so often, the

---

56 Plb. 2.35.8. Translation adapted from the revised edition (2010) of W.R. Paton's 1922 translation (Cambridge, Mass.: Harvard University Press).
57 Plut. *Mar.* 20–21.
58 Roman coins with *Spes*: e.g. *RIC* I Claudius 99, *RIC* III Antoninus Pius 431, *RIC* V Gallienus, sole reign 485.
59 Chains of utterance: Bakhtin 1986.

barbarians end up as mouth-pieces to Roman risk assessment strategies. After entering into negotiations with the emperor Aurelian, the ambassadors of the Juthungi offer the following eloquent reflection on the dangers of hope in warfare:

> But if anyone, uplifted by success in war, disdains reaching an accord, let him reflect that he is building on an insecure foundation, and that as a rule those who are not as strong as their success suggests and who, at the very height of their good fortune, turn away from the better course, pin their faith in nothing but hope, and because of this kind of foolishness they miss the pit-fall in front of them and deprecate the offer of a fortunate alliance. [...] On the other hand, the army that expects the unexpected and does not rely on hope but instead on sound reasoning and an abundance of power is the toughest opponent. It was with hope of this sort that we first divided our forces in two, and were beaten at the river rather by random chance than by your courage.[60]

6 Conclusion

This chapter has explored three themes which, naturally, constitute only some of the angles from which we can read the Greek and Roman perceptions and projections of the barbarians' hopes and motivations. They may, however, be seen as somewhat representative of the broad outlines of 'writing barbarian emotions', especially in the sense that they straddle the interlinking registers of ethnographicising writing, lighter literature, and etymological knowledge generation. At the same time, they gesture towards a variety of ideologically invested operations, such as explanations for historical causalities, Greco-Roman notions of civilizational development and cultural difference, and the moralising assessment of both individuals and essentialisingly understood population groups.

The motifs discussed separately above were also liable to be combined and merged in literary expositions of barbarian behaviour, which comes a long way towards explaining the epistemic appeal of the frequently described suicides of northern leaders such as Brennus, Decebalus, Julius Florus, Boudicca, Arbogast, and others —or indeed many non-individuated northerners.[61] The northern barbarian's suicide is almost predetermined by their φύσις: they act from faulty

---

60 Dexippus *BNJ* 100 F 6.6–7 ap. *Exc. de Legat.* 380–85, transl. J. McInerney at *BNJ* (Brill Online: http,//www.brillonline.nl/subscriber/entry?entry=bnj_a100; accessed 22 February 2012).
61 On the suicides of barbarians in the ethnographic register: e.g. Str. 3.4.7 on the Cantabrians, and cf. App. *Samn.* 6, *Celt.* 11.4 ap. *Exc. de leg.* 5; in iconography, e.g. the Pergamene statue groups of 'Dying Gauls'.

motivations— greed, anger or revenge being typical —and are unable to judge correctly the opportune moment for action or prepare for the unexpected; but being brave (sometimes with a reference to the belief in an afterlife or rebirth) they find it easy to end their life in a way that is suffused with pathos.

Hopes attributed to barbarians in Greco-Roman literature seem to have two primary fountainheads: the audience expectations about references to outgroup intentionality, and the conventions of the ethnographicising writing. Many northern barbarian groups —particularly the *Keltoi* and *Germanoi*— are frequently characterised through the fear they elicit in the Greeks and Romans. This poses the question: when you fear someone, are you more preoccupied with their intentions or motivations? Even hopes? An affirmative response seems to be supported by some sociological studies into how intergroup prejudice influences our theory of mind.[62] We also tend to expect more repulsive and emotively negative behaviour from our 'enemies' or groups about whom negative stereotypes have been primed.[63]

Such critics of the imperial order of power as Tacitus do imply here and there that giving a squarer deal to the provincials and conquered groups might be a sensible precaution,[64] but even these exercises in cultural criticism largely took for granted that the barbarians were prone to entertain avaricious plans and hoped for the reversal of the established Roman dominance. Such perceptions would in most cases have been only moderately useful tools for strategy assessment and risk management. In addition to this, they could have formed an obstacle to the acceptance of certain conquered groups into the officially sponsored networks of the empire, if these groups were commonly deemed to be potential turncoats. While almost all the 'true' Greeks (or Romans) were thought to hope for the same things —traitors and vengeful or greedy collaborators excluded— this blanket essentialism was even more uniform in the case of the barbarians: they all hoped for the same things because they were all alike.

Despite the literary stereotyping and demonstrable cases of actual hate speech, the ancient Greek and Roman theory of mind did, however, cover barbarians. Especially when explaining barbarians as narrative actors this was understandably quite necessary, even though it would be possible to maintain that in certain genres, such as classical drama, they were mostly depicted as reacting to

---

62 See the results of Hackel *et al.* 2014, 21.
63 Parker Tapias *et al.* 2007, 28, 32; cf. Hackel *et al.* 2014, 15–6, 21–2. See also Lateiner and Spatharas 2017, especially 2–4, 8, 14, 16, 29, 34, 40.
64 Criticism of the kind uttered through such barbarian mouthpieces as Tacitus' Calgacus (*Agr.* 30), Caractacus (*Ann.* 12.37), and Boudicca (*Ann.* 14.31–32, 35).

Greek action even when the original set-up derived from barbarian plans, such as in Aeschylus' *Persae*. For the most part, barbarians were perceived to have internally valid grounds for their hopes —meaning that 'madness' or 'foolishness' as a characteristic of barbarian action was for the most part used as a metaphor, not a diagnosis of pathology.[65] But their faulty reasoning meant that they had misidentified or misunderstood the reality upon which they founded their hopes; some barbarians could also misrepresent realities in stoking the predictable and manipulable hopes of their countrymen. In some cases, the barbarians' hopes only turn to be unrealisable after an unforeseen περιπέτεια swings divine favour back to support the Greeks or Romans after their acts of redemption: this is particularly true with Livy's impressive narrative of the Gallic invasion in Book 5.

References to barbarian hopes also vary in whether they fully inhabit the ethnographic register or not. To mention the northern barbarian hope for afterlife – and in many cases to then go on and associate this with their stereotypical fierceness in battle– belongs firmly into the 'ethnographicising' mode. On the other hand, referring to hopes or hope-like expectations of gain as motivators for action among barbarian groups does not necessarily need to fully partake in the ethnographic register, though it was used as a seemingly unchallenged *topos* in descriptions of barbarian hostility. Our sources from Cicero onwards treat it as an uncontroversial fact that groups subjugated to Romans would be vengeful and recalcitrant, and would try to seek revenge if the chance arose. These hopes, though deluded in their contents and inception, were something that had to be factored in: like natural forces and catastrophes or the insecurity of the seafaring pursuits —all of them circumstances which often required hope— barbarian upheavals were largely thought of something that could break out at any time and upset the expected order of things.

Of the three broad themes I have examined in this paper, the motif of barbarian hopes for plunder or land represents 'writing emotions' as both a reflection of cultural differences and as succour for collective shock and trauma, underpinned by the ancient theories of primitivism and civilisation. Hope for revenge, especially in the Roman literature, is a theme thoroughly enmeshed with the ideologies of the empire and the fear of the subaltern that can be approached with postcolonial theories in mind. Hope for a rebirth, on the other hand, is strongly connected with the old 'laws of the peoples' tradition and exhibits plentiful interfaces with the ethnographicising writing, as well. By looking at the hopes and hope-like expectations ascribed to the barbarians, it may be possible to discern that in addition to being treated as an emotion —with all the causations this

---

[65] But see Ahonen 2014, 85, 88. On perceiving intentionality: Reeder and Trafimov 2005, 108–9.

implies— hope could also be debated as a cultural standard, and even used as a help for conceptualising the spread of rationality within the humankind.

Hope was to many Greeks a deeply dangerous sentiment, clouding the rational and realistic assessment of facts and causalities, and making both individuals and communities vulnerable.[66] It could be argued that the barbarians offered an admonitory template for reflecting on the position of hope along the axis of cultural development. For the northerners, hope was an unreasonable and untimely expectation of a favourable but often immoral outcome. As with many other dangerous characteristics, it was within the register of ethnographicising writing that the strong, unadulterated forms of a vice could be examined and exemplified. If this could be linked into the epistemically comforting notion of Greeks (and Romans) constantly having an edge over the outsiders due to their 'civilised' or 'rational' distrust of such emotions as hope, then all the better.

Bibliography

Adler, E. 2011. *Valorizing the Barbarians: Enemy Speeches in Roman Historiography*, Austin.
Ahonen, M. 2014. *Mental Disorders in Ancient Philosophy*, Cham.
Ash, R. 2006. *Tacitus*, Bristol.
—— 2009. "The Great Escape: Tacitus on the Mutiny of the Usipi (Agricola 28)," in: C.S. Kraus/J. Marincola/C. Pelling (eds.), *Ancient Historiography and its Contexts: Studies in honour of A.J. Woodman*, Oxford, 275–93.
Bakhtin, M.M. 1986. "The Problem of Speech Genres," in: C. Emerson/M. Holquist (eds.), *M.M. Bakhtin, Speech Genres and Other Late Essays* (translated by V.W. McGee), Austin, 60–102.
Barr, D.J./Keysar, B. 2005. "Mindreading in an Exotic Case: The Normal Adult Human," in: B.F. Malle/S.D. Hodges (eds.), *Other Minds: How Humans Bridge the Divide between Self and Others*, New York/London, 271–83.
Barton, T. 1994. *Power and Knowledge: Astrology, Physiognomics, and Medicine under the Roman Empire*, Ann Arbor.
Bellen, H. 1985. *Metus Gallicus, metus Punicus: zum Furchmotiv in der römischen Republik*, Mainz.
Berger, P. 1992. "Le portrait des Celtes dans les *Histoires* de Polybe," in: *Ancient Society* 23, 105–126.
Boletsi, M. 2013. *Barbarism and Its Discontents*, Palo Alto.
Brunaux, C. 2006. *Les Druides: des philosophes chez les Barbares*, Paris.
Cairns, D. 2016. "Metaphors for Hope in Archaic and Classical Greek Poetry," in: R.R. Caston/R.A. Kaster, *Hope, Joy, and Affection in the Classical World*, Oxford/New York, 13–44.
Clark, M.E. 1983. "*Spes* in the Early Imperial Cult: 'The Hope of Augustus'," in: *Numen* 30, 80–105.
Dauge, Y.A. 1981. *Le Barbare: recherches sur la conception romaine de la barbarie et de la civilisation*, Brussels.
Dihle, A. 1982. *The Theory of Will in Classical Antiquity*, Berkeley.

---

66 Cf. Cairns 2016, 35–6.

Fantham, E. 2008. "With Malice Aforethought: The Ethics of *Malitia* on Stage and at Law," in: I. Sluiter/R.M. Rosen (eds.), *KAKOS: Badness and Anti-Value in Classical Antiquity*, Leiden/Boston, 319–34.

Gutsell, J.N./M. Inzlicht. 2012. "Intergroup Differences in the Sharing of Emotive States: Neural Evidence of an Empathy Gap," in: *Social Cognitive and Affective Neuroscience* 7, 596–603.

Hackel, L.M./C.E. Looser/J.J. Van Bavel. 2014. "Group Membership Alters the Threshold for Mind Perception: The Role of Social Identity, Collective Identification, and Intergroup Threat," in: *Journal of Experimental Social Psychology* 52, 15–23.

Harrell, S.E. 2003, "Marvelous *Andreia*, Politics, Geography, and Ethnicity in Herodotus' *Histories*," in: R.M. Rosen/I. Sluiter (eds.), *Andreia: Studies in Manliness and Courage in Classical Antiquity*, Leiden/Boston, 77–94.

Harris, W.V. 2001. *Restraining Rage: The Ideology of Anger Control in Classical Antiquity*, Cambridge, Mass./London.

Hornblower, J. 1981. *Hieronymus of Cardia*, Oxford.

Isaac, B. 2004. *The Invention of Racism in Classical Antiquity*, Princeton/Oxford.

Kerremans, B. 2016. "*Metus Gallicus, tumultus Cimbricus?* The Possible Promulgation of a *tumultus* in the Cimbrian War (105–101 BCE)," in: *Mnemosyne* 69, 822–41.

Konstan, D. 2006. *The Emotions of the Ancient Greeks: Studies in Aristotle and Classical Literature*, Toronto.

Lampinen, A. 2012. "Migrating Motifs of Northern Barbarism: Depicting Gauls and Germans in Imperial Literature," in: M. Kahlos (ed.), *The Faces of the Other: Religious Rivalry and Ethnic Encounters in the Later Roman World*, Turnhout, 199–235.

—— 2014. "Fragments from the 'Middle Ground' – Posidonius' Northern Ethnography," in: *Arctos* 48, 229–59.

Lateiner, D./D. Spatharas. 2017. "Ancient and Modern Modes of Understanding and Manipulating Disgust," in: D. Lateiner/D. Spatharas (eds.), *The Ancient Emotion of Disgust*, Oxford, 1–42.

Lovejoy, A.O./G. Boas. 1935, *Primitivism and Related Ideas in Antiquity*, Baltimore.

Marszal, J.R. 2000. "Ubiquitous Barbarians: Representations of the Gauls at Pergamon and Elsewhere," in: N. Thomson de Grummond/B. Ridgway (eds.), *From Pergamon to Sperlonga*, Berkeley, 191–234.

Memmi, A. 1974. *The Colonizer and the Colonized* (translated by H. Greenfeld), London.

Murphy, T. 2004. *Pliny the Elder's Natural History: The Empire in the Encyclopedia*, Oxford.

Nachtergael, G. 1977. *Les Galates en Grèce et les Sôteria de Delphes: recherches d'histoire et d'épigraphie hellénistiques*, Brussels.

Nenci, G. 1990. "L'Occidente 'Barbarico," in: W. Burkert/G. Nenci/O. Reverdin (eds.), *Hérodote et les peuples non Grecs*, Fondation Hardt, Vandoeuvres/Geneva, 301–18.

O'Gorman, E. 1993. "No Place like Rome: Identity and Difference in the *Germania* of Tacitus," in: *Ramus* 22, 135–54.

Otten, S./A. Mummendey 2000. "Valence-Dependent Probability of Ingroup Favouritism between Minimal Groups: An Integrative View on the Positive-Negative Asymmetry in Social Discrimination," in: D. Capozza/R. Brown (eds.), *Social Identity Processes: Trends in Theory and Research*, London, 33–48.

Parker Tapias, M./J. Glaser/D. Keltner/K. Vasquez/T. Wickens. 2007. "Emotion and Prejudice: Specific Emotions Towards Outgroups," in: *Group Processes and Intergroup Relations* 10, 27–39.

Pols, H. 2007. "Psychological Knowledge in a Colonial Context: Theories on the Nature of the 'Native Mind' in the Former Dutch East Indies," in: *History of Psychology* 10, 111–31.

Reeder, G.D./D. Trafimow. 2005. "Attributing Motives to Other People," in: B.F. Malle/S.D. Hodges (eds.), *Other Minds: How Humans Bridge the Divide between Self and Others*, New York/London, 106–23.

Rhodes, P.J. 2007. "The Impact of the Persian Wars on Classical Greece," in: E. Bridges/E. Hall/P.J. Rhodes (eds.), *Cultural Responses to the Persian Wars: Antiquity to the Third Millennium*, Oxford/New York, 31–45.

Romm, J.S. 2010. "Continents, Climates, and Cultures: Greek Theories of Global Structure," in: K.A. Raaflaub/R.J.A. Talbert (eds.), *Geography and Ethnography: Perceptions of the World in Pre-Modern Societies*, Chichester, 215–35.

Ros, M./C. Huici/A. Gómez. 2000. "Comparative Identity, Category Salience and Intergroup Relations," in: D. Capozza/R. Brown (eds.), *Social Identity Processes: Trends in Theory and Research*, 81–95, London.

Sassi, M.M. 2001. *The Science of Man in Ancient Greece* (translated by P. Tucker), Chicago/London.

Scaillet N./J.-P. Leyens. 2000. "From Incorrect Deductive Reasoning to Ingroup Favouritism," in: D. Capozza/R. Brown (eds.), *Social Identity Processes: Trends in Theory and Research*, London, 49–61.

Scodel, R. 2016. "Sunt Lacrimae Rerum," in: *CJ* 111, 219–30.

Syme, R. 1958. *Tacitus*, Oxford.

Todorov, T. 2010. *The Fears of the Barbarians: Beyond the Clash of Civilizations* (translated by A. Brown), Chicago/London.

Tomaschitz, K. 2002. *Die Wanderungen der Kelten in der antiken literarischen Überlieferung*, Wien.

Williams, J.H.C. 2001. *Beyond the Rubicon: Romans and Gauls in Republican Italy*, Oxford.

Wiśniewski, R. 2007. "Deep Woods and Vain Oracles: Druids, Pomponius Mela and Tacitus," in: *Palamedes* 2, 143–56.

Wolfram, H. 1997. *The Roman Empire and Its Germanic Peoples* (translated by T. Dunlap), Berkeley.

Woolf, G. 2011. *Tales of the Barbarians: Ethnography and Empire in the Roman West*, Chichester.

Yavetz, Z. 1998. "Latin Authors on Jews and Dacians," in: *Historia* 47, 77–107.

Keely Elizabeth Heuer
The Face of Hope: Isolated Heads in South Italian Visual Culture

Superficially, anthropomorphizing hope, unlike other abstract concepts, seems to have little interested Classical artists and their patrons. Personifications in Greek art are challenging for modern viewers (and presumably ancient ones as well) to recognize without either an inscription clearly identifying the figure or a mythological scene to provide logical context. No individuals are labeled as *Elpis* in surviving Graeco-Roman visual culture, yet one highly plausible instance of hope in physical form is found on a small red-figure neck-amphora attributed to the Owl Pillar Group, now in the British Museum.[1] (Figure 1) Wrapping around the body of the vase in a continuous frieze, the decoration begins with a draped woman rising from the earth who reaches towards a standing, beardless youth. He gazes towards her, wearing a pilos cap and chlamys while holding a mallet-like tool. Further to the right, a bearded male in a chiton and himation stands with a staff, facing a curious vessel on a low, rectangular base. From the mouth of the container emerges a tiny female head, her hair bound up in a saccos, like the woman emerging from the ground. This scene, based upon iconographic comparanda, has been interpreted as the anodos of Pandora in the presence of Hephaistos and Zeus, the latter of whom gazes at the infamous pithos, presumably in the act of commanding *Elpis* to remain inside the jar when Pandora later succumbs to her curiosity.[2] Noteworthy is the artist's choice to represent the embodiment of hope as a human head in isolation, rather than a complete, presumably winged figure, as the jar's contents were said to have been to fly. While effectively solving the dilemma of representing something outside of the viewer's sight contained in the solid vase, the painter devised a representation that reflects the inherent essence of *elpis* in its multifaceted uses in Archaic and Classical Greek, both positive and negative, as expectation, supposition based upon past evidence, and desire for a particular outcome.[3] In each of these aspects of *elpis*, it can exist only in a state of flux, where the full course of action is as yet unfulfilled

---
1 London F 147: *LCS* p. 667, no. 3.
2 Compare to the Attic volute-krater Oxford, Ashmolean Museum G 275 (*BAPD* 275165; *ARV2* 1562, 4) on which the similar figures are inscribed. See Neils 2006. Pandora's creation is recorded by Hesiod (*Works* 60–105). For the anodos of Pandora, refer to Harrison 1900, 106–108; Harrison 1908, 276–283; Robert 1914; Bérard 1974, 161–64.
3 For an excellent discussion of the multivalent nature of *elpis* in Archaic and Classical Greek literature, refer to Cairns 2016.

and incomplete, making future change possible, even if the odds are slim. Rather than representing *Elpis* as having a complete form, the norm in mainland Greek art for depicting the human body, the vase-painter perhaps chose to embody her as a truncated, even unfinished, entity to visualize her quintessential nature, perhaps inspired by the earlier iconographic traditions of Campania, the region of Italy surrounding the Bay of Naples, where his workshop was located. Starting in the mid 8th century B.C., this area was colonized by the Greeks and the Etruscans, one of the multiple indigenous peoples of pre-Roman Italy who used heads in a variety of media, starting as early as the third quarter of the 7th century B.C., including terracotta antefixes[4] and plastic appliques on bucchero vases.[5] (Figure 2) In fact, between the Archaic period and the late Hellenistic era, isolated heads, predominantly female, became one of the most prolific motifs in imagery produced throughout pre-Roman Italy, in both colonial Greek and indigenous spheres, particularly in sacral and funerary contexts, where certainly the positive aspects of *elpis*, were particularly relevant. The representation of *Elpis* as a female head on the Owl Pillar Group vase, likely buried in a tomb due to its excellent state of preservation, is thus perhaps not an anomaly, but rather provides crucial evidence regarding the iconographic meaning of this widespread cross-cultural phenomenon so distinctive to the multiethnic milieu of ancient Italy.

---

[4] Antefixes with female heads first appear ca. 640–630 B.C. at the Etruscan site of Poggio Civitate (Murlo). Over the course of the 6th century B.C., female heads on antefixes were framed by a "shell" and started to wear tall diadems and disc earrings. During the latter part of the 6th century B.C., Capua, the most important Etruscan settlement in Campania, became an important center for the manufacture of architectural terracottas, particularly antefixes decorated with various heads, including those of woman (maenads?) and satyrs, which were exported northward to Etruria and influenced antefixes in the Greek colonies of southern Italy. Within the Greek settlements of southern Italy and Sicily, the earliest antefixes featuring human and mythological heads date to 600 B.C. They became common in the mid 6th century B.C. and remained popular until the close of the 4th century. See Andrén 1940, cxxx–ccxlii; Winter 1974; Winter 1978; Wohl 1984, 117; *Enciclopedia dell'arte antica classica e orientale, Secundo Supplemento*, 1971–1994, vol. 1 (Rome, 1994), 242–52, s.v. "Antefissa" (M. Mertens-Horn); C. Marconi 2005; Winter 2009, 49–54, 85–88, 147, 157, 169–74, 223–36, 245–50, 311–17, 321–24, 344–50, 395–96, 400, 425–44.

[5] Profile and frontal male and female heads are frequently found on the bucchero pesante produced around Vulci, Orvieto, and Chiusi between the mid 6th to the early 5th century B.C. These appliques may decorate the bodies or rims of many shapes including chalices with high feet, oinochoai, hydriai, amphorae, kraters, and braziers. Such heads may be frontal or in profile. Refer to Donati 1967, 1968, and 1969.

Isolated heads in South Italian vase painting: Hope for the hereafter

The mid 5th century B.C. vases of the Owl Pillar Group, to which the *Elpis* vase belongs, were predecessors of the main production of red-figure vases in southern Italy that began around 440 B.C., first at Metaponto and soon after in Taranto.[6] How the technical knowledge for producing these vases traveled to southern Italy, a region that came to be known as Magna Graecia due to the numerous Greek settlements along its coastlines, is unknown. Hypotheses include the Athenian role in the establishment of the colony of Thurii in 443 B.C. and the flight of Attic artisans to promising new markets in the West with the onset of the Peloponnesian War that drastically reduced Attic vase exports to the region and encouraged the expansion of South Italian workshops to meet local demand for painted vases.[7] South Italian potters and painters reached their peak output between 350 and 320 B.C. before steadily declining in quality and quantity by the early 3rd century. South Italian vases are divided into five wares named after the regions in which they were manufactured (Lucanian, Apulian, Campanian, Paestan, and Sicilian), and while they were produced by Greeks, their largest numbers are found in Italic settlements or Greek colonies that by the 4th century B.C. had fallen under the control of native peoples. In South Italian vase-painting, the most frequent decoration is an isolated head, appearing as a primary or secondary motif on more than 7500 pieces, over one-third of the published corpus.[8] While isolated heads do occur on earlier Athenian vases, they are relatively rare and are concentrated in the oeuvre of select workshops. The earliest heads on South Italian vases coincide with the period at the end of the 5th century B.C.

---

6   For the Owl Pillar Group, see *LCS* 667–673; *LCS Suppl.* I 119; and *LCS Suppl.* 2 267.
7   For a summary of the different theories behind the transfer of the red-figure technique between Athens and southern Italy and relevant bibliography, refer to Heuer 2015, 81 n. 1. For early South Italian red-figure, turn to Denoyelle 1997; Silvestrelli 2005; Fontannaz 2005; Denoyelle and Iozzo 2009, 97–123; and Denoyelle 2014.
8   This statistic is derived from the vases in the catalogues of A.D. Trendall and the volumes of the *CVA* published through 2014. Shape often seems to have often determined the placement of heads on a vase's surface. Prior to 340 B.C., the motif played a primary role only on small-scale pieces and a secondary role on large vases, generally concentrated on the neck, shoulder, or a central band around the belly, after which it occurred as the main decoration on all vase shapes.

when South Italian vase-painters started to break away from Athenian models and tailored their work to local needs and interests.⁹

The image's frequency demonstrates its significance to western Greeks and their native neighbors, and it is striking nearly all of the heads' identities are ambiguous, with the exception of the small number depicting satyrs and Pan. Most heads are female, often wearing diadems, veils, or polos headdresses, as well as necklaces and earrings.¹⁰ (Figure 3) They appear identical to their full-length counterparts, both mortal and divine, and none are inscribed, except on the neck of Apulian volute-krater in London where it is identified as "Aura" (Breeze).¹¹ The paucity of epigraphic evidence is surprising as South Italian vase-painters otherwise generously label figures, particularly in mythological scenes. Even when female heads have distinctive attributes, such as being flanked by Erotes (Aphrodite?)¹², horns emerging from the forehead (Io?)¹³, or a quiver peeking out from behind the shoulder (Artemis?),¹⁴ their rarity prohibits the modern viewer from securely recognizing the attribute-less majority. Even when immortality is implied with polos crowns or a nimbus, the precise identity is unclear.¹⁵ Heads of generic youths or bearded men are similarly challenging.¹⁶ Heads of uncertain gender with attributes lead to various interpretations. For instance, heads wearing Phrygian caps have been labeled by scholars as Amazons, Orpheus, and even Paris, who sometimes wears such a headdress in South Italian vase-painting.¹⁷

---

9   Trendall 1990.
10   Cambitoglou 1954, 111–21; *RVAp II*, 445, 447–48, 456, 462–63, 473, 486, 601–2, 604–5, 647– 49; Schauenburg 1957, 210–12; Smith 1976, 50–51; Lehnert 1978; Kossatz-Deißmann 1985, 229– 39; Schauenburg 1989, 36–37.
11   B.M.F 277: *RVAp I* 8/5, p. 193.
12   For example, see Bari 872 from Canosa (*RVAp II* 18/43, p. 497) and Lecce 855, also from Canosa (*RVAp II* 29/186, p. 975; *CVA* Lecce 2 [Italy 6] pl. 59, 1–2; p. 35).
13   See Milan, Collezione Banca Intesa 115 (Once "H.A." Collection 306 — *RVAp II* 23/16, p. 728) and Ruvo 1092 (*RVAp II* 23/226, p. 753).
14   Such as on the volute krater by the Painter of Copenhagen 4223 formerly on the New York market at Ariadne Galleries (*RVAp Suppl.* 2 17/39–4, p. 121).
15   For examples of nimbus around heads, see Bologna 567 (*RVAp II* 23/19, p. 728; *CVA* Bologna 3 [Italy 12] pl. IV Dr 7, 3–4; p. 6) and St. Petersburg 354 (*RVAp II* 23/21, p.728). Female heads wearing polos crowns occur on Moa Museum no. 1729 (*CVA* Japan 2 pl. 51, 3–4, 52 and 53; p. 59–62) and Parma C. 96 (*RVAp I* 15/64 p. 408; *CVA* Parma 2 [Italy 46] pl. 3, 1–2; p. 3–4).
16   E.g. the heads of youths on Zurich 2636 (*LCS* p. 432, no. 518; *CVA* Zurich 1 [Switzerland 2] pl. 33, 7–9; p. 50–51) and Frankfurt ß 607 (*LCS* pg. 411, no. 343; *CVA* Frankfurt am Main 3 [Germany 50] pl. 33; p. 25–26).
17   For attempts to identify heads wearing Phrygian caps, turn to Schauenburg 1974, 171–72, 174–85; Schmidt 1975, 130–32; Schauenburg 1981, 468; Schauenburg 1982, 253–55; Schauenburg

Heads flanked by wings are identified alternately as Nike or the hermaphrodite/effeminate form of Eros, a common full-length figure in all South Italian wares.[18] The isolated heads' vague identities suggest either the meaning of the heads was so easily recognizable to their contemporary viewers that further iconographic or written identifiers were deemed unnecessary or the ambiguity was intentional, perhaps to allow for greater flexibility in interpretation and function dependent upon the user's ethnic and religious background in the cultural melting pot of pre-Roman Italy and Sicily.

Of the thousands of surviving vases decorated with heads, nearly all with known provenience come from a funerary context.[19] Not only did these vases serve as grave goods in Greek and Italic tombs, but the purely sepulchral function of many pieces is clear from the hole between the lower body and foot, rendering them useless as containers for the living. In the Greek settlement of Taranto, monumentalized vases with painted isolated heads were used to mark burials and served as means of funneling liquid offerings to the remains of the deceased below.[20] The nearly exclusive mortuary function of the vases provides an important clue to the iconographic meaning of the isolated heads as does the fact that the motif does not serve a narrative function on South Italian vases, unlike in Attic vase-painting, where the heads are often flanked by full-length figures, implying an anodos.[21] Rather, heads on vases made in southern Italy and Sicily appear to be wholly symbolic in nature. The sepulchral significance of the heads is further confirmed by the motif's use — heads are consistently paired with various types of figural scenes that make explicit reference to mortuary cult practices,

---

1984, 364; and Kossatz-Deißmann 1990, 517–520. Examples include St. Petersburg 406 (*RVAp II* 18/21 p. 490) and Warsaw 198951 (*LCS* p. 235, no. 59; *CVA* Warsaw 5 [Poland 8] pl. 32, 1–2; p. 26–27).
18   See examples of winged heads on Ruvo 425 (*RVAp I* 15, 42, p. 403) and Brussels R 252 (*RVAp II* 27/220, p. 886; *CVA* Brussels 2 [Belgium 2] IV D b pl. 7; 1a–b; p. 6). For the ambiguity of winged heads in South Italian vase-painting, see Cambitoglou 1954, 121; Schauenburg 1957, 212; Schauenburg 1962, 37; Schauenburg 1974, 169–86; Schauenburg 1981, 467–69; Schauenburg 1982, 250–55; and Schauenburg 1984, 155–57.
19   For a list of the few pieces found in sacral and civic contexts, see Heuer 2015, 82 n. 35.
20   Lippolis 1994, 109–28; Fontannaz 2005, 126.
21   Anodos scenes occur increasingly in Attic vase-painting of the second and third quarters of the fourth century B.C. particularly on pelikai, hydriai, stemless cups, lekanides, pyxides, kylikes, and kraters. For examples, refer to Cabinet des Médailles 472 (ARV^2 1489, 156) and London F 18 (ARV^2 1481, 1). Of the thousands of extant South Italian vases decorated with isolated heads, fewer than forty depict heads in the presence of full-length figures, which nearly always emerge from flowers and are flanked by Erotes, such as on the shoulder of Bari 872 (*RVAp* II 18/43 p. 497), a composition with no parallel in Attic vase painting or explanation in extant ancient literature.

mythological stories involving death, and Dionysian iconography, strongly suggesting that the motif embodied eschatological beliefs.

Heads regularly occur on vases in conjunction with depictions of mourners bearing offerings to funerary monuments of several types, a practice that began in the work of the Iliupersis Painter, active 370–355 B.C.[22] Most often the grave markers are a naiskos (a small, temple-like shrine containing a statue of the deceased and sometimes other family members or attendants), a rectangular stele on a stepped base, or an Ionic column. Typically, the heads appear directly above the funerary scene, on the necks of volute-kraters and the shoulders of amphorae and loutrophoroi, rising above the monument like an oversized akroterion, thereby emphasizing the vertical axis in the composition and visually connecting the two decorative components, as seen on the reverse of the Apulian loutrophoros Malibu 86.AE.680.[23] (Figure 4) The head regularly rises from a flower of varying species, often trumpet-shaped, or a leafy base, generally an acanthus calyx, a plant with extensive funerary connotations in the Greek and later Roman world.[24] Roughly symmetrical spiraling tendrils, often enhanced with flowers of various types or palmettes, surround the heads. The juxtaposition of the heads with vegetation suggests a correlation between the motif and the regenerative powers of nature, and the placement directly above a grave monument visually implies new life springing forth from death. Thus the combination of elements could well have been a potent expression of belief in (or at least desire for) an afterlife.

Around 380–370 B.C., heads began to be painted above mythological tableaux involving the demise of one or more individuals,[25] such as the death of Hippolytos due to his panicking chariot horses at the emergence of Poseidon's giant bull from the sea, depicted in the lower register on the obverse of a volute-krater

---

[22] The most extensive study of funerary monuments occurring on South Italian vases is Lohmann 1979.

[23] On occasion, heads may also appear in a dividing floral band around the middle of an amphora or loutrophoros' body or on the foot of a volute krater. For example, see the amphora Ruvo 423 (*RVAp* I 15/41, p. 403) and the volute krater St. Petersburg 420 (*RVAp* II 27/18, pp. 863–64).

[24] Acanthus appears on Attic marble anthemia stelai in the third quarter of the 5th century B.C. and is on funerary monuments painted on contemporary Classical Attic white-ground lekythoi, such as on Berlin 2680 (Oakley 2004, 123) and Athens, National Museum 14517 (*ARV*² 1373.13; *BAPD* 217642). For acanthus on grave stelai, refer to Kurtz and Boardman 1971, 124 and Froning 1985. Jucker (1961) hypothesized the funerary connotations of Roman portrait busts emerging from acanthus calyxes.

[25] One of the earliest examples is the name vase of the Cassandra Painter, the first Campanian vase painter, depicting Ajax dragging Cassandra from the altar (*LCS* p. 225, no. 1; *CVA* Capua [1] pl. 22, pp. 10–11).

attributed to the Darius Painter in London.[26] (Figure 4) The mythological subject matter found on South Italian vases with heads reflects the somber mood of funerary rites and at times may have served as parallels to the deceased's life as a means of heroization.[27] Certain scenes paired with heads, however, do appear to express a hope for the hereafter, particularly those in which an individual is spared from certain death, either through heroic intervention or the granting of immortality, which may involve a divine abduction. For example, on another of the Darius Painter's vases, a loutrophoros in New York, Persephone and Aphrodite plead for the life of Adonis on either side of an enthroned male deity, either Zeus or Hades, in the top register of the obverse.[28] (Figure 6) The link between the hero fatally gored by a boar and the funerary realm is underscored by the grave monument directly beneath the mythological scene and the head emerging from a flower above on the shoulder. Heads may also be painted in connection with representations of the Underworld and its inhabitants, further suggesting the motif's association with eschatological concepts.[29]

The types of heads on South Italian vases could reference cults practiced in southern Italy and Sicily known to have had promised benefits in the hereafter to their adherents and may even reflect religious beliefs, particularly those of indigenous peoples, that are otherwise lost to us due to the lack of surviving literary and epigraphic sources. For instance, at least to a Greek viewer, female heads could represent Persephone or even Aphrodite, who seems to have had chthonic associations in Magna Graecia.[30] Winged heads in this context, if interpreted by the ancient viewer as Nike, might symbolize victory over death, and even Eros, a popular figure on South Italian vases found in tombs, is shown to have a place in the Underworld on an Apulian volute-krater in the Hermitage.[31] Male heads might stand for Hades, ruler of the underworld, or even Dionysos, a vegetation god who not only rescued his mortal mother, Semele, from Hades, but also was a

---

26 British Museum F 279: *RVAp II* 18/17, p. 487; Taplin 2007, 137–138.
27 Giuliani 1995, 149–150, 155–56; Todisco 2002, 20–24.
28 New York, Metropolitan Museum of Art 11.210.3: *RVAp II* 18/20, p. 489.
29 Examples appear on Munch 3297 (*RVAp II* 18/282, p. 533) and Naples Stg. 11 (*RVAp Suppl.* 1 16/54, p. 424). For the comforting function of mythological images, refer to Schefold and Jung 1988, 324–26 and Geyer 1993, 448–50.
30 Jucker 1961, 197–208; Smith 1976; Sourvinou-Inwood 1978.
31 St. Petersburg inv. 1717 = St. 424: *RVAp II* 28/117, p. 930–31. Eros and Aphrodite are to the right of the palace of Hades and Persephone on the body of this vase.

resurrected being himself in variants of his myth.³² Dionysiac cult, which is clearly alluded to by the heads of Pan and satyrs on vases,³³ was particularly popular in Magna Graecia.³⁴ In fact, Dionysian imagery is the most common subject paired with isolated heads in South Italian vase-painting. Heads wearing Phrygian caps could plausibly have been understood as Orpheus, the supposed author of poems outlining an alternate cosmogony that became the foundation of Orphism, a mystery cult closely connected to Pythagorean philosophy, which focused on the birth, death, and rebirth of Dionysos and stressed the purification of humans' immortal souls though multiple reincarnations to reunite with the divine in the afterlife.³⁵

Other isolated heads in the sepulchral realm

Heads in various media uncovered in funerary and chthonic contexts in Etruria, southern Italy, and Sicily support the interpretation of the motif as a symbolic representation of a desired or anticipated afterlife. In a male burial at Thurii containing two of the famous so-called Orphic gold lamellae referencing Persephone's ability to guarantee salvation, two silver medallions decorated with a

---

32   Male heads wear ivy wreaths on four Paestan vases, strongly suggesting that these are depictions of Dionysos. See New York 65.11.18 (*RVP* 9/834, p. 223) and Cleveland 1989.73 (Trendall 1992; Denoyelle and Iozzo 2009, 132).
33   I know of ten examples of heads of Pan; for example, Vatican AA 2 inv. 18255 (*RVAp* I 8/13, p. 194) and Rizzo collection, Mandelieu, France (*RVAp Suppl.* 217/40–B, p. 507). Other than those of women, heads of satyrs of varying ages are the most common type of heads on South Italian vases, e.g. Copenhagen 88 (*RVAp* II 22/12, p. 651; *CVA* Copenhagen 6 [Denmark 6] pl. 254, 2a–b, p. 198), Trieste 1836 (*RVAp* II 22/38, p. 653), and Zurich 2548 (*RVAp* II 22/42, p. 653; *CVA* Zurich 1 [Switzerland 2] pl. 40, 3–4, p. 55).
34   For the cult of Dionysos in southern Italy and Sicily: Casadio 2009; Isler-Kerényi 2009; Cinquantaquattro *et al.* 2010; and Lombardo *et al.* 2011.
35   Some bibliography on Orphism: Rohde 1907, 335–61; Mead 1965; Orfismo in Magna Grecia 1975; Detienne 1979; Guthrie 1993; and Edmonds 2013. Ancient writers repeatedly tie Orphism in Magna Graecia to the Pythagorean movement (Herodotus 2.81; Diogenes Laertius 8.8). Pythagoras emigrated from Samos to Croton around 520 B.C. and is believed to have died in Metaponto at the end of the sixth century B.C. Pythagorean "clubhouses" were established throughout southern Italy and Sicily until ca. 450–415 B.C., when they were destroyed during an outbreak of civil unrest (Polybius 2.39). Orpheus' frequent presence in representations of the underworld in Apulian vase painting has been interpreted as evidence of Orphic beliefs (Schmidt 1975 and Pensa 1977).

female head surrounded by rays were placed on the deceased's chest.[36] As early as the 10th century B.C., roughly shaped three-dimensional stone heads marked graves in northern Apulia at Monte Saraceno, Troia, and Arpi.[37] Later, in the 4th and 3rd centuries B.C., heads carved in relief, sometimes in vegetal surrounds recalling those on South Italian vases, decorated hypogeum tombs such as those emerging from acanthus calyxes on pilaster capitals in the Medusa tomb at Arpi[38] and the two plaster busts, one male and one female, flanking the central funerary kline in the Tomb of the Reliefs at Cerveteri.[39] Painted heads likewise are found inside tombs, including a tomb in the Spinazzo necropolis at Paestum with a frontal head with short curly hair between a lion and panther[40] and female heads above the doorways to the side chambers of the François Tomb in Vulci.[41] During the second half of the 4th century B.C., isolated heads were carved on Etruscan stone sarcophagi, exemplified by the female heads with long blond hair flanked by palmettes on the corners of the lid of the Sarcophagus of Ramtha Huzcnai from Tarquinia[42] and the frontal heads with cropped hair emerging from blossoms in

---

36 This lamella, dated to the 4th century B.C., is now in the Museo Nazionale in Naples (inv. no. 11463). See Graf and Johnston 2007, 8–11; Zuntz 1971, 288–90. The inscribed gold lamellae, or tablets, connected with Orphic cult have been found in tombs in Lucania at Hipponium, Thurii, and Petelia. See Kern 1922; Pugliese Carratelli 1988, 162–70; Maddoli 1996, 495–96; Pugliese Carratelli 2003; Graf and Johnston 2007; and Bernabé and Jiménez San Cristóbal 2008. The texts give instructions to the deceased to successfully navigate the journey to a desired hereafter, culminating in a divine reunion, either with Dionysos or Persephone.
37 De Juliis 1984, 142–45; De Juliis 2009, 61–64.
38 Steingräber 1990, 79–80. For other examples in southern Italy, see Heuer 2015, 77 and von Mercklin 1962, 63–65.
39 Blanck and Proietti 1986, 20–21. By the early 3rd century B.C., sculpted isolated heads are found primarily on the exteriors, rather than the interiors, of Etruscan tombs, particularly in the rock-cut tombs of the southern Etruscan interior, especially at Sovana. The Tomba del Tifone at Sovana is the earliest, and it features a veiled female head rising from a background of tendrils and flowers in its pediment (Rosi 1925, 48; Oleson 1982, 55–56). Also at Sovana, the Tomba Pola and the Tomba Ildebranda, both dating to the late 3rd or early 2nd century B.C., have isolated heads in the column capitals of their facades (Rosi 1925, 48–50; Rosi 1927, 93–94; Oleson 1982, 49–50, 52–54). At Norchia, where rock-cut tombs are also frequent, frontal human heads in relief appear on the low-wide metopes of the so-called Doric tombs of the 3rd or 2nd century B.C. (Rosi 1925, 42–43; Rosi 1927, 93; von Hesberg 1981, 192; Oleson 1982, 50–51) Sculptured heads are also in the gables of the central hall and the central ceiling coffers of the side chambers in Tomb of the Volumnii in Perugia, begun in the 3rd century B.C. and further elaborated during the 2nd (von Gerkan and Messerschmidt 1942).
40 Rouveret 1990, 339; Rouveret and Pontrandolfo 1983, 125.
41 A head of Charun made of molded cement decorated the central coffer of the rear portion of the central chamber of the François Tomb. See Cristofani 1967, 194–196 and Roncalli 1987, 81–83.
42 Florence, Museo Archeologico: Herbig 1952, 26–27.

the gables of the lids of the sarcophagus of Ramtha Visnai and Arnth Tetnies from Vulci.[43] Around the same time, the motif appeared on cinerary urns produced in Chiusi, Volterra, and Perugia and continued to do so until the 1st century B.C. Usually these heads are carved in relief on the long sides of the chest, emerging from a leafy base, and are at times wreathed, veiled, flanked by wings, or wear a Phrygian cap.[44] (Figure 7) Semi-circular molded terracotta antefixes with frontal heads of different types served as decorative roofing elements on tomb monuments in Taranto and other Greek settlements in southern Italy;[45] one was even applied to the large terracotta slab closing the short end of Tomb 117 at Metaponto, corresponding to the location of the deceased's head.[46] Additional types of mold-made terracottas with isolated heads were grave goods, such as oscilla (suspended discs), semi-circular plaques[47], arulae (portable altars)[48], protomes, and busts[49], including a remarkable janiform bust of a young woman wearing a polos and a bearded man from a tomb at Locri Epizephryii, possibly representing Persephone and Hades.[50] Such self-supporting busts might also have served as

---

43 Boston, Museum of Fine Arts 1975.799: Herbig 1952, 13–14.
44 For example, Volterra no. 41, New York, Metropolitan Museum of Art 96.9.221, and Perugia, Necropoli del Palazzone, Inv. n. 152. Refer to Körte 1916, 199–200, 214–18; Dareggi 1972, 47–48; Sclafani 2010, 92–96. Also found in central Italian tombs are a series of silvered terracotta "stands" in the form of female heads that appear to have been produced in Falerii Veteres (modern Civita Castellana). See Ambrosini 1994.
45 The production of these antefixes intensified and diversified in Taranto during the 4th century B.C. One of the favored subjects appears to be the head of Pan and a female type that sometimes has bovine horns emerging from her temples, probably Io. Other recognizable heads of mythological figures are the river god Acheloös and Aphrodite, who has a winged Eros beside her. Male heads sometimes wear a petasos (Hermes?) or Phrygian helmet. Other heads of uncertain gender are covered by a lion skin (Herakles or Omphale, queen of Lydia?) or have short tousled hair. See Laviosa 1954, 217–50. The Etruscans, who also produced head antefixes, but of a different stylistic type, also seem to have used such architectural decoration in funerary contexts, as seen in the small building adjacent to the necropolis of Grotta Porcino at Vetralla, near Viterbo (Winter 1974, 151–54).
46 Metaponto 319201: Pugliese Carratelli 1996, 651–52.
47 A number of these come from tombs at Nola, a town in Campania under Etruscan influence (Claes 1981).
48 See van Buren 1918, 41–44; Jastrow 1946; van der Meijden 1993, 71, 177–81, 293–95, 309. Arulae are found in tombs and chthonic sanctuaries, and their molded reliefs are often funerary in subject matter, such as sirens and sphinxes.
49 Examples from graves in Taranto: Graepler 1997, 256, 259, 262, 273.
50 For protomes and busts as grave goods, see Kilmer 1977, 75–76; Lehnert 1978, 135; and Uhlenbrock 1988, 125, 129. For the janiform bust found at Locri Epizephyrii, refer to Orsi 1911, 68–70.

cenotaphs, illustrated by the so-called "Pot Burial" at Locri of the Classical period.[51]

Arulae, protomes, and busts are among the terracotta votive gifts dedicated to chthonic deities at sites in southern Italy and Sicily including the Sanctuary of the Chthonic Deities at San Biagio in Agrigento, the extramural Malophoros sanctuary at Selinunte, and the Mannella sanctuary at Locri Epizephyrii.[52] Protomes, which are not self-supporting and thus must either be suspended or leaned against a support, originated in Ionia during the mid 6th century B.C. and likely came to Sicily with exported perfume vases from Miletus.[53] Sicilian coroplasts soon after began replicating the type, and the practice was quickly adopted in various sites in Magna Graecia. (Figure 8) During the final decades of the 5th century B.C., protomes were extended in length to include the upper torso and arms, which may hold a variety of attributes or offerings, such as flowers, phiale, piglets, and cross-bar torches.[54] Experimentation with protomes likely led to the development of the shoulder bust in southern Italy, where the earliest examples, dating to the second half of the 6th century B.C., were discovered at Metaponto and Taranto.[55] In the following decades, busts were manufactured in Sicily, perhaps starting at Agrigento.[56] By the end of the century, busts appear in Etruria and areas under Etruscan influence, such as Campania and Latium, the earliest of which have clear iconographic ties with female protomes.[57] The Etruscan votive heads may be male or female, unlike the predominantly female protomes and busts of southern Italy and Sicily, and they were made until the 2nd century B.C.[58]

---

51 Kurtz and Boardman 1971, 259.
52 For isolated heads on terracotta votives found at Agrigento, see P. Marconi 1929, 579–80; P. Marconi 1933, 47; Kilmer 1977, 83–84, 101–9; and Uhlenbrock 1988, 125–26. For those from Selinunte, see Kilmer 1977, 73–74, 87–88, 115–16, 133–34; Uhlenbrock 1988, 20 n. 8 and 128; Wiederkehr Schuler 2004. For those at Locri Epizephyrii, see Zuntz 1971, 160–61; Kilmer 1977, 74, 89–91, 133–34; Barra Bagnasco 1986; Lattanzi 1987, 54–59; and Croissant 1992.
53 Zuntz 1971, 142; Kilmer 1977, 65; Croissant 1983; Uhlenbrock 1988, 19–20, 109, 146–50; Uhlenbrock 1989, 9.
54 Kilmer 1977, 95, 98; Lo Porto 1991, 84–85; Otto 1996, 177–78; Kurz 2005, 229–245.
55 Lo Porto 1991, 88–89; Bernabò Brea and Cavalier 2000, 115–17.
56 Kilmer 1977, 77–78.
57 The oldest votive heads come from Veii, where they were produced in significant number by the 5th century B.C. (Steingräber 1980, 226). Most terracotta busts produced in Lazio date after the early 4th century B.C. and seem to be directly inspired by the work of coroplasts in Magna Graecia and Sicily, such as the bust of Demetra from the Ariccia valley (località Casaletto), dated to the late 4th-early 3rd century B.C. (Rome, Museo Nazionale Romano, Terme di Diocleziano inv. 112376).
58 Steingräber 1980, 216, 228–29.

A further Etruscan variant is the "half-head," a molded head in profile with a flat back to allow it to stand upright.[59]

Isolated heads in South Italian sacral contexts: *Elpis* and divine favor

Votive gifts are either thank-offerings for benefits received from the divine or objects donated in hope of future assistance. In most instances, the circumstances behind the bequeathed object are impossible to determine without an inscription. However, whether the dedication was made either before or after the believed supernatural intervention, these transactions were predicated upon the principle that the god(s) will fulfill mortal requests as part of an exchange. In the past, it was erroneously assumed that terracotta protomes and busts, the majority of which come from votive deposits in sanctuaries, were a prime indicator of the cult's chthonic nature because of the objects' occasional presence in tombs.[60] While in certain instances, sanctuaries containing terracotta votives featuring heads do have clear structural or epigraphic evidence for a cult of Demeter and/or Persephone/Kore, such as the Thesmophorion of Bitalemi, there are a significant number dedicated to goddesses with no ties to the underworld, such as Athena and Hera.[61] These discoveries counter the idea that isolated heads are solely symbolic visual representations of a desire for life after death. Perhaps in sanctuaries, votive heads instead refer to the incomplete and unfulfilled nature of the wished-for results of the dedicator.

The head, as an individual's most readily identifiable body part, represents a figure's fundamental essence. Yet, when shown removed from the body, it may suggest a state of flux or a transition from one /state to another. In the case of isolated heads on South Italian vases and other grave goods, this shift is from mortal existence to the hereafter through death. Votive terracotta isolated heads are found in large numbers at sanctuaries dedicated to healing cults, where restored health is hoped-for and celebrated, and at those concerned with fertility and the continuation of life, including the preparation of young women for marriage and motherhood. These sacred sites, venerating a variety of goddesses including Hera, Aphrodite, and Kore-Persephone, became the locus of future

---

59 Steingräber 1980, 216, 222, 231.
60 Refer to Zuntz 1971, 143; Uhlenbrock 1988, 139–56; and Lippolis 2001.
61 Uhlenbrock 1988, 141, 146–48; Uhlenbrock 1989, 9–10.

brides' and mothers' desires for fulfilling marriages and the safe delivery of healthy children. Due to the high frequency of terracottas with isolated heads in Italian and Sicilian sanctuary, I present three case studies at Paestum, Locri, and Capua.

The 4th and 3rd century votive deposits of the Heraion at Foce del Sele near Paestum contain multiple busts, protomes, and floral thymiateria, a terracotta type originating at Paestum consisting of a female bust with a large open flower on the head, a reversal of the head emerging from a flower frequently seen on Apulian vases.[62] (Figure 9) The cult always seems to have been heavily concerned with the lives of women, but soon after the Lucanian conquest of Paestum at the end of the 5th century B.C., a new structure, known as the "Square Building," was constructed at the site.[63] The building, inspired by domestic architecture, contained objects connected with the feminine world, including several hundred loom-weights, leading to the hypothesis that the structure housed aristocratic girls who, as part of a period of initiation in preparation for marriage, wove the peplos given to Hera in the annual festival of the goddess.[64] Notably, it is in this structure that most of the very few South Italian vases decorated with isolated heads were discovered outside of a mortuary context.

Terracotta isolated heads across the Italian peninsula and Sicily are repeatedly uncovered in sanctuaries with proximity to water —a source of life— whether the ocean, rivers (as in the case of Foce del Sele), or springs, seen at the sanctuaries at San Biagio in Agrigento, Timmari, and Capodifiume.[65] Local nymphs were often worshipped at springs, and this practice may have led to the development of bridal preparation rites at these sites due to the double meaning of the term "nymphe." The rituals appear to revolve around purification as a girl transitioned into a bride, well illustrated by the Grotto Caruso located immediately outside the

---

62 Stoop 1960, 3–13; Uhlenbrock 1988, 291–92, 309–10; Dewailly 1997. Busts and floral thymiateria seen at Foce del Sele are found together in votive deposits of other southern Italian sanctuaries at Capua, Naples, Timmari, and Macchia di Rossano (Uhlenbrock 1988, 292). Similar floral figurines have also been found in an extramural sanctuary at Predio Maggiore on Lipari, the only examples of this terracotta type from Sicily (Bernabò Brea and Cavalier 2000, 118–21).
63 Zancani Montuoro, Schlaeger, and Stoop 1965; Greco and de La Genière 1996.
64 Cerchiai *et al.* 2002, 80.
65 For isolated heads on terracotta votives found at San Biagio at Agrigento, refer to Kilmer 1977, 83–84, 130–31, 133; Uhlenbrock 1988, 126; Cerchiai *et al.* 2002, 252. For those uncovered at Timmari, see Lo Porto 1991, 69, 75, 84–85, 88–89. See Ammerman 2002, 291 and Cipriani and Longo 1996, 237–39, 273 for the votives at the sanctuary at Capodifiume. Parallel phenomena are seen in central Italy as well (Steingräber 1980, 239–40, 242).

curtain walls of Locri Epizephyrii.[66] During the 5th and 4th centuries B.C., this cave containing a spring was enlarged and monumentalized for a cult of the nymphs and perhaps other gods related to nature, the chthonic realm, and regeneration including Persephone, Dionysos and Aphrodite. Inside the cave was a large basin of water (ca. 30–40 cm. deep), accessed via a staircase. Niches were carved into the cave walls to serve as repositories for lamps and votive gifts. In the center of the pool was an altar for offerings and a large submerged block.[67] The proposed ritual involved young women descending into the pool and perhaps sitting upon the block where they were washed in the spring's water, maybe even symbolically "married" to a chthonic groom.[68] The girls' descent into the cave's pool and subsequent ascent might have been viewed as a katabasis and anodos like that of Persephone. Votive gifts at the site include female heads and busts as well as grotto models, sometimes decorated with isolated heads in relief, and a distinctive series of terracotta plaques, often called "herms," which feature three frontal female heads across the top, generally assumed to represent the nymphs worshipped at the shrine.[69] Some of the plaques allude to the realm of Dionysos with thyrsoi and depictions of Pan in a cave.[70] On others, a man-faced bull appears below the nymphs' heads, perhaps representing Acheloös or another river god, who clearly has close connections with nymphs, the worship of water, and Greek concepts of fertility.[71] On several pieces, local folklore and water cult is blended with matrimony as the man-bull, in front of an altar, stands on a base inscribed with the name Euthymos, a victorious Locrian boxer whose two statues at Olympia and Locri were struck by lightning on the same day, causing the oracle at Delphi to decree the installation of his hero cult.[72] (Figure 10) He was said to have saved the people of neighboring Temesa from a daimon, who required the annual sacrifice of the most beautiful local maiden in recompense for the death of Polites, one of Odysseus' companions. In reward for his services, Euthymos received the parthenos as his bride. After a long life, he leapt into the local river and disappeared.[73]

Also connected with bridal preparation and water are the scenes of women, youths and Erotes on South Italian vases, which are repeatedly painted in

---

66 Barra Bagnasco 2001, 29–32; MacLachlan 2012, 345.
67 Costabile *et al.* 1991, 7–13; Larson 2001, 251–53.
68 Costabile *et al.* 1991, 103–5; Larson 2001, 254, 256; MacLachlan 2009, 206–7.
69 Costabile *et al.* 1991, 95–103; Larson 2001, 253–54.
70 Costabile *et al.* 1991, 156, 159–61; MacLachlan 2009, 212.
71 Costabile *et al.* 1991, 220–26; Oakley and Sinos 1993, 15.
72 Pliny *NH* 7.152; Costabile *et al.* 1991, 195–215; MacLachlan 2009, 212–14; Taylor 2009, 28.
73 Pausanias 6.6.4–10.

conjunction with isolated heads.⁷⁴ In a number of such tableaux, a youth courts a richly dressed woman, the bride, who is enthroned and/or attended by other women. In other instances, fountain houses and louteria (basins) are included in the scene. Maybe this iconographic combination was inspired by the dedication of terracotta isolated heads in various sanctuaries connected with coming-of-age rites for young women.

Thousands of votive terracotta heads, including some busts, were uncovered in mid 19th century excavations at the sanctuary of a mother goddess, often identified as Mater Matuta, at Fondo Patturelli outside ancient Capua (modern Santa Maria Capua Vetere). (Figure 11) Stylistically, they are dated to two main phases of production, the first between 423–304 B.C. and the second between 304–211 B.C., with a particular intensification of manufacture in the mid 4th century B.C.⁷⁵ The heads no longer have precise provenance, but they do appear to be connected with a cult focused upon both fertility and healing. Capua, established in the 9th century B.C., was a significant Etruscan settlement in Campania that provided a key point of contact with the Greeks in southern Italy and Sicily.⁷⁶ In the late 5th century, the city came under the control of the indigenous Campanians. The types of ex voto heads found in the Capuan deposits are comparable to those discovered in Etruscan, Faliscan, and Latin sanctuaries, a practice that began in the late 6th or early 5th century B.C.⁷⁷ These early central Italian votive heads, which terminate at the base of the neck and are self-supporting, have clear stylistic connections with Sicilian protomes of the period. Although predominantly mold-made, there is significant variety in their appearance including differences in gender, age, headdress types, jewelry worn, etc., with the finest examples close to portraiture.⁷⁸ Outside of Capua, these votive heads are often discovered in conjunction with terracotta statues of babies and swaddled infants, similar in

---

74   For example, Princeton 1989.29 by the Darius Painter (*RVAp Suppl.* 2 18/56b, pg. 149) and Urbana-Campaign 89.9.22 by the White Saccos Painter (*RVAp Suppl.* 2 29/J, pg. 354).
75   Bonghi Jovino 1965, 14–16, 21–25; Bedello 1974, 11, 19–25; Steingräber 1980, 241–42; Riis 1981, 18–24. Terracotta arulae, oscilla, and thymiateria decorated with isolated heads are also found in the votive deposits at Capua, although not nearly in the same amount as votive heads. See Tata 1990, 19–33, 39–52, 59–69.
76   For Capua's Etruscan phase, see D'Agostino 2004.
77   Brendel 1978, 393–94; Steingräber 1980, 217–22; Turfa 1994; Edlund-Berry 2008, 88–90. The earliest votive heads appear at the Portonaccio and Campetti sanctuaries of Veii and appear to have been influenced by architectural terracottas (Torelli and Pohl 1973, 227–48; Steingräber 1980, 238; Comella and Stefani 1990, 18–37; Turfa 2006, 98, 101; Nagy 2011, 117–19). For true shoulder busts, a rarer phenomenon in central Italy compared to Magna Graecia and Sicily, see Kilmer 1977, 203–54, 260–62, 265–67.
78   Steingräber 1980, 231–33.

appearance to the children held by depictions of the goddess carved from local stone and dedicated at the Fondo Patturelli sanctuary, as well as with terracotta statuettes of nursing mothers (kourotrophoroi), a motif that is rare in mainland Greek art. These types of ex votos imply the desire for future successful pregnancies and deliveries of healthy children.[79] Such heads in central Italy are also often associated with anatomical votives, in the form of limbs and various organs.[80] These objects, whose surviving numbers are in the thousands, have been interpreted as requests or thank-offerings for medical cures, with the dedicator providing an image of the affected part of the body.[81] Early scholarship interpreted the heads as representing maladies particularly affecting that part of the body such as migraine headaches,[82] but as the votive heads predate the proliferation of anatomical votives beginning in the last quarter of the 4th century B.C., they appear to be an independent practice, at least at first, and may have instead referred to the general well-being of an individual rather than a particular ailment.[83] Perhaps these votive heads served as a pars pro toto for the supplicant and were offered to the divine as a reminder to the deity of the dedicator's hopeful request, which could explain the many types of heads found at Capua and elsewhere in Italy.[84]

The similar functions of painted isolated heads and their three-dimensional terracotta counterparts as possible personifications of *elpis* during life's critical transitions (marriage, motherhood, recovery of health, and death) might be implied further by their many physical parallels. The types of heads are very similar, with an overwhelming majority being female, often wearing diadems, veils, or polos headdresses, as well as necklaces and earrings. Other heads found in both media are of youths, satyrs, Pan, Dionysos, Io, and those with wings or wearing Phrygian caps. The emergence of heads from flowers or acanthus calyxes and their surrounds of lush tendrils, particularly on Apulian vases, are comparable to

---

79   Steingräber 1980, 235; Smithers, 1993, 13–14, 29–30; Turfa 2006, 104.
80   Steingräber 1980, 235. Examples of sanctuaries where this phenomenon occurs includes the Ara della Regina in Tarquinia (Turfa 2006, 96–97; Comella 1982, 23–101, 104–61, 173–82, 186–91), a sanctuary at the necropolis of Sovana (Bianchi Bandinelli 1929, 36–37, 126–27, pl. 30; Steingräber 1980, 237; Pellegrini and Arcangeli 2007, 40–46), the Porta Nord at Vulci (Steingräber 1980, 237; Pautasso 1994), the Manganello sanctuary at Caere (Mengarelli 1935, 38–41; Steingräber 1980, 238; Nagy 2011, 121–124), and the Punta della Vipera sanctuary in Santa Marinella (Comella 2001, 25–51).
81   Edlund 1987; Turfa 2006, 104–106; Oberhelman 2014.
82   Stieda 1899, 236. Theory disputed in Steingräber 1980, 235–36.
83   Smithers 1993, 14; Turfa 2006, 105. The production of votive heads does dramatically increase at the time anatomical votives come into use in late 4th and early 3rd centuries (Steingräber 1980, 226–27).
84   Steingräber 1980, 236.

the vegetation around heads on some arulae and floral thymiateria.[85] (Figure 12) The occasional appearance of Erotes beside female heads is a further commonality as is the presence of a hand, either empty or holding an object, in front of the face, implying a body out of the viewer's sight.[86] Even the ambiguous identities of the majority of the heads is a shared trait, perhaps intended for greater flexibility of interpretation and function based on the object's context and the purchaser's intent, which would explain the terracottas' presence in sanctuaries dedicated to many different divinities.[87] Terracotta heads and busts without specific iconographic identifiers could additionally represent the object's dedicant.[88] As coroplasts, potters, and vase-painters would have worked in close proximity, it is not surprising that similarities in the representation of heads occur in their output.

Conclusion

The many thousands of extant objects depicting an isolated head produced on the Italian peninsula and Sicily between the Archaic and Hellenistic periods, most frequent on painted vases and molded terracottas, attest to the motif's extraordinary significance to Greeks and a wide range of Italic peoples. In southern Italy and Sicily, heads do not appear in the domestic sphere, but rather in tombs and sanctuaries, both contexts in which one can argue that *elpis*, as a blend of desire for a positive outcome and the expectation that such a result is plausible, played a significant role. While three-dimensional heads, often made of terracotta, were generally used as votive gifts by the living, two-dimensional heads, primarily painted on vases, were seen as fitting for the dead. Perhaps this distinction was due to the terracottas' tactile nature being unnecessary for the ephemeral souls of the deceased, who could no longer manipulate solid objects. The depiction of *Elpis* on the Owl Pillar Group vase as a female head in isolation, protruding from the mouth of the pithos (the single securely identifiable

---

85 Such as on the arulae Taranto 208342 and Capua inv. 530.
86 For the presence of Erotes, compare the neck of the Apulian volute-krater Ruvo 1092 with the fragmentary terracotta bust from the area of the Basilica at Paestum (Paestum Inv. 2630). For the presence of a hand in front of the face, see the Apulian plate in the Field Museum of Natural History in Chicago (inv. 182636) and the Campanian plaque in the British Museum (inv. 1867.0508.646).
87 Steingräber 1980, 242–45; Edlund-Berry 2008, 89; Nagy 2011, 124.
88 Huysecom-Haxhi and Muller 2007; Muller 2009; Ismaelli 2011, 219–23.

personification of the concept in Greek art) strongly suggests that for the Greek settlers and their Italic neighbors in pre-Roman Italy, the incomplete nature of a head apart from its body fittingly visualized the inherent conditions in which hope exists — a state in which change is likely and the complete course of action is as yet unfulfilled. The variety and seemingly intentional ambiguous identity of heads seen in South Italian vase-painting and votive terracottas allowed the necessary adaptability in meaning, dependent upon the ethnic and religious background of the viewer and the context of use, whether sacral or funerary.

Abbreviations

ARV^2 Beazley 1963
BAPD   *Beazley Archive Pottery Database* (www.beazley.ox.ac.uk)
CVA   *Corpus Vasorum Antiquorum*
LCS   Trendall 1967
LCS Suppl. 1   Trendall 1970
LCS Suppl. 2   Trendall 1973
RVAp I   Trendall and Cambitoglou 1978
RVAp II   Trendall and Cambitoglou 1982
RVAp Suppl. 1   Trendall and Cambitoglou 1983
RVAp Suppl. 2   Trendall and Cambitoglou 1991–92
RVP   Trendall 1987

Bibliography

Ambrosini, L. 1994. "'Sostegni' a testa femminile in ceramic argentata: Analisi di una produzione falisca a destinazione funeraria," in: *Archeologia Classica* 46, 109–168.
Ammerman, R.M. 2002. *Il Santuario di Santa Venera a Paestum II: The Votive Terracottas*, Ann Arbor.
Andrén, A. 1940. *Architectural Terracottas from Etrusco-Italic Temples*, 2 vols., Lund.
Barra Bagnasco, M. 1986. *Protomi in terracotta da Locri Epizefiri: Contributo allo studio della scultura arcaica in Magna Grecia*, Turin.
—— 2001. "Il culto delle acque a Locri Epizefiri: Contesti e documenti," in: S. Buzzi *et al.* (eds.), *Zona Archeologica: Festschrift für Hans Peter Isler zum 60. Geburtstag*, Bonn, 27–40.
Beazley, J.D. 1963. *Attic Red-Figure Vase Painters*, 2nd ed. 3 vols., Oxford.
Bedello, M. 1974. *Capua preromana. Terrecotte votive. Catalogo del Museo Provinciale Campano, Volume III – Testine e busti*, Florence.
Bedello Tata, M. 1990. *Capua preromana. Terracotte votive. Catalogo del Museo Provinciale Campano. Volume V – Oscilla, Thymiateria, Arulae*, Florence.
Bérard, C. 1974. *Anodoi: Essai sur l'imagerie des passages chthoniens*, Neuchâtel.
Bernabé, A./A.I. Jiménez San Cristóbal. 2008. *Instructions for the Netherworld: The Orphic Gold Tablets*, Leiden.
Bernabò Brea, L./M. Cavalier. 2000. *Meligunìs – Lipára Volume 10. Scoperte e scavi archeologici nell'area urbana e suburbana di Lipari*, Palermo.
Bianchi Bandinelli, R. 1929. *Sovana*, Florence.

Blanck, H./G. Proietti. 1986. *La tomba dei rilievi di Cerveteri,* Rome.
Bonghi Jovino, M. 1965. *Capua preromana. Terrecotte votive. Catalogo del Museo Provinciale Campano, Volume I – Teste Isolate e Mezzeteste,* Florence.
Brendel, O. 1978. *Etruscan Art,* New York.
Cairns, D. 2016. "Metaphors for Hope in Archaic and Classical Greek Poetry", in: R.R. Caston/R.A. Kaster (eds.), *Hope, Joy, and Affection in the Classical World,* 13–44, Oxford/New York.
Cambitoglou, A. 1954. "Groups of Apulian Red-Figured Vases Decorated with Heads of Women or Nike," in: *JHS* 74, 111–21.
Casadio, G. 2009. "Dionysus in Campania: Cumae," in: G. Casadio/P.A. Johnston (eds.), *Mystic Cults in Magna Graecia,* Austin, 33–45.
Cerchiai, L./L. Jannelli/F. Longo. 2002. *The Greek Cities of Magna Graecia and Sicily,* Los Angeles.
Cinquantaquattro, T./M. Lombardo/A. Alessio. 2010. *La vigna di Dioniso: vite, vino e culti in Magna Grecia,* Exh. cat., Museo Nazionale, Taranto.
Cipriani, M./F. Longo. 1996. *Poseidonia e i Lucani,* Naples.
Claes, M.-Chr. 1981. "Masques féminins de terre cuite d'usage funéraire en Italie méridionale à l'époque héllenistique," in: *Revue des Archéologues et Historiens d'Art de Louvain* 14, 7–29.
Comella, A. 1982. *Il deposito votivo presso l'Ara della Regina,* Rome.
—— 2001. *Il santuario di Punta della Vipera. Santa Marinella, Comune di Civitavecchia I. I materiali votive,* Rome.
Comella, A./G. Stefani. 1990. *Materiali votive del Sanctuario di Campetti a Veio. Scavi 1947 e 1969,* Rome.
Cristofani, M. 1967. "Ricerche sulle pitture della tomba François di Vulci. I fregi decorativi," in: *Dialoghi di Archeologia* 1, 2, 186–219.
Croissant, F. 1983. *Les protomés féminines archaïques,* Paris.
—— 1992. "Anatomie d'un style colonial: Les protomés féminines de Locres," in: *Revue archéologique,* 103–10.
Costabile, F./E. Lattanzi/P.E. Arias. 1991. *I ninfei di Locri Epizefiri,* Soveria Mannelli.
D'Agostino, B. 2004. "The Etruscans in Campania," in: G. Camporeale (ed.), *The Etruscans Outside Etruria,* Los Angeles, 236–51.
Dareggi, G. 1972. *Urne del territorio Perugino: Un gruppo inedito di cinerari etruschi ed etrusco-romani,* Rome.
De Juliis, E.M. 1984. "L'etá del Ferro," in: M. Mazzei (ed.), *La Daunia antica: Dalla preistoria all'altomedioevo,* Milan, 137–84.
—— 2009. *La rappresentazione figurata in Daunia,* Bari.
Denoyelle, M. 1997. "Attic or Non-Attic? The Case of the Pisticci Painter," in: J.H. Oakley/W.D.E. Coulson/O. Palagia (eds.), *Athenian Potters and Painters: The Conference Proceedings,* Oxford, 395–405.
—— 2014. "Hands at Work in Magna Graecia: The Amykos Painter and His Workshop," in: T.H. Carpenter/K.M. Lynch/E.G.D. Robinson (eds.), *The Italic People of Ancient Apulia: New Evidence from Pottery for Workshops, Markets, and Customs,* Cambridge, 116–29.
Detienne, M. 1979. *Dionysos Slain* (Translated by M. Muellner/L. Muellner), Baltimore.
Dewailly, M. 1997. "L'Héraion de Foce del Sele: quelques aspects du culte d'Héra à l'époque hellénistique d'après les terres cuites," in: J. de La Genière (ed.), *Héra images, espaces, cultes: ctes du colloque international du Centre de recherches archéologiques, de l'Université de Lille III et de l'Association P.R.A.C., Lille 29-30 novembre 1993,* Naples, 201–10.
Donati, L. 1967. "Buccheri decorati con teste plastiche umani: Zona di Vulci," in: *Studi etruschi* 35, 619–32.

—— 1968. "Buccheri decorati con teste plastiche umani: Zona di Chiusi," in: *Studi etruschi* 36, 319–55.
—— 1969. "Buccheri decorati con teste plastiche umani: Zona di Orvieto," in: *Studi etruschi* 37, 443–62.
Edlund, I. 1987. "Mens Sana in Corpore Sano: Healing Cults as a Political Factor in Etruscan Religion," in: T. Linders/G. Nordquist (eds.), *Gifts to the Gods: Proceedings of the Uppsala Symposium 1985*, Uppsala, 51–56.
Edlund-Berry, I. 2008. "Temples and the Etruscan Way of Religion," in: A. Ross (ed.), *From the Temple and the Tomb: Etruscan Treasures from Tuscany*, Dallas, 67–93.
Edmonds, R.G. 2013. *Redefining Ancient Orphism: A Study in Greek Religion*, Cambridge.
Fontannaz, D. 2005. "La Céramique proto-apulienne de Tarente: Problèmes et perspectives d'une 'recontextualisation,'" in: M. Denoyelle/E. Lippolis/M. Mazzei/C. Pouzadoux (eds.), *La Céramique apulienne: Bilan et perspectives*, Naples, 125–42.
Froning, H. 1985. "Zur Interpretation vegetabilischer Bekrönung klassischer und spätklassischer Grabstelen," in: *Archäologischer Anzeiger*, 218–29.
Geyer, A. 1993. "Geschichte als Mythos: Zu Alexanders 'Perserschlacht' auf apulischen Vasenbildern," in: *Jahrbuch des Deutschen Archäologischen Instituts* 108, 443–55.
Giuliani, L. 1995. *Tragik, Trauer und Trost: Bildervasen für eine apulische Totenfeier*, Berlin.
Graepler, D. 1997. *Tonfiguren in Grab: Fundkontexte hellenistischer Terrakotten aus der Nekropole von Tarent*, Munich.
Graf, F./S. Iles Johnston. 2007. *Ritual Texts for the Afterlife: Orpheus and the Bacchic Gold Tablets*, London.
Greco, G./J. de La Genière. 1996. "L'Heraion alla foce del Sele: continuità e trasformazioni dall'età greca all'età lucana," in: M. Cipriani/F. Longo (eds.), *I Greci in Occidente. Poseidonia e i Lucani*, Naples, 223–32.
Guthrie, K.S. 1993. *The Pythagorean Sourcebook and Library: An Anthology of Ancient Writings Which Relate to Pythagoras and Pythagorean Philosophy*, Grand Rapids.
Harrison, J.E. 1900. "Pandora's Box," in: *JHS* 20, 99–114.
—— 1908. *Prolegomena to the Study of Greek Religion*, 2nd ed., Cambridge.
Heuer, K. 2015. "Vases with Faces: Isolated Heads in South Italian Vase Painting," in: *Metropolitan Museum Journal* 50, 62–91.
Huysecom-Haxhi, S./A. Muller. 2007. "Déesses et/ou mortelles dans la plastique de terre cuite. Résoibses actuelles à une question ancienne," in: *Pallas* 75, 231–47.
Isler-Kerényi, C. 2009. "New Contributions of Dionysiac Iconography to the History of Religions in Greece and Italy," in: G. Casadio/P.A. Johnston (eds.), *Mystic Cults in Magna Graecia*, Austin, 61–72.
Ismaelli, T. 2011. *Archeologia del culto a Gela: il santuario del Predio Sola*, Bari.
Jastrow, E. 1946. "Two Terracotta Reliefs in American Museums," in: *AJA* 50, 67–80.
Jucker, H. 1961. *Das Bildnis in Blätterkelch: Geschichte und Bedeutung einer römischen Porträtform*, 2 vols., Lausanne/Olten.
Kern, O. 1922. *Orphicorum Fragmenta*, Berlin.
Kilmer, Martin F. 1977. *The Shoulder Bust in Sicily and Central Italy: A Catalogue and Materials for Dating*, Göteborg.
Körte, G. 1916. *I rilievi delle urne etrusche*. Volume Terzo, Berlin.
Kossatz-Deißmann, A. 1985. "Nachrichten aus Martin-von-Wagner-Museum Würzburg," in: *Archäologischer Anzeiger*, 229–39.
—— 1990. "Nachrichten aus Martin-von-Wagner-Museum Würzburg: Eine neue Phrygerkopf-Situla des Toledo-Malers," in: *Archäologischer Anzeiger*, 505–20.
Kurtz, D.C./J. Boardman. 1971. *Greek Burial Customs*, Ithaca, N.Y.

Kurz, U.Ch. 2005. "Büstenprotomen und Büste aus S. Maria d'Anglona," in: *Jahreshefte des Österreichischen Archäologischen Institutes in Wien* 74, 225–45.
Larson, J. 2001. *Greek Nymphs: Myth, Cult, Lore*, Oxford.
Lattanzi, E. (ed.) 1987. *Il Museo Nazionale di Reggio Calabria*, Rome.
Laviosa, C. 1954. "Le antefisse fittili di Taranto," in: *Archeologia classica* 6, 217–50.
Lehnert, P.A. 1978. "Female Heads on Greek, South Italian, and Sicilian Vases from the Sixth to the Third Century B.C. as Representations of Persephone/Kore." MA thesis, Michigan State University, East Lansing.
Lippolis, E. 1994. *Catalogo del Museo Nazionale Archeologico di Taranto*. Vol. 3, part 1, *Taranto, la necropolis: Aspetti e problem della documentazione archeological tra VII e I sec. a.C.*, Taranto.
—— 2001. "Culto e iconografie della coroplastica votive: Problemi interpretative a Taranto e nel mondo greco," in: *Mélanges de l'École française de Rome, Antiquité* 113, 225–55.
Lohmann, H. 1979. *Grabmäler auf Unteritalischen Vasen*, Berlin.
Lombardo, M./A. Siciliano/A. Alessio (eds.) 2011. *La vigna di Dioniso: vite, vino e culti in Magna Grecia: atti del quarantanovesimo Convegno di studi sulla Magna Grecia: Taranto, 24-28 settembre 2009*, Taranto.
Lo Porto, F.G. 1991. *Timmari. L'Abitato, le necropolis, la stipe votive*, Rome.
MacLachlan, B. 2009. "Women and Nymphs at the Grotta Caruso," in: G. Casadio /P.A. Johnston (eds.), *Mystic Cults in Magna Graecia*, 204–16, Austin.
—— 2012. "The Grave's a Fine and Funny Place: Chthonic Rituals and Comic Theater in the Greek West," in: K. Bosher (ed.), *Theater Outside Athens: Drama in Greek Sicily and South Italy*, 343–64, Cambridge.
Maddoli, G. 1996. "Cults and Religious Doctrines of the Western Greeks," in: *The Western Greeks* Exh. cat., Palazzo Grassi, Venice, ed. Giovanni Pugliese Carratelli, 481–98, Milan.
Marconi, C. 2005. "I Theoroi di Eschilo e le antefisse sileniche siceliote," in: *Sicilia antica* 2, 75–94.
Marconi, P. 1929. "Plastica agrigentina," in: *Dedalo* 3, 10, 579–99.
—— 1933. *Agrigento arcaica: Il santuario della divinità chtonie e il tempio detto di Vulcano*, Rome.
Mead, G.R.S. 1965. *Orpheus*. London.
Mengarelli, R. 1935. "Il tempio del Manganello a Caere," in: *Studi etruschi* 9, 83–94.
Muller, A. 2009. "Le tout ou la partie. Encore les protomés: dédicataires ou dédicantes?" in: *Kernos* Suppl. 23, 81–95.
Nagy, H. 2011. "Etruscan Votive Terracottas and their Archaeological Contexts: Preliminary Comments on Veii and Cerveteri," in: N. Thomson de Grummond/I. Edlund-Berry (eds.), *The Archaeology of Sanctuaries and Ritual in Etruria* (JRA Suppl. 31), 113–25. Portsmouth, Rhode Island, Journal of Roman Archaeology.
Neils, J. 2006. "The Girl in the Pithos: Hesiod's *Elpis*," in: J.M. Barringer/J.M. Hurwit (eds.), *Periklean Athens and Its Legacy: Problems and Perspectives*, 37–45, Austin.
Oakley, J.H. 2004. *Picturing Death in Classical Athens*, Cambridge.
Oakley, J.H./H.S. Rebecca 1993. *The Wedding in Ancient Athens*, Madison.
Oberhelman, S.M. 2014. "Anatomical Votive Reliefs as Evidence for Specialization at Healing Sanctuaries in the Ancient Mediterranean World," in: *Athens Journal of Health* March 2014, 47–62.
Oleson, J.P. 1982. *The Sources of Innovation in Later Etruscan Tomb Design (ca. 350-100 B.C.)*, Rome.
Orfismo in Magna Grecia: Atti del quattordicesimo convegno di studi sulla Magna Grecia, Taranto, 6–10 ottobre 1974. 1975, Naples.
Orsi, P. 1911. "Locri Epizephyrii," in: *Notizie degli savi di antichità*, suppl., 3–76.
Pautasso, A. 1994. *Il deposito votivo presso la Porta Nord a Vulci*, Rome.

Pellegrini, E./L. Arcangeli. 2007. *Gli etruschi a Sovana: Percorsi cultuali e riti magici*, Pitigliano.
Pensa, M. 1977. *Rappresentazioni dell'oltretomba nella ceramica apula*, Rome.
Pugliese Carratelli, G. (ed.) 1988. *Magna Grecia: Vita religiosa e cultura letteraria, filosofica e scientifica*, Milan.
—— (ed.) 1996. *The Western Greeks*. Exh. cat., Palazzo Grassi, Venice, Milan.
—— 2003. *Les Lamelles d'or orphiques: Instructions pour le voyage d'outre-tombe des initiés grecs* (translated by A.-P. Segonds and C. Luna), Paris.
Riis, P.J. 1981. *Etruscan Types of Heads: A Revised Chronology of the Archaic and Classical Terracottas of Etruscan Campania and Central Italy*, Copenhagen.
Robert, C. 1914. "Pandora," in: *Hermes* 49, 17–38.
Rohde, E. 1907. *Psyche: Seelencult und Unsterblichkeitsglaube der Griechen*, 4th ed., Tübingen.
Roncalli, F. 1987. "La decorazione pittorica," in: F. Buranelli (ed.), *La Tomba François di Vulci*, 79–110, Rome.
Rosi, G. 1925. "Sepulchral Architecture as Illustrated by the Rock Facades of Central Etruria: Part I," in: *JRS* 15, 1–59.
—— 1927. "Sepulchral Architecture as Illustrated by the Rock Facades of Central Etruria: Part II," in: *JRS* 17, 59–96.
Rouveret, A. 1990. "Tradizioni pittorische magnogreche," in: G. Pugliese Carratelli (ed.), *Magna Grecia: Arte e artigianato*, 317–50, Milan.
Rouveret, A./A. Pontrandolfo. 1983. "Pittura Funeraria in Lucania e Campania puntualizzazioni cronologiche e proposte di lettura," in: *Dialoghi di archeologia* ser. 3, 1, 1, 91–130.
Schauenburg, K. 1957. "Zur Symbolik unteritalischer Rankenmotive," in: *Mitteilungen des Deutschen Archäologischen Instituts, Römische Abteilung* 64, 198–221.
—— 1962. "Pan in Unteritalien," in: *Mitteilungen des Deutschen Archäologischen Instituts, Römische Abteilung* 69, 27–42.
—— 1974. "Bendis in Unteritalien?" in: *Jahrbuch des Deutschen Archäologischen Instituts* 89, 137–86.
—— 1981. "Zu unteritalischen Situlen," in: *Archäologischer Anzeiger*, 462–88.
—— 1982. "Arimaspen in Unteritalien" in: *Revue archéologique*, 249–62.
—— 1984. "Unterweltsbilder aus Grossgriechenland," in: *Mitteilungen des Deutschen Archäologischen Instituts, Römische Abteilung* 91, 359–87.
—— 1989. "Zur Grabsymbolik apulischer Vasen," in: *Jahrbuch des Deutschen Archäologischen Instituts* 104, 19–60.
Schefold, K./F. Jung. 1988. *Die Urkönige, Perseus, Bellerophon, Herakles, and Theseus in der klassischen und hellenistischen Kunst*, Munich.
Schmidt, M. 1975. "Orfeo e Orfismo nella pittura vascolare italiota," in: *Orfismo in Magna Grecia: Atti del quattordicesimo convegno di studi sulla Magna Grecia, Taranto 6–10 ottobre 1974*, 105–37, Naples.
Sclafani, M. 2010. *Urne fittili chiusine e perugine di età medio e tardo ellenistica*, Rome.
Silvestrelli, F. 2005. "Le fasi della ceramica a figure rosse nel kerameikos di Metaponto," in: M. Denoyelle/E. Lippolis/M. Mazzei/C. Pouzadoux (eds.), *La Céramique apulienne: Bilan et perspectives*, 113–23, Naples.
Smith, H.R.W. 1976. *Funerary Symbolism in Apulian Vase-painting*, Berkeley.
Smithers, S. 1993. "Images of Piety and Hope: Select Terracotta Votives from West-Central Italy," in: *Studia Varia from the J. Paul Getty Museum* 1, 13–32.
Sourvinou-Inwood, C. 1978. "Persephone and Aphrodite at Locri: A Model for Personality Definitions in Greek Religion," in: *JHS* 98, 101–21.

Steingräber, S. 1980. "Zum Phänomen der etruskisch-italischen Votiveköpfe," in: *Mitteilungen des Deutschen Archaeologischen Instituts, Römische Abteilung* 87, 215–53.

—— 1990. "Traditionelle und innovative Elemente in der frühhellenistischen Grabarchitektur und –malerei Unteritaliens," in: E. Schwinzer/S. Steingräber (eds.), *Kunst und Kultur in der Magna Graecia: Ihr Verhältnis zum griechischen Mutterland und zum italischen Umfeld. Referate vom Symposium des Deutschen Archäologen-Verbandes, Städtisches Schloss Rheydt, Mönchengladbach, 8.–10.1.1988*, 78–86, Tübingen.

Stieda, L. 1899. "Ueber alt-italische Weihgeschenke," in: *Mitteilungen des Deutschen Archaeologischen Instituts, Römische Abteilung* 14, 230–43.

Stoop, M.W. 1960. *Floral Figurines from South Italy*, Assen.

Taplin, O. 2007. *Pots and Plays: Interactions between Tragedy and Greek Vase-painting of the Fourth Century B.C.*, Los Angeles.

Taylor, R. 2009. "River Raptures: Containment and Control of Water in Greek and Roman Constructions of Identity," in: C. Kosso/A. Scott (eds.), *The Nature and Function of Water, Baths, Bathing, and Hygiene from Antiquity to the Renaissance*, 21–42, Leiden.

Todisco, L. 2002. *Teatro e spettacolo in Magna Grecia e in Sicilia: testi, immagini, architettura*, Milan.

Torelli, M./I. Pohl. 1973. "Veio: Scoperta di un piccolo santuario etrusco in Località Campetti," in: *Atti della Accademia Nazionale dei Lincei. Notizie degli Scavi di Antichità* 28, 40–258.

Trendall, A.D. 1967. *The Red-Figured Vases of Lucania, Campania, and Sicily*, Oxford.

—— 1970. *The Red-Figured Vases of Lucania, Campania, and Sicily*. First Supplement, London.

—— 1973. *The Red-Figured Vases of Lucania, Campania, and Sicily*. Second Supplement, London.

—— 1987. *The Red-Figured Vases of Paestum*, London.

—— 1990. "On the Divergence of South Italian from Attic Red-Figure Vase-Painting," in: J.-P. Descoeudres (ed.), *Greek Colonists and Native Populations*, 218–30, Canberra.

—— 1992. "A New Early Apulian *Phlyax* Vase," in: *Bulletin of the Cleveland Museum of Art* 79, 2–15.

Trendall, A.D./A. Cambitoglou. 1978. *The Red-Figured Vases of Apulia*. Vol. 1, *Early and Middle Apulian*, Oxford.

—— 1982. *The Red-Figured Vases of Apulia*. Vol. 2, *Late Apulian*, Oxford.

—— 1983. *First Supplement to the Red-Figured Vases of Apulia*, London.

—— 1991–92. *Second Supplement to the Red-Figured Vases of Apulia*, London.

Turfa, J.M. 1994. "Anatomical Votives and Italian Medical Traditions," in: R.D. De Puma/J.P. Small (eds.), *Murlo and the Etruscans: Art and Society in Ancient Etruria*, 224–40: Madison, Wisconsin.

—— 2006. "Votive Offerings in Etruscan Religion," in: N. Thomson de Grummond/E. Simon (eds.), *The Religion of the Etruscans*, 90–115: Austin.

Uhlenbrock, J. 1988. *Terracotta Protomai from Gela: A Discussion of Local Style in Archaic Sicily*, Rome.

—— 1989. "Concerning Some Archaic Terracotta Protomai from Naxos," in: *Xenia* 18, 9–24.

Van Buren, D. 1918. "Terracotta Arulae," in: *Memoirs of the American Academy in Rome* 2, 15–53.

Van der Meijden, H. 1993. *Terracotta-Arulae aus Sizilien und Unteritalien*, Amsterdam.

Von Gerkan, A./F. Messerschmidt. 1942. "Das Grab der Volumnier bei Perugia," in: *Mitteilungen des Deutschen Archaeologischen Instituts, Römische Abteilung* 57, 122–235.

Von Hesberg, H. 1981. "Die Aufnahme der dorischen Ordnung in Etrurien," in: *Die Aufnahme fremder Kultureinflüsse in Etrurien und das Problem des Retardierens in der etruskischen Kunst*, 189–97. Mannheim, Vorstand des Deutschen Archäologen-Verbandes e.V. and Archäologischen Seminar der Universität Mannheim.

Von Mercklin, E. 1962. *Antike Figuralkapitelle*, Berlin.

Wiederkehr Schuler, E. 2004. *Les protomés féminines du Sanctuaire de la Malophoros à Sélinonte*, Naples.
Winter, N.A. 1974. "Terracotta Representations of Human Heads Used as Architectural Decoration in the Archaic Period." PhD diss., Bryn Mawr College.
—— 1978. "Archaic Architectural Terracottas Decorated with Human Heads," in: *Mitteilungen des Deutschen Archaeologischen Instituts, Römische Abteilung* 85, 27–58.
—— 2009. *Symbols of Wealth and Power: Architectural Terracotta Decoration in Etruria and Central Italy, 640–510 B.C*, Ann Arbor.
Wohl, B.L. 1984. "Three Female Head Antefixes from Etruria," in: *J. Paul Getty Museum Journal* 12, 111–18.
Zancani Montuoro, P./H. Schlaeger/M.W. Stoop. 1965. "L'edificio quadrato nello Heraion alla foce del Sele," in: *Atti e memorie della Società Magna Grecia* series 2, 6, 23–195.
Zuntz, G. 1971. *Persephone: Three Essays on Religion and Thought in Magna Graecia*, Oxford.

Figures

Fig. 1: London, British Museum F 147 Red-figure amphora with the creation of Pandora, attributed to the Owl Pillar Group, ca. 450–425 B.C. (Photographs © The Trustees of the British Museum)

Fig. 2: London, British Museum 1877,0802.10 Painted Etruscan terracotta antefix molded with a female head in a shell-like border above from Capua, ca. 500–480 B.C. (Photograph © The Trustees of the British Museum)

Fig. 3: New York, Metropolitan Museum of Art 96.18.22 Apulian red-figure bell-krater with female head in profile to right, attributed to the Chevron Group, Archidamos Sub-Group, ca. 350–325 B.C. (Image © The Metropolitan Museum of Art)

Fig. 4: Malibu, Getty Villa 86.AE.680 Apulian red-figure loutrophoros with naiskos scene and head in floral setting above, attributed to the Painter of Louvre MNB 1148, ca. 330 B.C. (Digital image courtesy of the Getty's Open Content Program)

The Face of Hope: Isolated Heads in South Italian Visual Culture —— 323

Fig. 5: London, British Museum F 279 Apulian volute-krater with the death of Hippolytos and a head wearing a Phrygian cap above, attributed to the Darius Painter, ca. 340s B.C. (Photograph © The Trustees of the British Museum)

Fig. 6: New York, Metropolitan Museum of Art 11.210.3a,b Apulian loutrophoros with enthroned god (Zeus or Hades?) adjudicating between Aphrodite and Persephone regarding Adonis' fate, a grave stele surrounded by youths and women below, and a female head rising from a flower on the shoulder. Attributed to the Darius Painter, ca. 340–330 B.C. (Image © The Metropolitan Museum of Art)

Fig. 7: New York, Metropolitan Museum of Art 96.9.221 Etruscan terracotta cinerary urn featuring a frontal head with bovine ears and wearing a winged Phrygian cap and a reclining deceased female on the lid, 2nd century B.C. (Image © The Metropolitan Museum of Art)

Fig. 8: Gela, Museo Archeologico Regionale 7369, terracotta protome from Gela, Predio Sola extra-urban sanctuary (1959 excavation), ca. 510–500 B.C. (photograph courtesy Regione Siciliana, Assessorato dei Beni Culturali e dell'Identità Siciliana, Dipartimento dei Beni Culturali e dell'Identità Siciliana, Parco Archeologico e Ambientale di Gela)

Fig. 9: Paestum, Museo Archeologico Nazionale inv. 56492 Floral thymiaterion discovered in the Bothros I deposit at the Sanctuary of Hera at Foce del Sele, late 4th or early 3rd century B.C. (author's photograph)

Fig. 10: Reggio di Calabria, Museo Archeologico Nazionale inv. 110 Plaque from Grotta Caruso at Locri depicting three female heads above Euthymos in bull form next to an altar, 4th century B.C. (author's photograph)

Fig. 11: Capua, Museo Campano inv. 1036 Votive terracotta head likely from the sanctuary at Fondo Patturelli, second half 3rd century B.C. (author's photograph)

Fig. 12: Taranto, Museo Nazionale Archeologico inv. 208342 Terracotta arula from Taranto with a frontal female head surrounded by spiraling tendrils, second half of the 4th century B.C. (Photograph provided by the Ministero per i Beni Culturali, Soprintendenza per i Beni Archeologici della Puglia, Archivo fotografico, Taranto)

Olympia Bobou
Hope and the Sub-adult

Hope as an emotion associated with sub-adults, that is young people before the age of eighteen, is often found in the funerary record in the Hellenistic and Roman Greece. The child itself could be described as the hope of their parents,[1] but what was commonly expressed was the destruction of parental hopes through death. In most epigrams these hopes seemed to be left unspecified.

A good example of how parental hopes were not well-defined is an epigram from the city of Kios, at Bithynia. The area was colonized by Miletus, and thanks to its location by the mouth of the navigable river Askanios that joined lake Askanios to Propontis, it became a prosperous city.[2] Kios was destroyed by Philip V during the Second Macedonian War in 202, its people were sold into slavery, and its ruins were given to his son-in-law Prusias I, who renamed it Prusias-by-the-sea.[3]

The inscription has been dated with caution in the third/second centuries BC, therefore before the destruction and renaming of the city.[4] The epigram records how the parents of Asklepiodotos, a five-year-old, mourned and commemorated his death. It is possible to observe a clear and gendered distinction in the appropriate behaviours after the death of the child: the father was responsible for the burial arrangements, including the enclosure, the funerary marker bearing the son's image, and the altar, where the epigram itself was inscribed —all arrangements that have to do both with finances and showing the family's mourning to the community, to the outside world.

The poem contrasts the ways the two parents experienced their grief, the father by setting up the image of the dead son that could offer little comfort (κενὴν ὄνησιν ὀμμάτων), while the unfortunate mother cries. The adjective τάλαινα might even imply that the mother was the one who suffered the most emotionally

---

This paper is dedicated to the memory of my father.
1   For example, in *IG* II² 3964, ln. 2, T. Flavius Glaukias is the hope of his mother Athenais.
2   For the foundation and the relation of Kios to Miletos: Suk Fong Jim 2014, 223, and n. 69.
3   For the destruction of Kios: Polyb. 15.21; Brandis 1897, 507–539, esp. 518; Eckstein 2008, 148, 191.
4   For the epigram see Peek *GV* 661; Peek, *Grabgedichte* 231; Peres 2003, 249–250; Schlegelmilch 2009, 85–6, T4; Vérihlac 1978–1982, no. 164; Merkelbach 2000, 136–7; *SEG* 55 978. See also Parker 2005, 152–154 for the word ὄνησις translated as 'benefit,' instead of 'pleasure' as here.

from the death of Asklepiodotos. The text even describes her laments as sadder than those of the nightingale, a bird symbolizing mourning in Greek mythology.[5]

> Ἐπ' ὠκυμοίρῳ τοῦτον Ἀσκληπιοδότῳ
> πατὴρ Νόητος χῶσεν εὐερκῆ τάφον,
> καὶ ξεστὸν οἰκτρ[ο]ῦ παιδὸς ἀν<φὶ> σήματι
> ἔθηκε βωμόν, πενταέτους τε εἰκὼ τέκνου
> κενὴν ὄνησιν ὀμμάτων χαράξατο,
> τὴν πᾶσαν εἰς γῆν ἐλπίδων κρύψας χαράν·
> μήτηρ δὲ ἐν οἴκοις, ἁ τάλαινα, ὀδύρεται
> νικῶσα θρήνοις πενθίμην ἀηδόνα.

> Over Asklepiodotos, who died before his time,
> His father Noetos raised this well-surrounded mound,
> and placed the polished altar together with the funerary marker
> of the pitiable son and had engraved the empty delight to the eyes,
> the image of the five-year-old child.
> He hid all the joy of hopes in the ground;
> while his mother at home, the unfortunate one, cries
> and wins over the mourning nightingale with her laments.

What were the hopes that brought such joy to the parents of little Asklepiodotos, and then were cruelly dashed by death? In this paper, I want to explore how the emotion of hope associated with sub-adults, i.e. individuals before the age of 18, was specified in public contexts in the ancient Greco-Roman world through the use of funerary monuments (inscriptions and imagery), and votive and public inscriptions. Furthermore, I would like to explore the emotion of hope expressed in the letter of a young child, either a slave or an apprentice from the Athenian Agora.

Today, in some cultures, a common wish (and hope) upon a child's birth is for the longevity and good health of the infant.[6] Similarly in ancient Athens, adult hope was expressed from an early stage: the Athenians announced the birth of a boy by hanging a wreath outside their door: an olive wreath for boys, and a wool one for girls. The olive and the wool were directly connected with male and female achievements: for men, that of athletic victory at the Olympic Games, the

---

5   The nightingale was either Prokne or Philomela transformed; the most famous —and for us, complete— version of the myth is in Ov. *Met.* 6.424–674, but the myth was already known in some form to the Homeric poet, *Od.* 19.518–9. The sad song of the nightingale to be compared with mournful laments is also found in Hellenistic poetry, see Callim. *Hymn.* 5.94.

6   For example, in modern Greek, 'να σας ζήσει' is one of the most common congratulatory — and wishful— expressions upon the birth of a child.

most important of the Panhellenic Games, and the successful management of the household for women.⁷

In these cases parental hope is associated with expectation, since the child's future is unknown; however, there is also the strong desire for a positive future in which the children will perform their social roles to the best of their abilities. The combination of desire and anticipation creates an emotion that we can understand as hope: "To hope is to believe that something positive, which does not presently apply to one's life, could still materialize, and so we yearn for it."⁸

In the material record, almost always the emotion of hope associated with sub-adults is expressed by parents or guardians. The Athenian children just mentioned were too young to understand and express hope, as this particular emotion has a cognitive aspect and presupposes the ability to understand one's present position.⁹ In the epigrams and texts studied here, we will see how ἐλπίς was modulated in the public sphere, and was created through the combination of the expectation of a likely event and the desire for a positive outcome. Since the two parts were not necessarily always equal, this results in different nuances of ἐλπίς.

Most expressions of hope are known through funerary texts. The usual medium is an inscription or poem in the first person. There is enough evidence to suggest that the viewer of the funerary monument would read out the text, and so (sometimes) have a dialogue with, and/or take on the part of the speaking child, and speak out the child's regrets.¹⁰ This performance could offer insight into the deceased's life, and so create empathy towards his/her person, and ultimately, become part of the community of mourners that had set up his/her monument.¹¹

In a funerary monument from Perinthos we have a good example of the 'speaking child,' that can help us in our understanding of parental hopes. Perinthos was a colony of Samos, founded in 602 BC, on eastern Thrace on the coast of Marmara Sea. In the fourth century BC it had withstood a siege by Philip II of Macedon (340 BC), and had a long, successful life as a trading port, that probably culminated in its acquiring special status under Septimius Severus, and lasted

---

7   Golden 1990, 23; Cohen 2000, 38; Beaumont 2013, 195–206, 198.
8   Lazarus 1999, 653–678, esp. 653. For the connection between anticipation and desire for a future outcome see also Cairns 2016, DOI,10.1093/acprof,oso/9780190278298.003.0002 (consulted online on 18 July 2017).
9   See Cairns 2016 for the cognitive and affective aspects of hope as an emotion.
10 For the use of first-person in funerary inscriptions see Svenbro 1993, 43–46; Waters 2000, 114-15; Fantuzzi 2004, 283–349, 307. For the performative aspects of reading inscriptions see Chaniotis 2012, 91–129, esp. 101, 103, 104.
11 Chaniotis 2012, 104–106.

until Constantine I moved the capital of his empire to nearby Byzantium.[12] The monument and its inscriptions have been dated in the first-second centuries AD[13] therefore it was made during a time of prosperity for the city.

The epigrams were inscribed on a stele,[14] written on either side of a sculpted hermaic stele, and framed by palm branches. The image reinforced the ideas of victory and athleticism in the viewer, since both the hermaic stele and the palm branch have a long association with the world of the gymnasium and athletic victories. Low pillars or stelai had an athletic connotation from the classical period, for example in Athenian vases,[15] while the palm branch was a typical victory price (cf. Pausanias 8.48.2–3).

On the left of the herm was the following text:

Παῖδά με γυμνασίων ἐμπείραμον Ἑρμάωνος
καὶ τυχὸν ἱδρώτων ἄξιον Ἡρακλέους,
ἤδη που μέλλοντα παρὰ ξυστοῖο φιλάθλοις
καὐτὸν ἀριθμεῖσθαι τοῦ μεγάλου σταδίου,
ἥρπασεν ἡ πάντων φθονερὴ θεός, ἧς ὑπὸ νῆμα
κλήρῳ τῆς ἀδίκου κεκλίμεθ' ἔργα Τύχης.

Already as a child I was familiar with the gymnasia of Hermes and
perhaps capable of the toils of Herakles; already among the competitors of the xystus
I was counted among those of the great stadium, when the goddess who envies everything
grabbed me, under whose thread by lot we give way; this is the work of Tyche.

On the right:

Ἤδη γυμνασίοις ἠσκημένον, ἔντροφον ἄθλοις,
παῖδά με καὶ πάτρης ἐλπίδα καὶ πατέρος,
ἐγγὺς καὶ κοτίνῳ φθονερὸς κατεκοίμισεν Ἄδης,
ψευσάμενος τόσσους εἰς ἀρετὴν καμάτους.
Οὔνομά μοι Δωρᾶς, πατρὸς Διοκλεῖος, ἀπ' αὐτῶν
ἄθλων εἰς διδαχὴν τὰ αὐτὰ πονησαμένου
ἀλλά με πρηυτέρως πενθήσατε· καὶ γὰρ ἐς Ἄδην
ἔρχομαι ἡρώων οὐδενὶ λειπόμενος.

---

12 On Perinthos: von Bredow 2016: http://ezproxy-prd.bodleian.ox.ac.uk,2066/10.1163/1574-9347_bnp_e914230 (consulted online on 30 September 2016). On Philip II's siege: Gabriel 2010, 190–196. On its status under Septimius Severus: Rowan 2012, 102–104. Perinthos in the third-fourth centuries A.D.: Mennen 2011, 39.
13 Nigdelis 2000, 148–150; Sayar 1998, no. 214; Vérilhac 1978–1982, no. 66.
14 It was found in second use, incorporated in the walls of a house, Dumont 1892, no. 392, 74t.
15 For example, in the interior of a cup by the Euaion Painter, now at New York, Metropolitan Museum of Art inv. no. 96.18.119; or an oinochoe at the same museum, inv. no. 06.1021.171.

> Already trained in the gymnasium and acquainted with competitions, as a child I was the hope of my fatherland and my father
> And I was close to the olive wreath when the jealous Hades put me to sleep
> Belying so many toils for the sake of virtue.
> My name is Doras, my father Diokleios, at the end of the competitions,
> to instruct me at the same sport, he also toiled;
> But you have already mourned me; because I go to Hades
> without being far from any of the heroes.

The epigram emphasized the dashed hopes for further achievements after so many efforts. It highlighted built elements that were illustrated synoptically with the herm: the gymnasium, the xystus, the stadium, all places where the polis educated and trained its young citizens.[16] The use of the terms xystus and stadium specified where young Doras trained, and at which sport he was expected to win (something that was only hinted at by the depiction of the palm branches).

In this epigram ἐλπίδα is translated as hope, however, it is a hope grounded on hard work and earlier successes during training. The hope of his fatherland and his father for the victor's crown in athletic competitions for Doras was justified thanks to his previous toils, his training under his father, himself an athlete, and his talent. It is not simply the desire for a positive outcome, but also the expectation that, after this combination of factors, the outcome will be positive.

The ἐλπίδα felt by Doras' fatherland and father is closer to expectation than hope, even when there is a component of desire for a positive outcome. Doras' victory at athletic competitions was considered likely by all, until the boy's death destroyed their hopes for such a positive, desired event.

Thus, for the literate viewer the combination of text and image created a contrast between hope and disappointment, hard work and (bad) luck, expectation and negative outcome, and ultimately between life and death, all set against the backdrop of the polis, and the culture and education that befit its young citizens.

The text from Perinthos is not unique; it is, instead, a good example of the epigrams describing the hopes for athletic victories and achievements as a hope/expectation shared by the child's homeland. By sketching out a child's life and labours within a civic context and by showing the child's participation in activities that required sponsorship by members of the elite and that would glorify the name of the city, these privately commissioned monuments connected the world of the family with that of the polis.

---

16 For the gymnasium as educational centre in the Greco-roman world, see Kah and Scholz 2007; Scholz and Wiegandt 2015.

Other inscriptions stress, instead, hopes/expectations that revolve around the domestic sphere. An example from imperial-period Mysia, found at Demirkapi, and associated with the site of Hadrianoutherai ('Hadrian's Hunts'), a town founded by Hadrian,[17] shows how these hopes could be associated with young people. The inscription is dated in or after the second century AD.

Ποῦ σοφίης ἐρατῆς ἀγανὸν σθένος,
ἔγνομε Κλωθώ, ποῦ μοι Πειερίδων μου-
σοπόλος μελέτη; Δωδεκέτης ἔτι που
γὰρ ὑπὸ χθόνα καὶ βαρὺν Ἄδην κεῖμαι,
τὰς γονέων ψευσάμενος χάριτας· ἀντὶ
δέ μοι θαλάμοιο καὶ εὐιέρων ὑμεναίων
τύμβος καὶ στήλλη καὶ κόνις ἐκχθροτάτη·
πηοὶ μὲν τόδε σῆμα καὶ ὅσσ' ἐδύναντο θανόν-
τι τεῦξαν ἐμοί, Μοιρῶν νήμασι πειθόμενοι·
Ἀλλ' ἤδη δακρύων ἅλις, ὦ πάτερ, ὦ πανό[δυρ]-
τε ἀμμίον, ἴσχ' ἐπ' ἐμοὶ θρῆνον ἀεικέλιο[ν].

Where is the mild force of desirable knowledge, unjust Clotho?
Where is the study of the Pierides serving the Muses?
At twelve years of age, no more, I lie under the earth and grievous Hades
Having betrayed the favours of my parents.
For me, instead of a bridal chamber and holy songs of marriage, the tomb, and stele and most odious dust.
My parents, to honour me in death, made this monument and all that they could
Submitting to the threads of the Fates. But enough with the tears, oh, father,
Oh, most unhappy mother,[18] do not continue this unseemly lament for me.[19]

The name of the child was not mentioned, and the textual references to the works of the Muses and the bridal chamber and marriage songs could be found in epigrams for young men as for young women.[20] The achievements in studying the works of the Muses, allow us to identify the twelve-year-old as someone belonging to a cultured and educated elite; however, that is not the focus of the epigram.

What is betrayed in this epigram is not ἐλπίς but χάριτας, the favours, the kindness, the pleasure of the parents. However, the contrast between the bridal chamber and the sacred marriage songs with the tomb, the stele and the most

---

17 Or in nearby Miletopolis: *SEG* 19.728; Peek, *GV* I, 1584. For the association with Hadrianoutherai: *SEG* 57.1266; Merkelbach 2000, 104.
18 Following Merkelbach 2000, 2,104.
19 Vérilhac 1978–1982, no. 76.; Schwertheim 1980, no. 538, pl. 44.
20 For example epigram for Plaggon: *SEG* 12.193 = Peek, *GV* I 1820; epigram for Zenon: *IG* IX,1 879; epigram for Neikiadis: *IG* IX,2 316; for Aristogenes: Helly 1973, 212.

odious dust make clear that the former were the desired events, the latter what happened. The dissonance between what was socially accepted as the 'career path' of a cultured and well-bred young person, i.e. a good marriage, and their death, creates the impression of dashed hopes to the reader, even when ἐλπὶς itself is not mentioned.

Unlike the hopes mentioned in the epigram for Doras that were grounded on his training, the young person's study of the muses and knowledge did not necessarily mean that they would help him/her secure a suitable marriage partner. His/her parents' social status and wealth were more important factors in determining his/her worth in the marriage market. This means that in this case, the marriage that never happened was a highly likely event, yet the marriage to a suitable partner for such a cultured young person was a desired event. So the (dashed) ἐλπίς implied in the text is more hope than expectation.

This stele had another typical feature of most funerary monuments: while the epigram on a stele referred to prospective joys and achievements, the iconography of the monument emphasized instead the daily life of the family. The upper part of the stele has a bust portrait of the child placed in a deep recess in the stone, with a funerary banquet scene with a man, a woman, and a figure in small-scale in front of the seated female in a low relief underneath.

The banquet has a long tradition as a subject of funerary monuments, and as a scene, it could have had multiple meanings and values. It may have referred to the reunion of the family in the afterlife, and so potentially could be considered an image of hope. Other scholars, however, have argued that it could have referred to family dinners, and so the depiction on the monument replicated an idealised scene from a family's daily life. Another view is that the dinner served as a visible reminder of a family's wealth and status, especially when luxurious objects and servants were on display.[21] Like the portrait of the child is an image of him/herself as s/he was in life, the banquet scene may replicate a domestic scene.

In the stele from Mysia we see how the contrast between life and death is created through the different messages conveyed by the text and the image. The bust of the child and a scene that could refer either to the past (scene from daily life), or the future (belief in the afterlife and hope for reunion); in either case, the focus is on the shared experience of living as a family. The text, instead, concentrates on the lost hopes of the child and of his/her parents: hopes for a scholarly career, or at least for the enjoyment that comes from knowledge, and hopes for marriage. The two messages, textual and visual, are parallel, and give different (but complementary) information to the viewer.

---

21 On the funerary banquet see Draycott and Stamatopoulou 2016; Closterman 2015, 1–22.

A lot of the funerary monuments, however, that were made for children, focused on the children themselves, rather than their family life. In those cases, the scenes emphasized the sweetness and charm of the child, and depicted them in 'quaint' domestic settings. Sometimes we can also observe the incorporation of symbols and attributes in the iconography that refer to the child's death: snakes, downward torches and other emblems.[22] These reliefs usually give no visual definition to hope, in much the same way that the imagery on the relief from Mysia focused on the banquet scene and the portrait bust.

However, there are a few reliefs that give visual definition to hope for the future, and show how, for some parents, this was the primary emotion associated with the loss of a child. What is interesting about these reliefs is that there is no conformity in the way the image relates to the text, unlike the textual conformity of expressing dashed hopes.

The first is a stele from Rheneia, the small island that served as the burial ground for Delos from 534 BC.[23] The Hellenistic —and Roman— period funerary monuments in particular, are a testament to the cosmopolitan character of the island and the co-existence of people from the wider Mediterranean basin.[24]

The stele is for Themistokles, a boy whose family came from Antioch.[25] Themistokles is shown in a sketchily depicted gymnasium, indicated by a herm at the background, accompanied by a hunting dog and a slave that sits on the base of the herm and is visibly mourning. The text reads:

Ἀντιοχῆ Θεμίσωνος ἀεθλοφόρον κόνις ἥδε
κεύθει δωδεχετῆ παῖδα Θεμιστοκλέα,
ὅς βουλὰν καὶ θάρσος ἔχων ἴσ' ὁμονύμῳ ἀνδρί
[θ]νήσκει, τὴν Μοιρῶν οὐ προφυγὼν δύναμιν.

The dust here covers the twelve-year-old child Themistokles, winner at games, the son of Themison of Antioch, who was equal to the homonymous man in counsel and bravery. He dies unable to escape the power of Fates.

Both text and image emphasize Themistokles's athletic achievements: the (dashed) hope for victory at games is connected to the athletic iconography of the stele, and reinforces it. Similar to the second epigram discussed in this paper,

---

22   Kurtz and Boardman 1971, 234.
23   Külzer: http,//ezproxy-prd.bodleian.ox.ac.uk,2066/10.1163/1574-9347_bnp_e1021930 (consulted online on 27 September 2016).
24   On the cosmopolitan character of Delos see Zarmakoupi, 115–132.
25   Couilloud 1974, cat. No. 743; Vérhillac, no. 48; Schlegelmilch 2009, 77–8, cat. B5; Bobou 2015, 111.

that for Doras from Perinthos, where the palms and the herm referred to the world of the gymnasium, and the text recorded that the victories were expected but never realised, in the stele for Themistokles the text serves as a clarification to the image. The image may be powerful, but without the text, it is not possible to know whether the athletic victories alluded to by the various symbols are symbolic, expected or real.

Themistokles' successes in games and his wisdom mark the implied ἐλπίς of his parents as both belief in and expectation of a positive future that the fates destroyed, while the focus of these hopes/expectations was located in the public sphere. Victory at athletic events, wisdom, and bravery, were all necessary acts and virtues for making a young man an important and valuable member of his community.

Themistokles is also shown as older than his years. The poem clearly states that he was twelve years of age, yet his musculature is that of an older young man. He is accompanied also by a hunting dog. We do not know if Themistokles liked hunting; the text has no reference to other activities except athletic ones. The dog, though, marks him as an adolescent. Perhaps, considering his athletic activities and his twelve years of age, he was one of those precociously grown up boys; but it is just as likely (if not more likely) that he was deliberately shown as older than his years in the stele, to further emphasise the (dashed) hope for the kind of future man he would become.

The stele of Nikopolis is perhaps the best example of the use of prospective imagery.[26] The relief shows the image of a worldly young woman depicted with a toy dog and a servant that carries a fashionable hat. The text gives us a very different story:

Νικόπολι Σαραπίωνος, χαῖρε.
Αἱμύλα κωτίλλουσα τεοὺς γενέτας ἀτίταλλες
ἱεῖσα τραυλὴν γῆρυν ἀπὸ στόματος·
ἀλλά σε τὴν διετῆ κόλπων ἀπὸ μητέρος εἷλεν
ἀστεμφὴς Ἀΐδης, μείλιχε Νικόπολι·
χαῖρε, βρέφος, κούφη δὲ σέθεν περὶ σῶμα καλύπτοι
κόνις, Σαραπίωνος ὄβριμον θάλος.

With flattering chatter you amused your parents, so lovingly your little mouth twittered on. Yet, you, the two-year-old, cruel Hades took away from your mother's lap, sweet Nikopolis, Greetings, infant, may light earth cover your body, once strong sprig of Sarapion.

---

26 PM no. 392; Bobou 2015, 110.

Perhaps the grief-stricken parents of Nikopolis had bought an already-made stele,[27] but it is just as likely that the stele was commissioned on purpose. This is not as important, however, when thinking of the stele's function as a grave marker. What was significant was that it was a permanent memorial of Nikopolis; for the parents the image on the stone would have represented their daughter, and displayed their hopes that Nikopolis would have become a fashionable, strong young woman with all the markers of a wealthy upbringing (servant and dog). In this way, the image of the dead Nikopolis as a young woman, was an 'empty delight to the eyes' of her parents.

The text creates an added tension between reality (the death of a two-year-old) and hope (Nikopolis as a young adult). For the illiterate viewers of the stele, for whom the text would have been more a marker of wealth rather than a medium of imparting information, the dead girl would have been firmly fixed in their minds as a young woman of means and taste.

These two stelai, however, of Themistokles and Nikopolis, open a tempting possibility for us modern viewers of such monuments: that even in stelai where we have a seemingly typical imagery focusing on the child's daily life, we might be dealing with an image that represents expected hopes rather than actual reality.

For example a mid-fourth century BC stele from Athens for the girl Neiottion shows a seated pudgy girl holding a pet bird in her right hand looking down at her toy dog that jumps towards her.[28] At first glance this looks like a scene from a playful, happy childhood inside the house.

As a domestic scene one can also describe the depiction on the stele of a young girl from the second century BC: the girl is looking downwards, the seated mother is staring at her, two servants (in smaller scale) embrace each other and look down, while on a pillar behind the girl are a kalathos, a box and a snake. Although there are clear funerary connotations in the expressions, postures and symbols, the various objects (seat, kalathos, box) hint that the scene is taking place on the inside of the house rather than at the grave.

Considering that the Greeks rarely focused on the manner of death or the age of the deceased except in extraordinary cases,[29] it is likely that some of these stelai could be depicting images of the child as it would have been —not as it was at the

---

27 One could argue that this is the implication of the non-alignment between the text and the inscription.
28 Athens National Museum 2549; Schlegelmilch 2009, 45–46.
29 For example, death by accident or drowning. Recording the age became more popular from the second century BC onwards, but even then it was not the norm.

time of death. Obviously this cannot be proven, but should be considered a possibility.

The two stelai also show the interplay between hope and expectation in text and image: the epigram for Themistokles combines the two notions, but the image focuses on hope. In the epigram for Nikopolis there are no mentions of parental hopes or expectations, but the image gives us a representation of what kind of hopes they might have had for their daughter.

An epigram from the cult room of Artemis at Messene show how sub-adult experiences and hopes could be subordinated to adult, parental, ones. The cult room was part of the Asklepieion building complex at the centre of the city. Even though most of the rooms of the complex had political functions (bouleuterion / archives room), or were used as galleries showing the works of one of the most famous Messenian citizens, the sculptor Damophon, the goddess Artemis, and later the Theoi Sebastoi, were worshipped there.[30]

Inside the cult room of Artemis were found the statues of five young girls who had served as cult agents, as well as of three priestesses of the goddess; the statues of the girls date to the first centuries BC–AD, while those of the priestesses at the third century AD. Of these dedications, the one for the girl Mego is particularly important here: placed on a relatively high pedestal with a long inscription, it illuminates several aspects of the cult of Artemis at Messene.[31]

Τᾷ παρθένω τὰν παῖδα σοί με πότνια
Ὀρθεία Δαμόνικος ἠδ' ὁμευνέτις
Τιμαρχίς, ἐσθλοῦ πατρός, ἄνθεσαν Μεγὼ
τεὸν χερὶ κρατεύσασαν Ἄρτεμι βρέτας
ἄν τε πρὸ βωμῶν σῶν ἔτεινα λαμπάδα.
Εἴη δὲ κἀμὲ τὰν ἐπιπρεπέα χάριν
τεῖσαι γονεῦσιν. Ἔνδικον γὰρ ἔπλετο
καὶ παισὶ τιμᾶν φυτοσπόρους.

Damonikos and his wife Timarchis of noble father,
dedicated me the child Mego to you,
the virgin, the lady Ortheia,
having held in hand the statue
of Artemis and held up a torch
 before your altars.
May it be allowed that I show the appropriate gratitude

---

30 For the Asklepieion at Messene see Themelis 1998. For Damophon, see Themelis 1996, 154–187; Melfi 2016, 82–105.
31 For the statues at the *oikos* of Artemis: Connelly 2007, 147–157; Dillon 2010, 44; Bobou 2015, 59–62. For the statue of Mego, see also Schoch 2010, 242–245.

> to my parents.
> For it is right for the children too to honour
> those who gave them life.

The inscription explains Mego's particular choice of costume and attribute: she holds a representation of the archaic-looking image of the goddess in her hand, and wears distinctive clothes that seem to be the same as those of the other cult agents. She is represented in her role as cult agent taking part in the festival of Artemis.

Even though ἐλπίς is not mentioned in the text, the expression εἴη δὲ κἀμὲ τὰν ἐπιπρεπέα χάριν refers to a desired, future event, and as such can be interpreted as an expression of hope. This event does not depend upon Mego's abilities, education, or social standing, but rather fate, or the will of the gods, whatever power will allow Mego to grow old enough to return the favour shown to her by her parents.

What exactly does Mego hope to give to her parents in gratitude? That is not specified in the inscription; it is only presented as a just and appropriate thank-offering gift. Understanding the statue as part of a wider social and cultural framework can help us express some ideas about the possible gifts.

As we have seen earlier, a happy wedding day and a good marriage were considered important for all young people. For girls of elite families, especially, a successful marriage was one that united two upper-class, wealthy families, and created an alliance between them. Considering that such marriages were arranged by the parents, and not the future marriage partners, fulfilling this parental desire would be a way of honouring them, and showing them gratitude.

Another way to show gratitude and return the favour to one's parents was by taking care of them in their old age. This is expressed explicitly in a funerary epigram from Arkesine at Amorgos, where we read that the young man Philostorgos was raised "to be an anchor for [his mother's] old age". Even his name, 'the affectionate' is an expression of parental expectations and hopes.[32] Mego too could return the favour of her careful upbringing by taking care of her parents when they were old.

In addition to these potential, hoped-for gifts, I would like to propose another suggestion: that the favour that Mego is said to wish to return to her parents can be further specified, and situated within the broader culture of honours exchange in the period.

---

32 Chaniotis 2012, 104.

People, especially members of the elite, dedicated statues of themselves in sanctuaries from the very beginning of the use of monumental sculpture in the Greek world. Already, one of the very first statues that we have is that of Nikandre from Naxos, dedicated at the sanctuary of Artemis at Delos in the middle of the seventh century BC.[33]

Νικάνδρη μ' ἀνέθεκεν h(ε)κηβόλοι ἰοχεαίρηι κόρη Δεινο-
δίκηο τõ Ναχσίο ἔχσοχος ἀλ(λ)ήον Δεινομένεος δὲ κασιγνέτη
Φράχσο δ' ἄλοχος ν[ῦν].

Nikandre dedicated me to the far-shooter of arrows, the excellent daughter of Deinodikes of Naxos, the sister of Deinomenes, the wife of Phraxos.

Nikandre proudly proclaims her origin and familial connections in the inscription, and is at the beginning of a long line of members of the elite commemorating themselves or their family members in the guise of statuary dedications. However, most of these elites were men in the archaic and classical period.

From the fourth century BC onwards we see a rise in the number of statues dedicated by women for themselves and/or for family members. Two prominent examples are those of Aristaineta and Demokrite. Aristaineta put up statues of herself and her father at Delphi,[34] while Demokrite put up statues of herself and her son at the sanctuary of Amphiaraos at Oropos.[35] Men, of course, continued dedicating statues of themselves and of their family members in sanctuaries and other appropriate public spaces.

Thus, it is possible that Mego's parents also hoped for a statue in return for the statue they put up. Such an act would put them on a par with other elite families. It would create a statement about the kind of parents they had been, but also about the continuing power of their family.

The phrase used in the epigram 'it is just to honour' is also reminiscent of the language of honours in civic decrees,[36] in this case adjusted for a non-civic context.[37] This formulation shows humility and political savviness in adapting, not copying, the language of public honours.

---

[33] Dillon 2002, 9–11; Connelly 2007, 125–127.
[34] Dillon 2010, 37, 48–49; Scott 2014, 176.
[35] Dillon 2010, 49; Ma 2013, 188–189, 207, 221; Bobou 2015, 69.
[36] For example, IG II³ 1285, ln. 8: καθήκει δὲ τιμᾶν τοὺς ἀξίους; IG V,1 26, ln. 12–13: τὰς καταξίους τιμάς.
[37] See Ma 2013, 203 for an example of a statue of a father set up by the son at the sanctuary of Apollo at Kalymnos in gratitude for bringing up from infancy to adolescence.

If funerary and votive material reflects private, individual hopes and expectations, the speech by the Athenian Publius Aelius Isochrysus from the deme of Phlya reveals civic-oriented hopes for sub-adults. The speech was delivered during the festival of Theseus, a festival that was instituted in the first half of the fifth century BC (475 or 469 BC) when Kimon returned the bones of Theseus from Skyros to Athens. With the introduction of the *ephebeia*, the formal, military training and patrolling of Attica by the Athenian youths, during the archonship of Lycurgus, Theseus' festival became more prominent and probably included athletic competitions, as well as the customary procession and sacrifices.[38]

We are more familiar with the structure of the festival in the second century BC thanks to the epigraphic record. It was organised by an *agonothetes*, and comprised of a sacrifice to Theseus, races and other regular athletics (stadium, dolichos, wrestling, boxing etc), torch race, armed competitions, and equestrian competitions.[39] An *agonothetes* continued to be responsible for the organization of the games in the Roman imperial period (*IG* II² 1996, *IG* II² 2193, *IG* II² 2196, *IG* II² 2203), while thanks to the inscription put together by S. Follet and D. Peppas-Delmouzou we now know that the festival included a funeral oration to the Theseus on one of the days of the festival, and a speech to the *ephebes* delivered the following day.[40]

Publius Aelius Isochrysus was the agonothetes for the Theseia, as well as a gymnasiarch and archon of the *ephebes* in AD 184/5. His name reveals that he was a Roman citizen too, while he may have been related to an Aelius Isochrysus from Phlya, prytanes in or around AD 175.[41]

His speech had the stated purpose to incite the zeal of the *ephebes*, and to make them follow in Theseus' footsteps. Aelius Isochrysus reminds his audience that Theseus, while an *ephebe*, performed the feats that made him a hero and "in this way was of the greatest benefit to the citizens and the *ephebes*." The *ephebes* listening to the speech do not have to fight against monsters, but for virtue and

---

38 Even though Lycurgus institutionalized the *ephebeia*, the practice of providing young adults with military training is attested already in the fourth century BC (Xen., *Poroi*, 4.52, Aeschin. 1 49; 3. 167. Gehrke, http,//dx.doi.org/10.1163/1574-9347_bnp_e331340 (consulted online on 17 July 2017); Sommerstein 2010, 50–51. The Lycurgan reform dates in the mid-330s; the precise date is not known, with 336–35 and 334/3 BC being the most likely years when the law was passed. On the post-330s *ephebeia* see also: Kyle 1993, 40; Walker 1995, 101.
39 Bugh 1990, 20–37; Kennel 1999, 249–262; Kyle 1993, 40–41. The races were in the nude: *IG* II² 957: τοῦ γυμνικοῦ ἀγῶνος; for nude races see Miller 2004, 13–14.
40 Follet and Peppas-Delmouzou 2000, 11–17; *SEG* 50.155.
41 Meritt 1964, 168–227, esp. 220–222, no. 66; Meritt and Traill 1974, 282–283, no. 392; Follet and Peppas-Delmouzou 2000, 15.

in noble competition among each other. This is because the *ephebes* "carry the hopes of the city".

While an individual's hope for athletic victories and glory are promoted in the privately funded funerary monuments as the "hopes of the homeland", in this speech that was aimed directly at the city's youths, and was commissioned, written, and performed by a civic official, we see how 'the hope of the city' is expressed in a more abstract way. It is a struggle for virtue and a noble competition, an ἀγὼν τῆς ἀρετῆς, a word ordinarily used for athletic competitions. The association of virtue and athletics is taken out of the world of the gymnasium, and into the broader context of participating in civic life and working for the common benefit of the city.

This inscription, as well as that of the statue of Mego gives us an insight into the world of local elites and their hopes for their offspring, while the funerary inscriptions reveal the (dashed) hopes and expectations of members of the local elite and middle-class. My last example gives us an unparalleled view inside the world of the non-elites.

The letter of Lesis was written in a lead tablet and found inside a well in the Athenian Agora.[42] From the way the letters were written (carefully and not in a hurry), it has been suggested that they were written by a scribe, and not Lesis himself. The find location suggests that it was never delivered.

Lesis writes: Λῆσις ἐπιστέλλει Ξενοκλεῖ καὶ τῆι μητρὶ μηδαμῶς περιιδεν αὐτὸν ἀπολόμενον ἐν τῶι χαλκείωι, ἀλλὰ πρὸς τὸς δεσπότας αὐτο ἐλθεν καὶ ἐνευρέσθαι τι βέλτιον αὐτῶι. Ἀνθρώπωι γὰρ παραδέδομαι πάνυ πονηρῶι· μαστιγόμενος ἀπόλλυμαι δέδεμαι· προπηλακίζομαι· μᾶλλον μᾶλλον.

Lesis is sending (a letter) to Xenokles and to his mother by no means to overlook that he is perishing in the foundry but to come to his masters and find something better for him. For I have been handed over to a man thoroughly wicked; I am perishing from being whipped; I am tied up; I am treated like dirt-more and more!

His hope is that the recipients of his letter will act quickly, intercede with his masters and, they, in turn, will have him placed at a different work location with better work conditions.

There are two remarkable things in this document. The first is the rare glimpse of a non-elite's life from his own perspective. We do not know if Lesis was a slave or an apprentice. We have very little evidence for the apprenticeship

---

42 Harvey 2007, 49–50; Jordan 2000, 91–103; Harris 2004, 157–170; Ceccarelli 2013, 45–46.

system and the treatment of the apprentices in the classical period.[43] We are better informed for the Roman period, and the information shows that the conditions could be very harsh, with little differentiation in the treatment of slaves and apprentices, even though brutality against freeborn children was generally discouraged and not approved.[44] This means that, for us, and our understanding of hope, Lesis' legal status makes little difference.[45]

The second extraordinary thing is the hope expressed: for better work conditions. It is a modest hope –and perhaps a realistic one. If Lesis was an apprentice, then his appeal to his mother can be compared to a later one, that of another famous apprentice who suffered under his master: Lucian of Samosata. As Lucian himself recounts, after having been beaten at his uncle's studio on the first day of learning how to be a sculptor, he went back to his mother, who 'railed at her brother for his cruel treatment' (Lucian, *The dream* 4).[46] Unlike, Lucian, though, Lesis was not able to appeal directly to his mother, and had to use a letter. Perhaps, like later apprentices, his work place was in a place that was not close to him.[47]

But if Lesis was a slave, then it is possible to imagine a more complicated scenario: Lesis might have already seen how his mother's success in securing her own income might have eventually brought her her freedom,[48] or brought her in contact with Xenokles (who may be her new partner or owner). If, as some scholars have suggested, the letter was written by a scribe, then Lesis already had access to some funds himself to be able to hire a scribe.

Lesis creates a picture that conforms to social expectations, and is usually known to us through texts of slave owners. In the *Oeconomicus* by Xenophon, the slave owner and master is idealized and represented as just, fair, and having the welfare of his slaves in mind.[49]

In several slave narratives from North America from the mid-18th century onwards, we see the same phenomenon: the master is described as kind, attentive, providing them with shelter, material goods, and education. These narratives were heavily edited by white sponsors, and the slavery experience was presented

---

43 Wendrich, 2013, 186–191.
44 Laes 2013, 189–195.
45 See also Vlassopoulos in this volume.
46 Freu 2016, 183–199, 186.
47 For apprenticeships in remote locations or without the option of leaving before a set time, see Freu 2016, 186; Huebner 2013, 77.
48 For the possibilities of acquiring their freedom open to slaves in classical Athens, see Rihll 2011, 48–73, esp. 56–58.
49 Pomeroy 1994.

through a white man's lens.⁵⁰ As a result a whole class of masters appears as benevolent and having the slave's best interest's in mind, similar to the master presented by Xenophon in the *Oeconomicus*.

Lesis' letter shows the pervasiveness and dominance of the system, even the internalisation of the slave status: Lesis does not blame his masters for his situation; he blames the people to whom he was sent. He does not get in touch with his masters directly, but rather relies on the small family network he has. Even his hope does not include what we would expect: freedom.

Lesis' mental horizon for the hopes he could have was severely limited by his legal status.⁵¹ His letter is one the most poignant expressions of yearning for a positive change in the future, one that is not expected because of status, family connections, wealth, or other accomplishments, as in the previous examples. His hope is born out of desperation for his current situation, not out of pleasure or happiness or satisfaction with the present, as was the case with the hopes/expectations we saw expressed earlier.

His ἐλπίς, a word that is not expressed in his letter, is also a motivational force for making him act and seek out a scribe to write the letter for him. It also helps him suffer his current situation, as he hopes that, through his mother's aid, his life will change for the better. This hope, limited as it may seem to us, helps him 'sustain an appreciation of life', as Lazarus would put it.⁵²

In the private sphere, as we can see from Lesis' letter, hope could offer protection against despair; in the public sphere however, and especially in the funerary monuments, hope for the future was constructed and thought of in association with a positive present. It also had several nuances: sometimes a combination of yearning and expectation, sometimes simply the desire for something positive, sometimes just the anticipation of a successful event after hard work.

It is important to note again the disjunction between text and image; the imagery is grounded on the present, rather than the future, and works closely, but does not replicate the text, even when it touches upon it. For example, the image

---

50 The Oxford and Cambridge companions to slave narratives offer good introductions to the genre, its reception, and historical context: Ernest 2014; Fisch 2007. Already in what is perhaps the first of an African American slave narratives, that of Briton Hammon, the master is described as 'good old Master', a theme that appears often in the genre: see Sekora 1987, 482–515, esp. 486–487; for narratives of convicted slaves see Sekora 1987, 489–490.
51 Although one would like to hope that it was also tinged by pragmatism: that Lesis knew that a better apprenticeship and better training would lead to a well-paying job that would lead to freedom eventually.
52 Lazarus 1999, 655.

in the stele of Themistokles expands upon the 'victorious at games' adjective, without having any of the usual imagery of victory (palms and wreaths). It also shows the boy as older than his years. The stele of Themistokles also shows that more prospective images of sub-adults can be hidden in plain sight.

The evidence from other stelai reveals another characteristic relative to expressions of hope: hope for an afterlife is expressed through multivalent or ambiguous imagery such as that of the funerary banquet; explicit images are rare and could have perhaps been found on funerary paintings of tombs such as that of the hypogeum of the Octavii at Rome.

Like most of the evidence relating to the lives of children in the Graeco-Roman world, they present us with an adult view. The use of first-person in inscriptions lends immediacy to the texts and creates the impression that the children themselves shared these hopes. My focus has been on uncommon types of monuments, but these throw into sharper relief the common and expected forms of expression of hope, and reveal how it was culturally shaped. This means that children themselves probably shared these hopes —though to what extent will remain unknown.

Abbreviations

Pauly-Wissowa	Pauly, A., Wissowa, G., *Realencyclopädie der classischen Altertumswissenschaft* (Stuttgart: J. B. Metzler, 1893–1980)
New Pauly	Cancik, H., Schneider, H., Landfester, M., Salazar, Chr. F. (eds.) *Brill's New Pauly: Encyclopaedia of the Ancient World* (Leiden: Brill, 2006)
Peek *GV*	Peek, W. *Griechische Vers-Inscriften* (Berlin: Akademie-Verlag, 1955)
Peek, *Grabgedichte*	Peek, W., *Griechische Grabgedichte* (Berlin: Akademie-Verlag, 1960)
PM	Pfuhl, E., Möbius, H. *Die ostgriechischen Grabreliefs*. Mainz am Rhein: Von Zabern, 1977-1979
SEG	*Supplementum Epigraphicum Graecum*
ZPE	*Zeitschrift für Papyrologie und Epigraphik*

Bibliography

Beaumont, L. 2013. "Shifting Gender: Age and Social Status as Modifiers of Childhood Gender in Ancient Athens," in: J. Evans Grubbs/T. Parkin/R. Bell (eds.), *The Oxford Handbook of Childhood and Education in the Classical World*, 195–206, Oxford.

Bobou, O. 2015. *Children in the Hellenistic World: Statues and Representation*, Oxford.

Brandis, K.G. 1897. *S.v.* Bithynien, *Pauly-Wissowa* III.1, 507–539.

Bugh, G.R. 1990. "The Theseia in Late Hellenistic Athens," in: *ZPE* 83, 20–37.

Ceccarelli, P. 2013. *Ancient Greek Letter Writing: A Cultural History (600 BC–150 BC)*, Oxford.

Chaniotis, A. 2012. "Moving Stones: The Study of Emotions in Greek Inscriptions," in: A. Chaniotis (ed.), *Unveiling Emotions: Sources and Methods for the Study of Emotions in the Greek World*, 91–129, Stuttgart.
Closterman, W. 2015. "Family Meals: Banquet Imagery on Classical Athenian Funerary Reliefs," in: K.F. Daly/L. Ann Riccardi (eds.), *Cities called Athens: Studies honoring John McK. Camp II*, 1–22, Lanham, Maryland.
Cohen, D.A. 2006. *Pillars of Salt, Monuments of Grace: New England Crime Literature and the Popular Culture*, Amherst.
Cohen, E.E. 2000. *The Athenian Nation*, Princeton.
Connelly, J.B. 2007. *Portrait of a Priestess: Women and Ritual in Ancient Greece*, Princeton.
Couilloud, M.-Th. 1974. *Les monuments funéraires de Rhénée*. Exploration archéologique de Délos 30, Paris.
Dillon, M. 2002. *Girls and Women in Classical Greek Religion*, London/New York.
Dillon, S. 2010. *The Female Portrait Statue in the Greek World*, Cambridge.
Draycott, C.M./M. Stamatopoulou (eds.) 2016. *Dining and Death: Interdisciplinary Perspectives on the 'Funerary Banquet' in Ancient Art, Burial and Belief*: Colloquia Antiqua, 16, Leiden.
Dumont, A./Th. Homolle, 1892. *Mélanges d'archéologie et d'épigraphie*, Paris.
Eckstein, A.M. 2008. *Rome Enters the Greek East: From Anarchy to Hierarchy in the Hellenistic Mediterranean, 230–170 BC*, Oxford/New York.
Ernest, J. (ed.) 2014. *The Oxford Handbook of the African American Slave Narrative*, Oxford.
Fantuzzi, M. 2004. "The Epigram," in: M. Fantuzzi/R. Hunter (eds.), *Tradition and Innovation in Hellenistic Poetry*, 283–349, Cambridge.
Fisch, A. (ed.) 2007. *The Cambridge Companion to the African American Slave Narrative*, Cambridge.
Follet, S./D. Peppas-Delmouzou. 2000. "La légende de Thésée sous l'empereur Commode d'après le discours d'un éphèbe athénien (Ig II2 2291 a + 1125, complétés)", in: *Romanité et cité chrétienne. Permanences et mutations, intégration et exclusion du Ier au VIe siècle. Mélanges en l'honneur d'Yvette Duval*, ed. Françoise Prévôt, 11–17, Paris.
Freu, Ch. 2016. "*Disciplina, patrocinium, nomen*: The Benefits of Apprenticeship in the Roman World," in: A. Wilson/M. Flohr (eds.), *Urban Craftsmen and Traders in the Roman World*, 183–199, Oxford.
Gabriel, R.A. 2010. *Philip II of Macedonia: Greater Than Alexander*, Washington, DC.
Golden, M. 1990. *Children and Childhood in Classical Athens*, Baltimore.
Harris, E.M. 2004. "Notes on a Lead Letter from the Athenian Agora," in: *HSCP* 102, 157–170.
Harvey, F.D. 2007. " 'Help! I'm Dying Here': A Letter from a Slave," in: *ZPE* 163, 49–50.
Jordan, D.R. 2000. "*A Personal Letter Found in the Athenian Agora*," in: *Hesperia* 69, 91–103.
Helly, B. 1973. *Gonnoi 2. Les Inscriptions*, Amsterdam.
Huebner, S.R. 2013. *The Family in Roman Egypt: A Comparative Approach to Intergenerational Solidarity and Conflict*, Cambridge.
Kah, D./P. Scholz. 2007. *Das hellenistische Gymnasion*, Berlin.
Kennel, N.M. 1999. "Age Categories and Chronology in the Hellenistic Theseia," in: *Phoenix* 53, 249–262.
Kurtz, D.C./J. Boardman. 1971. *Greek Burial Customs*, Ithaca.
Kyle, D.G. 1993. *Athletics in Ancient Athens*, Leiden.
Laes, C. 2013. *Children in the Roman Empire: Outsiders Within*, Cambridge.
Lazarus, R.S. 1999. "Hope: An Emotion and a Vital Coping Resource Against Despair," in: *Social Research* 66, 653–678.
Ma, J. 2013. *Statues and Cities: Honorific Portraits and Civic Identity in the Hellenistic World*, Oxford.

Melfi, M. 2016. "Damophon of Messene in the Ionian Coast of Greece: Making, Re-making, and Updating Cult Statues in the Second Century BC," in: M. Melfi/O. Bobou (eds.), *Hellenistic Sanctuaries: Between Greece and Rome*, 82–105, Oxford.
Mennen, I. 2011. *Power and Status in the Roman Empire, AD 193–284*, Leiden.
Meritt, B.D. 1964. "Greek Inscriptions," in: *Hesperia* XXXIII, 168–227.
Meritt, B.D./J.S. Traill. 1974. *Inscriptions: The Athenian Councillors. Athenian Agora XV*, Princeton.
Merkelbach, R./J. Stauber. 2000. *Steinepigramme aus dem griechischen Osten 2. Die Nordküste Kleinasiens (Marmarameer und Pontos)*, Berlin.
Miller, S.G. 2004. *Ancient Greek Athletics*, Berkeley.
Nigdelis, P. 2000. "Από τη Ραιδεστό στη Θεσσαλονίκη: η τύχη μίας επιγραφής της Περίνθου," in: *Tekmeria* 5, 148–150.
Parker, R. 2005. "Τέκνων ὄνησις," in: *ZPE* 152, 152–154.
Peres, I. 2003. *Griechische Grabinschriften und neutestamentliche Eschatologie*, Tübingen.
Pomeroy, S.B. 1994. *Xenophon. Oeconomicus. A Social and Historical Commentary, with a New English Translation*, Oxford.
Rihll, T.E. 2011. "Classical Athens," in: K. Bradley/P. Cartledge (eds.), *The Cambridge World History of Slavery, Volume 1. The Ancient Mediterranean World*, 48–73, Cambridge.
Rowan, C. 2012. *Under Divine Auspices: Divine Ideology and the Visualisation of Imperial Power in the Severan Period*, Cambridge/New York.
Sayar, M.H. 1998. *Perinthos-Herakleia (Marmara Ereğlisi) und Umgebung. Geschichte, Testimonien, griechische und lateinische Inschriften. Philosophisch-historische Klasse. Denkschriften [DAW]*, 269, Vienna.
Schlegelmilch, S. 2009. *Bürger, Gott und Götterschützling: Kinderbilder der hellenistischen Kunst*, Berlin.
Scholz, P./D. Wiegandt. 2015. *Das kaiserzeitliche Gymnasion*, Berlin.
Schwertheim, E. 1980. *Die Inschriften von Kyzikos und Umgebung. Teil 1: Die Grabtexte. Die Inschriften griechischer Städte aus Kleinasien 18*, Vienna.
Scott, M. 2014. *Delphi: A History of the Center of the Ancient World*, Princeton.
Sekora, J. 1987. "Black Message/White Envelope: Genre, Authenticity, and Authority in the Antebellum Slave Narrative," in: *Callaloo* 32, 482–51.
Sommerstein, A.H. 2010. *The Tangled Ways of Zeus: And Other Studies in and Around Greek Tragedy*, Oxford.
Suk Fong Jim, Th. 2014. *Sharing with the Gods: Aparchai and Dekatai in Ancient Greece*, Oxford.
Svenbro, J. 1993. *Phrasikleia: An Anthropology of Reading in Ancient Greece*, Ithaca.
Themelis, P.G. 1996. "Damophon," in: O. Palaggia/J.J. Pollitt (eds.), *Personal Styles in Greek Sculpture*, 154–187, Cambridge.
—— 1998. *Αρχαία Μεσσήνη, ο χώρος και τα μνημεία*, Athens.
Vérihlac, L.M. 1978–1982. *Παῖδες Ἄωροι. Poésie funéraire*, Athens.
Walker, H.J. 1995. *Theseus and Athens*, Oxford.
Waters, W.A. 2000. *Poetry's Touch, On Lyric Address*, Ithaca.
Wendrich, W. (ed.) 2013. *Archaeology and Apprenticeship Body Knowledge, Identity, and Communities of Practice*, Tucson.
Zarmakoupi, M. 2015. "Hellenistic & Roman Delos, the City & its Emporion," in: *Archaeological Reports* 61, 115–132.

Electronic resources

von Bredow, I. (Bietigheim-Bissingen), "Perinthus", in: H. Cancik/H. Schneider (eds.), *Brill's New Pauly, Antiquity volumes*. Consulted online on 30 September 2016 http://ezproxy-prd.bodleian.ox.ac.uk,2066/10.1163/1574-9347_bnp_e914230

Cairns, D. 2016. "Metaphors for Hope in Archaic and Classical Poetry," in: R.R. Caston/R.A. Caster (eds.) *Hope, Joy, and Affection in the Classical World*, 13–44, Oxford.

Gehrke, H.-J., "Ephebeia", in: H. Cancik/H. Schneider (eds.), *Brill's New Pauly, Antiquity volumes*. Consulted online on 17 July 2017 http://dx.doi.org/10.1163/1574-9347_bnp_e331340

Külzer, A. (Vienna), "Rheneia", in: H. Cancik/H. Schneider (eds.), *Brill's New Pauly, Antiquity*. Consulted online on 27 September 2016 http://ezproxy-prd.bodleian.ox.ac.uk,2066/10.1163/1574-9347_bnp_e1021930

Angelos Chaniotis
Elpis in the Greek Epigraphic Evidence, from Rational Expectation to Dependence from Authority

1 Hope and cognition: *elpis* as justified expectation

In the early first century CE the city of Lykosoura honored Xenarchos and his wife for their benefactions. Among other things, they had donated the funds needed for restoration work in the temple of Despoina.¹ The relevant passage is not well preserved, but it is clear that the temple was about to collapse ([ὅτι ἔμε]λλεν [πεσ]εῖν ὁ ναὸς τᾶ[ς θε]ο[ῦ, and, although this would offend the gods (κατὰ τοὺς θεοὺς ἀτοπήματος), the enormous expenses could not be covered by the city. The impeding disaster is, unsurprisingly, called an ἀτύχημα. If there had been a lacuna on the stone just before ἀτύχημα, no editor would have ever though of restoring the participle ἐλπιζόμενον. This is, however, what the author of this text wrote: τὸ ἐλπιζόμενον ἀτύχημα.

We have been accustomed to associate ἐλπίζω and ἐλπίς with positive hopes. But a quick look at *LSJ* shows that ἐλπίζω can denote things that are feared of or things to be expected.² In the text of Lykosoura ἐλπίζω means to 'expect something based on observation and experience'. Anyone who saw the deplorable state of that building, expected it to collapse sooner or later.

I have selected this text for the introduction to my paper, because it highlights the cognitive aspect of the words ἐλπίζω and ἐλπίς, i.e. the connection of *elpis* with observation, experience, and knowledge. The inscription from Lykosoura points to the particularities of hope as a feeling. Usually defined as a positive attitude of the mind, hope is much closer connected with judgment and appraisal than other emotions; the expectation of a positive (or in this case of a

---

Abbreviations of epigraphic publications are those of the *Supplementum Epigraphicum Graecum*. I am very grateful to Dr. Henry Heitmann-Gordon (University of Munich) for proofreading the text.

1 *IG* V.2.515 B 4–7: [ὅτι ἔμε]λλεν [πεσ]εῖν ὁ ναὸς τᾶ[ς θε]ο[ῦ, καὶ χρ]ηματίζοντ[ας περὶ τοῦ] γ[ιγνομέν?]ου κατὰ τοὺς θεοὺς ἀτοπήματος [- - ca. 20 - -]ου πανμεγέθους ἀναλώματος, ὧν δηλουμένω[ν π]ερι[βλεπομένας τ]ᾶς πόλιος πρὸς τὸ ἐλπιζόμενον ἀτύχημα ...
2 See also Cairns 2016, 17–8.

negative) outcome in the future is based on passed experiences.³ Let us see, for instance, a document concerning the delimitation of the sacred land of Apollo at Delphi. The arbitrator knew that his decision would disappoint at least one of the parties to the conflict; his verdict might be falling short of the claimant's expectations ([ε]ἰ καί τι [δ]όξει τῆς ἑκατέρων ἐλπίδος ἀφηρῆ[σθαι]).⁴ The different expectations of the claimants had their roots in the particularly problematic documentation. The evidence was not clear (τὰ τεκμήρια ... ἀμφιβολίαν εἶχεν), and the names of locations in earlier delimitations had changed;⁵ hence, both parties were convinced that they had legitimate claims. Their *elpis* was rationally founded.

A third example: In Nero's oration at Isthmia (67 CE), with which the emperor granted freedom and exemption from taxation to the Greeks, the emperor characterized his gift as ἀπροσδόκητον, 'not anticipated', because of its dimensions, but also as μηδὲν ἀνέλπιστον, 'not beyond reasonable expectation'.⁶ Whoever knew of Nero's magnanimity should be prepared for extraordinary donations. Here, again, the underlying meaning of *elpis* is that of expectation based on observation and reason.

Similarly, the so-called hortatory formula in a decree of Olbia prescribes the publication of an honorific decree:

> in order that those who read it will be informed about this man's virtue and will zealously emulate the benefactions towards the fatherland, expecting that they will also deservingly receive the same eternal honors, worthy of their achievement.⁷

The expectation was, again, based on observation and experience.

This close connection of *elpis* with reasoning and cognition characterizes hope as an emotion. Hope is a particular emotion also because it is not a response

---

3 Cf. Thumiger 2016, 201–2 and 207–8, on *elpis* in Hippocratic medicine. See also the introduction to this volume by G. Kazantzidis and D. Spatharas.
4 *F.Delphes* III.4.295 L. 10.
5 *F.Delphes* III.4.295 L. 6–7: τὰ τ[εκμήρια τὰ περὶ τ]ινων μερῶν ἀμφιβολίαν εἶχε[ν καὶ αἱ] ὀνομασίαι τῶν τόπων αἱ ἐν τῷ τῶν ἱερομνημόνων ἀφ]ορισμῷ διὰ τὸ τοῦ [χρόνου] μῆ[κος οὐ]κέτι ὁμοίως γεινωσκόμεναι.
6 *IG* VII 2713 (Oliver, *Greek Constitutions* no. 296) LL. 9–12: ἀπροσδόκητον ὑμεῖν, ἄνδρες Ἕλληνες, δωρεάν, εἰ καὶ μηδὲν παρὰ τῆς ἐμῆς μεγαλοφροσύνης ἀνέλπιστον, χαρίζομαι, τοσαύτην, ὅσην οὐκ ἐχωρήσατε αἰτεῖσθαι.
7 *IOSPE* I²: ἀναγραφῆναι] δὲ τὸ ψήφισ[μα τοῦτο ἐν στήλῃ λευκο]λίθῳ καὶ ἀν[ατεθῆναι ἐν τῷ ἐπισημοτά]τῳ τῆς πόλε[ως τόπῳ εἰς τὸ τοὺς ἐντυγχά]νοντας αὐτ[ῇ μαθεῖν τὴν τοῦ ἀνδρὸς ἀρετήν?] καὶ ζηλωτὰς γε[νέσθαι τῶν εἰς τὴν πατρί]δα πραχθέντων [ἀγαθῶν - - -] ἐλπίζοντας καὶ α[ὐτοὺς κατὰ τὴν ἀξίω]σιν τῶν αὐτῶν αἰων[ίων τιμῶν τεύξεσθαι].

to what has occurred —in this respect it differs, e.g. from grief, joy, disgust, and anger—, but an attitude towards what lies in the future, sharing this feature, e.g., with some forms of fear. This is why one of the meanings listed in *LSJ* under ἐλπίζω is that of 'to fear'. We find the association of *elpis* with reasoning already in an early funerary epigram in Athens, the epigram for the war dead in Poteidaia (432 BCE). According to the epigram, those of the enemies who had not been killed, run away and sought protection in the city, "making the city-wall the most dependable/trustworthy hope of survival".[8] Reason, not irrational hope but also not blind fear, led the Poteidaians to seek protection behind the fortification wall of their city. In this case, *elpis* was an instantaneous response to a specific threat. But the same word could also designate a general attitude: self-confidence connected with a positive attitude towards the future.

2 Deceived hope and the arousal of empathy

The common meaning of *elpis* as justified expectation is important for the appreciation of grave epigrams and grave inscriptions that refer to deceived hopes caused by the premature death of a young person.[9] These texts were meant to express grief and to arouse the pity of the reader precisely because of a death that defied reason and deceived expectation. An epigram from Maionia (214/5 CE) lists the family members who paid their respects to Glykia, a girl: the parents, the brother, the maternal uncle and aunt, and the two grandmothers. The deceased girl, speaking from the grave, bitterly observes on the respects paid by her grandmothers: "this is an honor that I never expected to receive."[10] How can a girl ever reasonably expect to be buried by her grandmothers?

Precisely the fact that *elpis* requires reasoning makes the poet of a Hellenistic epigram from Gaza use the verb σφάλλειν, 'to miss the target', in connection with the hopes of a father that were cut short with his son's early death.[11]

That the unexpected, usually premature, death of an individual has deceived the hopes or expectations of the parents, the relatives, the community or the

---

8 *IG* I³ 1179 LL. 8–9: ἐχθρōν δ' οἱ μὲν ἔχοσι τάφο μέρος, ho̱[ὶ δὲ φυγόντες] | τεῖχος πιστοτάτεν heλπίδ' ἔθεντο [βίο].
9 See also the chapters by O. Bobou and K. Heuer in this volume.
10 *TAM* V.1.550: ἐ δέ τε μάμμε Τειμογενὶς καὶ Τύχη τὴν ἔγγονον ἐτείμησαν ἐμέν, ἣν οὔποτε ἤλπισα τεμμήν.
11 *SEG* VIII 269: ἔσφηλεν δ' ἐλπίδα τις νέμεσις. For this metaphor see Cairns 2016, 35.

deceased person is a widespread *topos* in epitaphs.[12] Two epigrams from Cyprus and Italy respectively exemplify its use. In both cases the deceased individual speaks from the grave and names the parents as the victims of the deceived hope: "my elderly parents have lost their only hope"[13] and "a horrible fate has deprived my parents of the expectations they had of me".[14]

Two epigrams from Tomis and Kallatis that derive from the same archetype underscore the vainness of human expectations when compared with the power of Fate:

> Men do not control anything; everything revolves under the power of the Fates. So, I too was eager to raise my child and to bring it up to fulfillment of the expectations; but the verdict of the Fates was faster than my design; for this reason I buried it.[15]

Starting with a gnomic phrase of general application (οὐδὲν ἐπ' ἀνθρώποις, Μοίραις δ' ὕπο πάντα κυ<κλ>εῖται), the poet associates the individual misfortune of a parent with a universal experience: men are powerless in front of fate. The reader is invited to feel empathy, precisely because he/she too is subject to this universal law. This does not prevent a father from having a design, a plan (βουλή), based on reasoning: to eagerly raise and educate a child, hoping to see the results of the efforts. Using the verbs σπεῦδον and ἔφθασεν, the poet creates the image of a race, doomed to be lost.

The topos of the deceived hope remained popular in epitaphs throughout the Hellenistic and Imperial periods.[16] But repetition may weaken the impact of a

---

12   Earliest attestation in the fragmentary epigram from Megara: *CEG* I 134 (ca. 500 BCE). See also e.g. *IG* II² 6626 (Athens, 4th cent. BCE); *I.Histriae* 231 (Histria, 4th cent. BCE). The association of *elpis* and deception in Greek poetry is discussed by Cairns 2016, 40–1.
13   *Salamine* XIII 192 (Salamis, 2nd cent. BCE): οἱ δ' ὀλέσαντες ἐλπίδα τὰν μούναν γηραλέοι γενέται.
14   *GV* 1576 (Capri, 1st cent. CE): ἄρτι δὲ καὶ γονέων ἐλπίδ' ἐμὴν στερέσας. Cf. *I.Tomis* 459 (2nd/3rd cent.): μοῖ[ρ'] ὀλοὴ γονέων δὲ ἐλπίδας ἐστέρισε.
15   *I.Tomis* 384 = *SEG* XLVIII 980 (Tomis, 4th cent. CE): οὐδὲν ἐπ' ἀνθρώποις, Μύραις δ' ὕπο πάντα κυκλεῖται. | καὶ γὰρ ἐγὼ σπεῦδον θρέψαι τέκνον καὶ εἰς ἐλπίδας ἄγεσθαι, ἀλλ' ἐμέο βουλὴν κρίσις ἔφθασεν, οὕνεκα τυμβῶ. *I.Kallatis* 148 (3rd/4th cent. CE): οὐδὲν ἐπ' ἀνθρώποις, Μοίραις δ' ὕπο πάντα κυ<κλ>εῖται· | καὶ γὰρ ἐγὼ σπεῦδον θρέψαι τέκνον καὶ εἰς ἐλπίδας ἄγε<σ>θαι, | ἀλλ' ἐμέο βουλὴν κρίσις ἔφθασαί τ' οὕνεκα τυμβῶ.
16   E.g., *IG* XII.2.489: τὴν πολλὴν γονέων ἐλπίδ' ἀπωσάμενος (Mytilene, undated); *CIRB* 130 = *GV* 1989: τὰς δ' ἀτελέστους ἐλπίδας οὐχ ὁσίη Μοῖρα κατεχθόνισεν (Pantikapaion, 1st cent. CE); *I.Thespiai* 1247: τίς ἐλπίδες οὐ[κ ἐδάκρυσεν] τὰς ἀτελῖς γονέων (Thespiai, 3rd cent. CE); *I.Knidos* 82: σοὶ γὰρ ἐς Ἅδαν ἦλθον ὁμοῦ ζωᾶς ἐλπίδες ἀμετέρας (Knidos, 1st cent. BCE); *GV* 292: οἱ δὲ γον<ῆε>ς μύρονται κεναῖς ἐλπ[ί]σι τειρόμενοι (Herakleia on the Latmos, Imperial period); *I.Smyrna* 552: ἐλπίσι λιφθείς (Smyrna, 1st/2nd cent. CE); *SEG* II 616: κενεαῖσι ... ἐπ' ἐλπίσιν

statement; it makes it trivial. The more individualized the fate of the deceased and the bereft, the stronger the empathy the passer-by might feel. It is for this reason that we find numerous variations and specifications of the topos of deceived *elpis*. For instance, in order to strengthen the feeling of loss, poets paint vivid images of precisely what has been lost. In the epigram for the eleven-year-old Pardalas (Athens, 1st/2nd cent.), the hopes that fate destroyed were the hopes of being educated and reward his parents.[17] In another epigram from Pergamon (3rd cent. CE), the expectations of the parents are spelled out: "we hoped to deliver our child to a beautiful wedding bed, see it in a wedding chamber and pay the dowry."[18] The specificity of the expectation makes the contrast between hope and deception more painful, exactly as in a Hellenistic epigram from Egypt: instead of seeing his own grandchildren, as hoped for, a man leaves his own children orphans.[19] A common expectation of parents is of course that of being taken care of by their children in old age. As a text from Delos asserts, "one should wish to die away from hateful fate, delighting in the hope of children to take care of one in the old age".[20]

Possibilities for variation are also offered by the use of images and metaphors. A good example is offered by the epigram for a girl from Sestos (1st cent. CE). The message is the same —death put an end to hopes and expectations— but the imagery and the vocabulary are unique. The poet used the vocabulary of transactions —the verbs ἐναλλάσσω ('give in exchange') and παρατίθημι ('give as deposit')— in order to highlight the deception and increase the feeling of loss: by burying their child the parents traded off every hope; and the girl deposited all her hopes with Hades.[21] No consolation is offered to either parents or deceased.

ἀνδρωθέντα (Teos, 1st cent. BCE). Other examples (mostly fragmentary): *IG* II² 13147 (Athens, 2nd/3rd cent. CE); *IG* IV 620 (Argos, Imperial period); *IG* V.2.180 (Tegea, undated); *SEG* IV 91 (Puteoli, 3rd cent. BCE); *SEG* LI 673 (Atrax, undated); *I.Thespiai* 1258 (Thespiai, undated); *I.Tomis* 175 (1st cent. BCE); *IGUR* 1231 (Rome, Imperial period); *IG* XIV 2431 (Forum Iulii, 2nd cent. CE); *I.Ephesos* 2101 (Ephesos, undated).

17 *IG* II² 11477: παιδείας γὰρ ἐγὼ πινυτῆς ἤλπιζα γενέσθαι καὶ χάριτ' ἂν δοῦναι μητρὶ καὶ πατέρι.
18 *IvP* II 586: [ἠ]λπίσαμεν τέκνον παστοῖσι καλοῖς ἀποδοῦναι καὶ ἐν θαλάμοισιν ἰδεῖν φερνήν τε ἀποδοῦναι.
19 *SEG* XXVI 1808: υἱῶν θ' ἕξειν τέκνα ποτ' ἤλπισα, νῦν δὲ λέλοιπα | ὄρφανα τῆς φιλίας πατρὸς ἐμειρόμενα.
20 *I.Délos* 1852 (1st cent. BCE): θνά[σκε]ιν εὐχέσθω τις ἀπεχθέος ἄνδιχα μοίρας, | τερπόμενος τέκνων ἐλπίδι γηροκόμωι. Cf. *SEG* XXVI 1622: ὃν ἀνέτρεφε[ν] ἐλπίδα γήρους (Zeugma, Imperial period).
21 *I.Sestos* 58: ἐλπίδα καί μοι πᾶσαν ἐνηλλάξαντο τοκῆες | κατθέμενοι τύμβῳ χερσὶν ἐῇσι νέκυν. | ἀλλά, πάτερ, λείπω καί σοι πολύδακρυ τεκοῦσα, | ἐλπίδας ὑμετέρας Ἄιδι παρθεμένη.

The poem leaves the reader with a feeling of loss and a sense of injustice and cheating.

Another technique used in order to arouse empathy is the use of metaphors that show the violent destruction of hope. In a text from Miletos (1st cent. BCE) the hopes are thrown into empty space (βέβληνται πολέων ἐλπίδες ἐς τὸ κενόν).²² When Chreste died shortly before her marriage in Pantikapaion, her father who had raised her 'poured his hopes in fire and ashes' (1st cent. CE).²³ In another epigram from Pantikapaion for a young woman who died just before the wedding, fate is blamed for burying under the earth unfulfilled expectations (1st cent. CE).²⁴

Interestingly, a common metaphor in connection with *elpis* is that of cutting or cutting short, as if hopes are growing organisms, trees or branches, that grow together with the young person. An epigram from Macedonia put it this way: "But Hades has not learned how to feel pity; when I was twelve years old he brought me under the earth, cutting the hopes of my parents."²⁵ Another epigram, this time for a girl, also from Macedonia uses the metaphor of cutting hair (*keiro*), probably alluding to the cutting of hair as a sign of mourning: "Envy and Plouton, you have plundered a golden flower and sheared the most noble hopes of the parents".²⁶ This is a stereotypical expression, found almost verbatim, also in a contemporary epigram from Thessaly for a man, probably of more mature age.²⁷ The epitaph of a young woman from Delos uses the related metaphor of breaking.²⁸

Another variation can be introduced by increasing the number of those who had an expectation, beyond the circle of the family, and including the whole community or the whole of Greece, as in a text from Pherai (fourth cent. BCE): "Hellas expected that a young athlete would adorn Thessaly with crowns."²⁹ The epigram for a young man educated in the gymnasium in Perinthos (1st/2nd cent. CE)

---

22 *GV* 2081. Cf. Cairns 2016, 34, for the metaphor of 'empty hopes' in Greek poetry.
23 *CIRB* 141 = *GV* 949: εἰς φλόγα καὶ σποδιὴν ἐλπίδας ἐξέχεεν.
24 *CIRB* 130 = *GV* 1989: τὰς δ' ἀτελέστους ἐλπίδας οὐχ ὁσίη Μοῖρα κατεχθόνισεν; ἀτέλεστος here refers to the *telos* of the woman, i.e. marriage.
25 *EAM* 193 LL. 6–8: Ἄιδης ... ἐλπίδας ἐκκόψας ἡμετέρων τοκέω[ν] (Archangelos, 1st/2nd cent. CE). Cf. *IGUR* III 1148: βάσκανε δαῖμον οἵας οὐχ ὁσίως ἐλπίδας ἐξέταμες (Rome, undated).
26 *I.Beroia* 404: ὦ Φθόνε καὶ Πλουτεῦ, συλήσας χρύσεον ἄνθος καὶ κείρας γονέων ἐλπίδας ἐσθλοτάτας (Beroia, 2nd cent. CE).
27 *SEG* XXXV 630: ὦ Φθόναι καὶ Πλουτεῦ, συλήσας χρύσεον ἄνθος καὶ κείρας ἰδίων ἐλπίδας ἀθλοτάτας (Larisa, 2nd cent. CE). In this case, γονέων (parents) became ἰδίων (family); the ancient mason turned ἐσθλοτάτας, possibly by mistake, to ἀθλοτάτας.
28 *GV* 759: [ἐλπίδα νῦν] ἔκλασε (2nd cent. BCE).
29 *SEG* XXIII 433: Ἑλλὰς | ἤλπισε κοσμήσειν Θεσσαλίαν στεφ[ά]νοις.

enlarges the community of mourners by calling him a 'hope of the fatherland and the father'.[30]

3 The people's expectations on the elite

From private funerary epigraphy, the *topos* of the deceived expectations was taken over by the authors of civic decrees in honor of deceased benefactors who had already provided evidence of their generosity and from whom a city could, therefore, have expected further services, but also for the offspring of elite families.[31] In Olbia (2nd/3rd cent. CE), a decree for Dados states: "he was being praised by all and he was expected to fulfill all the liturgies, in accordance with the status of his family, but he was mercilessly snatched away when all-conquering fate came upon him."[32]

At first sight, such decrees seem to be expressions of grief and media of consolation. By highlighting the contrast between expectation and loss, they appeal to the empathy of the contemporary readers. But their aim went beyond display and arousal of emotion. To understand these decrees and the position of *elpis* in them, we need to place them in the context of a strategy of communication between people and elite. In a number of sources, the death of a benefactor is assimilated with the death of a family member. E.g. when Herodes Atticus died in Athens, the burial which was being performed by his freedmen in Marathon was interrupted by the Athenian *ephebes*, who "seized the body with their own hands", brought it back to Athens in procession, and buried it there, near the stadium. All the Athenians attended the funeral lamenting the death of their

---

30   *I.Perinthos* 214: ἤδη γυμνασίοις ἠσκημένον, ἔντροφον ἄθλοις, | παῖδά με καὶ πάτρης ἐλπίδα καὶ πατέρος, | ἐνγὺς καὶ κοτίνῳ φθονερὸς κατεκοίμισεν Ἅδης, | ψευσάμενος τόσσους εἰς ἀρετὴν καμάτους. Cf. *I.Histriae* 267 (1st cent. BCE/CE).

31   See e.g. the honorary decree for T. Statilius Lamprias, offspring of an elite family: *IG* IV² 83 (Epidauros, 1st cent. CE): ἡρπασμένου ὑπὸ τοῦ δαίμονος ἀπὸ μ[ε]γίστων ἐλπίδων ἐν τῆι πρώτηι τοῦ βίου ἡλικίαι. Cf. *IG* V.1.1524 L. 20 (Gytheion, Imperial period).

32   *IOSPE* I² 52 LL. 5–10: ἐπαινούμενός τε ὑπὸ πάντων καὶ ἐλπιζόμενος πάσας τὰς λειτουργίας ἐκ[τ]ελέσειν κατὰ τὸ ἀξίωμα τοῦ γένους, ὑπὸ πάντα νεικωμένης εἱμαρμένης ἐπιστάσης ἀφηρπάγη καὶ τῶν γονέων καὶ τῆς πατρίδος ἀνηλεῶς. Cf. LL. 15–18: ἡ βουλὴ καὶ ὁ δῆμος στεφανοῖ χρυσῷ στεφάνωι Δάδον Τουμβάγου παῖδα ἐλπίδων ἀγαθῶν ἀντεχόμενον. Similar formulations in two other decrees from Olbia (Imperial period): *IOSPE* I² 46 LL. 4–7: ἐλπιζόμεν[ος πάσας τὰς λειτουργίας ἐκτε]λέσειν τῇ πατρίδι, ὑπ[ὸ το]ῦ βασκάνου [καὶ ἀπαραιτήτ]ου καὶ πάντα νεικῶ<ντ>ος Π<λ>ουτέ[ως ἀφηρπάγη]η; *IOSPE* I² 51 LL. 9–11: [καὶ ἀεὶ] πλείονας ὑπεχόμενος [ἐλπίδας, ὑ]πὸ τοῦ ἀπαραιτήτου δαί<μ>ο[νος ἀφηρπάγη]η.

benefactor "like children who have lost a good father" (χρηστοῦ πατρὸς χηρεύσαντες).³³ In this and in similar cases, the participation of the entire community in the funeral created the fiction of the orphaned people. By demonstrating the people's grief and gratitude, those who staged such public demonstrations of grief encouraged other members of the elite to follow the benefactor's model. This fiction of an intimate, family-like relation between the people and the elite was also manifested through honorary titles such as "the son of the people", 'the daughter of the people" etc. These titles created the illusion of a big family, in which the benefactors had to fulfil the role of a caring daughter, son, father or mother.³⁴ As part of this strategy, the *topos* of the deceived hope, deeply rooted in the expressions of grief by family members, contributed to the construction of the image of the city as a family, in which the city could have the same legitimate expectations of the wealthy elite as parents of their children.

Of course, when a young person, educated, wealthy, and prepared to take over the family traditions of benefactions, was dead, there was little to be expected of him. But by honoring him the communities encouraged others to live up to such hopes. This is explicitly stated, e.g., in a decree from Kolophon (2nd cent. BCE), which honors a man in order that "it becomes visible that the council and the people honor in a worthy manner the virtuous men and those who have given many specimens of their virtue and those 'who give the best hopes' (τὰς ἀρίστας ἐλπίδας διδόντας) for the future and that through such honors the council and the people encourage others to proceed to benefaction for all."³⁵

This strategy was, generally, successful, as we may judge from the contribution of benefactors to cities. But it also made the civic communities entirely dependent on the elite and its benefactions. The sources of communal hope were no longer the citizens but the notables. Precisely because of this feeling of dependence, from about the second century BCE on, benefactors were not only honored for their past services but also for a city's future expectations. A decree for a local statesman in Beroia (ca. 100 BCE) e.g. puts it this way: "he is worthy of honor

---

33   Philostr., *Vitae sophist*. XV, 20: ἀποθανόντος δὲ αὐτοῦ ἐν τῷ Μαραθῶνι καὶ ἐπισκήψαντος τοῖς ἀπελευθέροις ἐκεῖ θάπτειν Ἀθηναῖοι ταῖς τῶν ἐφήβων χερσίν ἁρπάσαντες ἐς ἄστυ ἤνεγκαν προαπαντῶντες τῷ λέχει πᾶσα ἡλικία δακρύοις ἅμα καὶ ἀνευφημοῦντες, ὅσα παῖδες χρηστοῦ πατρὸς χηρεύσαντες. See Chaniotis 2006, 224–5. For similar cases of interrupted funerals see Jones 1999.
34   Van Nijf 2013, 383–7. On these titles see Canali De Rossi 2007.
35   *SEG* XXXIX 1243: ἡ βουλὴ καὶ ὁ δῆμος φαίνηται τοὺς ἀγαθοὺς ἄνδρας καὶ πολλὰ δείγματα τῆς ἀρετῆς τεθικότας καὶ εἰς τὸν μέλλοντα χρόνον τὰς ἀρίστας ἐλπίδας διδόντας καὶ ἀξίως τειμῶντες καὶ προτρεπόμενοι διὰ τῶν <τ>οιού{ν}των ἐπὶ τὰς εὐεργεσίας τὰς κοινάς.

for many reasons, both for what is present and for what is expected".³⁶ When an association in Mantineia honored its benefactor Nikippa for her past services (ca. 64–61 BCE), it did so "in order that the association appears to be grateful and also that it has good hopes for the future".³⁷ In Amastris, a woman was honored for all her virtue and for giving a foretaste of what one could expect from her (98 CE).³⁸

That expectations, not services, justify honors is a radical change in the language of honorific decrees. The focus of the hope is shifted from the community, which may *have* hopes, to the benefactor who *is* a hope or *gives* hope.³⁹ These changes not only reflect the dependence of cities on benefactors; it also reflects a change in the perception of *elpis* and its use in public discourse. This change becomes more visible in the Imperial period.

4 Monarchical power as the source of *elpis*

Elpis is for the first time used in public documents (decrees, honorific inscriptions, letters) around 100 BCE. Then, from the reign of Augustus onwards, this word and its derivatives are continually invoked in documents concerning the relations between cities or provinces and the emperor. The vocabulary of *elpis* always appears in a particular context: that of the expectations a subordinate community has of a higher authority. The relevant passages refer to hopes that are entirely beyond the control and the power of citizen communities and depend on the goodwill and abilities of the emperor and his administration. *Elpis* now suggests weakness, subordination, loyalty, and trust.

The earliest attestation of this communicative function of *elpis* in the contacts between Greek communities and imperial power is to be found in the decree of

---

36 *I.Beroia* 2: διὰ πολλὰ καὶ ἐν τοῖς παροῦσιν ὧν τειμῆς ἄξιος καὶ ἐν τοῖς ἐλπιζομένοις.
37 *IG* V.2.265 LL. 38–41: ἵνα ... [φ]αίνηται ἁ σύ[ν]οδος εὐχάριστος οὖ[σα ἔχουσά τ]ε καὶ περὶ τῶν μελλόντων ἀγαθὰς ἐ[λ]πίδας.
38 Marek 1985, 159 no. 4: πάσας ἀρετᾶς καὶ ὧν προέδειξεν ἐλπίδων ἕνεκα.
39 Members of the elite being a hope: *I.Perinthos* 214 (Perinthos, 1st/2nd cent. CE): πάτρης ἐλπίδα; *I.Ancyra* 83 (Ankyra, ca. 150 CE): νέαν ἐλπίδα τῆς πατρίδος. Members of the elite giving hope: *I.Iasos* 90: τὰς μεγίστας παρεχόμενον ἐλπίδας τῶι δήμωι (Iasos, 1st cent. CE); *SEG* XXXIX 1243: τὰς ἀρίστας ἐλπίδας διδόντας (Kolophon, 2nd cent. CE); *IOSPE* I² 79 LL.16–7 (Olbia, early 1st cent. CE): προετρέψατο δὲ εἰς πλήονας ἐλπίδας τόν τε δᾶμον; *I.Napoli* I 44 L. 20 (letter of the benefactor of an association to his association): ἀλλὰ καὶ ἔτερα ὑμᾶς ἐλπίζειν παρ' ἐμοῦ (Neapolis, 194 CE); see also the inscriptions in notes 36 and 55.

the cities of Asia with which they honored Augustus by making his birthday the first day of the year (9 BCE).⁴⁰

> Born with this virtue, the Caesar has exceeded the hopes of those who anticipated (benefactions from him), not only surpassing in all good things all the benefactors before him but also leaving to future benefactors no hope to be compared with him.

A few years later (1 BCE), a decree of the cities of Asia in honor of Augustus' grandson Caius Caesar describes Augustus with a similar phraseology,

> his providence has not only fulfilled the hopes of all people but has also surpassed them. For earth and sea are pacified and the cities blossom with order, concord, and prosperity; there is vigour and produce of everything good. And as men are full of good hopes for the future and good spirit in the present, they - - - with contests, sacrifices and hymns ...⁴¹

The emperor is the sole agency for the fulfillment of the hopes of the empire's population and the only source of hopes for future bliss, exactly as in Nero's oration (note 7) *elpis* is directly associated with imperial magnanimity. Two more Greek decrees connect *elpis* with imperial power. In a decree of Assos for Caligula (37 CE)⁴² and a decree of Athens for Geta (209 CE)⁴³ the ascension of a new emperor is presented as the fulfillment of the humanity's hopes.

The close interdependence between *elpis* and imperial goodwill is a common feature of epigraphic texts in this period. The author of an honorific decree for an envoy of the Boiotians to Caligula (37 CE) describes the imperial letter is the

---

40 Most recent edition, based on copies found in Apameia, Eumeneia, Maionia, Metropolis and Priene in *I.Priene (2014)* 14 LL. 36–9: ἐν ᾗ καὶ γεννηθεὶς ὁ Καῖσαρ τὰς ἐλπίδας τῶν προλαβόντων ἐν ταῖς εὐεργεσίαις ὑπερέθηκεν, οὐ μόνον τοὺς πρὸ αὐτοῦ γεγονότας πᾶσι τοῖς ἀγαθοῖς ὑπερβαλόμενος, ἀλλ' οὐδ' ἐν τοῖς ἐσομένοις ἐλπίδ[α] τῆς συνκρίσεως ἀ[π]ολείπων.

41 *GIBM* 894 + *SEG* IV 201 LL. 7–14: οὗ (sc. Augustus') ἡ πρόνοια τὰς πάντων [ἐλπί|δ]ας οὐκ ἐπλήρωσε μόνον ἀλλὰ καὶ ὑπερῆρεν· εἰρηνεύο[υ|σ]ι μὲν γὰρ γῆ καὶ θάλαττα, πόλεις δὲ ἀνθοῦσιν εὐνομία[ι] ὁμονοίαι τε καὶ εὐετηρίαι, ἀκμή τε καὶ φορὰ παντός ἐστι[ν ἀ]γαθοῦ, ἐλπίδων μὲν χρηστῶν πρὸς τὸ μέλλον, εὐθυμία[ς | δ]ὲ εἰς τ[ὸ] παρὸν τῶν ἀνθρώπων ἐνπεπλησμένων, ἀγῶ[σ]ιν κά[ναθή]μασιν θυσίαις τε καὶ ὕμνοις τὴν ἑαυτῶν ---

42 *I.Assos* 26 LL. 5–7: ... ἐπεὶ ἡ κατ' εὐχὴν πᾶσιν ἀνθρώποις ἐλπισθεῖσα Γαΐου Καίσαρος Γερμανικοῦ Σεβαστοῦ ἡγεμονία κατήγγελται, οὐδὲν δὲ μέτρον χαρᾶς εὕρηκε ὁ κόσμος ("since the rule of Gaius Caesar Germanicus Augustus has been announced, a rule for which all men have hoped for in accordance with their prayers, the world cannot find a measure for its joy").

43 *IG* II² 1077 LL. 17–22: ἐπειδὴ ἡ ἱερωτάτη καὶ τελεω[τάτη πασ]ῶν [ἡ]μερῶν καὶ ὑπὸ πάντων ἐλπισθεῖσα διὰ τὴν ἀθάνατον ὁμόνοιαν τῶν ὁσίων βασιλέων ... ὑπὸ τῶν μεγάλω[ν βασιλέων κοινῶι κη]ρ[ύγμ]ατι πᾶσιν ἀν[θ]ρώποις δεδήλωται ... ("since through joint declaration of the great king the most sacred and most perfect of all days has been announced, the day that all had hoped for in view of the everlasting concord of the holy kings").

source of hopes.⁴⁴ In 126/127 CE an embassy of the Achaeans was sent to Hadrian, "begging him to accept the honors that they had voted for him with expectations" (ἐ]ν ἐλπ[ίδι ἐψηφισμένας).⁴⁵ Also the representatives of imperial authority, emperors and governors, exploited the motif of *elpis* in their texts, in order to stress the fact that the emperor was the source of hope.⁴⁶

5 A power that defies reason: *elpis* and the perception of the divine

This change in the use of *elpis* in the epigraphic material is connected with deep changes in society and communal organization —the rise of monarchy and the dependence of cities on benefactors. In the texts that concern the communication between the people and either benefactors or the imperial authority, *elpis* is used to highlight joy for benefactions that exceed reasonable expectations. The authors of religious texts, especially narratives of miracles, went one step further: they used *elpis* in contexts that allowed their audiences recognize the fact that divine power defies human reasoning. The crucial word in these contexts is the verb ἀπελπίζομαι/ἀφελπίζομαι, typically used to introduce sick people in accounts of healing miracles. A dedication from Philadelpheia (2nd/3rd cent. CE) was made by a man "about whom everyone had lost hope but was saved by" a deity, whose name is not preserved on the stone (ἀφελπισθεὶς ὑπὸ π[άντων καὶ] σωθεὶς ὑπ[ὸ - -]).⁴⁷ In Rome, two of the healing miracles of Asclepius (2nd cent. CE) introduce the healed men with the phrase ἀφηλπισμένῳ ὑπὸ παντὸς

---

44 IG 2711 LL. 68–9: ἤνεν{εν}κεν ἀπόκριμα πρὸς τὸ ἔθνος πάσης [φιλαν]θρωπίας καὶ ἐλπίδων ἀγαθῶν πλῆρες ("he brought to the federation a response which is full of benevolence and good hopes"); LL. 107–9: τὸ ἀπόκριμα καὶ πρὸς ἡμᾶς [τοῦ ν]έου Σεβαστοῦ διεκόμισεν πάσης ἐλπίδος [φι]λανθρωπίνης πλῆρες ("he brought to us the response of the new Augustus, full of every benevolent hope").
45 SEG XI 1198 (Olympia): ἐπειδὴ πρεσβεία ἐπέμφθη πρὸς τὸν] [θειότ]ατον Αὐτοκράτ[ορα Κα]ίσαρα Τραϊανὸν Ἀδριανὸν Σεβαστόν, δι' ἧς ἐδέοντο αὐτὸν οἱ Ἀχαιοὶ προσδέξασθαι τ]ὰς τειμὰς τὰς ὑπ' [αὐτῶν ἐ]ν ἐλπ[ίδι ἐψηφισμένας.
46 See e.g. an edict of the governor of Εγpt (68 CE): *I.Prose* 57 A LL. 16–21: ἵνα δὲ εὐθυμ[ότεροι πάντα ἐλπί[ζητε παρὰ τοῦ ἐπιλάμψαντος ἡμεῖν ἐπὶ σω]τηρίᾳ τοῦ παντὸς ἀν[θρώπων γένους εὐεργέτου Σεβαστοῦ Αὐτοκράτορος [Γ]άλβ[α τά τε πρὸς σωτηρίαν καὶ τὰ πρὸς ἀπόλαυσιν] καὶ γεινώσκη[τε] ὅτι [ἐφρόντισα τῶν πρὸς τὴν ὑμετέραν βοήθει]αν ἀνηκόντων; letter of the emperors Traianus Decius and Herennius Etruscus to Aphrodisias (250 CE): *IAPh2007* 8.114 LL. 14–5: συναύξειν ἑτοίμως ἔχοντες ὑμῶν καὶ τὰς πρὸς τὸ μέλλον ἐλπίδας.
47 TAM V.31647; cf. TAM V.3.1553: ἀφελπισθοῦσα ὑπὸ ἀνθρώπων.

ἀνθρώπου ("about whose healing everyone had given up hope").⁴⁸ When the unexpected healing occurred, the faith of the worshippers in divine power increased; this is why these narratives were inscribed on stone.

Christianity promoted further the transformation of *elpis* from reasonable expectation to expression of dependence by associating *elpis* with unconditional faith.⁴⁹ But the journey of *elpis* into the world of Christianity lies beyond the chronological limits of this study.

6 Conclusions: having *elpis*, being *elpis*, receiving *elpis*

Inscriptions are more than texts. They are monuments in public display. They are more evenly spread over the Greek world than literary texts, and they permit the examination of linguistic usage over long periods of time. For these reasons, epigraphic texts are suitable sources for the study of how terms of emotions are used in particular contexts and how this usage develops under the influence of social and cultural factors.

Most epigraphic attestations of *elpis* show the obvious: hopes and expectations are connected with cognition and judgment. When *elpis* motivates an athlete to continue fighting until the ultimate victory, it is because his hope is based on his training, his skills, and his strength.⁵⁰ In these cases, people *have* hopes,⁵¹

---

48 *IGUR* 148: ... Λουκίῳ πλευρειτικῷ • καὶ ἀφηλπισμένῳ • ὑπὸ παντὸς ἀνθρώπου ... καὶ ἐσώθη. ... αἷμα ἀναφέροντι Ἰουλιανῷ ἀφηλπισμένῳ ὑπὸ παντὸς ἀνθρώπου ... καὶ ἐσώθη. *Elpis* appears in a fragmentary context in the account of a miracle in the sanctuary of Amphiaraos in Oropos (late 4th cent. BCE): *I.Oropos* 301 = *SEG* XLVII 498. See also *IG* X.2.2.302 (Derriopos, 3rd cent. CE): a man dedicated a statue of Asclepius, full of hope (ἐλπίδας εὖ φορέων).
49 E.g. *IGLS* IV 1427 (Apamene, Syria, Late Antiquity): μ[ακ]άριος ἄνθρωπος ὁ ἐ[λπίζων] ἐπὶ [Κύ]ριον, κὲ οὐ μὴ ἀπω[λεῖται]; *SEG* VII 875 (Gerasa, 6th cent.): σῶσον τὸν δοῦλον σοῦ, ὁ θεός, τὸν ἐλπίζοντα ἐπί σε. For the association of πίστις and ἐλπίς see e.g. *IGLS* IV 1460/1461, 1732.
50 Honorific decree for Tiberius Claudius Rufus (Olympia, early 2nd cent. CE): *I.Olympia* 54 LL. 9–11: τάς τε γυμνασίας ἐν ὄψει τῶν ἑλληνοδικῶν κατὰ τὸ πάτριον τῶν ἀγώνων ἔθος ἀπέδωκεν ἐπιμελῶς, ὡς πρόδηλον εἶναι τὴν ἐλπίδα τῆς ἐπὶ τὸν ἱερώτατον στέφανον αὐτῶι ("he performed the he qualification exercises in front of the hellanodikai, in accordance with the ancestral custom of the contests, as he clearly had the hope to win the most sacred wreath"); LL. 24–7: καὶ ὅτι μέχρι νυκτός, ὡς ἄστρα καταλαβεῖν, διεκαρτέρησε, ὑπὸ τῆς περὶ τὴν νείκην ἐλπίδος ἐπὶ πλεῖστον ἀγωνίσεσθαι προτρεπόμενος ("he continued fighting until the night, until the stars appeared, being encouraged by the hope of victory to increase his efforts in the competition").
51 See e.g. an honorary decree for an educated man, who died young: *SEG* LXII L. 8: θαυμαστὰς ἔχων ἐλπίδ[ας] (Trikka, early 2nd cent.).

and they have them because of rational judgment. When parents expect a child to thrive and take care of them in old age, it is because of the care that they had shown raising it and the education that they had provided. The people of Tomis moved from the despair (δυσελπιστία) that was caused by the lack of sufficient guards to hope (εἰς βελτ[ε]ίονας ἐλπίδας), when they managed to recruit a force of guards.[52] It is because expectations are rooted in human efforts that in curses *elpis* means expectations connected with one's trade.[53] Deceived hopes could arouse grief and empathy in funerary contexts precisely because of the close connection between *elpis* and reason.

From around 100 BCE, *elpis* for the first time also appears in public documents in the context of negotiations between unequal partners. In this new usage, the ultimate sources of communal *elpis* are the emperor and the elite. *Elpis* appears in contexts that express a community's dependence on benefactors and the emperor. The most extreme manifestation of this perception is when a text from Ankyra (ca. 150 CE), calls the benefactor Tiberius Claudius Procillianus 'the new hope of the fatherland' (νέαν ἐλπίδα τῆς πατρίδος).[54]

In the same period, in religious contexts *elpis* is removed from the area of human cognition and is associated with unconditional faith that may even defy reason. *Elpis* is not an expectation rooted in human judgment; it can be viewed as faith given to humans by divine powers. This is directly stated in a record of divine justice from Lydia (3rd cent. CE). A man believed that by violating a sacred regulation he had caused his son's illness. As he reports, the gods 'punished my son Eumenes, son of Eumenes, and placed him in a state resembling death; but my Fortune gave me hope'.[55] In this text *elpis* is not a feeling that is aroused in an individual on the basis of judgment but a feeling that is given to him by an external power.

---

52   *I.Tomis* 2 (ca. 100 BCE).
53   See e.g. two *defixiones* from Athens (3rd cent. BCE): *DT* 72: καταδήω ... (names) τούτων τῶν ἀνδρῶν καὶ γυναικ[ῶ]ν καὶ ἐλπίδας ... καὶ ἐργασίας [ἁ]πάσας ("I bind the *elpides* of these men and these women ... and all their work"); *DT* 73: καταδήω Πάνφιλον καὶ ἐλπίδας τὰς Πανφίλου ἀπάσας καὶ ἐργασίας πάσας, Θουκλείδην, ἐλπίδας τὰς Θουκλείδου ("I bind Panphilos and the all the *elpides* of Panphilos and all his enterprises; Theokleides and the *elpides* of Theokleides"); cf. *IG* VII 2545: μήτ' ἐλπίδων ὄναιτο, μὴ τέκνων σπορᾶ[ς] (Thebes, 3rd/4th cent. CE); *IGBulg* III.1519: a dedication ὑπὲρ ἐλπίδος (Philippopolis, 3rd cent. CE).
54   *I.Ancyra* 83.
55   *SEG* XXXVIII 1236: ἐκό[λα]σαν Εὐμένην β' τὸν υἱὸν κὲ κατέθηκεν ἰσοθάνατον· ἡ δὲ ἐμὴ Τύχη ἐλπίδαν ἔδωκε.

Bibliography

Cairns, D. 2016. "Metaphors for Hope in Archaic and Classical Greek Poetry," in: R.R. Caston/R.A. Kaster (eds.), *Joy, Hope, and Affection in the Classical World*, 13–44, Oxford.

Canali De Rossi, F. 2007. *Filius publicus. Υἱὸς τῆς πόλεως e titoli affini in iscrizioni greche di età imperiale. Studi sul vocabolario dell'evergesia I*, Rome.

Chaniotis, A. 2006. "Rituals between Norms and Emotions: Rituals as Shared Experience and Memory," in: E. Stavrianopoulou (ed.), *Rituals and Communication in the Graeco-Roman World* (*Kernos* Suppl. 16), 211–38, Liège.

Jones, C.P. 1999. "Interrupted Funerals," in: *PAPhA* 143, 588–600.

Marek, C. 1985. "Katalog der Inschriften im Museum von Amasra. Mit Anhang: Die Inschriften von Amastris und die angebliche Pompeianische Ära der Stadt," in: *EA* 6, 133–56.

van Nijf, O. 2013. "Affective Politics: The Emotional Regime in the Imperial Greek City," in: A. Chaniotis/P. Ducrey (eds.), *Unveiling Emotions II. Emotions in Greece and Rome: Texts, Images, Material Culture*, 373–90, Stuttgart.

Thumiger, C. 2016. "Fear, Hope, and the Definition of Hippocratic Medicine," in: W.V. Harrris (ed.), *Popular Medicine in Graeco-Roman Antiquity: Explorations*, 198–214, Leiden.

List of Contributors

Antony Augoustakis is Professor of Classics at the University of Illinois at Urbana-Champaign, USA. His research interests include Latin imperial epic, Roman comedy and historiography, women in antiquity, classical reception, and gender theory. He is the author of *Motherhood and the Other: Fashioning Female Power in Flavian Epic* (Oxford 2010) and *Statius, Thebaid 8* (Oxford 2016). He is the editor of the *Brill Companion to Silius Italicus* (2010), *Ritual and Religion in Flavian Epic* (Oxford 2013), *Flavian Poetry and its Greek Past* (Brill 2014), *Oxford Readings in Flavian Epic* (Oxford 2016), and co-editor of the *Blackwell Companion to Terence* (2013) and *STARZ Spartacus: Reimagining an Icon on Screen* (Edinburgh 2016). He is the editor of *The Classical Journal*.

Olympia Bobou was educated first at the Aristotle University of Thessaloniki and then at the University of Oxford. She has held various teaching positions, as well as worked in the Cast Gallery of the Ashmolean Museum. She is currently working at the Palmyra Portraits Project at the University of Aarhus.

Angelos Chaniotis is Professor of Ancient History and Classics at the Institute for Advanced Study in Princeton. His research is dedicated to the study of society and culture in the Hellenistic World and the eastern provinces of the Roman Empire, examining subjects related to theatricality in public life, memory, identity, religion, and emotions. His most recent book is *Age of Conquests: The Greek World from Alexander to Hadrian*.

Nick Fisher is Professor Emeritus of Ancient History at Cardiff University. His recent publications include *Aeschines, Against Timarchos, Translated, with Introduction and 2 Commentary*, (Oxford University Press, 2001), two jointly edited volumes (with Hans van Wees), *Competition in the Ancient World* (Classical Press of Wales, 2011) and *'Aristocracy' in Antiquity* (Classical Press of Wales, 2015), a collection of articles on *charis* and social cohesion in Greek societies, and articles on Greek sexuality, athletics, violence and socialization, and emotions in Athenian oratory and tragedy.

Laurel Fulkerson is Associate Dean of the College of Arts and Sciences and Professor of Classics at The Florida State University. She studies Latin poetry and the emotions, and has recently written *No Regrets: Remorse in Classical Antiquity* (Oxford 2013). She is currently writing a monograph on the occurrence of hope in Greco-Roman antiquity.

Keely Heuer is an assistant professor of art history at the State University of New York at New Paltz. Her research focuses on the iconography of South Italian vases and cross-cultural interaction between Greeks and indigenous peoples in pre-Roman Italy.

Alexandre Johnston is currently in the final stages of a doctoral thesis on Sophoclean tragedy at the University of Edinburgh. From December 2017, he will hold a two-year Leverhulme postdoctoral fellowship at the Scuola Normale Superiore in Pisa, where he will be working on divine and human causation in Greek tragedy and modern thought.

George Kazantzidis (DPhil Oxford) is Assistant Professor of Latin Literature at the University of Patras. His research interests lie at the intersections between medicine and poetry, with special emphasis on the history of mental illness and the emotions. He has published articles on Callimachus, Cicero, Lucretius and the Hippocratic Corpus. Among his current research projects is a book length discussion of medicine and paradoxography in Greek and Roman antiquity.

Antti Lampinen obtained his PhD from the University of Turku (Finland) in 2013 with a thesis on the literary ethnographies of religion in Greek and Roman descriptions of northern peoples. Between 2015 and 2017 he was the Newton International Fellow in the School of Classics, University of St Andrews. In March 2017 he takes up the position of a Research Fellow of the Academy of Finland.

Donald Lateiner taught Greek, Latin, and Ancient History at Ohio Wesleyan University. His research addresses historiographical methods of Herodotus and Thucydides. Books include *The Historical Method of Herodotus* (1989) and *Sardonic Smile: Nonverbal Behavior in Homeric Epic* (1995), exploring body language and proxemics. He co-edited *Thucydides & Herodotus,* a volume (2012) on Thucydides' fraught relationship to Herodotos; and *The Ancient Emotion of Disgust* (2017). His current research concerns Plutarch's post-mortems, and senses and emotions in ancient novels.

Andreas N. Michalopoulos is Associate Professor of Latin at the National and Kapodistrian University of Athens. He is the author of: *Ancient Etymologies in Ovid's Metamorphoses: A Commented Lexicon* (Leeds, 2001), *Ovid, Heroides 16 and 17: Introduction, Text and Commentary* (Cambridge, 2006), *Ovid, Heroides 20 and 21: Introduction, Text, Translation, and Commentary* (Athens, 2013), *Roman Lyric Poetry: Horace Carmina* (Athens 2016, with Charilaos N. Michalopoulos), *Roman Love Elegy* (Athens 2016, with Charilaos N. Michalopoulos).

Sophia Papaioannou is Associate Professor of Latin Literature at the National and Kapodistrian University of Athens. Her research interests centre on the literature and culture of the Augustan and Early Imperial era, and on Roman comedy, and she has authored and edited several books and articles on the above topics.

Michael Paschalis is Emeritus Professor of Classics at the University of Crete. He has published over 100 articles and has written and (co-)edited 13 books on Hellenistic, Roman, and Modern Greek literature, the Ancient Novel, the literature of Late Antiquity, and the reception of the Classics in Modern Greek, Italian, English, and French literature.

Niall W. Slater (Dobbs Professor of Latin and Greek, Emory University) focuses on the ancient theatre and performance, prose fiction, and popular reception of classical literature. His books include *Spectator Politics: Metatheatre and Performance in Aristophanes* (Penn 2002); as well as translations for *The Birth of Comedy* (ed. J.S. Rusten, JHUP, 2011). Current work includes studies of Harley Granville Barker's Euripides productions and fragments of early Roman drama.

Dimos Spatharas teaches Greek at the University of Crete. He is the co-editor (with Donald Lateiner) of a recent volume on *The Ancient Emotion of Disgust* (Oxford, 2017) and has published several articles on the Attic orators, the Sophists, and ancient emotions. He has also produced a commentary on Isocrates' *Against Lochites*. He is currently working on persuasion and emotions and the representation of repulsiveness in Greek literature.

Andrew Stiles received a BA (Hons) and MPhil from the University of Sydney, and has recently submitted a DPhil at the University of Oxford. His research interests include the political, social, and religious history of the late Republic and early Principate, and the history of ideas in the ancient world, including conceptions of the future of Rome. He has articles published or forthcoming on Ovid, politics in the Augustan and Tiberian periods, and divination.

Natalia Tsoumpra obtained a BA (Hons) in Greek Philology from the Aristotle University of Thessaloniki, and an MPhil (2009) and DPhil (2014) from the University of Oxford. She wrote her PhD thesis on the topic of "Comic leadership and power dynamics in Aristophanes". In 2014 she joined the Glasgow University Classics department and has been working there as a Lecturer for the past two years. Her research interests lie in the field of Greek Old Comedy, and especially Aristophanes, while she is broadly interested in Greek drama, gender studies, performance theory, and myth and ritual. She is currently editing a volume on Costume in the comedies of Aristophanes (under consideration by Bloomsbury) and co-editing a volume on Morbid Laughter: exploring the comic dimensions of disease in Classical Antiquity (under contract with the Illinois Classical Studies).

Kostas Vlassopoulos is Assistant Professor of Ancient Greek History at the University of Crete. He is co-editor of the *Oxford Handbook of Greek and Roman Slaveries*, and the author of *Unthinking the Greek Polis: Ancient Greek History beyond Eurocentrism* (2007), *Politics: Antiquity and its Legacy* (2010) and *Greeks and Barbarians* (2013).

Index Rerum et Nominum

adventus: 261, 267–8 with n.36
Aeropagus: 7
Agrippina: 269–73
aidōs: 38–41
Alcibiades: 115 with n.20, 137–9, 144–5
anger: 4–5, 11–12, 47 n.45, 105 n.43, 108, 147, 186–7 with n.21, 203, 210, 284
anticipation: 4, 6–8, 10 n.21, 134–5, 140, 275 n.2, 331, 345, 352
Augustus: 26–7, 171–2 (*Spes Augusta*), 177, 185–7 with n.22, 214, 227 with n.32, 261–3, 266–7 with n.32
agency
– hope as a fallback emotion: 63–68, 167
– hope 'possessing' a person: 105–6
– hope as a drive to act: 50, 256
Alyattes: 134
ambition: 37–41, 49
anelpiston: 140–1
athumia: 141–2 with n.34
arrogance: 37–8, 211

barbarians: 16, 275–93
Bildung: 175
bravery: 69–74
Bloch, Ernest: 24 n.58, 111–12

Caesar: 278–9
Cairns, Douglas: 1, 4–5, 7–8, 13 n.28, 24 n.59, 35 n.3, 90 n.12
Calatinus, Atilius: 24–6, 161, 263–4 with n.22
calculation: 1–2, 14–6, 27–8, 72, 93, 134–7
children: 27–8, 100, 173–80, 253–5, 329–46
Christianity and hope as a virtue: 1–2, 71, 132 with n.3 and 7, 362
chthonic: 304–7

civitas: 226, 271
clementia: 187 with n.22
Cleon: 113, 141–3
coins: 265–6
comedy and fulfillment of hopes: 96–107, 153–67
consolation: 102–3, 138, 189–90, 271, 355–7
cowardice: 79, 106–7, 138
Croesus: 134–5

danger
– hope as a dangerous emotion/state of mind: 35, 49–50, 90, 112–4 with n.15, 132, 137 n.22, 142 n.34, 144, 167, 200
– hope as a comforter of danger: 122
daring/boldness (*tolme*): 38, 113, 121, 137–8, 145, 198
death
– and hope for afterlife: 277–9, 299–304
– causing frustration of hopes: 353–7
– funerary inscriptions: 329–46
Delphi: 36, 96, 135, 253–55, 280–1, 341
despair: 9–10, 24 n.59, 53–4, 63 n.33, 64–70, 94–5, 132, 141, 185–7, 193 with n.44, 216
Dickinson, Emily: 8, 53, 85
Diodotus: 41, 114, 141–3
deus ex machina: 97, 122
divination/oracles: 118–27, 180–1, 242–6
doxa: 13–14
dreams: 236–41

emotion scripts: 6, 153
endurance: 10, 55, 69–72, 74, 79
Epicureanism: 19–23, 199
exile and the occurrence of hope as a last-resort emotion: 97–8, 183–94

expectation (negative and positive): 4–11, 20 n.48, 27–9, 39–40, 44 n.37, 73–5, 91–3 with n.17, 99 n.29, 131–42, 171, 275–6, 291–3, 337–9, 351–3

fame (*kleos*): 21, 43
family: 37, 44, 55–7, 76–8, 177–81, 247–8, 268, 335–6, 341, 356–8
fate: 20 n.47, 37–8, 45, 81, 92, 100–3, 123, 157, 173–5, 189, 199, 208, 336–7, 354 with n.17
Feriale Cumanum: 268
fides: 24–26, 163, 201, 209, 263
Forum Holitorium: 26, 161–2 with n.22, 264–5
friendship: 67–73, 78–82, 192–3

Galba: 218–30
Germanicus: 263–73

hatred: 206–10
hedone: 11–13, 47
hope
– ambivalent concept: 2 with n.4, 7–8, 35–41, 71, 132–6, 167, 191–3
– bodily mapping of: 46–9
– cognitive vs. affective: 2–9, 93 with n.17, 131–4, 331 with n.10, 351–3
– metaphors for: 4, 9, 45–51, 90, 98
– personification of: 26, 133 n.8, 146, 161–4, 277, 312–4
– temple dedications to: 24, 161–3, 263–9
– worshipped as goddess: 24, 161–6, 171, 185–6, 264 (*Spes Vetus*)
– and chance/fortune: 20, 56, 103–4, 120, 167, 202, 207–8
– and deception: 121, 191–3
– and desire (*epithumia/ cupiditas*): 2–14
– and *eros*: 18–21, 41–9, 104–5, 114–7, 146, 171–2

– and fear: 10–11, 13 n.28, 16, 106–7 with n.51, 112 n.9, 113–4, 138, 188–9, 199–201
– and madness: 16–19, 22, 38, 61, 203 n.14, 207
– and religion: 24–26, 43–4, 118–22, 153–67, 189–90, 266–8, 308–13, 361–2
– as a collective emotion: 139, 146–7, 172, 221–2, 275–93, 353–9
– as a motivational force: 2–10
– vs. hopelessness: 9, 140
hopelessness
– and loss of faith in the gods: 53–82
– and dehumanization: 59–61
– and suicide: 68–9, 290
horme/ motus animi: 16
hubris: 62

illness
– and hope for recovery: 101–2, 247
– hope conceptualized as illness: 105
immortality: 43, 66, 206, 277–9, 300–4
imperial ideology
– and its investment in collective hope: 27–29, 173–180
– the emperor as a provider of hope: 186–8, 259–73, 359–61

kairos: 100, 282–9

lamentation: 64–7, 92, 100, 116, 198, 206, 211, 269, 330
Lazarus, Richard: 5, 191 n.40, 331 n.9, 345
leadership: 27, 117–8, 180, 190, 213–4, 229–30, 265–6
Lesis: 243–4, 343–6

manumission: 250–3
Mardonius: 136
Marxism: 111
material wealth: 280–4

Melian dialogue: 71, 122–3, 143–4
memory: 6, 12, 81, 203, 221–30
metempsychosis: 278

Nero: 15, 17, 216–8
Nicias: 119–22, 145

optimism: 4–5, 81, 116 n.26, 131 with n.1, 220
Otho: 225–6

pain (mental and physical): 8–13, 38–41, 47–9, 59–60,121
Pandora: 114 n.18, 132–3, 191 with n.37, 297
paratragedy
– and the use of hope as a comic device: 85–109
pater patriae: 189, 227 n.32, 260, 271
pathe/propatheiai: 10–14
pax Augusta: 177, 268 n.36
Pericles: 116–7, 137–8
pessimism
– vs. hopelessness: 214–6
– as a consequence of deceived hopes: 197–211
phantasia: 11, 17–18, 25
phrenes: 46–8
politics
– hope in modern: 1, 112–3
– hope in Greek and Roman: 27–29, 111–127, 136–45, 266–8
plot development: 153–4, 213–6

pragmatism: 118
prayer: 45, 96, 136, 158–60, 166, 204, 208, 287
promatheia: 38–41
Punic Wars: 163–7, 264

reason/*ratio*: 3–4, 16, 22, 70–1, 111–2, 122–3, 131–3
reversal: 68–9, 136, 154, 218, 284–9
revenge
– hope for: 11, 201–6, 284–8;
– hopelessness feeding a passion for revenge: 54–63

Sicilian expedition: 115–6, 144–5
sight/seeing: 43, 104–5, 115, 121
slaves/slavery: 155–7, 249–56, 278–9, 343–6
sophrosune: 289
spes Iuli: 178–9
Snyder, Charles: 3–4, 183 n.3
Stoicism: 12–16, 199–201
superstition: 112, 118–23

thumos: 14, 37, 46
Tiberius: 259–63
Tiger, Lionel: 9
Trilling, Lionel: 215
virtue/ *arete*: 24–5, 36–7, 69–70, 102

women: 54–68, 155–7, 208–11

Index Auctorum Antiquorum et Locorum

i. Literary sources

Aeschines
Against Timarchus
1.49: 342 n.39
1.171: 108 n.54
Against Ctesiphon
3.167: 342 n.39

Aeschylus
Agamemnon
11: 46 n.40
249: 42 n.28
992–997: 46 n.40
1030–1034: 46 n.40
1668: 97 n.26, 98
Choephori
194: 47 n.44
Persae
599: 106 n.47
744–750: 46 n.40
1027: 44 n.38
[*Prometheus vinctus*]
250: 142 n.33
537–538: 47 n.43
Septem
95–99: 123
Supplices
96–97: 105 n.43
Fragmenta
154a.19–21: 47 n.43

Alcman
3.61 *PMG*: 49 n.51

Ammianus Marcellinus
15.9.8: 278 n.18

Anthologia Palatina
7.425.3–4: 61 n.22

Antiatticista
λ. 2 (Valente 2015, 207): 85 n.2

Antiphanes
The Fuller (121 K–A): 98, 103

Appian
Celtica
11.4: 290 n.61
Samnitica
6: 290 n.61

Archilochus
105W: 44 n.38
122W: 44 n.38
196W: 49 n.51

Aristaenetus
Epistulae
2.4: 248 n.40

Aristophanes
Equites
30–34: 123 n.50
42–43: 126
47–48: 94 n.18
85–86: 123
167: 118 n.35
280–281: 126
339: 126 n.57
422–423: 118
424–425: 118

719–721: 118 n.35
739–740: 118 n.33
963: 126
964: 126
967–969: 125
997ff.: 124
1007–1009: 118
1015–1020: 124
1023–1024: 124
1025: 124
1027: 124
1121–1130: 125
1131–1132: 125
1141–1144: 125
1156–1157: 125
1162–1163: 118 n.33
1233: 124 n.52
1236–1246: 124 n.53
1237: 124 n.52
1240: 124 n.52
1240–1244: 86
1244: 88, 124
1244a: 87
1248: 124 n.51
1248–1249: 124
1253: 124 n.52
1262–1263: 125
1317: 126
1330: 126
1332: 126
1333: 126
1340–1343: 118 n.118
1346: 126 n.57
1349: 126 n.57
1385: 126
1388–1391: 126
Nubes
11: 88 n.9
24: 88 n.9

41: 88 n.9
11: 88 n.9
153: 88 n.8
161: 88 n.8
225: 89
289: 88 n.9
300: 88 n.9
314: 88 n.9
359: n.8
360: 891
379: 89 n.11
412: 88 n.9
439: 88 n.9
454: 88 n.9
470: 88 n.9
636: 88 n.9
737: 88 n.9
757: 102 n.37
1116: 88 n.9
1117: 88 n.9
1229: 88 n.9
1303: 88 n.9
1305: 88 n.9
1319–1320: 88 n.9
1499–1501: 89
1500: 96 n.22
1502: 89
Pax
782–784: 90 n.13
787–796: 91
Plutus
212–213: 97
Thesmophoriazusae
195–196: 93
869–870: 46 n.40, 47 n.44, 94
945–946: 94
946: 102 n.35
1009–1010: 96

Vespae
303–308: 90
1501: 90 n.13
Fragmenta
Gerytades (156.7–12 K–A): 87

Aristotle
De anima
403a 29–b1: 3 n.6
De memoria et reminiscentia
449b : 12
449b 27–28: 6
Ethica Nicomachea
1166a 25–26: 6
1166b 16: 6
Politica
1254a 9–13 : 235 n.4
[*Problemata*]
953a 11: 77 n.72
Rhetorica
1350b 8–16: 12
1369a 1–4: 14
1378a 31–33: 11
1378b 1–4: 57 n.8
1378b 2ff.: 12
1378b–1379b: 284 n.43
1382a 21–25: 114 n.15
1383a 17–18: 278 n.15
Topica
156a: 284 n.43

Arrian
Anabasis
1.3.2: 279 n.24

Artemidorus
Oneirocritica
1.13: 239 n.15
1.48: 237 n.9
2.8: 238 n.12
2.9: 238 n.14
2.12: 237 n.11
3.30: 239 n.16
4: 236 n.5
4.30: 237 n.8
4.64: 240 n.18

Asclepiodorus
Tactica
5.2: 132

Athenaeus
139B: 85 n.2
235E: 85 n.2

Augustine
De civitate Dei
4.18: 166 n.33

Augustus
Res Gestae
1.1: 227
3: 187 n.22
20.4: 267 n.32

Bacchylides
1.160–165: 46 n.40
1.163–165: n.44
3.57–58: 44 n.38
3.74: 47 n.43
3.75: 40 n.23, 42 n.31, 87 n.5
8.18: 42 n.31
13.121–140: 47
13.121–163: 47
13.157–158: 47

Fragmenta
10b.10: 48 n.47
20: 281 n.33
20b.8: 46 n.40, 47

Basilius Caesariensis
Epistulae
119.18: 248 n.40

Boethius
De Consolatione Philosophie
1.7: 192 n.41
1.7.26–27: 107 n.51

Caecilius
fr. 22 Ribbeck (=1 Guardi): 103

Caesar
Bellum Gallicum
6.13.18: 279 n.19
6.14.5: 278 n.18, 279
7.80.92: 15 n.33

Callimachus
Hymni
5.94: 330 n.6

Catullus
64.140: 20 n. 48
64.143–4: 20 n.48
64.177: 20 n.48
76.3: 167 n.33

Celsus
De Medicina
3.18.3: 17

Cicero
De amicitia
23: 192 n.43
De finibus
3.35: 189 n.28
De legibus
2.28: 25
2.11.28: 162 n.22, 263, 264 n.17
De natura deorum
3.13: 20 n.47
3.14: 263 n.17
3.46–47: 263 n.17
3.61: 263 n.17
3.88–89: 263 n.17
2.23.61: 24
De oratore
2.72: 284 n.44
Epistulae ad familiares
4.80: 188 n.26
7.28.2: 15 n.33
11.28.6: 27 n.69
12.23.2: 27
In Verrem
2.2.135: 10 n.20
2.3.6: 167 n.33
2.45: 10 n.20
Post reditum in senatu
7: 10 n.20
Pro Cluentio
176: 10 n.20
Pro Fonteio
33: 284 with n.44
36: 284
Pro lege Manilia: 265
Tusculanae disputationes
3.11: 17
3.24: 189 n.28
3.33: 190 n.31
3.63: 17

4.6.11: 16
4.15: 189 n.28
4.37.80: 171
4.80: 10 with 10 n.19

Clemens Alexandrinus
Stromateis
6.2.23: 104 n.40
Comica Adespota
fr. 1093.101 K–A: 105 n.44
Comparatio Menandri et Philistionis
47–48: 104, 108

Demosthenes
Philippic III
9.8: 102 n.37

Dexippus (*BNJ* 100)
fr. 6.6–7: 291 with n.60

Dio Cassius
50.10.3: 162 n.22, 265 n.23
55.13: 262 n.10
64.3.3: 222

Diogenes Laertius
Vitae Philosophorum
8.8: 304 n.35

Dionysius Halicarnassensis
Antiquitates Romanae
9.24.3–4: 264 n.20

Ennius
Annales
60–61: 165 n.30

Epicharmus
fr. 31 K–A: 85 n.2

fr. 34 K–A: 85 n.2
fr. 37 K–A: 85 n.2

Epictetus
Discourses
4.1.33–37: 255 n.53

Epicurus
Epistula ad Menoeceum
133–4: 23

Eubulus
Antiope (fr. 9 K–A): 97

Euripides
Andromache
262: 79 n.80
Alcestis
177–178: 95
Hecuba
53–54: 61
59–67: 61
74–75: 54 n.4
90–97: 54 n.4
153–168: 55
349–354: 73 n.56
349–366: 55
369–372: 55
487–491: 56 n.7
658: 56
678–80: 55–56
680: 44 n.38, 92
684–687: 57
688: 57
689–720: 56
708–805: 57 n.8
714–720: 61
721–722: 56
749–751: 57

753: 58 n.14
753–754: 58 n.14
756–757: 57
786–792: 57
787: 58 n.14
787–789: 58 n.14
812: 58 n.14
820–823: 58
841–851: 58 n.14
851: 58 n.14
898–901: 63 n.32
1024–1026: 61
1024–1034: 59
1035: 61
1049–1050: 61
1050–1053: 62
1051–1054: 62 n.27
1056–1058: 61
1066–1068: 61
1071–1074: 61
1075–1077: 61
1075–1078: 57 n.10
1077–1078: 61
1079–1082: 61
1099–1106: 59
1120–1121: 62 n.27
1121: 62
1161–1171: 62 n.27
1173: 61 n.24
1173–1175: 61
1256–1274: 59–60
1257: 62
1258: 62
1265: 61
1274: 62
1279: 68 n.44

Helen
1137–1143: 44 n.38

Heracles
53–59: 69 n.47
80–84: 69 n.47
81–84: 74 n.60
85–94: 69
87: 70 n.48
90–91: 70
105: 71 n.51
105–106: 70
143–150: 71
295–297: 71–72
307–311: 72, 74
315: 74
316–318: 72
339–347: 72
430: 69 n.47
458–461: 73
503–505: 73
503–507: 73
550–560: 69 n.47
565–573: 76
575–582: 76
629–635: 76
629–636: 81 n.86
655–662: 77 n.75
745–746: 74 n.61
746: 46 n.40
757–760: 74
763–773: 74–75
803–804: 75 n.63
801–806: 75
871–872: 74 n.62
877–879: 74 n.62
925: 76 n.70
940: 76
965–967: 76
966–967: 77 n.73
1063–1071: 71 n.52
1087–1088: 77

1119: 76 n.70
1127: 77
1142: 76 n.70
1146–1152: 78
1147–1150: 76
1151–1152: 77 n.75
1197–1202: 78
1229–1231: 78
1237: 76
1241: 78 n.77
1242–1245: 78
1248: 78
1254: 78
1279–1280: 76
1303–1305: 78
1303–1312: 77
1313: 78
1340: 80 n.84
1341–1345: 80 n.84
1347–1357: 80
1351: 74 n.60, 79
1352: 81
1357: 80, 81
1360–1364: 81
1367–1370: 76
1374–1377: 81
1377–1386: 80–81
1386–1388: 81
1392: 77
1403–1404: 81
1415: 81 n.87
1410–1417: 77 n.78, 80, 81 with n.87
1413–1414: 81
1419–1420: 81
1425: 81
1425–1428: 81
Heracleidae
433–434: 47 n.43
451–452: 96 with n.21

Hippolytus
38: 115 n.21
197: 93
682–683: 95
1120: 92 n.16
1120–1121: 44 n.38, 91
Ion
1450–4: 10 n.21
Iphigenia Aulidensis
511: 56 n.7
Medea
1035–1036: 47 n. 44
Orestes
977: 100
977–988: 44 n.38, 92
Phoenissae
3: 203 n.13
396: 97 n.26, 98
634–635: 203 n.13
Supplices
479: 59 n.15, 71, 142 n.33
Troades
98–100: 68
298–305: 63–64
342–347: 73 n.57
343–347: 64
349–353: 64
463–465: 64, 68
484–490: 73 n.57
505–510: 65
509: 68
613–614: 65
632–633: 65
680–683: 65
681–683: 46 n.40
701–707: 66
703–705: 66 n.35
833–837: 67
838–840: 66–67

1060–1080: 67
1121–1122: 66
1241–1245: 67
1251–1259: 68
1279–1281: 68
1280–1281: 68
1282–1283: 68
1289–1332: 68
Fragmenta
271.1: 87 n.5
301.1: 89 n.11
420.4–5K: 105 n.43
650: 59 n.15
700: 87
746a: 102

Frontinus
De aquis
1.5
1.6: 24, 264 n.21
1.19: 264 n.21
1.20: 264 n.21
2.65: 264 n.21
2.76: 264 n.21
2.76: 264 n.21

Galen
De placitis Hippocratis et Platonis
4.4.16–17: 13 n.26
Quomodo morbum simulantes sint deprehendendi
19.4–5: 248 n.40

Gerontius
Vita Melaniae
10: 245 n.32

Hellanicus of Lesbos
FGRHist 4 F 73: 278 n.16

Herodianus Grammaticus
II, p.927.12 L: 85 n.2

Herodotus
1.17–22: 134
1.22: 135
1.27.4: 134, 135
1.30.2: 135
1.50.1: 135
1.54.1: 135
1.56.1: 135
1.71.1: 135
1.75.2: 135
1.77: 134
1.77.4: 136
1.80.5: 135 n.15
1.105.4: 280 n.26
1.110.1: 134
1.141.2: 136
2.11.4: 135
2.13.3: 136
2.62.2: 135
2.81: 304 n.35
3.122: 135
3.39.4: 131
3.62: 135
3.122: 135
3.130.3: 136 n.16
4.1–4: 250 n.45
4.93.1: 277 n.11
4.94.1: 277 n.11
4.95.3: 278 n.12
4.135: 134
5.30: 135
5.35: 135
5.36: 135
6.5.1: 135
6.9.1: 136
7.237.1: 135

8.10: 134
8.10.2: 136
8.12: 11 n.21
8.136.3: 136
8.140α3: 136
9.61.3: 136

Hesiod
Opera
60–105: 297 n.2
90–105: 2, 114 n.18
95–98: 133 n.8
96: 185 n.15, 191 n.37
96–99: 191
498–501: 132, 133 n.8

Hippocrates
Prognosticon
7: 7

Historia Augusta (SHA)
Elagabalus
13: 164 n.21

Homer
Iliad
14.207: 105 n.42
21.583: 46 n.40
24.514: 49 n.52
Odyssey
5.291: 106 n.48
18.212: 48
19.518–519: 330 n.6
20.14: 61 n.22
21.157: 46 n.40
21.314–317: 7

Horace
Odes
1.35: 26
1.35.21–22: 163 n.26

Hymni homerici
Demeter
37: 47 n.4

Josephus
Bellum Judaicum
7.4.2: 285
7.76: 285 with n.45

Justin
Epitome of Pompeius Trogus
24.6.1: 280 n.27
24.6.4–5: 281 with n.30
24.6.10: 281 with n.31
24.7.9–8.1: 281 with n.32

Juvenal
9.125–134: 192 n.42

Libanius
Declamationes
26.28: 137 n.23
Epistulae
567: 148 n.40

Livy
praef. 10: 213
praef. 11: 213
2.51.2: 24, 264 n.20
6.6.18: 15
7.10.9: 10 n.20
8.13.17: 10 n.20
21.62.4: 162 n.22
24.47.15–16: 265 n.23

24.47.16: 162 n.22
25.7.6: 162 n.22, 265 n.23
25.57.5: 10 n.20
26.37.1: 10 n.20
38.17.16–17: 283 n.38

Longus
Daphnis et Chloe
29–31: 248 with n.41, 248 n.40

Lucan
De bello civili
1.450–462: 279 n.21
2.7–15: 19, 199

Lucian
Oneiros
4: 344

Lucretius
De rerum natura
1.271–76: 21–22, 22 n.53
1.273: 22
1.275: 22
1.586: 20
1.921–28: 21, 22 with n.53
1.922–3: 22 with n.53
1.923: 21, 22
1.924: 22 n.53
1.926–7: 21
1.927: 21
2.251: 20
2.302: 20
3.14: 24
3.61: 25
3.152–8: 18 n.41
3.252–3: 22 n.52
4.1061–1062: 18
4.1068: 20
4.1069: 17
4.1086–90: 18, 22 n.53, 191 n.39
6.30: 20

Lysias
Against Simon
3.2

Menander
Aspis
18: 99 n.29
322: 101
446–447: 101–102
447: 102 n.35
Epitrepontes
338–340: 100–101
538–566: 250–251 with n.46
Hērōs
40–49: 248 n.40
Kolax
fr. 57 Austin (B56 Arnott): 101 n.34
Naukleros
fr. 249 K–A (289 Koertel): 103
Sententiae
30: 158 n.14
31: 108
42: 158 n.14
51: 108, 158 n.14
213: 108
213a Pernigotti: 108 n.55
254: 108
Appendix 1.12/897 Pernigotti: 108 with n.56
Pap. V 1–2: 108
Pap. XIV 20/897 Pernigotti: 108
Sicyonioi
217: 100 n.29
251–254: 100
265: 100 n.31
286–287: 100

293–294: 100
416: 100
Fragmenta
fr. 351.1 Kock: 158 n.14
fr. 717 K–A [494 Koertel]: 102
fr. 782 K–A (=559 Koertel): 103
fr. 813.1 Kock: 158 n.14
fr. 859 K–A (=636 Koertel): 102–103
fr. 1063 K–A 3–14 [CGFPR 255]: 106

New Testament
Ephesians
2.12: 132 n.7

Nonius
392, 15 M. (682 L.): 103 n.38

Ovid
Amores
2.19.5: 20 n.48
Ars amatoria
3.478: 10 n.20
Epistulae ex Ponto
1.2.29–30: 185 n.15
1.2.59–62: 189 n.29
1.2.61–62: 189 nn.29, 30
1.2.61–64: 189
1.3.3–30: 190 n.32
1.3.5–6: 190 n.32
1.4.43–44: 190 n.34
1.5.86: 186 n.17
1.6.27f.: 186
1.6.27–44: 185
1.6.29–40: 185 n.15
1.6.41–44: 186
1.8.27: 186 n.17
1.9.17: 186 n.17
2.7.79f.: 187
2.8.71f: 191

3.3.91f.: 187 n.21
3.7.9f.: 192
3.7.21f.: 192
3.7.31f.: 192
4.6.15f.: 185, 193
4.6.49f.: 192
4.9.74: 186 n.17
4.12.41f.: 190 n.33
4.16.51: 186 n.17
16.105: 203 n.14
17.74: 203 n.14
18.175–176: 203 n.14
Fasti
1.285–286: 267 n.35
1.486: 10 n.20
2.55–56: 267 n.32
3.362: 10 n.20
4.905–942: 166 n.32
Heroides
9.42: 188 n.27
13.124: 188 n.27
18.178: 18, 191 n.39
Metamorphoses
3.417: 18
6.424–674: 331 n.6
Tristia
1.1.101f.: 189 n.30
1.1.20: 190 n.34
1.1.102f.: 188
1.2.3–4: 190 n.34
1.2.65–66: 186 n.17
1.2.71–71: 186 n.17, 187 n.17
1.3.3f.: 190
1.3.3–4: 190 n.31
1.3.21–24: 186 n.17
1.3.37–40: 190 n.34
1.3.89–98: 186 n.17
1.4.28: 186 n.17
1.5.77–78: 190 n.34

2.3.67f.: 190
2.3.67–68: 190 n.31
2.33–38: 190 n.34
2.33–42: 190 n.34
2.37–40: 190 n.34
2.103–110: 183 n.2
2.143–148: 185 n.10
2.145–148: 185
2.147–148: 189 n.29
2.153: 189 n.30
2.153–154: 189
2.181f.: 189
3.3: 186 n.17
3.5.43f.: 185 n.11
3.5.53f.: 186
4.3.11f.: 188 n.27, 189 n.30
4.3.63–70: 190 n.34
4.6.49f.: 193
4.9.13f.: 187
5.4.17f: 187 n.21 with n.22
5.8.21f.: 187 n.21
5.8.25ff.: 187 n.22
5.9.19: 186 n.17

Parthenius
Narrationum amatoriarum libellus
8.5: 283 n.40

Paul
Epistula ad Corinthios I
13: 132 n.3

Pausanias
6.6.4–6.610: 310 n.73
8.48.2–3: 332

Phaedrus
Fabulae
Appendix 20: 249 n.42

Philemon
Pancratiastes
fr. 56 K–A: 103–104
fr. 126 K–A: 105
fr. 197 K–A: 104 with n.39
fr.233 K: 108 n.57

Philochorus
FGrH 328 F 18: 80 n.83

Philodemus
De electionibus et fugis
xxiii. 7–13: 23

Philostratus
Vitae sophistarum
15.20: 358 n.34

Pindar
Olympian Odes
1.106–111: 45 n.39
1.108: 48 n.47
1.109: 45 n.39
3.11: 42
7.43–4: 40 n.22
12: 38 n.13, 39 n.13, 42
12.6–6a: 38 n.13
12.10–12a: 44 n.38
13: 45, 48, 50
13.63–64: 44, 44 n.36, 48
13.65–68: 44
13.83: 44, 92
13.104–106: 44
Pythian Odes
2.49–51 44 n.37
3: 45, 50
3.13: 42
3.19–25: 42
3.20: 46 n.41

3.22: 43
3.24: 42
3.25: 43
3.27: 43
3.27–31: 42 n.29
3.54: 43
3.59–60: 43 n.32
3.101–103: 45
3.110–111: 45
4.184–185: 47 n.44
4.201: 47
5.122–124: 45 n.39
8: 50
8.84–94: 47–48
8.88–94: 46
8.92: 48 n.47
10.59–60: 46, 47
10.60: 47 n.45
12.28–32: 44 n.38
Nemean Odes
3.26–31: 46 n.41, 47
3.69: 48 n.47
5.32: 47 n.45
6.1–7: 38 n.11
8.44: 43
10: 50
10.24: 45
10.24–28: 45
10.29: 46
10.29–33: 45
10.30: 45
10.31–33: 45
11: 36 n. 5, 48, 50
11.9–10: 49
11.11: 49
11.12: 49
11.15–16: 48, 49
11.17–21: 36
11.22: 36, 39, 40

11.24–26: 36
11.24–29: 36
11.27–28: 36
11.29–32: 37
11.33–37: 36
11.33–42: 37
11.37: 37
11.37–42: 37
11.41–44: 38
11.42: 38 n.11
11.42–44: 38
11.43: 38
11.43–45: 38 n.11
11.44–48: 38
11.45–6: 39
11.46: 40
11.47: 40, 42
11.48: 41, 49
12.6a: 90 n.12
Isthmian odes
1.36–40: 40 n.23
1.41–42: 40 n.23
1.52–54: 40 n.23
1.64–67: 40 n.23
1.64–68: 47 n.43
2.43: 46
5.56–58: 47 n.45
Fragmenta
123: 47
214: 46, 47 with n. 44
189: 90
Scholia
Σ *ad N.* 11.45–46: 50 n.55

Plato
Leges
644c–d: 278 n.15, 288 n.54
644c–645a: 13

Phaedrus
105 n.41
Respublica
439e–440a: 14

Plato Comicus
fr. 248: 94 n.18

Plautus
Bacchides
115–116: 165 n.31
144: 159
892–894: 165
Captivi
496: 154 n.8
Casina
47–48: 248 n.40
53: 155 n.9
312: 155 n.9
346: 155 n.9, 160
348–349: 160
973: 155 n.9
Cistellaria
596: 160
597: 160
Epidicus
124: 154 n.5
332: 153–154 with n.4
531: 154 n.7
Menaechmi
1081: 161
Mercator
866–7: 25, 164
Miles gloriosus
1209
Mostellaria
350: 25, 164
406: 153 n.4

Persa
251–253: 160
286: 154 n.5
Poenulus
1187–1188: 160
1208: 160
Pseudolus
709: 25, 164, 165
Rudens
92: 155
204: 155
222: 155
231: 155
246–247: 155
275: 155
303: 156
312: 156
359–362: 161 n.20
371–372: 161 n.20
400: 156
401: 156, 160
501: 167 n.33
552–553: 156
588–589: 161
589: 156
629–630: 156
635–637: 156
680: 156
968: 156
996: 156
1145: 156
1161: 157, 161
1175: 157
1195: 157
1414: 157

Pliny (the Elder)
Naturalis historia
7.152: 310 n.72f

Plutarch
Lives
Alcibiades
17.1–4: 115 n.20
Galba
18.2: 222
Marius
20–21: 289 n.57
Theseus
35: 80 n.83
Moralia
De fortuna Romanorum
323A: 162 n.22
Non posse suaviter vivi secundum Epicurum
1107C: 23 n.55
Questiones Romanae
281E: 162 n.22

Polybius
2.7.6–11: 280 n.26
2.17.3: 280 n.28
2.17.9–12: 280 n.28
2.22–34: 282 n.35
2.35.8: 288–289 with n.56
2.39: 304 n.35

Pomponius Mela
De situ orbis
2.2: 279 n.20
3.19: 279 n.20

Posidonius, *FGrHist* 87 (Edelstein–Kidd)
fr. 274: 283 with n.37

Publilius Syrus
672: 108 n.53

Quintilian
Insitutio Oratoria
6.2.4ff.: 284 n.44

Sallust
Bellum Catilinae
5.9–13.5: 2
54.2–3: 213

Sappho
fr. 31V: 18
fr. 130V: 49 n.51

Seneca (the Younger)
Agamemnon
284: 10 n.20
1668: 98
Apocolocynthosis
4.1: 224 n.26
De beneficiis
4.11.5: 10 n.20
7.1.7: 10 n.20
7.17: 192 n.41
De constantia sapientis
9.2: 10 n.19, 192 n.41
9.2: 15
De ira
1.1.2: 17
2.19.1–2: 284 n.43
4.15.1: 284 n.43
[De spe]
1: 191 n.38
Dialogi
9.2.7–9: 200 n.10
Epistulae
5.7: 107 n.51, 288 n.54
5.7–8: 11
5.7–9: 200
98.6: 200 n.10

101.4: 203 n.14
118.9: 16
Phaedra
492: 10 n.19
Phoenissae
516–517: 10 n.20
631: 10 n.20
Thyestes
348–9: 10. n.19
Troades
399: 10 n.9
425: 200 n.10

Simonides
1.5–6W: 108 n.56
259PMG: 44 n.38

Solon
13.33–6W
13.36W: 47 n.43, 87 n.6

Sophocles
Ajax
475–8: 29
478–479: 47 n.44
485: 56 n.7
646–649: 44 n.38
715: 44 n.38
803: 56 n.7
1052: 93
Antigone
330: 44 n.38
392: 44 n.38, 100 n.32
614: 41 n.25
615–617: 41
618–625: 41 n.25
Electra
48: 56 n.7

809–810: 46 n.40
1460–1461: 47 n.43
Oedipus Tyrannus
487–488: 87 n.5
1527: 106 n.47
Fragmenta
948N.: 108 n.56

Sortes Astrampsychi
242, 243–245, 248 n.39, 252

Sortes Sangallenses
242

Statius
Silvae
5.3.149–158: 197
Thebaid
1.239–247: 201
1.322–328: 202
1.382: 203
2.158–166 201–202
2.313–323: 203
2.319: 210
3.696–698: 205
4.13–15: 206
4.88–92: 204
4.712–716: 205
6.504–512: 205
6.513–517: 206
9.49–53: 206
10.907–910: 207
10.935–939: 207
11.648–651: 208
11.654–657: 208
11.669–672: 208
12.177–180: 209
12.334–338: 209
12.339–1240: 209

12.456–463: 210
12.635–638: 210
12.679: 211
12.797–809: 198–199

Stobaeus
2.7.10ff.: 13 n.26

Strabo
3.4.7: 290 n.61
7.1.4: 267 n.35
7.2.2: 283

Suetonius
Caligula
5–6: 270–271
Galba
2: 228
16.1: 222
12–15: 222 n.22
Nero
31: 17
Tiberius
13.2: 261 n.5
15: 261 n.6, 262 n.10

Tacitus
Agricola
15–16: 286 n.50
30: 291 n.64
Annales
1.3: 262 n.10, 267 n.33
1.4.2: 226 n.31
1.31: 269
1.33: 269
1.34: 269
1.55: 267 n.34
2.12.3: 10 n.20
2.25: 285 n.48

2.26: 267 n.35
2.41: 267 n.35
2.43: 269
2.47: 266 n.31
2.49: 25, 26, 162 n.22, 265
2.71: 269
2.82: 271 n.41
3.4: 269
3.6: 271–272 n.42
3.69.2: 10 n.20
4.50.3: 10 n.20
12.37: 291 n.64
14.31–32: 291 n.64
14.35: 277 n.5, 291 n.64
16.1: 17
16.3: 17
Germania
46: 287 with n.52
46.3: 10 n.20
Historiae
1.1: 220 n.15
1.1–1.11: 219 n.14
1.1–49: 26
1.1.1: 219
1.2: 217
1.2–3: 217 n.12
1.3: 218–219
1.4: 14–15
1.4.1–3: 221
1.4.3: 221
1.5: 221
1.5.1: 222
1.5.2: 222
1.6.1: 223
1.7: 223
1.7.3: 223
1.9.1: 223
1.11.3: 220 n.16, 219
1.12–1.20: 219 n.14

1.12.3: 225, 228
1.13.3: 225
1.13.4: 225
1.18: 222 n.22
1.19.1: 228
1.22: 225 n.29
1.23: 226
1.48: 229 n.35
1.49.2: 299
1.49.4: 229
1.57: 16 n.34
1.57.2: 224 n.28
1.62.2: 10 n.20
1.88.3: 224 n.28
2.2.1: 10 n.20
2.46.1: 16 n.34
4.1–37: 223 n.23
4.54: 286 with n.49
4.54–79: 223 n.23
4.59.1: 10 n.20
5.5: 279 n.25
5.14–26: 223 n.24
7.3: 223
15–16: 227

Theognis / *Theognidea*
639–640: 44 n.38
1135–1136: 185 n.15
1135–1150: 24 n.59

Thucydides
1.1: 127 n.61
1.11.1: 137
1.20.3–4: 137 n.24
1.22.4: 142
1.23.6: 113, 131
1.61.5: 138
1.69.5: 139
1.70.3: 113, 137

1.70.4: 137
1.70.5: 113
1.70.7: 137, 137 n.23
1.71.4: 141 n.32
1.76.3: 141
1.81: 146
1.81.6: 137, 138 n.26, 146
1.84: 146
1.84.2: 137 n.24
1.84.4: 146
1.84.6: 146
1.86: 146
1.88: 114
1.118.2: 114
1.135–138: 146
1.138.2: 137
1.138.3: 146
1.140.1: 136, 143 n.42
1.144.1: 138
2.7.1: 137
2.21.1: 137
2.24.3: 115
2.40.1: 116 n.27
2.42.4: 117, 138
2.42–43: 143 n.42
2.43.1: 117
2.43.5–6: 138
2.44.2: 138
2.47: 144 n.44
2.51.4: 117 n.31, 140
2.51.6: 117 n.31
2.54: 144 n.44
2.59.3: 138
2.62: 146
2.62.2: 138
2.62.5: 137, 143 n.42
2.64.1: 138 n.25
2.65.5–6: 138
2.65.9: 138

2.75.1: 137
2.77.5: 137
2.78.2: 137 n.22
2.88.3: 141
2.89.10: 10 n.21
2.95.101: 280 n.29
2.97.4: 280 n.29
2.98.3: 280 n.29
3.1–3: 142 n.38
3.2–3: 143
3.3.1: 142 with n. 38
3.3.3–6: 142 n.38
3.14.5: 139
3.30.1: 141
3.30.2: 140
3.38.2: 138 n.26
3.39.3: 137, 142 n.38
3.43.5–7: 49 n.55
3.45.1: 138 n.26
3.45.5: 41, 49 n.55, 71, 137 with n.24, 141, 142 with n.38, 146
3.45.5–6: 114
3.45.6: 141
3.45.7: 141
3.45.9: 144
3.46.1: 137, 141, 142
3.46.5–7: 141
3.57.4: 140
3.64.4: 141
3.82.2: 141
3.82.3: 139
3.82.4: 1
3.83: 132
3.83.2: 140
3.93.3: 141
3.97.2: 137
4.8.4: 139, 142 n.37
4.13.1: 142 n.37
4.17: 140

4.17.4: 47 n.43, 133 n.11. 140, 142 n.37
4.17.4–19: 116 n.26
4.18.4: 137 n.24
4.26.4.3: 141
4.28: 147 n.55
4.55.1: 140, 142 n.37, 147 n.55
4.59–64: 120 n.40
4.61.5: 147 n.53
4.65.4: 131, 142
4.76.5: 139
4.81.3: 139, 140
4.108.4: 41 n.24f., 143
5.14.1: 116 n.26, 139, 141
5.14.1–2: 143, 147 n.55
5.26: 144 n.44
5.69.1–2: 134 n.12, 141 n.31
5.87: 144 n.43
5.102: 43
5.102–103: 71
5.103: 71, 122, 137, 143 n.42, 144 n.44
5.103.1: 144
5.103.2: 122–123, 137
5.104: 143
5.111: 122
5.112.2: 143 with n.40, 144
5.113: 143 with n.40
5.113.1: 139
5.116.3: 144 n.42
6.3.20: 148
6.5.35: 148
6.5.42: 148
6.10.5: 136 n.21
6.11.6: 137 n.24
6.13.1: 43 n.32
6.13.3: 136 n.21
6.13–24: 43 n.32
6.15.2: 137, 144
6.16.6: 136 n.21
6.17.8 140, 142 n.37

6.23.3: 120 n.40
6.24.3: 43 n.32, 136 n.21, 137 n.24, 141, 144, 146
6.24.4: 136 n.21
6.30.2: 116 with n.24, 144, 144
6.30.2–6.31.1: 116
6.31.3: 115
6.31.4: 115
6.31.6: 115, 116 n.24, 144, 145
6.32.41: 145
6.33: 132
6.33.4: 139 n.28, 145
6.33.6: 139 n.28
6.33–34: 120 n.40
6.34.2: 139 n.28
6.34.6–8: 133 n.11
6.56.3: 137
6.65.4: 115
6.78.2: 137
6.86: 143 n.42
6.90.2–4: 144
6.90.3: 137, 139
6.104.1: 142
6.105: 141
7.4.4: 140
7.5.26–27: 148
7.18.2–3: 142 n.37, 147 n.55
7.24.3: 141
7.29.3f.: 280 n.29
7.41.3: 138 n.26
7.43.6: 133 n.11
7.47.2: 140
7.47.3–5: 119
7.48.2: 119, 147 n.51
7.48.3: 119
7.49.1: 119
7.49.4: 119
7.50: 144 n.44, 146
7.55.1: 141

7.60.6: 141
7.61: 145 n.49
7.61–64: 120, 121 n.43
7.61.2: 120, 137
7.61.3: 120
7.69.2: 122
7.71.7: 140–141
7.75.2: 121, 145
7.75.4: 121
7.76.1: 141
7.77.1: 121, 145
7.77.3: 121, 145
7.77.3–4: 121
7.77.4: 137, 145
7.79.3: 141
7.80.5: 137
7.86.5: 146 n.51
7.149: 146 n.53
8.1: 144 n.44
8.1.1: 119, 132 n.6, 140, 141
8.1.1–2: 138
8.1.2: 141, 147 n.55
8.2: 147
8.2.3–4: 142 n.37
8.2.4: 141
8.11: 147
8.11.3: 141, 142 n.37
8.54.1: 141
8.71.1: 142 n.37
8.76.3: 141
8.81.2: 137
8.89.2: 137
8.94.2: 142 n.37

Tibullus
2.6.19–28: 185 n.15
2.6.27: 20 n.48

Tragica Adespota
fr. 55 K–S: 87
fr. 61c: 97 n.24

Valerius Maximus
2.6.10–11: 279 with n.23

Velleius Paterculus
2.75: 262
2.94: 262 with n.16
2.94.2: 262 n.14
2.103: 260, 262, 263, 272
2.104: 262 n.9
2.112: 262 n.11
2.126: 263
2.129: 267 n.35
2.129.1–3: 272–273
2.192: 273 n.43

Virgil
Aeneid
1.33: 172
1.218: 10 n.20
1.267–277: 177
1.351: 17
1.556: 178
2.42: 180 n.18
2.281: 28
2.354: 185 n.11
3.103: 180
3.543: 180
4.265–276: 179
4.273: 27, 28
4.274: 178
4.305–306: 172
5.548–550: 176
5.548–603: 175
5.570–3: 28
5.570: 28
5.576: 176
5.596–603: 176 n.15
5.604–599: 173
5.613–617: 173
5.630–635: 174
5.644–652: 174
5.654–656: 175
5.657–658: 175
5.659–663: 175
5.667–674: 175
5.670–671: 180 n.18
5.679: 176
6.626–629: 173–174
6.364: 178
7.126: 181
7.365: 167 n.33
8.514: 181
9.257–289: 180
9.590–671: 179
9.634–635: 179–180
9.641: 180 n.19
9.641–644: 177
10.56: 181
10.426–509: 181
10.524: 178
11.49: 181
11.491: 28
12.132: 223 n.23
12.161–165: 179 n.16
12.166–168: 178–179
12.168: 28, 178
12.435: 180 n.19
12.435–440: 179
12.887–952: 181

Vita Aesopi
G29: 248 n.40

Xenophon
Hellenica
3.5.1: 147
4.2.3: 147
5.4.31: 146 n.50
7.2.10: 147
Poroi
4.52: 342 n.39

Zeno
SVF 1.51: 189 n.28
SVF 3.92: 189 n.28
Zonaras
8.15.4: 264 n.22
8.15.152: 264 n.22

ii. Epigraphic and papyrological sources

CEG (*Carmina Epigraphica Graeca: saeculorum VIII-V a. Chr. n.*. ed. P.A. Hansen, Berlin/New York, 1983)
I 134: 354 n.13

CIL (*Corpus Inscriptionum Latinarum*)
10.8375: 128 n.37

CIRB (*Corpus Inscriptionum Regni Bosporani*)
130 (=*GV* 1989): 354 n.17, 357 n.25
141 (=*GV* 949): 356 n.24

DT (*Defixionum Tabellae*, ed. Auguste Audollent, 1904, Reprint, Frankfurt, 1967)
72: 363 n.54
73: 363 n.54

FD III (N. Valmin, *Fouilles de Delphes*, III. *Épigraphie*. Fascicule 6: *Inscriptions du théâtre*, Paris, 1939)
4.295.6–7: 352 n.6
4.295.10: 352 n.5
6.38: 253 n.47

GIBM (*The Collection of Ancient Greek Inscriptions in the British Museum*)
894: 360 n.42

GV (Peek, W. *Griechische Vers-Inscriften*, Berlin: Akademie-Verlag, 1955)
292: 354 n.17
661: 229 n.5
759: 356 n.29
1576: 354 n.15
1584: 334 n.18
2081: 356 n.23

I. Ancyra
83: 359 n.40, 363 n.55

I. Assos
26.5–7: 360 n.43

I. Aph. (*The Inscriptions of Aphrodisias*)
2007 8.114.14-15: 361 n.47

I. Beroia
2: 359 n.37
404: 356 n.27

I.Délos
1852: 255 n.21

I. Ephesos
2101: 355 n.17

IG (*Inscriptiones Graece*)
IG i^3 1179. 8-9: 353 n.9
IG ii^2 957: 342 n.40
IG ii^2 1996: 342
IG ii^2 2193: 342
IG ii^2 2196: 342
IG ii^2 2203: 342
IG ii^2 2940: 246 n.33
IG ii^2 3964.2: 329 n.2
IG ii^2 6626: 354 n.13
IG ii^2 1077.17–22: 360 n.44
IG ii^2 11477: 355 n.18
IG ii^2 13147: 355 n.17
IG ii^3 1285.8: 342 n.37
IG iv 620: 355 n.17
IG iv^2 83: 357 n.32
IG v 1.26.12–13: 342 n.37
IG v 1.1524.20: 357 n.32
IG v 2.265.38-41 359 n.38
IG v 2.180: 355 n.17
IG v 2.515 B 4–7: 351 n.2
IG vii 2545: 363 n.54
IG vii 2713.9–12: 352 n.7
IG ix 2.316: 234 n.21
IG x 2.2.301: 362 n.49
IG xii 2.489: 354 n.17
IG xiv 2431: 355 n.17

IGBulg (*Inscriptiones Graecae in Bulgaria Repertae* 4 vols., Sofia, 1956–1966)
III. 1519: 363 n.54

IGLS (*Inscriptions grecques et latines de la Syrie*, ed. L. Jalabert/R. Mouterde, Paris, 1927-)
IV 1427: 362 n.50
IV 1460/1461, 1732: 362 n.50

IGUR (*Inscriptiones Graecae Urbis Romae*, ed. I. Moretti, Studi pubblicati dall'Istituto Italiano per la Storia Antica 17, Rome, 1968–1990)
IGUR 148: 363 n.49
IGUR 1231: 355 n.17
IGUR III 1148: 356 n.26

I. Histriae (*Inscriptiones Daciae et Scythiae Minoris Antiquae, Series Altera. Inscriptiones Histriae et Viciniae*, Bucharest, 1983)
231: 354 n.13
267: 357 n.31

I. Iasos
90: 359 n.40

I.Kallatis (A. Avram, *Inscription grecques et latines de Scythie Mineure. III. Callatis térritoire*, Bucarest-Paris, 1999)
148: 354 n.16

I.Knidos
82: 354 n.17

I.Napoli
I 44.20: 359 n.40

I.Olympia
54.9–11, 24–27: 362 n.51

I.Oropos
301 (=*SEG* 47 498): 362 n.49

IOSPE (*Inscriptiones antiquae orae septentrionalis Ponti Euxini*, ed. B. Latyschev, 2nd ed. Petropoli, 1916)
I^2 46.4–7: 357 n.33
I^2 51.9–11: 357 n.33
I^2 52.5–10, 15-18: 357 n.33
I^2 79.16–17: 359 n.40

I. Perinthos
214: 357 n.31, 359 n.40

I. Priene
360 *(2014)* 14: 360 n.41

I. Prose
57A.16–21: 361 n.47

I.Sestos
58: 355 n.22

I.Smyrna
552: 354 n.17

I.Thespiai
1247: 354 n.17
1258: 355 n.17

I.Tomis (*Inscriptiones Scythiae Minoris Graecae et Latinae*. II. *Tomis et territorium* m ed. I. Stoian, Bucarest, 1987)
2: 363 n.53
175: 355 n.17
384 (=*SEG* 48 980): 354 n.16

IvP (*Die Inschriften von Pergamon* II. *Altertümer von Pergamon* 8, 1–2, ed. Max Fränkel, Berlin, 1895)
586: 355 n.19

Lane, E.N. *Corpus Monumentorum Religionis Dei Menis* I. Leiden, 1971.
no. 80: 248 n.38

OGIS (=W. Dittenberger, *Orientis Graeci inscriptiones selectae*, 2 vols., Leipzig, 1903–1905)
765: 280 n.26

PM (=E. Pfuhl and H. Möbius, *Die ostgriechischen Grabreliefs*. Mainz am Rhein: Von Zabern, 1977–1979)
392: 337–338 with n.27

SGDI (H. Collitz et al., *Sammlung der griechischen Dialekt-Inschriften*, II. Epirus, Akarnanien, Aetolien, Göttingen, 1885–1899)
2171: 254 n.51

Papyri Oxyrhynchi
P.Oxy 3006.26: 108 n.53

SEG (Supplementum Epigraphicum Graecum)
SEG 2 616: 354 n.17
SEG 4 91: 355 n.17
SEG 4 201.7–14: 360 n.42
SEG 7 875: 362 n.50
SEG 8 269: 353 n.12
SEG 11 1198: 361 n.46
SEG 12 193 (=*GV* 1820): 334 n.21
SEG 19 728: 334 n.18
SEG 23 433: 356 n.30
SEG 26 1808: 255 n.20
SEG 26 1622: 355 n.21
SEG 35 630: 356 n.28
SEG 38 1236: 363 n.56
SEG 39 1243: 358 n.36, 359 n.40
SEG 39 1276: 247 n.36
SEG 50 155: 342 n.41
SEG 51 673: 355 n.17
SEG 55 978: 229 n.5
SEG 57 1266: 334 n.18

TAM (P. Herrmann (ed.), *Tituli Asiae Minoris*, V. *Tituli Lydiae, linguis Graeca et Latina conscripti.*
I: *Regio septentrionalis, ad orientem vergens*, Vienna, 1981)
1.442: 247 n.37
1.550: 353 n.11
3.1553: 361 n.48

www.ingramcontent.com/pod-product-compliance
Lightning Source LLC
Chambersburg PA
CBHW051555230426
43668CB00013B/1855